THE WACOUSTA SYNDROME

Explorations in the Canadian Langscape

This book is about Canada. More than that, it's about *our* creation of Canada. Taking as its point of departure an exhaustive documentation of social and cultural history, it works backwards from fact to ground, from text to context, in an attempt to elucidate the structures of consciousness that link and inform the diverse data of one particular communal experience. This book, then, is not just about Canada but about *being* Canadian; about our sense of ourselves and of the world we live in. Reflecting on its own methodology, it is also about the way we express or reveal or betray that sense in every gesture and preference: the language we use, the pictures we paint, the leaders we elect.

GAILE McGREGOR is a cultural analyst. She has studied literature, cultural history, and sociology at Carleton University, the universities of Western Ontario and Manitoba, and, most recently, York University. She lives in London, Ontario, and Otter Lake, Quebec.

GAILE McGREGOR

The Wacousta Syndrome

EXPLORATIONS IN THE
CANADIAN LANGSCAPE

UNIVERSITY OF TORONTO PRESS
TORONTO BUFFALO LONDON

© University of Toronto Press 1985
Toronto   Buffalo   London
Printed in Canada

ISBN 0-8020-2554-4 (cloth)
ISBN 0-8020-6570-8 (paper)

Canadian Cataloguing in Publication Data

McGregor, Gaile, 1943–
    The Wacousta syndrome
    Bibliography: p.
    Includes index.
    ISBN 0-8020-2554-4 (bound). – ISBN 0-8020-6570-8 (pbk.)
    1. Canada – Civilization. 2. Canadian literature.
    3. National characteristics, Canadian. I. Title.
    FC95.M24 1985   971   c85-098994-9
    F1021.M24 1985

49,296

This book has been published with the help of a grant to the University of Toronto
Press from the Andrew W. Mellon Foundation and block grants from the Canada
Council and the Ontario Arts Council.

Contents

Preface

This book was initially intended as a 'corollary' to a study of American cultural history. The sheer intractability of this preconceived format launched me on an unexpected intellectual journey that turned out to be a personal revelation. In discovering Canada, I also discovered what it meant to be a Canadian. Perhaps, though, re-covered would be a more appropriate term. Wacousta, after all, was made, not given. As in a sense were the 'hard facts' of our world-at-large. Hence my choice of title. The coinage 'langscape,' far from adventitious, is meant to underline the extent to which nature, like other aspects of reality, is not simply perceived but socially constructed. By mythicizing our environment we convert it into a body of symbols, a kind of code which – like all language – reveals the ability both to reflect *and* to coerce our experience of the world. Where the landscape is passive, morally neutral, and ultimately inaccessible, 'langscape' suggests a kind of accommodation or complicity between self and other. This book addresses the question of what this complicity comprises under *our* particular, perhaps peculiar, geo-cultural conditions.

Ironically, given its 'nationalistic' bias, it was written largely in the United States, during a period when I had severed all formal academic connections. This protracted double exile made me all the more dependent on and grateful for the interest and support of friends. In particular I would like to thank Leslie Miller, Jeff Lawrence, Gail Hartshorn, and Ann Davis for their encouragement, stimulation, and constructive criticism. I would also like to mention my editor, Gerry Hallowell of the University of Toronto Press. Without Gerry's well-honed pencil *The Wacousta Syndrome* would carry a good deal more unnecessary flab than it does. More crucial, without Gerry's active intercession and campaign on my behalf, it probably wouldn't have appeared at all. In this case thank-you hardly seems enough.

One last, very important pair of debts remains to be paid. This book, so long in the making, is jointly dedicated to my father, Leslie Stewart McGregor, whose Scottish common sense lurks behind my wildest flights of fancy, and to my husband, Norman Duke, whose wit and whimsy have done much to leaven the pomposity of my Scottish common sense.

A NOTE ON REFERENCING

Citations in parentheses in the text refer to 'Canadian' works listed in the 'Catalogue of Primary Sources' at the end of the book. Other material is referenced in notes at the end of each chapter; second and subsequent references to non-Canadian sources are enclosed in square brackets in the text. Abbreviations of periodical titles in the notes follow the usage of the *MLA* bibliography.

THE WACOUSTA SYNDROME

In a way, then, philosophy's beginning in history is the beginning each of us must make for *himself*: the ultimate assumption, made blatantly and audaciously by the early Greeks, that (a) there is a *cosmos*, not chaos – since all things compose an ordered whole, it makes sense to seek to know the principles defining that 'order,' and (b) man, as the possessor of '*logos*,' can cognitively apprehend and 'say' what that cosmos and its order are.

Richard M. Zaner

1

A View from the Fort

It has long been commonplace to compare Major John Richardson's *Wacousta* to the Leatherstocking novels of James Fenimore Cooper, and one would think that little could be gained by a revival of this somewhat shopworn critical perspective. The fact is, however, that the comparison has rarely been pursued beyond the most superficial levels.[1] In particular no one as yet has fully explored the cultural implications of the considerable differences these two writers display in the context of a single literary genre.

Without going into lengthy details about the characteristics of the American wilderness romance – plot structure, *dramatis personae*, thematic orientation, etc. – and its relationship to the European romance conventions established pre-eminently by Sir Walter Scott (all of which has been exhaustively documented in the corpus of Cooper criticism[2]), I would like to direct my examination of the Richardson/Cooper parallel primarily toward one important aspect of the genre: its location, in terms of both setting and moral/emotional co-ordinates, on the *interface* between civilization and the wilderness – not in a 'neutral territory' between the two, as Richard Chase terms it, for this, as Robert Lecker points out, would imply a fictional universe 'essentially devoid of antithesis' (A78), *but precisely on the line where those two realities and two states of mind come together*. In the truest sense the wilderness romance is thus, as Chase says, 'a kind of "border" fiction,'[3] for in its purest form it offers a paradigm for the pattern of feeling, attitude, or outlook that is deemed appropriate by its originating culture to the confrontations implicit in the 'border' condition. And this, of course, is what makes the contrast between Cooper and Richardson potentially so interesting. The differences may be idiosyncratic, but it is at least possible that their respective responses may encapsulate an essential divergence between cultures rather than merely between individuals. It is this possibility that is the ultimate concern of this study.

In terms of the wilderness/civilization dichotomy, the first and most obvious difference between Richardson and Cooper is in their handling of the landscape. Surprisingly enough for a genre which, by definition, explores a facet of man's relationship with nature, the descriptions of scenery in *Wacousta* are so rare and so scanty as to suggest that Richardson, to a large extent, doesn't 'see' the landscape at all. Indeed, throughout the novel he seldom surpasses, in either length or particulars, the brief and conventional set-pieces that serve as introductory material in a few chapters:

The sun was just rising above the horizon in all that peculiar softness of splendor which characterizes the early days of autumn ... (38)

It was that soft and hazy season, peculiar to the bland and beautiful autumn of Canada, when the golden light of heaven seems as if transmitted through a veil of tissue, and all of animate and inanimate nature, expanding and fructifying beneath its fostering influence, breathes the most delicious langour and voluptuous repose. (100)

At length came that terrible and eventful day, and, as if in mockery of those who saw no beauty in its golden beams, arrayed in all the gorgeous softness of its autumnal glory. (172)

These passages seem especially inadequate when compared, on the one hand, with Richardson's lengthy and detailed description of Madeline's apartments in the fort (249-52) and, on the other, with any of numerous landscape descriptions in Cooper. Cooper's diction and descriptive strategies are also largely conventional, of course, but in particularity, in vividness, and in versatility he far surpasses Richardson in evoking the physical scene[4]:

The long drought had ... changed its coat of verdure to a hue of brown, and, though the same localities were there, the view wanted the lively and cheering aspect of early summer. Even the heavens seemed to share in the dried appearance of the earth, for the sun was concealed by a haziness in the atmosphere, which looked like a thin smoke without a particle of moisture, if such a thing were possible. The blue sky was scarcely to be seen, though now and then there was a faint lighting up in spots, through which masses of rolling vapor could be discerned gathering around the horizon, as if nature were struggling to collect her floods for the relief of man.

The eye could range, in every direction, through the long and shadowed vistas of the trees ... the peaceful and slumbering scenery. Here and there a bird was heard fluttering among the branches of the beeches, and occasionally a squirrel dropped a nut, drawing the startled looks of the party, for a moment, to the place; but the instant the casual interruption ceased, the passing air was heard murmuring above their heads, along that verdant and undulating surface of forest, which spread itself unbroken, unless by stream or lake, over such a vast region of country. Across the tract of wilderness … it seemed as if the foot of man had never trodden, so breathing and deep was the silence in which it lay.

The difference here is significant enough to be seen as a difference in kind rather than merely degree. Nor is it simply a matter of execution. Cooper's skill in landscape description is certainly greater, but beyond this disparity it seems obvious that there is a basic variance in attitudes toward the ostensibly common subject matter. While the wilderness – nature – is a major component in the world of Cooper's books, in *Wacousta* it is barely evoked at all. It is *cited* – it is acknowledged as a formal *donnée* – but it is not a tangible entity to be seen, heard, tasted, felt. As Margot Northey points out, 'it has an abstract, symbolic quality' (22). For this reason, the theoretical wilderness/civilization dichotomy does not operate in the Canadian book in the same way that it does in the American wilderness romance. As a dichotomy implies two polar qualities, opposite in nature but equivalent in kind, the opposition between wilderness and civilization in Richardson (for certainly there still is opposition) is, rather, the opposition between centre and ground, between 'self' and 'not-self.'
   The corollary (or perhaps the cause) of this divergence is the fact that nature in Richardson's book, being simply a negation of 'self' rather than an autonomous entity, can be seen – when it is seen at all – only in negative terms:

When the eye turned woodward it fell heavily and without interest upon a dim and dusky point known to enter upon savage scenes and unexplored countries, whereas whenever it reposed upon the lake it was with an eagerness and energy that embraced the most vivid recollections of the past, and led the imagination buoyantly over every well-remembered scene that had previously been traversed, and which must be traversed again before the land of the European could be pressed once more. (244-5)

Nature, then, is here in a very real sense not merely ignored but denied. The result? Whatever common sense might suggest, the process of neutralization is far from producing neutrality. Once denuded of the tangible attributes (positive and/or negative) that make it comprehensible to the human mind, *Wacousta's* unknown and unknowable wilderness almost by default begins to accumulate increasingly sinister gothic overtones. These in turn exacerbate the sense of isolation, vulnerability, and entrapment already inherent in the pioneer's situation. They also tend to play up the more allegorical aspects of the story. The isolated fort, able only through 'art and laborious exertion' to push back the forest a short distance, and to maintain its safety-in-separation only under the 'protecting sweep of its cannon' (244), becomes a correlative for the beleaguered human psyche attempting to preserve its integrity in the face of an alien, encompassing nature. The landscape as a whole, conversely, comes to symbolize 'all the inscrutable, evil forces of life' (Northey 23). The woods in particular, for those held in unwilling thrall on its borders, presents itself as 'the gloomy and impenetrable walls of the prison-house.' In all this dismal scene, in fact, the 'bright lake' strikes the only positive note, representing as it does an escape route to the past, a sole 'portal through which happiness and liberty [can] be again secured' (245). The rest is inimical – like the gothic antagonist at his worst, not merely dangerous but *un*human.

The gothic face of the wilderness is not, of course, a new ingredient added by Richardson to the romance convention. Throughout the Leatherstocking tales, for instance, one finds numerous scenes in which the image of a hostile nature is employed as an effective means of intensifying the impact made by human brutality, thus heightening deliciously the reader's sense of the protagonists' vulnerability. Nor is the gothic component in Cooper limited merely to rhetorical or decorative functions. In *The Last of the Mohicans* in particular, the gothic overtones, as Thomas Philbrick points out, are pervasive enough that the setting at times evokes not merely a natural 'wasteland' but, more radically, a 'portal to the underworld,' a fantastic domain characterized by 'nightmarish confusions and deceptions.'[5] Such a landscape is obviously no more benign than the haunted element that forms a backdrop to *Wacousta*. If, indeed, one compares Philbrick's article to Marcia Kline's discussion of Richardson it is obvious that the two books, whatever their substantive differences, *come across as remarkably similar in tone*. Leaving aside simple matters of fact, the following description could be equally applicable to either:

The atmosphere – fearful and pregnant with danger – is sustained throughout the book. When day finally dawns in this first chapter, after thirty-five pages of mysterious thumps, bumps, and whoops in the night, the first thing it reveals is the body of a British soldier, unwittingly killed by one of his fellow officers in the effort to beat off the unknown foe. By far the greater part of the action is set at night, which augments the fear, and day or night there are Indians skulking around, each one 'like some dark spirit moving cautiously in its course of secret destruction, and watching the moment when he might pounce unnoticed upon his unprepared victim.' (Kline 19-20)

Having noted all this, however, it must be said that there is still a significant difference between the two writers. Most important is the fact that in Cooper *the dawn that follows the gothic night truly does offer a promise of renewal*, counterbalancing the terrors of the darkness rather than merely spotlighting their horrid effects. Seemingly untouched by the recurrent threat of violence that lurks behind her Janus-like visage, Cooper's nature is always ready to reassume 'her mildest and most captivating form' [*Mohicans* 171]. Nor does the beauty thus displayed – 'The mountains ... green and fresh and lovely; tempered with the milder light, or softened in shadow' – signal merely the amoral indifference of an alien element without relevance for man, as it seems, on its rare appearances, to do in Richardson ('the sun shone in yellow lustre, and all nature smiled and wore an air of calm, as if the accursed deed had had the sanction of heaven' 267). In the person of Leatherstocking, Cooper is always ready to remind us that whatever dangers the wilderness may offer in gothic guise, in her equally tangible beneficent mood nature is also a temple for worship, an inspiration, a moral exemplar, a sanctuary where man can 'at any instant open his heart to God without having to strip it of the cares and wickednesses of the settlements.'[6] In Richardson, in contrast, nature has only the one, terrible face. Indeed, as Northey indicates, 'in *Wacousta* a profound fear of nature often seems to override any other response' (23). The gothic mood, consequently, is not merely a function of particular circumstances that may be confronted and overcome by human courage and will; instead it becomes an inseparable part of the human condition.

This one-sided view of nature implies certain problems for the book. On the most obvious level, it may be the strongly urged hostility of nature that is ultimately responsible for Richardson's failure to deal effectively with the circumlocutions of his plot. The British in the book are tied by an invisible umbilical cord to their fort: 'to have crossed the ravine, or ventured out of reach of the cannon of the fort, would have been to seal the destruction of the detachment. But the officer to whom their security was entrusted, although he had his own particular views for venturing thus far, knew also at what point to stop' (116). We can almost see the string that measures the radius of their circle! What is more significant, however, is that Richardson himself seems to suffer the same limitations as his characters. Certainly the fact that a full fifteen chapters – almost two hundred pages – elapse before we are given any explanation about those mysterious events in the forest that provide the impetus for the entire plot suggests that he is as reluctant to venture into the wilderness as are the over-imaginative soldiers with their fancies of Indians behind every tree (see 117). Throughout the book it is the view from the fort that dominates. Those parts of the story that take place outside the garrison are kept at a distance, filtered through the consciousness of the non-combatants, *told* rather than *shown* to the reader. This not only makes the book seem irritatingly uneven, but at times the retrospective or 'distanced' narration makes it difficult for the reader to follow what is happening.

A second problem links both structure and theme, and it is here that *Wacousta*'s variant view of nature begins actually to run counter to the basic impulses of the romance form. It has already been mentioned that the opposition is established in terms of centre and ground, rather than in terms of a polarity. The resulting structure – circular rather than linear, static rather than dynamic – thus lacks the sense of movement, of process, that draws the reader into Cooper's fictional world. In Cooper the polar states – civilization and wilderness – still maintain their integrity, but not in terms of a fixed location. Instead, like the classic 'string of beads,' a series of discrete 'scenes' (using the word in its original, graphic sense) is deployed along the linear linkage of a flight-and-pursuit plotline; the graphic correlative for the action, in other words, is a series of clearings through the middle of a dense, shadowy forest.[7]

The advantages of this technique are considerable. For one thing, by placing the civilized protagonists in the closest possible proximity to the towering majesty of nature, Cooper brings the fundamental thematic opposition into high relief. Even more important, he recapitulates structurally the psycho-symbolic movement that typifies and energizes the conventional romance form. In Cooper's wilderness romances, according to a mythic pattern, man does not merely 'confront' nature but makes a spiritual journey *through* it, enduring its gothic aspect as a kind of 'dark night of the soul' that must be traversed before reconciliation can be achieved with the sources of life and fertility that it – or 'she' – alone may offer.

This brings us to a third problem that Richardson's limited view of nature entails for the success of *Wacousta*. By denying both the desirability and the possibility of a true journey into the wilderness, effecting reconciliation with nature, Richardson also denies the reader one of the most important of the *dramatis personae* of the wilderness romance, the primitive or 'natural' man who serves as mediator between the civilized world and the wilderness 'other': the Leatherstocking figure without whose assistance – both protection from nature's dark side and education about her beneficence – the journey may not be accomplished. The loss is significant, in practical terms if nothing else. By deleting the type from his cast, Richardson ignored a resource that was probably the single most important factor in Cooper's success. Delighted by his apparent symbolic resolution of their age-old dilemma, their historic perplexity about man's relation to nature (a deep-cutting conflict in the American psyche since Roger Morton denied the wilderness was a hideous waste and raised a maypole at Merry-mount), generations of American readers and critics have imputed to Natty Bumppo a kind of numen that has transformed him into an archetype. Charles Brady, in 'Myth-maker and Christian Romancer,' for instance, describes him as a 'semi-divine hero,' a 'Herakles wrestling against death on behalf of a series of clean-cut young American Admetuses and their Alcestises,' a 'young god ... an embodied conscience for America.'[8] Other critics are even more specific in imputing an overtly 'messianic' function to him; against the background of the Edenic myth that irradiated America's self-image from the beginning, he serves, they say, as a symbolic redemption for the public guilt resulting from the pioneers' mutilation of the landscape. 'Beset with ... remorse,' says Warren Walker, 'Americans ... were provided a measure of atonement in the spectacle of the white man, in the person of the frontiersman, being offered up on the same altar of progress with the red man and the buffalo.'[9] Whether as mediator or scapegoat, however, Natty was invariably associated with the energized interface between man and nature, and his role provided for the novels an emotional focus of considerable power. In overlooking this role, it would seem that Richardson missed out on one of the most interesting potentialities of his chosen genre.

It is possible to claim that the Indian girl, Oucanasta, serves Natty's function in *Wacousta*. Weighing against such an attribution, however – even leaving aside the problem that as an individual this character remains shadowy and ill defined, without the power to stir any notable response[10] – is the fact that the Indian, in terms of romance conventions, generally represents a force of nature (good or evil), and as such is associated with *one* term of the dichotomy rather than mediating between *two* poles. Only a hybrid figure like Leatherstocking can properly straddle the interface: 'removed from nearly all the temptations of civilized life, placed in the best associations of that which is deemed savage, and favorably disposed by nature to improve such advantages, it appeared to the writer that his hero was a fit subject to represent the better qualities of both conditions [that is, civilization and savagery] without pushing either to extremes,' Cooper tells us in his preface to the Leatherstocking Series.[11] Without such a mediator Richardson denies completely the reconciliation of opposites which is at the heart of the symbolic model embodied in the wilderness romance.

It is important, on the other hand, to view this discrepancy in its proper perspective. Was the distortion of the conventional pattern simply a flaw of judgment or a lapse of taste on Richardson's part? Certainly the view of nature that underlies the lapse is not an uncommon one in Canadian literature. Many critics have noted the prevalence of the gothic face. 'Nature,' says Northrop Frye, 'is seen by the poet, first as unconsciousness, then as a kind of existence which is cruel and meaningless . Nature is consistently sinister and menacing in Canadian poetry' (B141-2). '[T]his was a world of frozen corpses, dead gophers, dead children, and the ever-present feeling of menace, not from an enemy set over against you but from everything surrounding you,' writes Margaret Atwood (F30). 'Canadians ... exhibit a "terror of the soul" at the utter indifference of Nature to the values and efforts of puny men,' Kline adds. 'In their work, this terror manifests itself in the fear – or even the conviction – that the geographic realities of the New World mountains and forests are not symbols of that metaphor for moral goodness, Nature, but symbols instead of Chaos and Indifference' (47).

The discovery that a negative response to nature is common among Canadian writers is, admittedly, neither new nor revolutionary. As yet, however, no one has satisfactorily explained the causes or noted the ramifications of these recurrent images of a hostile wilderness – or, in fact, fully traced the extent to which such an image, mediated and mutated, pervades and dominates not just

Canadian literature but Canadian culture as a whole. Such an explanation is crucial to an understanding of what Richardson's novel implies in terms of its cultural context. If, for instance, the Canadian response to nature, as most of these critics seem to suggest, is simply a reorientation of the same ambivalence that has historically coloured the American view, with Canadian writers merely emphasizing the negative pole, the darker face, a little more strongly and consistently, then the phenomenon is interesting but not particularly surprising. But if the characteristic Canadian response – as Kline implies, at least with respect to literature[12] – differs not just in degree but in kind, moving beyond ambivalence entirely to the unidimensionally negative view illustrated in *Wacousta*, then Richardson's problems – his inability to reconcile the emotional necessity of maintaining an absolute discontinuity between fort and forest with a literary form implying, even demanding, mediation between the two – were not idiosyncratic but symptomatic of the cultural setting out of which he wrote.

The fact is, leaving Richardson aside for the moment, there is plenty of evidence in the Canadian corpus to suggest that our national response to the environment *has* been almost completely negative. This does not mean that it has necessarily been simple. Rather it seems to have progressed through a number of distinct stages (all of which persisted as minor strains even after the appearance of later developments that *seemed* to alter both the mode and the mood of its characteristic expression), attaining its fullest and most complex form by the end of the nineteenth century. Because of the nature of the material, this development is revealed most strikingly not in literature but in art. A useful first step in delineating the morphology of the Canadian 'langscape,' therefore, would perhaps be an examination of how nature has been depicted in Canadian painting. The only consideration that might militate against this cross-disciplinary approach is the question of whether we can validly translate visual data into 'psychological' (that is, verbal) facts. Fortunately there is greater continuity between these purportedly diverse levels of experience than may at first appear.

The art of the eighteenth and nineteenth centuries is, to be sure, representational; that is, formally object-oriented. The apparent concern with mimesis should not, however, mislead us about the extent to which the artists' predispositions determine not only *what* but *how* we see. As Ronald Rees points out, 'landscape paintings reveal more about the artist's attitudes toward the landscape than they do about the landscape itself. Subjectivity of vision, the dictates of artistic convention, and concern for imaginative rather than literal truth preclude paintings which are mirror images of the environment' (259). Perhaps, though, the emphasis on 'attitudes' is a little misleading. What Rees fails to emphasize here is the surprising extent to which purely public factors shape not only the dictates of convention but the supposed 'subjectivity of vision' as well. Both the artist's explicit preferences and, more important, the largely unconscious expectations that shape not merely the forms he imposes *on* his raw material but the way that raw material 'composes' itself (presents itself to his eye as potential subject matter) are synthesized from the stock of aesthetic alternatives already available in his cultural milieu. This is true, indeed, of *all* the arts. A writer is said to develop his own style, but the possible *directions* for this development are already laid down for him. '[T]he choice of, and afterwards the responsibility for, a mode of writing point to the presence of Freedom, but this Freedom has not the same limits at different moments of History,' says Roland Barthes. 'It is not granted to the writer to choose his mode of writing from a kind of non-temporal store of literary forms. It is under the pressure of History and Tradition that the possible modes of writing for a given writer are established.'[13] We may thus expect to find that the literature of a community will not only express common ideas, values, attitudes (whether by celebrating or denying them) but that similar visions will tend to be expressed by way of similar forms. In painting, further, where the formal component is even more highly visible, we should be able to discern these relationships – to infer the 'historical' determinants – with even greater ease.

If we turn to early Canadian art we will soon realize the truth of this claim. These visual documents yield relatively little hard information about the landscape the artist is presumably looking at, but the covert messages to be inferred even from ostensibly divergent formal qualities are both surprisingly consistent *and* fully consonant with other known aspects of the cultural matrix. Certainly there is little 'naturalism' to camouflage the communal/subjective element. What, then, can we learn about the mood of colonial Canada from its painting?

During the first years of the Maritime colonies, 'wild' nature, judging by the art produced, might scarcely have existed at all. As Mary Sparling tells us:

The first visual record available to the British public of Halifax had been Moses Harris's town plan published in October 1749 ... The overriding impression it gives is one of regularity, order and safety (which is of course exactly what Cornwallis, acting for the British government, set out to achieve). Riding at anchor in front of the settlement is a ship flying the British flag; cleared from the surrounding forest is an organized community displaying the flag from its principal fort; identified as existing facilities are the buildings from which order and regularity are dispensed, the governor's house, the barracks and fort. Next to come, surrounding the parade square, are the church, the court house and the prison. Streets are laid out in orderly rows; lots are marked out as subdivisions. Surrounding the whole is a palisade, guarded by five forts. Everything was shown to be organized – at least within the settlement.

However accurate that may have been, outside the palisade was another story, one that Harris did not record. He chose not to portray the natural forest and its inhabitants, the

Micmac Indians. Why was this? Very simply both were dangerous, both were untamed ... Obviously Moses Harris, naturalist, stayed within the palisade and drew only those aspects of the natural world which could be isolated (i.e., pinned, pressed or stuffed), identified and thereby controlled ... Even though endless forest vistas awaited his pencil ... he gave his viewers only the clearing in the forest, and of Nova Scotia's flora and fauna only individual specimens – a dwarf apple, a country cherry, a beetle and a porcupine. (8-9)

Other artists during the period followed the same pattern. *A New Map of Nova Scotia* (1750) by Thomas Jefferys, according to Sparling, celebrates 'the civilizing hand of European man, not untamed nature,' while a series of drawings by Richard Short (views of the town of Halifax as it was in 1759, later transformed into paintings by British artist Dominic Serres) are notable for their depiction of unallayed 'order and prosperity' (10, 15). It is not until the nineteenth century that we are taken out into the countryside: it is only then that 'it is safe to do so; the Indians have long since ended their resistance to the British. Untamed nature remained a challenge only to the Indians, the sportsman, the farmer and the fisherman.' However, Sparling emphasizes, the art of this period 'did not include any observations of *their* connections with nature' (25); even after the early xenophobia diminishes, it is definitely only the domesticated, pastoral face of nature that the artist allows himself to 'see.' Later, after European fashions in landscape painting have encouraged a taste for more rugged natural landscapes, the *illusion* of domestication is still maintained by constant reminders of the human presence. 'Paul Sanby's *Scale Force, Cumberland* ... is an excellent example of a genre which while presenting an awesome aspect of nature, always included human figures somewhere in the scene. To give a sense of scale certainly, but also implying that man by the very fact of his having chosen to be there, is in control' (21). The art of the eastern colonies is modelled almost without exception on the practice of such 'absentee' commentators as Sanby; the wilderness is denied as firmly in early visual documents as it is in *Wacousta*.

In the west, first impressions were a little different, although in the long run the implications for the Canadian view of nature are similar. If the original Maritime colonist was so intimidated by the wilderness that he apparently blocked it from his consciousness, one would expect that the early visitors to the Pacific coast, where nature is characterized by a more spectacular but equally intimidating kind of desolation, would deny the vision even more strenuously. At first glance this does not seem to be the case. Although in many pieces landscape is treated as incidental or supplementary to a pictorial theme (see Tippett and Cole 18-20) or to the informative function of the travel literature they often accompanied, some early paintings actually do seem to make an attempt to depict the wilderness. The *way* it is depicted, though, implies a repulsion as intense as that which we sense in Richardson's book. *Resolution and Discovery in Nootka Sound* (1778) by John Webber, William Ellis's *View of Ship Cove in King George's Sound, on the N.W. Coast of America* (1778), and *Friendly Cove, Nootka Sound*, an engraving done by James Heath (after H. Humphries and William Alexander) for Captain George Vancouver's *A Voyage of Discovery* (1798), for instance, are all remarkably similar treatments of a scene wherein a diminutive British ship at anchor appears to be almost completely hemmed in by a dense, forbidding wall of forest and/or mountains. The effect of this composition is claustrophobic in the extreme. 'Terrifying and desolate in its overpowering presence, the terrain is an inhospitable barrier to man. The ships and sailors, even the natives, are active only on the coastal fringe. The rocks and the forest rear up as walls, overwhelming the fragile human endeavour' (Tippett and Cole 19). Here again is nature as the alien 'other.'

To complete our survey of first responses, the prairie region of Canada, despite its later date of settlement, would seem to have posed even greater problems for the beholder. Judging by the corpus, the great plains, predictably enough, resisted aesthetic expropriation more strenuously than almost any other area. Why predictably? Given the natural paranoia of man on the brink of the unknown, limitless space is almost certain to be more intimidating than even the most monumental mountain. And space is *the* identifying feature of the Canadian interior. Space – set forth in all its nakedness – is also virtually unpaintable. In consequence, early painters of the prairie were not merely induced but constrained to favour those pictorial techniques that would allow them to delimit what Rees calls the 'terrible grandeur' of horizontal expanse. Some ignored the 'real' landscape entirely, searching out 'the valleys and the carpets of early summer wild flowers which for a short season, to quote Paul Kane, "enamelled" the plains.' Others habitually filled 'the immediate foreground of [their] drawings or paintings with human and/or animal subjects, using the landscape merely as background' (263). More subtly, there was also a general tendency either to obscure the horizon with smoke or cloud (as in H.J. Ware, *Forcing a Passage through Burning Prairie* [1847], Paul Kane, *Buffalo at Sunset* [1851-6], and F.A. Verner, *Indian Encampment at Sunset* [1873]), or to establish a vantage point so low to the ground that even very slight swells of land cut off the view (see W.G.R. Hind's *Camping on the Prairie* and *Buffalo on the Prairie* [both 1862]). Cumulatively all these practices reveal a striking consistency of effect. We might go so far as to say, in fact, that the identifying feature of this body of work is, paradoxically, a short focus. No matter *what* the intrinsic quality of the landscape confronted, the early Canadian artist, it seems, was bound and determined to ignore the power of nature out beyond human reach. Why? The obvious conjecture is that the early Canadian artist was simply repelled by what he saw 'out there.'

It might be argued that a predominantly negative response to nature is predictable in the colonial situation; that the unfamiliarity of the environment coupled with their own insecurities would inevitably tend to make settlers more aware of the threatening aspects of the wilderness – that the Canadian, in other words, was in no wise unique. If this were true, though – if the apparently spontaneous sense of alienation were in fact merely a natural stage *all* colonists go through – we should expect, first of all, to find a similar reaction among the *American* colonists, and secondly, to find the Canadian response becoming more positive as the landscape becomes more familiar. Significantly, such would *not* seem to be the case. Even a cursory survey reveals that a substantial number of early American responses to the New World convey an image not of 'wilderness' but of 'garden.' Leaving aside realities, the reason for this (by Canadian standards) anomalously felicitous perception of the untamed landscape is not hard to find. Buoyed by national prosperity and titillated by the crumbling of feudal socio-religious certainties, the renaissance Englishman was not merely ready but predisposed to glamourize the newly discovered Americas. The essential conservatism of the communal imagination, on the other hand, inclined him to do so by way of ready-to-hand stocks of imagery. It was hence almost inevitable, as Richard Slotkin points out, that the first views of America should be set forth 'in the conventional terms of utopian treatise-fiction, arcadian poetry, and the chivalric romance-epic.'[14] Under the influence of Protestant millennialism, moreover, to these classical conventions were soon added the paradisial images of Christian tradition. The resulting synthesis combined Eden with 'Arcadia ... Elysium, Atlantis ... Tirananogue ... the fragrant bower where the Hesperides stood watch over the golden apples' and all the other 'enchanted gardens' of antiquity to produce a vision of abundance and felicity such as 'Centuries of longing and revery' could scarcely have conceived.[15]

The romanticized vision of the New World was not reserved only for those utopian dreamers who contemplated its promise from afar. As Slotkin observes, to such a degree did expectations control perception that the 'explorers and conquerers themselves tended to see the landscape of America through lenses colored by their reading of romance-epics and pastoral verse' [31]. Early eyewitness descriptions of the new land, in both words and paint, were in consequence most often formulated in the conventional celebratory terms produced by the European imagination. Captains Amadas and Barlow, for instance, reported that when they first entered the coastal waters of North Carolina 'we smelt so sweet and so strong a smell, as if we had bene in the midst of some delicate garden abounding with all kinds of odoriferous flowers,' and later colonists tended to employ the same edenic motif: America, they said, was the 'paradise of the world'; 'heaven and earth never agreed better to frame a place for man's habitation'; it was 'a good land, a land flowing with milk and honey'; it was a land of 'extream fruitfulness' where 'no Seed is Sowed ... but it thrives.'[16]

The response was not *solely* or even primarily positive, of course: the Puritan fear and distrust of the natural environment, as of the natural man, is axiomatic, and even after the weakening of the religious basis for viewing the wilderness as hostile, ambivalence is still a very noticeable ingredient in the American attitude. If St John de Crevecoeur finds the wilderness beautiful and the savage life in some ways enticing, the perception makes nature seem all the more dangerous to him: 'I dread ... the imperceptible charm,' he says repeatedly.[17] In spite of this, however, it is obvious that the appealing side of nature seized and held the American imagination, even *after* the natural disillusionments of the colonization process had plenty of time to work their effects, in a way that it never – early or late – managed to do in Canada. Certainly there is little evidence in early Canadian painting that the untransformed wilderness appeared to be anything like a garden.

If the expected parallel with the colonial American response fails to support the thesis that the initial alienation was simply a function of unfamiliarity, so too does the assumption that it would automatically decrease as the colonial situation became more secure and comfortable.[18] During the nineteenth century, Canadian landscape art *appears* to express a more positive view of nature, in the sense at least that nature is made to seem more familiar, less overtly threatening, but to a large extent this is an illusion fostered by the adaptation in Canada, as in the United States, of European theories of landscape painting, especially the theories of the sublime and the picturesque which, as interpreted in the work of Salvator Rosa and Claude Lorraine, simultaneously made wild nature fashionable and offered a model for responding to it properly. Despite the widespread acceptance by Canadian painters of both the conventions and the subject matter characteristic of this trend, however, there is striking evidence that the vision of a menacing nature was as strong, as *exclusive* even, as in the earlier period when the wilderness was rarely allowed to show its face at all.

The problem doesn't really emerge at the level of individual works, and this is perhaps why the uniqueness of the Canadian vision has not been generally recognized. There are, to be sure, numerous paintings that seem to illustrate the threatening aspect of nature fairly directly – paintings like Lucius O'Brien's *Wagon Road on the Fraser* (1887) and John A. Fraser's *Fraser River Line of the C.P.R.* (1886), in which the works of man are diminished almost to the point of absurdity by either the towering grandeur or the menacing bulk of mountains squatting hugely against the skyline; paintings like *The Rogers Pass* (1886), also by the latter artist, where a dark, sinister-looking forest appears as an impenetrable barrier between the viewer and the sunlit peaks; paintings like Ebenezer Birrell's *Good Friends* (1830) and Homer Watson's *On the Grand*

River at Doon (ca 1881) that show domestic animals ringed in by bush (only a fragile line of rail fence seems to be keeping it from closing in on them) or weighed down by the shadow of a looming wooded hill; paintings, especially, like Daniel Fowler's *A Wanderer in the Woodland* (1888), Lucius O'Brien's *A British Columbian Forest* (1888), or Allan Edson's *Autumn Forest* series (ca 1874), where human figures are dwarfed, diminished, sometimes almost lost amid the towering trees and luxuriant underbrush – but none of these subjects or treatments is outside the normal range for the conventions of the period. If we survey nineteenth-century Canadian paintings, it appears, indeed, that nature in general was depicted here as (if anything) *less* wild than either current British fashions or American practices would dictate; that it was the picturesque which was the favoured mode, and most Canadian artists tended (in relative terms) to *avoid* the extremes associated with the sublime. It is not in the area of individual preferences in subject matter or explicit treatments of the man/ nature relation that we find the best evidence for communal response, in any case. Only by examining the *cumulative* effects of certain trends in composition can we gauge the direction and extent of significant divergence from prevailing norms.

The moment we invoke 'trends' we unfortunately invoke as well a whole host of methodological problems. For all that colonial Canada was in world terms a very small puddle, its artists were still numerous and prolific enough to make any sort of exhaustive breakdown of the corpus impractical for present purposes. Any survey that lends itself to the kind of broad generalizations we are dealing with here is necessarily going to be both superficial and subjective. Notwithstanding these limitations, however, there is something to be said for the holistic approach. Stipulating that it is the forest and not the trees to which we are mainly addressing ourselves, a quick scan of Canadian painting of the period seems clearly to indicate – what closer scrutiny obscures – that certain characteristics were widespread and consistent enough to be identified as markers of a truly indigenous pattern of response.

1 There are usually signs of human activity in the fore-to-middle ground but actual human figures tend to be dwarfed in scale and in impact in relation to their environment. Modes of transportation are featured in a strikingly large number of paintings. These features would seem to indicate a *desire* to dominate the environment symbolically by focusing on the human element, but a general fear or suspicion that it is the human who is dominated instead. The preoccupation with transportation implies a preoccupation with escape.

2 In a great many paintings there is a definite compositional break between the fore-to-middle ground and the background (by a change in colour tones, degree of definition, or lighting; by cutting the picture plane horizontally with a water

line, road, etc.; or by telescoping the foreground abruptly onto the background), with visual focus and significant detail largely limited to the former. This suggests a denial of meaningful relation between man and nature-as-panorama, nature in the broadest sense.

3 In a high proportion of paintings the background is left relatively indistinct – depicted as vague, highly stylized, and/or undifferentiated – or is obscured by atmospheric conditions such as cloud or mist. Again this signals a dislike for panoramic nature, and an attempt to limit visually the suggestion of unmanageable distance.

4 The horizon is raised or hidden by features in the fore-to-middle ground. In the case of forest scenes, for instance, it is usually only the first rank of trees that is differentiated to any extent; the succeeding ranks blend almost immediately into a diffuse wall that frustrates any attempt to see *beyond* or *through* them. Even if there are no tangible obstacles to vision, the vantage point is generally kept so low that there is no possibility of moving very far out into the landscape; we are quickly brought to a halt. There are very few paintings of the period, in fact, that have any great depth of field at all. Once again, 'natural' recession is carefully countered by composition.

5 The sense of depth is even further delimited in many paintings by the arrangement and treatment of geographical features. Various common combinations of light and texture, for example, have the property of making mountain masses or cliffs seem to loom forward rather than receding. This exacerbates the claustrophobic effect of the shortened focus.

6 In an unusual number of paintings the general atmosphere is ominous. Even when neither the weather nor the physical environment seems to contain any overt threat, the colour tones and lighting often convey an impression of gloom or a vaguely sinister unreality. This, added to the perspectival features, underlines our clear sense that the scene viewed is viewed, albeit covertly, as inimical to the viewer.

What does all this mean? Even admitting that there is a demonstrable bias at work, is there any way we can establish that it is significant rather than merely circumstantial? As with individual works, *all* of these general characteristics, alone or in combination, can be 'explained' in terms of conventional schools of painting. But to explain is not to explain away. If nothing else, the preponderance of *these particular* characteristics rather than any of the other possibilities offered by current fashions would seem at least suggestive. And if we go one step further and compare, in the same general terms, this body of work with more or less contemporary American paintings of the same basic style and subject matter, the suspicion that the Canadian response is collectively deviant in mood if not in detail is quickly confirmed.

On the assumption that any truly significant divergence should catalyse functionally equivalent adjustments across the board, I will for convenience limit this comparison to a few basic motifs and standard compositions. Taking a lead from our Canadian findings, the first thing we might look at is the use of the panoramic viewpoint. Here the results are gratifying. On the American side the practice of combining almost illimitable recession with a sense of visual domination was common enough during the nineteenth century to be considered as much of a norm as foreshortening evidently was for the Canadian. What is more interesting, when we compare the ways almost identical pictorial conventions were employed in each country, even when formal resemblance is stipulated critical differences still remain. In both countries one of the most popular compositions in the 'panoramic' mode was the framed prospect. So different is the usage in each case, however, that the respective products would seem almost to represent different species. Where the American version (and here the classic example would be James Smillies' *Kaaterskill Clove* [1865], where three travellers on a tree-fringed rocky ledge look out over an expansive vista to a river valley nestled among distant, low, rolling hills, or Asher Durand's famous painting – aptly entitled *Kindred Spirits* [1849] – of fellow artist Thomas Cole and his friend, poet William Cullen Bryant) almost always comprises an overt celebration of man-in-nature, or at least symbolically asserts the ascendancy of the viewer over the vista, the substantially more mundane Canadian equivalent is an urban or semi-urban scene like Thomas Davies' *Montreal* (1812) or Robert Whale's *General View of Hamilton* (1853) – both compositionally similar to Smillies' painting (though the length and elevation of the vantage point are reduced) but focused on man-made rather than natural objects. The fact that the cityscape was the *only* variant of the basic composition that found any real favour north of the border (dozens of similar studies were done of other cities and villages[19]) suggests that, for all their reliance on American models, Canadian painters were captives of their own conditioning. Repelled by raw nature, they proved incapable of handling the panoramic perspective unless the scene surveyed were fully domesticated.

Looking further, we find more of the same. Divergence in other respects is generally somewhat more subtle, but propensities are psychologically consistent right down the line. In the depiction of waterways, for instance, painters on each side of the border diverged not only along national lines but in accordance with the same pro- and anti-panoramic orientations revealed in their handling of the vista. In the United States a river was most often employed – in combination with a long and usually elevated vantage point – to draw the eye into and across the landscape. Alexander Wyant's *The Mohawk Valley* (1866), where the serpentine river twisting off into the distance gives depth and definition to a heavily wooded valley bottom, and Thomas Cole's *The Ox Bow* (1808) exemplify the mode; in both of these, as in numerous like paintings, the view is *along* the river, not merely penetrating but laying claim to the distance, opening up the countryside like a lush, compliant woman. In Canada the case is quite different. Where the waterway is inviting, it leads out from, not into the picture. Where it penetrates, it is not inviting. The keynote is almost invariably reticence, not aggressiveness. In some paintings – like Otto Jacob's *Lac des deux montagnes* (1860) and John A. Fraser's *A Shot in the Dawn* (1873) – far from eliciting even visual entry, a river or narrow lake bisects the canvas horizontally such that a raised bank of foliage radically restricts the depth of field. In other cases – like C.P. Forrest's *Grande Coupement, French River, Lake Huron* (1822) – the *initial* view is along the river, but is quickly pinched off by high-banked, bulky curves. The most common technique, however, is to establish the viewer at ground level, looking upstream, so that the path of the water appears to terminate abruptly at the top of a small rapids or falls with a solid wall of hills or woods looming up behind it. Versions of this arrangement appear in F.A. Verner's *Indian Camp* (1876) and Thomas Davies' *The Falls of Ste Anne* (1790), among others. The effect of all these compositional variations is, of course, to avoid entirely the 'opening up,' the sense of distance, that is typical of so many American river scenes.

A similar but even more telling distinction may be detected in the respective treatments of another popular theme, the waterfall. Again it comes down to perspective. In American variants, the viewer is usually placed above and at a considerable distance back from the falls, so that he gets a sense of both the vertical drop *and* the horizontal panorama behind it. Representative pieces in both mood and vantage would include Frederick Church's *Cotopaxi* (1862), Sanford Gifford's *Kaaterskill Falls* (1862), and, especially, Thomas Cole's *Mountain Landscape with Waterfall* (1840), where our view extends all the way from the rugged little river valley below the falls right up over the top of the ridge to the chain of humped hills receding into the distance. On the Canadian side of the border, in contrast, waterfalls are typically seem from below and at relatively short range. The human figures, usually diminutive and almost always placed at or near the base of the falls, often seem to be trapped in the bottom of a deep bowl, and although the viewer usually looks *down* on these figures (diminishing them even further), we share their perspective in looking *up* at the falls. The classic example of this is Lucius O'Brien's *Kakabeka Falls* (1882), where the massy cliffs hemming in both sides of the river add to the oppressive effect. Thomas Davies' *Montmorency Falls* (1791), being more stylized, is less oppressive, although the bowl effect is actually more striking, while in Joseph Légaré's *Les chutes de Saint-Férreol* (ca 1840), where the closure is less explicit, a dark, densely wooded hillside weighs down upon and almost overwhelms the figures below. Whatever the specifics of style or content, however, it is a fact that none of these, and few Canadian waterfall paintings in general, allows the viewer to see much beyond the rim.[20]

Turning to larger geographic features we also find striking contrasts between Canadian and American mountainscapes. In the United States, nineteenth-century painters generally tended to focus on the valleys *below* (Albert Bierstadt, *Yosemite Valley* [after 1860]; William Sontag, *Mountain Landscape* [1854]) or the pass or gap *through* the mountains (Thomas Cole, *In the Catskills* [1827]), usually accentuating both the accessibility and the desirability of the space 'beyond' through the use of heightened and dramatic lighting. In Canadian art, however, mountains are typically made to appear as symbolic or actual barriers to human penetration. In some of the more extreme cases – like David Thompson's *No. 2 Nelson's Mountains South* (1810) or W.G.R. Hind's *Foot of the Rocky Mountains* (1862) – they form an apparently solid wall extending across the whole width of the picture plane. Even when the effect of absolute impassibility is mitigated somewhat, it is more often than not the *bulk* of a mountain or group of mountains – rather than a route around or a path through – which dominates the middle of the canvas. If this weren't enough, the claustrophobic effect is exacerbated by the fact that these focal formations often shoot up with rather unnatural abruptness behind a lake or river, seemingly at no great distance, such that it is inevitably the sheer *obtrusiveness* of the geography that communicates itself to the viewer above any other feature. The obstacle posed by the mountain, in other words, is clearly implied to be much more than merely physical. One of the most notable examples of this effect is provided by Cornelius Krieghoff's *Owl's Head, Memphremagog* (1859), where the complacent weight of the garishly coloured hill against the grey sky is in ominous contrast to the flimsy boat on the choppy lake below, but variations on the same format were produced by a great many Canadian painters.[21] John A. Fraser, indeed, seems to have favoured this composition over any other. Again there is a subtle but important difference to be discerned between the practice of the two countries: where Americans typically emphasized the 'romantic' aspects of alpine scenes, Canadian artists most often presented the mountainscape in a predominantly inimical mood.

On the whole, it seems obvious from all these discrepancies in approach that even within the confines of a putatively identical range of subjects and stylistic conventions there is, as Kline says of Canadian and American writers, 'some very basic cleavage in the way ... [they] see and confront the natural world' (42). The American view is not, admittedly, as wholly simplistic and untroubled as these comparisons may make it seem: for every moment that nature seems paradisial there is always another in which it becomes 'A waste and howling wilderness,/ Where none inhabited/ But hellish fiends, and brutish men/ That devils worshiped.'[22] It is, however, a view in which both possibilities, if they are not reconciled, at least co-exist in a kind of dynamic tension. The Canadian view of nature, in contrast – although camouflaged by the visible persistence at the level of theory, technique, and diction of unassimilated but influential ideas imported from outside – seems to repudiate entirely the possibility that nature is benevolent, maternal: a 'garden.'

Rereading this last sentence, one becomes aware of just how complex a 'simple' response can be. If the conceptual ambivalence characteristic of American views of nature is largely lacking in the Canadian version, there is still a profound and disturbing split between response and expression. The fact is, despite the seeming homogeneousness of their deepest intuitions, Canadians did continue for a long time to work in genres and use conventions fostered by quite different and even conflicting attitudes to the environment. The full ironies of this situation are illuminated in a deceptively simple little fable by Charles G.D. Roberts. *The Heart of the Ancient Wood* may, in fact, be said to provide a paradigm for the irreconcilability of the Canadian's *real* and *assumed* relationship with nature.

To begin with, this book offers (or appears to offer) two opposing responses to the wilderness. On the one side is the child/woman Miranda, an innocent, untutored creature who is as much at home in the woods – and in some essential ways, as unhuman – as Hawthorne's Pearl. Deer and moose are her friends and protectors; a bear is her adoptive mother. For her there is no danger in the wilderness, only freedom and beauty. On the other side is ranged all the rest of humanity, from the two ruffians who try to rob her to the noble hunter who comes to court her. And although they may differ radically in motives and personal worth, all members of this group are by definition adversaries of nature. Even young Dave, who claims that the wilderness offers the only kind of life he could stand – ' "'way in the woods, with the shadows, an' the silence, an' the trees, an' the sky, an' the clean smells"' – believes that he must kill or be killed out there, and for him the forest echoes with ' "whispers you can't never understand"' (160).

On the surface, then, we appear to have those same two possibilities that comprise the American's ambivalent vision: benevolent Mother Nature, a source of health and inspiration for those who are pure in heart, versus the gothic wilderness, an arena for violence. Roberts's fictional treatment of the alternatives, however, undercuts the ultimate viability of Miranda's romantic brand of primitivism as sharply as the hostile Canadian landscape so often undercuts the pastoral diction of nineteenth-century poetry.[23] For one thing – to combat the implication that the hostility of the wilderness is a state of mind, that simply 'thinking positively' can neutralize its dangers and turn it into a happy, wholesome, Walt Disney world – Roberts demonstrates clearly that the menace imputed to the forest is very real, regardless of whether man is frightened, unafraid, or simply oblivious:

From the mossy crotch of an old ash tree, slanting over the trail, a pair of pale, yellow-green eyes, with fine black slits for pupils, watched the traveller's march ... [The animal] itched fiercely to drop upon the man's bowed neck, just where it showed, red and defenceless, between the gaudy bundle and the rim of the brown hat. But the wild-cat, the lesser lynx, was heir to a ferocity well tempered with discretion, and the old lumberman slouched onward unharmed, all ignorant of that green gleam of hate playing upon his neck. (10-11)

Secondly, Roberts establishes quite unequivocally that even Miranda's brave new world is not 'really' the light-filled, loving, fairytale forest she believes it to be. Indeed, it is only by a stubborn disregard for the facts that she can manage to maintain the naive illusion of its benefice:

Miranda ... regarded the folk of the ancient wood as a gentle people, living for the most part in a voiceless amity. Her seeing eyes quite failed to see the unceasing tragedy of the stillness. She did not guess that the furtive folk, whom she watched about their business, went always with fear at their side and death lying in wait at every turn. She little dreamed that, for most of them, the very price of life itself was the ceaseless extinguishing of life. (124)

Then, finally, he illustrates dramatically that this flawed vision – a childish form of wishful thinking, and as such a dangerous delusion to carry into adult life – must be relinquished if Miranda is to attain her full humanity. The only way, in other words, that the girl can hold on to her innocent dream-wilderness, the only way she can continue to refuse to 'see' the cruel reality at the heart of nature, is to deny her own kind. And in the end, of course, Miranda does 'see':

It chanced that Miranda, not far off, had heard the roar with which Kroof had rushed to the attack. The fury of it had brought her in haste to the spot, surprised and apprehensive. She recognized Dave's rifle and hunting-shirt under the hemlock tree, and her heart melted in a horrible fear. Then she saw Dave high up in the beech tree, his bare shoulders gleaming through the russet leaves. She saw Kroof, now not three feet from her prey. She saw the hate in the beast's eyes and open jaws. (272)

Miranda, at this moment of recognition, makes her choice instinctively; she shoots her erstwhile 'mother,' the bear.

Roberts's tale – despite the illusory effect of imported fashions in art and literature – may well contain the final verdict on nature as far as Canadians are concerned; the uncomfortable message that somehow seems to make its presence known no matter how conventional the vehicle. Whatever the wilderness may be to its own creatures, it implies, it is a foolish fancy to believe that for the human it is or ever can be anything but totally alien – and therefore dangerous. Miranda returns with Dave to the 'real' world, "way down onto the Meramichi, where [he] can git a good job surveyin' lumber' (275). She will not live in the forest any more.

NOTES

1 Focusing on the degraded figure of the Indian in *The Pioneers* and conveniently ignoring *The Last of the Mohicans* and *The Prairie* (although both of these also appeared before *Wacousta*) Waterston claimed patriotically that 'Richardson's novel pre-dated Cooper's in glamourizing the Indian' (21). Admittedly, Richardson's Pontiac is a fairly respectable example of the *classic* Noble Savage – stern, stoical, and statesmanlike – who declaimed his way through numerous American literary works of the late eighteenth and early nineteenth centuries, reaching fullest development in Washington Irving and William Gilmore Simms, but nowhere among the wooden Indians of *Wacousta* is there one to rival in glamour or emotional appeal the romantic figure of, say, Uncas in *The Last of the Mohicans*.

2 See, for instance, Joel Porte, *The Romance in America: Studies in Cooper, Poe, Hawthorne, Melville and James* (Wesleyan U. 1968).

3 Chase, *The American Novel and Its Tradition* (Anchor 1956) 19

4 See Blake Nevius, *Cooper's Landscapes: An Essay on the Picturesque Vision* (Berkeley 1976) for a useful discussion and evaluation of his technique. Quotations from James Fenimore Cooper, *The Pioneers, or The Sources of the Susquehanna* (Signet 1964) 379; *The Last of the Mohicans* (Washington Square 1957) 390

5 Philbrick, '*The Last of the Mohicans* and the Sounds of Discord,' *AL* 43, 1 (1971) 32-3

6 *The Prairie* (Signet 1964) 260. Leatherstocking's 'pantheism' is not as vociferous or as romanticized in the first three novels of the series, but the positive influence of nature was not only a *donnée* but a major theme of the whole series.

7 See Nevius for a full discussion of the visual aspects of this structure; also Donald Ringe, *The Pictorial Mode: Space and Time in the Art of Bryant, Irving and Cooper* (Kentucky U. 1971).

8 In *American Classics Reconsidered: A Christian Appraisal*, ed. Harold G. Gardiner (Scribner 1958) 91, 92, 95

9 Walker, *James Fenimore Cooper: An Introduction and Interpretation* (Barnes & Noble 1962) 37

10 Compare Richardson's scant characterization in chap. 17 with Cooper's vivid and detailed description of Uncas in chap. 6 of *Mohicans*.

11 Reprinted in *The Deerslayer* (Washington Square 1961) xv

12 'Across the border the tradition is monolithic: nowhere is there a joyful affirmation of wild nature' (Kline 53).

13 Barthes, *Writing Degree Zero + Elements of Semiology*, trans. Annette Lavers and Colin Smith resp. (joint ed. Beacon Press 1970) 16

14 Slotkin, *Regeneration through Violence: The Mythology of the American Frontier, 1600-1860* (Wesleyan U. 1973) 29-30

15 Leo Marx, *The Machine in the Garden: Technology and the Pastoral Ideal in America* (Oxford 1964) 40

16 From 'Reports of the Voyage of Captains Amadas and Barlow, 1584,' in Howard Mumford Jones, *The Frontier in American Fiction* (Jerusalem 1956) 118-19; Charles L. Sanford *The Quest for Paradise: Europe and the American Moral Imagination* (Illinois U. 1961) 83, 84; Roy Harvey Pearce, ed., *Colonial American Writing* (Holt, Rinehart & Winston 1969) 511

17 J. Hector St John de Crèvecoeur, 'Distresses of a Frontier Man' (Letter XII), *Letters from an American Farmer, and Sketches of Eighteenth Century America* (Signet 1963), esp. 207 ff

18 A complicating factor for any discussion of trends is the idea put forth by a number of critics – in contrast to the theory that familiarity should mitigate the apparent sense of alienation – that the process was actually *reversed*; that far from being weakened, the vision of a hostile nature seemed rather to take a *stronger* hold on the Canadian imagination throughout the nineteenth century as the conventional romantic view became 'increasingly affected by Darwinism, [by a view] of nature red in tooth and claw' (Frye B243; see also A.G. Bailey, esp. 192, fn 11, for an elaboration of this view). I would maintain, however, that since this development operated primarily at the most superficial levels of convention and idiom, it produced only a peculiarly stylized (and thus 'safe') version of nature's 'hostility' that may easily be distinguished from the less conscious and therefore less contrived response to be inferred from a cumulative overview of the literature. As will be seen, this deeper response does not reveal either a systematic weakening (based on familiarity) *or* a significant increase (based on literary Darwinism) in the degree of alienation felt by Canadians toward nature; rather, base attitudes seem to have been remarkably consistent (despite idiomatic differences) from the colonial period well into the twentieth century. If Darwinian theories enjoyed a considerable vogue in Canada it was thus likely a *result* rather than a *cause* of the country's idiosyncratic vision.

19 A partial listing would include George Heriot, *Quebec from the North Bank of the Charles* (1807); E. Walsh, *View of the City of Montreal from the Mountain* (1811); James Gray and J. Gleadah, *York from Gibralter Point* (1828); James Pattison Cockburn, *View of Quebec with Timber Depot* (ca 1828-30); T. Young and N. Currier, *General View of the City of Toronto* (1835); W.H. Bartlett, *Kingston, Lake Ontario* (1840); John Poad Drake, *Montreal from the St Lawrence River* (1849); James Duncan, *Montreal from the Mountain* (1850); Eden Whitefield, *Montreal, Canada East, from the Mountain* (1852); E.M. Richardson, *Inner Harbour, Victoria* (ca 1864).

20 The numerous other examples include C.J. Way, *Niagara in the Time of the Red Man* (1880); R.C. Todd, *The Ice Cone, Montmorency Falls* (ca 1845); W.S. Hunter, Jr, *The Chasm, Chaudiére Falls* (1855); H.J. Warre, *Falls of the Peloos River* (1848);

James Gray and J. Gleadah, *General View of the Falls of Niagara* (1828); G.B. Fisher (aquatints by J.W. Edy), *The St Ann's or Grand River* and *The Falls of Chaudiére* (1785); Joseph Dynes, *Falls of Montmorency, Meeting of the Sleighs* (ca 1840); William Armstrong, *The Kakabeka Falls* (nd).

21 Otto Jacobi's *Canadian Autumn* (1870); Allan Edson's *Mount Orford and the Owl's Head from Lake Memphramagog* (1870); Henry Sandham's *On an Eastern Salmon Stream* (1874)

22 Michael Wigglesworth, 'God's Controversy with New England,' in Henry Nash Smith, *Virgin Land: The American West as Symbol and Myth* (Vintage 1950) 4

23 Zezulka claims that because 'the vision [of Goldsmith and other Canadian pastoral poets] celebrates the imposition of a human form on the wilderness ... the use of language more appropriate to the domesticated landscape of England is quite appropriate' (233), but it is obvious from this overview of responses to the wilderness that Canadians felt imposed upon much more than imposing. The use of pastoral conventions with their concomitant naive optimism, therefore, actually reflected ironically on the Canadian's attempt to come to terms with his relationship with nature. For this reason as much as for reasons of decorum and aesthetic unity the pastoral mode proved an unfortunate liability for poets attempting to communicate the Canadian experience.

2

Circum Locutions

Once recognized, the characteristic Canadian response seems omnipresent in all aspects of Canadian cultural history. Certainly it has provided a persistent and surprisingly homogeneous substratum through Canadian writing of many different kinds right from the beginning. Richardson was not, in fact, atypical. Far from finding that paradisial garden, the image of which dominated for so many centuries European visions of the New World,[1] Canada's first visitors – judging by their reports – were almost universally repelled by their encounters with the land. On the west coast, as Maria Tippett and Douglas Cole describe it, 'Vancouver found no pleasure ... Anchored along the coast in June, 1792, he despaired of the scene about him. "Our residence here," he wrote, "was truly forlorn." John Meares, a trader, found that the coast was almost totally without variety; it was nothing but "immense ranges of mountains or impenetrable forests." His partner, George Dixon, simply condemned it as "dreary and inhospitable"' (16). Was this negativity simply the result of inappropriate expectations? Possibly. At least in part. But longer acquaintance seems to have made little difference to the refrain. As in the visual documents produced during the period, the almost sole image of nature to be gleaned from nineteenth-century travel literature is a hostile one. Despite his presumably greater familiarity with the attributes of the new, wild, northern territory, Simon Fraser's response to the landscape of the interior in 1807 'parallel[ed] Vancouver's reaction to Desolation Sound': '"I scarcely ever saw any thing so dreary ... and seldom so dangerous in any country; and at present while I am writing this, whatever way I turn, mountains upon mountains, whose summits are covered with eternal snows, close to the gloomy scene"' (Tippett and Cole 25-6). Reactions to the prairie, though somewhat less dramatic in tone, convey – covertly – an even *greater* sense of alienation. 'These great plains appear to be given by Providence to the Red Man for ever, as the wilds and sands of Africa are given to the Arabians,' writes David Thompson in 1798 (A103). 'It is difficult to convey an adequate idea of these dreary solitudes ... which require tedious weeks to traverse,' echoes John Lambert half a century later (151). Even allowing for the very real hardships endured by these travellers, this is a *long* way from Rousseauistic enthusiasm.

It is, of course, the palpable *absence* of Rousseau that, more than any other factor, renders these comments so historically interesting. As with nineteenth-century painting, the attitude to which this written documentation testifies is in marked contrast to that associated not merely with early adventurers but also with later interior explorers in the United States, where, even after the frontiersman had provided ample evidence that he was *not* commonly anything like the 'natural nobleman' that the European romantic imagination had conjured – after the destructiveness and profligacy of the pioneering movement had become too blatant to ignore[2] – the tone of the response still continued (quite irrationally) to be dominated by a wish-fulfilling motif of paradise regained.[3] The difference is not limited to travel journals. While superficially dominated by the same idiom, the same genre conventions, Canadian literary writing both before and after Richardson yields surprisingly little of that passionate idealization of nature which, at least until the latter decades of the nineteenth century, served as a virtual *donnée* among both poets and romancers south of the border. More important, it showed little of the diffuse quasi-mysticism by means of which these latter sought not merely to normalize but to expropriate the otherness of the environment. Where the American typically imaged the wilderness as a repository, a spawning ground, for some specifically human value – as a temple or cradle, a schoolroom or arena – the Canadian seemed reluctant or unable to get past its immanence, the obtrusive *thereness* of the thing-in-itself. Indeed, until relatively recently, the verbal as much as the visual response to the landscape has tended, whatever its conventional vehicle, to reveal nothing so much as the viewer's *apprehension* about his environment. As a result, if viewed holistically like the painting, nineteenth- and early twentieth-century Canadian literature covertly yields (as, indeed, according to Douglas Jones, so many of our critics have already observed) 'a picture of irresolution, of isolation and frustration, of exile, [suggesting that] ... a kind of cultural schizophrenia, a division between ... conscious aspirations and ... unconscious convictions' provided a common ground for almost all our early writers (A14).

Part of this negativity, at least in the earlier period, may simply signal a temperamental bias in the colonists themselves. Certainly it is true, as David Stouck points out with respect to Susanna Moodie, that because the true seekers-after-Eden (those desiring a really radical break with their past) gravitated toward the United States, many who came to this country were armed with quite different motives than those we associate with 'the American dream': more pragmatic, modest if not downright sceptical, on the whole less naively hopeful. The Moodies, he says, like the United Empire Loyalists before them and like great numbers of people since, came to Canada not with a dream of carving individual empires, but with the modest hope of salvaging a way of life threatened at home ... Like so many of the genteel poor from England and Scotland the Moodies sought in Canada a refuge, a way of saving pride in the face of ever dwindling economic and social circumstances. The contrast to the creative and forward-looking American experience in the eighteenth and nineteenth centuries is absolutely crucial to understanding a distinctively Canadian imaginative tradition. Seeking a haven in which to preserve customs threatened at home is imaginatively at the opposite pole from rejecting the old order and emigrating in order to begin life anew. (B470-1)

Without denying that this circumstance probably did contribute to the despairing note one so often detects in our early writing (one might wish to point out that there is plenty of evidence in early American letters that homesickness was a large part of *their* immigrant experience too, but it is undoubtedly true that a myth of abundance, of futurity, of participation in a noble experience, perhaps even a divine mission, offsets such pangs to a considerable degree), I would still claim that it was the landscape itself that crystallized and exacerbated the doubts these reluctant pioneers brought with them, and the landscape, therefore, that tended to collect and focus all their displaced fears. Far from the *diffused* negativity one might expect as a reaction to disappointment or unbearable nostalgia, what we find in our early literature is what we might call a 'limited' (that is, structured) ambivalence centring quite precisely on that same interface that caused Richardson so much anxiety. As a result, paralleling to a remarkable extent several features we have seen to be characteristic of Canadian landscape painting, Canadian writing, both literary and non-literary, is marked throughout its first century and beyond by a small number of distinct though complementary modes of depicting nature.

The simplest kind of reaction to an inhospitable landscape is, of course, an overt negativity of the kind evinced by Vancouver, and examples of such outspoken derogation are not hard to find. In 1769, for instance, Frances Brooke, in the persona of Emily Montague, an English belle temporarily domiciled at Quebec, writes of Canada: '"I no longer wonder the elegant arts are unknown here; the rigour of the climate suspends the very powers of the understanding"' (90). More than fifty years later, Anna Brownell Jameson not only complains, predictably, of the unprecedented rigours of the winter ('When I look out upon the bleak, shrouded, changeless scene, there is something so awfully silent, fixed, and immutable in its aspect, that it is enough to disturb one's faith in the everlasting revolutions of the seasons' 67) but finds the summer, with its stifling heat, its voracious mosquitoes, and its disorderly jungle-like fecundity, to be almost beyond human endurance as well ('Immediately on the border of the road so-called, was the wild, tangled, untrodden thicket, as impervious to the foot as the road was impassable, rich with vegetation, variegated verdure, and flowers of loveliest dye, but the haunt of the rattlesnake, and all manner of creeping and living things not pleasant to encounter, or even to think of' 81). And M. Allerdale Grainger's 1908 portrait of the early west coast logging industry in *Woodsmen of the West* provides an even more uniformly negative view of nature:

I hate isolation. To set out alone on a long trip makes me feel like the small child who, lingering behind, screams from fear of being abandoned ... Making camp by oneself in bad weather, in a bad country, is a dismal thing to look forward to. As Carter talked my mind pictured, in nightmare hues, the upper reaches of the Inlet: the gloomy lowering roof of clouds, hanging across the water; the steep-to shores, black walls of cliff streaked and splashed with dreary whiteness of snow; the dark, quiet sea; and the ever-present threat of storm, a threat almost visible to the eyes in that scene of misery. That was the Inlet at peace – unstable peace – the peace of a few short hours. Then there was the Inlet disturbed: the cloud mass dragging past the mountain slopes, tailing wisps of mist; the sea all ridged with the white tops of waves in the path of a wind slanting from cliff to cliff across the bends of the Inlet. How depressing the thought ... (119)

Straightforward negative responses like these are not, however, as common as one might expect. Significantly enough, all three of the writers cited here were visitors to Canada, rather than committed residents[4]; perhaps they had less need to deny or disguise their intimation of nature's menace. For whatever reasons, rather than expressing overt hostility native Canadian writers have been more likely to demonstrate one (or a combination) of the following patterns of response.

SIMPLE AVOIDANCE

Like those first artists of the Maritimes who did not, seemingly, 'notice' the wilderness outside their fortressed communities, there were many even among the explorers, whose business it was actually to enter into and describe the wilderness, who apparently avoided to a great extent having to focus on nature *qua* nature at all. Such wilful myopia may seem strange if not impossible under the circumstances, but, as Ronald Rees points out, 'Functional seeing, as is commonly acknowledged, is usually fleeting, the observer seeing only as much as is necessary for his practical needs' (268). Repulsive to European-trained sensibilities, the Canadian landscape seems to have been devoid of intrinsic interest for many early travellers; such explorers as Sir Alexander Mackenzie and, to a lesser extent, Fraser, consequently concentrate on plot rather than setting in their narratives. '[R]eferences to flora and fauna, to Indian customs and habits, and to natural scenery ... appear ... scanty and inadequate,' says Roy

Daniells of Mackenzie (21). 'They seldom allow digressions on Indian habits or on scenery or animals to divert their tales from being unremitting accounts of the hardships and difficulties they faced, and their modes of overcoming those obstacles,' adds T.D. MacLulich (B61). For the reader of these journals, therefore, the land itself, which ostensibly provided the reason for their explorations, remains surprisingly indistinct. Henry Kelsey's laconic 1691 diary is in many ways representative: 'August ye 20th To day we pitcht to ye outtermost Edge of ye woods this plain affords Nothing but short Round sticky grass & Buffillo' (in D. Harrison E3). From the pages of documents such as these little beyond the human activity emerges.

A similar avoidance pattern can be observed in early Canadian literature. Even when writing specifically about the frontier, many authors of 'popular' fiction managed to ignore the landscape almost entirely. William Kirby's historical romance, *The Golden Dog*, set in 1748 Quebec, contains scarcely a single landscape reference of even the most conventional kind – a lack that seems particularly striking when one compares the book to similar works (such as *The Spy*) by Cooper. More surprisingly, even relatively realistic publications purporting to portray life in pioneer society, such as John Galt's semi-satirical *Bogle Corbet*, often dismiss the environing wilderness with a few token references of no greater consequence or vitality than Richardson's half-hearted offerings:

On the one side rolled the majestic St Lawrence, and from time to time its mighty rapids, tumbling and roaring, and tumultuous – horizontal cataracts -were objects of attractive admiration; and on the other the primeval forest, with a narrow strip of cleared land between, stood like the arborous wall of Paradise, with, here and there at long intervals, a narrow vista into the green Eden of new settlements beyond. The landscape is, however, solitary, and, to say the truth, is to the emigrant a little saddening. It lacks the social cheerfulness of villages. (45)

Well into the twentieth century, the lighter varieties of Canadian fiction tended to minimize direct reference to nature. As Laurence Ricou indicates in his discussion of prairie novels, landscape is more often than not just a shadowy diffuse backdrop to the action. Gilbert Parker's settings 'are generally slight and vague,' he says, quoting an example 'typical for its use of undescriptive adjectives like "lovely," its use of [a] sea image to suggest vastness, the occurrence of the romantic notion that the northern air promotes physical and moral health, and the total lack of any attempt to relate the vastness and invigorating air to the immediate characters and action.' John McLean's novels, on the other hand, appeal 'more directly to the cult of the primitive,' but, Ricou points out, his 'primitivism is totally cultural, with scarcely any reference to the physical wilderness.' And in Ralph Connor's 'highly didactic novels,' despite overt claims about the west as 'a land of infinite possibility,' 'landscape is seldom significant ... and descriptions of it are characterized by shallow, romantic ecstasy' (B14-15). In almost all Canadian 'westerns,' in fact, although the landscape is conventionally cited for its moral qualities (as Connor in *The Sky Pilot* cites the influence of the rugged prairie environment as the specific means by which the members of his 'Company of the Noble Seven' are enabled to achieve their full stature, morally and physically: 'freed from the restraints of custom and surrounding, [they] soon shed all that was superficial in their make-up and stood forth in the naked simplicity of their native manhood' J.L. Thompson A167), it is rarely seen or felt as a real presence.

Popular fiction is not alone in ignoring the landscape. A writer as thoughtful, and as significant in Canadian literary history, as Frederick Philip Grove made this practice the basis of his entire aesthetic. Eschewing mimesis, Grove chose the oblique or distanced vision above any other perspective on the world. He did so, moreover, quite deliberately. Why? Whatever covert motives one might be tempted to infer,[5] on the surface at least Grove disclaimed strenuously the *value* of drawing from nature. The superimposition of a 'perfectly irrelevant actuality,' he said, would destroy a character's literary validity: 'From a type and a symbol, he would have become an individual; he would have been drained of the truth that lived in him; he would have become a mere fact' (A260-1). Before he could create a fictional world, in other words, the writer had first to *uncreate* the reality. The same precept applied doubly when it came to painting in the background. For all their verisimilitude, the landscapes of Grove's novels were, he claimed, almost entirely 'the product of [his] mind' (A373). For Grove, as much as for any 'popular' novelist of his time, 'real' nature was inconsequential if not invisible.

To turn inward for inspiration is not, of course, a necessarily objectionable strategy, and indeed characterizes the stance of many of the world's greatest writers. There is, however, typically an element of strain in the Canadian response – a hint of dissimulation, awkwardness, or bluster – that in many cases makes what is missing seem as obtrusive as what we are actually shown. For one thing, though there is nothing intrinsically wrong with an anthropocentric focus, when a writer purports to be reproducing real experience in a real landscape we may be excused for being dissatisfied when that landscape, though loudly and lengthily eulogized, fails to materialize. What it comes down to is not so much a question of the author's choice of subject matter as a seemingly involuntary mechanism of psychic compartmentalization. As with the painters' careful segregation of foreground and background, there simply seems to be in early Canadian writers a reluctance to view the human element *in actual contact with* the inhuman one, whatever their chosen genre or even their own conscious intentions might demand.

This leads to a number of different problems. If, on the one hand, the 'real' landscape is avoided, since few writers are as capable as Grove of filling the gap with a credible landscape of their own imagining, there is often a disconcerting sense of 'placelessness' in even ostensibly realistic writing which detracts from its effectiveness considerably. Lacking the background, there is no matrix, no larger structure, no 'intellectual or imaginative framework,' as Dick Harrison puts it, to give definition to the events that are reported: 'Lizzie McFadden's diary is typical of pioneer accounts in that things seem to happen to her in a kind of vacuum in the new land' (B173). If, on the other hand, the 'real' landscape *is* overtly confronted the writer often experiences great difficulty bringing man (even symbolically) into any sort of viable relation with it. In this sense, the practice of many late-nineteenth-century 'nature' writers, as paradoxical as it may sound, is actually a simple inversion of the explorers' practice of ignoring the scenery almost entirely. Again this can have unfortunate results. There is patently nothing wrong with taking nature, in and by itself, as a literary subject, but when the writer claims to be concerned quite specifically with man-*in*-nature and then *fails to place him there* there is obviously an ambivalence, an unconfronted fear, underlying his whole vision. Such a split between intention and performance is by no means rare in Canadian writing. The poet Archibald Lampman was a prime example. 'He pretended to judge writers by their knowledge of the human heart and literary works by their power to create a living world of living people,' says W.E. Collin. But if 'we come to his own work with those same criteria, what power, what knowledge do we find? "The human" is singularly absent' (64). Similarly, although Charles G.D. Roberts claimed explicitly that the point of his stories was to demonstrate the moral and spiritual relevance of animal experience to man, a tangible sense of anxiety pervades his writing whenever it is necessary to introduce human characters, good *or* bad, into the wild kingdom. These writers did not avoid nature, but they *did* avoid, as much as the Lizzie McFaddens, the relation between nature and man. *Both* responses comprise a kind of evasive manoeuvre.

CONVENTIONALIZATION

Despite its *relative* paucity there are, to be sure, many examples of landscape description in the Canadian corpus that escape falling into either of these extremes. A second strategy often employed by writers to distance themselves from the natural world entails the transformation of the wilderness, by superimposing prefabricated conventions on the world of natural fact, into something entirely different and, while still 'formally' exotic, more comprehensible. Most attempts to capture in words the impact of the Canadian landscape during the nineteenth century tend to be overwhelmingly 'literary,' slavishly imitative of models approved by Britain's late-eighteenth-century cult of sensibility and, to a lesser extent, later romantic canons. Many of these essays are so far from experienced reality as to make one suspect that the writers did not 'see' the unruly element at all; what they saw was what they expected and wished to see: reassuringly familiar 'compositions' in the picturesque or sublime style. The conventionalization process, a major mode (although with some variation in idiom[6]) until the mid-twentieth century, consequently offered what was essentially another means of avoiding real confrontation.

This response may be detected even among the early explorers. Most of their narratives, as we might expect, tend to be predominantly pragmatic and circumstantial in tone, but when some particularly striking scene catches their attention it is to the conventional literary models that they usually turn:

I found the country almost inaccessible, by reason of masses of rock, which were scattered in all directions: some were as large as houses, and lay as if they had been first thrown into the air, and then suffered to fall into their present posture. By a circuitous route, I at last ascended the mountain, from one side of which they had fallen; the whole body was fractured, and separated by large chasms. In some places, parts of the mountains, of half an acre surface, were raised above the general level. It was a scene for the warfare of the Titans, or for that of Milton's angels. (Alexander Henry 61)

This last is one of the more admirable passages of its type. The diction, while conventional, is vigorous and suited in tone to the scene under consideration. All too often the image evoked, even if it escapes the facile artificiality of Galt's 'primeval forest ... like the arborous wall of Paradise,' has more in common with the contrived gothic fantasy of Salvator Rosa's Italian alpine scenes than with the more ponderous grandeur of Canadian mountainscapes. Furthermore, the reliance on conventional diction often prevented viewers from dealing adequately with natural features not specifically enshrined by current vogues. Mackenzie, as noted, tends to ignore the landscape entirely – with one significant exception. When he reaches the park belt of northern Manitoba he becomes suddenly and effusively preoccupied with the aesthetic qualities of the region. Why? As Dick Harrison observes, 'from the terms he uses, "romantic," "ravishing," "wood," "lawn," "stately forests," terms which might have come from an eighteenth-century topographical poem, it is clear that [this particular] scene lends itself to familiar conventions of landscape description. It is therefore easier to see, respond to, and record' (E5).

Unfortunately, in the experience of early visitors to Canada this congruence between language and landscape is rare. In many cases the conditioned vision actually limits rather than merely shapes the response. Confronted with an unconventional landscape the traveller either doesn't pay any attention to it or reacts with repugnance. William Keating, whose *Narrative* is both more concerned with scenery than was common in travel literature of the period *and* substantially more conventional in tone, not only dismisses the prairie out of hand for its unfashionable monotony ('The flatness of surface that almost universally prevails throughout the valley of the Red River, may be regarded as a defect in its natural character' 140) but proves able to appreciate waterfalls *only* to the extent that they approximate the romantic ideal:

The characters which we admire in the scenery of the Winnipeek, are the immense volume of waters, the extreme rapidity of the current, the great variety of form which the cascades and falls present, and the incomparable wildness of the rocky scenery which produces these falls, and which contrasts by its gloom, its immoveable and unchangeable features, with the bright dazzling effect of the silvery sheet of water, passing from a smooth and unruffled expanse, to a broken and foaming cataract. It is in the effect of the rocky bed of the Winnipeek, that its numerous falls surpass all others which we have seen; the cataract of Niagara, which far exceeds them in volume, is uniform and monotonous in comparison; the horizontal ledges of secondary rocks of the latter are as far inferior in picturesque effect to the dark water-worn granite and sienite of the former, as the height of the bluffs at Niagara exceeds that of the rocky banks of the Winnipeek. (141)

The sheer size of features in the Canadian landscape, rather than adding to the sublimity, was obviously felt to be a negative feature.

The difficulties of achieving verisimilitude with the imported diction was not a problem that bothered, or even occurred to, the majority of writers at the time. Among the poets in particular, verisimilitude was not in any case considered a significant criterion, according to the forms and traditions (such as the popular pastoral mode) in which they attempted to work. Most prose writers too, limited as they were in their actual confrontations with the wilderness, were not likely aware of the discrepancy between idiom and actuality. Nor, despite vestigial gropings toward realism in Europe, is this indifference necessarily a sign that they were either out of date or irredeemably 'provincial'; one must be careful not to let hindsight influence one's judgment. The fact is, even in Europe, as Erich Auerbach points out, experiments with the realistic mode were still tentative: 'Until toward the end of the nineteenth century the most important works which undertook to treat contemporary social subjects seriously at all still remained in the genres of semi-fantasy or of idyl or at least in the narrow realm of the local.'[7] It seems unreasonable, considering this historical context, to expect to find any significant degree of realism in Canada. In Canada, moreover, the use of conventions to structure experience would seem to be further justified by the extent to which so much of the land was in *fact*, not just in imagination, an amorphous mass inherently resistant to both humanization and aesthetic ordering. The protagonist in Duncan Campbell Scott's story 'Vengeance Is Mine,' for instance, characterizes his northern environment as almost mythically formless: 'the land, which had risen without violence, pressed from beneath the surface of the waters ... extended on all sides, the mere essential earth without the form of hill or valley' (A87). It may easily be argued that such a setting not only invites but demands some sort of extrinsic definition. Notwithstanding these objections, it's still possible to claim that at least some of the problems posed by nineteenth-century Canadian literature were, in fact, rooted quite specifically in its mimetic dimension – or lack of it.

One important consideration is the extent to which excessive conventionalization delimits not only the literary expression but the observer's actual ability to come to terms with his environment. The ramifications of this phenomenon go far deeper than questions of 'taste,' of having one's capacity to 'appreciate' native scenery undermined. Even if we refrain from using twentieth-century standards of self-validating realism, it seems obvious that the wilful confounding of fact and fantasy, when the latter is imposed upon rather than emerging from the former, can, especially in a colonial setting, be culturally debilitating, even dangerous. In the first place there is the clichéed but nonetheless valid objection that reliance on an imported idiom is bound to militate against the development of a more authentic native voice. More important, there is also the problem of its immediate effect on communal morale. As Dick Harrison (quoting Marshall McLuhan) points out, the literary response, inasmuch as it forms and reinforces the personal response, may actually hamper the individual colonist's process of adaptation by '"blanket[ing] perception and suppress[ing] awareness ... indispensable to survival"' (E162). Even if one concedes that a literature need not be 'realistic' in any formal sense, one would surely wish to claim that a major function of art is to provide models whereby its auditors may better comprehend their environment. If a given literature actually militates against such a comprehension it is hard not to see this as a practical drawback if not an aesthetic flaw. Consider the following quotation from H.Y. Hind's *Report on the Exploration of the Country between Lake Superior and the Red River Settlement.*

It must be seen at sunrise, when the vast plain suddenly flashes with rose-coloured light, as the first rays of the sun sparkle in the dew on the long rich grass ... It must be seen at noon-day, when refraction swells into the forms of distant hill ranges the ancient beaches ... when each willow bush is magnified into a grove, each far distant clump of aspens, not seen before, into wide forests, and the outline of wooded river banks, far beyond unassisted vision, rise into view. It must be seen at sunset ... [with its] colours blending and separating with the gentle roll of the long grass, seemingly magnified towards the horizon into the distant heaving swell of a parti-coloured sea. It must be seen, too, by moonlight, when the summits of the low green grass waves are tipped with silver ... Finally, it must be seen at night, when the distant prairies are in a blaze, thirty, fifty, or seventy miles away; when the fire reaches clumps of aspen, and the forked tips of the flames magnified by refraction, flash and quiver in the horizon, and the reflected light from rolling clouds of smoke above tell of the havoc which is raging below. (194-5)

The image evoked here is a stunning one, but what use will this glowing rhetoric serve when the colonist has to confront the *unmediated* reality of a prairie fire, not glinting poetically on the nighttime horizon but actually bearing down on his house? Is it likely that he will be psychologically prepared for the pioneer experience if the only expectations he has are based on almost wholly artificial renditions such as this? When W.A. Fraser speaks in the *Canadian Magazine* (1899) of 'God's own garden' and assures the prospective westward traveller that when he reaches the prairies he will 'roll down those jewelled hills, all set with ruby, and amethyst, and pearl flowers, like a boy' (158), are we not justified in feeling that he is betraying both his subject and his reader? Such set-pieces, as Wallace Stegner remarks of western memoirs he has read, hardly give one much of an idea of – or prepare one for – 'how it feels to ride sixty or eighty miles on a freezing and exhausted pony, or how cold thirty below is when a fifty-mile wind is driving it into your face, or how demoralizing it is to be lost in a freezing fog where north, south, east, west, even up and down, swim and shift before the slitted and frost-stuck eyes' (138).

One may, of course, hold to a hermetic definition of literature, repudiating practical considerations as proper criteria for gauging its worth. Even if we limit our discussion to the purely aesthetic effects, however, the tendency to conventionalization may still be seen as having been a negative influence in Canada. Part of the problem was simply a failure on the part of early writers to achieve an adequate integration of their borrowed ingredients. As A.J.M. Smith says of Charles Mair, 'his verse suffers from the load of poetic diction carried over from his reading of the popular English and American poets – Byron, Tennyson, Poe, and Bryant – and it is very uneven in quality' (A9). More serious is the inability of the superimposed conventions to 'contain' or 'subdue' satisfactorily the reality to which they are applied. If the poems or romances were *purely* literary performances, no discrepancy need ever have arisen, but because these writers – out of avowed patriotism – tried to cut and tailor Canadian experience to fit imported moulds, they ran the constant danger that the rude face of the wilderness would suddenly thrust itself into their polished gardens. As a result, much nineteenth-century Canadian writing, and especially poetry, has a kind of strained undercurrent, visible in sudden disconcerting glimpses or equally disquieting ambiguities of tone, that accords ill with its decorous surface. As Northrop Frye points out, even in the most conventional of our nineteenth-century poets 'there are likely to be the most startling flashes of menace and fear. A placid poem of Charles G.D. Roberts about mowing is suddenly punctuated by the line "The crying knives glide on; the green swath lies"' (C95). Whatever the author's intent, such outbursts belie the ostensibly bucolic mood of the landscape on which he meditates.

A number of critics have claimed that the major source of such tension in at least the Confederation poets was the irreconcilability of different aspects of their borrowings, and particularly of 'the romantic Christian world spirit and the Darwinian germ of life' (Djwa A140). One might speculate, however, that Canadian concern with the ethical problems posed by Darwinian theory signalled a more than merely academic interest; that both the attempt by such poets as Lampman and Scott to transcend the Darwinian world by means of a more positive romantic world vision *and* their inability to do so with any consistency were rooted in the fact that they perceived something in Canadian nature that gave an uncomfortable immediacy to the most disturbing aspects of the amoral universe implied by Darwin. It was largely *because* of this immediacy that the conventions in which they sought to take refuge from their intimations of vulnerability proved inadequate; they were simply not 'real' enough to dominate the greater vigour of the very real objects of their fear. When something like this happens we are no longer talking merely of a lack of accord between literary expression and external reality, but of a chasm splitting apart different aspects of the writer's own vision. The conventionalization process was, in a sense, both a consequence and a cause of this chasm.

We see this problem in its most extreme form in the writing of Susanna Moodie, a woman who, when it came to expressing her perceptions of the Canadian landscape, was at once extremely 'literary' and (more covertly) authentically personal. Perhaps, though, this is a little misleading. To a great extent, if we judge by her books, Mrs Moodie avoided looking too hard or too often at nature in the broader sense at all. The few panoramic views confronted in *Roughing It in the Bush* are typically obscured by the intensity of her emotional response: 'The spectacle floated dimly on my sight – my eyes were blinded with tears – blinded by the excess of beauty' (22); 'words are perfectly inadequate to describe the impression it made upon my mind – the emotions it produced. The only homage I was capable of offering at such a shrine was tears' (29). When she does attempt landscape description, however, it is always in pre-eminently conventional terms. At the same time, her failure to dominate her language (the fluctuating narrative tone, the unevenness of the writing, the abrupt transitions between high and low styles; see McCarthy, especially 94) demonstrates vividly the strength of affect associated with such confrontations. The result is not a happy one. Moodie's determined attempt to control her response – to minimize her sense of menace – by clinging to safe, consoling, Wordsworthian conventions is unable to withstand the impact of the landscape itself. As Margaret Atwood points out, 'Again and again we find her gazing at the sublime natural goings-on in the misty distance – sunsets, mountains, spectacular views – only to be brought up short by disagreeable things in her immediate foreground, such as bugs, swamps, tree roots and other immigrants. Nature the Sublime can be approached but never reached, and Nature the Divine Mother hardly functions at all' (F51). Moodie, in other words, is totally incapable of sustaining either the selective focus or the degree of detachment her imported idiom assumes.

The question arises as to what Susanna Moodie's experience implies for the Canadian experience as a whole. Two points, I think, must be borne in mind. Firstly, if we look closely at *Roughing It in the Bush* it seems obvious that the failure of the conventional response does indeed signal something more serious than the kind of relatively minor stylistic problems we have imputed to the poetry of the period. Indeed, in Moodie's writing the discrepancy between language and vision seems above all to reflect a serious inbuilt ambivalence, a kind of psychic dislocation so deep and so anxiety-ridden that the cumulative effect of the book, going far beyond occasional unevenness, is almost wholly one of confusion and despair. Secondly, if we examine other nineteenth-century literary productions it becomes apparent that Moodie's response, although perhaps more extreme than most, was in many ways typical of her contemporaries. In truth – and this is the crux of conventionalization – we would seem to be dealing here not merely with a typical case of colonial cultural dependency, soon outgrown, but with a kind of self-perpetuating 'double bind' or vicious cycle spawning conceptual problems that reverberate far beyond the level simply of literary expression or style. Even aside from the predictable influence of nostalgia, the average immigrant typically finds the familiar idiom of 'home' all the more attractive as a means of escaping from or attempting to transform his unmediated vision. Unfortunately, this withdrawal in itself exacerbates his sense of alienation.

The fact is that Wordsworthian diction, with its implications of a beautiful, benevolent nature, could only emphasize by contrast the harsh and threatening aspects of Canada. The more exquisitely enamelled the face of the wilderness is made to appear, the more conscious one becomes of the possibility that violence lurks just below the surface. As a result, while the imported models *seem* to offer the observer a refuge, the very act of employing the romantic idiom tends to accentuate the more problematic aspects of the experience. As William Gairdner describes it, 'the whole Shaftesburian tradition of innate sensibility in the 18th century, and the later romantic canon stimulated by Wordsworth and his definition of poetry as "the spontaneous overflow of powerful feeling"' leads to an association of *feeling* (defined as 'a means of understanding more comprehensive than reason') with *intelligence* itself. Thus, 'to feel strongly [is] to comprehend, to "grasp the significance of" ... something. And what significance? Why, the ultimate significance, the essence, which, since it is particular in every case, can only be grasped by complete identification of the perceiver with the perceived' (39). Paradoxically, then, the very convention seized upon by writers such as Moodie to distance them from an unpleasant reality insists upon a more intense empathy with the very element they wished to avoid. (The same problem arises with later conventions, like the American-derived frontier ideology that dominated Canadian thought in the 1920s and 1930s, discussed below.) It's hardly surprising, therefore, that the attempt to conventionalize the landscape produced disquieting undertones in literature. Indeed, the image of nature that emerges from much nineteenth-century Canadian writing is similar to that evoked by Anna Jameson's beautiful island:

We breakfasted on an island almost covered with flowers, some gorgeous, and strange, and unknown, and others sweet and familiar ...

[Later] Old Solomon asked me once or twice how I felt; and I thought his anxiety for my health was caused by the rain; but no: – he told me that on the island where we had dined he had observed a great quantity of a certain plant which, if only touched, causes a dreadful eruption and ulcer all over the body. I asked why he had not shown it to me and warned me against it? and he assured me that such warning would only have increased the danger, for when there is any knowledge or apprehension of it existing in the mind, the very air blowing from it sometimes infects the frame. (163-4)

DOMESTICATION

Yet another avoidance strategy involves an attempt, largely by means of a selective focus, to dominate the landscape symbolically by humanizing it. In this mode nature is usually treated somewhat more realistically (side-stepping the problems of conventionalization) but instead of dwelling on its exotic or dangerous features the writer limits his attention specifically to those aspects that are amenable to human control and relevant to human culture.

At its most basic, domestication may simply comprise a kind of counting over of unassimilated features in the environment. This is certainly the tack taken in most of the early travel narratives, with their enumerations and measurements, their plethora of scientific facts and figures, their deliberate de-emphasis of 'scenery' in favour of an evaluation of economic potential. Henry Ellis's (1746-7) and James Isham's (1743-9) observations on Hudson Bay, for instance, are simply compilations of hard data: notes on the variety and distribution of vegetation and wildlife, geographic observations, meteorological information. Later explorers tend to be somewhat more discursive, but the pragmatic intent still dominates their journals and reports. 'The soil is rich and deep, and [there is] much vegetable mould from the annual decay of the leaves of the Forest Trees, and the Grass of the Meadows,' observes David Thompson of the prairies early in the nineteenth century. 'Civilization will no doubt extend over these low hills; they are well adapted for raising of cattle; and when the wolves are destroyed, also for sheep' (A98).

Such an approach is not unexpected in view of the practical motives behind such expeditions. Compared to the overt romanticism and stylistic extravagance common to so much American travel literature of similar vintage, however, the restraint and factual emphasis seem at least mildly anomalous. And when one notes that a strikingly similar approach can be observed not only in documentary writing but in many works of more explicit literary intent, it seems plausible to speculate that a 'domestic' perspective, like the other strategies discussed, derives from and reflects on certain peculiarities of the Canadian response. To domesticate is admittedly not necessarily to evade, of course. If we examine the phenomenon more closely, and with careful attention to the Canadian context, we will see that in practice symbolic domestication is typically attended by as much strain as the conventionalization process.

Straddling the line between the literary and the pragmatic, Catharine Parr Traill offers a particularly instructive demonstration of this strategy in *The Backwoods of Canada* and *The Canadian Settler's Guide*. In both books (though more confidently in the second) the author's determination not to be depressed or intimidated by her circumstances effects an apparent transformation of the wilderness into a kitchen garden. Despite her ostensible control over her 'fictional' universe, however, it is here – far more than in any of the travel narratives – that we catch a glimpse of the uncertainties that those interminable catalogues of facts favoured by our explorers may perhaps hide. Notwithstanding Traill's expressed didactic intent, we get the strong impression that one of the major functions of such chapters as 'Canadian Wild Flowers' is to assert and reinforce, almost ritualistically, her feelings of ease and familiarity with the landscape she wishes to dominate by *cutting nature down to size*. This is surely domestication par excellence. It seems useful, therefore, to consider Traill's technique in some detail.

Two things are involved here, relating respectively to perception (what one 'sees') and cognition (how one assimilates it). On the simplest level Traill's preference for the near and the small is merely a functional equivalent to the foreshortened focus preferred by so many Canadian landscape painters and, as such, finds parallels in the work of many other Canadian writers. When A.J.M. Smith comments that 'the best passages of Mair's poems afford some delightfully precise close-ups of the Canadian woodlands and their flowers, animals, and insects ... [which] reveal in [him] an eye for the tiny realities of nature that many better poets might envy' (A9), he implies that this poet's facility with the short view is an idiosyncratic feature. The truth is, however, the relative confidence and competence demonstrated by Mair when working in what is essentially a lapidary mode is a characteristic shared by numerous of his literary colleagues. As Frye points out, 'Nature in Canadian poetry ... has little of the vagueness of great open spaces in it: that is very seldom material that the imagination can use. One finds rather an intent and closely focussed vision' (C93). Traill's emphasis on the foreground is therefore no more than predictable.

Going beyond perspective to her specific choice of, and attitude toward, her subject matter, however, it is notable that Traill concentrates almost exclusively not merely on what is *close* but on what is *safe*: those aspects of nature that can be controlled, manipulated, *used*. Such a narrowing of the imaginative range, especially when we consider that she is purportedly describing life in the wilderness, would seem to reveal something more than simply a dislike for the unaesthetic 'vagueness of open spaces.' Here, in fact, we get clear inklings of the covert message almost always carried by the domestication strategy in Canadian literature. Not only do Traill's botanical preoccupations save her from having to contemplate the larger and more unmanageable aspects of her environment, but her assumed proprietary relationship also provides a means of mitigating – indeed, of denying altogether – the more disturbing because 'irrational' aspects of that initial unmediated reaction to the wilderness. It is thus the *absence* of any sign of the pioneer's quite natural anxiety vis-à-vis his environment that is one of the most significant features of Traill's work, inasmuch as it violates our expectations. 'Imagine their first confrontations with such immense solitude!' says Gairdner. 'Men who had been used to seeing fences, a pathway, a clearing, now saw only solid virgin forest. The associations are easy, for the forest hid within it wild, dangerous animals ... Thus, the backwoods came to equal not only resistance to cultivation because of its stumps, weeds, and the beasts which ate the crops, but more importantly because of resistance to peace of mind, silence, darkness, and the threat of death' (36-7). In the face of such associations it's hardly surprising that Canadians in imaging nature should (in Gairdner's words) look 'to their fears before they looked to their need for beauty' (37). But this predictable reaction to a hostile environment is exactly what we *don't* find in Traill's memoirs. Far from 'looking to her fears,' she quite determinedly looks *away* from them. She comments blandly on the pioneers' obsession with axework, but 'never once suggests that these men wage war against nature because, having been transplanted from an ancient, vertical class culture in which all immediate surroundings bore the imprint of human life, they quite naturally reacted against the overwhelming emptiness of the Canadian wilds' (Gairdner 36) – because, in other words, they were simply *afraid* of the forest. The domestication strategy proved attractive to writers like Traill precisely because it allowed them to ignore not only the *objects* that were alien and threatening but also all those darker and more problematic *feelings* that so devastatingly belied the response they thought the environment *should* evoke in a normal, healthy observer.

Are we, however, not going too far in imputing to Traill this kind of disguised paranoia? As Clara Thomas notes in an introduction to *The Backwoods of Canada*, 'In Mrs. Traill's writing, sturdy adaptability to the emigrant's condition, acceptance of the present, and optimism for the future dominate' (c7): may we not simply accept these qualities at face value? Despite the contrast between the sunny tone of this book and Susanna Moodie's neurotic confusions, we would be misled if we were to accept an over-simplified view of Traill. For one thing, the cheerful and homely kitchen-garden image of nature is not the only possibility we are allowed to consider in *The Backwoods of Canada* – although it is the final one. As a matter of fact, a close reading hints at a *progression* in attitude with interesting implications for popular impressions of Traill's untroubled, commonsensical vision.

In the earlier chapters Traill's reaction to the landscape seems as conventional and as conventionally expressed as her sister Susanna's:

Sometimes the high lands are suddenly enveloped in dense clouds of mist, which are in constant motion, rolling along in shadowy billows, now tinted with rosy light, now white and fleecy, or bright as silver, as they catch the sunbeams. So rapid are the changes that take place on this fog-bank that perhaps the next time I raise my eyes I behold the scene changed as if by magic. The misty curtain is slowly drawn up, as if by invisible hands, and the wild, wooded mountains partially revealed, with their bold, rocky shores and sweeping bays. At other times the vapoury volume, dividing, moves along the valleys and deep ravines like lofty pillars of smoke, or hangs in snowy draperies among the dark forest pines. (16)

Even at this early stage, however, the author finds the impact of nature a little too overwhelming for comfort: 'Though I cannot but dwell with feelings of wonder and admiration on the majesty and power of this mighty river, I begin to grow weary of its immensity, and long for a nearer view of the shore; but at present we see nothing more than long lines of pine-clad hills ... huge mountains divested of verdure bound our view' (17). The closer she comes to the wilderness, the less able she is to maintain her conventional stance, and with her arrival at the Peterborough district which is to be her home the vision splits apart entirely. On the one hand, overlooking the panoramic landscape from a distance, she offers a generalized picture in the most glowing terms imaginable: 'These plains form a beautiful natural park, finely diversified with hill and dale, covered with a lovely green sward, enamelled with a variety of the most exquisite flowers, and planted, as if by Nature's own hand, with groups of feathery pines, oaks, balsams, poplars, and silver birches' (42). In stark contrast, she describes her actual entrance into this 'parkland' in terms reminiscent of nightmare:

my husband bought a passage in the skiff as I was unable to walk any farther. An angry, growling consent was extorted from the surly Charon, and we hastily entered the frail bark, which seemed hardly calculated to convey us in safety to the opposite shore. I could not help indulging in a feeling of indescribable fear as I listened to the torrent of profane invective that burst forth continually from the lips of the boatman. Once or twice we were in danger of being overset by the boughs of the pines and cedars which had fallen into the water near the banks. Right glad was I when we reached the opposite shores; but here a new trouble arose: there was yet more untracked wood to cross ... At the distance of every few yards our path was obstructed by fallen trees, mostly hemlock, spruce, or cedar, the branches of which are so thickly interwoven that it is scarcely possible to separate them, or force a passage through the tangled thicket which they form. (39)

Significantly, it is only *after* the shock of this confrontation that Traill takes refuge in the cheerful, short-range, domesticated view of the wilderness that dominates the tone of the rest of the book. It seems likely that she healed the disconcertingly divided vision in the only way possible: by being careful henceforth not to 'see' too much.

It is precisely because the inconsistencies in Traill's vision reveal her so vividly as an evolving rather than a static personality that *The Backwoods of Canada* is such an interesting document. Indeed, this young woman's encounter with the wilderness and subsequent change of attitude in many ways provides a paradigm for the national experience. In the first place, the resort to domestication is always a secondary effect, subsequent to an initial shock of recognition. Secondly, the 'kitchen garden' is *created*, by an act of will, rather than merely perceived. These facts add a degree of psychological complexity to the Canadian vision at an early stage, notwithstanding its apparent 'typically colonial' crudeness. This unrecognized substratum has important consequences for literary developments later on. More important for the present discussion, however, Traill's method of accommodating the wilderness demonstrates a crucial difference between the Canadian version of 'domestication' and what is more generally implied by that term. A useful comparison is offered by the Robinson Crusoe story, a prototype for the journey into the wilderness that catalyses self-discovery. MacLulich claims that Traill's experience diverges from the original fable most significantly in so far as, rather than returning home in the end, she (unlike Mrs Moodie, the inflexible sister who clings to inappropriate behaviour and expectations) succeeds in turning the place of exile into a *new* home, and thus 'lives happily ever after' (A125). A more important distinction between the European (and American) version of this tale and the Canadian one, though, lies in the fact that the true Crusoe figure literally *transforms* his environment through his industry and ingenuity while the Canadian settler, whether Traill or Moodie, is incapable of effecting any such change (the wilderness is impervious to his most determined depredations; the forest grows back as fast as he can cut it down); he therefore has the alternatives only of running away (like Moodie) or of transforming *himself*.

This last point underlines the reason why the wishful insistence upon a humanized nature, aside from inviting a rather too facile literary response to experience, often causes a degree of anxiety even beyond that spawned by the conventionalization process. Unless one believes in the individual's power, at least potentially, to dominate nature (which the Canadian apparently has great difficulty with), one can achieve only the merest *illusion* of control. This particular illusion, furthermore, to a much greater extent than the more distanced 'poetic' stance, is in constant danger of being undermined by the demonstrable recalcitrance of reality. Indeed, the position implied by the 'kitchen garden' view of the world is often not even symbolically convincing. In spite of Ricou's assertion of the symbolic house on the prairie as a triumph of human will ('The urge to erect something in the prairie emptiness, of no matter what material – bricks, or paint, or words – is the urge of man to assert his presence in a forbidding land. The building of a vertical equivalent to man, it seems, allows man to take the measure of his achievement, to insist on his determination to endure.' B8), the fact is that at any distance at all such fragile vertical gestures are inevitably dwarfed by the horizontal immensity of the land in much the same way that horizontal gestures, like roads and railways, are so easily dwarfed in landscape paintings by Canada's vertical grandeur.[8] For another thing, the position is not really an emotionally satisfactory one either. If nature is at best indifferent and at worst overtly hostile, the rural landscape, connoting as it does that phase of man's development when he is most dependent on the beneficence of the inhuman, most vulnerable to the incalculable accidents of geography and climate, can surely offer small solace. Given the inescapable physical facts of a country like Canada, the more important the 'land' is perceived to be – the stronger the hold of the pastoral myth – the more covert anxiety the juxtaposition between man and nature is bound to generate.

This is possibly the reason that the pastoral mode reveals even more ambiguity in Quebec, where the rural idyll was for almost two centuries enshrined not merely as a secular myth but as a sacred trust enjoined upon an entire culture. As early as *Maria Chapdelaine* the landscape seems to be compulsively associated with pain and frustration, the forest evoking, in Beverly Rasporich's words, 'a vague Thanatos yearning towards self-obliteration' (454). Even when the conscious intent of the author is celebratory, odd cross-currents persist. Antoine Gérin-Lajoie's *Jean Rivard, le défricheur* (one of the earlier *romans du terroir*), while explicitly formulated 'to convince nineteenth-century readers that the survival of Québec depended upon the domesticating, if not the civilizing, of nature' (Blodgett A177) betrays a certain uneasiness about the beneficence of the supposed '*paradis terrestre*' when, in a dream, the protagonist images his endeavour in terms suggesting a military expedition. Man and nature, it would seem, are in Canada most easily imaged at odds. This propensity belies entirely the traditional mediating function of the pastoral. What is worse, it also undercuts the capacity of the domestic strategy to function effectively as an evasive manoeuvre. As Barbara Thompson Godard suggests in her discussion of Ringuet's *Trente arpents*, while the literary emphasis on a (real or symbolic) process of domestication might serve to distract the pioneer temporarily from the encompassing menace of the wilderness, there is a covert but strong anti-pastoral bias embedded in the Canadian communal vision that in the long run must militate against any attempt to idealize the rural.

Ringuet has more clearly drawn the lesson to be found in all the 'realistic' novels of the land, behind Ostenso's *Wild Geese* as well as the trilogy of Germaine Guèvremont. In trying to possess the land as is necessary for civilizing it, the farmer or woodsman has given himself utterly into the hands of nature: he has placed himself on a turning wheel of the seasons, which moves down to decay and death annually even as it moves up to birth. Writers until then had confidently believed in a Christian God immanent in this nature and dominating it as well, mitigating this effect and providing a promise of life and communion on another plane. Ringuet and Grove [in such novels as *Fruits of the Earth*] indicate that this cult of the land has all along been that of a primitive and vengeful god. (234-5)

The unadmitted but omnipresent threat suggested by this description perhaps explains why in Canada even an ostensibly domesticated nature is rarely conceived in traditional terms of maternal warmth and fertility. Instead, Canadian nature, so often associated with images of violence and cruelty, tends to be incarnated in such exaggeratedly masculine personae as the monstrous antagonist of Martha Ostenso's *Wild Geese*: Caleb Gare, a man who is explicitly characterized as 'a spiritual counterpart of the land, as harsh, as demanding, as tyrannical as the very soil from which he drew his existence' (33). This is a far cry from 'Mother Nature'! – a fact that will prove to have important ramifications for later developments in the characteristic Canadian vision. Notwithstanding such problematic associations, symbolic domestication, along with the simpler ploys of avoidance and conventionalization, continued to structure the Canadian's perception of, and relationship with, the landscape throughout the nineteenth century and beyond.

NOTES

1 See, for instance, Richard Ruland, *America in Modern European Literature: From Image to Metaphor* (NYU 1976).
2 To a large extent, Cooper's *The Pioneers*, with its vivid recreation of a pigeon shoot and its continual lament for the lost trees, is a diatribe against this phenomenon, rather than a celebration of frontier life.
3 For a full discussion of the brutality and waste entailed by the westward movement, and the paradoxical persistence of romantic expectations in the face of these inimical characteristics, see esp. Arthur K. Moore, *The Frontier Mind* (U. Kentucky 1957).
4 Grainger returned to Canada after his 1908 marriage in England, and settled

permanently in British Columbia, but the book was conceived before he made this commitment; his point of view was that of a footloose young Englishman, adventuring his way around the world.

5 In this respect it is noteworthy that despite his public affectation of an 'intimate love of nature' (Stouck A20), Grove's most *natural* response to the natural environment seems to have been a deeply ingrained sense of alienation. No one, for instance, ever suffered as much bad weather as does the protagonist of the pseudo-autobiography *In Search of Myself*. With provocative implications for his avowed anti-naturalism, the key image offered by this book in illustration of the writer's felt relationship with the landscape is the recurrent one of a man driving through threatening weather down a progressively degenerating road bordered by forest or swamp, apparently unable either to turn around or to surmount the obstacles ahead.

6 See the discussion of the impact of F.J. Turner's wilderness thesis on Canadian thought, below, 50 ff.

7 Auerbach, *Mimesis: The Representation of Reality in Western Literature*, trans. Willard R. Trask (Princeton 1968) 452-3

8 See, for instance, Lucius O'Brien's *Through the Rocky Mountains, a Pass on the Canadian Highway* (1887).

3

The Frontier Antithesis

The question we must address now is *why* the characteristic Canadian patterns of response should be so different from those of our neighbours. While Americans have generally viewed nature as a source of inspiration, natural wisdom, moral health, and so on, Canadian writers seemingly do not even like to look upon the face of the wilderness. How do we account for this divergence? One of the simplest explanations might be geographical. Nature seems more hostile to the Canadian because it *is* more hostile. In response to this possibility Marcia Kline points out, quite plausibly, that the United States contains many equally inclement areas. 'The climate of Upper Canada is fairly cold in the winter – the Great Lakes region averages about twenty degrees [fahrenheit] – but very little of its populated region lies north of the northern part of New York State, Vermont, New Hampshire, or Michigan. Toronto, for example, is on approximately the same latitude as Portland, Maine, and Windsor, across the river from Detroit, is much farther south than that' (15). Despite its initial attractiveness, this argument does not turn out on closer scrutiny to be a particularly convincing one.

For one thing, from the colonist's point of view 'weather' *per se* is not the only, or even the most important, aspect of 'nature' to be taken into consideration. He knows, if we with our supermarkets and 'agribusiness' have forgotten, that in a subsistence existence it is not merely temperature or precipitation or seasonal variation but the physical reality of the land itself – the ease with which it can be penetrated, subdued, cultivated, *humanized* – that is ultimately going to establish the critical controls on his failure or success. One need only recall Robert Beverly's complaint that the garden-like fecundity of the Virginian landscape was so great as to make the settlers slothful and indolent,[1] or even Samuel Purchas's more restrained comments on the natural abundance of New England,[2] and then think of the Canadian Shield with its skimpy topsoil and infinity of rock to realize the relatively great difficulties with which a great many Canadians must have been confronted as soon as they attempted to penetrate any distance into the interior in consequence of the sheer recalcitrance of the terrain. Even if he endured the weather, the Canadian colonist – like the early Nova Scotians of Thomas Raddall's 'A Harp in the Willows' – was as likely as not to discover that his land was finally unfarmable.[3]

Even if we limit ourselves to the single factor of weather, moreover, the case still reveals a number of flaws. Although many of the northern extremities of the United States may challenge the southerly parts of Canada in severity of climate, the American sense of identity, the national mythos, evokes an image drawn from the more temperate regions comprising the geographical bulk of the country. 'With its Mississippi winding into the warm South, and the Western plains sweeping across to the mountains and the promise of California, the American landscape has always provided an escape route from the specific limitations of "home"' (Stouck A9). Secondly, even in cases involving some degree of physical contiguity, generalized comparison can be misleading. Degree of latitude is only one factor in determining climate, and while it is difficult to know exactly what Kline means by the 'Great Lakes region,' one does not have to travel very far inland before the moderating effect of these bodies of water dissipates abruptly. The weather, even in southern Ontario, is just not as homogeneous as Kline's summary implies. Finally, once certain climatic extremes are approached, even a relatively minor difference may be felt in human terms as major – the straw that breaks the camel's back. Certainly the impression one gets from reading such pioneer writers as Moodie and Traill, or visitors like Jameson, is that, regardless of actual, measurable temperature and snowfall, the Canadian winter was *experienced* as unbearably harsh and, especially, long – just as the summer *seemed* to be an eternity of insects and infernal heat. One interesting piece of evidence for a divergence in subjective if not objective conditions north and south of the border is the fact that most of the older houses in small towns in southern Ontario tend to be smug, solid-looking structures in stone and brick, while in northern New York just across the border the majority are frame. One can undoubtedly come up with historical and/or economic explanations for this phenomenon, but inasmuch as architectural styles express more than a merely pragmatic choice one may infer quite a different concept of 'shelter' from a brick house than a wooden one. It would seem that the Canadian settler at least *perceived* nature as being more of a threat than did his neighbour.

The perception of a relatively harsher face of nature also tended to accentuate the problems inherent in the second significant difference between Canada and the United States: the historical contexts that provided a background to the colonization process in the two countries. Even more than physical tools, culturally shaped expectations and patterns of thought, by determining the directions and limitations of psychological adaptability, affect the mode of a man's relationship with the environment (I implied something of this sort above when I noted the possibly detrimental effects of continued reliance on an imported idiom). A 'successful' colonist (defined as one who comes to feel 'at home' in his new circumstances) must be equipped not only with the means to dominate his surroundings physically but also with the capacity to comprehend his experience and either translate it satisfactorily into terms of reference provided by his old environment or transform it into something new but compatible with his previous experience. The tools by which this latter feat is accomplished at least initially are provided by the conceptual vocabulary he brings with him to the new world. And herein lies the difference between the Canadian and the American.

What we're talking about here are *time frames*. Under the influence of the millennial expectations of the seventeenth century, the early American colonist, borrowing concepts from scriptural explication, tended to interpret the empirical environment predominantly in terms of signs or types of supernatural events.[4] In its original usage, a *type*, according to Ursula Brumm, comprised 'the meanings of model, parallel, and prophecy.' Typology thus provided 'a pattern for construing the world's events as leading toward redemption.' In its purest sense, it was a mode of interpreting Old Testament figures and phenomena as shadows or 'umbra' pre-figuring New Testament antitypes, or 'veritas.' In colonial America, however, this mode of thought came to be 'applied unconsciously to new secular situations,' such that, by process of association, the entire world became charged with cosmic significance and every human life was seen as part of a cosmic conflict between the forces of Good and Evil. In particular, the New England Puritans delighted in a typological self-identification with the Israelites in their exodus from Egypt. This conception on the one hand lent them 'the strength and endurance necessary for their trials on the stony soil of New England in the face of the dangers of the wilderness.'[5] On the other hand, the wilderness, in the context of these biblical associations, became 'so surcharged with historic, cultic, and mythical connotations, and so accented theologically and ethically, as to yield in a generalized or abstracted fashion the following four concepts or motifs, which we ... find recurring in various combinations throughout post-biblical history: (a) the wilderness as a moral waste but a potential paradise, (b) the wilderness as a place of testing or even punishment, (c) the wilderness as the experience or occasion of nuptial (covenantal) bliss, and (d) the wilderness as a place of refuge (protection) or contemplation (renewal).'[6] The American colonist thus found ready to hand in his cultural baggage a model of the man/nature relation flexible enough to allow for both positive *and* negative aspects of his response, and dramatic enough to encompass the full extremes of the New World environment.

In contrast, the simplistic Shaftesbury-Wordsworthian image of nature which had come to dominate cultural expectations by the time English Canadians were attempting to come to terms with the wilderness experience was inadequate for comprehending the colonial situation. The impact of nature was too frightening to be seen as potentially benevolent and too immediate to be aesthetically distanced (see Frye, especially B145-56). And since the late-eighteenth, early-nineteenth-century cultural milieu did not offer any appropriate alternative models, the result was that the man/nature relation in Canada became, quite simply, a conceptual impossibility.

Beyond these two fairly obvious differences, the geographical and historical factors also combined in Canada to produce a final cultural difference that in many ways summarizes and exemplifies the basic divergence. Although both countries shared a role as 'frontier' societies, the concept of 'frontier' has had quite different implications in each case.

This has not been generally recognized. Revealing yet another characteristic split between covert and overt response, twentieth-century Canadians in quest of a national identity have made extensive use of the imported American theory of frontier influence. This theory, formulated in classic form in 1893 by Frederick Jackson Turner, a Wisconsin historian, promulgated a view of the west as 'a great crucible, the original melting pot in which the European was stripped down to his vital human essences, these essences then being collected to form a new and better being – the American' (Cross 2). Concomitantly confronted with the demands of a rigorous environment and freed from the constrictions of European civilization, the pioneer would first revert temporarily to savagery, but then he would emerge from his ordeal stronger, healthier, more self-sufficient: an individualist and a democrat. The frontier thus offered what Turner called a 'perennial rebirth'[7]; the colonist went there specifically 'to re-capture that Renaissance condition where each man was potentially able to realize his broadest ambitions' (Stouck A9). Whether this romantic view of the effects of the frontier condition was ever more than a nostalgic fantasy concocted well after the fact has been seriously questioned even with reference to the United States,[8] but there at least, as Arthur K. Moore points out in his examination of the gap between the myth and the reality of settlement in Kentucky (see chapter 2, note 3), the vision has a certain psychological plausibility in that it did provide both a primary model for behaviour and an influential formula for interpreting it retroactively. In Canada, largely because of the relative impotence of the 'garden' myth which played so great a part in developing the American's self-identification with Adam,[9] even the *symbolic* relevance of the frontier is debatable.

The question of relevance did not stop a good many eminent Canadian historians – A.R.M. Lower, A.L. Burt, Walter N. Sage, Frank Underhill among them – from jumping on the 'frontierism' bandwagon, especially during the twenties.[10] These men did not by any means swallow Turner whole,[11] but they did adopt a number of the basic methodological premises implicit in his thesis as a point of departure for interpreting political history. In particular they followed him in addressing themselves not to imperial relations, the traditional concern of the Canadian historian, but to 'the way in which British political institutions and attitudes to politics had been profoundly altered in North America by a different environment' (Berger 147). This perspective inevitably effected a shift in the terms by which the county imaged itself. As Carl Berger notes in his discussion of a series of lectures delivered by John Dafoe at Columbia University in 1933-4 entitled *Canada: An American Nation*, despite their reservations, once historians began to emphasize the common background of the two countries there was a tendency toward a general conflation:

The crucial events in Canadian experience became analogous to decisive episodes in American history: the Rebellion of 1837 in Upper Canada, for example, appeared as an abortive northern version of the Jacksonian assault on privilege. The immediate effect of looking at Canadian history in terms of these identities was to blur the distinctions that had previously been emphasized between a British tradition and American republicanism. Similarly the word 'Americanization' came to connote not deliberate imitation or influence, but similar responses to the American continent and modern industrial life generally. (Berger 148)

As a result of this conceptual reorientation, by the second quarter of the century Canadians had come to define themselves in largely American terms.

The effects of the continental viewpoint were, of course, felt far beyond academic circles. Indeed, the environmentalist emphasis had even greater ramifications at a popular level. An uncritical acceptance of the Turner view of frontier society on the part of the public soon began to bear fruit in terms of changes in mass culture. The most important of these was an 'official' sanctification of nature. Smitten (at least superficially) with America's mythicization of its pioneer forebears, Canadians embraced enthusiastically a romantic cult of primitivistic wilderness-worship that expressed itself in such diverse phenomena as 'the creation of wilderness parks, like Algonquin and Garibaldi ... children's woodcraft camps ... Grey Owl ... the animal stories of Ernest Thompson Seton and Charles G.D. Roberts . the summer cottaging movement, [and] the art of Emily Carr and the group of seven' (Cole 69). The impact of this development was incalculable. Although Turner himself, as it turned out, had only a relatively minor long-run influence on Canadian historiography, assumptions spawned by the frontier thesis about the character of the Canadian people were, seemingly, assimilated beyond extrication into the national self-consciousness. As a result, the environmental perspective *still* exerts a disproportionate influence on Canadian thinking.[12] Marcia Kline, for instance, while departing substantially from earlier interpretations of the cultural implications of the relationship between the frontier phenomenon and Canadian history still accepts the fundamental *concept* as relevant. While historians like Underhill tended to use the frontier ideology to emphasize 'the similarity of Canadian and American development and ... the difference between European and North American political patterns' (Cross 3), Kline, comparing the writings of Moodie and Traill with a similar description of life in the Michigan settlements (*A New Home – Who'll Follow?*, by Caroline Kirkland), uses it to explain a point of *departure* in Canadian and American attitudes toward nature: 'the Kirklands' reaction to settlement life sounds, initially, every bit as negative as the Canadians',' says Kline, but the former acknowledge a 'compensating power of the wilderness' which the latter do not (32-3, 34). She does *not*, however, question the hypothesis that the frontier actually functions in essentially the way Turner claims, in Canada as in the United States, differing from Underhill *et al.* only in putting forth the idea that the Turner effect was viewed differently in Canada; that here, for political reasons, it was seen as a negative effect rather than a positive one:

The quality that Mrs. Kirkland praises as the compensating power of the wilderness is exactly the same quality of forest life that Mrs. Moodie terms ultra republicanism – and categorically rejects. The two women both see the trials and disadvantages of settlement life, and neither minimizes them in her book. But in those conditions, Mrs. Moodie sees only the discontinuity of accepted civilized patterns of life. Mrs. Kirkland, however, seeing beyond the discontinuity, strikes a note that is reminiscent of the essays in *The Home Book of the Picturesque*: obviously her point, relative to the essayists, is toned down considerably, but what they both have in common is the idea that the wilderness that was so abundant in America has some special ability to gratify needs, inherent in human nature, that civilization does not have. (34-5)

There is a problem here. The question that should be asked is not whether the democratization process effected by the wilderness was viewed as positive or negative by Canadians, but whether the Turner scenario accurately reflects the historical situation in this country at all. Certainly the startling discrepancy that emerges when we set the loud public protestations of woodsiness against more covert aspects of communal response suggests that the frontier perspective may, notwithstanding its apparent popularity, ultimately be a distorting one. The truth is, although numerous Canadian writers and artists have gone out of their way to tout the northern wilderness as a sanctuary from the 'decadent and sterile values of the "South"' (Mitcham B35), in most cases, at the level of symbol anyway, the wilderness they actually *portray* seems monstrous rather than inviting. If we look more closely, in fact, it would seem that while the intentional and especially the rhetorical levels of such productions are dominated by a specifically American vision – a B-movie image of Canada as 'God's country,' a primitive snow-covered wilderness where one goes to find moral, physical, and spiritual rejuvenation (see Pierre Berton's *Hollywood's*

Canada) – the more spontaneous elements, from modes of composition to iconography, tend to communicate something quite different.

This phenomenon – a kind of normalized duplicity – is simply a later version of the uneasy juxtaposition of Wordsworthian idiom with 'Darwinian' experience. Because it is *our* idiom, however, it's difficult for us to see the discrepancies it entails. If we penetrate below the surface similarities, there doesn't really seem to be much danger (or possibility) of the Canadian *turning into* an American, but at the same time we seem to be afflicted with an Americanized self-consciousness. At a 1976 conference in Banff, Alberta called 'Crossing Frontiers,' the papers presented made it clear that the Americans tended to think of Canadian experience as simply an extension of their own ('the West for Fiedler is paradoxically placeless,' says Rosemary Sullivan in her summing up, 150), and although the Canadians present made a point of disclaiming this blanket assumption, judging by their collective contribution they lacked any clear alternative view or even unanimity about where exactly the sensed differences lay. Things have changed little since then. For all our restiveness, self-definition continues to elude us. Why? For one thing, because the quest itself makes us nervous. Like the hometown boy in the big city, we are afraid that even the most modest display of chauvinism would brand us as parochial. For another thing, we simply don't have the conceptual tools. We have measured ourselves against an imported yardstick for far too long. Despite concerted attempts to naturalize the school curriculum during the seventies, if only because of its omnipresence as part of a general cultural ambience Canadians are necessarily on much more *intimate* terms with American literature than with their own. What is more insidious, even when they are addressing themselves specifically to the work of Canadian writers, Canadian critics for the most part employ American critical concepts, diction, and ideology as their basic analytic tools. Indeed, even when we wax nationalistic we tend to use an imported idiom, as, for instance, the Tish group (among others) adopted the rhetoric of the 1960s American counter-culture to rationalize their rebellion against what they saw as 'American' cultural homogenization. As Robert Kroetsch points out, the Canadian writer's 'particular predicament' thus lies in the fact that although 'he works with a language, within a literature, that appears to be authentically his own, and not a borrowing,' he is betrayed by the very sociolinguistic tradition from which he derives his sense of uniqueness. '[J]ust as there was in the Latin word a concealed Greek experience,' the Canadian's 'word,' unbeknownst, drags along with it an alien experience that undermines the coherence and integrity of his voice (143).

To object to this state of affairs is not merely a matter of patriotism. The seemingly incurable tendency for Canadians to get stuck at the level of language, confounding rhetoric with reality, is an intellectual handicap we can ill afford. To borrow the old adage about history, to be oblivious to the duplicity of one's own myths is to be fooled by them, condemned, in a sense, to act them out over and over again. Less fancifully, in so far as metaphor, normalized, always tends to become generative as well as descriptive, the inappropriate modelling of a communal psyche not only retards self-understanding but actually spawns inappropriate behaviour, misdirected efforts, radical disjunctions of social ends and means. [13] Ignorance is *not* bliss, in other words. Why, then, do Canadians insist on *imposing* rather than *deriving* meaning from experience? More – why don't they even appear to notice the discrepancy? Part of it at least is purely circumstantial: the gross surficial similarities between both the peoples and the cultures of the two countries make it unlikely that we would even look for differences. Part too, though, has to do with the basic assumptions underlying our inherited intellectual traditions, the kinds of messages we are conditioned to infer from our 'readings' of culture. In Western society we have an unfortunate inclination, as Terry Fenton says of artists in particular, to be 'obsessed with "meaning,"' subscribing most naturally to the notion that '"form" … is a kind of "delivery system" for "content."' We consequently give little credence to the possibility that circumstances may arise when 'implicit "formal" content conflicts with explicit information.' The truth is, as Fenton emphasizes – and indeed as we have observed in our survey of early Canadian cultural artifacts – that 'forms and conventions speak in art. When they're taken for granted, all too often they speak against inspiration.' To be more specific, when used unreflectively to tell a given story they reveal a disconcerting 'tendency to tell a different, and often contradictory, story of their own' (82). This entails obvious problems for the creator. More important for the present discussion, it also has important implications for us as readers. *Without extracting that contradictory story we cannot claim to have educed the 'true' – that is, the full – meaning of the text.* The contradictory story that emerges most commonly from Canadian writing concerns our feelings about ourselves and our relation to the world. Which brings us back to Turner. The *real* relevance of the wilderness mythos to Canada can be seen only if we pay attention to what its proponents *show* us unconsciously, rather than giving too much weight to what they *say* they are doing.

The Group of Seven provides a striking demonstration of how wide the gap between intentions and results can be. Ardently pro-nature in their articulated stance, these artists yet produced collectively a version of the Canadian landscape which, at least in the view of many of their contemporaries, was at best harsh and somewhat disturbing, and at worst evoked the quality of nightmare. As Ann Davis points out:

Critics on both sides of the fence, those who opposed and those who supported the Seven, frequently saw in their work feelings of terror and violence. Of those who admired the Group, Augustus Bridle described Lismer's and Varley's over-reproduced pine trees as 'terrified'; Barker Fairley felt that Thomson was 'tragic-minded' ... Hugh MacLennan admired Thomson because he exposed the 'essential violence of the Canadian landscape.' Nor did critics unfriendly to the Seven lag behind in identifying the fearful aspects of their work. Hector Charlesworth planted the seed of dissension in the ear of the Member of Parliament who chastised the Group for being detrimental to Canada's foreign image because he felt that their work was likely to discourage immigration. These critics, then, saw the Group's representation of nature as antagonistic. (A433-4)

Those of us who have grown up in classrooms with Tom Thomson and A.Y. Jackson reproductions on the wall may find this reaction somewhat extreme, simply attributing such evocations of terror to the unfamiliarity of both the subject matter ('wild' nature) and the sensationalizing tendencies of the Art Nouveau style. If we look a little more carefully at the Group's work, however, we will have to conclude that much of the imputed ambiguity is *in* the paintings themselves.

It's not just a case of *what* they painted, either. Pieces like J.E.H. MacDonald's *The Elements* (1916) and Frederick Varley's *Stormy Weather, Georgian Bay* (ca 1920), with their tattered landscapes and broiling skies, certainly address themselves explicitly to the inimical face of nature, but even more significant is the fact that many of the peculiarities of composition observed in nineteenth-century art persist in the collective oeuvre. The shallowness of the picture plane, for instance. Frye has commented that 'the best paintings of Thomson and the Group of Seven have a horizon-focussed perspective' (B10), but even in those works which take as their *subject* a panoramic view the apparent expansion into space is more often than not denied vigorously on the level of technique. In Thomson's *Tamaracks* (1916), to cite only one fairly typical example, although we can see the blue hills beyond the lake clearly through the spaces between the trees in the foreground, the illusion of distance is countered by the way the crude brushwork pulls all colour planes into alignment, calling attention to surficial relations. In many other pieces the anti-panoramic stance (despite Frye's claims) is not merely implicit in technical preferences but quite overt. The escarpment in Thomson's *Purple Hill* (1916) is fully as wall-like as David Thompson's mountains, mentioned earlier. With similar implications, the tapestry-like woods in numerous paintings by Lawren Harris (*Algoma Woodland* [1919] and *Algoma Forest* [1920]) and Arthur Lismer (*Forest, Algoma* [1922], *Canadian Jungle* [1946], even *Sunlight in a Wood* [1922], with its oddly opaque light rays) are depicted as solid impenetrable barriers. The cumulative effect of such works is *not* one of openness or invitation.

Even in ostensibly benign landscapes there is often a strong hint of disquiet. In MacDonald's *The Tangled Garden* (1916) the grotesque profusion of the vegetation, combined with the garish colours and the low perspective, makes it seem as if nature is rising up and overwhelming the human element represented by the insubstantial-looking house in the background. In A.Y. Jackson's *The Edge of the Maple Wood* (1910), although the overt subject is a domesticated rural scene, the tree shadows falling on the foreground from 'behind' the viewer's vantage point make one feel as though the wilderness is at one's back, looming over one. The covert message carried by the same artist's *Winter, Charlevoix County* (1933) is even more provocative. This pastoral landscape, where a winding track leads the eye across rolling farmland toward a half-hidden village nestled against the foothills, looks innocuous enough until one notices the peculiar effect achieved by its juxtaposition in J. Russell Harper's *Painting in Canada* (366-7) with Harris's *Above Lake Superior* (ca 1922) and Lismer's *Cathedral Mountain* (1928). As modest and unthreatening as it may appear in isolation, in this company the central humped hill of Jackson's painting seems to echo oddly both the shape and the placement of Harris's starkly aggressive mountain and, even more so, Lismer's overtly forbidding craggy peak. Considering what has been said about the Canadian artist's apparent preoccupation with the *obtrusiveness* of mountains, this replication makes it seem, despite the radical change in style, as though not merely the vision but the basic iconography of Canadian nature painting remained unchanged in the twentieth century.

Judging by these features, it would seem that the Group, no less than their colonial predecessors, whatever they might *say* about the effects of nature actually *saw* something there that was far from wholesome. As Frye says of Thomson, 'Griffins and gorgons have no place in [his work] ... but the incubus is there, in the twist of stumps and sprawling rocks, the strident colouring, the scarecrow evergreens. In several pictures one has the feeling of something not quite emerging which is all the more sinister for its concealment' (B200). This sense of 'something not quite emerging,' the ineradicable impression of intangible threat, perhaps explains why even those Group of Seven paintings that seem on the surface quite unambiguous tend to have a queer 'haunted' quality. Certainly it suggests a reason for the covert ambivalence which, reading between the lines of their letters and journals, we may impute to their physical confrontations with their subject matter. As Wyndham Lewis says of Jackson, nature is *not* approached as something kindly and comfortable but as the 'Nature-as-Enemy' that is known to the explorer: 'His painting expeditions are as it were *campaigning seasons*, rather than the breathless rendezvous of a "nature lover" with the object of his cult' (298). It was clearly just as difficult for these apologists of the great outdoors actually to *enter* the wilderness as it was for Richardson and Moodie and Traill.

Interestingly enough, in at least some Group of Seven works we can see evidence of the same kind of covert avoidance strategies that we attributed to nineteenth-century literature in the last chapter. Lawren Harris provides a classic example. His Theosophical mysticism, though in theory irradiating the landscape with spiritual value, in practice only dehumanizes it more. Far from celebrating his subject matter for its own intrinsic appeal, he seems to want to distance himself from what he feels to be an alien environment by transforming it into geometry. As long as any representational element remains at all, the transformation effected is never wholly successful, however. Typically, in fact, Harris's paintings show clear signs of both his initial (though unadmitted) unease *and* his progressive recoil from the unruly reality. Even when his work becomes almost overwhelmingly cerebral the sense of threat is still unmistakable. In *North Shore, Lake Superior* (1926), for instance, we are given a landscape that is not merely alien but repellent. Intellectualized and abstracted, the blatantly phallic tree stump dominating the foreground connotes all the violence of the masculine mode without any of its life-giving sexuality. Bathed in a cold mystic light that simply by virtue of its aggressive unearthliness devalues the contingent, the mutable, the material, this painting is at once an expression of the artist's vision of nature's menace and an attempt – at least symbolically – to control it.

Harris's reaction, though perhaps extreme, is not unusual. Even outside the Group there is ample evidence in art of the period of the tension between the Canadian's desire for and fear of reconciliation with nature. Deeply rooted in rural Ontario, Carl Schaefer nevertheless both domesticated and – by means of his pictorial reticence, his subordination of subject to composition, his cool, painterly style – distanced his 'beloved' landscape. David Milne, fascinated by the syntax of 'appearing,' deconstructed it. Emily Carr's retreat was less obvious but in some ways even more radical. The ambivalence she demonstrated, in fact, might almost be taken as prototypical. In her journal she often speaks of her wish to get close to nature, to assimilate it, to capture in her work 'the vastness, the wildness, the Western breath of go-to-the-devil-if-you-don't-like-it, the eternal big spaceness of it' (A5). If we turn to the paintings themselves, however, it becomes obvious that her spontaneous response to the wilderness was not nearly as positive as she herself seemed, consciously, to believe. As George Woodcock points out, 'In a painting like *Old Time Coast Village* (ca 1928) the poles and the longhouses are stylized shapes of light above a luminous curve of beach, but all is trapped and overshadowed by the dense green darkness of the surrounding forest, its trees stylized into cowled and terrifying presences. The Indians feared the rain forest, which their imagination populated with menacing spirits, and in *Old Time Coast Village* locality and fear are darkly combined in a compelling and strangely visceral nightmare' (F42).

How could anyone claim to love nature and then image it like this? If we return to the journals with a slightly more sceptical eye we soon realize that however much she *thought* she wanted to celebrate nature, Carr, like Harris (whom she greatly admired), actually tried to use art as a means of escaping from its crudeness and animality. 'Half of painting is listening for the "eloquent dumb great Mother" (nature) to speak,' she says. 'The other half is having clear enough consciousness to see God in all' (32). 'I find that raising my eyes slightly above what I am regarding so that the thing is a little out of focus seems to bring the spiritual into clearer vision, as though there were something lifting the material up to the spiritual, bathing it in the above glory' (48). With such an attitude it's no wonder that her later work becomes increasingly stylized, the emphasis on object replaced by an emphasis on depiction. Some pieces, as Terry Fenton describes it, are 'composed entirely of writhing, undulating, curling and zigzagging lines' (53). Even though nature remains her ostensible 'subject,' Carr, instead of reproducing is *un*-creating the world, replacing it with a vision culled from her own depths. In *Reforestation* (1936), for instance, though we still sense the hard recalcitrance of the skeletal trees beneath the surface, the entire landscape has been subdued and softened by the artist's egocentricity, the thrusting organic forms so completely obscured by the insistent rhythm of the brushwork that they resemble swatches of material or appear, like Christmas trees, to be swathed in angel hair or tinsel.

The question that arises here (as with respect to the tendency toward conventionalization discussed in the last chapter) is whether there is any reason why this kind of aesthetic transformation need be regretted. Again the answer is no – and yes. It all depends on whether the discrepancy occurs between art and 'reality' or *within* the artist's own vision. In the latter case there is always a danger of incoherence. Even in Carr's case, while we cannot regret what she did achieve, one wonders what might have happened – how much more, how much differently, if not how much better, she might have painted – if she hadn't been wracked with self-doubts and conflicting impulses. For all her rhapsodies, Carr was never entirely happy with the direction her semi-mystical yearnings seemed to impel her. Raw nature was repulsive and even frightening at times, but at other times its beauty made her regret her incapacity to achieve a closer relation. A journal entry for May 1936, for instance, reveals vividly the discomfort she had begun to feel with Harris's cerebral approach to nature. 'I have missed the contact with Lawren bitterly ... He opened his door a crack and I peeked in. I went just a little way in and found it was a fair garden, serene and beautiful but *cold*. When I touched the lovely flowers they were wax. They had not the exquisite feel of live petals and no smell. I was frightened and ran out of his garden and the door shut and I grabbed the homely, sunwarmed weeds and simple wild flowers that grew outside the gate and held them tight' (238). Carr, it seems – more honest perhaps than Harris – was unable to rest easy with evasions. She wanted the 'reality' of nature. At the same time there was something that wouldn't *let* her truly give herself up to the landscape no matter how much she desired it. Why? This brings us back to Turner again.

The fact is, the basic conflict demonstrated by Emily Carr and the Group of

Seven was both, in a sense, a consequence of the popular attempt to define Canada in terms of the frontier theory and a clear indication of how wrong-headed that imputation was. The frontier did *not* play a positive role in the Canadian experience. To pretend that it did – or should – could only exacerbate the problems of coming to terms with nature. Nor was the difference, as Kline implies, simply a matter of Tory recoil from all signs of emergent republicanism. Indeed, Kline and all the other frontierists (whether pro or con) have generally mistaken a cause for an effect: Canadians, they say, historically favoured law and order, and etiquette, and decent social stratification because of the continued influence of British social and political mores, and if they – the Canadians – reacted negatively to the wilderness it was simply because, as Turner himself claimed, it was a disorderly element that threatened these *a priori* values. If one looks at the phenomenon in light of the patterns of response to be inferred from Canadian arts and letters, however, it seems far more likely that the influence worked the other way around; that Canadians moving west, rather than looking for Renaissance freedom ('an alternative to conventional society' Moss D12), typically spearheaded their migration with an advance guard of 'missionaries to build churches, surveyors to divide up the land into homestead sections, Mounties to maintain order, and troops to tidy away the Indians and Métis' (Wood 199) *because of* their fear of an unbuffered encounter with the wilderness. That is to say, hostility to the wilderness may well have been a cause rather than a result of their dependence on British forms. In any case, an examination of Canadian history and geography soon demonstrates that, whatever effects attended the westward movement in the United States, the environmental influences simply did not – indeed, could not – function in Canada in accordance with Turner's model.

The reason for this, rather than being political as Kline implies, is rooted in the essential difference between a 'western' and a 'northern' frontier. A western frontier, depending on one's perspective, is the *limit of knowledge* or the *limit of control*, and as such denotes a temporary and arbitrary boundary that may not only be transcended but actually redefined – moved, advanced, or even eradicated – by human effort. To 'go beyond' a western frontier, therefore, is both a commendable achievement in public terms and an exhilarating experience on the private level. A northern frontier, in contrast, denotes the *limits of endurance*. It is, in brief, an intangible but ineradicable line between the 'self' and the 'other,' between what is and is not humanly possible. While the western frontier is simply a culturally defined interface, the northern frontier is an existential one.

This subtle but crucial distinction is shown vividly in two stories that deal ostensibly with the same aspect of the man/nature relation. In both 'To Build a Fire' by Jack London and 'Snow' by Frederick Philip Grove the protagonists are frozen to death, but there is a fundamental difference in the way the authors, one American, one Canadian, seem to interpret the common fate. In the former story, the man's death is directly attributable to a human failing: he did not have enough imagination to foresee and thus forestall his predicament. The implication is that the hostile environment *could*, potentially, be conquered if one were only strong and smart enough. This is the view fostered by a western frontier. In Grove's story, however, the man's death is seen much more fatalistically as an ever-present possibility for those who live close to the frontier; it is only a matter of circumstance that this particular individual made the one fatal step over the invisible boundary between safety and death. No human quality – or lack of it – was responsible; no human quality – no moral status, no physical capacity or act of will – could have saved him.

A similar pattern emerges from Wallace Stegner's fictionalized memoir, *Wolf Willow*, a book which, more than any other single document, literary or otherwise, testifies that the Canadian attitude toward the pioneering experience was different from his American cohort's. Stegner himself is apparently not fully conscious of the implications of his work. As with the Group of Seven, he simply seems to take it for granted that the American frontier tradition, if not altogether healthy or rational as a behavioural prescription for modern times, at least provides a viable standard for explaining the culture of the early Canadian west. '[I]t was the cowboy tradition, the horseback culture,' he says, 'that impressed itself as image, as romance, and as ethical system upon boys like me' (134). The real message, however, emerges between the lines. The central *story* he elects to tell – the one incident he chooses to illuminate the broader meaning of his memoir – turns out to be a demonstration not of Turneresque pioneer conquest but of the inevitability of man's *defeat* by the land. Were it not that he never draws such a conclusion explicitly, one might be tempted to believe that the 'education' of Stegner's young hero was deliberately intended as a means of dramatizing the foolishness of trying to use the American myth of the west as a model for Canada, not merely in a technological present-day that renders the pioneer stance *ipso facto* obsolete, but right from the beginning. Rusty Cullen, who comes to the prairie fresh from England, starts out full of typical romantic illusions. He is far from impervious to the threatening aspect of the landscape ('he felt in every deceptive snow-shadow and every pulse of the Northern Lights and every movement of the night wind the presence of something ancient and terrible, to which the brief stir and warmth of life were totally alien' 163), but, like a Jack London protagonist, he is convinced that the 'answer to the challenge' is for a man 'to be invincibly strong, indefinitely enduring, uncompromisingly self-reliant, to depend on no one, to contain within himself every strength and every skill' (164). *Un*like the London hero, however, by the end of the story, having barely survived a winter so catastrophic that 'it changed the way of life of the region' (137), he comes to see exactly how helpless man really is when 'thwarted by a blind force of nature, a meteorological freak, a mere condition of wind and cold' (190). The attitude he *now* evinces is pragmatic, not romantic; Canadian, not American: 'The Rusty Cullen who sat among them was a different boy, outside and inside, from the one who had set out ... He thought he knew enough not to want to distinguish himself by heroic deeds: singlehanded walks to the North Pole, incredible journeys, rescues, what not. Given his way, he did not think that he would ever want to do anything alone again, not in this country. Even a trip to the privy was something a man might want to take in company' (219). Rusty has learned first fear, then caution. This – not Turner's individualistic ultra-republicanization process – is what a *northern* frontier does to one.

Stegner's story is more than just a cautionary tale. Cullen's experience is figuratively, if not literally, representative of the Canadian experience as a whole. So, too, is his reaction. It is vulnerability, not opportunity, that the frontier most often suggests in this country. This is partly because it is *in fact* a dangerous place to be. Our *sense* of that danger, moreover, is exacerbated by the particular *shape* it takes. Northern man in close proximity to nature does not, as in the mythic American west, simply have the wilderness on one side and civilization on the other with a free choice between the two. The frontier is by definition all around him, a precondition of his whole imaginative being.[14] And Canada, as the archetypal incarnation of the northern nation, is like nothing so much as a collection of beads loosely and tenuously strung out along the fragile, essential threads of river, railroad, and highway. Small wonder that all of these have gathered so many symbolic connotations, figured so prominently in so many diverse aspects of Canadian culture.[15] Small wonder, too, that the pioneer has typically chosen to buttress his westward advance with as many of the trappings of civilization as possible. The order imposed by human institutions offers the only chance he has of maintaining his integrity, staying on the right side of the fatal line – resisting the life-denying menace of natural chaos.[16] It is a recognition of this home truth that produces that peculiarly Canadian nature-paranoia Frye characterizes as 'the garrison mentality.' It also accounts for the evident (and, to the continentalists, odd) fact that in Canada the culture hero is not the gunslinger, triumphing over opposition by a demonstration of natural prowess and anarchistic individual will, but rather the Law itself: impersonal, all-embracing, pre-eminently social. 'The archetypal scene south of the border might show the lone hero confronting his foes at high noon; but a typical scene in western Canadian fiction shows the American desperado surrendering his six-shooter at the quiet, firm command of a Canadian Mountie' (Wood 199).[17] The contrast between these two encounters exemplifies the contrast between egocentric and objective, personal and impersonal political modes. This is the ultimate difference between Canada and the United States. 'Not life, liberty and the pursuit of happiness, but peace, order, and good government are what the national government of Canada guarantees' (Morton B68).

All of this sounds very British, of course: Mounties, law, good government. What, one might ask, of Quebec? If any historical figure on *either* side of the border epitomizes the accommodation of man to the wilderness, surely it is the voyageur or coureur de bois. As one popular historian puts it, 'Over the Saint Lawrence canoe route the French brought their mystic piety, their thirst for adventure and for knowledge of what lay beyond the next hill ... They were almost free of racial arrogance ... [and] were quite willing to marry in the Indian camps' (Howard 26). Such assessments obviously strike a note in diametric opposition to the nature-paranoia we have been tracing. Does this mean that all our inferences about the 'typical' Canadian world vision are relevant only to English Canada? For a number of important reasons, I would claim not. Despite the surficial differences between the two literatures, there are, as will emerge later, a number of equally striking similarities on almost every level from narrative patterns through to preferential themes. The foregoing discussion, moreover, far from underlining the bases of ir-reconcilable divergence, actually hints at the reasons why French-Canadian and English-Canadian literatures are more profoundly alike than is generally supposed.

The fact is, although the terms of reference are different, the *structure* of the French-Canadian image of the relation between 'self' and 'other' is virtually identical to that developed in English Canada. This is not as unlikely as it sounds. Despite the obvious (and perhaps overemphasized) political, cultural, and religious contrasts, the *practical* experiences of the two people were not all that disparate. Voyageurs notwithstanding, the true communal mythos of the French Canadian has always been based on a pastoral ideal, and a primitive pastoral at that. The rural context, especially in so far as it becomes crucial to self-definition, has an unfortunate tendency, as noted, to highlight one's dependence on an unpredictable nature. It is hardly surprising, therefore, that the *romans du terroir* should reveal a great deal of antipathy toward the landscape even as they eulogize the pastoral tradition; indeed, there is ample evidence that the French view of nature has historically been even more anxiety-ridden than the English one.

If we look a little more closely at the voyageur tradition as viewed from *inside* French culture, moreover, we will find that the special case actually reinforces such a conclusion. Even in his heyday the voyageur – his joie de vivre increasingly tainted with recklessness, irresponsibility, even (especially in so far as he was identified with the liquor trade) outright corruption – was far from representing the conscious aspirations of the general population of New France. More licentious than liberated, he was anathema to both sacred and secular ideals. Dangerous at home for its challenge to domestic security, his notorious self-indulgence, carried into the pays d'en haut, was – as Jack Warwick points out in *The Long Journey* – equally inimical to the public purposes of a community explicitly enjoined 'to confer the benefits of Christian civilization on the savages' (19). If the habitant might secretly envy his independent cousin, therefore, he was bound to feel considerable guilt for doing so. And this ambivalence in turn carried over to secondary associations. Linked as he was with subversion and irreligion, the voyageur's real and symbolic links with nature could only help make the wilderness seem more, rather than less, threatening, if not in physical then certainly in spiritual terms.

Given the character as well as the practical circumstances of the early settlers, then, it seems obvious that there were excellent reasons why the French Canadian should have felt the alienness and omnipresence of nature just as intensely as his English counterpart. It is appropriate, in fact, that Willa Cather (as John Ditsky reports) traced the North American seige mentality to its symbolic roots in 'a citadel, a Rock, Quebec.' 'The ancestral home of the French-Canadian imagination,' Ditsky adds, 'is a cabin around which snow swirls constantly' (216). This is an image that Rusty Cullen – or Susanna Moodie, for that matter – would find familiar. It is also an image that seemingly haunts the Québécois imagination even today. In Jacques Godbout's *Le couteau sur la table*, the incessant circling of the narrative, compulsively wrenched back as it is to the claustrophobic discomforts of a storm-bound present, not only echoes the protagonist's sense of his cultural situation as hopelessly stultifying but, in the felt obtrusiveness of the blizzard outside his room, also makes it seem as though nature itself (as Emily Montague complained more than two centuries earlier) must inevitably overwhelm and extinguish the puny efforts of a merely human will:

A sudden storm has flattened the city: a few hours have transformed streets into soft fields of snow. Huge nests of snow cling to the forks of trees on the windward side, garland passers-by with identical hats: asexual beings advance in a sort of white fog, fighting the wind, straining their whole bodies in an effort that the ice under foot promptly nullifies. Silent.
These people are silent all winter. When summer comes, they've forgotten how to speak. The fight is very simple: not to be cold. (36)

Surely no culture with such a sense of its powerlessness in the face of natural forces could be said to *identify* with a figure like the voyageur. This is no doubt why, as Warwick notes, though Americans such as the historian Francis Parkman might make much of the romantic frontier type, 'the *coureur de bois* occupies surprisingly little space in French-Canadian literature' (106); why 'in the literary schools of the nineteenth and early twentieth centuries the journey was less admired than the farm, which represented the official side of order and stability' (78) – why, indeed, even in more recent productions an anti-primitivistic bias seems at least covertly to dominate. In Yves Thériault's

Agaguk, for instance, the 'natural' man – in this case the Eskimo – is portrayed, for all Thériault's apparent approval, as dangerous, a killer, wholly inimical to the very idea of community.[18] What all this adds up to is the clear certainty that the French Canadian has experienced nature in much the same way as the more overtly hag-ridden English.

The parallels to be drawn between the two cultures do not stop here. Even after the west was won and nature ostensibly 'tamed' (or at least pushed back to the city limits), English Canada's communal paranoia was reinforced, possibly even augmented, by fear of its powerful neighbour to the south. Sociologist John Porter connects a number of recurrent cultural themes including 'negativism, lack of commitment, withdrawal from social issues, and a feeling of resignation' with a 'fear of being "swallowed up"' (266). The sense of engulfment, of being totally surrounded by an alien element, thus becomes generalized into an existential norm, and symbolic echoes between diverse but apparently homologous kinds of experience – like sympathetic vibrations – intensify and confirm the type response until it frees itself of necessity from causal connection to become an unentailed (that is, *a priori*) item of self-definition. The same process can be seen to have taken place in Quebec – and to an even greater degree. After the British victory in 1759 and the Treaty of Paris in 1763, as Hilda Neatby describes it, 'The ties with the mother country, so much more and completely a mother than Britain had been to any of her active and sometimes ungainly offspring, were severed. One more journey direct to France could be taken, by British permission in a British ship, and then no more except by special permit from London and London officials, separated from the Canadians on the St Lawrence by many barriers of which language was only one' (3). Quebec was thus set adrift from both her past and her future. In Jean LeMoyne's words, 'From being a small, precarious, and neglected colony on the bottom rung of the provincial ladder, we were suddenly conquered, isolated, and surrounded by foreigners.' The result was that Quebec 'began to fear everything outside itself and to develop a radical xenophobia' (174).[19] Even apart from the nature-paranoia shared by both cultures, then, the image of engulfment epitomizes the French-Canadian historical experience quite as much as the English-Canadian one. It is not surprising that it should spawn a similar iconography in art and literature.

Having made this point, it is tempting to go one step further. Quebec, although the most considerable, is not the *only* discrete cultural entity within Canada. It's no accident that the country has been described as a mosaic rather than a melting pot – although it's difficult to say with any degree of confidence whether the condition connoted by this figure is ultimately a cause or a consequence of the Canadian character.[20] W.L. Morton claimed that the operative factor was a political tradition common to both French and English: 'The monarchy ... subsumed a heterogeneous and conservative society governed in freedom under law ... where the republic would have leveled the diversities and made uniform the various groups by breaking them down into individuals' (B63). While this is true, it's perhaps not the whole truth. Rather than saying that ethnic and other groups have maintained their autonomy because a particular political philosophy fostered such a condition, we might equally well say that that political philosophy remained powerful, despite the all-too-immanent example of our southern neighbours, because a prevailing if tacit mythos strengthened the tendency for self-identified groups to be insular, isolated, and self-referencing. Whatever the case may be (and the influence probably worked *both* ways in reality), Canada *is* a collection of discrete social particles. As Woodcock remarks, 'It might be a metaphorical exaggeration to describe [the country] as a land of invisible ghettos, but certainly it is, both historically and geographically, a country of minorities that have never achieved assimilation' (E21).

The point, of course, is that here we have our engulfment image again. The only difference is that now we are talking about *multiple* solitudes rather than only one or two – a distinction that doesn't affect the validity of the comparison. The implications are provocative. Whether we speak of a ghetto or a garrison – or an entire embattled culture, for that matter – we invoke the same kind of relationship between 'self' and 'other,' 'we' and 'they' (or 'it'). These units, of whatever size, are mutually reflective. The relationship of parts to whole in Canada, in other words, is much like that between the members of a set of Chinese boxes. In contrast to the United States, where an ideal of assimilation makes it impossible for any group to remain distinct unless it defines itself in terms specifically *counter* to the broader cultural ambience, the smaller socio-political units in this country take the *same* basic form as those by which they are contained. This may be why, in Canada, we find that the literatures of even quite narrowly defined sub-groups (ethnic minorities like Rudy Wiebe's Mennonites and Adele Wiseman's Winnipeg Jews; regional ones like Hodgins's islanders and Kroetsch's Albertans), rather than demonstrating a contrapuntal or antagonistic relationship with 'mainstream' literature or with each other, actually tend to yield a surprising number of functionally equivalent and structurally similar patterns of perception and response. This is not to say that there are not important differences between these sub-groups, but because of a fundamental identity of stance they offer an unusually good basis of comparison.

This phenomenon has already been noted with respect to Canada's Jewish sub-group. Michael Greenstein, for one, takes the 'Jewish metaphor' invoked by Frye in his celebrated discussion of 'garrison mentality' in the conclusion to the *Literary History of Canada* as a jumping-off point to establish strong parallels within the two (that is, Jewish and 'mainstream') traditions: 'Linguistically, "garrison" is related to such terms as "garret" and "avant garde," both descriptive of the defenses of the isolated artist's imagination against society; conceptually, Frye's closely knit and beleaguered society with its unquestionable moral and social values also characterizes the ghetto. When Frye suggests that "novelists of our day studying the impact of Montreal or Westmount write of a psychological [garrison]" ... it becomes clear that his metaphor is interchangeable with the ghetto mentality of Montreal's Jewish writers' (121). Unfortunately for the success of what could have been a most fruitful line of inquiry, when we progress beyond the first page of Greenstein's essay we realize that his inclusion of, and emphasis on, Saul Bellow as a 'Canadian' Jew leads to a certain amount of confusion about what, specifically, this 'ghetto mentality' implies. Notwithstanding his few childhood years in Montreal, Bellow is *not* a Canadian by either conscious identification or unconscious inclination. In comparing Bellow with European practitioners of the 'novel of enclosure' such as Kafka and Beckett, Frederick Karl points out – with considerable relevance to our present subject – that 'Herzog is a hero of enclosures, but American-style, which frequently means that enclosed space eventually expands toward new horizons. With their spatial orientation American writers have rarely been at home with enclosure; when the theme does occur, it is a stage onward, part of a temporary process. Enclosure, for Herzog, [as for his creator,] is attached to his sickness, not to a viable alternative culture.'[21] If we leave aside Greenstein's determinedly extra-national stance, however, we realize that the base intuition of resemblance with which this critic presumably began is valid. If, instead of Herzog, we focus on a more typically 'Canadian' Jewish protagonist like, say, Mordecai Richler's Joshua Shapiro – a man who is apparently so strongly, albeit unconsciously, identified with the underdog image characteristic of the ghetto mentality that after he has to all intents and purposes 'escaped' from his entrapment by virtue of professional success, marriage to an aristocratic gentile, and cosmopolitan lifestyle, he ends up (in *Joshua Then and Now*) precipitating his own 're-ghetto-ization' by a disastrous self-identification (in jest!) with an even more downtrodden and despised minority, the homosexuals – we see quite clearly the kind of 'psychological garrison' that Greenstein, following Frye, has cited: that is, the self-projected garrison which, by definition, cannot be transcended. What is more important, though the Jewish sub-group, being both larger and more explicitly defined, is easier to analyse than most others, it will become clear in this book that attitudes and responses are remarkably consistent across the board. The Jewish case may, indeed, be taken as in some sort a paradigm of the national situation. The full ramifications of this interesting fact will not be appreciated until we have progressed a little further. In the meantime, let us merely accept as a provisional assumption that the 'northern' values implicit in the confrontation between Mountie and gunslinger, if not the terms by which this is imaged, are characteristic not merely of any given sub-group, no matter how large, but of Canada as a whole.

NOTES

1 See excerpts from *The History and Present State of Virginia* (1705) in Roy Harvey Pearce, ed., *Colonial American Writing* (Holt, Rinehart & Winston 1969), esp. 516. Leo Marx discusses Beverly's response in *The Machine in the Garden* (Oxford 1964) 87 ff.

2 '[S]uch luxuriant plentie and admirable raritie of Trees, Shrubs, Hearbs: such fertilitie of soyle, insinuation of seas, multiplicitie of Rivers, safetie of Ports, healthfulnesse of ayre, opportunities of habitation, materialls for action, objects for contemplation, haps in present, hopes of future, worlds of varietie in that diversified world.' In Pearce, *ibid.*, 22

3 As Douglas Jones summarizes it, 'they arrived in Nova Scotia in November 1783, three thousand men, women, and children determined to settle a section of that rocky coast simply because it had been given to them. They were warned against the attempt, but settle it they did, during one terrible winter, sawing logs at a sawmill several miles away, hauling the lumber by water, from which it emerged coated with ice, and erecting homes in December and mid-January. They established themselves until spring, when a forest fire drove them into the sea. From the shore they watched their winter's work and all they possessed reduced to a smoking ruin. Anyway, as the melting snow had revealed, no one could have farmed that patch of rock, sand, and bush and they had all been farmers, plantation owners, in the south' (A35).

4 This description applies more to the Puritan settlers than the aristocratic adventurers of the Virginia Company, but the ideas involved were so much an ingrained element of the general seventeenth-century world view, with its apocalyptic vision of human history, that the trends noted may be considered as broadly influential beyond the Puritan camp. Certainly the southerner employed much the same imagery to describe his New World experience (see Pearce, *Colonial American Writing*), and his expectations (judging by, for instance, the wording of the Letters of Patent issued for Virginia in 1610) were quite congruous with the Puritan concept of Divine Mission.

5 Brumm, *American Thought and Religious Typology*, trans. John Hoagland (Rutgers 1970) 19, 23, 18, 46

6 George Williams, *Wilderness and Paradise in Christian Thought* (Harper 1962) 18

7 George Rogers Taylor, ed., *The Turner Thesis: Concerning the Role of the Frontier in American History* (Heath 1972) 4

8 See, for instance, the range of critical reactions to Turner's thesis in Taylor.

9 For the classic discussion of this phenomenon, see R.W.B. Lewis, *The American Adam: Innocence, Tragedy and Tradition in the Nineteenth Century* (U. Chicago 1955).

10 Although Lower went further than most of his colleagues in embracing the wilderness ethos, his reaction was in many ways typical of the period. In Carl Berger's words, 'This experience of the North was one of the crucial episodes in Lower's intellectual development and he was to return to it again and again. His attachment to the wilds sometimes expressed itself as a pantheistic feeling for the mystery of the forest, at other times as a simple enjoyment in the physical exertion

that came from canoeing or chopping wood. "To go into the 'bush' in the spring, soft from a city winter," he wrote in 1932, "and come out hard as nails in the fall, rejoicing in your ability to carry a canoe over a two-mile portage without setting it down, or to paddle at racing speed up the length of a twenty-mile lake ... to learn tolerance of others with whom you must live at very close range, to acquire the adaptableness and self-reliance which only the woods and their counterpart, the sea, impart: these are matters which must leave their mark [upon countless Canadians]." Lower's response to the North affected both the history he would write as well as the style of life he would lead' (115).

11 'Turner's generalizations about the role of the frontier had ... only an indirect and modified influence on the writing of the history of Canada since 1920. Innis had rejected it outright; Underhill had fused the frontier approach with the broader Beardsian notion of the class and sectional bases of parties; and [even] Lower had been at pains to note that, while North American democracy had a forest birth, its survival was conditional on the existence of certain institutions and laws of self-government' (Berger 174-5).

12 See, for instance, Wilfred Eggleston's *The Frontier and Canadian Letters*.

13 If the reader is inclined to doubt this contention, Part II of *Metaphor and Thought*, ed. Andrew Ortony (Cambridge 1979), examines from several different perspectives the generative function of metaphor with respect particularly to the public domain. In 'Generative Metaphor and Social Policy' (254-83) Donald Schön discusses the problems that arise when the tacit 'frames' that underlie and generate social programs are inappropriate, inconsistent ('frame conflict'), or inadequately understood. More farreaching, in 'The Conduit Metaphor' (284-324) Michael Reddy, contrasting the current almost wholly dehumanized model of language (which, by reducing the exchange of information to a matter merely of motive plus message – water flowing through a pipe – localizes all expenditures of energy in the speaker or writer) with a more radically subjective 'toolmakers' paradigm (which explicitly implicates readers and listeners in the 'difficult and highly creative task of reconstruction and hypothesis testing'), demonstrates how an ill-conceived metaphor can not only bias but hamper cultural development. 'The difference in viewpoint here between the conduit metaphor and the toolmakers paradigm is serious, if not profound ... We neglect the crucial human ability to reconstruct thought patterns on the basis of signals and this ability founders. After all, "extraction" is a trivial process, which does not require teaching past the most rudimentary level. We have therefore, in fact, less culture – or certainly no more culture – than other, less mechanically inclined, ages have had ... I am suggesting, then, that, in the same way that "urban renewal" misled the policymakers discussed in Schön's paper, the conduit metaphor is leading us down a technological and social blind alley' (310).

14 According to Frye, the psychological groundwork for the Canadian's traditional propensity to visualize himself totally surrounded by an alien element was laid

before he even set foot on the shores of this country. 'The image of being swallowed by the leviathan is an almost inevitable one for Canada: the whole process of coming to the country by ship from Europe, through the Strait of Belle Isle and the Gulf of Saint Lawrence and then up the great river, suggests it, again a marked contrast to the United States, with its relatively straight north-south coastline' (D36-7).

15 Canadian historian Donald Creighton, for instance, built his entire view of Canadian history around the great river, both dream and actuality, which led the Canadian voyageur into the heart of the continent: 'In his three most important works ... Creighton's subject forms itself around the central image of the river – the river of Canada – and the hero who grasped its meaning and embarked upon the immense journey to possess and subdue the inland kingdom to which the river was the key' (Kilbourn B93). Dreams notwithstanding, the river was still a natural rather than a man-made phenomenon, and in consequence – ironically enough – the more important it was perceived to be the greater its potential to stimulate anxiety in those who were dependent on it. This too is an aspect that comes across clearly in Creighton's work. Especially in *The Commercial Empire of the Saint Lawrence*, as Berger points out, 'the river was a colossal presence, men were Lilliputians in comparison. Living on its shores and responding to its dictates, they were but frail instruments of its purposes. Ultimately their hopes were dashed on its rocks.' In consequence, 'The feeling that pervaded Creighton's narrative had much in common with that evoked by the paintings of the Group of Seven' (214).

16 See W.L. Morton B for a discussion of the unavoidable physical dependence on a civilized base that distinguishes the maritime and northern frontier from the western one.

17 For more on the dichotomy of values implied by the gunslinger/Mountie contrast, see Dick Harrison A and C. In the latter especially, Harrison makes a point of discriminating between the 'true' Canadian Mountie and the Mountie as recreated by outsiders. As Robert Thacker summarizes it in a review article, 'Harrison reiterates his previously-published notion that the Mountie in fiction reflects an author's nationality, since the writer's cultural assumptions are revealed by the way in which he depicts the Mountie. Thus Canadians such as Ralph Connor presented Mounties who most closely resembled actual Mounted Policemen. His Corporal Cameron is ... a symbol of empire, or imperial hegemony, and so is protected by the ideals he represents. The British Mountie, seen in the writing of Roger Pocock and John Mackie, was presented in somewhat different light; he was invariably a black sheep from a good family, out to spend some time in the territories, and was often a confused amalgamation of soldier-mountie. The key difference, however, is that such figures were usually presented as protecting the empire, rather than being protected by it, like the Canadian Mountie. Not surprisingly, American writers were the most inaccurate because of the influence of their own West on the popular imagination. Authors such as James Oliver Curwood, often with scanty knowledge of the North West, portrayed Mounties as American sheriffs in scarlet, officers who

often acted as if above the law' (553-4). We will be returning to the problem of home-grown versus imported folk heroes in chapter lo, below.

18 As Jeannette Urbas describes it, 'Thériault has chosen to stress, if not distort, those aspects of Eskimo life that fit into his own personal artistic vision and the fictional universe he creates as a result of it. He places a high priority on closeness to nature which he often equates with violence and the rejection of all restraint. Animal-like behaviour is not reprehensible in itself, nor is the release of elemental passions as is suggested by the little tales inserted into the larger framework of the story; such as, the stories of the man who murders another to obtain his furs, as well as the long-lost husband who comes home and kills one of his usurpers and several children in order to re-establish himself. None of these reinforces the idea of brotherhood and mutual help, of cooperation and kindness which would seem to be necessary for survival in this harsh environment' (81).

19 The xenophobic tendency, while rooted in the quite natural feelings of insecurity and cultural alienation consequent upon a catastrophic military defeat, was exacerbated by developments within the church in post-conquest Quebec. As H.J. Hanham describes it, 'when French Canada was cut off from France the consequences were much the same for the church in Canada as they were for the Dutch Reformed Church in South Africa when the Cape was cut off from Holland by the British occupation. An official church establishment was maintained by the government but it lacked the capacity for intellectual and spiritual renewal. The church had to be remade from below, not in the image of the church of the mother country but in the image of the peasant society which supplied it with priests and beliefs' (13). The result of this 'remaking' was a conservative anti-intellectual bias that strongly militated against change.

20 See Allan Smith for a discussion of the sources and implications of the mosaic metaphor. He points out the extent to which this concept is much more 'an idealization' than an accurate representation of Canadian social reality. In so far as it represents covert aspects of self-image, though, like most ideological rhetoric, the metaphor, he allows, 'however much it deals in distortion, may still reflect something fundamental in the character of the society to whose mystique it attempts to give expression' (247).

21 Karl, 'Enclosure, the Adversary Culture, and the Nature of the Novel,' *Mosaic* 7, 2 (1974) 12

4

Re Definition

All of this seems on the whole to add up to a rather negative picture of Canada. Not only do we hate nature (which is a disconcerting discovery for anyone nurtured on the voyageurs, Tom Thomson, and the Boy Scouts) – not only are we evidently a bunch of sissies who much prefer sitting around the stockade playing euchre to going out and killing a few Indians – but most of our fiction and poetry and painting seems to specialize in telling us one thing while showing us another. The fact is, though, that the twentieth century has witnessed the emergence of a distinctive and potentially powerful literature that owes much of its character specifically to the peculiarities of the historical Canadian view of the man/nature relation. Indeed, if we trace our way back through the network of connections it can be seen that nearly every unique feature of our communal voice may be attributed to the covert persistence of this type response. If we *seem* to have moved a long way beyond Major Richardson, it is only because the iconography of the initial dislocation has in most cases been converted, by a process similar to the structuralist's transformational grammar of myth, into secondary patterns – idiosyncratic ways of 'seeing' – that diverge radically from the original mode and in some cases actually appear to invert it. Paradoxically, once this process of conversion has taken place, even nature can be redeemed.

Does this seem implausible? One need only look at some of Lévi-Strauss's ethnological studies to realize the deviousness of the mythopoeic process, of which the phenomenon cited here is a part or form.[1] The particular development that took place in Canada can, however, be explained in quite simple, commonsensical terms. If the Canadian had merely *disliked* his environment things may have been different, but because his recoil was so extreme – because he withdrew himself from it so completely – nature became to a large extent demythicized, invisible. This development meant that after a while the landscape became a kind of *tabula rasa*, neutralized to a degree that has been impossible since the primitive first projected the spirits of his ancestors into the trees: *usable* again. The Canadian wilderness and its symbolic correlatives, having largely escaped being typed or tainted by the enervating sentimentality of the nineteenth century, is thus able to offer contemporary writers a far more flexible aesthetic tool than the American one, now irrevocably tied to the nostalgic image of a mutilated Garden, and as such enshrined too firmly in the national pantheon to be capable of carrying any but the simplest and most traditional thematic implications. In the United States today, it is for instance almost impossible for a serious writer to make 'straight' (that is, non-ironic) use of a noble savage figure, steeped as it is in a century's worth of bathetic sub-literary clichés. In Canada, however, the Indian still offers a wide range of possibilities, from the realism of Hubert Evans's *The Mist on the River* and Matt Cohen's *Wooden Hunters* to the ambiguous primitivism of W.O. Mitchell's *The Vanishing Point*, David Williams's *The Burning Wood*, and – quintessentially – Rudy Wiebe's *The Temptations of Big Bear*. Similarly, the land itself, largely saved by Canadian avoidance strategies from the constrictions of too broadly assumed emotional connotations, sustains an evocative versatility that would be hard to duplicate.

Does this mean that nature has simply gone from being a negative symbol in the nineteenth century to a positive one in the twentieth? Not at all. In the first place, the negative *response* is still there, even though the confrontation that originally stimulated it has been generally transformed or displaced. This response, moreover, out of sheer habit has a tendency simply to recreate its conventional object unless the context exerts a specific force that would counter the impulse. Even at a distance of a century and more from colonial hardship, it's not difficult to find overtly negative views of the environment in the casual usage of Canadian writers. Patricia Blondal's image of the prairie as inhuman and oppressive is one that recurs so frequently, with small variations to allow for change in locale, as to have become a stereotype: 'the sun pressed low and red against the dust-dark air, an unhealthy bloated clot of fire that transformed the world into some freakish Martian landscape in which there was no ocean, no distant England, only Manitoba ... reeling beneath the constant gray night, the voracious wind' (26). Clark Blaise's identification of nature with decay and disorder also expresses what has evidently become a common, perhaps habitual association for Canadians to make. 'The whole saucer-shaped field was humming with dragonflies and mosquitoes ... The smell was faintly of cooking gas and human waste, but mainly a totality of every potential putrefaction in nature that I'd never thought of defining. It could have been the end of the world' (69). Conventional or not, this is as uninviting a landscape as we could find anywhere in print a century earlier.

Recent treatments do not always stop short at simple naturalistic negativity, either. Robert Harlow's *Scann*, for instance, goes far beyond these relatively restrained expressions of distaste for what 'really is' out there. By focusing not merely on the 'unconscious horror' of the landscape but on the suffering it causes, this book, as Northrop Frye says of his hypothetical Canadian poet, begins to 'animate nature with an evil or at least sinister power' (B140). The wolverine, which (to an even greater extent than the debilitating cold or the snow or the more radical violence of the ice) seems to represent the natural impulse in Scann's fictional universe, is shown as in some sense an avatar or archetype of inhuman irrationality, the ultimate opponent, so determined to consume the human protagonists that it cannot be dislodged from its victim even after it is dead. John Moss claims that this implacable antagonism, far from being wilful, has the 'inexorability of an unknowing force, an indifferent continuum beyond man's power to withstand or fully comprehend' (D119). The evidence of the book itself clearly indicates, however, that at least in the eyes of the trapper who engages it in mortal combat, the creature, and by extension nature itself, is possessed of an extreme and fully conscious malevolence. The landscape Harlow evokes is consequently just as dangerous, as demonic, as the nightmare forest we glimpse between the lines of nineteenth-century literature.

We must be careful, on the other hand, not to misinterpret what such survivals as this mean. Granted that threatening landscapes are still relatively easy to find (and Harlow is far from exceptional), there is nevertheless a subtle but important difference between nineteenth- and twentieth-century versions of man/nature antagonism. The key phrase is 'in the eyes of the trapper.' Even when they deliberately invoke its negative symbolic potential, contemporary Canadian writers have generally made it quite clear that they are aware that nature *in itself* is, in Moss's words, 'amoral, impassive, indifferent' (D111), lacking both hostility *and* benevolence. The imputation of evil to the landscape, when not purely a poetic device, thus tends, at least in our best and most conscious literary productions, to be attributable to the protagonist or persona rather than to the writer himself. The response, in other words, is *explored* rather than merely *expressed*. This displacement allows such secondary developments as the explicit exploitation of the pathetic fallacy as a means of illuminating the tension between 'self' and 'other.' In Earle Birney's 'David,' for instance, although the wilderness for a while *seems* actively malevolent with its stony fangs and thirsting lichens and vulture-hawk, we are made to realize by the final emblematic image of the stone finger beckoning in a 'wide indifferent sky' that this malevolence exists only in the mind of the alienated human observer. As Richard Robillard points out, 'Bob projects his shock and panic *into* nature' (17, italics added). The significance of this is considerable. As long as the distinction between subjective and objective is sustained, the Canadian fear of the environment may be aesthetically distanced, *used* instead of merely reflected, a manoeuvre that is effective on the level of both technique and theme.

With this distance comes freedom. Nature *qua* nature may continue to be negative, but it may be many other things just as easily. Most important, perhaps, it can, as mentioned, be used not as a fixed symbolic counter but as a means of exploring alternatives. The virtual *tabula rasa*, in other words, now presents itself ready to hand as a code, a language waiting to be uttered, but one that remains staunchly resistant to assigned meanings. As a result of this flexibility, at least for the last half century the Canadian literary landscape, re-cognized as psycho-setting, has demonstrated a consistent significatory potential that energizes even ostensibly realistic works like Sinclair Ross's *As for Me and My House*, developing in the sixties into the full-blown surrealism of, for instance, Roch Carrier's *La guerre, yes sir!*. In the latter book, interestingly, the snow, which for both Grove (in novels such as *Settlers of the Marsh*) and Ross serves in a fairly straightforward way as a reflection or projection of ambivalent subjective states (especially in relation to the interface, or Horizon), now – recapitulating some of the techniques of Quebec's surrealist-inspired Automatist painters (see Davis c) – becomes simultaneously an ambiguous moral ground against which the action stands in high relief; an insulating, isolating cocoon; and an obliterating blanket that obscures pre-existent relation and distinction of all sorts. This development is in a sense exemplary. Snow has always exerted a strange fascination for the Canadian, if only because of its doomful connotations. 'In a literal way,' says Robert Kroetsch, 'the snow-filled Canadian night is – The clean sweep. The subtle fear. The wipe-out. The peculiar promise of a terrifying yet easy death' (F51). Converted to the recent more complex mode, however, snow can connote all this *and* much more besides.[2] As Frye points out with respect to David Milne's painting, in fact, snow, along with other ambient effects, becomes less a 'thing seen' than a control on the conditions for 'seeing': 'rain, fog, snow and mist play an important role ... their function is not to blur the outlines but to soften them down so as to increase the sense of a purified visual pattern. Rain, which is very difficult to paint, has the paradoxical quality of bringing objects nearer by partly veiling them: it decreases the sunlight sense of hard objective fact, not by making things look unreal, but by making them seem less conventionalized' (B206). Weather, stylized as 'atmosphere,' thus becomes a major tool for directing or undercutting or qualifying or even *exploding* simple semantic meaning. The same might be said of the landscape as a whole. The very value of the psycho-setting resides in its ability to *swallow* divergent realities, something substantially more difficult and important than the accretion of *extra* meaning by a verbal construct through, say, simple metaphor or irony.[3]

This new ability of the landscape naturally makes it an important resource for the symbolist writer. The prime example of this genre is Sheila Watson's *The Double Hook*, but even in more occasional usage – such as Ernest Buckler's *The Mountain and the Valley* – the value of a demythicized nature is amply demonstrated by a certain unexpected subtlety, a resistance to simplistic aesthetic/symbolic solutions to the human dilemma. There is nothing overtly radical in Buckler's use of the Mountain and the Valley as structural correlatives for two states of mind, two life possibilities, but it is specifically because, in Canada, these environmental features have to a significant extent escaped from or even inverted their traditional symbolic implications and values that David Canaan's alternatives seem so complex. Certainly the full impact of the ambiguity of his final vision on the mountain would be lost if it were not echoed in the shifting valuations of Buckler's setting (see chapter 7, pp 167-8 below). The possibilities do not stop here. Even more important than the advantage offered by such a landscape to traditional but relatively specialized modes like symbolism and surrealism is its role in developing a new and distinctively Canadian style of writing that, following up the parallel with developments in art, might be said to lie somewhere between abstract impressionism and magic realism. Pre-eminently exemplified in Rudy Wiebe's work, this style invokes a setting that is simultaneously abstracted into its formal essence – emphasizing graphic pattern – and irradiated with a numinous but largely unmoral (unfocused, enigmatic) emotional quality such that it subsumes both the stark immutable 'reality' of a mathematical equation and the haunting insinuation of a psychic emanation:

The grass shimmered in the morning air along the line between sky and land. Out of that line the lodges developed, another feature of the land forming against space, against shouldered hills and an ultimate suggestion of mountains. But more ancient than the blue-green hills were these lodges, their weathered poles reaching swallowtail through smoke-blackened vents, out from the smoke grey and rubbed white of their base clutching at, rooted down squatly into the earth. From that scattered grey and whitish line a shape spread, dark and gradually bumbling up until it broke apart, flaring wide into pieces whose running sound was the beating of the earth itself as they grew larger, gigantic, their shadows passing over like hawks or eagles. Horses and men drumming over the land. (H123-4)

Even aside from its implicit exploration of the man/nature relation (note again the emphasis on horizon, a motif that runs like a thread through Canadian literature), this technique provides Wiebe and others with a unique and effective means of elucidating their material – manipulating point of view, backdropping character development, suggesting thematic ramifications – to counteract the increasing evasiveness of their narrators: this development will be discussed more fully in chapters 10 and 11. The main point here, though, is that it is to a large extent the *a priori* invisibility of the Canadian landscape that makes possible individualistic usages like this. Nature really has been redeemed.

How does this tie in with other developments in the Canadian vision? The appearance of a new multivalent image of nature is actually more important for what it reveals about the underlying mythopoeic mechanism than it is in itself. The phenomenon, in other words, should be considered as a symptom rather than a cause, a technical development secondary and subsidiary to the real nexus of critical change. The factor that has been of primary importance in the evolution of our contemporary world view is not the *object* of our apprehension – the landscape – but the *mode* of that relation, *considered as a prototype for our relation not merely with nature but with the world at large*. Both the structure and the focus of our vision have, in other words, been not merely influenced but in a sense *determined* by our idiosyncratic experience of the self/other interface. How? It all comes down to the fact that the habit of apprehending the landscape has the effect of turning the viewer's attention back upon himself habitually, no matter what may be 'out there.' 'In the landscape there was nothing to distract us,' says Grove, 'except perhaps an occasional mirage. All about lay the featureless prairie, stretching away to the distant horizon, utterly flat. The fact threw us back on the immediate then-and-there and ourselves' (A274-5).

This mechanism, although superficially simple and even predictable (to avoid looking in the direction of a potentially unpleasant 'other,' one would naturally keep a short focus, avoid vistas, stay inside the garrison), implies something a little more complex, and certainly more far-reaching, than the avoidance strategies listed in chapter 2. Although the retreat from nature – the 'Wacousta syndrome' – provides a kind of prototype for responses on other levels, the recoil we are talking about here – and this is the point that must be stressed – operates quite independently of any specific stimulus. Two factors are involved in this development. In the first place, the tendency to generalization arises simply as a kind of corollary to the transformative process we have observed. Neutralization does open up the symbolic potential of the landscape, it is true, but on the psychological level it has some less laudable effects as well. *Too* extensively demythicized the environment tends simply to become a kind of void that resists *all* human connection. This is what happens in Canada. Wiebe describes the effect vividly when he tells how he and his father became lost one day driving across the prairie: 'The grass crunched as dry as crumbs and in every direction the earth so flat another two steps would place me at the horizon, looking into the abyss of the universe. There is too much here, the line of sky and grass rolls in upon you and silences you thin, too impossibly thin to remain in any part recognizably yourself' (E26). The key to the significance of this experience is found in his next sentence: '*The space must be broken somehow or it uses you up*' (italics added). Demythicized and largely unutterable, the landscape is simply so vast, so formless, that the human subject, in so far as he actually confronts this emptiness, has no choice, as Hugh Hood demonstrates in *White Figure, White Ground*, but to withdraw himself in terror:

The movement of the sky and the pulse of his body merged hideously and he felt a terrible fear, desolation, insignificance. He felt the world turning under him, and felt that he was clinging, infinitesimal himself, to a tiny ball spinning in an immensity. He had a horrified intuition that he might fall off.

He couldn't come out here again.

He gave a desperate groan, rolling over and burying his face in the hot sand, shutting out the sky, clutching and digging, trying to get back inside. (86)

When diffuse fear replaces more localized fears, the impulse to recoil becomes stronger, more automatic, less *object-oriented* almost as a matter of course.

The development does not stop here, however. As long as we are talking about an actual empirical inside/outside situation we are still limiting ourselves to the personal and the particular, the peculiarities of character and the explication of motive and behaviour. By the time the transformation runs its whole course what started out as the observable result of specific, isolable causes becomes internalized as, in a sense, an ideogrammatic representation of self-in-the-world, a means of *creating* experience rather than merely responding to it. The fact is, inasmuch as a mode of vision is unconscious and spontaneous, it tends to become conventionalized; to crystallize into patterns that are fixed, simple, and self-replicating. These patterns, once generated, begin not only to subsume all functionally equivalent future experience but to impose themselves on any 'free' – that is, unstructured, unsystematized – experiential phenomena that manifest themselves in the subject's perceptual set, such that these incline to express themselves in a compatible form whatever their actual content. This is not as far-fetched as it may seem. If we consider the evidence of cultural artifacts, it seems obvious that cognitive systems, like cultural systems, are (at least in part) regulated by a mechanism Jean Piaget calls *assimilation*. 'Psychologically ... considered, assimilation is the process whereby a function, once exercised, presses toward repetition, and in "reproducing" its own activity ... So assimilation, the process or activity common to all forms of life, is the source of that continual relating, setting up of correspondences, establishing of functional connections, and ... which finally gives rise to those general schemata we called structures.'[4] As a result of this mechanism, even generations removed from the real wilderness the *form*, if no longer always the *content*, of Canadian consciousness is still derived explicitly from the peculiar relation between the northerner and his environment. The resulting structure, in both graphic and logical variants,[5] permeates Canadian art and literature.

What, specifically, is this critical structure? We should be able to infer the answer from what we have already observed of historical and cultural trends in Canada. There is only one obvious graphic correlative for man in an apprehended environment. The prototypical 'function' that presses for replication may thus be discerned even in very early responses. Indeed, the following excerpt from W.H. Keating's account of his western travels in 1823 contains a fully developed prescription for the pattern we are seeking:

If we except the margin of the river and those of its tributary streams, which are fringed with trees and shrubbery, there is very little to interrupt the simplicity and uniformity of scenery; scarcely is there an undulation to variegate the prospect, save what is afforded by an optical illusion that *makes the traveller fancy himself in the centre of a basin, and surrounded by an amphitheatre of rising ground at no great distance, which constantly eludes his approach.* (139-40)

'The centre of a basin.' A provocative choice of words! Keating speaks of an *optical* illusion, but we may assume that here as elsewhere at least part of the stimulus shaping his perceptions is emotional. Be that as it may, what is particularly pertinent is obviously the strong sense of being *contained* – physically, not just mentally. We have seen this before, of course. Aside from demonstrating a suggestive similarity in point of view with many of the landscape paintings discussed earlier, not to mention the ghetto/engulfment image associated with the Canadian mosaic, Keating's description of his experience evokes visually a striking analogy to the circular figure-and-ground structure that was a significant formal characteristic of Richardson's novel. It would thus seem that Richardson's perspective was not as idiosyncratic as it might have seemed. Given the Canadian mode of response – the recoil from otherness – the vaguely claustrophobic effect of even an ostensibly neutral landscape *always* tends to exert a centripetal influence on the imagination. This common orientation, in turn, affects many aspects of our communal expression. Most strikingly, our art (including literature) tends to become introspective and introverted – though not necessarily (or only) in the conventional sense of those terms. How does this orientation manifest itself? With respect to literature in particular an inward turning may, at its most basic, simply signal an increased tendency toward egocentricity, whether this is expressed in an obsessive concern with one's private *feelings,* as in Susanna Moodie, or an overemphasis on one's public *role,* as in Mackenzie's *Voyages* ('As for the characters in the story,' Roy Daniells tells us, 'there is only one, Alexander Mackenzie. The voyageurs are barely named, the Indians barely numbered' 21). More significantly, however, it tends to focus attention on profound problems of identity. And this is the starting point for some of the most interesting developments in recent Canadian writing.

In itself the quest for identity is obviously not unique to Canada. In the context of Canadian culture, however, it tends to take on certain distinctive characteristics. For one thing, when man's consciousness is dominated by a pattern of response inimical to the usual process of self-definition by means of polarity, it becomes necessary to depart from those narrative forms that entail a polarized world view. In most Western literary conventions, the typical protagonist-in-search-of-himself has simply to determine his location in the range between two opposing values or qualities, and either eliminate one alternative (if the extremes are set forth in evaluative terms: good/bad) or, perhaps with the help of a mediator like Leatherstocking, reconcile, at least symbolically, the best of both worlds. Linear narrative patterns like this will *not* serve to comprehend the Canadian protagonist's plight. One example: the opposition set up by Shakespeare in *The Tempest*, as Leo Marx demonstrates in *The Machine in the Garden*, has traditionally been viewed as a paradigm for the human condition, with the self (Prospero) suspended between the beautiful and the brutal aspects of nature.[6] When Canadian critics play with this model, though, something interesting happens. 'The Prospero-Caliban antithesis is ultimately the division each individual carries within himself,' says Max Dorsinville (13). What has happened to Ariel? Mediation is impossible if one term in the polarity is unthinkable. Being in figurative terms centrally isolated and in generalized opposition to an alien, encompassing 'other,' the Canadian protagonist is thus faced with the problem of developing new conceptual modes before his quest can even be initiated.[7] Nor is this the extent of his problems. The reorientation of relations from a linear to a non-linear form also tends to dislocate a great many of the traditional symbolic correlations associated with a polarized response. As a result, all the moral/emotional dimensions of the Canadian fictional universe, not just the connotations of the landscape itself, are characteristically enigmatic and shifting. The 'self,' losing all the definition provided by the idealized categories against which it was traditionally measured, becomes – just as much as the 'non-self,' nature – a largely unknown quality. Confronted with this disquieting circumstance one has no choice but to devote oneself, as Dermot McCarthy says of Susanna Moodie, to 'the rough work of fashioning a self, a mask, a fictional "I"' (9). Kroetsch implies that the act of *un*-creating identity is a willed stance of the Canadian writer (145). Quite counter to this, our preferred iconography hints that the landscape of our dreams will, in Kroetsch's own words, un-conceal, dis-close, dis-cover us *whether we wish it or not*.

At this point we begin to notice an interesting thing about the Canadian mode of response. This description of the breakdown of traditional categories and the consequent freeing of the self from its culturally predetermined identity is strongly suggestive of certain basic elements in existential philosophy. Denying the reliability of all externally validated claims about the meaning of man's relation to the universe, the existentialists assert that it is '*only by destroying the vital lie of character*' that one can become fully liberated, fully enlightened, fully human. As Ernest Becker describes it:

The self must be destroyed, brought down to nothing, in order for self-transcendence to begin. Then the self can begin to relate itself to powers beyond itself. It has to thrash around in its finitude, it has to 'die,' in order to question that finitude, in order to see beyond it ... to infinitude, to absolute transcendence, to the Ultimate Power of Creation which made finite creatures. Our modern understanding of psycho-dynamics confirms that this progression is very logical: if you admit that you are a creature, you accomplish one basic thing: you demolish all your unconscious power linkages or supports ... [E]ach child grounds himself in some power that transcends him. Usually it is a combination of his parents, his social group, and the symbols of his society and nation ... Once you expose the basic weakness and emptiness of the person, his helplessness, then you are forced to re-examine the whole problem of power linkages. You have to think about reforging them to a real source of creative and generative power.[8]

The liberation of the self entailed by Canadian perceptual patterns is, therefore, according to this accounting, not only a potentially positive psychological development but also very much in the mainstream of twentieth-century intellectual trends.

This is not the only point of resemblance that can be identified in this context. The image of the external world we have seen bodied forth in Canadian literary tradition is also quite consonant with the type of world implied by the existentialist vision. The 'fear and loathing' we have noted beneath the Canadian's cheerful Wordsworthian diction or muscular Christian outdoorsiness, for instance, is equivalent to the 'nausea' experienced by Sartre as a result of his constant and unavoidable awareness of the pointlessness, the total formlessness of life[9]; the concomitant sense of alienation is similar to Camus' concept of the 'absurd,' a phrase coined to denote the condition of man in confrontation with 'the ineffable strangeness of reality, the plethora of alien things in Nature that have no relation to the self.'[10] The apparent resemblances between the typical Canadian response and the classic existentialist world view are thus quite striking. Indeed, even aside from the natural and 'accidental' preponderance in both fiction and poetry of images of the world as either absurd or horrifying (this effect, inasmuch as it goes well beyond the traditional negative-nature theme cited by Frye *et al.*, is particularly noticeable in such French-Canadian writers as Carrier, Hébert, Blais, and Aquin, but the same nightmare vision also characterizes the work of many recent English authors, including – in different degrees - Findley, Gibson, Helwig, LePan), much Canadian literature of the last two decades seems to propound basic tenets of existentialist theory quite explicitly and deliberately. In Jack Hodgins's treatment of the Genesis myth in *The Invention of the World*, for instance, there is an echo of Kierkegaard almost too striking to be coincidental. As Gregor Malantschuk describes it, Kierkegaard connects the Fall with the development of human awareness, and further equates Original Sin and the feelings of guilt/fear that such self-awareness inevitably involves:

In his original state man ... is bound to nature, living only in the present, in the moment. The new state begins through the human individual's capacity to rise, through reflection, above nature, and to view the future as a possibility which both attracts him and frightens him ... Since possibility always concerns the future with its drawing power and its uncertainty, the state of the individual corresponding to possibility will be anxiety, which both desires and fears possibility.

Through his experience of anxiety and possibility, which are the distinguishing marks of freedom, the individual moves away from the original 'immediate unity with his natural condition,' where he lived in innocence and ignorance, and moves in the direction of knowledge and guilt.[11]

This Kierkegaardian vision, equating awareness with distress, is strongly suggestive of the version of the Fall that Hodgins presents symbolically in his description of the Year of the Mist that came to the village of Carrigdhoun. Before this catastrophic occurrence, the villagers of the tiny Irish hamlet had lived in a state of blissful unselfconsciousness: most notably, they had been absolutely free from any sense of fear. After the coming of the Mist, however, 'they'd learned to create worlds for themselves out of their imaginations,' and by the end of the year 'the fear-disease had taken root' (106). This fear-disease, signalling the beginning of sin in Carrigdhoun, would seem virtually identical to Kierkegaard's 'anxiety.'

These resemblances should not, on the other hand, blind us to the fact that there are other, significant elements in Hodgins's myth that conflict with Kierkegaard's view. To begin with, although Kierkegaard implies that the achievement of self-knowledge entails a progression *away from* bestial ignorance and therefore, although painful, is ultimately positive, Hodgins, by associating it with fog, suggests that this new awareness was *false* knowledge, delusion: the world that the villagers saw after the mist lifted 'was only the pale counterfeit of the world they remembered seeing before' (106). Secondly, while Kierkegaard insists that the destruction of the self, the recognition of guilt, is only a preliminary step in order for 'the self [to] begin to relate itself to powers beyond itself,' Hodgins's Fall into the absurd world is non-reversible and non-transformable. No *felix culpa*, indeed it seems to have no redeeming promises to offer at all. Nora O'Sullivan's sudden fearful realization of her own mortality, for instance, is not a positive step toward ultimate enlightenment but merely a confirmation of the horror of the post-lapserian condition: 'Within a few days the thing that was growing in her went out of control and ate out her insides like a ravenous hyena, killing her before she had time to tell anyone about the terrible pain' (107).

This point of divergence underlines what seems to be a fairly critical difference between the Canadian vision and classic existentialism. The realization of an absurd and alien universe – a central facet of most variations of existentialist philosophy – is certainly there in Canadian literature; the image of the stripped-down self is also evident, though in the Canadian corpus the stripping-down generally comes across simply as the automatic and not necessarily positive consequence of a particular perceptual mode, rather than a volitional step toward enlightenment. What is *not* there is any strongly felt possibility of the kind of escape implied by the passages quoted above. For Kierkegaard the recognition of the absolute insignificance, in cosmic terms, of human existence merely opens the way for a non-rational 'leap of faith' to Christianity that allows – indeed automatically entails – transcendence of the apparent chasm man otherwise encounters as an insurmountable barrier between his limited self and his unlimited non-human environment. Kierkegaard claims, in other words, that when man is stripped of the consolations of rationality – when he has nothing left at all – then he has no choice *except* to believe, not despite but *because of* the absurdity of his belief. For Kierkegaard the shattering confrontation with the absurd is simply a starting place. 'Only when one truly despairs does he go beyond despair . It is this experience of despair that prepares him for the crisis of inwardness that leads to the religious leap' [Glicksberg 23].

This kind of hopeful assertion is not idiosyncratic. Even those later, more consistently pessimistic and firmly secular existentialists who endorse Nietzsche's proclamation that God is dead still generally suggest the possibility of *some* sort of transcendence or transformation of the absurd dilemma, albeit a more naturalistic one. When Jupiter in Sartre's *Les mouches* upbraids Orestes for his avowed intention of revealing to the people of Argos the true pointlessness of their human condition, the latter, who is clearly Sartre's spokesman in the play, replies in a positive vein reminiscent of Kierkegaard that 'human life begins on the far side of despair.'[12] Lacking Kierkegaard's explicit focus and external referents, the nature of Sartre's promised redemption is not made very clear either in this play or elsewhere, nor, in fact, is the optimistic coda nearly as convincing in this writer's work as the preliminary bleak vision of human hopelessness. Even if we leave aside such problems, however, it is questionable whether *any* kind of transcendence – religious, social, or merely 'symbolic' – is imaginatively viable in the context of the Canadian world view. In Hodgins's fictional universe, for example, life is a closed system, a *box*, from which – as from the reception hall that stands as its symbolic correlative at the end of the novel – there is only one exit, under the aegis of the Horseman, death.

It is possible (and only human), of course, to euphemize this finale, as Becker does, but the nursery rhyme echo evoked by his choice of closing words quite pointedly undercuts both the redemptive implications of the so-called House of Revelations, where the departed have ostensibly gone, and the religious rhetoric that has historically provided man with this kind of consolation. Hodgins's point is not that his protagonists are among the damned. Indeed, by the time they make their ambiguous exit both Maggie and Wade have 'paid their dues,' come to terms with the existential vision (Wade through a subterranean confrontation with his own mortality, as represented by his döppelganger, the same Horseman who carries him off at the end of the story; Maggie by her realization, as she looks down at the island from an airplane on the way home from her pilgrimage to Ireland, that human endeavour must seem utterly insignificant in the face of an indifferent and all-encompassing nature), but there is no suggestion that their respective epiphanies provide any way out of the dilemma. Hodgins, for one, seems to deny firmly the possibility of a 'leap.'

Hodgins's stance is not a surprising one. There are several aspects of the Canadian response that work to preclude the possibility of transcendence. Even aside from the fact that a typically gothic mode of relation to the wilderness exacerbates one's fear of the other side of *any* wall, whether of logs or of flesh, the tendency for the Canadian to visualize his situation in terms of centre-ground works against a convincing conceptualization of the movement implied by the Kierkegaardian solution. If the 'self,' in other words, is always perceived in explicit opposition to a diffuse, absolutely alien 'other,' subsuming not just nature but the totality of non-human reality, including God, then 'out there' simply becomes the direction of undifferentiated danger. The 'leap' outward from the self here-and-now – even if this is equated with 'upward to God' or 'forward beyond history' – is not, therefore, even in abstract terms easily reconcilable with the dynamics of the Canadian vision. This is probably at least part of the reason why there is virtually no native Canadian science fiction.[13] It is also why, despite the tantalizing similarities of stance and tone, it is dangerous to try to fit Canadian literature too exclusively into an unmodified existentialist framework. There *is* an overlap, but the coincidence is only partial. Even leaving Kierkegaard and his Christianity aside as a special case, a problem is implied by the very terms of reference spawned by the existentialist idiom. '[T]hough a deep gulf divides man from his non-human world,' says Arturo Fallico, 'the break is neither radical nor "given"; it is more in the nature of a polarity than a duality. After the ratiocinative mind has done its worst to deepen the gulf, the mind's primordial union with its world at its very foundations remains patient and undisturbed.'[14] As we have seen, the Canadian viewpoint does *not* generally lend itself to an authentically polarized model such as this terminology entails.

Even on a more naturalistic level, the Canadian response to nature itself militates not just against Christian Kierkegaardian-type redemption but against other kinds of transformation as well. In the United States, twentieth-century man has by and large been able to withstand the encroachments of post-Nietszchean nihilism due to the fact that a naive pantheism residual in the native character has encouraged the vague conviction that some sort of union with nature – whether by way of full-blown Emersonian oriental-cum-platonic mysticism or simpler Whitmanesque 'sympathy' – can provide a symbolic/emotional or even a 'real' means of transcending human mortality and isolation. The impact of the existentialist dilemma has thus been deflected or at least softened into something more academic than immediate. The garden myth, which continued to play a central role in America's self-image even after the inevitable covert decay of the Christian ethos, reinforced this particular habit of thought. Even if one does not believe in the possibility of 'leaping' forward, ascending upward to the angels, one can still hope to return, by means of the aforementioned union with nature, to the primeval source, re-achieving the purportedly blissful innocence and wholeness of an animal past.[15]

For the Canadian, however, the backward movement, just as much as the forward one, suggests an unpleasant if not impossible endeavour. Again Hodgins' book illuminates the distinction. In contrast with the traditional image of Eden, the pre-mist, pre-lapserian village of Carrigdhoun is barren, open, abstract: as free of vegetative excess as of irrational emotion. When the villagers are forced after the mist to leave this peaceful haven for Vancouver Island, moreover, it is made clear that their Fall – attended with all the anxiety and trauma mythically imputed to that particular eviction – is *into* rather than *away from* nature:

In all that ragged company, only Jems the Cripple found the strength to cry out his dismay when they'd arrived at the land. The others were silently aghast or too exhausted to care. Gathered, huddled in the little clearing on the high sudden precipice above the sea, they watched Keneally out of eyes like dark smudges. 'Jaysus,' Jems the Cripple said, 'the trees!' And all of them, who on their journey had felt themselves driven already to an incredible sense of smallness, looked up, up, at the giants that stood thicker and taller than the highest church spire they'd ever seen. And one by one ... they went down on their knees on the damp floor of fir needles and cones. 'Mother of God!' someone said. 'The trees!' As if they hoped that all of this was just one more mirage created by their conjurer-leader. (115-16)

One can hardly wish to 'return' to a garden that, rather than being associated with a prior state of happy innocence, is an after-effect of – a punishment for – the Fall.

What Hodgins has produced here is a total inversion of the traditional American westering myth (the view of the pioneer movement as approximating

in some fashion the reattainment of Paradise) and the Turner thesis of social
value that grew out of it – which is no more than one might expect given our
survey. Hodgins's novel in fact might be viewed as paradigmatic. Even leaving
aside the rather blatant implications of the Keneally legend that provides a
symbolic matrix for the story, Maggie Donovan, moving out of the mountains
and forests of her childhood down to the coastal town, recapitulates exactly the
characteristic movement of the Canadian imagination *toward the human
centre*. Familiar? Of course. This is Catharine Parr Traill, looking for her
kitchen garden. More strikingly, it is also Jerome Martell, the charismatic hero
of Hugh MacLennan's *The Watch that Ends the Night*, who as a child fled *out* of
the wilderness, downriver from the primitive logging camp where he was born
(a setting described almost entirely in terms of alienation and violence and
perversions of human feeling) to the city where he could find safety, love, a
name. '"[I]t's always seemed to me an incredible privilege to belong to
civilization,"' he says later (244). In tacit rebuttal not only of Turner but of
every would-be nature-nurtured American Adam from Huckleberry Finn to
Hemingway's Nick Adams, this is a man who knows just how stark and brutal
life in the woods can be. It is also *us*! Martell's attitude, his *orientation*, is one
that Canadians in general – despite their much-touted wilderness bravado – are
not merely inclined but preconditioned to share. Even aside from the explicit
paranoia observed above, this is why, outside of a few exceptions like Ethel
Wilson's *Swamp Angel*, and Fred Bodsworth's wildlife stories, and – although
even these, as we will see later, reveal a number of ambiguities – the novels of
W.O. Mitchell, the pastoral idyll is rarely invoked with any success in Canada.
'Rural interludes traditionally represent an awakening to consciousness of
urban characters,' says Moss, but, he continues, in the Canadian practice, even
when a movement out into the countryside plays a pivotal role in the plot of a
novel, the conventional conjunction of landscape and enlightenment often
seems more arbitrary than real, or absent altogether: 'Human and geophysical
realities do not converge. There is no reciprocity, no mutual illumination of
complementary conditions. Instead, there is the residual effect of opposing
conditions, where one acts as a spotlight on some particular aspect of the other'
(D119).

One especially striking example cited by Moss is from Gabrielle Roy's
Alexandre Chenevert, caissier. Like many twentieth-century fictional protagonists, the title character of this work, a bank clerk in Montreal, is oppressed by
the pettiness and pointlessness of urban existence. In Ben-Zion Shek's words,
he 'experiences feelings of alienation vis-à-vis the Metropolis, the economic
institution in which he works, and the culture of a minority which presses in on
him, a member of the majority French-speaking group' (185). In response to the
'overwhelming feeling of non-being' because of his involuntary isolation
Chenevert seeks exactly that brand of compensation so frequently exploited in

American fiction of similar ilk: a return to nature. At first the result is exactly what one might expect. Arriving at Lac Vert he is initially disoriented but before long he begins to develop an exhilarating sense of freedom and well-being. 'From confusion there is a sudden climb to contentment, *élan*, and love of life. The traveller has reached a plateau of satisfaction with God and the world. He takes pleasure in hearing the sound of rain on his cabin roof, welcomes the affection of the farmer's dog and abandons himself to the ancient dream of Robinson Crusoe' (Warwick 88). All very predictable. Where the conventional pattern would stop here, however, Chenevert's process of self-confrontation goes a crucial step further. Despite, or perhaps because of, the pleasure he has found during the interlude he is in the end brought to reject his fantasies of pioneering because his intuition tells him these are founded on an illusion that, just as much as the impersonal city, ultimately lacks the power to satisfy his hunger for 'life.' Cutting short his holiday, he returns with some relief to familiar terrain. 'To the solitude of the country, he prefers in the end that of the city, in spring, when windows open and one innocently enters the lives of others' (Shek 189).

Departures from explicitly invoked convention reveal more than simple conformity ever can. Such divergence from the pastoral pattern as Moss notes here thus not only violates our expectations (which may or may not be an aesthetic problem) but strongly supports the hypothesis that the Canadian simply does not believe that the landscape offers either moral lessons *or* an escape from the self. If we are not easily persuaded to leap blindly into the void, neither will we risk ourselves by placing our emotional dependence on an idealized garden that we can scarcely even conceive. From the Canadian perspective, if there *is* a garden at all, it is in all probability like the gardens of Sylvia Fraser's *Pandora* – a 'poison pocket' full of plants so deadly that even to 'say them aloud would poison [one's] mouth' or a carefully preserved 'Wilde Corner' in the park, with a flasher in the bushes (17, 48-51). In such a world transcendence by way of nature is not only unlikely, but dangerous. The whole idea of *exploration*, consequently, far from being the national obsession it has proven for the United States (space opera is just another version of the western, of course), is in this country, on the rare occasions it is even considered, generally presented as a tragic experience. In Matt Cohen's 'Columbus and the Fat Lady,' for instance, the lust for discovery is quite explicitly self-destructive; a sickness if not (as the Spanish priests who try to exorcise the explorer's demons obviously believe) a mortal sin. Similarly, the cumulative impression made by the 'true' exploration stories in Farley Mowat's *Top of the World* trilogy is one of a stubborn foolhardiness for which nature was wont to exact an exceedingly stiff price. Hodgins's version of the Fall into the garden, in other words, is neither eccentric nor rare. In total opposition to the American dream of regaining paradise, the Canadian's concern (as Douglas Jones recognizes in

Butterfly on Rock) is more typically with accommodating himself to the expulsion.

An apparent acceptance of life as a closed system and a suspicion (if not a fear) of proposed modes of breaking out are thus common characteristics of Canadian literature. The Canadian existentialist, that is, almost always stops short of the optimistic coda to his vision of the absurd. He lives, in spirit if not in fact, in a narrow corridor surrounded – hemmed in – by oppressive ranks of vaguely sinister hills. 'I don't know why I hated the hills,' says Edward McCourt's Stephen Venner, in an attempt to unravel the complexities of his own peculiar confrontation with the existentialist dilemma in *The Wooden Sword*: 'Most boys I knew liked hills. Something to climb. But to me they were alive. Alive and remote and frightening. Watching me all the time. Whenever I did something I knew I shouldn't, I thought that the hills were watching. God's spies...' (71). Venner is not alone in his sense of being spied upon by possibly unfriendly, certainly alien, eyes. In Watson's *The Double Hook* this watching 'other' is such a strongly felt presence that it becomes personified as Coyote, the morally ambivalent, humanly incomprehensible trickster-god of the Plains Indians. Indeed, in Watson's book the entire landscape is animated with a sensed but unseen menace ('Mist rising from the land and pressing in. Twigs cracking like bone. The loose boulder and the downdrop. The fear of dying somewhere alone, caught against a tree or knocked over in an inch of water.' 42) which communicates itself as a uniquely vivid objectification of man's anxiety-ridden awareness of his own mortality. From such a landscape there is no exit. Like a horse tied to his master by bonds much stronger than fences and bridles, a person, as William comments in this novel, 'only escapes in circles no matter how far the rope spins' (132). Here is that ubiquitous structure again.

What about Martell's 'civilization,' though? If nature shuts us in, doesn't the city – Prospero's arts – offer a way out? We mustn't be deluded by the fact that our sense of the existential trap is often imaged as an anti-westering myth into forgetting that at least by the mid-twentieth century the recoil, the introspective impulse that characterizes the type Canadian response to the environment, is no longer necessarily linked to a hostile landscape, but represents a generalized stance vis-à-vis the entire external world. In so far as the city – like the more primitive fort – signifies a gathering together of humans for mutual comfort it may stand for something positive, but in so far as it is 'setting,' that is, the realm of the transpersonal, it is just as alien as – indeed, an exact moral/emotional equivalent to – the 'real' wilderness that Richardson was so intimidated by. John Martens, one of David Helwig's protagonists, makes this identification explicit. When, lost in the heart of London, he recalls a story he heard as a child about a trapper lost in the northern Ontario woods, the anecdote strikes him forcefully as emblematic of his own situation. 'The landscape here was as anonymous and hostile as that forest,' he muses: 'blocks of flats that all looked the same, closed circles of acquaintanceship' (A10). Martens – an outcast, an amnesiac, a self-created double agent – though an extreme case, in some ways (as discussed further in the next chapter) epitomizes the Canadian condition. In any case, it is certainly true that his conflation of city and wilderness – not only opposites but active antagonists in the polarized American vision – is characteristically Canadian.

Landscape and cityscape thus mirror each other quite oddly in Canadian literature. Indeed it is not uncommon for one to be depicted specifically and extensively in terms of its conventional alter. E.J. Pratt, for instance, not only endows natural creatures with the attributes of machinery but makes machines into living animals. In an early poem, 'The Shark,' he gives his subject a fin 'Like a piece of sheet-iron ... with a knife-edge' (5). Later, in 'The Submarine,' he reciprocates by calling the man-made craft a 'tiger-shark' and turning its encounter with the troopship into a battle between two great predators of the sea (89–94). In Dunkirk, the Nazi tanks are seen as 'multipedes,' while the bombers are 'great Birds' (306, 308). This is not an idiosyncratic usage. Some of Earle Birney's imagery is almost identical. Flying fish in the poem by that name 'flash into the alien air/ toward the dry and blinding sky/ stall and fall and soar and then/ flicker back' (59). In 'And the Earth Grow Young Again,' alternately, planes are 'monstrous kites,' 'revenging raptors' (80). At least one implication would seem to be that the natural and the artful are in some sense interchangeable.

This raises some interesting questions. The technique employed by these poets, considered in a world context, is by no means original, or even, taken at face value, particularly radical. What is notable, however, is the way the poetry in which these images appear diverges from convention not in method but in *effect*. In traditional terms, the yoking of animate and inanimate, nature and civilization, is almost always done to convey a moral message. Value is underlined by the ironic juxtaposition of one reality with its opposite. Wallace Stevens' jar on the hill in Tennessee, giving meaning to the environing wilderness. Or – especially during the neo-primitivistic sixties and early seventies – visions of nature evoked to underline the sterility of the modern city. In Canadian practice, however, the moral framework is rarely that simple. Even in Birney, who tends to fluctuate between the naive primitivism of 'Eagle Island' and the outright nature-paranoia of 'Bushed,' it is difficult to find an unambiguous conclusion. 'And the Earth Grow Young Again' is fairly typical in that although the poet's *overt* message is that the natural predator is preferable to the man-made one ('By Christ I wish that fuselage/ of greater girth [than the osprey's] had never raged/ nor should storm up again/ from this too artful earth' 81), the violence associated directly with nature, along with the reverse imagery that connects the birds indirectly with the war, tends to undercut, at least a little, the authority of the ending. In Pratt the ambiguity is even more deeply embedded. Indeed, to a large extent this ambiguity becomes his subject. Is it the iceberg (both beautiful *and* brutal, cathedral *and* claw) or the human arrogance embodied in the *Titanic* which causes that disaster? Is the cachalot meant to be a positive symbol, an emblem of human heroism, for his battle against the 'collective' evil of the kraken, or simply an image of the violence in nature that threatens (and defeats) mankind? Pratt's moral vision has been amply documented by critics such as Sandra Djwa, so it is enough to point out here the extent to which the shifting moral associations of both art and nature in his poetry are typical of the Canadian vision as a whole.

The result of this kind of moral confusion is, of course, to exacerbate one's anxiety about what is 'out there.' The twentieth-century setting, like Richardson's gothic wilderness, is to be feared and avoided not so much because it offers recognizable dangers as simply because it is unknown, *unknowable*. This equation perhaps explains why, far beyond Hodgins, fog seems to play such an important role in the Canadian imagination, recurring as a critical (that is, reverberatory or subsumptive) image less frequently but often with even more provocative effect than snow. Norman Duncan described the type experience back in the nineteenth century:

Fog and night, coalescing, reduced the circumference of things material to a yet narrowing circle of black water. The feel of the fog was like the touch of a cold, wet hand in the dark. The night was heavy; it was, to the confusion of all sense, *falling*; it seemed to have been strangely vested with the properties of density and weight; it was, in truth, like a great pall descending, oppressing, stifling. Here is an awesome mystery; for the night was no substance; the mist, also, is impalpable! The fog, like the dark, is a hiding-place for shadowy terrors; it covers up familiar places – headlands and hills and coves and starry heavens – and secludes, in known vacancy, all the fantastic monsters that enter into and possess the imaginings of children in lonely times. (169-70)

Something that reduces circumference, weighs in on one. Something impalpable yet impenetrable that swallows up every conjecture one might project on it, yet refuses either to confirm or to refute. It's easy to see why Canadian writers would seize on this image. It provides such a trenchant correlative for our sense of our own condition. Besides, it's so *flexible*. It can be made to suggest almost any circumstance, any mood one wishes, while at the same time covertly carrying as its ultimate message the news of man's absolute limitation. It doesn't even always have to be negative. Timothy Findley exploits its most horrific potential in *The Wars* when his protagonist gets lost in a waterlogged, corpse-covered battleground where stinking mud sucks at his legs and stinking fog, saturated with chlorine gas, comes down 'like a muffler over his face': 'when Robert's eyes had cleared, he cast a single look back to where [he] ... had been. He saw that the whole field was filled with floating shapes. The only sounds were the sounds of feeding and of wings' (80, 82). This is otherness at its most inhuman. In Kroetsch's *But We Are Exiles*, however, the fog, as if it were not the negation but the *totality* of landscape, the ultimate Canadian psycho-setting, actually reflects the human centre back in on itself.

Johnny Louttit had come around from the side of the house on the house barge and was waving to get attention in the pilot-house and pointing forward into the fog.

Abraham straightened up from his hand of cards and looked. 'There's an iceberg up there and we're going to ram it head on and lose all hands before we can get the lifeboat down.'

'There's a dust storm heading this way,' Mud said. 'A good old Saskatchewan dust storm.'

'A plague of grasshoppers,' Pottle said. 'Whipped on by a herd of galloping polar bears.'

They all strained to see into the fog. Straining, they could here and there see eddies where there had seemed to be only stillness before. They were afloat in a pool of water that was somehow suspended in a world of fog. 'You make out anything?' Peter asked.

Abraham folded shut his hand of cards. 'Look.'

Peter turned his head quickly to where Abraham pointed straight ahead.

'It's a neon sign. The government just opened a big beer-parlour on a sandbar, and they want us to be the first customers.' (67-8)

From one point of view the 'box' makes a mockery of human aspirations. From another, a demythicized landscape says that anything is possible – at least 'inside.' Canadian literature in the twentieth century has largely addressed itself to the task of negotiating if not often actually reconciling these two extremes.

NOTES

1 In one of his simpler formulations Lévi-Strauss claims that logical relations between nature and culture are explored in myth by means of the food categories raw and cooked. This is fairly straightforward. Many of his other interpretations are considerably less so. The 'code' he finds embedded in the Oedipus myth, for instance, purportedly substitutes cases of over- and under-estimation of kinship bonds for the alternatives of chthonic and non-chthonic origins.

2 Interestingly, in recent usage snow can be ambiguous even when it is indubitably fatal. In Gwendolyn MacEwen's story 'Noman,' a young immigrant with romantic fancies about snow ('it was a kind of heavenly confetti, ambrosia or manna, and he rushed out half-mad at the first snowfall and lost himself in the sweet salt cold' 76) is, predictably, frozen to death. The mode of his death, however, raises some questions about the *meaning* of that fate: 'She *was* surprised, though not totally, to find

Grigori lying there ... with his Mediterranean hair all aflurry from the wind and his absolutely naked stone dead body wedged somehow into the snow drift, and his arms outstretched at his sides as if he'd been making his last angel./ But what really got her was the smile on his face' (80).

3 The distinction I want to make here will perhaps be a little clearer if we look at Sigurd Burkhardt's discussion of the function of ambiguity in poetic language. 'For Empson, ambiguity became all but synonymous with the essential quality of poetry; it meant complexity, associative and connotative richness, texture, and the possibility of irony ... By exploiting the ambiguity of words the poet could ironically undercut the surface meanings of his statements, could avail himself fully of the entire field of meanings which a word has and is. I want to shift the stress of Empson's analysis a little. He made us aware that one word can – and in great poetry commonly does – have *many meanings*; I would rather insist on the converse, that many meanings can have *one word*. For the poet, the ambiguous word is the crux of the problem of creating a medium for him to work in. If meanings are primary and words only their signs, then ambiguous words are false; each meaning should have its word, as each sound should have its letter. But if the reverse is true and words are primary – if, that is, they are the corporeal entities the poet requires – then ambiguity is something quite different: it is the fracturing of a pristine unity by the analytic conceptualizations of prose. The poet must assume that where there is one word there must, in some sense, be unity of meaning, no matter what prose usage may have done to break it. The pun is the extreme form of this assumption, positing unity of meaning even for purely accidental homophones, such as the sound shifts of a language will happen to produce.

'Ambiguity, then, becomes a test case for the poet; in so far as he can vanquish it – not by splitting the word, but by fusing its meanings – he has succeeded in making language into a true medium' (*Shakespearian Meanings* [Princeton 1968] 32-3). If we take 'language' in the semiotic sense to mean any expressive system, any set of significatory elements, we may say that the landscape, in so far as it is used by Canadian writers as vehicle as well as setting, has achieved exactly this poetic fusion.

4 Piaget, *Structuralism*, trans. & ed. Chaninah Maschler (Harper & Row 1970) 71

5 These aspects are quite naturally interchangeable since, as J. Bronowski points out, 'in our society, we express logical relations as structure, and we express structure as shape.' Furthermore, because 'no design exists in isolation from others,' we may expect to find 'a unity among the things we make, a unity of purpose and of action, which shapes their design toward the image of an age.' *The Visionary Eye: Essays in the Arts, Literature, and Science* (MIT 1978) 41, 42-3

6 See 'Shakespeare's American Fable' in Marx, *The Machine in the Garden: Technology and the Pastoral Ideal in America* (Oxford 1964) 34-72.

7 See Kattan for an intriguing discussion of the extent to which Canada and the United States represent polar opposites in their respective relations to the

imaginative dimensions implied by space and time, and the effect this has had on linear/non-linear thinking. We will discuss this further in chapter 11.

8 Becker, *The Denial of Death* (Free Press 1975) 88, 89-90

9 Sartre's view of existence as nauseating is expressed most explicitly in the semi-surrealistic early novel, *The Diary of Antoine Roquentin*, but it is a motif that runs through – indeed, predominates in – almost all his works.

10 Charles I. Glicksberg, *The Tragic Vision in Twentieth-Century Literature* (Delta 1970) 55

11 Malantschuk, *Kierkegaard's Thought*, ed. and trans. H.V. Hong & E.H. Hong (Princeton 1974) 259-60, quoting from Soren Kierkegaard, *The Concept of Anxiety [Dread]*, trans. Walter Howie (Princeton 1957) 37

12 In William V. Spanos, ed., *A Casebook on Existentialism* (Crowell 1966) 50

13 John Robert Colombo's *Other Canadas* is purportedly an anthology of Canadian science fiction, but, as Terence Green points out, his criteria are so loose as to be meaningless. 'Colombo includes nearly everything to either the concept of Canadian (former Canadians as well as non-Canadians when their work is set in Canada, qualify) or to the concept of science fiction (film script of NFB's *Universe*; poetry)' (3-4).

14 Fallico, *Art & Existentialism* (Prentice-Hall 1962) 6

15 The relationship between the mythic and historical past is discussed more fully below, in chapter 11.

5

The House of Revelations

Now that we have traced the historical development that structured the contemporary Canadian imagination, it remains to examine the way these characteristic structures enter into our present-day communal expression. Not surprisingly, the phenomenon may be observed in its purest form in art rather than literature – although no critic has yet documented the trend. As with nineteenth-century landscape painting it is possible to explicate the work of Canadian artists almost solely in terms of international movements. When we examine the corpus holistically, though, it can be seen that certain features, certain peculiarities of stance and concern, unify the practice of quite radically different schools while cumulatively demonstrating a number of significant divergences, at least in emphasis, from their ostensible foreign models.

Like contemporaneous writers, many Canadian artists of even recent decades have continued merely to transliterate their experience of the landscape in fairly traditional and straightforward ways. As might be expected, moreover, the *kind* of landscape they seem to see is generally consistent with earlier visions. Notwithstanding George Woodcock's comment that his work 'involves a deep penetration into many aspects of the British Columbian environment' (F42), Jack Shadbolt's view of the Pacific coast, for instance, seems very similar to Emily Carr's. This similarity of tone if not execution is demonstrated particularly strikingly in the large triptych entitled *The Way In* (1973), where the only proffered entry into the grotesque profusion of the rainforest is dark, narrow, and altogether forbidding. In a different mood but with complementary implications is the work of another west coast artist, Toni Onley, whose cool monumental landscapes (in Michael Greenwood's words) typically reflect 'the antiquity and immense endurance of the land as a reality against which the span of human existence is infinitesimal' (A15). This vision demonstrates considerable kinship with the type response delineated in the last chapter.

Even with non-representational artists one can often make fairly direct connections between perception and expression. Discussing the 'big attack' colour-painting of Kenneth Lochhead (whom Ronald Rees describes as 'the first pictorial artist in the West to explore the metaphorical possibilities of the prairie … as an empty, meaningless landscape' 275), David Thompson, for instance, draws our attention to a degree of consonance between idiom and subject matter that has generally been obscured by the explicit 'Americanness' of the work in question. 'The prairie is of a flatness and endlessness that make even its cities look like arbitrary interruptions of the dominant horizontal,' he says. If these pieces strike closer to an American norm 'in [their] command of scale and the totality of the colour-field than is usual in Canadian painting, [then,] one might say paradoxically that it was for Canadian reasons' (72). On a more specific level, habitual negativity toward the environment may also be seen as responsible at least indirectly for the continued prevalence of such composition-al features as the shortened focus and segregation of 'life-spaces' that Philip Fry finds in the work of prairie sculptor Don Proch.

The strong horizon is both the visual and emotional framework in which incidents of prairie experience take place. What one sees and, more importantly, what one knows about what one sees, is situated in that context, not through its visual relation to the actual horizon but through its relationship to the horizon of consciousness. What one does see clearly are the details – the grass under one's feet, the faces of friends, the hands that work the soil, machines, signs that give directions and establish orientation. Unlike the city, the flatland does not easily afford a visual context of human scale. The eye jumps from the microscopic to the macroscopic, from the grain of wheat to the big sky. Rather than being perceived within a set of visual relations, various things are seen in isolation. (46)

From these few examples it would seem there is a remarkable similarity between the writers and the artists of contemporary Canada vis-à-vis both the base vision of the world from which they start *and* their spontaneous reactions to this.

More interesting than such more or less conventional responses as these, however, are those visual documents reflecting a *secondary* stage of develop-ment, wherein the idiosyncratic self/other relation reveals itself only covertly, having been translated into purely formal elements. In this stage, if the landscape is evoked at all it is with duplicity. As object it still retains its own autonomy but as *vehicle* it is pure projection, a correlative for or ideogrammatic representation of those cognitive structures that are both prior and consequent to its manifested existence. 'I see nature,' says Shadbolt, 'when sections of it are brought into micro-focus, transforming itself into emblems – a stylized synthesis with abstractly memorable overtones. I don't know what it signifies but I know acutely what it feels like' (A29). The reason why it is difficult to say what it signifies is, of course, that what it signifies – thus transformed – is simply self, *being*: that is, *being-in*. This is where it all starts and ends.

The terms of expression at this level are exactly what we might predict. I said above that art in Canada tends to be introverted; as far as the plastic arts are concerned this is certainly the case. Almost across the board we can detect a centripetal impulse. Compositions tend to be *centred*, not merely with respect to the positioning of components but dynamically, with respect to the internal tensions of the visual gestalt. This may be achieved by explicit means – as in Shadbolt's *Winter Theme No. 7* (1961), where an unruly cluster of quasi-organic shapes are 'pinned' to a rigid geometric framework that strictly delimits any tendency the components might have to fly apart – or it may be something as subtle as the central 'squeezing' of Jack Bush's *School Tie* (1958) and *Pink Blossom* (1965); the contrast in Roy Kiyooka's *Barometer* (1964) between the sharp, bright, rigid central strip and the soft, dark shapes that envelope it; the disproportionate authority of the tiny pink target in the middle section of John Meredith's triptych *Seeker* (1966); the strain at the point of cleavage in Michael Snow's *Beach-hcaeb* (1963); or the sizzle of the lightning-like filament down the centre of Harold Town's *Great Divide* (1965). One of the more intriguing examples of this orientation is Paul-Emile Borduas' *Expansion rayonnante* (1956). Notwithstanding its title, this explosion seems more of an *im*-plosion, since the thick layers of oleaginous white paint seem to be superimposed and encroaching upon the dark centre. Also, most of the 'rays' are broader and blunter toward the canvas edges, tapering to the middle like darts. Whatever the particular idiom, though, in all these cases, and indeed in a surprising proportion of contemporary Canadian paintings in general, the reference is clearly internalized.

Moving from composition to content we see that the controversial response is reflected not merely in orientation but more specifically in aspects of iconography. The structural propensities noted above, in other words, show up not merely in the artist's implied attitude toward his material but in the actual forms with which he chooses to image it. Most notable among the patterns of preference to be discerned (because it echoes most explicitly the prototypical figure/ground ideogram) is a recurrent 'containment' motif. This turns up in many different guises depending on the school as well as the personal biases of the artist, but all share the common denominator of a roughly geometric focal 'enclosure' and an inside/outside (instead of vertical or horizontal) organization of pictorial space. Variants may range anywhere from the quiet irony of Roy Kiyooka's *The Bridge* (1965) to the overt emotionalism of Joyce Wieland's assemblage, *Young Woman's Blues* (1964) with its 'boxed' ego peering wistfully out at the world through a cloudy heart-shaped window, but some of the most interesting are those that mirror the existential dilemma by reproducing not merely the inside/outside discontinuity with its attendant strain but also the human/inhuman (animate/inanimate) dichotomy. Gordon Rayner's *Aquarium* (1962) is a good example of this.[1] As the title suggests, the dynamic elements of the composition are 'boxed' into a small, rigid, rectangular space at the lower right of the picture. This 'aquarium,' interestingly enough, while it straddles the horizon between the contrasting flat red/mottled grey-blue planes that fill the rest of the space, internalizes its referents to an extent that makes it equally recalcitrant to both. The yellow echoes inside and outside the box, far from suggesting any sort of transcendence, only serve to accentuate the impression of 'edges' or 'boundaries.' A similar and perhaps even more intense effect is achieved in Ted Godwin's *'G' Corners* (1964). Here lively white vermiform shapes are crowded into a narrow red box that seems to 'protect' them from a diffusely energized, subtly oppressive blue-grey ground.

The question arises at this point as to what extent these trends really are idiosyncratic to Canada. Certainly none of the features mentioned could be seen, in themselves, as unique. As Edward Lucie-Smith points out, indeed, 'The bold central image has become one of the trademarks of the new American painting – one of the things that differentiates it from European art.'[2] But even aside from the fact that the centring tendency seems far less ubiquitous, less exclusive south of the border (one need only think, for example, of the paintings in the Rothko Room of the Tate Gallery, in which, in Hugh Adams's words, 'Each area of colour seems to expand spatially, and appears to bleed over the edge of the canvas,'[3] or of de Kooning's energetic gestural works), such central images as do appear in general tend to evoke quite a different mood than those we observe in Canada. For one thing, they typically seem self-assertive rather than introspective; the sense of *strain* associated with the Canadian version is therefore almost entirely absent. Some, like Franz Kline's enormous black-on-white ideograms, not only overlap the edges of the canvas but resonate with striking if inexplicit hints of extrinsic validation. Most important of all, there does not seem to be in American works the insistence on the absoluteness of the discontinuity between inside and outside that we have been discussing. This can be illustrated by comparing a few works from each country having in common a strong, central, circular motif – the prototypical correlative for the containment theme.

Art McKay's *Flux* (1964) and Ronald Bloore's *Painting* (1961) are typical of Canada in that in both of them the *closure* is complete. In the former the radiating texture of the red circle at first suggests an opening out, but any extrovertive tendency is strictly delimited by the fine but definite, doubled light/dark outline that accentuates the integrity of the form. In Bloore's work, similarly, the white circle is broken, uneven, hinting initially that it may be breached or transcended, but this possibility is firmly denied by the heavy green-black border that seals off the vulnerable edge from the 'outside.' The American handling of the motif is quite different. In Kenneth Nolan's 'target' paintings (ca 1962) the series of relatively sharp inner rings are – provocatively enough – typically encapsulated in a fuzzy outer ring that appears to mediate between figure and ground. In Jasper John's *White Target with Four Faces* (1957), alternately, the central form itself is a closed one, but the viewer's reference point is obviously the row of half-obscured faces that look out from above and behind the board on which the target is mounted. In the light of contrasts like these, I think we are justified in saying – as with the nineteenth-century landscape paintings – that although Canadians are using the same basic idiom, what they do with it is significantly different.

Containment is not the only, or indeed the ultimate, expression of the Canadian's sense of his relation with the universe – although it is probably the most *basic* form. An allied theme with somewhat more complex psychological implications is hinted at in the recurrent motif of 'framing.' With this motif there is still an effect of 'boxed' experience, a distinction between inside and outside, but with this difference: that the line dividing these life spaces is not existential but self-evidently arbitrary, imposed, *constructed*.[4] Examples are boundless. In William Ronald's *Ontario Place* (1971), typically enough, intricate, oozy, quasi-organic shapes are crudely but definitively boxed in by a broad, sketchily striped, rectangular framework. Similarly, in John Meredith's 1962 *Painting #1*, large, naive, semi-geometric doodles are dominated, pulled into focus, by a superimposed red-and-pink barred square. These two pieces establish not only the type composition but, what is more important, the impression of control-achieved-only-by-an-act-of-will which is probably the single most important feature of the mode. In Gordon Rayner's *Magnetewan* (1965) this effect of precarious order is even more obvious. Here a central oily cluster, though focused on a red-edged black blob of great vividness and authority, seems almost to merge into the mottled, washy background. Any tendency to diffusion is checked, however, by the thin but self-assertive red frame overlying the central grouping. Despite minor differences in these works, the pattern of perception and response is surprisingly consistent. The *ultimate* exemplar for the framing motif, on the other hand, is perhaps Henry Bonli's *Orange Field* (1962). In this painting the emphasis is entirely on the frame; there is no overt content *except* the framework, so the message is undiluted. What is this message? One of the most interesting things about a frame is that – unlike, for the most part, simple containment – it doesn't always appear to 'mean' the same thing. Although certain *general* psychological or emotional concomitants do seem to be among the identifying marks of the species, the implied experiential correlatives would seem to be variable.

In at least some variants – like Otto Rogers's boxed landscapes, for instance – the intent would seem merely to be to control by containing some aspect of otherness. In such cases, moreover – as we might expect from the foregoing chapters – the object contained usually seems at least subtly inimical. This holds even for overtly positive views like Rogers's. In *Sunset Stillness* (1967), for instance, diffuse multiple bordering in darker tones of green and brown frames a light-flooded landscape. The initial impression is peaceful and nostalgic. Despite the conventions connoted by the title, however, the heavy quiescence of the scene, accentuated by the frontalism, the virtual symmetry, and especially the turgid, slightly squashed shapes of the sun and tree that form a double focus for the composition, makes it seem as if the canvas is saturated rather than radiant with light. The overall effect is subtly stultifying, mysterious, perhaps even vaguely sinister. *Sunset Stillness* would thus seem – despite the surficial dominance of a reassuring pastoral idiom – to hint at the same kind of reality as we are given, much more poignantly, in Michael Snow's *Lac Clair* (1960). The 'lake' of this painting, which might be taken as an emblem of nature in general, is, quite explicitly, opaque rather than clear (the irony of the title only serves to underline the discrepancy between expectations and actuality), and thus totally inaccessible to human penetration or comprehension. The only way the artist can deal with it is by framing it, 'wrapping it up' with rigid brackets of brown paper tape.

In pictures like these two, framing would seem primarily to represent a means of defusing the threat (overt or covert) of the inhuman world 'out there.' The implications of this are similar to the work of a group of British Columbia artists who styled themselves the N.E. Thing Co. This group, among other things, during the seventies set itself, as Charlotte Townsend describes it, quite literally to 'bag' the environment, 'putting the green, rocky, Pacific coast, blue water and toy boats into bags of clear vinyl' (77). Bagging, like framing, is obviously a kind of self-protective ritual. The uncontrollable must be at least symbolically controlled, or contained. 'Polythene, a sensuous but cool medium,' Townsend continues, comes 'between people and their environment' (78). Joyce Wieland's transformation of geopolitical reality into 'quilted images' ('a soft downy protection from the harsh realities of land and climate,' in Greenwood's words) does the same thing (c71). So, in a purely formal sense, does the frame.

In other cases – superficially similar but psychologically distinct – the purpose of framing would seem to be not so much the domination of real external menace as the distancing of emotional threats by displacing what should be contiguous with the self into the external realm. Claude Breeze's *The Home Viewer No. 1: Mother and Child* (1967) – a painting of war victims contained in a television screen – is clearly an example of this. It could be argued that what is being framed is simply the war, but the choice of subjects (mother with dead baby), the blatantly satirical implications of the television set, and the general sentimentalization indicate that what is being distanced here (immorally, Breeze implies) is the viewer's own response, his 'natural' impulse toward self-identification. A similar effect is achieved in Jack Chambers's *Regatta No. 1* (1968). This piece, based on a boating accident, juxtaposes positive and negative photographs of the victim with the framed picture of a happy middle class family and newsreel footage of a boat race. In addition to the framing of components, Chambers, as Barry Lord describes it, 'has then covered the whole work with layers of coloured plastic. These dull, slightly tinted shields, put the pictures at a psychic distance from us, just as if we had turned on the six o'clock TV news and heard about the drowning' (230). Again the viewer is protected from imaginative participation.

This last example, significantly enough, reveals one feature that Breeze's relatively simple treatment lacks. Chambers's mode of composition suggests not merely the viewer's detachment, but a horizontal compartmentalization as well. This is an important development. Even more than the single frame, the juxtaposition of multiple frames – another common Canadian usage – represents particularly well the Canadian's fear less of 'things' than of 'relation.' Tom Forrestall's 'cut-out' paintings demonstrate the technique in its most basic form. Especially in his compound works – linked sets of separate paintings, each firmly and assertively bordered – the compartmentalization of such normally contiguous elements as, say, bird/sky and water suggests the traditional Canadian anxiety about 'horizon,' and the desire to keep separate not so much physical as psychic spaces. The effect is particularly striking when human figures are involved. As Pat Murphy points out, 'the separateness implied by human existence, is particularly symbolized in those Forrestalls which show one or more individuals over against objects of nature … [like] the self-portrait of the artist, larger than life, looking out from one end of an elongated gessoed board [while] at the other end is a waterfall' (43).

The technique of multiple framing can, to be sure, produce much more complex compositions than this. Although Forrestall's vision is in a sense exemplary, the device lends itself to many different variations. In Greg Curnoe's *Spring on the Ridgeway* (1964), for instance, the pictorial space is chopped up by means of frames into a series of telescoped layers. The woman in this assemblage is not only separated from the picture's interior by the window through which (with her back to the viewer) she stares, but further cut off by the truncation of her head and legs, 'masked' by the protruding panel and curtains, and insulated from the 'outside' by a number of explicit verbal and visual borders. In Shadbolt's *Man of Symbols* (1971), the motif is reduced to more purely iconic terms. The shaman figure of the title is himself a mandala (that is, ritually 'centred'), while the symbolic forms over which he presides are all neatly boxed. In Wieland's *Boat Tragedy* (1964), finally, the segmentation is temporal rather than spatial. This strip-style narrative painting starts with the panorama, zooms in for a close-up of the blank white sail, and then backs off for a long view of the accident. Both the incident itself and the natural energies it suggests are distanced and defused by the compartmentalizing process.

From all these examples it would seem as though the 'frame' – an arbitrary and rigid structure imposed on experience – comprises, along with the 'enclosure,' the basic Canadian iconography. These, in other words, are the two specific images (formally related by virtue of their mutual source in the figure/ground archetype, and sometimes interchangeable), by means of which the Canadian consciousness most often and most naturally expresses its sense of self. If we move from art to 'reality,' the most obvious symbolic correlative for *both* aspects of the motif is the house. The fact, then, that houses have played such an important role in Canadian letters is a clear indication that the imagination expresses itself not merely in *compatible* ways in art and writing, but in terms of *identical* patterns. The literary house thus provides us with a good jumping-off place for our examination of the more complex structures characteristic of Canadian writing in recent decades.

In its most archetypal sense a house connotes, quite simply, protection. In the context of a northern frontier it is therefore important, as Dick Harrison points out, 'that Jason Currie's house in *The Stone Angel* is one of a "half a dozen decent brick houses" in Manawaka. It is equally important that the Connor house in *A Bird in the House* is "sparsely windowed as some crusador's embattled fortress in a heathen wilderness"' (E186). Harrison's own concern is more with the paranoia signalled by these fortress-like residences (such houses 'embody a reaction of hostility and fear toward the environment,' he says), but the fact is, to the extent that the landscape really *is* inimical, their insisted-upon impregnability must be seen as not merely a critical but a positive feature. Especially in a country like Canada, in other words, the house not only can be but often is an image of perfect comfort, peace, security. To the extent that its strength and integrity are underlined, in fact, the house image can even be used to transform the menacing forces of nature into a positive symbol, in so far as they are *outside*, giving point and focus to the human world within. 'The brilliant conceit of the hammering rain building the barn in which the poet and her companion have taken refuge, "Shaping a separate/ World for the dry and the warm," conveys with great imaginative power [her] vision of nature cooperating harmoniously if dialectically with man in order to create a home,' says John Ower of Dorothy Roberts's poem 'Rain Builds.' 'In the atmosphere of physical and emotional security which is paradoxically provided by the rain-lashed barn, the poet's momentary vision of ... a savage at the mercy of a hostile nature, serves merely to increase her sense of prosperity, safety and fulfillment' (86). The house is thus both literally and figuratively the single most important item of man's worldly equipage.

Protection is by no means *all* that the house provides, however. On an even more important level of signification, because the house is man-made it can come to seem an image not merely of external shelter but of inner strength. In doing so, it moves quite naturally beyond its association with the ego's outer shell to become an icon of *self*, a manifestation of or correlative for character, not merely in the simple social sense that Susan Jackel points out ('the provision of shelter on the prairies was equivalent to proclaiming one's social status' 48) but more profoundly, in the sense that it images the needs/hopes/visions that comprise the most important (if ofttimes only wishful) stratum of personal identity. We need only think of the log house that strikes the unhappily rootless protagonist of Laurence's *The Diviners* 'like the spirit of God between the eyes': 'Land. A river. Log house nearly a century old, built by great pioneering couple, Simon and Sarah Cooper. History. Ancestors' (414). This dwelling, with all it represents, is both an outward emblem of Morag's lifelong quest and, in the context of the story's 'present,' the sign – especially in so far as its dilapidated condition conflicts explicitly with her fantasies of hominess – that this quest must be abandoned or at least redefined in order for her to recognize and realize her true self.

This last point suggests a rather critical qualification we must make. As one might expect of any object or image that carries such a weight of latent symbolic meaning, the house evokes not merely positive associations but negative ones as well. Indeed, it is perhaps simply because by definition it *is* positive – that is, *necessary* – that the house is often viewed ambivalently. 'The self is eternally divided in its attitudes to the forms and spaces it inhabits,' says John Wilson Foster – 'simultaneously needing, fearing, desiring and despising them' (6). The iconic representations of those spaces themselves therefore tend to localize a good deal of strong if inexplicit emotion. This is evident even in the wholly formalized structures of art. In Borduas' *L'étoile noire* (1957), for instance, the way the containment motif is handled reveals quite clearly the anxiety that it generates. The passive black areas in this painting are not only 'contained' by the more vigorously applied white, but seemingly crowded – squeezed – by the ridged edges of a surrounding element that is too aggressive to be felt as merely matrix or ground. As Barry Lord points out, moreover, 'the slight traces of brown on white reinforce a sense of strain' (163). Borduas' reaction is not an anomalous one. Charles Gagnon's *Homage to John Cage* (1963), to give only one further example, communicates exactly the same covert concern, though by quite different means. In this painting a crudely coloured green ground is 'contained' on two sides by a rough framework comprising broad, washy, uneven patches of translucent white. The important feature to note is an obtrusive spatter effect at the interface between the green and the white that emphasizes strikingly the tensions – indeed, frictions – that the juxtaposition of spaces entails.

While these works demonstrate the *presence* of ambivalence, it still remains for a more realistic idiom to delineate the actual concomitants of this feeling. Clare MacCulloch hints at the existential dilemma involved when she claims that, if the 'primary image of Pre-Romanticism is a church; [and] of Romanticism a tree,' the emblem 'of Canadian neo-Romanticism [is] a cave or cage' (20). Leaving aside the question of why MacCulloch would want to apply a 'Romantic' label at all to a body of work for which even in her own telling it is so inapposite, the duality cited here points to the essential duplicity of – and problem implied by – the house symbol, the fact that it can be seen as connoting either protection *or* imprisonment.

Actually (as we might have expected) what is involved in the Canadian context is a little more complicated than the simple dichotomy the cave/cage pairing suggests. If we look at the paintings and drawings of Christiane Pflug – an oeuvre that illustrates with particular poignancy the complex associations commonly accrued to the framing/containment theme in Canada – we can see that the ego is torn on a number of levels. As Ann Davis points out, three symbols are important in Pflug: 'windows, cages, and, finally, toys or small animals' (B9). These may be taken, respectively, to represent three different aspects of the type Canadian response to the idea of a house. Firstly, there is the fairly straightforward ambivalence which, by virtue of the Canadian's *a priori* uncertainty about transcendence, typically arises even when the containment is perceived in relatively neutral terms. In Davis's words, 'The window symbol, sometimes represented by a door ... or by a mirror ... has the advantage of a dual nature: it can point inward or outward, or even, on occasion, in both directions ... This very identification of a window or door frame suggests a distinction between here and there, between mine and theirs ... The window symbol can thus represent a reaching out, a creative extension, or a fear of the exterior' (B9). Secondly, there is the equally straightforward negativity conventionally represented by a cage, whether this latter is explicit or merely suggested by the placement of furniture. Thirdly, and perhaps most interestingly, there is a more profound kind of ambivalence which seems to be catalysed *after* and perhaps even *because* the negative image has been evoked. On the one hand, the dolls and birds (alive or dead) associated with Pflug's 'cages' demonstrate vividly the dangers of dehumanization consequent upon entrapment. On the other, however, the fact that the urban skyline itself is often imaged as a cage suggests that the 'trap' may be *outside*, rather than inside the personal space represented by the house. This interpretation is supported by such paintings as *The Kitchen Door in Winter* II (1964), where a large doll stares dejectedly *in* through the bars of a kitchen door, with winter at her back. As Davis points out, Pflug's subject is obviously 'the life/death interface' rather than just inside/outside in a physical sense (B11), but she seems to have little confidence in her ability to tell one side from the other.

Pflug's response is in a sense exemplary – and this is something which must be borne in mind. In Canadian literature, even when the demonic aspect of the house is evoked, the wish to escape tends to be undercut by a persistent fear of what is 'out there.' As Francis Teague indicates, in Canadian usage even *explicit* images of imprisonment – of which we find many, especially in drama – are not as invariably negative as the conventional (especially American) associations would imply, nor, as a group, do they suggest 'that freedom is necessarily a solution that will give the characters happy lives.'[5] Both the good house and the bad house, cave and cage, are consequently inclined – like the landscape itself – to resist simple typing. Indeed the house symbol often resonates in odd ways that neither the author nor the reader expects.

This slipperiness does not, of course, prevent the house from being *used*, frequently and with considerable effect. Its appeal to the Canadian imagination is just too great to be resisted. Its more problematic associations remain for the most part safely tucked away below the surface, in any case. The gap between overt and covert connotations, furthermore, reflects the idiom/vision split in Canadian consciousness with an aptness which, if not recognized, is certainly felt. Symbolic houses – or, to translate the image into its most basic terms, architectural spaces – are hence scattered across the literary landscape in great abundance. They are often negative. They are usually at least superficially conventional. Their most frequent role is to mirror the Canadian ego as his portrait does Dorian Gray. How? Even in its cave role the house has an incomparable reflective potential. In Sinclair Ross's short story 'The Painted Door,' for instance, the author's use of woody creaks and groans and rattles to accentuate the house's vulnerability in the face of the storm underlines vividly the young wife's susceptibility as she is battered by her tumultuous emotions. In its cage role, the associations are even more blatant – and more useful. Most often linked with either unhealthy introspection or hubristic fantasy, the cage-house – or its close relation, the tomb-house – symbolizes not so much externally imposed isolation as those varieties of egocentricity which shrivel or shatter the spirit. In the first category we would find, for instance, both the House of Bentley, with its inner fastness, Philip's study, and the mortuary Rachel Cameron grows up in, which, as Dick Harrison puts it, 'makes explicit the sense of something moribund in the heavy propriety of all the brick houses on Laurence's prairie' (E186). Here also would be Anne Hébert's *Les chambres de bois*, with its message that 'The enclosed space, be it tomb or *château*, is symbolic of a soul closed in upon itself, of a stultified inner existence, of a neurotic self-obsession' (Mezei A33). In the second category, alternately, we would have to place Keneally's House of Revelations; Alf Dobble's splendiferous but never to be finished resort hotel – billed as 'the Switzerland of America' (171) – in *Tay John*; and, pre-eminently, all the ill-fated dream-houses of Grove's monomaniacal pioneers: 'Abe Spalding's vision of Spalding Hall dominating the prairie, John Elliott's patriarchal vision of generations growing up around him, Niels Lindstedt's vision of domestic purity' (Harrison E137). Harrison's description of the last of these suggests just how, by means of its progressive implication in a character's inner life, such an iconic structure can be made over the course of a book to seem not brick and board, or even (in naturalistic terms) the mere product of ambition, but an actual emanation of its master's soul, the very type and manifestation of his psychic condition:

> When Niels brings Clara home as his wife, she refers to his house as 'the famous White Range Line House.' Its fame has spread partly because the house is remarkable in itself. The most imposing in the district, with a kitchen and four rooms fifteen by eighteen feet, Niels's house is part of a grand vision, meant to embody visibly his dreams of plenty and domestic comfort. When Ellen will not marry him and complete the dream, the house becomes a hollow mockery, and when the horror of his marriage to Clara grows upon him, the house becomes a demonic parody of his dream. (E133)

Once this kind of equation is set up, it becomes easy to exploit the parallels as a means of underlining theme, counterpointing construction with the evolution of a personal vision, or using 'the decay of [an] actual house as an image of the decay of [a character] and his dream' (Harrison E133).

This sort of usage, to be sure, invokes only the most superficial strata of signification, the most uncomplicated kind of metaphorical function. Beyond its obvious conventional roles, the house symbol in Canadian literature can also be and often is used as a conceptual tool to aid in the exploration of transpersonal meaning, the delicate but critical questions of fate and the human condition. Exploited effectively the house symbol, in other words, rises above simple metaphor to become generative, to body confrontation, 'to form double-exposures.' Thus extended, the iconic structure, as E.D. Blodgett says of Alice Munro's houses, is no longer 'predominantly a frame that extends and reflects the character ... [but] is related to character as a problem and process' (B112). This level, too, is presupposed in the practice of our artists. As Dennis Young says of Michael Snow, the 'preoccupation with framing, evident in so much of his work, is richly symbolic of the artist who keeps seeking the limits ... of art and who is constantly testing himself against those limits, not out of a sense of rebellion or hostility but as the compulsive exploration of a first-rate intellect' (in Withrow 116).

Seeking the limits. This is, in a sense, where all Canadian literature starts. With Spit Delaney's obsessive search for the '*dividing line,*' the line '*Between what is and what isn't*' (Hodgins B7-8).[6] Delaney himself is fixated on the seashore, but the house, representing as it does a more personal kind of limit, border, boundary – the line *around* (which is, after all, the most critical kind of *between*) – provides an even better basis for imaging the quest for definition. Besides, it's inescapable. The house symbol, whether present or absent, is bodied forth by the very mode of our being. The house symbol, moreover, provides what *must* be our essential terms of reference in its covert confirmation of our fear-knowledge that it is not the arbitration of absolutes that is critical (or possible) for us so much as the shape, location, feel of the interface. Delaney, self-identified in dreams with a beached dolphin, a marooned starfish, some kind of legless creature shrivelling in the sun at the edge of the ocean, is for all his evident exemplary status less the archetypal Canadian, therefore, than Catherine in *Les chambres de bois*, pacing nervously between two windows, 'trembling with cold, continually comparing the courtyard and the street in a grave and mysterious game, as if her whole life suddenly hung on some elusive balance' (109). As this last quotation indicates, on the other hand, house or no house the game of brinksmanship is far from being a simple one. Even in Hébert's tale, where the concomitants of in and out are both obvious and (for the Canadian context) unusually clear-cut, there is a certain amount of ambiguity entailed by (for instance) the author's alignment of art with the timeless indoor realm, the wood-panelled chambers where Michel and Lia, defying the seasons, 'create their own exclusive kind of weather, motionless and retrospective' (78); the realm, ultimately, of death. We will come back to this later. In the meantime, let it merely be pointed out that the 'house' in the book – icon, artifact, psycho-setting, and metaphysical model – provides the standard of definition (like art itself?) whether one is inside *or* out.

The implications of all this are obvious. If the Canadian is commonly seen in terms of houses, with all the emphasis on autonomy, self-containment, and limitation that that particular image implies, one would expect to find in our cultural artifacts, and especially in literature, evidence of preoccupation with the plight of the isolated ego. When we examine the corpus this is exactly what we do find. Human isolation (its causes, its effects, the possibilities for a cure) is, in a sense, *the* Canadian subject. Even in art we find an intimation of this concern. A striking number of Harold Town's works, for instance, present enigmatic solo personae who also rebuff or repel or evade the viewer. And Town is far from an anomaly. Indeed, the figures to be found in Canadian canvases of recent decades are almost without exception both solitary and unknowable. They exude reticence; in a great many cases their faces are actually hidden. They have their backs to us (Ernst Lindner's *The Window* [1969], Greg Curnoe's *Spring on the Ridgeway* [1964]); their faces are masked (Ken Danby's *At the Crease* [1972], Alex Colville's *January* [1971]); or they are seen only indirectly, reflected in mirrors or polished surfaces (both D.P. Brown and Christopher Pratt use this device frequently). If presented in traditional frontal fashion they tend, as Davis says of Pflug's sitters, to remain stubbornly 'hidden behind their unseeing eyes or sullen, uniformly downturned mouths' (B52). Even in crowds there is very little suggestion of interaction. Michael Snow's walking woman is iconic: eternally replicated, but sharp-edged, eternally alone. In *Blind* (1967) she is sandwiched between layers of mesh. In *Beach-hcaeb* (1963) she turns her back on herself, literally wrenching apart from her alter ego. Snow notwithstanding, the real prototype for the Canadian ego is Jean-Paul Lemieux' *L'orpheline* (1951). This figure (which appears in many variations in Lemieux' work) is, as

Lord points out, always shown standing by itself, staring meekly, arms hanging limp and loose, 'engulfed in the immense landscape.' 'This is an art that tells us that people are alone, futile, orphaned in the world,' he concludes (168).

In literature even more, the isolated figure seems almost some kind of norm. A random survey turns up dozens of them: some self-perceived, others seen only from the outside; some – like Engel's Lou and Van Herk's Judith - complacent, even enthusiastic about independence, but many more distressed, even anguished, by their estrangement from the world. Lowry's consul. Hébert's Elisabeth d'Aulnières Tassy Rolland. Laurence's Rachel Cameron. Bodsworth's Ashley Morden. Wiseman's Hoda, ostracized by her fat and her innocence and her poverty. Atwood's reluctantly objectified Marian McAlpin. Encapsuled. Beleaguered. Engulfed. Canadian exemplars.

Or is this just the 'modern condition'?

I think not. There is something distinctive about the Canadian version of the theme of isolation, if only in the sheer ubiquitousness seemingly attributed to the state. Again it is largely a question of emphasis, of course. The idiom is certainly familiar enough. 'We are all in the same time zone and more or less in the same place,' muses Audrey Thomas's Mrs Blood, 'and yet we do not exist at this tense/relaxing moment for anyone other than ourselves' (14). Familiar indeed – and yet there *is* a difference. In traditional literature such words would merely identify the conventional eccentric, a misanthrope (like George Eliot's Silas Marner) whose attitude is both socially and self- destructive. The wilful isolate, in other words, is in the traditional view an exception, an anomaly, who must be either assimilated into or purged from the community. In more recent usage the base terms of reference and especially the moral assumptions commonly brought to bear on the matter have changed, perhaps even inverted, but I would maintain that that one critical fact still holds true. Though the existentialists in particular make estrangement the most fundamental concomitant of human existence, the man who *confronts* his isolation is still the exceptional man, the anti-hero, the rare individual whose terrible integrity sets him apart from his comfortably deluded and less than fully human fellows.[7] With respect to her own literary context, however, Mrs Blood represents not the exception but the rule. The absoluteness of this woman's aloneness as she waits out the term of her doomed pregnancy, insulated from all meaningful contact by the 'dull ooze of fear' to which she awakens every morning (90), does not, in other words, set her apart from the common run as in any way abnormal or unusual. Mrs Blood is, in fact, simply one of Snow's replicated women. There are (if we can judge by the country's novels) a virtual army of such in Canada. Even the normal *illusions* of communion are hence extremely rare. The world is a kind of Dantesque limbo in which we all wander like lost and wordless ghosts. 'It was like a tunnel through which you walked not knowing your destination. Everyone remained a stranger. At night – the Zeppelins came. There was a sense of silent menace'; *The Wars* (94). 'He was overcome by a feeling of loneliness, of how full of loneliness the world was. What concentration of pain had produced the diamond-hard glitter in her eyes? And the boy in patent leather shoes – a waiter perhaps? – was there no one he could turn to, was there no better prospect for him than the mirroring blankness of a plate-glass window?'; *The Deserter* (36). 'I suffer, you suffer, she suffers, he suffered'; *A Candle to Light the Sun* (60).

What is particularly dreadful about these portraits of mass isolation is their almost invariable implication that the suffering is not accidental, or temporary, or curable at all, but inherent in the very facts of human existence. *There is no way to get outside the prison of the self, ever,* they seem to say. Certainly this is the conclusion to which Marie-Claire Blais points in *La belle bête* when she surrounds her characters with actual and metaphorical mirrors. Admittedly, on the face of it the denizens of Blais' world would seem to be to blame for their own egocentricity: without exception they are selfish, foolish, mad. Notwithstanding the token nod to naturalistic 'character development,' however, the aura of doom that surrounds this little community strongly suggests that theirs is a universal rather than a merely personal dilemma. No matter *where* he looks, the intimation is, man remains incapable of 'seeing' any reality except his own face. Indeed, even nature, imaged here by the lake, is subjectively 'real' only in so far as it reflects the viewer back on himself. The message seems quite explicit. The figure is wholly, not merely selectively, debarred from his ground. Inaccessible, he is also – unfortunately – insensible. A fair price for safety? Perhaps. But if *La belle bête* tells us anything it is that such security may itself be a snare and a source of delusions. In a wholly solipsistic world, a world where centre and circumference are indistinguishable, there is considerable doubt whether even the ego – the one factor we might assume to be certain – lacking extrinsic definition, can lay claim to anything more than merely provisional, that is, 'formal' identity. 'Am I a mirror or am I Patrice?' asks the idiot of Blais' terrible little tale. 'Everything in his mind was confused. He had lived so long with mirrors, in front of mirrors, inside mirrors. All his memories were superimposed, as in a nightmare' (110). There is at least a possibility, in other words, that the isolation inherent in the human condition is, ultimately, annihilation.

What, though, of other people? Notwithstanding the almost unanimous agreement among existentialists and phenomenologists about the futility of the individual's attempt to 'know' the world in any *objective* sense ('Consciousness is always perspectival and essentially incapable of the total synthesis of horizons which would enable us to be aware of something from all times and places – that is ... from the overarching view presupposed in the classical ontology'[8]), at least some modern philosophers have intimated that if any possibility of escaping solipsism exists, it is through inter-*personal* relations, that is, in *subjectivity*.

Because of the fundamental homology of all human experience, in other words, it is deemed possible for the individual, through a leap of sympathy, to achieve self-identification with the 'other.' Not only is 'knowledge of the social,' as Merleau-Ponty claims, 'self-knowledge' [in McCleary 109], but vice versa. Do Canadians, with their qualms about transcendence, really find it possible to believe in even this limited kind of exchange, however? If any such potential does exist, it is certainly not seen as easy or natural. For one thing, because of their implication in the generalized realm of the transpersonal, 'other people' quite as much as other things tend to be viewed in Canada quite simply as dangerous. Even those who are closest to us, our literature implies, are liable at any moment to turn on us; display a new and alien aspect that seems utterly incomprehensible, even sinister. Such an experience can be more or less shattering depending on the context, of course. When Elisabeth's husband in *Kamouraska* reveals on his deathbed that unbeknownst to her he has secretly believed his wife a murderess throughout the whole eighteen years of their domestic intimacy, the revelation in a sense retroactively negates the whole basis of their relation, but when Dunstan Ramsay's mother in *Fifth Business* erupts into violence, the irrationality of her behaviour undermines his capacity to trust reality on any level at all:

I pondered [her loving] words before I went to sleep. How could I reconcile this motherliness with the screeching fury who had pursued me around the kitchen with a whip, flogging me until she was gorged with – what? Vengeance? What was it? Once, when I was in my thirties and reading Freud for the first time I thought I knew. I am not so sure I know now. But what I knew then was that nobody – not even my mother – was to be trusted in a strange world that showed very little of itself on the surface. (33-4)

Such shocks of recognition occur relatively rarely, but the fact that the potential is there makes human relationship seem a very risky business.

The problems don't stop here, moreover. Even above and beyond the *danger* of the undertaking there is considerable evidence that many of our authors are secretly convinced that real intersubjectivity is, in the long run, impossible. One may make the attempt at communication, but *it just doesn't work.* As Dennis Brown says of Susan Musgrave's poetry, 'When the "I" persona reaches out for [the] "you" it abruptly vanishes: untouchable, inaudible, invisible, it retreats "into the only darkness/animals come from"' (60). This is perhaps why the isolates of Canadian literature tend to appear not merely singly but in *sets*: couples, families, whole communities of mutually exclusive individuals pursuing their erratic paths through life with as much awareness of the other selves they circle, touch, collide with, as electrons, but without in most cases the electron's stabilizing centre. Surveying the corpus it would seem, in fact, that counter especially to the pattern of recent American 'existentialist' fiction it is more often than not primarily the *collective* aspects or concomitants of isolation – the exigencies of group membership rather than merely the suffering of the alienated individual – that are viewed as comprising the central and critical problem to be addressed by Canadian writing. Poetry, by its very nature, tends to emphasize the personal, but novels certainly abound in which not only the ubiquitousness but the specifically social – that is, role-related – implications of relational breakdown may be detected as a premise if not a major theme. Raymond Knister's *White Narcissus*. Blondal's *A Candle to Light the Sun*. Ross's *As for Me and My House*. John Moss implies there is something exceptional about the Bentley ménage when he tells us that the image of 'the two horses ... Philip discovered ... frozen on their feet against a fence, their backsides to the wind, suggests much about the Bentleys' moribund union' (D115), but in truth the Bentleys are more typical than not. Indeed, Hooker's vision of his household in Findley's *The Last of the Crazy People* may be taken as a paradigm for the whole world as it seems to be seen by Canadian eyes. 'Mother is upstairs and won't come down. You live in the library. Rosetta won't look at me. Iris has secrets. And Papa sits with his back to everything. What does it mean?' (204). What it means is that isolation is endemic in the Canadian universe, a public rather than personal phenomenon, *not consequent upon but prior to any individual case*.

This brings us back to a point we touched on earlier, that it is possible that John Martens of Helwig's *The Day before Tomorrow* may be the prototypical Canadian protagonist – more, that the book itself, at least in terms of the pattern it presents, the questions (if not the answers) it poses, for all its slightness provides some not merely interesting but critical sidelights on our emerging conceptions of the prototypical Canadian novel. Certainly it is one of the most intriguing portraits of aggregate isolation to be found in the corpus. As such, it reveals a number of features that may be seen as characteristic of the Canadian treatment of this characteristically Canadian theme. It employs a multi-voice narrative technique, thus underlining the irreconcilability of separate viewpoints. It alternates between first- and third-person modes in order to underline the difficulty (perhaps impossibility) of synthesizing subjective and objective experience. Finally, and most pertinent to the present discussion, it elucidates the inside/outside theme by simultaneously illuminating homology and discontinuity between three separate centres of consciousness. It gives us three characters, in other words, who are both *alike* and *alone*. Despite their formal relation they are separated by ignorance, presumption, and a total inability to empathize. Despite their mutual exclusiveness they are shown to be radically similar in their shared isolation.

This last point may not be immediately evident. Martens, who is half spy and half madman, at first strikes us as (quite literally) the odd-man-out, an anomaly, a complete deviant. When, however, he is set in the context of his ostensibly 'normal' wife and brother – she wrapped in God-fixated silence since the moment of her child's death; he complacent, self-centred, absurdly self-important with his adolescent fantasies of revolution – we realize that the difference between these people is only one of degree; that Martens's amnesia, his paranoia, his complete inability to step outside his own frazzled psyche, are only a more extreme version of a general malaise. Far from being capable of the phenomenologist's imaginative leap, these people *as a group* are firmly shut up inside their own heads. Under the circumstances, any kind of intersubjective relation must be at best a lucky accident, at worst self-deceptive, dangerous, delusory. And this is the last and most important element in Helwig's treatment of the major theme of isolation: a demonstration of what happens when we are stripped of our comforting conventional modes of prepackaging experience – and of how threatening otherness can seem when confronted by one so dis-illusioned.

He stared at the man who sat across from him, trying to find something in the features of the face that would tell him what he should feel. It was a round face, at first a friendly face, but there was something, perhaps the fact that one eye was larger than the other... There was a small wart on the side of his face. He looked again. The man smiled.

Was the smile a prelude to an action? An attack? It was clear that the man was important to him, was an essential contact, or perhaps an enemy, the man he most had to fear. (84)

If isolation is the common state of affairs, there remains the questions of whether and how much this limits individual freedom. Balanced against the impression of fatedness entailed by the apparent universality of the condition, there is an indication in at least some treatments that isolation is to a large extent self-caused. 'I make boxes for myself,' Morag tells her friend in *The Diviners* (188). Too much insistence on this point, however, creates difficulties. Even aside from the covert conflict between the deterministic implications of the patterned response and the apparent autonomy of individual characters, assertions of responsibility, of control, are only going to be believable if we can also believe in these characters' capacity to break out. But *do* we believe that? Rachel Cameron can light out for the territories, certainly, but do we believe that when she gets there she will suddenly be transformed into a new person: spontaneous, outgoing, unafraid? The problem once more comes down to the duplicity of houses. Those aspects of personality that produce isolation can, like more tangible kinds of walls, function as either a constraint, or a defence, or, as is often the case in Canadian literature, both at once. In *The Lonely Passion of Judith Hearne*, says Moss, 'Judith is not at middle age an alcoholic spinster, vulnerable, disillusioned, unfulfilled, by chance or bad luck or poor timing. She is alone and afraid and the walls of her prison are *the flaws and the strengths of her own personality*. Her incapacitating humility before an ignorant God derives from the confusion of pride and compassion that she has helplessly cultivated within herself as a means, in her mind, of survival' (D23, italics added). If one's strengths and weaknesses are so inextricably bound together, however – if one's defence is also one's doom – it is difficult to see how escape is possible *in fact*, no matter what freedom one may have in theory.

This is an important point. Lest my attempt a few pages back to differentiate the Canadian usage from the more general modern pattern remains unconvincing, here is the one factor that establishes the divergence beyond doubt. The thing is, the European existentialist hero and to an even greater extent his American romantic-existentialist counterpart are by definition wholly, not merely relatively, self-created; wholly, not merely relatively, responsible for their own 'authenticity.' Thus, when Yossarian of *Catch-22* escapes to Switzerland, and when Chief Bromden of *One Flew over the Cuckoo's Nest* heads for the Hook River, and – even more significant for the present discussion – when Ralph Ellison's Invisible Man decides to emerge from his cellar at the end of the book, ending his isolation by a sheer act of will, we view these acts not merely as symptoms of character development but as signs of radical, self-willed metamorphosis. The typical Canadian protagonist, in contrast, is capable only of tiny transformations, slight swervings from the path of his personal history, changes not of kind but only of degree. He is free within limits, but the *mode* of that freedom, the terms of reference by which it is structured, framed, contained, is – like the 'net' surrounding Douglas LePan's young swordsman – both inescapable and inescapably fixed.

This explains why the most extreme acts of self-assertion, the most concerted attempts at self-invention, often turn out in Canada to exacerbate rather than cure – or even compensate for – a character's isolation. One of the most exhaustive demonstrations of this particular tendency is found in Graeme Gibson's *Communion*. Notwithstanding its clearly ironic title, this novel is peopled solely by radical isolates, a group of men who, beyond the obvious behavioural stigmata of their shared condition (making love to statues in the cemetery; huddling in the corner in the subway so as not to brush accidentally against anyone; living in a basement like an animal, stripped of dignity, strength, even memory), are defined largely in terms of their individual fantasies or personal myths. It is, moreover, specifically in the collision between these fantasy worlds and the 'real' world that each discovers, painfully, the narrow limits of his being. Peter Walters, for instance, is forced to the appalled recognition that his bestial sexual fantasies, far from being shared and augmented by his partner as they invariably are in his daydreams, are likely to win him only the label of pervert. Fripp comes face to face with the woman with whom, as a by-product of his voyeurism, he has invented an elaborate relationship, and can think of nothing to say except, feebly, 'Are there any, do you have any odd jobs, you know... work around the house' (79). Felix Oswald, most disastrously of all, attempts to set free the sick white husky which has come to symbolize his own entrapment, but – foreshadowing his own death when, at the end of the book, he in turn is placed in jeopardy by events set in motion by someone else's fantasy – manages only to kill the wretched beast, accidentally running it over when it frantically tries to get back in the car. Obviously this is a world where the imagination offers little hope of salvation, being fully as treacherous as any other aspect of human existence.

Gibson's book, in fact, is almost a tract on human limitation. Even aside from the insistent example of these replicated individual collisions with an inimical reality, his narrative technique in itself mirrors effectively the base structures of the Canadian vision. By returning repeatedly to key words and phrases, whole passages replayed with only slight variations over and over throughout the text, he produces an effect of incessant circling. By means of this purely verbal strategy he is thus able to get across the idea that the protagonists of his story, attempting repeatedly to force their way free of the cage of identity, are just as repeatedly brought up short by the intransigence of their self-created myths. With every circuit, every rebound to centre, we can actually see the psychological walls around them getting thicker, harder, more resistant to change or penetration. This novel is not merely an exploration of the *effects* of human isolation, therefore, but a powerful demonstration of the extent to which the ostensibly liberating process of self-definition actually involves the (for good or ill) creation and/or reinforcement of personal limits. And that, of course, is at root what the whole Canadian preoccupation with the isolation theme is all about: the phenomenology of human limitation.

This brings us to what is possibly the most crucial feature of the Canadian 'langscape.' Speaking of Hugh MacLennan, Warren Stevenson identifies as central a 'theme of individual self-awareness, worked out in terms of a contrast between two types of persons, those who learn to come to terms with what [the author] calls "the ultimate solitude" and those who don't' (53-4). This ultimate solitude – the final limitation of which every other human limitation is only a pale copy – is, of course, death. If the Canadian is concerned about the invisible walls that surround him in life, he is even more obsessed with the immanence, necessity, and experience of dying. This peculiarity, indeed, is perhaps our most notable mark of identity. As Margaret Atwood puts it, 'the central European experience is sex and the central mystery "what goes on in the bedroom" ... the central American experience is killing and the central mystery is "what goes on in the forest" (or in the slum streets), [but] the central Canadian experience is death and the central mystery is "what goes on in the coffin"' (F222).

Even aside from its connection with the isolation theme, the death obsession is predictable. On the simplest level, death is usually viewed primarily as a concomitant of the natural, animal part of man. When man conquers nature –

either physically, as a pioneer, or figuratively, by transforming it through myth into explicitly human terms – he is thus symbolically conquering his own death. Part of the reason that the landscape is perceived most naturally as inimical in Canada is undoubtedly related to the fact that without the transformative power of some sort of transcendent philosophy, nature tends to be seen in pre-eminently morbid terms. At the same time, its association with universal processes of decay and destruction reinforces the negative connotations it already carries. It is inevitable, in other words, that 'creatures who [assess] their true puniness in the face of the overwhelmingness and majesty of the universe' should, in Ernest Becker's words, be uncomfortably 'alive to the *panic* inherent in creation.' This in turn must inevitably produce an abnormal sensitivity to those aspects of nature that exacerbate one's sense of horror:

Panic is fittingly King of the Grotesque. What are we to make of a creation in which the routine activity is for organisms to be tearing others apart with teeth of all types – biting, grinding flesh, plant stalks, bones between molars, pushing the pulp greedily down the gullet with delight, incorporating its essence into one's own organization, and then excreting with foul stench and gasses the residue. Everyone racing out to incorporate others who are edible to him. The mosquitoes bloating themselves on blood, the maggots, the killer-bees attacking with a fury and a demonism, sharks continuing to tear and swallow while their own innards are being torn out. Creation is a nightmare spectacular taking place on a planet that has been soaked for hundreds of millions of years in the blood of all its creatures.[9]

With this vision lurking in the background it is small wonder that Canadian writers seem almost spontaneously to image nature as bloodstained, pungent with rot, or otherwise replete with death. 'Groundwood is spongy, silver birchsticks CRACK they break sometimes,' thinks Peter Such's Beothuk as he traverses the wet forest, irresistibly drawn to a vision of corpses. 'Old woman's bones their silver skins slip off, wet red rotwood under his moccasins. His moccasins in the wet turn red' (12).

Nature and death, death and nature. The fact is, this is an association so deeply engrained in the Canadian consciousness – not taught, but *absorbed*, seemingly without effort or awareness, during childhood ('She has seen dead gophers, run over by cars or shot, their guts redly squashed out on the road' Laurence B16; 'I did not listen because I had heard [about gangrene] before, along with the difference between getting bitten by a rattlesnake and a cobra ... and between the size of the bites made by lions and grizzly bears' MacLennan B56; 'No morality in nature accounted for catbirds or that putrid meat was sweet to vultures or that some birds killed while others sang and sipped nectar ... Painted buntings that we fed were related to the buzzards we'd seen on the highway, tearing the flesh of spattered dogs.' Blaise 12; 'Lilka learned to think of them not as tragedies but as normal and intrinsic links in the chain of life by which one group, the flesh-eaters, could live only if others died' Bodsworth 343) – that it seems to underlay our whole literature with a substratum of fatality, for the most part invisible but prone to pop out at odd moments in unexpected glimpses and sinister little hints. The corollary to this insistent undertone is, of course, an equally obtrusive sense of *human* corporeality. And this, whether as cause or result, is what energizes finally the Canadian's preoccupation with the *dividing line*, his fascination with and anxiety about frontiers, his frenzied attempts to define the interface between 'self' and 'other.' 'There is no protection, unless it is in knowing,' says Munro's Del Jordan. 'I wanted death pinned down and isolated behind a wall of particular facts and circumstances, not floating around loose, ignored but powerful, waiting to get in anywhere' (D39).

Death, then, as a special and in a sense exemplary kind of limitation is an element which (as symbol or reality, event or condition) turns up with almost monotonous regularity in Canadian literature.[10] Suggesting what would seem to be an almost astonishingly persistent morbid strain in the Canadian imagination, it is in fact difficult to *find* a book in the corpus in which nobody dies, or remembers death, or meditates on death at some length. This does not mean that death is treated in this country as purely conventional or propaedeutic. For the Canadian death is simply too *real* to be wholly intellectualized; too personal, too serious to be either distanced as pure ideal *or* reduced to the occasional and the contingent. This bias in itself both signals and explains what would seem to be the key characterizing feature of our national usage – not the fact or even the predominance of death in our productions but the *way* it is presented: its obtrusiveness, its palpability, its immanence. 'So far you have read of the deaths of 557,017 people,' says Timothy Findley in *The Wars*, 'one of whom was killed by a streetcar, one of whom died of bronchitis, and one of whom died in a barn with her rabbits' (158).

This invocation of statistics may, on the other hand, be just a little misleading. Findley's strategy with this quotation – his offsetting of public with private facts – points up yet another important aspect of the Canadian's death obsession. Despite an ofttimes grotesquely quantitative approach to the subject, it is usually not only or even primarily the frequency with which death occurs – that is, the sheer number of fatalities – that tends to be *stressed* in Canadian literature. The suddenness, the senselessness, the absolutely inexplicable randomness of its strike claims somewhat more attention, but even this is a little aside from the point. Judging by the oeuvre, in fact, what would seem to be by far of greatest concern to Canadian writers is a sense of death's 'embeddedness' in human experience; the fear, perhaps the conviction, that death is not merely an *end* to life, an isolated event, but somehow essentially, and horribly, *contiguous* with it. This feeling is something more than simply another variant of the nature-paranoia we have already examined. It is quite distinct, too, from the kind of submerged Manichaeism that Sandra Djwa imputes to the poet in *E.J. Pratt: The Evolutionary Vision* – although the experiential or even metaphysical dualism invoked by her discussion is also, as we have seen, a strong element (latent if not generally fully realized) in the Canadian vision as a whole. What I am talking about here is the explicit sense that death is not just immanent but omnipresent; *that the whole of life is nothing but a process of dying*. The Canadian, in other words, is secretly convinced, with Abraham of Adele Wiseman's *The Sacrifice*, that 'death is sown in all of us when we are conceived, and grows within the womb of life, feeding on it, until one day it bursts out' (144).

This disquieting message is conveyed quite overtly in Canadian literature by, for one thing, the constant association, directly or indirectly, of death with sex[11] and, even more, with birth. (We will be examining different aspects of this phenomenon in chapters 6 and 7 below.) On a symbolic level, moreover, the same association is evidenced by the tendency of Canadian writers to conflate and even invert the values inherent in conventional life/death imagery ('frequent symbols of vitality and abundance, such as the sun and the sea, become more often symbols of paralysis and death, the Medusa sun, the capacious tombs of the sea'[12]). Perhaps one of the most unusual illustrations of this particular theme, though, is Matt Cohen's short story, 'Keeping Fit,' where a young man actually *runs* from life into death. In this fable it is not the fact that the protagonist dies that shocks us but the *way* he does it: the ease with which he slips over the threshold; the lack of catastrophe, or struggle, or strangeness; the explicit mention of 'an imperceptible transition' with its clear implication that death is simply the logical extension to life (A66). Based on such peculiar usages as this it is tempting to apply to Canadian literature as a whole the observations made by Margot Northey (citing Nancy Bailey) on Carrier's *La guerre, yes sir!*, that it 'is not simply a tale about death, but ... presents a battle between life and death in which the two forces are often surprisingly confused' (82).

Such 'confusion' can have dire consequences. Enforced recognition that life cannot, finally, be separated from death any more than a house can be subtracted from its own walls must inevitably exacerbate man's sense of vulnerability if only because it frustrates his ability to rationalize unpleasant aspects of his experience. Here is yet another point of divergence between the Canadian and the American. The Revolution was not merely a repudiation of the parent culture, but a denial of history altogether. The American's recurrent neo-primitivistic nature worship, therefore, is paradoxically possible only because he has *freed* himself from nature; symbolically asserted his immunity to *process*. America's self-defining myth of Paradise Regained, in other words, is, as Ihab Hassan points out, 'essentially a timeless vision.' The corollary to this odd state of affairs is that the American, in addition to his naive faith in a Walt Disney version of the wilderness, also has a rather distinctive attitude toward death. In short, he refuses to believe in it. His whole sense of his place in the scheme of things is, in fact, as Hassan says, predicated upon 'an old dream: not freedom, not power, not even love, but the dream of immortality' [325]. In Canada the entire complex of associations is reversed. In complete contradistinction to the American's gleeful (or agonized) evasions, therefore, the most basic *donnée* of Canadian literature is simply *awareness of death* – that mortal fear or 'darkness of the soul' that Coyote embodies in *The Double Hook* (see Moss D177) – and the most obvious point of departure for the fictional journey the question of *how we can live with that donnée*.

What does this mean in terms of actual literary production? In the first place death is rarely, outside of a relatively small body of deliberately 'popular' fiction, invoked simply as pure sensation à la Sam Peckinpah, or as a wish-fulfilling fantasy of personal power (such a usage requires that the subject can distance himself from his *own* death enough to block empathy with the victim), or even in the playful way exemplified by the classic murder mystery as something abstract and hypothetical, the unknown quantity in a cold equation. Death in Canadian fiction (and to a lesser extent, poetry) tends to function, rather, as either a focus or a vehicle for serious moral and/or philosophical questions. If we conflate the whole corpus, in fact, we can see our literature as offering, cumulatively, a complete course in the theoretical and, far more important, practical (that is, personal) meaning of death. This is, of course, yet another version of the game called 'exploring the interface.'

How is this program carried out in practice? Lesson one is simply that everyone is going to die – and it may happen at any time. Lesson two, more significantly, is that although the *condition* is a universal one, the event is not: every man is alone at the moment of his death. This last fact, paradoxically, is illustrated with particular vividness in books that ostensibly deal with circumstances where, by definition, men are dying together. Canadian war novels, consequently, tend to diverge from conventions of the genre in some rather interesting ways. Perhaps this is why there are so few of them. In any case, the phenomenon is worth examining a little more closely.

In traditional usage, war stories tend to emphasize the social. Even celebrations of individual heroism, as in epic or romantic works, are celebrations of heroism put to the service of social ends.[13] In realistic treatments the implications are even more blatant. In Stephen Crane's *The Red Badge of Courage*, for instance, the young protagonist's encounter with death – the corpse in the wood – has the effect of motivating him to return to his 'duty,' to reintegrate himself into the group. The whole incident, in fact, as Hassan points out, illuminates 'the conflict between social and instinctive behavior, ideal choice and biological necessity' [43]. This is a typical thematic concern of war stories – and typically the social wins out. Indeed, even in explicitly ironic versions of the war novel from Hemingway's *Farewell to Arms* to Heller's *Catch-22* the emphasis on loyalty to the group, on the mystique of comradeship, on the importance of mutual support and sympathy in shared adversity (even if it is shown to be ultimately futile) remains much the same. The only thing that has changed is that the critical 'they' against whom 'we' are defined is now generally not the enemy but the bureaucratic politico-military machine.

In Canadian war novels, in contrast, the whole sense of 'we' tends to disappear. In Colin McDougall's *Execution*, for instance, the focal incident, rather than any aspect of *common* experience, is the exemplary trial and punishment – the ritual isolation, in other words – of an unfortunate young soldier accidentally implicated in black marketeering. In Charles Yale Harrison's *Generals Die in Bed* the message is even more explicit: here the experience of war is not merely asocial but *anti*-social, and anti-social, moreover, in a distinctly anti-conventional way. 'Out on rest we behaved like human beings; here we are merely soldiers. We know what soldiering means. It means saving your own skin and getting a bellyful as often as possible... that and nothing else. *Camaraderie – esprit de corps* – good fellowship – these are words for journalists to use, not for us. Here in the line they do not exist. We fight among ourselves' (91). Later novels dealing with the war, either centrally or peripherally, tend to take the same line. War is a condition that *alienates* man from his fellows, rather than the reverse. Armies are not really groups at all, but only collections of isolates caught up in a common fate. '[T]here were one or two who tried to dress one another's wounds but most were sitting separate, staring into space' (Findley E118). The speaker here, Robert Ross of *The Wars*, is in that sense Canada's version of the prototypical soldier. Starting out as a fairly normal young fellow, with conventionally adolescent ideas of heroism and a laudable sense of duty, he is driven more and more in on himself by his despairing recognition of waste, brutality, and human obtuseness until, in the end, he dies despised and misunderstood, burned beyond recognition during a 'traitorous' attempt to rescue a herd of horses from the front lines: *alone*.

The implications of all this are provocative. Even aside from the attitude toward war that one may infer from this group of books (far more cynical than the traditional-realistic or even the existentialist-ironic versions), the almost exclusive emphasis on individual experience conveys clearly that there is no comfort to be gained from either the *idea* that one is dying for a cause (the social rationale) or the *fact* that one is dying in company. As I said above, *death is by definition the ultimate isolation*. The death of comrades cannot in any way mitigate that. Indeed, as Peter Such's elegiac tale of the last of the Beothuks reveals, the group-death can only exacerbate one's despair by taking away the small consolation of knowing at the moment of death that at least one's acts and words may live on in the minds of companions or kin. In *Riverrun*, which details the death of a whole race, the individual deaths shown are the loneliest imaginable. Nonosabasut dies encircled by alien white faces, knowing that 'He, one of the last tall People, will die down and it will be these around him who will tread down the People's forest' (82). Demasduit dies in exile from her family and tribe; her total alienation is underlined by the fact that at the moment of death the white man's document, formal and official, takes over the narrative burden. Shawnadithit, most tragic of all, is fully aware as she waits despairingly for death to overtake her that she, the very last, will have no one to mourn her, no one to give her the rites that alone can grant her spirit surcease. Her fate also illustrates quite pointedly the vanity of all man's attempts to find or invent some sort of social compensation for his death. 'Her grave, originally in the Church of England cemetery on the Southside, St John's, was lost when the cemetery made way for a city street' (145).

Such's vision here is sombre, but not exceptional. It would seem, in fact, to be a vision that Canadian literature for the most part simply assumes. We do find the occasional (generally unsuccessful) attempt – like MacLennan's in *The Watch that Ends the Night* – to transform death into something a little more palatable *without* recourse to traditional religious solutions with their transcendent implications, but we rarely find the more facile sorts of evasions typical of much American writing. Indeed, even when treated in an explicitly comic idiom – as in Kroetsch's novels – death is virtually never trivialized in Canadian literature. Jeremy Sadness's plunge into the abyss in *Gone Indian*, for instance, is not (as the bare outline of the story might tend to suggest) simply a conventional ironic commentary on his naive quest for the noble savage but a serious response to the question of whether ideals may not – despite, or perhaps even *because of* their 'absurdity' – be worth more to a man than mere physical survival. Death for a Canadian, in other words, is no laughing matter. Nor, on the other hand – the well-documented gothic undertones notwithstanding – is it wholly evil, negating all that is human and debilitating the will. Atwood's invocation of a 'victim mentality' (discussed in chapter 8) tends to obscure this fact. To recognize death, to accept death, to assume death, even to be obsessed with death is not necessarily to be a victim. One can attempt to keep one's house in order even if one is well aware that it is only a prison cell. If the Canadian's preoccupation with mortality makes death seem in some ways the most important event in life, it does not deny him the possibility of confronting it, of living within the limits it sets, with wisdom and with dignity. And if his sense of isolation exacerbates his sense of the poignancy of his fate, it does not diminish his stature thereby, but merely conveys to him the sad truth that if he is to come to terms with his death he must do so as an individual. Death in Canadian literature, in other words, is more typically treated as a means than an end. Far from merely tolling the common doom, death becomes *the* exemplary occasion.

This, of course, explains why death, far beyond its sheer obtrusiveness, tends to be both thematically *and* structurally critical in much Canadian literature. There is scarcely a novel in the corpus, in fact, in which death is not a beginning, a focus of energies, a critical nexus, an apotheosis or finale. Death can backdrop or colour or counterpoint or frame. Often death is the glue that holds a whole book together. In *La guerre, yes sir!*, for instance, Corriveau's funeral 'contains' the whole story as in the end his coffin expands to contain the whole world. For the poets, death generally seems to invite a more intimate approach, which makes it both a more and a less complicated thing. (Consider only the difference between A.J.M. Smith's cool metaphysical speculations and Irving Layton's apocalyptic but intensely personal vision in 'A Tall Man Executes a Jig' of the dying snake with its 'intestine like a small red valise' offering up a 'last silent scream' 385.) For them, as much as for the novelists, however, death can be and often is both object and vehicle of speculation. Pratt's usage is among the more conventional (his 'persistent ... topic – sudden news of death – with its associated ideas of a metamorphosed world' is very similar to the common novelistic plot of using a parent's death as the jumping-off point for a quest of some kind; see G. Warkentin 22), but even in such an idiosyncratic vision as is implied by James Reaney's explorations of mortality in *The Red Heart* there still tends to be an insistent sense that death – dying – is fundamental, absolutely primary, whether it is localized in specific human experience or as abstract and pervasive as the forces conjured by the image of the ticktock heart-sun. Above all, whether in novel or poem, death tends to be presented in terms that demand the reader's active involvement rather than merely his contemplation. It thus functions as a kind of pedagogical aid by means of which, paradoxically, we are offered lessons on living, that is, living in the context of death.

In numerous books the didactic function is quite overt. Death is not merely a hypothetical framework or a symbolic turning point but an actual physical fact which the protagonists must learn to deal with. Occasionally it is death-once-removed – the death of a neighbour, foreshadowing but distinct from one's own – that provides the impetus, and in these cases the response tends to be diffused, circuitous, philosophical; a testing of available resources, alternate modes of structuring response. In Carrier's *La guerre, yes sir!* Corriveau's funeral provides occasion for posing the crucial question whether death gives point to life ('The villagers were alive ... and all the time they were praying for Corriveau's salvation, it was their own joy in being alive that they proclaimed in their sad prayers' 48) or simply negates it ('What was the use of having been a child with blue eyes, of having learned about life, its names, its colours, its laws, painfully as though it were against nature? ... Everything was as useless as tears.' 94). Even where the perspective is *formally* public, as here, however, the focus is still on the individual. Death is seen from a *multiple* viewpoint, not a common one. And in the majority of Canadian novels it is not the public death, the *representative* death which is considered at all, but death as a unique event, personal and private.[14]

In *The Watch that Ends the Night* it is *death of the other* that must be confronted. Through the example of Jerome Martell (who has himself come back from the dead), George Stewart must learn to accept his wife's terminal illness as inevitable but unregrettable, the defining line that endows each individual existence with its shape and meaning. Unfortunately, the process of enlightenment as shown here is somewhat less than totally convincing. MacLennan's harping on the largeness of Catherine's soul, her strength of will and vitality, the energy of her paintings, makes the discrepancy between man's spirit and his corporeality, his potential and his fate, seem absolutely rather than just apparently unbridgeable, at least without the superaddition of a transforming third factor – and all the more unbearable for being that way. Far from solving the problem he poses, consequently, MacLennan in a sense only evades it. 'When the tension between the ideal and the actual finally becomes intolerable,' says Catherine Ross of one of MacLennan's other books, 'a possible response to the resulting despair is repudiation of this foundering world in favour of some transcendental reality: the quest for the ideal, frustrated in this world by sin and the perversity of human nature, is transferred to the spiritual world' (A5-6). There is nothing *intrinsically* wrong with this sort of manoeuvre. Since *The Watch that Ends the Night* seems to insist that the only acceptable solution is a solution framed in wholly human terms, however, the spiritualization that takes place at the end of this particular novel with Martell's invocation of the Christ-principle inherent in 'humanity' can hardly help but seem a bit of a cheat.[15] What is worse, it doesn't work in a purely literary sense either. George's final affirmation is far weaker, far less credible than his earlier anger, resentment, confusion, and fear. Nevertheless, *The Watch that Ends the Night* is a powerful study of the effects of death on those who have to live in its shadow – and in a sense its aesthetic flaws, its covert evasions, make it even more interesting as a demonstration of man's attempts to reconcile himself to an unacceptable fate.

Death of the other is not, to be sure, the worst thing a man has to face. Though the mode is less frequent than studies focusing on deaths of loved ones, Canadian literature also offers a number of explicit exemplars for the art of dying which focus in a direct and unmediated fashion on the *death of the self*. Margaret Laurence's *The Stone Angel* is one of the most effective of these. This is in some ways a very deceptive book. Most critics – Atwood, Thomas, Jones, among others – focus on the 'wilderness of pride' theme, seeing as the core of the novel the growth of self-knowledge in the protagonist, and the climax the triumphant moment shortly before her death when she recognizes and regrets the tragic inflexibility that has kept her cut off from human contact all her life. This element is obviously there – at least part of the meaning of Hagar's story certainly concerns the human need for community (see chapter 12) – but neither Hagar's experience nor the final message of the book is simple enough to be wholly comprehended in any summary so pat. Laurence herself said in an interview that 'The final, almost grace, that is given to her in the very last moments of her life is that she realizes that, although she has survived with pride and that this is her triumph and her strength, her terrible tragedy has been the inability to give or to receive affection and love and the inability to allow herself to experience joy' (C. Thomas A68). On the evidence of the book itself, however, we might just as well reverse this and say Hagar realizes that although she has been unable to give or receive love, *she has survived with pride*. Pride, in other words, is both her weakness *and* her strength. In the end it is this *double* fact that she must recognize and accept, for it is this that defines her existential limitations. Certainly it is important that she should learn to acknowledge her failing faculties and the inevitability of dependency; to admit to the tears and the memory lapses and the childish outbursts of rage: this is all part of coming to terms with her mortality, accepting her impending fate. It is equally important, however, that despite this growing awareness she should resist annihilation with every ounce of will, *'flail against the thing'* (76) as long as she has breath. Hagar, in other words, must learn to know and accept her *whole* self, without either evasion of responsibility *or* undue recrimination. And this, in fact, is what she manages to do. In the last incident of the book, though quite aware after all her recent insights into the disastrous effects of her lifelong independence that she is being foolish to insist on holding her own glass of water, she nevertheless reacts in her accustomed fashion. As the tart but fond tone of these final sentences reveals, moreover – and this is the really important point – *without* rationalizing the act as she once might have done, Hagar *is able to forgive herself for the irrationality of her behaviour.* '"I can't help it – it's my nature,"' she says (235). For Hagar, coming to terms with the limitations of mortality is coming to terms with – *not* just repudiating – the limitations of the self.

Death of the other. Death of the self. If we stipulate that mass death is either abstracted into setting or treated as multiples of one, typically imaged as an aggregate rather than a common fate, then these two mark the polarities of possibility. It would be a mistake, on the other hand, to infer that either Laurence or MacLennan – though between them they do illustrate quite strikingly a number of important, recurrent patterns of response – offers any sort of definitive model for or demonstration of the way death is 'typically' treated in Canadian literature. If the subject is dictated by convention, that is, the approach most definitely is not. Of the two books, *The Stone Angel* may perhaps be considered as slightly more exemplary, especially in so far as it ties death explicitly into the general isolation theme, but even works very similar to Laurence's in terms of base vision can diverge considerably when it comes to detailing either the process of dying or the individual reaction. Death, after all, is a very personal thing. Thus, although Matt Cohen's novel *The Disinherited* begins with what would seem to be an almost identical combination of back- and foreground factors, focusing as it does on the death of a man alienated from his family by stubbornness and pride, when it comes down to specifics Richard Thomas shows little of Hagar's capacity for understanding *or* her will to resist. Death in this case seems to be a kind of gradual creeping paralysis in the face of which one can do little except succumb. As a result, despite the fact that both the actual physical process of dying and the associated mental development are in Cohen's book presented in more detail and at considerably greater length, Richard's death has less impact as either event or symbol than Hagar's. Part of this is due to the diffusing effect of the double focus of the plot (leaving aside the flashbacks, even in the 'present' segments attention is divided between what Richard feels dying and what his family, especially his estranged son Erik, feel as they wait), but part of it too would seem simply due to a different, and in many ways equally effective projection of (what is in fact unknowable) what it is like to die. Interestingly enough, though Richard's last vision may be explained simply as an involuntary, pain-associated return to the occasion of his original heart attack in the woods, Cohen's choice of imagery to convey the moment of death also has some interesting resonances in terms of other themes we have discussed. 'Falling. The forest rising all around, swallowing the light. Leaves and earth' (209).

If there is no real unanimity about what death 'means' on an individual level, may we at least cull from the corpus enough shared assumptions to construct what we might call a Canadian 'philosophy' of death? I would say not. This is hardly surprising. If we look to the existentialists again as a point of comparison, we see that even here, among men who at least in broad terms share a common intellectual stance, there is considerable disagreement on this most crucial aspect of the human condition. In Heidegger's view, since life is already given over to death, the only way one can escape from anxiety is to 'take death upon oneself.' 'The authentic *being toward death* arouses us and makes for a new life. It is similar to the old precept – in order to live one has to die – in the sense, however, that one has to become aware of the essential finitude of existence. Thus, Heidegger ... summons man to change his life, to live "authentically." It is only in the realization of our existence as essentially and necessarily "being toward death" that man can rise above the petty day-to-day life to become truly himself and truly free.'[16] This type of affirmation is one that has appealed to a number of Canadians. Frye, for instance, embraces death explicitly as 'the only event in which the genuinely heroic aspect of human life emerges' ('Without death, the struggle would only seem unending and hopeless' D33), and there is at least a hint of this same attitude in Laurence's intimation that for Hagar the act of dying, if not death itself, offers a means to self-validation. Others, in contrast – and here would be the impulse behind both

Hagar's *'flail against the thing'* and George Stewart's covert rage – seem more inclined toward Sartre's view that death, far from being something noble lifting man above the merely human and contingent, is solely and simply absurd. '[D]eath is never that which gives meaning to life,' he says: 'it is, on the contrary, that which actually deprives life of all significance. If we have to die, our life has no sense because our problems do not receive any kind of solution and because the very meaning of the problems remains undetermined.'[17] Most Canadian writers, however, seem to fall somewhere short of these extremes, electing for a compromise position or, like Carrier's *habitants*, waffling between the two. If any existentialist philosopher speaks for the Canadian view, therefore, it would probably be Karl Jaspers. '[T]here is no one stable attitude to death,' he says, 'which can be considered as the only correct one: death transforms itself with me.' Consequently, 'it is no contradiction when man clings to life with every particle of his being, and still, while loving life with its contradictions and absurdities, desires death; when he seems to despair at the thought of death, and at the same time, contemplating death, becomes aware of his true being; when he sees death as a friend and as a foe, avoids it and at the same time longs for it.'[18]

Such vacillation, though perhaps 'natural' for a private individual, might seem to invite certain problems when carried over into art, a level of experience that generally implies a higher degree of order and consistency. In fact, however, the lack of a consensual intellectual mould to tuck all their ideas into has made it possible for Canadian writers to deal with death in a much more immediate and authentic way. While some associated elements – the recognition of and fascination with 'limits,' the acknowledgment of the inevitability of isolation – are, as we have seen, constant enough to be considered as *données*, any decision on how to respond or deal with the inescapable fact of death is and must be, it is implied, a purely individual matter. In *Les chambres de bois*, though Catherine (out of shame for her crude peasant vitality) almost succumbs to her husband's fatal vision of a cool and languid beauty untouched by time or the sun, in the end she wrenches herself back from the very brink of death and flees the silent rooms for the wide unordered expanses of sky and ocean. In Findley's *The Last of the Crazy People*, on the other hand, young Hooker, compelled by his horrified recognition that the alienation of everyone around him is so extreme as to comprise a kind of living death, but without true death's pain-killing oblivion, gives himself up to death, becomes its servant – commits the only valid self-sacrifice possible in a world without God, a world full of silence: not martyrdom but murder. One may, in other words, opt with equal plausibility for life *or* for death.

The one point on which both of these very different books seem to agree is that 'being toward death' has its own coherence, a sense of fitness and inevitability that makes a man one with his actions. One's only choice when it comes right down to it is, as Findley says of Hooker's plight, 'to do that thing that simply must be done' (B145). Is it, then, simply a kind of determinism that is implied? Yes – and no. It may more accurately be described as a fundamentally aesthetic view of existence that imputes to life – to lives – the same kind of self-referenced order, the 'rigorous necessity within ... internal constitution'[19] that we often attribute to art. It's the 'self-reference' that is important in this formulation, of course. If man is *determined*, so the Canadian seems to believe, it is not so much by extrinsic factors (if the perception of an absolute discontinuity between 'self' and 'other' militates against belief in transcendence, it also implies that one will not naturally think in terms of supernatural influence – intervention from the outside in – either providential or demonic), but by patterns, propensities, inclinations carried within the self like seeds. In Catherine's case, for instance, the return to life is signalled by a sudden upsurge of sensual awareness, that is, awareness of things *outside* – 'the tiled roof ... glistening, its salmon pink colour touched with watery light,' the 'thought of juicy watermelons,' the aroma of geraniums rising 'like incense to the sun' (122–3) – but these elements call to her only because she carries an answering life-force within her, as signalled by her recurrent association with colour, her warmth, her stubborn preference – even while most fully under Michel's spell – for '"the daylight and summertime"' (73), her rebellious desire '"to run until [she is] breathless, barefoot through the puddles"' (52). In *The Last of the Crazy People*, similarly, though Graeme Gibson talks of 'the logic of the book' (B145), it is clear the 'logic' that inexorably impels the final action – both the fly buzz of panic that opens up the chasm and the 'fearful thought' that closes it again (271) – is Hooker's, not merely the author's. This is why Findley calls the climax an 'orgasm' (B145). Because it comes from inside.

This sense of self-impulsion, connoting as it does both free will and necessity, is the basis of the mythopoeic impulse in Canada. The 'box' in which the Canadian resides is, paradoxically, both existential *and* arbitrary, natural *and* self-created, container *and* frame. The box is definitely there, though. We may take that as given. It now remains to see how we *respond* to our intimations of mortality.

NOTES

1 Interestingly, Rayner's painting provides a striking visual correlative for Jacques Godbout's novel by the same name.
2 Lucie-Smith, *Late Modern: The Visual Arts since 1945* (Oxford 1975) 42
3 Adams, *Modern Painting* (Phaedon 1979) 56
4 In this connection we might note Scott Symons's description of the Canadian flag: 'that "maple leaf" ... it is the Crushed Cube. That's it – the all-Canadian Cube, flattened. With its guts bashed splat. It's us all right – but us squashed. A flag for

Cubes castrated. Boxed in with red at either end, and set on a virgin field of white. Boxed in, flat' (79).

5 'The number of Canadian plays concerned with various kinds of imprisonment suggests the concern Canadian dramatists feel about the individual who is trapped by a situation and seeks to free himself from it. The situation may be of his own creation, as in *General Confession*, or he may be a victim of circumstances, as in *Listen to the Wind*. Yet Canadian drama cannot be catalogued as claustrophobic, for in these plays imprisonment is not always viewed negatively. In *No Scandal in Spain*, imprisonment is clearly the right choice for the officer to make. In *Lake Doré*, the alternative to imprisonment is suicide. Certainly *Creeps* does not suggest that freedom is necessarily a solution which will give the characters happy lives. In that play, as in *Fortune and Men's Eyes* and *The Ecstasy of Rita Joe*, there does not seem to be any possibility for a "happy ending"' (Teague 121).

6 In view of the existentialist echoes observed in Hodgins in the last chapter, it is interesting that Delaney apparently comes to accept that the disintegration of his life – the loss of his job, the breakup of his marriage – is in some way conducive, perhaps even necessary, to the achievement of his quest. '*Okay! Okay you son of a bitch! I'm stripped now, okay, now where is that god-damned line?*' (23).

7 See Colin Wilson, *The Outsider* (Picador 1978), for a discussion of the influence of the existentialist concept of estrangement on modern literature; also Ihab Hassan, *Radical Innocence: Studies in the Contemporary American Novel* (Princeton 1961), for an examination of the slightly different ways in which American writers have treated the standard existentialist themes. I have argued elsewhere that the difference between American and European usages is greater than Hassan admits, the American version of the existentialist anti-hero being far more romantic than his European counterpart.

8 Richard C. McCleary, 'Introduction' to Maurice Merleau-Ponty, *Signs*, trans. Richard McCleary (Northwestern U. 1964) xiii

9 Becker, *The Denial of Death* (Free Press 1975) 282

10 Although space precludes any exhaustive compilation of evidence for this contention, a random survey of the criticism will attest to the fact that death is not merely an important ingredient of the Canadian fictional universe but one of the cornerstones on which it is erected, the single feature that unifies the work of writers otherwise quite diverse in both vision and style. For a representative range of opinion see, for instance, Dawson on Blais (esp. 59), Pesandro on Laurence (esp. 83), Davey on Godfrey (F, esp. 127), St Pierre on Davies (esp. 127), Djwa on Pratt (esp. A27).

11 Roch Carrier's characters, for instance, seem almost irresistibly drawn to morbid fancies at tender moments. David Bond cites as an example the occasion in *La guerre, yes sir!* when, on the verge of making love to Amélie, Arthur becomes obsessed with the thought of the dead Corriveau (see Bond 124), but the equation between sex and death is, in fact, constant throughout Carrier's trilogy, particularly in *Floralie, où es-tu?* with its juxtaposition of honeymoon/wilderness ordeal.

12 Douglas Jones discussing T.E. Farley's thesis submitted at Carleton University in 1968, 'Love and Death in Canadian Poetry' (A14)

13 See Paul Zweig, *The Adventurer* (Basic Books 1974).

14 In Quebec literature death is such a grotesquely dominant motif that individual deaths actually lose some of their impact. This makes the approach as a whole *seem* more general and philosophical than is typical of English Canada. Part of the apparent difference in emphasis represents a real, if only relative, deviation (undoubtedly due on the one hand to the more direct European influence and on the other to the fact that in recent decades the revolt against political-cultural engulfment has produced more extreme versions of the type response) but part, too, is an illusion fostered by the choice of narrative vehicles which, with their unmistakable echoes of fairytale and fable, have the curious impersonality of folk forms of literature but *without* the familiarity of myth.

15 MacLennan himself later recognized the extent to which his (wishful?) intimations of divinity were working at odds with the intellectual underpinnings of this novel, undermining its emotional coherence. 'In *The Watch that Ends the Night* my intuitions were forcing me to utter something socially blasphemous in those years. They were asserting that God had not been outmoded by the Christian Church, Bertrand Russell, the social scientists and modern education. My brain did not grasp this, and that was why I had so many hang-ups. Not even when I finished the novel had I reached the place where I could say, regardless of whether anyone laughed at me or not, "I believe in God – and that is what scares me." In the God manifest in evolution, which I am told some geneticists now question? Yes' (A119).

16 Jacques Choron, *Death and Western Thought* (Collier 1963) 236-7

17 Sartre, *L'être et le néant* (Gallimard 1955) 624, in Choron 244

18 Jaspers, *Philosophie* (Springer 1932) II-230, in Choron 228

19 Arturo Fallico, *Art & Existentialism* (Prentice-Hall 1962) 2

6

Harlequin Romances

We have noted in connection with *La belle bête* that self-obsession may lead to self-annihilation. Introspection is one thing; radical solipsism is something else. If inside and outside are exclusively and eternally mutually reflective, the point comes when the images cancel each other out. This is why, as a first step, knowledge of one's limits – including death – is important: it provides at least a negative standard against which the self may be measured. It is not enough, however. One needs positive standards as well. Normally these are inferred from cues embedded in the communal myth system, but when a culture's modes of self-reference are dislocated, new models of every sort must be evolved. One of the most fundamental stages of this refurbishing involves the development of a new, more appropriate set of exemplary (in the sense recent anthropologists have imputed to the kinship model[1]) cultural roles and relations.

If life is a closed system – if, under *normal* circumstances, man is hedged about by invisible walls that seem destined to foil his attempts to get outside himself, to merge with or even simply to touch some larger reality – the question still remains whether there might be some special circumstances, some magical means whereby he might at least temporarily break out of his isolation. The romantic would claim that there are, indeed, certain psychic states that facilitate communion even though estrangement be the common lot. 'Mystical' translation is one of these. In a de-mythicized universe, however, the answer is likely to invoke instead some kind of interpersonal relation. One of the commonest resorts of alienated modern man, therefore, has been the glorification of love, not merely as a source of forgetfulness, a stopgap against the yawning chasm of existential isolation, but as an actual means – in theory at least – of transcending the limited human condition. As Ernest Becker, quoting Otto Rand, describes it:

[M]odern man edged himself into an impossible situation. He still needed to feel heroic, to know that his life mattered in the scheme of things ... he still had to merge himself with some higher, self-absorbing meaning, in trust and in gratitude ... If he no longer had God, how was he to do this? One of the first ways that occurred to him ... was the 'romantic solution': he fixed his urge to cosmic heroism onto *another person* in the form of a love object. The self-glorification that he needed in his innermost nature he now looked for in the love partner. The love partner becomes the divine ideal within which to fulfill one's life. All spiritual and moral needs now become focussed in one individual. Spirituality, which once referred to another dimension of things, is now brought down to this earth and given form in another individual human being. Salvation itself is no longer referred to an abstraction like God but can be sought 'in the beatification of the other.' We could call this 'transference beatification.' Man now lives in a 'cosmology of two.'[2]

Attractive as it may sound, the romantic solution unfortunately implies problems even at the best of times. As Becker points out, the expectations are simply unreasonable. 'How can a human be a god-like "everything" to another?' he asks. 'No human relationship can bear the burden of godhood, and the attempt has to take its toll in some way on both parties' [166]. A love affair – even, or perhaps especially, a love affair nourished on the uplifting sentiments of *Lorna Doone* and *Jane Eyre* and *Le Grand Meaulnes* – as Marian Engel points out in *The Honeyman Festival*, is at the very least bound to deflate somewhat under the impact of the mundane realities of cohabitation (see 74-5). At worst the disillusionment engendered by such deflation can trigger, by way of reaction, a mutual antipathy all the more excruciating because of the consolation that *by definition* is supposed to inhere in the romantic union. Canadian literature yields so many examples of this kind of backlash as to suggest that especially in a setting like this one, where the conditions already seem unusually conducive to isolation, it is the more radical possibility which is the most likely to ensue. Patricia Blondal's *A Candle to Light the Sun*, indeed, suggests that the recoil is wellnigh inevitable. Virtually every marriage mentioned in this book is a case study in communication breakdown: the mismatched Newmans; the Backhouses, driven apart by his irrational jealousy; the brittle, aristocratic Rushforths. And then of course there are the Rosses, perfection-loving Gavin and Sir Richard's golden daughter, the fairytale couple who – radically estranged since the moment of their child's death, bound by mutual pain yet cocooned in separate silence – not only give the lie to the idea of fortune's favour but demonstrate poignantly how even the truest love can sour:

He watched her go, the crown of gold hair glistening through the trees. Proud. The head proud. And we cannot speak. He closed his eyes ... The not-speaking is her sanity. One word and there is nothing left. Yet he wished he could make her smile, just once as she used to when she was a girl cutting up through the district like a healthy animal, laughing at everyone and everything. But how, with the barrier of sanity a thin bright shell holding off smiles as well as grief? He wondered if this were love's end always, the ultimate, to know there was no giving of happiness, that it grew always within, solitary and incommunicable, and that, having none himself, he could not spark it from her. His love was worthless, like Sir Richard's boxes of old gold mine stocks. (70)

In such circumstances, far from being a haven, love – with its empty yet enticing promises – can only mock hope with its impotence. No escape route this, but a far crueller trap than unloved and *unillusioned* loneliness. 'That's what marriage is,' Elisabeth d'Aulnières concludes bitterly in *Kamouraska*. 'One fear shared by two, one need to be consoled, one empty caress in the darkness' (18).

This is not the worst of it, either. If merely human love must necessarily fail of its mythic capacity to span the gap between individuals, to the extent that it is associated with sex it actually becomes a destructive force. It is not simply a moral matter – the association of lust with corruption glimpsed, for instance, in the poems of James Reaney's *The Red Heart* with its demonic vision of 'seething secret life in the "scrotal city"' (see Woodman, especially 86-7) – but a profound ambivalence rooted in the very terms of existence. The fly in the ointment is, as Becker points out, the inescapable fact that 'Sex is of the body, and the body is of death' [162]. Rather than enabling an individual to transcend his mortality, in other words, love merely makes him more agonizingly aware of it. Small wonder in a death-obsessed culture like Canada's that love should tend to be associated with fatality of one kind or another.

Some writers, like Leonard Cohen, simply sidestep the issue by avoiding ultimate consummation. 'To Cohen,' says Frank Davey, 'lovers are involved in impossible quests for perfection and purity; to imagine this quest ever fulfilled would be to sell out to society and embrace domesticity, mediocrity, and anonymity, to emulate not Christ but "just some Joseph looking for a manger"' (F69). If we read between the lines of Cohen's poetry, however, there are intimations – especially in the predilection for richly textured surfaces, intricate stanzaic patterns, and ornate romantic imagery that seems to evince a wish to translate the disorder of life into the static (and thus less threatening) beauty of art – that his evasiveness may have some deeper cause than simply a dislike for the humdrum. And avoidance of this sort is not as much of a common resort as one might expect. For all its problematic associations, sex, while generally treated less explicitly in Canada than is common in American fiction of the last two decades, is, as John Moss has observed, a fairly noticeable ingredient of modern through contemporary Canadian literature. It *is* problematic, though – almost invariably. The extent to which these problems are related directly to the connection with corporeality that Becker draws so trenchantly is, moreover, demonstrated by the disquietingly frequent associations made by our writers not merely between sex and negative emotional reactions, from disappointment through to disgust, but between sex and personal catastrophe: madness, violence, or death.

In some cases, admittedly, this association may be passed off as concomitant with exceptional conditions. In F.P. Grove's *Settlers of the Marsh*, for instance, both the breakdown of the marriage and the climactic disaster may be blamed directly on either Niels's unnatural innocence or Clara's lack of it. In either case, though, these are patently not normal people. When she begins her terrible program of revenge, flaunting her lovers deliberately before her husband to repay him for his guilt-ridden recoil from her, she is no less mad than he is at the height of the murderous rage that results in her death. If one surveys the corpus as a whole, however, it is clearly *not* just the special case that ends disastrously. In Dennis Sears's *The Lark in the Clear Air*, a generally limpid reminiscence of rural adolescence, a young girl falls off a bridge to her death almost immediately following and perhaps even (it is implied) *because of* her loss of virginity. ' "But she was as sure-footed as a deer; she wouldn't miss her step,"' cries the young protagonist (her lover) in the extremity of his outrage and despair. '"Perhaps her eyes were on a cloud,"' replies his uncle ambiguously (117). The toils of sin? It doesn't seem likely. The seduction is hardly painted in terms of Victorian morality, and young Holly seems implausible as a modern version of Hardy's poor doomed Tess. Besides, in Canadian literature marriage is no guarantee of safety, moral or otherwise, and quantitatively speaking may in fact imply an even greater degree of danger. *The Last of the Crazy People*, with its 'atmosphere of denied sexuality, guilt, and accusation' (as the back-cover blurb would have it), outside of the fact that the events are filtered through the mind of a child paints a by no means unusual picture (for Canada) of conjugal relations:

He thought about his mother and their troubles.

Some of the happenings which made up the trouble took place behind his back. For instance, quite often he heard arguing, and very often he knew that someone, somewhere, was crying. And many times, too, he was taken for sudden walks by Iris who was the Negro maid. Sometimes he would hear such phrases as 'I can't, oh, I can't....' and 'Don't make me do that....' from faraway upstairs. For two months in the autumn he had barely seen his mother, and then, from December to February, he did not see her at all. But he heard her. Weeping... crying... complaining... making noises that he did not understand. In March she went to the hospital, and in April she came home. She had given birth to a dead child. (11)

Whether the participants are married or unmarried, sex in this setting seems perceived as at best diffusely dangerous, and at worst absolutely deadly. '[T]his was what I expected sexual communication to be,' says Alice Munro's Del Jordan' – a flash of insanity, a dreamlike, ruthless, contemptuous breakthrough in a world of decent appearances' (D135).

In recent French-Canadian literature the lethal potential of sex is given even greater emphasis. The characteristic effect, in contrast to the more subtle (albeit unsettling) insinuations of the English oeuvre, is frenzied, nightmarish, flamboyantly grotesque. More telling, it is specifically and monotonously cautionary. Going far beyond occasional or covert usage, indeed, one of the most dominant and fully realized themes in the collective corpus, as Joan Coldwell says of Marie-Claire Blais' *La belle bête*, concerns 'the essential destructiveness of human love' (66). Across the board, the link between concupiscence and death is thus asserted not merely as metaphor but as an inescapable figment or facet of existential reality. The result is to make sex seem, more often than not, less an expression of affection than an act of war. Anne Hébert's *Kamouraska* is typical in this regard. As her husband lays dying, Elisabeth d'Aulnières, now Mme Rolland, is impelled by the subtle violence of her relation with this man to relive the more overt violence of her younger days, the brutalization she suffered at the hands of her first husband and her consequent successful attempt to fashion her lover into a tool of her revenge. 'It fills me with awe and despair, both at once,' she says. 'To make him my own, like my very own hand. Be with him at every deed of his wonderful manly strength ... To kill my husband with him' (198).

In other writers the association is generally made somewhat more indirectly, but the implications are much the same. In Hubert Aquin's novels, for instance, sexual passion (in Leonard Sugden's words) is characteristically likened to 'fulgaration, explosion, or crisis'; repeatedly imaged in terms of 'motion, spasm, convulsion, jolting, fury, exaltation, cries (of ecstasy or death), madness and delirium.' Even more significantly, 'Since sexuality is ... inherently violent and related to physical dominance,' his work also reveals strong 'sadistic nuances which recur continually along with rape and murder as major themes. Such events,' Sugden continues, 'take place when delirium breaks through. In human relations, the presence of the "Other" (be it a sex partner) already constitutes a threat' (81, 83). In Roch Carrier's trilogy, it is the sex/death correlation that energizes the entire text, permeating the level of language as well as the more explicit aspects of plot and theme. Carrier gives the equation another whole dimension, moreover, through his introduction of and emphasis on the transcendent third factor of religion. This manoeuvre, invoking as it does the additional (homologous/antithetical) bivalencies of spirit/flesh and heaven/ hell, makes it possible for the author to carry an extremely heavy weight of signification in a simple, dramatic verbal vehicle. This effect is most pronounced in *Floralie, où es-tu?*, a novel (if one can adequately encompass Carrier's odd mixture of naturalism and allegory within any such term) which uses structural replication between diverse elements of theme to set up a complex vertical resonance that more than counters the horizontal simplicity, the almost crude sparseness of the text. On the surface we have a poignant but fairly straightforward exploration of the gap between Floralie's hopeful expectations of her honeymoon and the actual brutality of the marital consummation.[3] Co-extensive with this 'story,' both paralleling and extending its implications, is a more clearly 'fabulous' stratum wherein the author exploits the striking, structurally analogous discrepancy between the conventional idea of the wedding journey (night of love) and the nightmare journeys that Anthelme and Floralie, lost and separated, must make through the wilderness before they can find each other again (dark night of the soul). Finally, moving further into abstraction, we have the grandest irony of all: the radical contrast between the Church's purported lifegiving capacity and its demonstrated destructive effects, not merely on the private level ('Floralie had to accept that the most precious joy that life had given her was wicked' 101) but even more on the level of public function, as its self-appointed role as communal refuge is undermined drastically by the catastrophic climax of the book:

Father Nombrillet's sermon was interrupted by a cry. A fire had broken out among the pilgrims. Springing up from the earth, the fire took hold of clothes and held on. The pilgrims wept, pushed, shouted and hit one another. The fire tore off their clothes and scratched their faces. Impressed by Father Nombrillet's words a pious man had forgotten the lantern in his hand and it had fallen, spattering oil on a woman in front of him. Seized by the flames she had dropped her own lantern. They prayed and cursed and hit and trampled. They tore, but the human wall was impassable.

'God puts to the test those whom he has chosen,' shouted Father Nombrillet.

The walls of the chapel opened and the flaming roof gave way and fell onto piles of blazing flesh. (104-5)

The implications of this apotheosis are not as simplistic as the obvious ironic reading may make it appear. Accepting the Church's culpability for its failure to *save*, one might still question what it was that actually caused this 'accident.' Are these pilgrims devoured by the flames of their own life-denying fanaticism? Does the fire perhaps represent the fires of lust which the Church, for all its efforts, is unable to staunch? Or is it merely life itself, purposeless, insensible, full of suffering, devouring the individual before he has time to do more than cry out in pain? Notwithstanding these ambiguities, it still must be obvious that the implicit causal connection made between the initial sexual act and the ensuing horrors indicates a profound discomfort with the idea of sexual relations *per se*.

The Québécois vision, while admittedly extreme, is not a special case. The implications of Carrier's psycho-drama are not, despite the radical difference in style, unlike those contained in Sears's story mentioned above. Notwithstanding the contrast in tone between French and English versions, in fact, Canadian literature as a whole shows a remarkable propensity for such a view. There is evidently a strong covert anxiety in the country (differing from the 'natural' response Becker describes if not in kind at least – if we can judge by the anomalous literary effects – in degree) about the flesh and its urgencies such that what normally seems deadly only by virtue of the associations it carries becomes, in frequent literary usage, depicted as deadly in fact. Such a propensity would militate against the romantic solution even if nothing else were involved. Quite aside from the basic and intrinsic problems implied by sex, however, the Canadian ambience introduces a number of *further* peculiar complications into the romantic arena which are all its own.

In chapter 4 we saw that due to the peculiar cognitive structures which developed as a secondary effect of the Wacousta syndrome there is a proclivity in Canadian literature for the traditional categories of thought to shift, re-orient, even break down completely. One of the most striking examples of this phenomenon, aside from (although directly connected with) the complex recasting of symbolic values associated with nature, is the tendency toward an inversion of sex roles. The typical protagonist in most non-Canadian Western literature, for formal reasons as much as for reasons of authorship, is masculine, while nature is generally presented in feminine terms. This conventional attribution is part cause, part consequence of the fact that, as Gloria Onley points out, 'in the patriarchy ... women have been the "ground" against which the "figures" of men have emerged' (49). In Canada, however, nature – as noted in passing at the end of chapter 2 – often has specifically masculine associations.

Is this anomalous usage really common enough to be considered a trend, though? The answer, I think, is indubitably yes. 'Mother Nature' is singularly absent from the Canadian scene. Even in cases where writers have continued to use the conventional 'she' – as Pratt does, for instance, in *Towards the Last Spike* when he characterizes the Canadian Shield as a great dormant lizard ('This folded reptile was asleep or dead:/ So motionless, she seemed stone dead' 369) – the landscape so designated tends to be portrayed in terms of qualities, like coldness and hardness, which are traditionally imputed to masculinity. At times, indeed, the covert contrast in such cases between the land's nominal femininity and the felt reality conveyed by the author's treatment of it is striking enough to make the conventional attribution seem a proof rather than an exception to the rule. In *The Burning Wood*, most notably, David Williams uses a self-consciously Faulknerian idiom to depict nature as a raped female ('So

*it's little wonder she this land has turned cold unyearning inviolate though
ravished any woman would who is plowed for profit'* 158), but his handling of
the Sundance, the climactic scene in the book, would seem to have an
implication totally opposite to that carried by his rhetoric. In this incident the
young protagonist-in-search-of-enlightenment, led by the conventional Indian
helper (Spirit of Nature), must make his way, like the classic questing prince,
through a wilderness so dense as to seem magical ('they had to stoop beneath the
cover of spreading bushes which felt as durable as grillework and almost as
pliable ... The farther they went the lower and tighter the lattice grew.' 121-2).
The fairytale echoes here are unmistakable. When Williams's young quester
finally accomplishes his qualifying task, however, what he finds in the heart of
the enchanted kingdom on the other side of the thicket is not Sleeping Beauty,
the anima figure, but the pre-eminently masculine symbol of the Sundance
pole.[4] For all that Williams *wants* to see nature as feminine, therefore, it would
seem that his unconscious response betrays his conscious intentions. In Canada
nature is just *not* naturally perceived as warm and maternal.

The masculinization of the landscape does not take place solely at a covert
level, either. There are plenty of instances where the atypical attribution seems
to be made quite explicitly. As mentioned above, for example, those *personif-
ications* of nature that turn up in Canadian literature, in marked contrast to such
gentle spirits as Rima of *Green Mansions* (the Anglo-American version of
Roberts's *The Heart of the Ancient Wood*), are likely to be unequivocally
masculine, not merely when the landscape is overtly hostile, as in Ostenso's
Wild Geese, but in almost every mood and mode. The personifying figure can
even be a positive one, although more typically he is morally ambivalent. He
can turn up in realistic fiction (the protagonist of Raddall's *The Nymph and the
Lamp*, for instance, has strong nature associations: 'men spoke of him as
"Carney – you know, Carney of Marina,"' as if he were part of the place like one
of the wild ponies on the dunes' 11), but his most memorable incarnations are in
books with a significant fantasy component. One example of this type is
Hodgins's Donal Brendan Keneally (discussed in greater detail below); an even
more striking version is the central character in Howard O'Hagan's *Tay John* – a
strange mythic creature, half-white, half-Indian, who, appropriately enough,
both emerged out of the earth (the grave of his dead mother) and in the end
returned to it again: 'just walked down, the toboggan behind him, under the
snow and into the ground' (264).

Generally notable for their size and strength, as well as for occasional fits of
irrational ferocity, these figures tend to carry a perceptible numen. More
significant, though not without their own peculiar sense of morality, they are
typically implicated in a kind of violence which is not merely anti-social but
explicitly sexual. O'Hagan's hero, for instance, is both – by report – a rapist and
a kidnapper. His culpability, on the other hand, would seem to be at least partly

offset by the eager complicity of his female victims. Tay John, in other words, is both dangerous *and* fascinating. He is also in a sense surreal. Eminently physical, yet 'having something of the abstract about him' (83), he literally incarnates – as one of the other characters in the book remarks, bringing together in a single symbol both his associations with nature and his exemplification of primitive masculine force – 'the totem pole' (237). It is hardly surprising that the Canadian symbolic ego, set in dramatic opposition to an 'other' objectified in these particular terms, would – whatever the ostensible sex of its various literary personae – become feminine in temperament and function: emotional, passive, and vulnerable. Indeed, given the iconographic preferences noted in the last chapter, the shift seems inevitable. As Otto Rank points out, woman's psychology – like, it would appear, the representative Canadian's – 'can be designated as insideness, in contra-distinction to man's centrifugal outsideness.'[5]

Returning to Richardson's novel with which this investigation opened, we can see the pattern in its prototypical form. Wacousta, the Indianized English officer whose original identity has been obliterated by the effects of the wilderness, is presented as an almost grotesquely masculine figure (he actually grew larger and stronger, we are told, when he 'went over' to nature, although he was a mature man at the time), while the inmates of the fort are portrayed in strikingly feminine terms. Charles Haldimar, for instance (whose symbolic associations with the garrison are underlined by the fact that he seems literally *tied* to the place; doomed – like the sea captain's wife – to pace the walls incessantly in suspenseful anticipation of the return of his more active compatriots), is not only described as having the appearance of a 'frail and delicate woman' (83), but associated repeatedly with such conventionally feminine affectations as swooning, nervous debilitation, and paroxysms of tears.[6] Indeed, both his effeminacy and his somewhat peculiar relationship with his sister and Sir Everard Valletort are enough at odds with convention to create what a number of critics perceive as an emotional and aesthetic flaw in the book (normal sexuality, says Moss, is, 'in this effete triangle, replaced by bonds of filial devotion which are a crude disguise for incipient incest, homosexuality, and impotence' D47[7]). If nothing else, however, Richardson's lengthy passages on Charles's girlish beauty and sensitivity provide a blatant foil to Wacousta's exaggerated masculinity.

Instead of Mother Nature versus a paternalistic military establishment, therefore, *Wacousta* seems to pit a feminine garrison against a masculine gothic landscape. The action of the novel, moreover, reinforces this basic inversion. Establishing the tone right from the beginning of the book, Wacousta's midnight intrusion into Colonel de Haldimar's bedroom, with its suggestion of secret violation and its traumatic after-effects, seems almost like a kind of rape. The ultimate stage in the feminization of the garrison, however, occurs when

Wacousta breaks the flagpole in effecting his escape. This fantastic act of violence, appropriately directed toward the flag as a symbol of both military power and civil order, whatever it lacks on the level of verisimilitude[8] not only demonstrates the impotence of civilized man in the face of the wilderness but, at a deeper level, unquestionably suggests a symbolic castration.

Again there is the possibility that Richardson represents an idiosyncratic case; the particular elements of the novel on which I have focused here are certainly grotesque enough in his handling to make one resist generalization. The fact is, though, that in Canadian literature of both the nineteenth and the twentieth centuries, ample examples may be found to confirm that the pattern of inversion is a pervasive one. 'A Legend of the Lake,' a nineteenth-century story by Harriet V. Cheney, for instance, inverts entirely the conventional pattern of sexual implication found in the wilderness romance. Where normally the genre, influenced strongly by the gothic mode, focuses on a weak, vulnerable young girl, lost in the wilderness and threatened by libidinous savages, Cheney's story relates the fate of an aristocratic young *man* who becomes lost in the woods and is seduced, against his will, by an Indian *girl*. A similar role reversal is demonstrated by Gilbert Parker's *The Seats of the Mighty*, where for almost the first twenty-six chapters – considerably more than half the book – the protagonist, Major Robert Stobo, while overtly described in the conventional terms of a romantic hero, is locked in a dungeon, passive and impotent, while the heroine takes the active role of plotting his escape. His effeminacy is reinforced, moreover, first by his implied relationship with the villain, Doltaire (in tones strikingly reminiscent of the gothic heroine, Stobo exclaims repeatedly upon the magnetic attraction exerted by Doltaire's fascinating and repellent satanic personality: 'to this hour his handsome face, with its shadows and shifting lights, haunts me, charms me' 22), and second by the implication that Alixe's desire to free him extends *only* to the alleviation of his physical situation, and not to a rekindling of the 'masculine' spirit prerequisite to the aggressive role which she, by default, has assumed ('"Thou has two jails",' she says, '"and the one wherein I lock thee safe is warm and full of light"' 35).

The pattern continues to manifest itself in modern literature as well – and in surprisingly similar terms. Hodgins's Wade Cameron, for instance, not only reveals a peculiarly feminine and narcissistic sense of self ('[H]is mother told him he was a little old to be showing off legs and chest like a brand new youth. But he liked the air, he said, he liked to be aware of himself. He smirked, smiled, grinned, and ran fingers through the curled hairs on his belly' 130), but, reinforcing the impression on a more covert level, is also self-identified with the fortress that he has built as a tourist attraction, and particularly with its tiny dungeon. 'Barely large enough for a man to stretch out in ... a semi-circular space surrounded by big smooth speckled beach stones cemented together, with a thick plank door on iron hinges and no window at all' (130-1), this womb-like space is explicitly indicated by Wade's alter ego, the Horseman, as a focal centre for psychic introversion: 'It would feel like a pretty small world. There'd be nothing in it but yourself. Or what you thought was yourself' (159). These implications about Wade's symbolic sexual identification are echoed in the passive role he plays in relation to his sometime-inamorata, Virginia.

The inverted 'wilderness journey' motif, too, may be as easily recognized in the twentieth as in the nineteenth century. On his picaresque questing through the surrealistic landscape of rural Alberta, Hazard Lepage, the protagonist of Kroetsch's *The Studhorse Man*, becomes progressively less self-actuated as he is helplessly propelled – by fate and the wishes of the stronger-willed women he encounters – through a series of bizarre impositions from a reluctant seduction by a museum curator (appropriately named P. Cockburn) through to his sexual enslavement by an ugly but insatiable widow, and climaxing with the necrophilic rape of his 'dead' body by his aging, virginal fiancée, Martha Proudfoot. The symbolic function of Hazard's quest, in fact, seems to be totally opposite to the goal of the traditional fairytale: the affirmation of the masculine principle as the basis of social order through the symbolic marriage of the successful hero to the passive, waiting princess.[9] Instead of marriage at the end of his journey, Hazard finds only death – significantly enough, through the agency of his stallion, Poseidon, the correlative of his masculinity. If the message isn't clear enough, Poseidon's own fate is in a sense a mirror image of his master's. He, unlike Hazard, does win his harem, but only by symbolically betraying his sexuality, perverting it to the end of sterility by servicing the mares whose urine is to be used in the manufacture of birth control pills.

If the Canadian literary hero seems to demonstrate a distinctly feminine aspect, the next obvious question is whether Canadian heroines show a reciprocal development of masculine characteristics. The answer to this is not as obvious as one might expect. There are a few anomalously dominant women in Canadian fiction – the strong-willed Valkyrian mother of Grove's *In Search of Myself* is an example – but, somewhat surprisingly in view of the feminization of the hero, the conventional overly possessive mother and tyrannical wife are not as visible in this country as in the United States where, as Geoffrey Gorer points out in his study, *The American People*, these stereotypes are pervasive.[10] More common on this side of the border, on the other hand, is a slightly different kind of dominant stereotype, that of the woman as sexual predator. Extreme cases would include Jerome Martell's mother in *The Watch that Ends the Night*[11] and, even more excessively, the title figure of John Mills's novel, *Skevington's Daughter*, a notable grotesque whose remarkable strength of will and prodigious sexual appetite reach their fullest expression in the seduction and – it is hinted – eventual murder of her father ('How men fear us!' she crows to her correspondent, 170). The usage is not, however, limited to such idiosyncratic and extravagant examples as these. In somewhat less virulent form, in fact, the same essential character can be identified in numerous more or less realistic versions throughout the Canadian corpus: Elisabeth d'Aulnières; Ainslie of *The Edible Woman*; Barbara Kramer in Matt Cohen's short story, 'Our Passion Lit the Night'; most notably perhaps, Lady Barbara d'Orsey of Findley's *The Wars* ('"Barbara standing at the foot of the bed. Someone else doing all the talking. Barbara with her flowers. Her freesia. Emanations. There they are on the mantle. And she was like that cold white vase and never said a word. She stood and watched them dying like a stone. Ariadne and Dionysus. Well – it's not a bad analogy. Yes? Deserted by one god – she took up another. Every year Dionysus was destroyed and every year he was born again from the ashes"' 104–5). We should be careful not to make too much of this particular recurrence, though. The mankiller is always a peripheral figure, and (whatever the usage may imply *covertly* about the Canadian psyche) as such does not provide very convincing evidence for a *general* shift in conventional sexual roles.

On the other hand, it does seem as though *something* a little peculiar is going on. Perhaps a different approach is required.

If – as with our survey of paintings in the last chapter – we look for more subtle kinds of indicators, relative rather than absolute differences, cumulative evidence of a divergence in emphasis rather than exceptional cases, we will have a better chance of proving our point. The fact is, taken as a group, in comparison at least with traditional, and especially romantic, conceptions of 'normal' femininity, Canadian literary heroines do generally exhibit stronger personalities, a greater degree of individuality, and more autonomy of action than might conventionally be considered appropriate, and there are certainly moments when this relative authority seems to be perceived as slightly subversive. In McCourt's *The Wooden Sword*, for instance, although the protagonist's wife does not on the surface appear to be either particularly aggressive or, with respect to her role as student-protégé-bride of a university teacher, unconventional, her husband seems to feel – and the author to agree – that in her essential self she is somehow anomalously masculine:

Her eyes were bright with unshed tears. Again it occurred to him that he had never seen Ruth cry ... She was like a man that way. Perhaps he would tell her some time that she was like a man that way. She would be pleased. Once, before they were married, she had said to him, face grave, brow slightly puckered, 'Tell me, Steven, am I masculine or feminine?' He had answered, thinking to please her and because he really believed, 'All woman, Ruth, body and mind. The most feminine person I've ever known.' But she hadn't been pleased; she'd been annoyed a little. He thought now that what she wanted to believe of herself was no mere freakish seeking after individuality; she knew herself better than he did. Her capacity for silence, for isolation, the moods of sullen, seemingly unprompted depression with the subtle undertones of sombre independence and strength, above all, her inability, or perhaps reluctance, to shed tears even when stricken – these things were not characteristic of woman. (197-8)

In some respects, then, the Canadian heroine, while no militant feminist or matriarchal harridan, does tend to display a certain 'masculine' dominance, an instinctive confidence and self-reliance, a capacity to control her own life and her own self to a degree slightly at odds with conventional feminine norms. The result of this is that the world of Canadian fiction is full of women who, if hardly anomalous taken as individuals, are in at least relative terms stronger and more dynamic characters than their masculine peers: Lady Diana of Robertson Davies' *Fifth Business* ('I do not want to make Diana seem crafty in my record of this conversation, but I must say that she had a great gift for getting her own way. *She* had strong ideas on what the future held for us, and I had none.' 82); Mrs Newman of Patricia Blondal's *A Candle to Light the Sun* ('A lesser lady, he knew, could make it clear that she was superior to her present. It was a kind of monumental dignity with Muriel Newman that she should not. The wind as she blows. They put iron in those women. Where she is there are no savages. It's in her eyes, home.' 52); Narah Hale of Wayland Drew's *The Wabeno Feast* ('In a town like Sable Creek she was a continuing event. Large boned, tanned, her blonde hair flowing, she crossed and re-crossed the town as if it were the domain of a Saxon queen.' 12); Del Jordan of Munro's *Lives of Girls and Women* ('I felt amazement, not that I was fighting with Garnet but that anybody could have made such a mistake, to think he had real power over me ... it seemed to me impossible that he should not understand that all the powers I granted him were in play, that he himself was – in play, that I meant to keep him sewed up in his golden lover's skin forever.' 197); even, despite her physical debility, Catherine of MacLennan's *The Watch that Ends the Night* ('This Catherine was ambitious. This Catherine was also strangely solitary in her core and – I dare say this now – there were days when she seemed totally to exclude me because of this communion she had established with color and form. Yes, she was also ruthless. All artists are.' 25). The lineup is an impressive and (demonstrating a significant divergence from the American attitude toward dominant females) for the most part an attractive one.

For all her apparent superiority, however – and this is an important point – the Canadian female doesn't usually feel particularly comfortable with her dominance. Her ascendancy, indeed, is made more often than not to seem an accidental rather than an intentional state of affairs, a trick of fate or, more likely, the consequence of some strange inner quirk of personality that simply 'grew' in her, unnoticed and unwanted. The covert ambivalence signalled by this attitude, the writer's seeming uncertainty about his/her heroine's normality, is hinted at in certain peculiarities of the Canadian *Bildungsroman*. Just as

Wallace Stegner in *Wolf Willow* recalls a 'contemptible' but – despite the ultra-masculine (that is, American) ideals that he shared unquestioningly with his contemporaries – seemingly *inherent* effeminacy that did much to make his boyhood miserable ('I found early that I could shine in class, and I always had a piece to speak in school entertainments, and teachers found me reliable at cleaning blackboards, but teachers were women, and school was a woman's world, the booby prize for those not capable of being men.' 132), the women who turn up in Canadian literature often speak of having had problems during adolescence adjusting themselves to what they had been taught to regard as a 'normal' sexual identity. Marian Engel seems to view this confusion as a concomitant, quite simply, of contemporary culture: the malaise of the 'times.' 'I failed so early to distinguish God's masculinity from my own femininity, ill-defined as it was by my red cardigans and Kitty Higgins bows,' says the protagonist of *The Glassy Sea*, 'that I became, in spite of my instincts, which are on the whole as passive as any man could wish, a woman of my own generation' (22). If we turn to *Lives of Girls and Women*, however, we see clearly the disconcerting truth that lurks *behind* Engel's timely concern about 'the fall-out from the battle of the sexes' (157) (as if that were a specifically localized phenomenon), that *it is not a question of cultural pressures perverting 'feminine' instincts, but of 'unfeminine' instincts asserting themselves despite cultural pressures.* '[A]bout this time I started to read an article in a magazine, on the subject of the basic difference between the male and female habits of thought,' says Del:

The author was a famous New York psychiatrist, a disciple of Freud. He said that the difference between the male and female modes of thought were easily illustrated by the thoughts of a boy and girl, sitting on a park bench, looking at a full moon. The boy thinks of the universe, its immensity and mystery; the girl thinks 'I must wash my hair.' When I read this I was frantically upset; I had to put the magazine down. It was clear to me at once that I was not thinking as the girl thought; the full moon would never as long as I lived remind me to wash my hair. (150)

The Canadian heroine, then, is strong not merely without trying to be but in a sense against her own will. No wonder she is often uneasy, self-conscious, confused to an extent that she feels (with Morag of *The Diviners*) 'totally inadequate and yet frightened of a strength she knows she possesses' (186). She is trapped between what she knows of herself and what she thinks she should be if she is to find happiness. 'I did not want to be like my mother, with her virginal brusqueness, her innocence,' Del protests. 'I wanted men to love me, *and* I wanted to think of the universe when I looked at the moon' (150).

With all this, we might well single out the protagonist of P.K. Page's *The Sun and the Moon* as the archetypal Canadian heroine. Kirstin has the supranormal talent of projecting her personality into an external source, animate or inanimate, and taking it over; 'possessing' it, in the the parlance of witchcraft. As a consequence of this strange power, she finds that she is – almost inadvertently – 'devouring' her fiancé, Carl; draining away his vitality, his will, his entire personality 'like a leech, a vampire ... the moon eclipsing the sun' (99). '"It is as if I have surrendered my being to an alien force and it has made me less,"' says Carl (98). Kirstin, like many other Canadian heroines, thus plays a dominant role *by nature rather than by choice*, and quite despite her own generally more conventional loyalties and preferences.

This last observation raises an interesting question about the inversion pattern as it appears in Canadian literature. Viewed from a traditional and, especially, an American standpoint, a symbolic sexual inversion or loss of sexual identity usually connotes an abnormality, a moral or spiritual sickness of some kind, which must be cured before psychic balance is restored. Hemingway uses the motif frequently. Brett, the heroine of *The Sun Also Rises*, for instance, despite her 'good form,' ultimately seems, in the judgment of the book, an emotional cripple, since she cannot grow her hair out for her young lover, Romero, and become 'womanly.' Her incapacity, like Jake's physical wound, is, moreover, seemingly offered as a symbolic correlative for the general sterility and corruption of the whole post-war world. In Canadian literature, however – and this is an important distinction to make – there is at least some indication that since *the whole fundamental pattern of response is inverted*, the reversal of sexual roles is perceived as *normal*, rather than perverse or ironic. When Aritha Van Herk's Judith gets *her* hair cut before returning to the farm, for instance, the act is clearly presented as a symbol of her repudiation of the vanity and artifice of her 'unnatural' life in the city. The moral dynamic of this book would seem, in fact, completely opposite to that which actuates Hemingway's universe. Such a shift of modes is not without precedent, at least in individual cases. In the second half of *Don Quixote* – to give a classic example – there is a realignment of the moral authority of variant levels of experience such that rather than appearance (the Don's foolish romantic delusions) being undercut ironically by sober reality, it is the reality which is finally undercut, but heroically rather than ironically, by the *surreality* of the Don's ennobling vision. It is thus quite possible that a fundamental reorientation of the moral dimension of the Canadian fictional universe could transform and validate a conventionally negative symbolic pattern. Such a thesis would account for the otherwise anomalous fact that in many Canadian novels we find variants of sex role inversion (dominant female/submissive male) treated in such a matter of fact way that they hardly seem exceptional, let alone a detriment to community morale.

A development like this does not merely affect roles, of course, but, even more so, relations. As far as marital modes are concerned, the reorientation of the basic psycho-sexual paradigm would seem to have the effect of undermining our capacity to believe in even the theoretical viability of the institution. Conventional matches tend to be depicted in Canadian literature as unworkable *in esse*, regardless of intent, either because the man is too weak or the woman too strong or both. In *The Diviners*, for instance, it is clear to the reader from the beginning that Morag's marriage to Brooke is doomed. His need for an adoring acolyte to confirm him in his role as 'man' without in any way testing or threatening the reality of that role allows her no space to grow, no freedom to be her own person – and eventually, though reluctantly, even she has to recognize this. 'His terrible need for someone who could bring him light, lightness, release, relief. How could you fight that? How could you withdraw from the terrors of the cave in which he lived almost always alone? But what if remaining there meant to be chained to that image of yourself which he must have and which must forever be distorted?' (257). The answer is obvious.

In Atwood's *The Edible Woman* the problem is similar. Peter, like Brooke too engrossed in his own needs to see what is before him, *objectifies* Marian, turns her into an idealized and wholly synthetic version of 'fiancée' that has virtually no relevance to her own essential self. The interesting thing about this book, though, is that it makes explicit what is only implicit in *The Diviners*: that the inevitable revolt against dehumanization – against the whole conventional submissive wifely role, in fact – is in a sense *forced upon* the heroine by the radical obtuseness of her masculine partner not merely without her conscious connivance but even against all her own efforts. Marian is not as much of an innocent as the early Morag, nor does Peter have the age or experience advantage of Brooke, but nevertheless, having offered only token resistance to his manipulation, she embraces passivity as willingly as the most childlike of child brides. 'Somewhere else, arrangements were being gradually made ... it was all being taken care of, there was nothing for her to do. She was floating, letting the current hold her up, trusting to it to take her where she was going' (114-15). Marian, in other words, *wants* to believe that the conventional male-dominant mode will work, will provide the security she lacks in herself and lay all her confusions to rest. The day finally arrives, however, when the increasing feeling of unreality becomes unbearable. 'Looking down, she became aware of ... the body that was sitting in [the bath], somehow no longer quite her own. All at once she was afraid that she was dissolving, coming apart layer by layer like a piece of cardboard in a gutter puddle' (227-8). Alarmed and alerted by her intimations of disaster, when Peter at the climactic party tries to take her picture (the ultimate objectification), she flees in terror from him, and from the whole mode of relation that he has imposed upon her.

This particular pattern – perhaps inevitably, given the Canadian psyche – is a common one in recent Canadian fiction, especially that written by women. (In male writers, as we shall see, the same impulse is present, but tends to be expressed in more indirect terms.) The heroine of Van Herk's *Judith* is more wholly self-actuated in her rejection of the feminine stereotype (it is significant that she is unable to express her sexuality, to submit to her new lover, until she has proven her symbolic ascendancy by taking over from him the chore of castrating the young pigs), while Rita/Sister Pelagia/Peggy, the nun turned housewife of Engel's *The Glassy Sea*, is less so, but both still present variants on a single basic theme that may be summarized as follows: (1) a woman (often very young and/or inexperienced) is coerced into the kind of traditional relationship she has been taught to believe holds her only chance for happiness; (2) her partner, incapable of dealing with the demands that might be made on him by a 'real' person, attempts, not without the co-operation of the victim, to turn her into a doll, remake her entirely in terms of his own (usually childish) expectations and needs; (3) the woman, unable finally to relinquish the hard kernel of identity that he finds so threatening, has no choice but to withdraw from the relationship.

If the negative version of the marital mode is interesting, the positive one – illuminating the functional realignment necessitated by the fundamental inversion of sex roles – is even more so. Quite contrary to the traditional and especially the American model, in a great many Canadian novels it is the *relinquishment* rather than the rediscovery or reassertion of a protagonist's masculinity that signals the achievement of emotional/aesthetic equilibrium. Somewhat surprisingly (since the implications of this pattern are even more radically subversive than those carried by the simple marriage breakdown), in this category male writers predominate – perhaps because the *illusion* of normality is more fully maintained. Sinclair Ross's *As for Me and My House* provides an exemplary demonstration of the type approach. As with the negative version, three stages of development may be discerned: (1) the conventional marriage falls apart; (2) a crisis occurs that reorients the habitual mode of relation between the couple; (3) the man's *acceptance* of his new involuntary passiveness signals the basis for a permanent reconciliation. Because it represents such an important – and in American terms peculiar – aspect of the Canadian response, the pattern is worth examining in some detail.

Philip Bentley, Ross's protagonist, is (even allowing for possible narrative bias) unmistakably the locus of the relational problems in this book. On the other hand, he is far from a simple or obvious character. In earlier parts of the novel we get the clear impression that he suffers a certain amount of discomfort with or at least ambivalence toward the traditional concomitants of his masculine role, but both the reasons for and the implications of this are revealed only indirectly. One thing is certain, though: the roots of Philip's dilemma lie in his childhood. He is the bastard son of a young student preacher who died before he was born, and the tension in the story centres largely on his obsession with this dead and unknown father:

[H]e made a hero of his father, and in lonely, childish defiance of his surroundings, resolved to be another like him.

It became a kind of worship in which there was an effort perhaps to maintain his own self-respect, a belief in his own importance. He was the son of this hero: that was some compensation, at least, for being the son also of a common waitress. In his taking sides it never seems to have occurred to him that if these two were really as he thought, then the moral responsibility for his existence could hardly have been where he placed it. But he was just a boy then, and even now he feels a situation better than he can think his way through it. And his father all this time belonged to the escape world of his imagination, and his mother to the drab, sometimes sordid reality of the restaurant. (30)

The escape into fantasy described here is, to be sure, a fairly common ploy among unhappy children. The psychic disequilibrium caused by Philip's unreasonable hero-worship is not, however, limited in its effects to his felt relations with the past. His unnatural preoccupation with the paternal mode and his desire to emulate his father at all costs lead him, despite the unsuitability of his artistic temperament, to become a minister. Later, when his failure on this level becomes increasingly difficult to live with, he puts all his energies into a rather pitiful attempt to become a 'real' father to the tough young orphan, Steve. Meanwhile, his own marriage, symbolized by his wife's 'useless' garden, is withering into ruin. Only when Philip gives up his insistence on the masculine role along with his official connections with the patriarchal religion, can life be restored. At the end of the book, having finally surrendered himself to the feminine will, he seems to submerge his entire being into the dumb, passive presence which is, although genetically *his*, in terms of the felt relational dynamics his wife's child:

He doesn't look like Philip yet [she says], but Philip I'll swear is starting to look like him. It's in the eyes, a stillness, a freshness, a vacancy of beginning.

'Another Philip?' the first one says. 'With so many names to pick and choose from you don't need that again. Two of us in the same house you'll get mixed up. Sometimes you won't know which of us is which.'

That's right Philip. I want it so. (164-5)[12]

It might be objected, of course, that Philip's original orientation is so extreme that the final shift toward feminine dominance merely realigns the normal balance between polarities. There are numerous cases, however, where the shift to the feminine is clearly a shift away from the medial norm. In this respect it is interesting to examine the relational model offered by Thomas Raddall's *The Nymph and the Lamp*. Aside from anything else, this book encapsulates particularly vividly the typical Canadian view of nature. The central setting is a barren little island huddled in the stormy sea off the Canadian Atlantic coast, its dunes riddled with the bones of ship-wrecked sailors whose ghosts haunt the night and whose voices can still be heard in the incessant moaning of the wind. In such a landscape, man can hope to achieve little more than 'a small wooden oasis in a desolation of sand and spire-grass' (105), a flimsy garrison wherein to barricade himself against the beseiging elements. Ultimately, however, the fortress becomes more prison than protection. As Isobel Jardin discovers, the winter on Marina inevitably transforms each isolated inhabitant into 'a primitive creature in a lost corner of the world, the prey of phantoms, a prisoner of the weather and the sea – and of the dark' (192).

With a setting so classically 'northern,' it is not surprising that this book should reveal something of the characteristic Canadian form. At first sight, however, this would not seem to be the case – not if sexual inversion is indeed a key element. Matthew Carney, in spite of his gentle and retiring personality, is almost archetypally masculine; alternately, Isobel when he meets her is passive and submissive and vulnerable, a traditionally feminine figure. Their courtship, moreover, also follows a conventional romantic pattern: falling in love almost at first sight, he pursues and captures her, carrying her off to his eminently masculine (that is, primitive) domain. Here, however, the pattern breaks down. Almost at once Isobel has second thoughts about the 'marriage,'[13] and although after a short probationary period of platonic isolation the couple is reconciled for a brief romantic interlude, her early misgivings are eventually justified: for no apparent reason the relationship simply disintegrates. Ultimately Isobel's discontent, her feeling of alienation from her increasingly remote lover, lead her to leave the island, and him, for what she thinks of as forever.

This is not the end of the story, though. Skipping over Isobel's adventures on her own, we now come to the final twist that makes this book such an odd but revealing commentary on the Canadian sexual mode. Suddenly and by accident, Isobel finds out the real cause of Carney's remoteness; he is going blind – and this one factor transforms entirely her attitude toward the marriage. Although they were unable to relate to one another satisfactorily in terms of *conventional* male/female roles, now that Matthew must be *dependent* rather than her master, a reconciliation may take place:

Skane stared at her. 'Look here, you don't mean you'd chuck everything that's good in life to go back to that barren heap and be a – a lamp for Carney?'

She threw back her head and smiled. 'Yes – yes, that's it. A lamp for Carney! I've always dreamed of being loved by some man utterly – completely – absolutely – as Matthew has loved me. But love by itself wasn't enough. All my life I've wanted – I've craved to have someone need me absolutely and completely.' (310)

Again – the masculine force must be relinquished, subsumed in the feminine strength and will, before equilibrium can be achieved. Is this, then, a marital norm for Canada? Comparing these 'happy endings' with the negative feminist version, there would certainly seem to be more than a hint that a general shift in attitudes toward what comprises 'normal' sexual relations has indeed taken place.

Designating the female-dominant marriage as the type relational model in Canadian literature does not, of course, mean that it is necessarily always the pattern that appears. It must not be forgotten what we noted above, that Canadian attitudes, as distinctive and as influential as they might be in imprinting certain aspects of our literary forms, are always held in the context of a pervasive, convincing, and officially 'approved' American world view which is in many ways inconsistent with our own less clearly articulated vision. As a result, although the non-ironic dominant female/submissive male model may represent a genuine felt response for the Canadian writer, on an intellectual level, judged according to American standards, it is not always an *acceptable* one. This conflict frequently produces an aesthetic dilemma which manifests itself in a lack of coherence between different aspects of the fictional world such that the resolution is less than totally emotionally satisfying. In Page's book, discussed above, for instance, because Kirstin feels strongly that Carl *should* be the dominant partner, the Sun, she is forced to deny her own nature, fragmenting her personality irretrievably. Her 'real' self is projected into the trees (a symbolic mating with the true masculine force, Nature?), while Carl is left to marry a soulless husk, no longer a threat, but also no longer capable of either pain or joy. This unnatural solution is obviously unfair to *both* the parties involved.

In other cases, the accommodation made by artists in response to their uneasiness with the inversion of relational modes is less drastic. In McCourt's *The Wooden Sword*, for instance, the author simply truncates the pattern. Although Steven Venner's neurotic condition is clearly the result of a futile and self-destructive attempt to live up to his father's conventional expectations of heroic masculinity, and although – as mentioned above – his perception of his wife as a dominant personality seems to invite his dependence, the expected inversion does not take place. Instead of allowing his protagonist to relinquish his inappropriate role model and assume a passive stance as the situation would seem to demand, McCourt arbitrarily lets Venner 'confront' his bogeys in a dream and, by means of a particularly unconvincing symbolic mechanism,[14] make peace with them. His reconciliation with his wife is, therefore, a result rather than a cause of his cure, and the ending, instead of denying actually reaffirms his (childish) concept of masculinity: '"Happy?" she said after a while. "Happy," he said. "They gave me back my sword"' (155).

Another means of evading the implications of the sexual inversion involves simply the superimposition on the base pattern of either an authorial commentary or a dramatic incident affirming the conventionality of the marital roles. Hugh Hood does this in *White Figure, White Ground,* apparently trying to obscure the fact that the entire movement of the book is toward a submission of the protagonist to his wife's feminine will (it is upon her urging that he gives up his profound but dangerous quest for the aesthetic absolute in order to become once more the 'good charming second-rate funny guy, with a nice sense for decorating walls' that she feels secure with; sacrificing, as it were, the child of his mind to give her a child of his body, 219) by superadding a climactic lovemaking scene in which the man plays an almost oppressively traditional masculine role. The somewhat mawkish, D.H. Lawrencian style of this scene is out of place with the crisp, concrete prose of the rest of the book, just as the relational mode is incompatible with the book's dynamics as a whole. [15]

Attempts like these to deny or obscure the base pattern do not, however, hide the fact that it is surprisingly omnipresent in Canadian literature. Because of the obvious efforts to resist or disguise it (particularly by male writers) we cannot, perhaps, call it a *norm,* since this implies public consensual legitimation. On the other hand it is equally obvious that it doesn't just signal an idiosyncratic response on the part of a few individuals. Like many of the other features to be discussed in this book, in fact, though the tendency to sex inversion is not a *recognized* element in our national self-image, it is general enough to be seen as an important characteristic of what we might call the Canadian un-consciousness. Though the pattern of relation implied is largely antithetical to our *overt* (that is, American) value/belief system, in other words, it is obviously a real component of *covert culture* in this country. As Bowron, Marx, and Rose describe it:

In any society men tend to ignore or repress certain commonly learned attitudes and behaviour patterns, much as an individual may ignore or repress certain personal experiences or motives. In the case of covert culture, the repressed traits are more or less common to members of a society, and they are probably transmitted in the same informal ways that the basic elements of the overt culture are transmitted. The covert traits are not more 'true' or 'real' than the overt traits [but] they are equally representative of people's attitudes and behaviors. The distinction lies in the degree of acknowledgment (to self and others) and the degree of repression. If one were to suggest to a representative member of a society that his behavior, or that of his community, exhibits a particular characteristic of covert culture, he might be expected to scoff at the idea, and even reject it heatedly.

... We may assume we are in the presence of covert culture when we note a pattern of inconsistent or seemingly illogical behavior. When most people in a given society or sub-society adhere to inconsistencies in their actions, when they resist with emotion any attempts to reconcile their actions with their expressed beliefs ... then presumably we are dealing with covert culture.

... It consists ... of parts of culture that happen to be seriously inconsistent with other parts of culture and so get driven underground. [16]

Covert and overt culture, then, exist side by side, making it possible to accommodate simultaneously in one perceptual 'set' what may be totally incongruous points of view. Much more interesting than those strategies for obscuring or denying the symbolic sexual inversion, therefore, are those rare cases which encapsulate the *total* picture; where the writer manages to achieve a structure which (like many myths) holds *both* possibilities in suspension. An example of this is Grove's *Settlers of the Marsh*.

In this novel, typically enough, we find in the basic passiveness of Niels's relationships with Clara and Ellen an inverted echo of the romance form wherein the heroine, static and submissive, is caught up between the opposing modes of action represented by the hero and the villain. This subversive level is not immediately apparent, however. On the surface of Grove's intention, Niels simply appears as a giant of a man who, in the best traditions of the western masculine ideal, has a dream of conquering the wilderness. His downfall, moreover – again in the best western traditions – is precipitated quite specifically by his desertion of that dream for domestication. In the simplest terms, that is, Niels, like Sampson, is ruined by woman. Notwithstanding the contributory factor of his own naiveté, the catastrophe in this book is clearly ascribable – at least on the surficial level of signification – to the combined effects of Ellen's unfeminine fear of pregnancy and Clara's equally unfeminine sexual aggression. Correspondingly, the solution on this level is apparently achieved through a realignment of the relational dynamics in accordance with proper, conventional male/female roles. After the tragedy of Niels's misguided marriage and the murder he is driven to commit, Ellen ostensibly realizes her mistake, recognizes her true womanly needs, and – despite the brutal example of her mother's experience – accepts conjugality as her 'natural' lot in life.

Lurking behind this optimistic 'American' fable is an equally compelling 'Canadian' vision. On the covert level, it is not Ellen's sexual terrors at all, but Niels's dreams of conquest, of asserting his will, above all of a wife interchangeable with the loving, self-effacing mother of his memory, that create the basic imbalance in the emotional dynamic of the book. It is not, therefore, until he symbolically relinquishes the masculine aggressiveness that led to the murder of the faithless Clara by killing his treasured horse, thus surrendering to Ellen for once and for all his male prerogatives of initiating and structuring action, that the offence against order may be considered expiated. In this covert reading, the final reconciliation scene takes on an entirely different meaning. Rather than supporting the suggestion that the resolution depends upon Ellen's arbitrary change of heart (a change which is somewhat less than convincing being merely *told* rather than *shown* to us), the book now, by pointedly reiterating for a second time *almost exactly the same words* that Ellen spoke on the occasion of Niels's first proposal ('"The bush hides,"' she says. '"... I wish I had a vista through it, out on the plains, to the horizon. I want to see wide, open, level spaces. Let us go to the slough ..."'; see 95, 215), seems to insist that she has *not* changed at all in her fear of the (feminine) enclosed bower and her (masculine) desire to dominate the horizon. Grove's book thus offers as simultaneous, viable possibilities both the overt and covert patterns of sexual relation in Canada.

Dominant female/submissive male: this would seem to be the only kind of marriage that 'works' in the Canadian context. On the other hand, whatever the universality of the initial *impulse*, it would be misleading to suggest that there has been anything like a unanimous rush to take advantage, even covertly, of this particular kind of solution to our common relational problems. Often, indeed, if the 'new marriage' tends to hover intangibly at the level of felt possibility, at the level of action, rather than just being camouflaged, it is resisted altogether. One may speculate that many women writers (who presumably share the same kind of extrinsic pressures as their heroines) may feel too guilty to indulge easily what their upbringing tells them is unnatural misanthropy, while men, for obvious reasons, would tend to feel threatened by the recognitions that the pattern localizes. Even above and beyond this understandable general reticence, moreover, it is a fact that outside of a very few special cases like Thériault's *Agaguk* (where the relationship with nature insisted upon by the author seems to implicate the protagonist with 'other' rather than 'self'[17]) the successful female-dominant marriage doesn't appear to be a significant factor in Quebec literature at all.

Why the discrepancy? It could, of course, simply indicate that Quebec has escaped from the initial sexual inversion syndrome entirely, thus undermining my thesis of cross-cultural identity. If we examine the oeuvre, though, this would seem patently not to be the case. Certainly there are plenty of strong women in recent Québécois writing. *And* plenty of bad marriages. More significant, there are plenty of *failed* marriages. Indeed, the theme of marital breakdown is not only common in French as in English Canada, but tends to be treated in strikingly similar terms on both sides of the linguistic borderline. Hébert's *Les chambres de bois* provides an interesting example. Although the marriage between Catherine and Michel is handled much less naturalistically than the Morag/Brooke, Marian/Peter relations, the underlying pattern of development is almost identical. When Michel first agrees to marry her, Catherine – naive, uneducated, scarcely more than a child – is both grateful for his condescension and overawed by his sophistication. As a result she gives herself entirely into his hands, not merely allowing but actively participating in his program to subdue her energy, bleach away her rude colour, turn her from a warm and vital woman with the capacity to threaten his own detachment into a beautiful but lifeless work of art ('[A]ll day she worked hard at becoming what Michel wanted her to be,' says Hébert. 'Set like a bas-relief against the woodwork, she read or sewed until it was time for the evening meal' 61, 63).

Finally, though not until she is brought almost to the point of death, Catherine – as noted in chapter 5 – flees in desperation from the tomb-like, wood-panelled apartment where her husband has incarcerated her. Only then can she come back to life. Whatever the difference in style between Hébert and her English colleagues, Catherine, Morag, and Marian McAlpin are obviously sisters under the skin.

This poses an interesting problem. If the Québécois/e suffers from the same ambivalence about sex roles as the rest of his/her countrymen, why does the inverted marital mode, which would seem to be a natural corollary, fail to appear? The answer is simple. If we examine both fictional and non-fictional documentation, it seems possible that the tendency toward covert sexual inversion is even more deep-seated in French culture than it is in English Canada. The female-dominant marriage may thus seem too real, too immediately threatening, to be easily embraced as an imaginative possibility. The reason for this odd state of affairs (which, as Gordon Sheppard points out, is rooted in Quebec's history) is actually twofold. The first element has to do with the irreconcilability of a strong patriarchal ideal with an equally strong impulse toward uxoriousness catalyzed by the religio-pastoral myth of the land:

The terrible, guilty secret of the French-Canadian people is the weakness of their men and the strength of their women. They have the Conquest, the Church, and themselves to thank for that. Together, the Conquest and the Church humbled the French-Canadian men, making most of them weak, miserable, seldom capable of generosity or tenderness; while their women, used to conquest and supported by a Church that made a hero of the Virgin Mary and fellow-women out of celibate priests, became the splendid rocks of this society – which humbled the men still more. (Sheppard 192)

The result of this development was already to stimulate considerable ambivalence by making the feminine influence seem both more valuable *and*, because of the power involved, more fearful as well. This was only the beginning, though. While this mythicization of the *abstract* female was going on, the Church, anxious to stem any natural drives that might threaten the stability of the isolated and involuted Québécois culture, was waging war on sexuality in any form. Procreation was a duty, but enjoyment of the process – love, in other words – was explicitly sinful. In consequence, in Jean LeMoyne's words, the Québécois 'multiplied greatly though rejecting the flesh ... When [they] loved [they] did so with a defective intimacy that made the need of woman become something forbidden. And [they] deceived [them]selves by entering into a union in which the wife was the mother' (190). Considering this combination of contradictory pressures, it is not surprising that woman would be viewed with a jaundiced eye. It is also not surprising that French-Canadian writers should find it difficult to envision a successful – that is, wholesome, stable, mutually beneficial – marriage of *any* kind. What we generally find when we encounter the overt female-dominant marriage in French-Canadian literature, therefore, far from equilibrium, is catastrophe.

How does this fit in with the patterns observed elsewhere? Interestingly enough, as in most areas of comparison if we examine this phenomenon closely we will see that what it represents is not so much a departure from the English-Canadian usage as an exaggeration or distortion of it. Surficial images of contentment notwithstanding, even in the examples cited it is possible to pick up disquieting hints of a more sinister aspect to submission than the foregoing discussion might indicate. Are Niels and Mr Bentley really better off for their relinquishments, or only broken? Would Carl have been happier if he'd simply allowed himself to be eclipsed? The unpalatable truth skirted here emerges quite unmistakably in Philip Child's fiction. Granted that most of this author's heroes win through in the end, the formula by which they are enabled to do so, with its implication that 'to embrace suffering and death purges guilt and legitimizes sex' (Duffy B51), makes it clear that the submission involved is always submission to life-denying forces. This is the point at which the Québécois parts company with his opposite number. Where Journay in Child's *Village of Souls* can expect, finally, to achieve true happiness with his Anne once he has 'pursued her through a demonically hostile wilderness, a treacherous morass,' in other words, the French Canadian, stricken with the suspicion that Euridice and her demon-lover, the death god, are in collusion, feels compelled to repudiate Child's optimistic dénouement, denying in effect that any Orpheus so entrapped has any chance of emerging from Hades intact.

We see this response at work in André Langevin's *Poussière sur la ville*, a novel offering what should be, in abstract form, an absolutely classic demonstration of the Canadian predilection for the female-dominant marriage. Not only does the protagonist of this book habitually accede to the wishes of his more independent and aggressive young wife – not only is he dominated on a *practical* level – but it is specifically her 'unfeminine' strength which, though he knows he *should* find it repulsive, most fascinates him. 'After our marriage I felt I had come to love Madeleine better because I knew her better,' he says. '... I discovered what ferocity boiled under her outward indifference, what eagerness to try anything, to know everything. I even learned that sometimes her will could not be broken. Madeleine had cruel strength, not often shown but always there, restless like a big mastiff who may someday run rabid. Hidden in her was quite a different person who did not belong to me, and whom I could never conquer ... it was the basic Madeleine' (12-13). These words give us a very clear picture of their object. Here is no regretful or reluctant self-possession such as a Morag might confess to. Here, rather, is a woman who wilfully and consistently asserts her powers against her partner, who glories in her own unbridled vitality. Indeed, inasmuch as she is associated throughout the book with images of 'nature,' of 'wildness,' Madeleine is symbolically masculinized in a sense far more profound than the typically self-uncertain English-Canadian heroine ever could be. It is perhaps because of this that she cannot be redeemed – that the 'unnatural' marriage she dominates is doomed.[18] In any case, as it turns out, Madeleine, having sought corruption as a means both of defiance and of self-definition, dies by her own hand, while her husband, young Dr Dubois, is both emotionally devastated and professionally ruined. The community at large sees his failure as a punishment for his 'unnatural' refusal to assert himself to keep his wife from betraying him, but the book makes it clear that from the first moment of his sexual enthralment Dubois has been acting under a fatal compulsion that makes his downfall certain.

So much for the inversion solution to the problem of marital relation. The fact is, it just doesn't work for the Quebec psyche, seemingly posing far too much of a threat to personal survival to be considered even on a symbolic level. As a result of this apparently spontaneous reactivity, if there is any image of sexual equilibrium to be found in Quebec literature at all it is not the inverted or any other kind of marriage but the narcissistic self-love that is symbolized by, among other things, the union of siblings. The relationship between Michel and Lia in *Les chambres de bois* is one example of this. Even more extremely, as noted above, *La belle bête* is an extended study of solipsism. Self-love is hardly a solution to *relational* problems, of course. Although one might find some mythic justification for the radical recoil in the story of Adam's original androgyny that we find in apocryphal and rabbinical writing, in Quebec literature there is little sign that either the incest motif or its symbolic equivalent is meant to signal a return to pre-historic psychic wholeness. Indeed, as the two texts cited indicate, in Québécois usage the *kind* of equilibrium that narcissism offers seems in the end, just as much as submission to the female, inevitably to entail destruction of the self: madness or death. In offering the inverted marriage as an at least potential resolution, the English-Canadian oeuvre, it seems, has an optimistic coda, a 'way out' – albeit a problematic one – that the French-Canadian vision simply doesn't allow for.

Potential is, to be sure, by definition something only vestigially realized. As already noted, many if not all of the protagonists of English-Canadian fiction in practice find it just as difficult to come to terms with available marital modes, traditional *or* inverted, as their French-Canadian counterparts. Rationalization and fancy footwork obfuscate the problem to some extent, but the felt inadequacy of both conventional and unconventional solutions would lead us to expect some alternate kind of resolution to be catalysed on a different level. At the very least, the marital mode *per se* being implicitly devalued, we would expect that alternate emotional arrangements would thrust themselves forward willy-nilly in reaction to the vacuum. But what are the alternatives? The only thing that can be set against 'marriage' is 'no-marriage.' Is there, then, a narcissistic impulse to be found in English-Canadian literature as well? Certainly there is precedent for it in *Wacousta*. Despite this early model, however, the fact is that the English response, though psychologically consonant with the French one, is once again less extreme. The only thematically important or central incest and/or androgyny motif (outside of Robertson Davies' bearded lady and a few others of her rather specialized ilk whom we will consider in a later chapter) that I can think of in recent English-language fiction is Clark Blaise's *Lunar Attractions*, where the young protagonist receives his sexual initiation at the hands of a homosexual and transvestite youth who has been masquerading as both brother and sister, predator and victim. There are some similarities to the Québécois pattern to be discerned in this novel (and it is interesting that Blaise's family background is in part French-Canadian, although, having spent his childhood in the United States, he now writes in English), but notwithstanding the characteristic association of sex with (a) role inversion, (b) madness, and (c) death (the symbolic androgyne is later killed by one of his/her disgruntled victims), there are at least two points that seem to set Blaise's version apart from, say, Hébert's. In the first place, the narcissistic impulse is imputed to a figure who is clearly not an alternate 'self' but radically 'other.' In the second place, and consequent on the first factor, the sexual confusion is indicated as the *cause* rather than the *result* of the protagonist's trauma. Even in Blaise, therefore, the extremity of recoil signalled by narcissism is not (except perhaps as an adolescent aberration) associated with the protagonist himself. Narcissism *per se* is not, then, perceived as a likely alternative, or even a particularly virulent threat, in English Canada. In gross terms, on the other hand, the implications of the English oeuvre are by no means as divergent from the ostensibly more radical French as might appear on the surface. If the conventional marriage is unfeasible (which it almost invariably is), and if the inverted marriage is repugnant (which is often the case), the only alternative if not self-love is *no love*: celibacy and self-elected isolation.

This brings us back to where we were at the end of the last chapter, though with one small modification. Once we start differentiating our protagonists along sex lines, we see that there is in fact an important distinction to be made between male and female isolates. The former, almost always in our literature, are losers. They may go mad, like Helwig's John Martens or W.O. Michell's Saint Sammy. They may die, like Harold Horwood's 'White Eskimo' or Drummond McKay, the misanthropic fur trader of Wayland Drew's *The Wabeno Feast*. Or they may simply succumb in the end, more or less reluctantly, to a stronger and more aggressive woman, as Davies' Dunstan Ramsay is seduced in his old age by the satanic Liesl. But they always lose. There just doesn't seem to be any other possibility for them, according to the relational dynamics of their literary context. Despite Rosemary Sullivan's contention that, woman being the 'unknown chaos' in Kroetsch's vision, '*man holds on to the known and safe by resisting her*' (A91, italics added), Hazard Lepage in fact only has two alternatives, neither of them 'safe.' He can surrender his masculine integrity to Martha, or he can surrender his life. Women, on the other hand, seem to be gifted by the Canadian imagination with the ability to survive quite well – indeed *better* than ever – by themselves, without masculine support. Canadian literature consequently is full of female 'survivors,' women making it on their own; not just the 'powerful, negative old women' that Atwood associates with Hecate (F205)[19] – although even these, as the earlier discussion of Hagar should indicate, are as a group far from being as unequivocally negative as Atwood implies – but a surprising number of apparently well-adjusted, relatively young women as well. To *choose* isolation, to be alone *voluntarily*, does not necessarily come naturally or easily to them, indoctrinated as they are with conventional values, but once they free themselves of destructive attachments and learn their own strengths these women, though they may end up as Hecates a few years down the line, for the time being at least demonstrate a degree of self-knowledge and psychic wholeness, combined with an ability to live in the world, that is singularly absent from a large proportion of their masculine counterparts. Morag of *The Diviners* and Rita/Peggy/Sister Pelagia of *The Glassy Sea* are classic examples. Each emerges from a demeaning marriage to find a new identity and sense of self-worth by non-sexual means, in the one case through her writing and in the other through her vocation.

Is this healthy, though? Isn't the retreat from sex in these cases as much of an evasion of 'life' as the narcissistic recoil? I would say not. For one thing, within the fictional worlds of these novels it seems healthy; far healthier, in any case, than the alternatives that are available. Certainly there is little sign that either of these particular women is, in Atwood's words, a frustrated Diana or Venus struggling to free herself 'of the rigid Hecate stereotype in which she finds herself shut like a moth in a chrysalis' (F210). If Canadian female protagonists like Laurence's Stacey (*The Fire-Dwellers*) and Engel's Minn (*The Honeyman Festival*) do, as Atwood claims, tend to think of themselves as encased in alien bodies, distorted by fat, pregnancy, or, in other cases, old age, it is less likely that here we have a 'loving, potentially beautiful woman trapped inside a negative shell' than simply another manifestation of the Canadian obsession with housings, with the inside/outside interface, with mortality. In the end I can only repeat what has already been said: isolation, according to the Canadian mythos, is by no means an wholly negative thing. What is important is how one comes to terms with it. And these women, it seems to me, do a surprisingly good job.

What about the men, though? Even leaving aside the relational problem, if we are capable of producing a Morag and a Sister Pelagia does it nevertheless not argue some kind of national neurosis that so many of our fictional males seem either helpless or doomed? Perhaps. The kind of identity crisis occasioned by the Canadian experience is obviously not going to be weathered without strain. If our literature is any indication, women, able to deal with both the psychic dislocation and the anxiety it stimulates in a more direct fashion, may be less susceptible to its more destructive effects. One other point to consider, though, is this. If the Canadian symbolic ego is, as I said at the beginning of this chapter, feminine, then the 'female survivor' is not simply *woman* but in a sense represents the Canadian *everyman*. At the very least, then, she stands as an icon of hope for the beleaguered ego. If she is strong enough to be herself, unaided, who knows what else she may achieve. In the last story of *Spit Delaney's Island*, Hodgins' protagonist meets an itinerant poet who seems to be able to see right into his head. '"Come on up with me, Spit Delaney,"' she says, '"come walking with me on the mountains. Learn to see. Don't go back to your puddles"' (198). Spit is too timid to take her up on this offer, but the knowledge that she exists, the belief that she has found the key to survival, has been an inspiration to him ever since.

I could go up there yet, to see. I should, to see for myself. She just might still be there … I like to imagine her stumbling into a camp of wild and desperate soldiers laying plans to set the island afloat and liberate us all from something. They tell me the mountains on other islands in other parts of the world are just swarming with these secret armies and escaped convicts, with passwords and smuggled-in machine guns and whispered meetings. Not us, as far as I know, but I still like to think of her coming into a group of them, being caught by their lookout. They would kill the Crotch [her boyfriend] right away, of course, but she'd become one of them, and even more than that, she'd become a leader, too, in no time at all. Maybe she's up there now, somewhere, plotting my freedom for me. (199)

NOTES

1 In 'Hypothesis on Kinship and Culture' Francis L.K. Hsu, for instance, demonstrates convincingly (by linking differential cultural attributes with specific modes of familial relation) that 'interaction patterns in a kinship system' are intimately connected with 'the characteristic modes of behavior in the wider society of which that kinship system forms a part.' Introduction to *Kinship and Culture*, ed. Hsu (Aldine 1971) 6

2 Becker, *The Denial of Death* (Free Press 1975) 160-1; he quotes from Otto Rank, *Beyond Psychology* (Dover 1958) 168, *Psychology and the Soul* (Perpetua 1961) 192, and *Will Therapy and Truth and Reality* (Knopf 1963) 303.

3 'Riding off with his bride, Anthyme whips his horse into a frenzied gallop, while Floralie, frightened by the speed of the horse and apprehensive of Anthyme's sexual

passions, thinks of the times horses have run wild in her village, causing havoc. The beat of Anthyme's heart is compared to a galloping horse, and Anthyme brutally consummates the marriage as the horse drags the buggy through the forest' (Bond 121).

4 Even aside from the explicit connections made by Williams between the pole and the sun and the buffalo, themselves properly masculine symbols, its essentially phallic nature is underlined by Thomas Singletree's earlier off-colour remark, 'You can bet yer long Sun Dance pole' (120). The female (anima) figure is not absent from the Sun Dance entirely, as it seems obvious that Williams intends Thomas's sister, Lulu, to represent this aspect, but Lulu – as discussed more fully in chapter 8 – is not a representative of nature at all in the sense that the Sun Dance pole is, being quite explicitly associated with 'human' space, the encampment or, more significantly, the back seat of a car.

5 *Beyond Psychology*, 250

6 It is interesting that in James Reaney's drama-workshop adaptation of the novel Charles has been changed quite openly into a female, Charlotte de Haldimar.

7 Robert Lecker (A77, 85) and Marcia Kline also discuss this issue.

8 The empirical implausibility apparently bothered some readers so much that Richardson was moved to attempt (rather unconvincingly) a 'scientific' justification in the 'Introduction' to the 1851 edition.

9 In this mode the princess is not an intentional individual, but merely a symbolic token, an acquisition by means of which the questing hero establishes his sovereignty.

10 'The clinging mother is the great emotional menace in American psychological life, the counterpart to the heavy domineering father in England and on the Continent ... the fear of ... vampire-like possession – the hidden fear that one may oneself have been so possessed – is one of the components in the very strong ambivalence American men feel toward women.' *The American People: A Study in National Character* (Norton 1964) 64

11 'She was absolute ruler of the kitchen, and more than once she drove men out of it by throwing boiling water at them or threatening them with a carving knife,' but 'Cyclically, this man-hating female required a man, and when she wanted one she took him' (174, 176).

12 Because Mrs Bentley is the narrator of this book, there is the possibility that we are given a distorted view of the situation; that the marriage breakdown and relational problems are due to her failure rather than his. Even if this were the case, however, the essential pattern remains. Disequilibrium is brought into equilibrium through the surrender of the masculine to the feminine will.

13 In spite of Matthew's fully honourable intentions, due to technical difficulties and a shortness of time the marriage was never actually legitimized; this irregularity obviously presages its eventual breakdown.

14 Venner, recovering from his amnesia, relives his traumatic wartime failure of nerve,

but since neither his understanding nor, apparently, his 'masculine' values seem to be significantly altered, it is hard to see what justification there is for the symbolic 'forgiveness' he obtains from his betrayed comrades. It thus seems a rather contrived solution.

15 An interesting sidelight on Hood's reluctance to carry his protagonist's covert feminization through to its logical conclusion is afforded by the pseudo-memoir, *The Swing in the Garden*, where the narrator speaks in peculiarly positive terms of the childhood experience of being spanked and humiliated in public by an older girl. He claims that the occasion had a beneficial effect on his character simply because it gave him a saner appreciation of male-female relations ('My lucky/unlucky encounter with ... Marianne freed me from [an] element of masculinist folly. I learned with pain and tears that a woman could overmaster my will.'), but the extent to which he found the event not merely educational but *enjoyable* (I 'followed her around like a puppy during the rest of our stay at the Point. Sometimes I courted her disapproval in the half-conscious hope that she might punish me again.') argues for a dimension of motivation that his articulated recollection hardly skirts. A passage on the following page, with considerable significance for our thesis of a Canadian propensity for sex-role inversion, makes the implication explicit: 'I've done this myself: modelled a dress, high-heeled shoes, a girdle and bra, before a mirror and before my wife, to shouts of her charmed, delighted laughter. This isn't transvestism, fetishism, an impairment of sex, or anything at all like it. It's an exhilarated, delightful awareness of our *likeness* to women' (148-9).

16 Bernard Bowron, Leo Marx, and Arnold Rose, 'Literature and Covert Culture,' *AQ* 9 (1957) 377-8

17 One of the first indications of Agaguk's alignment, aside from his voluntary self-exile from the community, is the fact that he openly *challenges* nature, as an equal: '"The wind!" he cried. "It is stronger than I am. Nothing must be stronger than I am."' 'He repeated it, his body trembling.' '"You hear me? Nothing!"' (12).

18 As Jack Warwick remarks, 'The entire novel, both in action and in comment, indicates that the freedom sought by Madeleine is absolute. This is why she cannot even accept the engagements of her own nature, in the way that a lover like Thomas Clarey can. Her freedom is "une liberté quasi animale" ... and not easily compatible with even a society of two persons ... Consequently, her eventual suicide merely ratifies what we have known all through the novel: a person like Madeleine cannot exist in reality' (125).

19 Atwood exclaims repeatedly on the fact that 'most of the strong and vividly-portrayed female characters in Canadian literature' are 'malevolent, sinister or life-denying' old women ('there is a bumper crop of sinister Hecate-crones. What can account for this? Where do all the Crones come from? They seem to appear fully aged out of nowhere, having skipped two of the usual phases of the Triple Goddess' F199), but in fact she gives very few convincing examples to prove her contention, concentrating instead on the younger women ('failed Venuses') who, having opted for independence, she presumes to be taking Hecate as a *model*.

7

Farewell, Charles Atlas

In the last chapter, although we focused primarily on patterns of relation between real men and women, I also indicated that these patterns can and must be assessed in the context of some sort of idealized roles. Beyond a loose association with active and passive modes, however, we have not yet defined precisely what the idealization of male and female implies.

On the simplest level these roles correspond to the unconscious, imprinted images that C.G. Jung calls archetypes: 'an hereditary factor of primordial origin engraved in the living organic system of ... man.'[1] Less contentiously, they correspond to the abstract categories *implicit* in Jung's schema. The distinction is an important one. Being general rather than particular, ideal rather than real, it is dangerous to use such conceptions prescriptively with respect to the wide variations possible in actual – and fully 'normal' – human relationships. Where they do prove useful is in providing an effective symbolic shorthand to delineate a basic dichotomy in human experience: two contrasting principles or styles of action which Richard Slotkin, following J.L. Henderson, identifies as *Moira* and *Themis* – 'the unconscious and the conscious, the dream or impulse and the rational idea, the inchoate desire and the knowledge of responsibility, the gratification-world presided over by the mother and the world of laws and reasons ruled by the father.'[2] As this catalogue implies, these principles, far from arbitrary, comprise a theoretical polarity against which nearly every kind of human activity and thought can be measured. As Robert Scholes points out, 'It is in the differentiation of the sexes that we learn our earliest and deepest lesson about sameness and difference. Sexual differentiation is the basis not only of our social systems, but of our logic as well.'[3] Our model of the world, therefore, tends to be constructed not merely in binary terms but in the *specific* terms of male-female oppositions.

In the light of such far-reaching implications it is easy to see why any reorientation of attitudes toward sex roles would be an important one. Location in terms of the Moira/Themis polarity is in a sense the key aspect of any cultural signature. This means, among other things, that marriage – as an emblem for unifications and reconciliations of all kinds – may be considered as offering a microcosmic reflection of relational patterns on mesocosmic (public, especially political) and macrocosmic (religious and quasi-religious) planes as well. To put it more simply, a society's attitudes toward marriage, and beyond marriage toward familial relations in general, more often than not have both a metaphorical *and* a direct bearing on its entire world view. Aside from its intrinsic interest, this interrelation of conceptual levels provides us with an incomparable analytic tool. With respect to the task at hand, the principle of structural replication not merely allows but enjoins the conclusion that the endemic sex role inversions and distortions in Canadian literature, more than a quirk of the imagination, are almost certainly diagnostic of broader patterns of psycho-social development.

Before we can tackle the question of our uniqueness, it is of course important to understand what comprises a norm. In *ideal* terms, the Moira/Themis dichotomy should be held in some sort of balance on all levels of experience, a dynamic tension between the creative but disorderly elements of Moira and the civilizing powers of Themis. In fact, this rarely happens. Or at least it rarely happens in modern societies. In many primitive religions, including those of most American Indians, the image of 'creative divinity' – conceived as a conjunction between the dark, dumb, passive earth and the bright, active energy of the sun or the sky – was 'distinctly sexual, combining both paternal and maternal aspects' [Slotkin 45]. In later Christian tradition, however, woman being viewed as inferior if not inherently evil, the mother's place in the pantheon was taken over by the asexual holy ghost.[4] Concomitant with this shift, the patriarchal mode came to dominate meso- and macrocosmic interrelations as well. Metaphorically linking all three levels, from the Middle Ages through the Renaissance God was most commonly identified with 'the political king, the authority father,' and the concept of a political monarchy was used to model man's relation to the universe as a whole.[5]

In the New World the dislocation went one step further. Especially after the American Revolution confirmed the symbolic break with European Christendom, a complex of political and cultural changes altered the relational dynamics not merely within but *between* experiential levels such that, although the patriarchal mode still remained the 'official' mode with respect to religion, the pattern definitely lost its ascendancy elsewhere. The key factor in this orientation was the mesocosmic repudiation of the monarchy, but this in turn – engendering as it did both guilt feelings and an impulse toward self-justification – also affected attitudes toward other kinds of 'familial' relations. '[T]he England of the textbooks,' Gorer tells us, 'became the monster of oppression and tyranny, and the throwing off of the English allegiance was stripped of nearly all the ambivalence which had accompanied the historical act; to reject authority became a praiseworthy and specifically American act, and the sanctions of society were added to the individual motives for rejecting the family authority personified in the father.'[6] On the meso- and microcosmic levels the father figure thus became discredited as both symbol and model.

This discrediting of the father did not, however, simply produce an across-the-board inversion from patriarchal to matriarchal values, as might have been expected. For one thing, as long as the culture remained by definition Christian, the rejection of the political/private father had to be disguised or compartmentalized lest it reflect subversively on the God-father. For another, by the mid-nineteenth century the mother had begun to collect a number of rather ambiguous connotations too. As Gorer points out, the default of the father as moral authority gave the American mother a much more central role in family discipline, and this in turn led to a cycle of resentment-guilt-increased resentment on the part of her menfolk. Adding to this particular source of ambivalence, moreover, the *symbolic* mother, nature, has also played a rather peculiar role in the American conscience in the last hundred and fifty years. The process of nostalgic sentimentalization that took place during the nineteenth century, once the real dangers of the wilderness were pushed back to a safe distance, tended to divest nature of her earlier ambiguity and transform her into a purely positive symbol. On the other hand, this very sanctification tended to stimulate guilt for the continuing rape perpetrated by the nation's westward thrust. The mother was thus both an essential source of spiritual health and a threat to peace of mind. The resulting complex of inconsistent attitudes could not easily be integrated. One result of this uncertainty about both parental figures, as Leslie Fiedler points out, is the seeming inability of the American writer to deal convincingly in literature with mature heterosexual relations. [7] Indeed, the most persuasive symbolic ego for the American is perhaps Cooper's Leatherstocking. Like Adam not just before the Fall but even before the 'gift' of Eve – parentless, childless, womanless – in D.H. Lawrence's words he is 'alone, and final in his race ... stark, abstract, beyond emotion.'[8] Ambivalence toward familial relations in America is solved to a large extent simply by avoiding them.

In Canada, in contrast, as suggested above, the basic symbolic associations of Moira/Themis are inverted: nature becomes a masculine force; society – the 'I' – by default becomes feminine. And this fundamental inversion naturally causes dislocations on other levels. One important point to note, however, is that changed conditions do not simply manifest their effects in terms of a *tabula rasa*. The Canadian response must be seen in the context of both the traditional Christian mode and the modified American one. As might be expected from our survey of patterns of marital relation, though, it is distinct from and somewhat more complex than either of these.

On the macrocosmic level, the acceptance of an 'official' patriarchal God plus the vision of a masculine nature tends to merge both male and female external functions into the one generalized, hostile 'other' already noted. In this sense, at a secondary stage the two-gender classification system (which Canada shares with other Indo-European cultures) begins to break down, or at least to shift its referents in the direction of the Oriental mode of classification in terms of the more basic categories of 'soul' and 'no soul' (animate/non-animate, personal/impersonal).[9] Because of the strong emotional connotations of the primary associations, however, 'outside' still tends to be attributed with specifically masculine characteristics. God, if he is explicitly evoked at all, thus tends to become an intimidating Blakean Nobodaddy figure. As such He is almost invariably seen as dangerous; indifferent if not overtly inimical to human interests. The former view predominates when the response is primarily intellectual. E.J. Pratt's concept of the Panjandrum in 'The Truant,' for instance, simply subsumes the totality of inhuman – that is, anti-human – forces that surround and threaten the individual all his life. In Frye's words:

He is the mechanical power of the universe: he controls the stars, the movement of matter, the automatic instincts of living things, even reason and consciousness. It infuriates him that something in the human soul should elude him, and as he screams at man in the 'shrillest tenor' which is the voice of tyranny, he gradually takes on the outlines of Satan the accuser. What he has to accuse man of is his mortality. As far as we can see, everything man does, however heroic, vanishes and leaves not a rack behind. The Panjandrum should know, for he was in the 'grey shape with the paleolithic face' that sank the *Titanic*, in the mechanical mantrap sprung at Dunkirk, even in the 'leopards full of okra pods' in The Great Feud. He was certainly in the Iroquois torturing Brébeuf, knowing that they could kill anything that could die. (xxxiv)

Despite his fearsomeness (which in any case is clearly in the eyes of the beholder), this is God at his most distant. Indeed, the Panjandrum has no reality in Himself at all, but is merely a personification of one aspect of life, a wholly demythicized (Darwinian) version of natural processes which is blind, dumb, relentless, amoral. Many other Canadians are less detached than Pratt, using the concept of God to re-mythicize the universe; focus or localize their diffuse fears of otherness. To Roch Carrier's Québécois, for instance, He is something both immediate and personal, an oppressor much like all the other 'big guys' who cheat the little guys out of not merely their happiness, but their very lives (c23). Diverging radically from Pratt's version of cold, mechanical indifference, in fact, one of the basic themes of Carrier's fiction – and (undoubtedly as a reaction against the extravagance of the Church's promises on His behalf) of contemporary French-Canadian literature in general – is the theme of 'God's' malignance, 'His' betrayal of mankind. Although his books and stories, like much of Pratt's poetry, may simply be viewed 'as allegories of man in a world where he is subject to inhuman and cruel forces such as death and the passing of time' (Bond 127), therefore, Carrier's examples of divine cruelty have none of the abstract quality of Pratt's Panjandrum (or sharks, or icebergs, or even Indians); here, indeed, God's malevolence is as obtrusive an element of everyman's personal reality as it is of the general human condition. 'It is no coincidence that, having watched the procession of twenty-one little monsters in their wheel-barrows, followed by an assortment of lame and halt, Philibert starts pulling the legs off grasshoppers,' says David Bond: 'he is merely imitating a God who allows, or practices, the mutilation of men' (127-8).

Pratt notwithstanding, the latter is the view of God that actually dominates the Canadian vision, even outside of the relatively unsophisticated purview of rural Quebec. The reason for this is not hard to find. If the original gothic invoked emblems of supernatural horror as correlatives for the unthinkable evil and anguish of the human heart (the Dark Romantics, as G.R. Thompson points out, suffered 'a sense of nameless guilt combined with a suspicion that the external world was a delusive projection of the mind'[10]), the perception that one is living in a 'real' gothic universe, a universe in which any deity is by definition implicated with life-denying forces of every kind, can easily trigger an opposite effect: that is, the invocation of specifically human (internal) images of evil to objectify an undoubted but ineffable 'other.' The result of this largely unconscious conflation is, among other things, a tendency for Canadians to anthropomorphize God far beyond what conventional practice would sanction; to identify Him almost wholly, that is, with human behaviour, human characteristics – and especially those more inexplicable aspects of personality such as wilful cruelty and destructiveness. This in turn, by making Him seem less distant, naturally exacerbates the sense of threat. '"What do you think of a God that asks for blood?"' demands Del Jordan's mother in Lives of Girls and Women. '"Blood, blood, blood. Listen to their hymns, that's all they're ever about. What about a God who's not satisfied until he has got someone hanging on a cross for six hours, nine hours, whatever it was? ... Ordinary people wouldn't be so bloodthirsty"' (89). Notwithstanding the fact that they are both inimical, this God is at the other end of the emotional scale from Pratt's Panjandrum.

Addie's view is not an unusual one. For all that the current fashion is to deplore the Calvinist vision that was such a significant component of our national heritage, in fact God is presented with surprising frequency in Canadian literature as somehow simply synonymous with pain. Man's enemy. The antagonist. Making matters worse, He apparently shares human perverseness without sharing human limitations. Or human accessibility. Indeed, far more frightening than the brutality with which He tends to be associated is the enigma of His contradictory nature, the irrationality or at least absolute alienness of His motives. This aspect appears most vividly in reminiscences of childhood. In Sylvia Fraser's *Pandora*, for instance, the thought of God – typically enough – inevitably arises in connection with ugliness, suffering, emotional or physical violence. The thing that really bothers the young protagonist the most, however, is the sudden suspicion (stimulated by her own perverse impulse to stamp on the ants she has been 'helping') that '*Sometimes* GOD likes to play God' too (120). The same kind of association is made (albeit more covertly) in W.O. Mitchell's *Who Has Seen the Wind*. Throughout the course of this novel, God – 'all grapes and bloody' (23) – comes somehow to be linked in Brian's mind not only with the prairie, a meadowlark, a dewdrop, but with a dead pigeon, a mutilated gopher, a two-headed calf, and a mad old man living in a piano box as well. Young Morag in *The Diviners* expresses her disquiet more straightforwardly. She herself fears God, we are told in an early Memorybank Movie, quite simply because He 'is the one who decides which people have got to die, and when. Mrs. McKee in Sunday school says God is LOVE, but this is baloney. He is mean and gets mad at people for no reason at all, and Morag wouldn't trust him as far as she can spit' (77).

For the average Canadian, if we can judge by our literature, it would thus seem as though God, when acknowledged at all, has an unfortunate tendency to take on the attributes of, at best, a cruel and capricious master (see *The Double Hook* 77) and at worst a kind of Super-Hitler. This being the case it is revealing but hardly surprising that even those who *begin* in our fiction as believers almost invariably end up losing their faith, either gradually, as they come to suspect that the deity is at least indirectly implicated in their pains and humiliations, or – most commonly – through some sudden, traumatic recognition of His irrelevance if not oppugnance to humanity. '*Hell, how could there be a God in a world like this in which those who are dying are the ones who deserve most to live,*' ponders Fred Bodsworth's Ashley Morden as he huddles in the belly of a half-disabled bomber (89). Morden is far from alone. The distrust is so pervasive, indeed, that even when God is 'officially' accepted as 'good,' He tends to be set forth in decidedly ambiguous terms. In David Williams's *The Burning Wood*, for instance, He is explicitly identified as a super-being who 'can topple your wall with a single word ... [as] he did to the people in Jericho' (113). Considering the Canadian's mystical identification with the house symbol, this image of penetration, of invasion of the sealed self by some alien force, is bound to be a disturbing one.

If these direct responses were not enough to substantiate our postulate, the bias toward an evil God in the Canadian vision is supported as well by the ambiguous treatment in Canadian literature of God's earthly representatives. The phenomenon is not merely a quantitative one. Indeed, the *kind* of negativity commonly associated with the pastoral calling has even more interesting implications than the mere fact of its ubiquitousness. There are, to be sure, a few examples of those two most conventional types of comic clergymen, the bumbling saint and the smooth-talking charlatan. In Mitchell's *The Vanishing Point*, for instance, we find not one but *both* of these stereotypes: the neurotic and mercenary faith healer, the Reverend Heally Richards, versus the well-meaning but totally ineffectual Reverend Bob G. Dingle. More often, however, pastors in Canadian fiction are condemned for qualities that might be seen as *intrinsic* to their priestly roles – and in particular a lack of tolerance – rather than for any failure to play these roles properly.

Again we have to allow for some differences. On an overt level, simply because the Church has been *in fact* such a strong force for social repression and polical conservatism in Quebec, the reaction against institutionalized religion *seems* much more extreme in avant-garde Québécois writing. Marie-Claire Blais' *Les manuscrits de Pauline Archange*, for instance, is even more virulently anti-clerical than Carrier's fiction with her grim scenes of religious retreats and convent schools where naughty children are deprived of food, worked like navvies, made to sit for hours without being able to use the toilet, threatened with incarceration in a cell full of rats, above all, dunned incessantly with reminders of their innate and incorrigible corruption, the shame of their flesh ('one acquires the habit of living with a body [that is] slighted and humiliated ... the eye of memory ... [captures] forever the image of a young girl sobbing on her knees beside her bloodstained bed, while the nun standing near her seems to be hiding in her round, magnanimous eyes the murderer, the incurable monster whose thoughts one can read. "Give me something, Mother, it's running all down my legs..." "It's a punishment from God, do the best you can with toilet paper." "You must flatten your chest with a wide elastic so as not to tempt the devil." "You must wear a corset and pull your stomach in against your spine"' 83). If we make allowances for the political component in the French-Canadian view of the Church (as opposed to the individual churchman), however, we will see that the attitude toward the ministry to be inferred from Blais' vision is by no means specific to Quebec.[11] Indeed, if clerical cruelty in English-language literature seems in general neither quite so grotesque nor so pervasive, this probably reflects only the greater degree of compartmentalization possible in a Protestant setting. The negativity attributed to the pastoral role is actually equally intense in both cultures. Many of the terms of reference – the emphasis on personal rather than professional failings, failings in the area of *feeling* rather than function, for instance – are also similar. Contrary to what we might expect, moreover, for all that it lacks the revolutionary fervour of the Quebec counter-culture and the anti-institutional bias which this naturally entails, when it comes to specific, individual problem-parsons, English-language literature presents its exemplars in much more intimate detail. In this sense, then, it is English-language literature that yields us our prototypical Canadian clergyman.

Who is he? If we examine the corpus, we'll see that his identifying characteristic is – significantly enough – an almost total lack of the more feminine of Christian virtues, compassion and charity. His intentions may be good, in other words, but because his religious assumptions make no allowance for the human element, the results are almost always deplorable. The Reverend Amasa Dempster in Robertson Davies' Deptford trilogy, for instance, commonly ties up his demented wife and prays over her; to his son he gives only the *word* of the Bible (forcing him to learn ten verses each day) rather than its *spirit*. Paul, retrospectively in *World of Wonders*, asserts that 'my father wasn't a tyrant; he truly wanted to protect me against evil' (23), but against this is the fact that after being raped and kidnapped as a boy, he was more afraid of being returned home in his 'soiled' condition than of any further abuse that his kidnappers might offer:

They assumed that I was aching to return to my loving family, whereas I was frightened of what my father would do when he found out what had happened in the privy, and what the retribution would be for having stolen fifteen cents, a crime of the uttermost seriousness in my father's eyes.

My father was no brute, and I think he hated beating me, but he knew his duty. 'He that spareth his rod hateth his son; but he that loveth him chasteneth him betimes'; this was part of the prayer that always preceded a beating and he laid the rod on hard, while my mother wept. (47)

Duty is the key word here! The motivating force behind almost all the flawed pastors of Canadian fiction, in fact, is not a willed malice but a misguided sense of duty.

Interestingly enough, considering what I said above about inter-systemic homology, the failures of these men as ministers – a reflection perhaps of God's perceived failure as a kind of super-Father – are almost always manifested in terms of warped familial relations. In Bodsworth's *The Atonement of Ashley Morden*, the protagonist's minister-father, disappointed that his son has decided to study medicine instead of becoming a missionary, refuses to give the impoverished young man even a roof over his head. '"I cannot continue providing him with free support while he hoards money to buy a godless education,"' he says. '"In the future, son ... you shall pay your mother ten dollars a week board money or live elsewhere. I must demand this to insure that no contribution of mine is turned to a purpose that I regard as sinful"' (173). Conveniently identifying his own will with the will of God, he is totally oblivious to any obligations beyond those ostensibly entailed by his religion. The grandfather in Williams's *The Burning Wood* suffers from a similar lack of perspective. Although not a minister in any official sense, his formal connections with the church as well as his total commitment to religion give him the status in his community of a religious leader. Like the Reverend Morden, however, he reads into the demands of Christian duty only what he wants – in this case support for his paranoid hatred of the 'godless' Indians. Bram Cardiff is at root no more cruel or inhuman than Paul Dempster's father, but his particular brand of narrow-mindedness, providing him – among other things – with a 'religious' justification for his unreasonable expectations of his grandson, inevitably produces cruelty as a side-effect.

The important aspect of these paternal failings is, of course, the extent to which they typify not merely private but public aspects of the pastoral role. Deacon Block of Rudy Wiebe's *Peace Shall Destroy Many*, an even more extreme case, demonstrates clearly the broad ramifications of the familial model considered as a kind of prototype for or mirror of behaviour and attitudes on many different levels. Again racial prejudice is used to signal a general failure of love, but Block's rigidity – his immovable moral certitude, his neurotic fear of contamination, his obsession with rules – is revealed to be a far greater sin against life than Bran's blustering intolerance. Indeed, as Patricia Morley points out, the deacon's incessant talk 'about the community's cleanness and peace, about the security of seclusion' is nothing more than a mask for spiritual sterility, just as his rock-like strength of will, once heralded as the mainstay of the community, is actually a 'demonic inversion of the Pauline metaphor for Christ' (A69, 68). The rock reference, on the other hand, points even more tellingly to Peter than to Christ, for just as the apostle was the father of the Church, Block is in a very real sense 'father' to the whole Mennonite settlement. It is appropriate, therefore, that the spiritually deadening effect of his influence on a public level should be echoed and underlined by his daughter's tragic fate.

Elizabeth Block, in the present of the novel, is a faded spinster of thirty-three. When she was younger her father had forbidden her marriage to a Mennonite neighbour because of his illegitimate birth, and now her life consists of nothing but endless, backbreaking labour. When, desperate for love, she seduces and becomes impregnated by a half-breed farmhand, Block, unyielding, orders her out of his house. Before he can enforce this sentence, however, the girl dies – bleeding away her life as the deacon over the years has drained away her spirit. Her brother at first believes that both the miscarriage and the death have been caused by the inordinate physical demands of the harvest, but the doctor denies that. '"People don't die from working,"' he says. '"It was ... an internal disorder that got out of control"' (147-8). The context makes the implication obvious. Under Deacon Block's 'godly' rule, the community – his public children – is dying just as surely as Elizabeth from a lack of that brotherly love which should have been its lifeblood.

If nothing else it seems evident from these examples that the role of pastor (as God's stand-in) is – paradoxically, considering the traditional connotations of the word – totally incompatible with the role of father; with any humanized role, in fact. In Laurence's *The Diviners*, when Royland tells Morag that in his earlier life he had been a preacher, therefore, we are not surprised that this is a confession he makes with shame rather than pride:

I thought ... that I had the revealed Word. God was talking to me, sure as hell, and probably to no one else. At meetings I used to give 'em real fire-and-brimstone. Strong men wept. I'm not kidding. Must've been a godawful sight, eh? I never saw it. I mean, I never saw it that way. Well, I was married then. You never knew I'd been married, did you? I'd married young, just before the Call came upon me. Well, for all them years I was death on every such thing as drink, tobacco, dances, cards, lace curtains, any dress that looked like anything but a gunny sack, and so on and so forth. My wife led a life which was filled with nothing pleasant in any way at all. I even quit making love with her. I burned, yeh, but virtuously. (240)

Royland does not recognize his failure until after his wife drowns herself. Appropriately in terms of the typical Canadian pattern of response, however, once he repudiates his role as the voice of Nobodaddy, he is then able to become a *true* spiritual guide, a Diviner.

If relations with God the Father are perceived in negative terms, this also affects the Canadian view of the mediating role. As a result, although there are a number of striking symbolic crucifixions in Canadian literature, these generally come across quite ambiguously. Father Rorty of *Tay John*, for instance, sees not the love but only the violence of the sacrificial act. '"Beauty affronts the world by its violence,"' he says. '"Its violence draws man and affrights him. Without the Cross our Saviour's life would not be beautiful. It is from His agony, not from His words, that the leaves of the poplar-tree are never still"' (188). In the end, moreover, the crucifixion that he himself seeks and finds in a life-denying flight from his own human passions reinforces the demonic suggestions of his religious vision. Scourged and beaten throughout his last night by the terrible fury of a mountain blizzard, when he is found the birds have already 'eaten into the soft flesh of the belly' (221). The Promethean echo here is an appropriate one, with its connotations of the tyrant-god, Zeus. It also, however, transforms quite significantly the implications – especially the question of volition and purpose – of the original act. [12]

In *The Mountain and the Valley*, Buckler offers an even more complex Imitation of Christ. This book as a whole seems to recapitulate biblical history, with David Canaan representing the total body of God's chosen people, albeit (considering the associations of his name) in their unredeemed form. There is a fall, closely followed by a falling out of brothers, and as a result of this incident David carries throughout his long period of spiritual exile both a visible mark and a debilitating weakness which, like original sin itself, alienates him from human relation. Buckler's recapitulation of the Old Testament does not, however, seem to offer even the limited affirmations of the original. The keel tree of the Canaans' ark brings death instead of safety. And in David's climactic scene in the last chapter, the expected symbolic triumph fails, at least in part, to convince us.

One element that clearly undercuts David's messianic epiphany on the mountain is the fact that although there is certainly a suggestion of a symbolic tree and a crucifixion thereon, the context in which this episode takes place seems to imply that the protagonist has embraced his doom as an *escape from* rather than *on behalf* of the human community. 'Suddenly there were all the voices of all things everywhere at all times as they *might* have been ... He heard all the crushing screaming challenge of the infinite permutations of the possible... the billion raised to the billionth power... / He screamed, "Stop, stop..."/ ... And then he put his arms about the great pine' (297). Even more damaging than the dubiousness of his motivations, moreover, is his *response* to the transcendent vision that he is given in this climactic moment. Embracing all space and time, he is – as is appropriate to his symbolic role – at first filled with love for everyone but, as though Buckler were juxtaposing with this emblematic episode yet another passage from the Bible, Christ's temptation on the mountain, in the end David becomes fixated upon the image of his own generosity and success, and falls into a rather puerile wishful fantasy.

I will ask Chris to come live with us, and he'll know that I forgave him long long ago. And Anna. How could I have ever thought that Anna and I could ever grow away from each other? (The morning of my first trip to the mountain, the Christmas tree, the blindman's bluff...) How proud she will be when she hears what I have done ...

He could hear his voice saying to her on the phone, 'What do you think, Anna – my book won the prize!' Then the line would be still, because they'd both be crying; then they'd both be laughing at each other crying... Oh, Anna, Anna...

And then he heard the beating of his heart. (300)

The ending, as far as David the individual is concerned, is perhaps not as unambiguously negative as these quotations may make it sound. On the other hand, the ambiguity itself undercuts the symbolic mimesis in terms at least of the traditional religious mode. This is not an icon of Christ triumphant but, rather, an image of a Christ who fails.

It's not difficult to suggest reasons for these ambiguous crucifixions. Even beyond the difficulties of making mediation with a hostile God seem like a good idea at all (remember the Canadian's natural distrust of transcendence), there is a further problem posed with respect to literary adaptations of such specifically Christian symbolic action, and this involves the identity of the mediator himself. While under the circumstances one might well be delighted to welcome a mediator *if* one were sure where his loyalties lay, any doubt on this count merely adds another turn to the screw. In the traditional terms of his incarnation, Christ is in some peculiar way only half man, the other half being God. So whose side is he really on? The answers offered by Canadian literature to this critical question are generally ambivalent ones. In Leonard Cohen's *Beautiful Losers*, Charles Axis (even aside from the suggestive classical allusions to the original Atlas, the name is an obvious pseudonym for Christ Crucified, the *axis mundi*) is, according to F., humanity's hero against the supernatural 'other.' '"The Fat! The Fat! He's one of us!"' he cries. '"Charles Axis is on our side! He's with us against Blue Beetle and Ibis and Wonder Woman! ... Charles Axis is all compassion, he's our sacrifice! He calls the thin but he means both the fat and the thin"' (91-2). Alas for F., however, the church of Charles Axis turns out in the end to be nothing but a delusion and a snare. Despite his faithful observance of all the appropriate rituals, he still gets sand kicked in his face – by Charles Axis, 'the worst nuisance on the beach' (93).

What if the Christ figure is desacralized? This is what happens in *The Watch that Ends the Night*. Isolated and ill in a foreign country, Jerome Martell has a palliative vision of Jesus which reveals to him the messiah's essential humanity. 'He wasn't the Jesus of the churches. He wasn't the Jesus who had died for our sins. He was simply a man who had died outwardly as I had died inwardly' (330). Following this experience, moreover, Jerome himself, as Douglas Jones points out, having become 'the figure of such a Jesus, of the man who has died and risen again,' is enabled not merely to 'heal' Catherine after her dangerous operation but, more important, to serve as an exemplar for George in his desperate search for a way to come to terms with the horror of his wife's impending death (A160). Martell is an exception in Canadian literature, though. In most cases even would-be messiahs without a hint of divinity about them are presented very ambiguously. Morley Callaghan's *More Joy in Heaven* provides a striking example. When Kip Caley, a reformed criminal, is released from prison he is lionized by a public that sees him not only as the very type of the prodigal son but as a kind of symbol for man's triumph over his own nature: '"Someone who stands for all the good resolutions we ever made"' (66). On the simplest level Callaghan's novel is the story of Caley's rise and fall; the high hopes he formulates in response to all the adulation and his subsequent bitter disillusionment when he is dropped by his admirers as soon as the novelty wears off. One of the most interesting aspects of the book, however, is the peculiarly equivocal messianic parallel that Callaghan establishes right from the beginning by having Caley's release take place on Christmas morning (lest we miss the clue, one of the excited reporters refers to it as '"Your birthday"' 19): equivocal not so much because Caley fails in his ambition to 'do good' by becoming a member of the parole board or even because this man to whom the love of his fellows has seemed so important ends up in his frustration shooting a policeman as 'one final, anarchistic rejection of the force he felt to be the only thing that held people together' (151) – both these elements are important, but *More Joy in Heaven* is something more than just an ironic inversion of the Christ story – as because of the specific terms in which Callaghan sets forth the idealized messianic role.

Caley, we are told, had wanted to be 'the mediator between the law and those who break the law' (149-50). Because of the Christian parallel we naturally interpret this to mean 'between God and the sinners of His world.' But 'the law' here is represented by the arch-Calvinist, Judge Ford, a man just as rigid, as misanthropic, as obsessed with *order* as Deacon Block ('"justice is like a pattern – the pattern of the common good. It's up to me to see that the pattern isn't broken."' 91). Despite the fact, then, that the 'official' representative of God in this novel, Father Butler, is a good and charitable man (one of the few in the Canadian corpus), it would seem that Callaghan's *covert* view of divinity is somewhat less positive than the overt level of the book would suggest. This perhaps explains why we feel that it is not merely Caley's naive presumption that has caused him to fail as a mediator (for, in fact, he *does* mediate between exactly those two elements he earlier designated as his special concern, though not – as Christ – by bestowing life but by dealing death), but some sinister influence built into the mediating role itself. Even leaving aside the hovering presence of Nobodaddy, mediation – going 'between' – is *always* seen in Canada as potentially dangerous.

How, other than being suspicious of preachers, does the Canadian respond to his intimations of an angry God? One might think that fear of the Father and distrust of the Son would simply produce an inversion – a resurgence of matriarchalism in some form. This is patently not the case, however – nor is it likely to be. As Robert Graves points out, 'The Goddess is no townswoman: she is the Lady of the Wild Things, haunting the wooded hill-tops.'[13] Even aside from the difficulty of placing a benevolent feminine deity in what is perceived as a hostile masculine landscape, the urbanized modern age (American wishful primitivism notwithstanding) is perhaps irrevocably inimical to this particular archaic conception.[14] For another thing – and the importance of this point must not be underestimated – our response, as idiosyncratic as it might appear in symbolic manifestation, is still 'officially' contained within the conventional Western Christian world vision. Despite this, the reorientation of the macroscopic mode is *covertly* responsible for some of the most interesting and unique features of our national oeuvre. Fear, even sublimated fear, makes one far more sensitive to the *possibilities* of divinity than does officially worshipful complacency. The concept of God may be true or false, but it is hard to dismiss it as purely propaedeutic. Thus it is that even in books in which God himself plays no overt part, the pervasive influence of the *religious attitude* tends to manifest itself quite strikingly. Apart from direct effects like the character stereotypes discussed above, our characteristic concern with/distrust of the supernatural underlays many ostensibly conventional works with an odd seriousness, almost a sense of doom ('The terrible and sad things the principal characters sometimes endure seem parts of an ominous pattern building to completion, beyond their control or understanding,' says John Moss of Matt Cohen's novel *Wooden Hunters*, BVI), which tends to materialize unexpectedly in brief transient glimpses of a horrid incongruity lurking behind the rational surfaces of things. As a result of this disquieting propensity, like Graeme Gibson's Lucan Crackell, to the extent that we enter imaginatively into the fictional universe we cannot help feeling as though we are afflicted with omens. The fact is, beleaguered by God and unconvinced by resurrections ('Jesus Christ is risen today they sang at Sunday School, celebrating the daffodils,' says the narrator of Atwood's *Surfacing*, 'but people are not onions ... they stay under' 104), Canadians find it very easy to identify with Lucan's kind of paranoia. Certainly the fragmented headlines that punctuate his stream of consciousness throughout *Five Legs* could easily provide a subliminal choral accompaniment to much of our literature. 'SAVE! SAVE! NOBODY WALKS AWAY FROM HERE.' 'REPENT or be DAMNED.' 'THERE IS NO EASTER!' So much for the Heavenly Father!

If the macrocosm is radically deranged, a significant shift is evident in the values associated with the Canadian mesocosm as well. The problem on this level is that if nature is a threat, then society needs the paternalistic ordering power of Themis (the Mounties, the army) for protection. This, as noted in chapter 3, already creates difficulties through its irreconcilability with the anti-paternal American ideals of democratization. Even worse, since the menace we are being protected from is *also* masculine, there is a felt danger of our protectors and our enemies coalescing somehow. The father, in other words, no matter what his formal allegiances, equals nature equals danger. The figure who emerges from this disturbing equation can thus all too easily turn out to be Colonel Haldimar of *Wacousta*, whose tyrannical assertion of patriarchal authority on both public and private levels not only seems (symbolically) to set him at odds with the femininely oriented garrison, but actually *does* establish him as their enemy. Even aside from his behaviour in the present of the novel, it is made abundantly clear that it was his early betrayal of his friend (not only stealing his beloved fiancée but subsequently, by lies and trickery, hounding him right out of the army, branding him indelibly traitor and coward) which is alone responsible for the whole horrible ordeal that his children must undergo. When the father inside is as much of a threat – as fully tainted with violence and irrationality – as the demonic masculine element outside, the garrison is indeed doubly vulnerable.

What is the solution? The situation, one would think, should be alleviated by the fact that for much of our history the symbolic authority figure has not been a king but a queen. Even this identification, however, creates its own internal contradictions. The problems emerge vividly in Wiebe's *The Temptations of*

Big Bear, where the image of the benevolent Grandmother is undercut from both the white *and* the Indian points of view.

First of all, because the strongly patriarchal mythology of the British makes it difficult for them to accept an unqualifiedly feminine presence as their ultimate authority, in official presentation the Queen is – must be – firmly subjugated to the symbolic dominion of a Father God. Especially in the context of the attitudes discussed above this invocation can hardly help but complicate an already complicated situation. '"She is our Mother under The Great Spirit. Good,"' says Big Bear. '"Under the Spirit as missionary McDougall there says? Or the other one says, Lacombe? Or as I say?"' (23). Even more problematic is the inconsistency revealed by 'her' conduct. The Indians, who unlike the whites still perceive nature as feminine, could perhaps accept authority quite readily in a maternal guise ('"The White Queen is our Mother. Good. I am not a disobedient child. She will feed us when we are hungry."' 23) if it were not for the fact that her revealed function in their lands is not the expected one of succour but, rather, a masculine attempt to impose straight lines on the earth, divide it into neat, arbitrary sections. '"No one can choose for only himself a piece of the Mother Earth,"' Big Bear points out (28). The Queen's apparent delusion that she can do so, therefore, makes it obvious that she is an imposter in the maternal role. '"I say I am fed by the Mother Earth,"' he concludes, in the light of these ambiguities. '"The only water I will be touched by comes from above, the rain from The Only One who makes the grass grow and the rivers run and the buffalo feed there and drink so that I and my children live. That we have life!"' (23). The Queen, it seems, is not really a true feminine symbol at all.

Faced with these sorts of inconsistencies, the Canadian typically tends to avoid even looking too closely at the mesocosm for fear of losing his bearings entirely. Too much is confused, precarious on this level. Politics are incomprehensible. International crises, in MacLennan's words, appear 'like gigantic mystery plays in which obscure and absolutely irrational passions are handled by politicians, and viewed by the public, in a form of ritual akin to primitive religious rites' (B245). The Mountie, while theoretically incorruptible, is not one of us.[15] There are no clear party lines, no ideological certitudes. Indeed, as Atwood reveals in *Surfacing*, even the 'Americans' who kill the animals and violate the sanctities of the land, turn out all too often to be ourselves; crucifying the heron, fighting nature (what other choice do we have?), raising the water level to drown the garden. It is one of the more ambiguous aspects of our national behaviour. With all this, no wonder the Canadian persona often seems to feel – like Raddall's Nova Scotians in *His Majesty's Yankees*, caught helplessly between the equal menaces of the British and the American armies – that it is very difficult to tell friend from foe. No wonder, too, that he tends to distrust *all* authority, *all* official structures and roles: to avoid the political arena altogether.

Instinctive anti-establishmentarianism? Yes, in a sense. Revolutionary? Definitely not. What we have here isn't just the exaggerated fear of institutionalized repression and regimentation that the ultra-individualistic American so often manifests. As in the world of Kafka's novels, the Canadian's paranoia does not relate 'to the absolute power of the rationality of the State over individuals' but – echoing our attitude toward God – 'to the lack of communication between them.'[16] The state, in other words, is simply *alien*, and that's what makes it dangerous. In marked contrast to the American's horrified vision of a monolithic man-eating machine (like the 'Combine' of Ken Kesey's *One Flew over the Cuckoo's Nest*) systematically depersonalizing and homogenizing the populace, 'society' in Canada is viewed as fearful specifically because it is *not* machine-like, predictable, mechanical, but, rather – as Zéraffa says of the power structure against which K. is pitted in Kafka's *The Trial* – 'prey to confusion and disorder' [131]. There is thus a frequent sense in Canadian literature that the public world is somehow demonic, an utterly foreign element (as Munro describes Uncle Benny's world in *Lives of Girls and Women*) 'lying alongside our world ... like a troubling reflection, the same but never at all the same. In that world people could go down in quicksand, be vanquished by ghosts or terrible ordinary cities; luck and wickedness were gigantic and unpredictable; nothing was deserved, anything might happen' (22).

Such a vision is naturally bound to influence a writer's choice of vehicle. The novel of public life, of social forces, of political intrigue on the grand scale – the panoramic or epic form so beloved by the Americans (Dos Passos, Dreiser, Steinbeck; more recently, in diverse fashion, Wouk, Drury, Caldwell, Clavell, and so on ad infinitem) – is virtually unknown in this country. Indeed, in complete contradistinction to Auerbach's dictum that 'the serious realism of modern times cannot represent man otherwise than as embedded in a total reality, political, social, and economic,'[17] the Canadian writer tends more often than not to isolate his characters on an 'island' of one sort or another. As a result, as Dick Harrison points out with respect to the prairie novel, where we would expect to find Auerbach's 'total reality' there is typically only a vacuum:

Once we begin to look for what is missing from prairie realism we discover some surprising gaps. During the 1930's two national political parties were formed in Saskatchewan and Alberta, yet with the exception of McCourt's *Music at the Close*, these novels give us practically nothing of the very active political life of the time. And where are such staples of prairie life as the cooperatives, grain growers' associations, and other farm organizations? Where is the Prairie Farm Rehabilitation Administration? The radio? The *Winnipeg Free Press*? Where, in effect, is the outside world? (E181)

The novels on which Harrison comments here are not anomalous. In Canada, in fact, even fiction that *purports* to deal with social subjects almost always turns out on closer examination (as Robert McDougall says of Morley Callaghan) to be 'preeminantly concerned with personal values and "inscape"' (224). We will be examining this aspect further in chapter 12, but in the meantime we might merely note that the primary characteristic of the mesocosm in Canadian literature is simply its absence.

But is this, perhaps, too sweeping a statement?

The question arises inevitably as to whether Quebec, where so many writers have been self-identified with revolutionary or at least radical politics in the last two decades, can be included in this case under the general prescription. 'So closely tied are literature and politics in Québec that certain dates burn like beacons, illuminating the cultural landscape,' claims Kathy Mezei. 'As Gilles Marcotte has said, "la littérature fait le pays, et le pays fait la littérature"' (B32). If this is true we could hardly claim that French-Canadian literature lacks a public dimension. When we examine the oeuvre itself, however, we get the sense that the mesocosmic realm seems just as alien to the Québécois as it is to his English counterpart. Whatever the political motives of these writers as individuals, the world they depict in their books is one in which political activity is futile, irrational, or – more often, surprisingly enough – missing altogether.

It comes down to a question of perspective. Roch Carrier's works, for instance, have radical political *implications* but they cannot be classified as being *about* politics. If what we are shown is a kind of war, there are no clear sides, no ideological solutions: just the 'little guy' against everything else. 'Carrier's novels are a protest against all the forces that have enslaved Quebec and prevented her from freely fulfilling her destiny,' says David Bond. 'It is not so much the Church itself which Carrier attacks as a symbolic representation of all the forces of darkness, superstition and fear which would hamper the development of a people. It is all "official" explanations and justifications of Quebec's misfortunes' (121). Margot Northey makes a similar distinction. 'The enemy is ... nebulous, wearing many faces besides that of the *maudit anglais* . The threat is also a matter of modern technological society stamping out indigenous cultural mores and desires, of massive, impersonal forces acting against the villagers' feebler human particularities and peculiarities' (81). The socio-political background to Carrier's books, in other words, is exactly that: a *background*, every bit as 'hazy and terrifying' as Uncle Benny's vision of the public world.

The ramifications of this view are considerable. However much one would *like* to act, the only way to combat such a diffuse 'enemy' is not to politicize but simply to withdraw. Carrier's protagonists, therefore, are just as isolated, as paranoid and impotent, as the alienated individuals who wander their way through English fiction. Philibert's experience of the urban environment to which he flees from the death-saturated rural setting is not only generally correlative with but almost identical to the wilderness-like London experienced by David Helwig's John Martens:

The streets ran right across the city, stretched out, crossed one another, made knots, formed letters that could only be deciphered from the sky, proliferated like jungle vines.

All at once a street had moved imperceptibly, another had twisted, trembling gently, and it seemed to Philibert that the immense hand of the city was closing up. He would be crushed between these streets that looked so much alike, with their names that all sounded the same and their uniform houses. (B33)

The catastrophic conclusion to this novel, leaving a bleeding Philibert trapped under an overturned car with 'His heart [like] a little berry between big iron fingers' (100), suggests that if one *does* get mixed up in the public realm, the inevitable result is pain and disaster.

We find similar implications in other recent Quebec writers, even when their explicit *subject* is revolution. When Hubert Aquin sets up a parallel in *Prochain épisode* between the desire/necessity of recreating one's country (*pays, terre*) and the process of writing, the writer-revolutionary's inability to control his fictional reality (he 'breaks with the coherence of domination and begins a Hamlet-like monologue interrupted at each word,' says Mezei B41) naturally reflects on his political efficacy as well. Indeed, though revolution provides a kind of psycho-setting to this book, it seems as if the protagonist is a mere pawn of irrational forces; acted upon rather than acting; *in* the political landscape, but not of it. This ambiguity perhaps explains why, as Leonard Sugden points out, while Aquin has been considered by many as 'among the most intelligent apologists of Quebec's independence ... others have seen in his revolutionary stance mere literary bravado consumed in defeatism and even the signs of a counter-revolutionary impulse' (73). Aquin's ambivalent response, however, is, despite the *conscious* political intent commonly claimed by the Québécois artist, in many ways even more typical than Carrier's. Like Aquin's, post-sixties Quebec fiction, far from expressing the spirit of reform 'that brought the P.Q. to power, has borrowed other "voices" that express a colonial situation – the voices of dispossession, schizophrenia, mutilation and death' (Victor-Lévy Beaulieu cited in Mezei B50).[18] Sugden's comments on Aquin's introvertive tendencies may thus be extended to cover a large proportion of the recent French-Canadian oeuvre: 'In Aquin's novels, social and political realities are only seen on the rhetorical plane ... Social revolution is seen almost entirely from the viewpoint of a narrator's individual reactions, his own anguish and search for personal fulfillment . [He insists] upon focusing his novels on the interaction of equal human partners largely outside of any family context and often to the exclusion of the entire Quebec social frame' (74-5). Judging by this there is a far greater covert consensus among both English and French-Canadian writers about the dangers of the mesocosmic realm than the *apparent* extreme politicization of the latter would suggest. Indeed the frequent explicit conflation in Québécois fiction of revolutionary activity with sex, and of both with death (a strategy used not only by Aquin but also by Godbout, Jasmin, and others), besides further denigrating the possibility of love, casts such an air of fatality and irrationality over the whole area of French-Canadian politics as to place it definitively beyond the reach of human comprehension or control.

The Canadian writer does not, then, generally focus on public life *per se* at all, but directs his fictional explorations almost entirely toward private experience. It is hence in the microcosm that the reorientation of archetypes tends to show its primary effects. To the extent that one level is always at least implicitly a metaphor in literature for all other levels of human action, the resulting vision is not, of course, lacking in broader significance. The Canadian fictional universe, however, is generally conceptualized in terms of purely domestic interaction. And this is why patterns of familial relation are so important for our understanding of Canadian culture as a whole.

We have already surveyed the spectrum of marital modes. These naturally exhibit the greatest and most direct relationship with the inverted Moira/ Themis polarity. What, though, of other linkages, such as parent-child, child-parent? The fact is that the immediate focus of Canadian writing is quite preponderantly upon the horizontal level. Probably because of the confusions inherent in the shifting values of meso-and macrocosmic realities, vertical relationships seem to suggest mainly disturbing possibilities. This is not to say that vertical relationships do not appear at all. Indeed, in a peculiar way, it is in these relationships that some of the most strongly felt psychic-emotional energies seem to inhere. Vertical relations *qua* relations, however, are generally presented in a very ambiguous light.

Father figures, even aside from all those flawed parsons, are – not surprisingly – often overtly negative. Ostenso's Caleb Gare, a brutal domestic tyrant who uses his family as beasts of burden, terrorizing them, forbidding them all pleasures, cutting them off from any hope of escape into a more bearable future in order to support his greed for land and profit, is perhaps an extreme example, but even stripped of Gare's demonic energies, the fathers in Canadian literature – like nature itself – tend to be associated with cruelty and violence. In Sylvia Fraser's brilliant novel of childhood, *Pandora*, Lyle Cragg is a brutal husband, a terrifying and unpredictable presence to his children: 'Pandora's father is tall and fleshy with a bald head and glistening steel-rimmed eyes: Pandora's father smells of blood and rage' (18). The reason for his fearsome aspect is not hard to find. Through a transference equivalent to that by means of which the Canadian fictional pastor tends to identify himself with the cold, hard righteousness of the Christian God, Mr Cragg, going one step further, is self-identified as His rival and enemy. At Pandora's christening, offended by his wife's devout transports, 'The father glares at Christ on the ceiling. Splintered notes stick in his craw, and he grinds them between his molars as he stiff-arms the spirit-sodden child that is now also animal-sodden.

Cuckold of a deadman!' (10). This is an uncomfortable image indeed.

In French-Canadian literature the habitual association of violence with the paternal role is so deeply engrained that it seems more often than not to be assumed – accepted – quite casually as a natural and even proper aspect of things. When Arsène in *La guerre, yes sir!* beats his son ('He would have liked [the boy] to understand, but he knew that gentleness is never effective. So he buried his boot in Philibert's behind and repeated the action until his leg was tired.' 15), Philibert, though resentful, is not surprised, simply viewing himself resignedly as 'like all the boys in the village' (16). The father who emerges from the pages of Claire Martin's autobiographical *Dans un gant de fer* dominates his family so completely by both physical and psychological means that they are kept in a constant humiliating state of fear which in itself is 'the hardest thing of all to forgive' (292). In Marie-Claire Blais' reconstructions of childhood, similarly, paternal brutality is so endemic, so inevitable, that it becomes one of the defining features of her young protagonists' world. 'On "the nights of the big whippings," as Jacob called them, the father whipped all the children who happened to be in the room, going from one to another in a crazed, waltzing stupor' (B43).

Mothers in Canadian literature – again as might be expected – are more variable and certainly less threatening as a group. Especially when coupled explicitly with strong father figures, in fact, they tend to fade into the background. The mothers of Mitchell's *The Vanishing Point* and Laurence's *The Stone Angel* die in childbirth, as does, in more spectacular fashion, Keneally's mother in *The Invention of the World*. Paul Dempster's mother in Davies' Deptford trilogy becomes gently deranged after he is born. A generation later in the same series, David Staunton's mother, Leola, is revealed as a pretty vapid woman who fails utterly to live up to the expectations of her more sophisticated husband and bright children. Mrs Morden in *The Atonement of Ashley Morden* is a sympathetic figure, but helpless to resist openly in any way her strong-willed husband. The most she can do for her son is secretly to return to him the board money the Reverend makes him pay. In *Les manuscrits de Pauline Archange* the mother is austere, melancholy, possessed by the image of her own encroaching death as she is wasted by some inherent weakness of her woman's flesh that the daughter-narrator sees 'reflected in the extreme poverty of her energies, in the smudges under her eyes, in the savage attacks of vomiting that left her drained of consciousness on her bed' (17). In Munro's *Lives of Girls and Women*, the protagonist's mother herself is a strong enough personality, but *her* mother, the grandmother, fulfils strikingly the expected role at one remove: ' "She was a religious fanatic," says my mother of this kneeling woman, who at other times is discovered flat on her back and weeping – for reasons my mother does not go into – with a damp cloth pressed to her forehead. Once in the last demented stages of Christianity she wandered down to the barn and tried to hide a little bull calf in the hay, when the butcher's men were coming' (63). The pattern is not limited to the Christian family, either. In Adele Wiseman's *The Sacrifice* – a novel in which, characteristically enough, the father is implicated in his son's death by the sheer weight of his mythic existence – the mother seems a figure totally drained of vitality. Never fully recovering from the shock of losing her two oldest sons, 'Sarah began, almost imperceptibly at first, but in Abraham's eyes at least more clearly, to fade away. It was as though a long tiredness was creeping over her, wrapping her up in its filminess ... Her life had become like a long conversation ... to which she was even now forgetting to listen' (133).

At this point a problem arises. The type combination of aggressive male and passive female seems to run entirely counter to the exemplary mode of dominant female/passive male isolated above. Such a conflict naturally generates a great deal of tension, and may in itself be responsible for much of the ambiguity that seems to inhere in the familial model. It also, one would think, presents a problem for the writer. If our inherited conceptual vocabulary offers two diametrically opposed versions of the masculine role, how does one decide which is appropriate? Perhaps, indeed, the apparent indeterminacy of this role militates against the entire foregoing attempt to establish *the* prototypical Canadian pattern of relations. If we examine the evidence, however, we will see not only that the theoretical conflict tends to be sidestepped in practice, but that the choice of masculine mode, far from being arbitrary, a mere toss-up, as the co-existence of alternate possibilities seems to imply, is generally directly related to the particular relational dynamics of a given novel. What it comes down to is this: if a male character appears as a (real or potential) sexual partner, he tends to be either weak (bad) or passive (good); if he appears primarily as a father, on the other hand, he is typically both dominant and negative.

What about all the strong mothers to be found in the corpus? – Addie Jordan of *Lives of Girls and Women*, Mrs Ramsay in *Fifth Business*, Brian's mother in *Who Has Seen the Wind*, among others. These women are all presented as being much stronger than their easy-going, likeable menfolks, despite the fact that since these books are narrated from the child's point of view the latter are, presumably, presented in paternal mode. The key to this apparent inconsistency lies in the protagonist's emotional perspective. Oddly enough, in the Canadian fictional family, perhaps because of the irreconcilability of different aspects of male and female roles, the child almost always seems to be fixated on one parent to the near exclusion of the other. In the three examples cited here, as in most Canadian novels with a strong mother figure, it is the maternal relation which is the most important and (generally) problematic. In terms of the *emotional* rather than the *formal* relational dynamics of these books, the father, being of less importance in the child's quest for identity, is consequently treated more as a kind of appendage to his wife than as an exemplar of the parental role. When it is the paternal relation that focuses the protagonist's anxieties, on the other hand, the mother is almost always retiring. It isn't a matter of which parent the child *identifies* with – indeed, the strong parent, and especially the strong father, is almost always explicitly imaged as 'other' – but of which accrues the most numen. In Clarke Blaise's *Lunar Attractions*, for instance, it is the mother – fastidious, sensitive, cultured – with whom the young boy feels the most empathy rather than the pre-eminently physical and apparently invulnerable father ('In those years I felt myself on special terms with "Mac," the ninety-eight pound weakling of the Charles Atlas ads. My father looked like Charles Atlas.' 11), but it is the *father* who obsesses him, embarrasses and puzzles and repels him with his patent alienness, the mysteries of the male mind and body that seem to the child not only strange but enormously threatening – and in consequence endlessly fascinating:

I used to worry about my father's little warts – like dripping on a sand castle. Did they hurt him? Did they rub? Once I even touched them, and he gave my wrist a vicious wrench ... [He also had] a slablike mole on the side of his navel, like a hardened excrescence [sic] ... Of other parts between his navel and kneecap, I have no knowledge. We were a circumspect family, very formal with each other. I remember only one occasion of quasi-nudity. I was climbing the stairs in a duplex we inhabited – I was in junior high, then. The bathroom stood at the top of the stairs. My naked father was propped against the lavatory, shaving before the mirror, buttocks to the open door. And between his legs, halfway to the knees, something incredibly thick and dark was hanging. Before he could hear me, I quickly turned and went back downstairs. (19)

In some ways the pattern of antipathetic fathers paired with retiring mothers seems not unlike the familial model to be found in American culture as described by Gorer. However, even aside from the fact that the American mother, rather than demonstrating a genuine passiveness, usually seems to be effaced because she is covertly perceived as threatening (too *strong*, in other words), the Canadian version of the family reveals three important differences. In the first place, while the perceived negativity of the American father is typically rooted in his imputed foolishness or ineffectuality – Willy Loman in Arthur Miller's *Death of a Salesman* – the Canadian father, as we have seen, is feared more often than not precisely because he *is* so potent. Secondly, and more important, while the American filial role is relatively simple and static, the Canadian one is duplicitous, shifting, subject to transformation. In the United States the son's ambivalence toward and need to free himself from the father, whether – as in most nineteenth-century versions – encapsulated behind a facade of overtly affirming, 'officially approved' Christian filial piety or – as is more common in the twentieth century – simply acknowledged as natural and inevitable, typically plays its part in the maturation process, is transcended and forgotten. Outside of the *Bildungsroman*, the father is consequently curiously absent from American (non-Jewish) literature, at least as a significant factor in the emotional lives of its protagonists. In Canada, in contrast, the father is not only hated and feared for his superior strength, but desired for the very same reason. Even if he is vanquished in approved American style, therefore, he is rarely just left behind. Indeed, much of Canadian literature is energized by a *double* impulse, to deny *and* to confirm heredity. Thirdly and finally, since in the 'absence' of the father it may just as easily be the mother who plays the ambiguous dominant role in the Canadian fictional family, this flight/quest motif can technically be focused on either the male *or* the female parent. Because the mother has no *inherent* connections with inimical 'otherness,' either God or nature, such as the father has, she can theoretically be more easily assimilated, but because she is implicated with *him* (by analogy when dominant, by simple association when passive), she too tends to accrue in the child's eyes a disturbing aura of mystery. 'Parents,' by definition, are simply another species, not always overtly fearsome (though young David Greenwood of *Lunar Attractions* has a nervous breakdown when he becomes convinced that his parents are enemy spies or even extraterrestials, his reaction is somewhat extreme) but inevitably perplexing. 'Occasionally, from afar and with a disturbed respect, we did look at our parents,' says Blais' Pauline Archange, 'much as we gave ourselves up, on summer evenings, to a timorous contemplation of the policemen walking their beats beneath the streetlights, our fascinated eyes riveted on the white truncheons with which they always played, one hand behind their backs. Such beings were an alien way of life, their habits mysterious and incomprehensible; it would have been futile to seek to understand them' (B10-11). The object of filial obsession in Canada, therefore, is not just the father but the archetypal *parent*.

The complications do not end here. If there is a perceptible impulse toward some kind of reconciliation to balance the initial recoil from parental 'otherness,' this is not in general realized in terms of reoriented familial relations. Lorna Irvine in her study of mothers and daughters in Canadian fiction asserts that a 'translation of oppressive ancestral laws into dynamic legacies' may be achieved by such means as the metaphorical transference of the female role from one generation to the next (56). Against this view, however, the examples she herself uses – especially her descriptions of the self-destructive hostility felt by daughters from and toward their mothers – are so strikingly biased toward the negative aspect, the alienation, that the transferences, if they take place at all, would seem to be forced ones. The fact is, for Canadians a 'real' parent, even the less overtly menacing mother, always seems to present a real psychic danger. The tendency in Canadian literature, therefore, is *not* toward familial reconciliation in any naturalistic sense, but, rather, toward a definitive separation – more often than not symbolized by the parent's death. What, then, of the second stage of the double movement mentioned above? Typically the Canadian writer aesthetically compartmentalizes the mutually exclusive phases of the filial repulsion/attraction syndrome by differentiating explicitly between the real parent and the parent as idea. The prototypical double movement hence juxtaposes a protagonist's recoil from his 'real' mother or father with an attempt not merely to find but in a sense to *create* an 'ideal' parent for himself.

The base pattern appears in two related but distinct variants. The first involves an actual repudiation of the parental figure in favour of someone else. Matt Cohen's *The Disinherited* offers an interesting example of this particular structure, containing as it does not merely one attempt at father substitution but two parallel (in a sense homologous, in another sense inverted) cases.

Richard Thomas, whose death is the focal incident in this novel, has two 'sons.' The first, Brian, is a foster child who is so emotionally committed to his step-family that when his real mother and her husband come to claim him as a young child, hurt and angry, radically disoriented by the urban environment, he ends up burning down his new home and seriously injuring himself in the process. His reunion with the Thomases after this traumatic episode not only confirms the child's emotional dependency, but catalyses an intense and narrowly focused identification with the adoptive father. 'When they took him back to the farm, Brian had trusted neither Erik nor Miranda, but had wanted to be with Richard all the time ... He was willing to play with Erik and accept food from Miranda, but it was Richard he needed' (74-5). As he grows up the psychological bonding rooted in this period only becomes more complete. By the time of Richard's death, indeed, he has wishfully turned himself into the heir that the old man has always wanted: dutiful, dedicated to the land, devoted to his 'father.' Somehow he has even acquired a family resemblance, seemingly almost by an act of will. Unfortunately, Brian's devotion is wasted. Richard Thomas, perversely, is fixated only on Erik, the child of his flesh. He thus virtually ignores all the eager efforts of the other. '"He treats you like a slave,"' says Brian's wife, Nancy. '"You live on the farm and you work there every day for twenty years. When he passes you in the yard or ... asks you to pass the salt he never recognizes you more than a dog. And now that he's dying he doesn't even think of you, he only wants to make sure [of] his precious son"' (77). These hard words cannot deflect Brian's affections – even though he does recognize, and bitterly resent, their truth. Richard is simply 'father' as far as he is concerned.

Ironically, as it turns out, Richard's love is just as misplaced as Brian's. Erik, the son he does want, is a young academic who desires nothing more than to repudiate his birthright – not just the farm his father threatens to give him (despite all common sense, his wife's advice, and Brian's obvious moral rights), but the whole way of life it represents. In token of this, as the old man lies in the hospital awaiting death Erik spends his time trying to find a substitute not merely for the *person* who is his father but, seemingly, for the paternal *principle* the aggressive Richard so strikingly represents. Experimenting variously with Rose Garrett (the young fortune-teller who, combining sex and sensitivity, epitomizes the archetypal female) and Norman Nemo Zeller (the old man in the hospital whose ironic detachment suggests a rejection of familial relation and emotional involvement altogether), he finally makes a symbolic identification with the great uncle whose journals he has inherited – significantly enough, an exemplary embodiment of the passive-male mode: poetic, sexually ambivalent, a natural-born victim – and, by passing on the ancestral ring to the young, nameless, pregnant girl he has picked up, simultaneously frees himself from and reconciles himself with both past and future, affirming his 'familial' connections while in a sense displacing them to an impersonal and perhaps wholly abstract realm. Paradoxically, it is Brian, the foundling who wanted but could never have a real father, who will *be* one himself (right after the funeral Nancy announces that they are going to start a family), while Erik, who had Richard but didn't want him, can apparently play the paternal role only at one step removed.

In isolation these peculiar – and peculiarly disparate – father/son relations may easily seem anomalous, but if we look further in the corpus we will see that the modes of response illuminated here are characteristic of the Canadian domestic scene as a whole. We have already mentioned Philip Bentley's propensity to downplay his real but unsatisfactory waitress-mother in favour of a much idealized absentee father. The emotional dynamics are strikingly similar in Blondal's *A Candle to Light the Sun* where both plot and theme revolve around the futile efforts of the young protagonist, another illegitimate child, to distance himself from his brutal stepfather by 'proving' his fantasized kinship with the town doctor. Other versions approach the substitution theme somewhat more obliquely. A major motif in Robertson Davies' Deptford trilogy, for instance, concerns the attempt by each of the three protagonists (Dunstan Ramsay, Paul Dempster, and David Staunton) to escape the parents who 'represent his natural background, not in the sense that they are his biological parents, but in that they represent the *milieu* he is born to,' and replace them *metaphorically* with '"parents in art,"' the male and female aspects he contains within himself (Davy 129). In *The Diviners*, conversely, Morag must learn that it is Christie, who has always seemed too oppressively real to her, and *not* the mythical 'parent in art,' Piper Gunn, who is her ideal father. She doesn't need to go to Sutherland to find her history, she discovers, because she already holds it, in Christie's tales, *inside* her head: '"It's a deep land here, all right ... "' she tells her Scottish lover. '"But it's not mine, except a long way back. I always thought it was the land of my ancestors, but it is not." "What is, then?" "Christie's real country. Where I was born"' (390-1).

This last example brings up a curious point. Christie is not Morag's biological father, although he has been her 'official' one, so her final recognition of him still reflects the pattern of relational dynamics outlined here. If we look further, though, we will find many other Canadian books in which – seemingly contrary to our thesis about the unassimilability of the 'real' father – the protagonist, like Morag, belatedly recognizes a parent's worth. In Aritha Van Herk's *Judith*, for example, the young heroine realizes after her father's death that she has made a mistake in rejecting the life he wanted for her in favour of an effete, unnatural existence in the city, so she uses her inheritance to buy a farm. If it is too late to become reconciled with the man himself, she can at least be reconciled with the principles for which he stood. ' "What should I have done with his money?"' she defensively demands of an incredulous neighbour. ' "Gone to Hawaii like every other city slicker?" You don't know, she thought. It's all I've got left of him, it's all that's left of anything . If I don't do it now I never will and I'll never do anything at all, and I'll never please him' (27). Far from controverting our base prescription, however, the mode of response detailed here, whatever may *appear*, actually confirms it. This, in fact, is the second major variant of the real parent/ideal parent flight/quest motif mentioned above.

The key phrase in the foregoing summary is 'after her father's death.' If we reflect a moment on the emotional dynamics of Van Herk's novel we will see that the real and the ideal, though *apparently* conflated in a single father figure, are actually still as carefully compartmentalized as they are in any of the other books examined in connection with this theme. In Canadian literature – and this is the crucial point – the dead parent is, in both symbolic and psychological terms, an entirely different entity from the parent alive. The parental death in Canadian literature is typically not, therefore – as it might be perceived in terms of the American familial mode – simply a conclusion, a climax, a resolution: a final liberation from the past.[19] It is, rather, a *turning point* in the protagonist's process of individuation. As on the mesocosmic level, Themis is loved and needed as intensely as he is hated and feared. After the parents are dead, consequently, they – and in particular the father, who was perceived so negatively in life – can often become transformed from a threat into a symbol of hope. This catalyses the resolution that cannot be achieved in terms of either the physical father *or* the fantasy family of Brian's wishful imaginings. How? Unlike either of these unsatisfactory alternatives the image of the *symbolic* father, the 'real' but dead father, has the unique capability of both liberating the protagonist *from* and affirming him *in* his ancestral identity. Here, then, is where the true quest begins. Boy Staunton's grotesque death impels his son into a Jungian journey back into childhood in *The Manticore*. Alexander MacDonald, the painter-protagonist of Hugh Hood's *White Figure, White Ground*, embarks on a real/symbolic expedition into his family's history in order to reconstruct the father whose overweening presence he had so resented in life. The protagonist of *Surfacing*, in search of her lost father, journeys even more deeply and traumatically into her primaeval roots. The pilgrimage into the past will be discussed more fully in chapter 11. The point to note here, however, is the extent to which such journeys both realize and illuminate the complex pattern of parental/filial relations implicit in *all* versions of the father substitution theme. Whether he is killed or simply repudiated, it is only after the 'real' father is out of the way that the important second phase of the double movement – the search for the *essential* father – can commence.

Hypothetical quests notwithstanding, the bias against real parents entails serious problems when one comes to deal with real families, of course. As the foregoing examples demonstrate, *any* kind of vertical relationship in Canadian literature is almost bound to be problematic. Indeed the masculinization of nature (by rendering ambiguous our exemplary marital model, but even more by evoking a threatening patriarchal God as the ultimate epitomization of 'otherness') and the consequent association of sex with death makes the whole concept of 'family' seem an untenable one. As a result, not merely the relation with parents (who may be seen as overtly dangerous) but even, perhaps through some sort of transference, the relation with children typically appears to focus a considerable degree of anxiety. The child symbol is also connected with the problems of aesthetic creation, which will be discussed in a later chapter, but on one level at least the repudiation of fatherhood/motherhood is a correlative for the repudiation of the father/mother. It thus becomes significant that Canadian literature presents so many childbirth disasters as well as a considerable number of lost (dead) children; real, adopted, and imaginary. *The Vanishing Point*, for instance, juxtaposes Carlyle's frantic search for his lost Indian pupil ('Jesus, dear Jesus, I'll find you, little lost lamb, Virginia!') with the earlier loss of his own wife and daughter. Both Atwood's *Surfacing* and Audrey Thomas's *Blown Figures*, on the other hand, focus on a woman's *internal* quest for/escape from her lost (miscarried/aborted) baby. Mrs Bentley of *As for Me and My House* also lost a child, as did Ethel Wilson's Maggie, along with a husband. In both *A Candle to Light the Sun* and Helwig's *The Day before Tomorrow* the death of an infant literally stops time for the bereaved mothers, signalling not merely the end of the marital relationship but the end of their capacity to relate at all. What John Martens says of his wife is true of both of them: 'Margaret was destroyed. Nothing less dramatic would be true. She has not fully existed since that morning ... We would never have another child, that was clear ... [for] she was entirely shut up in herself' (54-5). In Drew's *The Wabeno Feast* a schoolboy is killed by poisonous gas in an industrial accident. In Engel's *The Glassy Sea* Peggy's son, a hydrocephalic, begins the slow, painful process of dying the moment he is born. In Findley's *The Wars* another hydrocephalic is killed falling from her wheelchair. In Horwood's *White Eskimo* the hero's adopted daughter, a young Indian girl, is literally run to death by authorities who want to incarcerate her in a boarding school. The list of fatalities seems incredible.

Perhaps even the child never conceived in Laurence's *A Jest of God* should be included here. And Joshua's dead uncle/alter ego in *The Burning Wood* is a kind of lost child too. It seems, in fact, that (outside of reminiscences about the protagonists' *own* childhoods) the focal unit in Canadian literature, especially recently, more often than not comprises at most a unit of two. Perhaps this implies something about the fertility of the inverted marriage. Perhaps it simply reflects our suspicion that isolation is not merely a widespread but an essential condition.[20] Certainly it indicates a feeling that beyond the base unit (which already presents problems enough) relations inevitably become strained and complicated; the family fragments and dies. Grove's powerful portraits of failed dynasties illustrate poignantly the felt impossibility of familial continuity in the Canadian setting.

If the army of lost children weren't enough to establish our pattern beyond cavil, in the relatively few cases in the Canadian fictional universe where the family *is* physically intact, the filial/parental relation is almost always shown to be destructive to one or the other party, and often to both. Findley's *The Wars* provides an instructive example. In the earlier parts of this book we see only Mrs Ross's cruelty – her callousness toward Robert after his beloved sister dies, her refusal to come and see him off when he is leaving for overseas ('"I know what you want to do. I know you're going to go away and be a soldier. Well – you can go to hell. I'm not responsible. I'm just another stranger."' 28). Later, however, we realize that her apparent lack of normal maternal feeling is rooted in an *over*-sensitivity rather than the reverse. She simply can't stand the emotional demands that familial relations entail. 'The fact of being loved was difficult: almost intolerable,' she thinks. 'Being loved was letting others feed from your resources – all you had of life was put in jeopardy' (136). We also come to see that this women's 'selfish' impulse to self-protection is neither unnecessary nor irrational. For all her disavowals, the whole time her son is in danger Mrs Ross, suffering increasingly from depression, insomnia, general disorientation, becomes progressively more divorced from reality. When she receives the news that he is missing in action, her withdrawal is suddenly and catastrophically completed; she not only breaks down emotionally but also becomes blind.

Children, being more vulnerable, are even more liable than their parents to sustain damage when familial relations are unstable or unwholesome. This may suggest why, although the childish centre of consciousness is a not uncommon device in Canadian literature (I will examine some of the reasons for this in chapter 10), the mode generally entails a number of effects inconsistent with more conventional usage. Because the sinister, or at least ambiguous, undertones are often obscured by the reader's expectations if not by disparate aspects of their own fictional vehicles, however, this peculiarity has not been generally recognized. Eli Mandel, for instance, sees the predominance of the child particularly in regional literature solely in terms of a traditional primitivistic or pastoral or (as it is sometimes called with relation to art) 'populist' vision.

> Why the Child figure? One obvious reason is that from the adult's point of view the child's vision is a vision of innocence, of a lost Eden; another way of putting this is that the child's vision – again from the adult's point of view – is of home ... [of] the *first* place, the *first* vision of things, the *first* clarity of things. Not realism, then, but rather what in painting is called magic realism, the qualities we associate with Alex Colville's paintings. Perhaps not incidentally, Ron Bloore, one of a regional school of painters, speaks of Colville as a regionalist, presumably because Colville's work evokes with extraordinary clarity objects, people, places in a design at once objective and dream-like. It is precisely the magical clarity, mistaken for accuracy, that we find in Mitchell's superb descriptions of how a boy becomes aware of objects throughout *Who Has Seen the Wind*. (A50)

It is interesting that Mandel cites Colville here – although the association has implications quite different from those he recognizes. While Colville has indeed been compared in the past to regionalists such as Andrew Wyeth, an American painter whose work is pre-eminently characterized by a self-conscious and nostalgic rusticity, the comparison, as Terry Fenton points out, is 'only superficially apt.'[21] Even aside from the numerous technical differences that Fenton cites, Colville's rural landscape is not – whatever Mandel may imply – anything like Wyeth's 'vison of innocence.' Demonstrating a striking congruence in tenor with the whole Canadian oeuvre, in fact, Colville's work (in Michael Greenwood's words) is 'tragic, heavy-laden with the deep presentiment of fate that the Spanish writer Unamuno recognized as a not exceptional condition of the modern psyche and described in the title of his book, *The Tragic Sense of Life*' (36). Does this mean that Mandel makes a mistake when he draws the comparison? Not at all. As we will see in chapter 10, the 'magical clarity' on which he comments is a key stylistic feature of Canadian literature as it is of Canadian art. His only mistake is in thinking it has anything to do with a lost Eden. Colville's painting in fact offers an illuminating parallel with the Canadian child's-eye view of the world specifically because *the child's vision in this country is typically as tragic as his.*

We see this clearly enough if we turn an unbiased eye on the fiction itself. Rosemary Sullivan comments of Marie-Claire Blais' adolescent protagonists that 'they are inevitably maimed or destroyed by the process of maturation – they die of disease or are "crucified by the cupidity" of an adult world where the familiar contents are frustration, suicide, and omnipresent death' (B120), but the 'gothic' world painted by Blais is by no means limited to Quebec. The childhood worlds of *The Last of the Crazy People* and *Lunar Attractions*, for instance, are as nightmarish – as *literally* lethal – as anything we could find in literature. Even more revealingly, there is a decidedly ambiguous aspect even to *Who Has Seen the Wind*, a novel commonly cited as the epitome of Canadian pastoral idylls. In support of this contention it is worth quoting at some length from Warren Tallman's classic essay 'Wolf in the Snow':

Throughout *Who Has Seen the Wind* we are shown [Brian's] growing consciousness of the grim passive cruelty of the prairie and of the only somewhat less grim cruelties of the community. The prairie doesn't care and the townspeople care too much, but in all of the wrong ways. Mitchell would have us understand that Brian attains insight into deep permanent forces of man and nature and so becomes reconciled to the problems of his existence. But if the winds and gods of the prairie and the town are shown ministering to the evolution of a troubled boy's consciousness, there are many reasons to question the nature of their influence. For what Brian actually discovers and enters into is somewhat uneasy communication with a hierarchy of odd and withdrawn persons, most of them caught up as he is in attempting to resolve the dilemma of their alienation from the community ...

It is all but impossible to accept Mitchell's inference that contact with these persons serves to reconcile Brian's consciousness to the 'realities of birth, hunger, satiety, eternity, death.' What he learns, if anything, is that the kinds of suffering which afflict those who are completely alienated from the community are far more damaging than the kinds of suffering which afflict those who are only partly alienated. It isn't surprising that the two most vivid portraits in the novel are those of young Ben and old Sammy, the two most severely withdrawn of all the persons presented. Young Ben appears to Brian in unexpected places and at unpredictable moments with all the suddenness of a hallucination projected from Brian's unconscious. To be Brian in the kind of community Mitchell represents is to be not far from young Ben. And what is old Sammy in his age and insanity but young Ben later on and farther out on the road leading away from contact with other human beings. What but negative lessons can Brian learn from such dissociated beings – so grim a school of lives! (234-5)

Tallman's analysis hardly evokes a 'vision of lost innocence,' does it? The fact is, Brian's world, as innocuous as it may superficially appear, is not merely consonant but contiguous with Colville's doomful landscape. It is fitting that our last glimpse into the boy's mind at the end of the book finds him counting over the deaths he has known. Negative or not, the ultimate lesson the child must learn in the Canadian setting concerns his isolation, not his relation with a family; the lesson, in other words, of his own mortality.

So much for vertical relationships. What are the other possibilities? I mentioned above the unit of two, but, as we saw in the last chapter, marriage – at least *traditional* marriage – is not generally viewed as a likely possibility. *All* traditional modes of relation, in fact, if not ruled out are at least undermined, rendered difficult and even dangerous. If they are to find any sort of antidote to their existential isolation, Canadians, it seems, cannot merely assume the bonds of kinship as an invariable given, either pro *or* con, but must forge new hopes, new securities, perhaps even new fears, from a network of merely *potential* - that is, shifting and largely undefined – roles and relations.

NOTES

1 Jung, 'Marriage as a Psychological Relationship,' *The Portable Jung*, ed. Joseph Campbell (Viking 1971) 172

2 Slotkin, *Regeneration through Violence: The Mythology of the American Frontier, 1600-1860* (Wesleyan U. 1973) 11

3 Scholes, *Structuralism in Literature* (Yale 1974) 197

4 The anima figure was not totally dispossessed, of course. Among some early Christian and gnostic sects she survived – underground, as it were – as *Sophia Sapienta*, emerging once more around the eleventh-twelfth centuries in the cult of the Blessed Virgin and the 'religion' of courtly love. The patriarchal mode, however, certainly dominated mainstream Christianity. For further discussion of Christian misogyny see Edwin Honig, *Dark Conceit: The Making of Allegory* (London 1959), esp. 31-2. For more on subversive survivals, see Jung, *Psychology and Religion* (Yale 1973), esp. 89.

5 See Alan Watts, 'Western Mythology: Its Dissolution and Transformation' in *Myths, Dreams, and Religion*, ed. Joseph Campbell (Dutton 1970) 9-25.

6 Gorer, *The American People: A Study in National Character* (Norton 1964) 30-1. It is true that since the mid-nineteenth century there has been ample evidence of an analogous tendency toward the discrediting of the father's authority in Europe as well, but even aside from the fact that most of the major spokesmen for this trend – like Nietzsche – have consciously been playing a revolutionary and thus counter-cultural role, it must be obvious that there is a great difference between working deliberately to free oneself from what is viewed as a stultifying tradition and accepting that freedom simply as a *donnée*.

7 See Leslie Fiedler, 'Montana: Or the End of Jean-Jacques Rousseau' and 'Adolescence and Maturity in the American Novel' in *The End of Innocence: Essays on Culture and Politics* (Beacon Press 1955).

8 D.H. Lawrence, *Studies in Classic American Literature* (Viking 1964) 59

9 See Otto Rank, 'Female Psychology and Masculine Ideology' in *Beyond Psychology* (Dover 1958), esp. 245.

10 Thompson, 'Introduction: Romanticism and the Gothic Tradition' in *The Gothic Imagination: Essays in Dark Romanticism* (Washington State U. 1974) 5

11 The question arises whether the mutual anti-clerical reaction may be seen, quite simply, as a direct consequence of the repressive influence of established religion in both French and English Canada, rather than implying any special view of 'God' at all. As Ronald Sutherland has pointed out in 'The Calvinist-Jansenist Pantomime'

and elsewhere, inasmuch as both theological traditions have their roots in St Augustine, there is a similar strain of moral rigorousness and puritanism in both cultures. I am perfectly willing to agree that this is so. Nevertheless I would claim that while the Old Testament bias and especially the emphasis on an angry God common to these sects undoubtedly reinforced the tendency to localize fear in a Nobodaddy figure, in itself the theological background does not explain the intensity or the *mode* of the reaction, especially in English Canada where the 'Church' as either institution or social influence is largely ignored and the negative affect projected on individuals of a very specific type.

12 It is interesting to compare this with Birney's 'Vancouver Lights' where he says explicitly 'No one slew Prometheus. Himself he chained/ and consumed his own bright liver' (720). The implication here is clearly that the messianic figure, even aside from being potentially dangerous to the community, is above all dangerous to himself. I will examine this element further in chapter 9.

13 Graves, *The White Goddess* (Faber & Faber 1961) 481

14 It might be argued that the greatly increased interest during the last decade among both academics and writers in Jung, with his emphasis on the anima and the Great Mother, in opposition to the more male-oriented Freud, may in fact testify to a limited resurgence of the authority of the feminine principle, symbolically if not in practice. The Freud/Jung dichotomy will be discussed further in chapter 11.

15 In Patricia Blondal's *A Candle To Light the Sun*, for instance, one of the protagonists, unable to communicate with the police the intangible but (to him) utterly incontrovertible truths rooted in shared experience, community knowledge, suddenly sees the significance of the law officer's detachment:

'Is that why they move you around?' [he asks]

'Move me?'

'The R.C.M.P. So that you never get to be part of a place. The town closed the case.'

'That's why. Now look, if you think of anything else, give me a call.'

'So that you can't change. You're always the same man with a different name.' (300)

16 Michel Zéraffa, *Fictions: The Novel and Social Reality*, trans. Catherine & Tom Burns (Penguin 1976) 130

17 Auerbach, *Mimesis: The Representation of Reality in Western Literature*, trans. Willard R. Trask (Princeton 1968) 463

18 According to Michèle Lalonde the 'irresponsibility' demonstrated by Quebec fiction is quite consistent with and possibly a direct result of the political situation in the province. 'It is disconcerting that violence should have appeared on the scene before the intelligentsia, which had barely given up its belief in Federalism, had had time enough to articulate effectively the terms of the ... struggle for decolonization. In order to have the fact of the bombs sink into our national conscience (which had hardly emerged from the confessional), it was necessary to precipitate the process of politicization and exculpation that at that point had barely begun; for the same

reason, it was necessary to administer large doses of theoretical justifications in an effort to exorcise the moral anguish ... engendered by the "problem" of terrorist violence ... [B]ecause of this obsession with terrorist-style violence and its Marxistic or Maoistic rationalization, little attempt was made to envisage other means, outside the political arena, of unequivocally rejecting the colonizer and resolving our alienation. This paralleled a considerable loss of contact with the popular mentality. Actually the fantastically accelerated phenomenon of religious disaffection ... gave no proof whatever that the people of Quebec had automatically become more highly political or suddenly more receptive to ... guerrilla warfare, and so on. This was clearly shown in the October Crisis, with its enormous undercurrents of collective guilt, together with the symptoms of depression and the swing to the right that followed it ... It is also quite striking that the most audacious spokesmen for *Partis pris* ... finally turned their revolutionary tactics towards fields of cannabis and daisies, of naturalistic mysticism, "peace and love" movements, and universal poetic liberation. This is not very far removed from *Refus global*, which makes us wonder whether revolutions in Quebec can only be spiritual in nature and very personal and interior even then' (in Shouldice 88-9). Under such conditions as this it is not surprising that the literature produced after the fact should reflect feelings of helplessness and unease. It is significant that Claude Jasmin's novel *Ethel et le terroriste*, despite the fact that the author has stated explicitly that he drew on his observations of real people and situations, and that his aim, far from fantasizing, was to understand the psychology and behaviour of the terrorists – essentially mimetic, in other words – offers us a protagonist who is just as ineffectual, as confused, as Aquin's and Carrier's characters. As Jeannette Urbas describes it, 'Paul threw a bomb, but he admits that he was not following any definite theory, nor was he deeply convinced of the validity of his deed. He repeats what he has been told by the Movement that it was necessary to act against his own people in order to show them that they do not have the right to collaborate. The lack of any carefully-thought-out commitment is revealed in the terms he uses to describe himself. He sees himself as a puppet and a robot, a creature without a will of his own manipulated by others. He refers to himself derogatorily as a "conspirator made of chocolate." Even the leaders of the Movement are not consciously in control of their destinies: they are phoney, made of rubber, "papier-maché puppets" that bend to the prejudices of the working-class' (141).

19 In *Survival* Atwood offers a somewhat oversimplified but nevertheless penetrating analysis of this fundamental difference between Canadian and American modes of handling familial relations. 'In American literature the family is something the hero must repudiate and leave; it is the structure he rebels against, thereby defining his own freedom, his own Frontier. *You Can't Go Home Again*, as the Thomas Wolfe novel has it. Once you're out, you must forge your own life, your own private America, out of whatever new materials you can find. An American "family" scene that's repeated over and over is the hero at the train station, lighting out for the Territory. Sons must *by definition* transcend their fathers, in the process rejecting

them. The family, then, is something you come from and get rid of (unless you're from the South; then you commit suicide because you *can't* get rid of it).

'In Canadian literature the family is handled quite differently. If in England the family is a mansion you live in, and if in America it's a skin you shed, then in Canada it's a trap in which you're caught' (131).

20 Otto Rank claims that the urge to procreate is a direct consequence of the recognition of one's own mortality and the compensatory development of a sense of *racial* identity: 'as male or female cells we not only have to procreate but we want to, in order to survive at least collectively' (*Beyond Psychology* 228). Reversing the order of this sequence, we might speculate whether the development of a psychological block to the idea of commonality, of merging with a group, may throw a culture back to the primitive stage at which procreation, with its inevitable associations of corporeality, is viewed as a threat to individual survival.

21 'Local colour and nostalgic description count for far less in Colville's art; colour and a kind of simplified modelling count for much more. Like Lemieux, his figures have a frozen, monumental presence, and his pictures are governed by a stillness reminiscent of Piero della Francesca, which is not characteristic of Wyeth. While Colville isn't a flat colourist like Lemieux, he uses strong, graphic design as a framework for a sense of light which bathes volume and space in a mysterious ambiance. This makes him – despite his provincial associations – less of a populist' (Fenton & Wilkin 101).

8

Fool-Saints and 'Noble' Savages

Felix crouches at the edge, on a sandbank, with a mountain of filthy snow and salt on the other side. Clearly pressed into the wet sand there are the tracks of animals, exquisite icons, he doesn't know what they are, he touches them with his finger. He doesn't know what they mean ... All about him there are signs, strange birds chase each other on an empty sky, he threads through husks of summer plants, their pods open and dry like insects. He does not want them to touch him. The snow is melting, the river grows. Even here, all around him, there are animals. They watch him pass. He doesn't know. (68)

As noted, Graeme Gibson's characters are typically wrapped up in private fantasies. Notwithstanding, there are moments when the world we glimpse through the eyes of his purported deviates seems suddenly so familiar, for all its distortion, that it's as if he has managed to distil something from the common 'langscape' of which we ourselves are hardly aware. The passage quoted above embodies one of those moments. The fact is, Canadians are fascinated by animals. Like Gibson's Felix Oswald, we are haunted by the sense that they carry a crucial message for us, that their superficial 'ordinariness' may at any moment dissolve to reveal some elusive and critical life truth. This intimation is an ambivalent one, however. As a result, though many of our writers have demonstrated a predilection for animal stories, anecdotes, imagery, it's not always clear what they mean to imply by their allusions.

One thing seems certain. The iconic animal signifies something quite different in Canada from what it does in the United States. For the American, more often than not the animal is simply an object – whether antagonist or prey, a means merely by which he may demonstrate his pioneer prowess, a token of his ascendancy over the wilderness. Indeed, as James Polk points out in his comparison of Faulkner's classic story 'The Bear' with Ernest Thompson Seton's *The Biography of a Grizzly*, even in less simplistic treatments in the United States the animal tends to resolve itself 'into a personal symbol illuminating the life of the seeing "I"' (A53). In Canada, on the other hand, the animal is granted a phenomenological status that puts it beyond the reach of the kind of easy imaginative appropriation that such strategies entail. In Alden Nowlan's poem 'Hunters,' for instance, the narrative stance (in Atwood's words) 'hovers tantalizingly between sympathy for the bear and potential fear of it; at any rate, *the bear is real for the narrator in a way that it is not for the Americans*' (F79, italics added).

Even above and beyond this unAmerican intransigence, the Canadian literary animal tends to have a *personal* significance for the human auditor quite different from the abstract numen of Faulkner's totemic beast. This is evident from the fact that Canadians seem to find it more difficult to relate imaginatively to the human aggressor than to his prey. More important (for such a tendency is characteristic as well of certain kinds of popular fiction outside Canada) this preference is *generalized*, apparently unrelated to specific moral questions. It does not, for instance, seem to make any difference whether the act of killing is justified or purely gratuitous. If Nowlan's Sunday hunters are objectionable because of an unsportsmanlike attitude that trivializes – demeans – both the animals and themselves ('He might/as well have bought it and perhaps he did:/guides trap and sell them out by weight/to hunters who don't want to hunt' 32), the *serious* killer mythicized by Hemingway is equally foreign to the Canadian's sense of self. When Richard Thomas in *The Disinherited* sees a movie about bullfighting, he is 'pleased ... to see how many people it took to weaken the bull enough for the matador. The matador himself, making his fancy passes over a half-dead animal, hadn't impressed him at all' (2). Even *need* doesn't seem to change the situation much. As Allison Mitcham points out, despite the fact that Pierre in Gabrielle Roy's *La montagne secrète* is starving, 'He is ... guilt-ridden during his pursuit of the caribou for food because he is obsessed with the perception that [the animal] is closely related to him – his brother as he says' (A26). Lest we write off Pierre as superstitious or over-sensitive, this sort of reflex seems well-nigh universal in Canada – even when it goes against more conscious aspects of self-image. The protagonist's father in *The Watch that Ends the Night* is typical. Theoretically obsessed with warfare, weapons, human and non-human killers, in practice he is as incapable as Pierre of divorcing himself from the point of view of the prey.

[H]is real occupation was ... reading boys' books and battle stories and anything he could find dealing with the habits of snakes, soldiers, sailors and savage beasts. His favorite killer among humans was Genghis Khan, among reptiles the African black mamba, and among animals the Canadian grizzly bear, which he insisted could break the back of a lion if it got in the first blow. He was also the gentlest man I ever knew. He never saw a man die a violent death, he never struck a person in his life and the only animal he ever killed was a groundhog that ate Mother's asparagus. The look of reproach in the eyes of the dying animal haunted him for years, and though rifles and muskets were suspended all over our house, he never bought much ammunition for them and when he did so his targets were bottles and tin cans which he pretended were enemy battleships. He infested our property with traps for skunks, muskrats, otters, squirrels and groundhogs, but when he caught them he always released them. (64-5)

The prevalence of Mr Stewart's type of response perhaps explains the rather peculiar phenomenon observed by Polk whereby 'Sympathetic identification with the hunted is sustained in Canadian animal stories even when the narrator is also the hunter' (A54).

What lies behind such an idiosyncracy? Patricia Morley suggests that our motives might include 'a romantic attraction to the underdog ... humanitarian sensitivity, a mystical feeling for the oneness of creation' (B29). Considering what has already been said about the Canadian feeling for the 'oneness of creation,' we may, I think, dismiss this last possibility, but it is at least theoretically possible that our interest is romantic, humanitarian, in a word, *sentimental*. If this is the case, we are not as far from the Americans as the foregoing observations may suggest. The Sierra Club and the National Rifle Association are simply two sides of the same coin. American-style ecology consciousness generally boils down to a matter of distanced (or retrospective) idealization, compounded with a large dollop of guilt. The identification such a stance implies, however, is almost wholly specious. As Ann Douglas points out, sentimentalism 'asserts that the values a society's activity denies are precisely the ones it cherishes; it attempts to deal with the phenomenon of cultural bifurcation by the manipulation of nostalgia. Sentimentalism provides a way to protest a power to which one has already in part capitulated.'[1]

To what extent is this an operative factor in the Canadian response? Morley notwithstanding, there are good reasons for thinking that the 'romantic' component is minimal. For one thing, animals in Canadian literature are typically no more 'good' or 'cute' than nature is benevolent and motherly. *The Heart of the Ancient Wood*, examined above, is far from anomalous. Indeed, both in the early stories of Roberts and Seton *and*, almost without exception, in the work of their literary descendants, the approach, if biased toward the animal, is not merely realistic but explicitly anti-sentimental. The lesson Lilka must learn in Fred Bodsworth's *The Atonement of Ashley Morden*, for instance, if less traumatic is substantively reminiscent of Miranda's experience. '[S]he began to acquire ... a more intimate insight into the forest as it really was – the intrinsic ruthlessness of its unending struggle for survival, the life-and-death pitting of wits and brawn between the hunters and the hunted. And despite her love for all of them, Lilka saw the struggle as neither good nor bad, right nor wrong, but simply nature as it was' (382). Note the reference to 'love.' Objectivity does not debar feeling. The *kind* of identification felt with animals in this country, however, is significantly different from the Sierra Clubber's proprietary affection. Although there is an almost total absence of Walt Disney-type anthropomorphism in Canadian literature ('a writer would think twice before turning an Ontario wolf and a Jasper Park grizzly into miniature persons with shoes, hats, and big vocabularies,' says Polk B9), the intangible but inescapable message we derive is that animals are somehow contiguous with 'self' rather than 'other.'

Timothy Findley's *The Wars* provides an instructive example. On the surface the conventional guilt motive seems to offer an adequate explanation for the protagonist's behaviour. Before he leaves for the war, Robert Ross is clearly on the side of the hunters. He has inherited from his father a romantic ideal of chivalry, a boy's yearning for greatness and adventure. If nothing else, his concern with getting an appropriate sidearm – a motif that runs through the whole period of his training and transshipment – pointedly signals his conscious alignment. So far we seem set up for a fully conventional treatment of a fully conventional ironic theme. The climax when it comes, moreover, seems quite predictable, a sudden, traumatic change of heart rooted specifically in the protagonist's recognition of the suffering – symbolized by (though not limited to) the dumb suffering of the draft animals in his charge – that the 'heroic' stance entails. His shift of allegiance in the end from his human co-predators to the helpless creatures that are their prey, his desertion and (doomed) attempt to rescue a herd of trapped animals from the front lines, may therefore be seen primarily as an act of atonement for his complicity in the brutality of war:

The barns were a heap of burning rubble ... All the horses and mules were either dead or were dying. It appeared that only Robert had survived.

He got out the Webley, meaning to shoot the animals not yet dead, when he paused for the barest moment looking at the whole scene laid out before him and his anger rose to such a pitch that he feared he was going to go over into madness. He ... thought: 'If an animal had done this – we would call it mad and shoot it' and at that precise moment Captain Leather rose to his knees and began to struggle to his feet. Robert shot him between the eyes.

It took him half-an-hour to kill the mules and horses. Then he tore the lapels from his uniform and left the battlefield. (178)

Read in this way, Robert's moment of truth, though it has far more catastrophic results, is not substantially different from Hemingway's Nick Adams' realization, as he lies wounded in Italy, of the emptiness of patriotic slogans and his decision to make a 'separate peace.'[2]

This is not the whole implication of Findley's story, however. There are odd undertones, emotional loose ends, that we can't tuck away quite so neatly. At that moment when Robert makes his fateful choice, walks away from the battle, it seems less like a departure than as if, in some mysterious way, he has come home. Appropriately enough, it is here, at this moment, that the novel begins. 'She was standing in the middle of the railroad tracks. Her head was bowed and her right front hoof was raised as if she rested ... Lying beside her there was a dog with its head between its paws and its ears erect and listening ... She greeted him with a snuffling noise and looked around to watch him as he adjusted her saddle and tightened her cinch. The dog, in the meantime, had got to his feet and was wagging his tail. *It was as if both dog and horse had been waiting for Robert to come for them'* (9, italics added). Rodwell, the naturalist who kills himself when he is unable to stop a group of fear-crazed soldiers from torturing rats, perhaps sensed something of this when he included Robert in his sketchbook. 'Of maybe a hundred sketches, Robert's was the only human form. Modified and mutated – he was one with the others' (138). There is more than a slight suggestion in this book, in fact, that Robert Ross – and in numerous aspects of character and experience, this man resembles closely the type Canadian protagonist – is not merely making a symbolic repudiation, a gesture of defiance, by going off with the horses but *has belonged with the animals all along.*

The fact is, humanitarian *sympathy*, even when tacitly energized by a post-sixties American-style communal sense of guilt-by-association for the rape of the land, entails a kind of detachment that neither Robert Ross nor the average Canadian seems capable of achieving. This becomes clear when we see that the fictional Canadian is characteristically fascinated by the animal victim even, or particularly, when its suffering is caused not by man but by an accident of fate for which no one need feel the slightest complicity or guilt. In Marian Engel's *The Glassy Sea*, for instance, the protagonist is so obsessed with an old horse's death that it comes to seem a kind of negative epiphany for her. 'I dreamed about it, night after night,' she says, 'a white horse and a thunderbolt coming down and the blinkered thing not knowing: oh, it bothered me' (14). Such a feeling – an overpowering and apparently spontaneous sense not merely of sympathy but of *empathy* with the damaged beast – may be glimpsed in incident after incident throughout the corpus. Aside from anything else, the usage seems to indicate that the animal is not, as it is for the Americans, a symbol of nature, but, rather, nature's victim – just as we ourselves are.

It seems clear, then, that for the Canadian the animal kingdom represents in an important sense man's own condition. The helplessness of the animal, its inability to withstand predators, accidents, even its own savage nature, is ours.[3] Animal symbols consequently may be and are used for a much wider range of signification in Canadian than in American literature, serving a variety of narrative functions from the simple thematic counterpoint provided by the recurring motifs of dead or mutilated animals in *Who Has Seen the Wind* through the more complex invocations of animal-as-alter-ego we find in *The Studhorse Man* to the diffuse animal imagery which, reverberant with intimations of existential terror in its unbearable conflation of predator and prey, is a common feature of the contemporary French-Canadian oeuvre.[4] The question is, what does this tendency to empathetic – rather than merely sympathetic – identification reveal about the Canadian self-image? Margaret Atwood's popular study, *Survival*, suggests that the psychological ground to the response is both simple and negative, signalling the presence of a pervasive 'victim mentality.' Canadians, she says, 'feel threatened and nearly extinct as a nation, and suffer also from life-denying experience as individuals.' Their spontaneous identification with the hunted in animal stories is therefore simply 'the expression of a deep-seated cultural fear' triggered by the recognition of a homologous life situation. For the Canadian, as for the Canadian animal, 'bare survival is the main aim in life, failure as an individual is inevitable, and extinction as a species is a distinct possibility' (79). Our affinity with animals thus signals nothing more profound than the fact that like attracts like.

Is the situation really as straightforward as Atwood's confident analysis implies? Certainly there is ample evidence that a victim mentality *is* in fact an important component of the Canadian psychological profile. With such a world view as we established in earlier chapters it would perhaps be more surprising if this were *not* the case. It is consequently hard to dodge the conviction that our concern with animals is, as Atwood claims, connected directly with a kind of communal paranoia, perhaps even outright masochism. This somewhat unpalatable conclusion is reinforced, moreover, when we note how frequently it turns out to be not merely the vulnerability of the animal but its actual suffering that makes it a locus of emotional energy in Canadian fiction. In Graeme Gibson's *Five Legs*, for instance, anecdotes about deformed or crippled animals are juxtaposed consistently with such images of human entrapment as the Girl in the Iron Lung ('SHE WILL NEVER GET OUT' 107). In *Communion* the association is made even more directly through Felix's self-identification with the sick, caged husky. Other elements in other books, however, seem to hint that this is not *all* the Canadian sees in animals; that if the animal *qua* victim is in some ways an irresistible image of 'self,' there are other and perhaps more important sides to the animal symbol that the too-exclusive focus on a victim mentality may obscure.

One possibility glossed over in Atwood's approach is that the animal, besides demonstrating the omnipresence of suffering and death (a message to which we are already all too well attuned), actually teaches us something about *living*. This is what Morley would claim. 'I have no quarrel with the word "survival" or the experience it connotes as a theme central to Canadian literature and life,' she says. 'My quarrel is with Atwood's extremely negative interpretation of the concept. She speaks of "bare" survival, "grim" survival ... in terms of an inner-directed will to fail. I believe that survival under difficult conditions is a positive, an affirmative act' (B22). Morley's determination to grind this particular axe leads her to stress the superficial sweetness and light a little too much in her readings of Canadian literature, closing her eyes to any ambiguous undertones. She is right, however, when she hints that there is more than one way to respond to a victim's lot. And it is the *way* one fails, not the fact of failure that is important. As Polk says of Seton's grizzlies, in fact, it is quite possible that the real importance to us of the exemplary animal lies in its 'struggle to survive and heroically accept a defeat which is inevitable' (A53). The animal, in other words, shows us how to live as long or at least as well as we can, *and* how to come to terms with the inescapable fact of death.

What particular lessons are we offered in this regard? In Aritha Van Herk's *Judith*, the pigs obviously represent some standard of 'naturalness.' Their response to Judith and Judith's response to them, progressing from initial nervousness to a kind of embarrassed love, affords a means of charting also her progress in shedding her self-destructive and artificial city identity: 'Layer by layer she shed the accumulation of those years, the thickness between herself and her surface growing smaller and smaller each day until she could feel through her skin the push of bones, their angular fragility. And she lost her stiffness, the jerky awareness that had carved her movements for so long, fluid and shapely she slid around the pigs, moved between them like a sorceress' (146-7). Van Herk's tale, despite the total absence of an idealized landscape (all we see of the farm itself is mud and snow), is a little too close in emphasis to the American back-to-nature myth to be truly representative, however. More often than this kind of romantic celebration of spontaneousness, literary animals are seen in Canadian fiction as presenting some kind of specifically *moral* lesson for the human auditors.

This emphasis can be traced all the way back to Roberts and Seton. The animal story, says Robert MacDonald, 'is part of a popular revolt against Darwinian determinism, and is an affirmation of man's need for ... spiritual values. The animal world provides models of virtue, and exemplifies the order of nature. The works of Seton and Roberts are thus celebrations of rational, ethical animals, who ... rise above instinct' (18). Hold on a moment, though. Is not the imputation of 'virtue' to 'the order of nature' just as contrary and, in a different way, as romantic as Van Herk's more modern brand of primitivism? Yes – and to the extent that the animals of Seton and Roberts are mythicized, transformed into 'symbols of a more perfect world,' as MacDonald puts it (27), they strike us today as rather naive creations.[5] Once one scrapes away the rhetoric, however, this tendency toward idealism is a much less noticeable feature of early Canadian animal stories than MacDonald would suggest. Indeed, even in Roberts and Seton the *kind* of moral lesson to be inferred is similar at root to the wholly realistic brand of 'morality' offered by Fred Bodsworth's recent, more sophisticated productions.

What does this morality comprise? We find the basic themes presented explicitly in *The Atonement of Ashley Morden*. There are two kinds of animals, Bodsworth says: wolves and doves. *Both* (in contradistinction to the popular stereotypes) have aggressive instincts, and both have different mechanisms for regulating these. With the latter group, since killing is a slow business, it is largely a matter of the defeated individual's ability to flee beyond his conqueror's territory ('[T]he weak ones – the small birds, the rabbits – could fight this way without doing much harm to each other, because they had little in the way of weapons with which to fight. They could fight to the death only if they were penned up unnaturally in cages ... only if the vanquished was kept constantly available for repeated attacks of the victor.' 352). With the former, on the other hand, unnecessary destruction is averted by means of an inhibition against aggression toward any individual who has ritually submitted ('"They are all the same... birds, mammals, any of them with weapons that are capable of swift and widespread killing. All the defeated one has to do is offer the victor a clean, wide-open killing opportunity and it immediately produces a psychological block in the victor that prevents it from completing the kill."' 454-5). Humans having unnaturally acquired their weapons combine the worst of both groups. They are as lethal as the wolves but lack the 'ethical' imprint that would forbid the persecution of those who are weaker or simply less aggressive than themselves. There is ample evidence to suggest that Bodsworth's view represents a consensual one for Canadians. When Peter Such relates in *Riverrun* how white furriers attacking a Beothuk encampment catch one member of the group without her snowshoes and knife her through the chest as she kneels 'with her robe drawn open to show she [is] a woman' (29), we find the incident despicable but unsurprising. We have no difficulty at all, it would seem, believing that humans are to their own detriment more destructive than any animal.

'To their own detriment.' This brings us to an important point. Leaving aside the purely didactic content of Bodsworth's fable, what we have here, for all that it is couched in moral terms (the 'clean' kill of nature versus fire-bombing, Nazi concentration camps, and biological warfare), is actually something quite pragmatic: hints on how to survive in the 'wilds,' a simple and valuable object lesson. If at a primary level of signification the animal kingdom provides an effective symbolic correlative for 'a savage, meaningless world, "red in tooth and claw,"' a secondary and perhaps more important function of the animal-symbol is the exemplification of a *safe*, rather than merely an ethical life-stance.

Bodsworth's novel makes this point succinctly. The arch-aggressor, Roger Dork, is killed by the wolf while the meek, retiring Ashley Morden survives to win the girl. Bodsworth's vision is not an unusual one. For the Canadian, the kind of defensive strategies commonly observed in animal behaviour – flight, concealment, disguise, submissiveness, passive non-resistance, and so on –

almost always seem to represent the best chance for survival. It is hence a defensive stance rather than American-style heroism that we find touted most often in Canadian writing. '[I]t is the retreat and not the resistance which Pratt celebrates,' says Douglas Jones (A115); 'Birney tends to walk with vigilance through a world of strangers, where courage and ingenuity are primarily defensive' (126); 'Only when he is prepared to accept his final, if not immediate engulfment, shall [man] find comfort, love, communion ... This is the burden of Miss Macpherson's "Ark Overwhelmed"' (127). We could extend this list to include a goodly proportion of Canada's best writers. Indeed, if one examines the corpus as a whole, it seems clear that assumption of a victim position is *not*, as Atwood seems to infer, commonly viewed by Canadians in a negative light at all. When the 'other' is by definition unbeatable, submission is not masochistic but sensible. 'Canadian experience teaches two clear lessons,' says historian W. L. Morton. 'One is that the only real victories are the victories over defeat ... And our experience teaches also that what is important is not to have triumphed, but to have endured' (A112). If a disturbing number of the inhabitants of the Canadian literary universe are 'losers,' therefore, it's perhaps simply because, in Stephen Scobie's words, 'they have *chosen* to be' (C7). With all this we can understand why many of the animals offered by recent Canadian writers as either exemplars or emblems of 'self,' rather than the beautiful, deadly predators preferred by the romantic, tend to be small and shy and peaceable: Souster's hibernating groundhog or Purdy's Beavers of Renfrew with their 'secret of staying completely still.' As Helwig's John Martens demonstrates so vividly, theirs is the experience to which the Canadian can best relate:

When I'd wake after a nightmare, I'd search for some comforting thought to lead me back toward sleep. It was hard, at first, to find the right thing. Most of the things would draw me back toward the past, toward memories that I wasn't yet strong enough to sustain. Finally, I found a perfect method. I'd imagine that I was an animal, a sort of groundhog, but nothing that specific, just something small and furry and brown curled up in the darkness under the earth. I'd imagine layers of earth above me and the snow above that, but I wouldn't imagine the light shining on the snow. When I reached the snow, I'd start back down through all the whiteness of the snow, then the earth with roots and larvae buried there, then myself passing the winter. (A170)

The Canadian as groundhog: here is where we find what is probably, after the sex inversion (to which it is, of course, intimately linked), the key to one of the most crucial aspects of the national character. Does this seem improbable? Even if there weren't detectable peculiarities in our usage, the sheer ubiquitousness of the animal symbol in both prose and poetry would tend to suggest that it represents something more than merely an interesting but minor sidelight to our national literary practice. The *way* it is used, however – the kind of emotional authority it exerts and, most important, the particular values with which it is associated – makes it invaluable to us as a diagnostic tool. Far from being simply a peripheral or subsidiary motif, the animal symbol both reflects *and* elucidates some of the most striking idiosyncracies of our communal self-image. The fact is, if meekness is viewed as a survival trait in Canada, this explains, *without* requiring improbable (not to mention unpalatable) postulates of nation-wide masochism, the phenomenon noted (usually with disapproval) by numerous critics: our fascination with what we might call a *passive role model*. Here is the first and most basic of those new exemplary modes I predicted. Which brings us, finally, to the real point of this chapter. As hinted in the title, one of the most interesting versions of this figure – indeed, judging by both the frequency with which he is invoked and the amount of numen he carries, a virtual prototype for the species – is the 'fool-saint' or holy innocent.

Normally the appearance of a fool-saint in literature would signal a primitivistic bias (either romantic or ironic), but in the Canadian version we can detect a slight but significant departure from convention. Again it is a question of emphasis. In traditional practice the fool-saint is valued primarily for his/her instinctive 'goodness,' and certainly there is a strong element of this in the Canadian usage. Robertson Davies' Mrs Dempster, for instance, is not only shown in her amorality to be more charitable than the good Christians of the town (giving away her belongings, submitting to the sexual needs of the tramp), but is associated, at least in Dunstan's mind, with the truly miraculous. First she apparently brings his brother back from death; later – appearing to him in a vision at the moment of his wounding in battle – she symbolically presides over his own improbable recovery. Since she is explicitly conflated with the little Virgin he glimpses in the ruins on that crucial occasion, moreover, her efficacy, it is implied, is not merely natural in derivation but divine. Even in Mrs Dempster's case, however, it is not this particular aspect of her character – her holiness – that seems of primary importance to her exemplary function. Indeed, sidestepping the supernatural element that he himself has invoked, Davies brings the whole question of miracles down to the level of subjective experience. And at this level, if we examine the evidence of the text, for all Dunstan's academic fascination with saints and personal fascination with the little Madonna, what really seems to intrigue him about Mrs Dempster is her capacity to be *happy*:

[T]ied up in a rotten little house without a friend except me, [she] seemed to live in a world of trust that had nothing of the stricken, lifeless, unreal quality of religion about it. She knew she was in disgrace with the world, but did not feel disgraced; she knew she was jeered at, but felt no humiliation. She lived by a light that arose from within; I could not comprehend it, except that it seemed to be somewhat akin to the splendours I found in books, though not in any way bookish. It was as though she were an exile from a world that saw things her way, and though she was sorry Deptford did not understand her she was not resentful. When you got past her shyness she had quite positive opinions, but the queerest thing about her was that she had no fear. (a48)

The fool-saint, passive, peaceful, *accepting*, thus seems, even more than the animal (whose inherent dumbness is something to which we cannot very well aspire), to hold the secret for escaping from the terrors of the existential world.

We see this phenomenon even more clearly in Adele Wiseman's *Crackpot*. Fat Hoda, who is in many ways a representative Canadian protagonist, afflicted by flesh, frustrated in every effort at communication, baffled and frightened by the irrationalities of existence, only becomes less happy, less hopeful, as she gains maturity. Her father, blind Danile, on the other hand, for all his helplessness is able to remain cheerful despite the sordidness and uncertainty of the life they are forced to lead. It is not, Wiseman makes clear, that his saintliness wins him divine protection (the misfortunes he has to weather make a mockery of this particular piece of folklore), nor that in his innocence – like the 'dumb' fairytale hero – he instinctively makes the right choices, performs the tasks that are 'rationally' impossible, wins through by sheer hunch to the treasure that is the object of the quest. No, indeed. Though both Danile's goodness and his ostensible 'foolish wisdom' are conventionally underlined in the book, the only reason he survives is because there has always been someone to take care of him. What his saintliness does do, however, is to protect him from *awareness* of his miserable state. His innocence, a kind of spiritual blindness that parallels his physical disability, is simply a kind of protective armour. 'It would take a bludgeon,' thinks Hoda '... to break its way through that amazingly tough shell of softness, in which the most obvious revelation of the truth lost its shape and disappeared' (171). Thus, although Danile lives in a 'dark abyss,' he does not know it (179). His imperfect awareness makes it possible for him to create a 'great myth' out of 'inner pattern,' and in doing so, to impose his personal order on 'the fragments of a disordered world' (78, 92). Even aside from his exemplification of the 'safe' submissive stance, it is this capacity for ignorant faith that makes the fool-saint such an apposite role model for the Canadian. Victim and survivor both, this unlikely creature is not merely our most plausible but our most attractive alter ego.

Or is he?

Just to complicate things, there is another whole side to this picture that must be considered. As much as his innocence appeals to our Canadian impulse to withdraw into the self, the fool-saint's very pliancy seems suspect to us. Most important, perhaps, is the fact that the mode is so blatantly inconsistent with our conditioned allegiance to an American value system. According to frontier mythology, passiveness is effeminate, cowardly, despicable – perhaps even subversive.[6] This circumstance – another version of the idiom/vision split – has obvious consequences if not for the deep-seatedness of our tendency toward self-identification with the passive exemplar, at least for our *feelings* about that tendency. Given the context, in fact, moral/emotional conflict is almost inevitable. How do Canadians respond to such conflict? We find a paradigmatic demonstration in the novels of Morley Callaghan, particularly *The Loved and the Lost*. Inasmuch as Peggy Sanderson shares many of the features of the conventional fool-saint – she is serenely self-contained, totally oblivious to evil and danger, wholly instinctual – Jim McAlpine's response to her, a chaotic mixture of fascination and repugnance, mirrors strikingly our own ambivalence about the kind of experience, the kind of life-stance she represents.

To mirror is not to resolve, of course. Even aesthetically. More questions are raised than answered, both in and by this novel. In the foreground is simply the question of whether or not the girl's innocence is genuine. Jim himself is unable to decide one way or the other. Indeed, his vacillation on this point provides the primary dynamic of the book. The worm in the apple – at least on this level – is sex. For reasons slightly different on each side of the border (the American, terrified that he will be robbed of his individuality by domesticity, fears that sex will turn to love – that is, permanent involvement – while the Canadian, if anything, fears that it won't), North Americans find it difficult to believe that sex is *ever* really innocent. Everything Peggy does, therefore, seems to Jim to have a double meaning. 'Her own life could be blameless. But was there another side to her nature suggested by her actions? Blamelessness could be carried too far – it could have dreadful consequences. When he had tried to kiss her, she had been blameless; she had merely turned her head away. But it could have been taken as a coy gesture' (48-9). Jim is not as sceptical as the black bandleader Wagstaffe with his Browningesque resentment of her promiscuous smiles ('"You think she offers it just for you, and then you see it's no more for you than the next guy. A bum is a bum in my race as well as yours. A girl ought to have some discrimination, not make it cheap."' 103); he is, moreover, motivated to trust her ('He wanted to believe completely in her own pure feeling' 65). Nevertheless, Peggy seems so alien to him that he has almost as much difficulty as her more casual acquaintances taking her at face value. 'The point is,' says Edmund Wilson, 'that none of these people can rise to the level of believing that such a person as she exists' (61).

The problems don't end here. Even if we accept that the innocence is real enough, Callaghan raises the further and even more serious question whether the quality is in ultimate terms beneficial. Peggy's 'serenity' at times makes her callous, which detracts considerably from her emotional if not moral authority. More to the point, it also makes her stupid. In life, unpleasant realities do not go away simply because one refuses to acknowledge them. In life, in fact, the ostrich stance is more likely than not to facilitate the growth of social malignancy. And Peggy's case is no exception. For all its short-term efficacy as a 'shield,' her obtuseness, as the book makes clear, is not merely contributory to, but very possibly a sole cause for the near-riot that erupts when her detractors and protectors clash. More serious, to the extent that it invites misunderstanding, it is very possibly a major factor in her own rape. Does this mean that pure-mindedness, tolerance, and disinterest are in themselves worthless, an opening if not an invitation to evil? Callaghan himself, as Stephen Scobie writes in his paper on Canadian 'saints,' seems ultimately unsure:

The issue is not really one of Peggy's naivety, or lack of prudence ... but to what extent Peggy really does explore the dark areas of human consciousness about death, madness, and sexuality. Callaghan's refusal, for whatever reason, to give us any extended insight into Peggy's mind, makes this very difficult to decide. Peggy's vision of the reality she is accepting is actually very superficial: she refuses to accept the undercurrents of hate and violence which are visible even to McAlpine at first glance. When the violence finally does erupt, Peggy runs. She is shocked and horrified by the fight at the cafe, and afterwards she is fully prepared to deny her own vision ... [She thus] dies deeply compromised. After her death, McAlpine (and Callaghan too?) attempt to ignore (or are simply unaware of?) this change, and talk of Peggy entirely as she was before the essential shallowness of her position had been revealed. To repeat: a saint can go beyond the intellect but not stop short of it. There is no virtue in facing something that you don't even know is there. (c8-9)

Scobie's own view is flawed by his failure to recognize the at least potential iconic value of Peggy's passiveness – as his insistence on the importance of 'facing things' reveals, he has a tendency to confuse our home-grown saint with the more militant (that is, heroic) American version – but nevertheless, and perhaps all the more effectively for that flaw, he puts his finger on some of the obvious difficulties presented by this figure in Canadian literature despite, or because of, its evident appeal to the Canadian imagination.

If this were as far as it went, the phenomenon of the Canadian fool-saint would be interesting but hardly exceptional. The philosophical implications of 'innocence' have been and no doubt will continue to be a staple of literature far beyond these shores. Other, more covert aspects of the Canadian practice, however, seem to indicate that the archetype localizes even more deep-seated anxiety here than Callaghan's fairly rational treatment of the problem implies. Never mind whether the saint is *admirable* or not, the Canadian seems unsure about the extent to which his 'holy' innocent – and by extension himself – must be seen as actually monstrous, an abomination, rather than somebody merely pitiable. On the most basic level, there is a persistent question about whether, ultimately, the creature is wholesome or diseased. Even apart from the fact that a significant number of explicitly saintly figures seem to suffer some sort of physical disability like Danile's blindness, many of the sick or crippled individuals found in Canadian literature not only demonstrate the same quirks of personality and attitude as the saint (thus reflecting on his moral status simply by association), but also catalyse the same mixture of attraction and repugnance in the protagonists who warily circle their quiescent centres.

The ambiguity entailed by the attribution of unusual numen to the physically disabled is not always readily apparent. George Stewart of *The Watch that Ends the Night* both pities his semi-invalid wife for her increasing debility and admires the courage and serenity she exhibits in facing it. In Catherine's case, however, the equation between a physical weakness and a spiritual strength is literal. She *is* a beautiful and courageous woman, and her illness makes her *more* rather than less so. She herself hints at both the source of her equanimity *and* the reason for her husband's fascination in her description of Martell's adopted mother: '"People like her are the strongest in the world. They ask so little for themselves that almost nothing can be taken away from them. And they accept so much that almost nothing can be added heavy enough to break them"' (215). Suffering, in other words, is conducive to peace of mind. Though it seems paradoxical at first, it is actually quite *rational*, therefore, that George should laud the 'strength' of a woman who is to all outward intents a kind of cripple. In other cases, though, both the handicapped subjects and the observer's reaction are presented far more equivocally. In contrast to *The Watch*, where George's negative feelings surface only briefly and vestigially,[7] in Mordecai Richler's *St Urbain's Horseman* the inherent duplicity of the cripple symbol is exploited quite openly as an element of theme. On the one hand, Jake claims to be disgusted by the sensationalization of the sick and maimed (the amputees who paint with their toes, the girl who cooks from an iron lung, the colostomized actor who is proclaimed as having 'triumphed' over cancer) because the public adulation of these disadvantaged individuals perversely obscures the fact that health *is* preferable to disease. Beneath this ostentatious disapproval, though, his fascination with the handicapped has yet another side which, in terms of Richler's moral dynamic, is considerably less defensible. 'Sadly,' Moss points out, 'there is perhaps a touch of jealousy in Jake's response' (ab160). Hypocrisy aside, the extent to which the reader is implicated in Jake's ambivalence suggests that in such a setting it is difficult to hold up the cripple as an unmixed symbol, either positive or negative.

In some ways, of course, Richler's handling of this theme is just as conventional as MacLennan's. Notwithstanding his evident conviction that his protagonist's attitude is in some way reprehensible, any ambiguity localized in the figure of the cripple is pinned to – explained away by – a quite unexceptionable moral scheme. On the surface it would seem that these people are adulated (both overtly by the public and *covertly* by Jake) solely because of what may be seen as 'heroic' qualities – their battle *against* rather than submission to an unkind fate. Jake's envy of the amputees, for instance, is clearly traceable to his awareness, in Moss's words, that 'he has not been able to surmount obstacles within his own personality of a much less dramatic nature' (Ab 160). On the other hand, the mere fact that sick and mutilated individuals recur with such implausible frequency in Richler's works (*The Apprenticeship of Duddy Kravitz* is also full of them, from Wonder-Boy Dingle through to Duddy's paraplegic partner), and that they carry such a tangible if inexplicit burden of significance, would seem to hint that there is something more involved – whether quirk of vision or more basic emotional idiosyncracy – than the conventional reading may imply.

The same thing might be said of Canadian literature as a whole. Not only is it oddly overburdened with mutilations and amputations (Dunstan Ramsay, Pandora's father, Joseph of *La guerre, yes sir!*, and the trapper in *Scann*, to instance only a few, are all missing one or more parts), not to mention wasting ailments (old Esau of *The Vanishing Point*, Pauline Archange's mother, Jules Tonnerre in *The Diviners*, Rahel in *Crackpot*), but the victims of these various disabilities are not in general viewed as conventional usage would dictate. For one thing, they are more likely to be envied, even feared, than pitied. The anomalous response is often disguised by superficial sympathy, mockery, or disgust, but it may be clearly discerned in the tendency to attribute the handicapped with either secret wisdom (as in the case of Jerry Quirk, the armless, legless schoolteacher who becomes Keneally's mentor) or a magical capacity for survival (without, seemingly, any effort on his own part, Harlow's trapper, for instance, exerts some mysterious influence that makes his sworn enemy rescue him from the wilderness at the risk even of his own life). This fact alone already strikes a peculiar note. Secondly, Richler notwithstanding, the focus for this envy is, quite specifically, their helplessness rather than any 'heroic' attempt at compensatory self-assertion. As Carrier's Philibert watches the procession of deformed children going to the church to be blessed, for instance, he is struck by the conviction that it is he, the healthy one, who is unlucky, not they with their 'blissful' smiles and 'lifeless eyes.' 'He wished he could be taken for a ride in a wheelbarrow like those worms with children's heads. But nobody ever took him for a walk. He was condemned always to walk on his own legs. It wasn't fair' (B19). The cripple in Canadian literature thus becomes iconic for almost exactly the same reason as the saint, because his externally imposed impotence in one way or another protects him from the vicissitudes of life: the necessity of striving and the inevitability of failure. At the same time, because he is by definition abnormal, diseased, or deformed, he both symbolizes and exacerbates our self-disgust for our identification with the passive stance. And this in turn adds further ambiguity to the figure of the fool-saint who exemplifies this stance.

The ambiguities don't stop here. If the moral/emotional authority of the fool-saint is undercut by his association with physical debility, he is even more severely compromised by imputations about the soundness of his mental state. In traditional terms the figure is by definition simple-minded anyway, but in Canada there is a tendency for this kind of mild congenital condition to be extended into outright insanity. Mrs Dempster, Dunstan's little Madonna, ends up in an asylum. Saint Sammy of *Who Has Heard the Wind*, for all his imputed harmony with the powers of nature, is a lunatic living in a piano box out on the prairie. Even more striking, Father Dowling, the compassionate priest of Callaghan's *Such Is My Beloved*, becomes mad, it is implied, as a direct result of his saintliness. Unable to find any 'way out of the clash between the law of the Church and his personal gospel of love ... He can merely withdraw from the troubled world into the sanctuary of his own now deranged mind' (Watt 122). As in the case of physical ailments, moreover, the associations become so entrenched that there is a tendency to infer tacit connections even with deranged individuals who have no hint of holiness about them.

In some cases, this kind of cross-referencing is harmless, of course. Just as Catherine's example could only reflect well on the saintly ideal, if 'madness' is shown to be a positive feature the damage is minimal. Alice Munro's 'The Dance of the Happy Shades,' a story detailing the discomfort felt by a group of suburban mothers when, due to the gaucheness of the local music teacher, their children's annual party-recital is infiltrated by a group of retarded youngsters, is a prime example. Not only does it turn out that one of these 'handicapped' children has a natural genius for music that far outstrips the plodding efforts of their own offspring, but, as the title implies with what Rae McCarthy MacDonald calls 'illuminating irony,' we are made to realize before the end of the story that 'Miss Marsalles and the "idiot" children, though strictly excluded from "the world" are, nonetheless, happy ghosts who know a measure of feeling and freedom lost to the nervous mothers in their social garrison' (367). Munro's message here is thus quite similar to, say, Wiseman's in *Crackpot*. If life itself is (in MacDonald's words) cruel and deforming, then it is both reasonable and possible to claim that those 'who appear to adapt or cope and survive' may be 'more deformed in an internal, spiritual way, than those who are clearly retarded or maimed and unable to enter the struggle'; further, that 'obviously defective people seem better off and freer than those who have found acceptance in a "normal" world' (369). The situation is rarely perceived in such simple terms, however. Even leaving aside the ambiguities that even a Danile presents, to the extent that madness in its more virulent forms may be far more destructive than the simple retardation that marks its nearer bounds (we need only think of *La belle bête* for a devastating example), *any* tendency that underlines the association between derangement and the saintly role must needs affect our view of the latter.

If these built-in problems weren't enough, again the 'American' ideology that haunts our literary landscape like a kind of ghost of Christmas past, reminding us of our aberrations, adds further complications to our response. If, according to the frontier mythos, the victim stance is *in general* a reprehensible one, the madman in particular has nevertheless acquired a certain numen in the last few decades in the American novel. At first sight this seems to reveal an existentialist leaning. In European terms the madman, exemplifying as he does the hopelessness of the human condition, is the anti-hero par excellence. 'Anti-heroic fiction,' says Michael Woolf, 'reflects a view of reality that grew out of ... the realization that the individual's capacity to effect changes or to control the direction of his own experience was severely limited. The individual was revealed as powerless, buffeted by forces too massive, too nightmarish. Society no longer seemed to have an accessible logic, was no longer hospitable to man.' So far this sounds much like the picture we have evolved of the Canadian vision, does it not? There is more: 'Clearly there is no obvious manner in which heroic action can be framed convincingly within [such a version] of reality ... In this view the only possibility is simple survival and even this is rendered precarious. The qualities necessary to obtain that objective are hardly heroic – stoic patience and a capacity to bear the pressures emanating from a nightmarish environment.'[8] Surely any literary practice based on a world view like this has to be consonant with our own. The problem is, though, that same American dislike for admitting limits mentioned in our discussion of existentialism above works covertly to counteract the base terms of the articulated vision. Even when the American specifically invokes a universe that entails limitation as a *general* condition, he is inclined to cling to the illusion that heroic action is possible on at least an *individual* basis. As a result, the American literary madman and his Canadian cousin are actually miles apart.

How? In the first place, in many American novels the 'madman' isn't really mad at all. It is, rather, a mad or even sinister society that has labelled him thus, perhaps because his particular brand of sanity (he is almost invariably a good old-fashioned individualist) threatens the orderly operation of the modern state. Secondly, even if he *is* truly deranged from a clinical point of view, his 'unreasonable' and 'antisocial' behaviour provides a clear moral standard for the world in which he operates. Like Mrs Dempster and Peggy Sanderson, in other words, he is commonly 'wiser,' certainly kinder and more tolerant – more *Christian* – than his neighbours. In contrast to the Canadian handling of this motif, however, the American writer rarely finds anything the least bit morally equivocal about this unsane innocence. Thirdly, and most importantly, the American madman – as we might expect – is dynamic rather than passive, refractory rather than resigned. Randle Patrick McMurphy of Ken Kesey's *One Flew over the Cuckoo's Nest* is the perfect example.[9] Such a figure, says Woolf, 'projects the possibility of a prevailing human vitality in defiance, albeit doomed defiance, of the enveloping anti-humanistic forces' [262-3].

This is a long way from blind Danile. The American madman, in fact, isn't a real victim at all. Like McMurphy he may be powerless in practical terms, but his madness, typically expressed as action rather than merely attitude, provides him with a means of asserting his individual freedom (which for the American comprises the essence of his identity) at least negatively, in pain and violence, despite, or perhaps even because of, its utter impossibility from any sane point of view. As Ihab Hassan says of Faulkner's Joe Christmas on the one hand and Ellison's Invisible Man on the other, if the 'madman' appears to be possessed by a perverse self-destructiveness, it is only because he repudiates the world as mirror. His victory consists of his refusal to believe that his life is trivial, a mere statistic. He will not accept invisibility as his natural state. 'The trick is to say the "yes" which accomplishes the expressive "no."'[10] Where the Canadian madman does actually exemplify that 'stoic patience' Woolf talks about, therefore, the American version stands for a mode of response not merely divergent but diametrically opposed. As a consequence, the charisma accrued by this figure during recent decades can only add to our ambivalence toward the home-grown fool-saint.

A complicated picture? Indeed. This is still not the whole of it, either. If these more or less naturalistic associations did not present enough problems, the fool-saint reveals yet one further, more covert affiliation in Canadian literature that hints at a complexity of signification even beyond that of the ambiguous cripples and madmen with whom he is obviously felt to share a family resemblance. Although it requires a far more devious logic to unravel the relation, we frequently find our holy innocent associated as well with the circus, carnival, or sideshow. The question is, what does this last, rather odd affinity mean.

On the surface at least, some of the connections suggested seem to be fairly straightforward ones. If we examine individual cases, though, we soon realize that the answer is not as easy to pin down as one might expect. Indeed, we seem to be confronted – again – with evidence of a deep-seated ambivalence. Like most basic forms of the role model, the carnie, in other words, presents a number of different and even mutually irreconcilable faces. To the extent that he is perceived as on the one hand a natural 'victim' (Boris Rataploffsky, the strong man in Carrier's *Il est par là, le soleil,* for instance, is, as David Bond points out, 'an ironic embodiment of the "little man" ... [since although] he is, in fact, a giant with great strength ... it is a purely passive strength, which allows him to endure ill-treatment rather than impelling him to rebel' 124) and on the other grotesque, *freakish,* in psychological if not physical terms, we might consider him as merely representing a variation on the cripple symbol, all the more poignant both for the trappings of fantasy surrounding him *and* for the implication of his complicity in his own exploitation and degradation. This particular emphasis, with its ambiguous if not overtly negative moral/

emotional connotation, is certainly the aspect that seems to dominate in Davies' Deptford trilogy, where Mrs Dempster, the original fool-saint, is associated (by contiguity) with the little Madonna, who (inasmuch as she inspires Ramsay's interest in hagiography) is in turn associated with St Wilgefortis, the bearded lady, who (by virtue of her physical peculiarity) is in turn associated with the explicitly abnormal denizens of Paul Dempster/Magnus Eisengrim's carnie experience. In other cases, though, the ramifications are more obscure. In *The Loved and the Lost*, Peggy Sanderson reminds Jim McAlpine for some reason of a little circus he stumbled upon by accident in Paris ('[A] door opened and we stepped into bright lights. Well, it was a little amphitheatre with the benches filled with people ... and down there in the toy arena were a couple of clowns in their pirouette costumes dancing around; a girl in a silver dress was riding a white horse; someone was leading an elephant across the arena. All this was going on down there under a brilliant white light. Everything was so white and clean and fantastically surprising and so wonderfully innocent and happy' 77), but although both the original event and the retrospective association obviously carry an unusual significance for him, in terms of the text itself the author's reasons for invoking such an image are left provocatively unclear. Are we meant to conclude that Peggy's saintliness is as illusory, as fraudulent, as a circus performer's? Perhaps. But, if so, we are hard pressed to explain the fact (seemingly running completely counter to the conclusion we might normally infer from the book's catastrophic ending) that the chance encounter was apparently a positive one for the protagonist, suggesting as it did an oasis of light and joy in the middle of the dark chaos of war. It would thus seem that there is little consensus (at least on conscious levels) about what the circus association implies for our communal mythology. Notwithstanding the ambiguousness of his referents, however, it *is* clear that the carnie persona of the fool-saint, like his original, is perceived as somehow embodying an important lesson for the Canadian, albeit a lesson his auditors are ill equipped to comprehend. Johnnie Backstrom's perceptions of the fatally wounded rodeo clown in Robert Kroetsch's *The Words of My Roaring* may, in fact, be taken as representative of the response typically evoked by this exemplary confrontation:

I was bending over [him] ... His bulbous nose had come off, showing a human nose that wasn't painted or anything, except that blood was coming from it. He was bleeding pretty freely somewhere beneath his torn clown's costume; the red was stained a cleaner red ...

Another thing I noticed, [he] was very thin. His costume was baggy and had billowed when he ran, but he was skin and bones. The only thing that moved on him now was his eyelids; they kept opening and staring in a sleepy confused way, and all the make-up, the white paint and the black and yellow, was smudged with sweat and dust and the blood from his nose. Then he tried to say something. His mouth moved small inside the smile that was painted on his face. He kept trying to say something to me, a perfect stranger, but he couldn't make it. He tried to raise a hand and point but couldn't and I wanted to point for him but I didn't know where.

'The kid is all right,' I said. I thought maybe that was it. 'You saved him,' I said. 'Just a sprained ankle.'

But that wasn't it, apparently; he kept trying to point, kept trying to tell us all something. (107-8)

Does this mean that the fool-saint as clown/freak must remain an enigma to us? It's important, of course, to distinguish between intrinsic and extrinsic ambiguity. Actually, for all Backstrom's (and perhaps even Kroetsch's) uncertainty about the significance of this figure, with the advantage of the broader perspective afforded by the foregoing chapters we can see why such a character should localize so much ambivalent (and inarticulate) emotional energy. In a sense, he summarizes the whole gamut of Canadian preoccupations. With his carnival associations, he is by definition a social outcast, an isolate. Either costume and make-up or actual deformities of the flesh, moreover, can be used as a physical correlative for the existential chasm between 'self' and 'other,' the absolute discontinuity between inside and outside. The recurrence of these motifs in connection with the carnie, therefore, hints at both the difficulty of human communication and the more serious problem of man's agonized sense that he is alienated from and trapped within his corporeal nature. Most important, the more or less radical abnormality of the clown/freak also reflects the Canadian's discomfort with his own 'abnormal' responses to experience.

In this regard it is interesting to note how often sexual ambivalence is associated with the carnie version of the saint typos. It is particularly significant that, going well beyond predictable deviancies like promiscuousness or homosexuality or even sado-masochism, we find a number of cases where androgyny (real or symbolic) is a central motif. The best-known example of this is the hermaphroditic saint who serves as the icon for Dunstan Ramsay's life quest, but a perhaps more intriguing (because more extensively developed) version is Gwendolyn MacEwen's Julian the Magician, an oddly inverted Christ figure who is also a sideshow conjurer. Although normal in a physical sense, Julian is by choice *psychically* trans-sexual. '"I can navigate in both female and male territory as freely as grass,"' he says. '"[I can] anticipate both female and male qualities in all things"' (121). We have already mentioned an incest/androgyny motif in connection with the French-Canadian treatment of familial relations, but the freak's sexual peculiarities are grounded outside and perhaps in opposition to the domestic arena. The question is, then, what exactly does the association mean.

In conventional terms, literary emphasis on an expressed ambivalence of this type may be interpreted in different ways according to whether the hermaphrodite is perceived as alter ego or 'other.' In the latter instance – and this, interestingly, is the interpretation stressed by the American critic, Leslie Fiedler – the audience's fascination is rooted in a perverse desire for self-transcendence that hides a wish for self-annihilation ('[A]bnormality arouses in some "normal" beholders a temptation to go beyond looking to *knowing* in the full carnal sense the ultimate other. That desire is itself felt as freaky, however, since it implies not only a longing for degradation but a dream of breeching the last taboo against miscegenation'[11]). In the former case, in contrast – and this, predictably, is the aspect emphasized by such Canadian critics as E.B. Gose (with respect to MacEwen's Julian) and Nancy Bjerring (with respect to Davies' St Wilgefortis) – the appeal of androgyny is that, in Jungian terms, it symbolizes the healthy union of the sundered halves of the psyche. If we look more closely, however, it seems apparent that the motif as used in this country commonly connotes a bit of both views, the negative American superimposed on or underlying the formally positive Canadian version. The morally ambiguous, freaky and/or saintly hermaphrodite hence provides an incomparably useful means of objectifying our national ambivalence toward the reorientation of sex roles and relations we have observed.

If the clown/freak fool-saint serves so many diverse symbolic functions in the Canadian langscape, this does not, of course, obscure the fact that his *primary* association is still with the victim. Theoretically this only means he is passive, powerless, vulnerable by definition. In practice, the creature all too frequently turns out to be not merely a potential, but an inevitable loser. Although, that is, some of the homelier versions of the fool-saint manage to escape, perhaps because we are trying symbolically to purge such a subversive element from our consciousness or merely to punish ourselves vicariously for our own aberration-by-association ('People who seek to become victims are not christlike,' says George Bowering in explanation for Mrs Blood's self-castigation; 'they are guilty, guilty-feeling' D88), the more radical varieties of this role model almost invariably get killed off or at the very least incarcerated in asylums. It's possible they embody too blatantly a message that can only be approached in the most oblique terms. In any case, this fact in itself exacerbates the already considerable problems associated with the prototype since we end up with a sense of inexorable doom (it is significant, for instance, that Jim McAlpine, comparing Peggy to Joan of Arc, emphasizes exactly this element of fatedness: 'Joan had to die, he thought with a sharp pang, simply because she was what she was' 144), which runs entirely counter to the initial implication that the passive stance is the 'safest' one. Like many of the significatory elements that typify Canadian culture, in fact, the fool/saint does not neutralize tensions so much as body them forth.

Not surprisingly, the instances where the passive exemplar seems least ambiguous are those that entail a *context* consonant rather than in conflict with its moral/emotional implications. Because the tacit American standard of reference reflects so badly on the submissive stance, in other words, the fictional world must offer some sort of quasi-philosophical rationalization, explicit or implicit, individual or communal, for the numen accrued by the role model. Less ambiguous does not necessarily mean less problematic, of course. Depending on the associations of the context in question, in fact, the passive response may be projected in individual literary works as either more positive or more negative than the free-floating ambivalent prototype tends to be. Since traditional Church-dominated French-Canadian culture prescribes submission, for instance, the attitude of the fool-saint is typically seen as less *abnormal* in French than in English Canada, but since this circumstance is viewed by most recent Québécois writers as unfortunate, both cause and concomitant of cultural and personal subjugation, it is generally deplored as self-destructive. As Beverly Rasporich puts it, 'the French Canadian is trapped not only by the hopeless profanity of his environment, but trapped as well by his love of sacrifice and death' (464). In English Canada, if writers are not hampered by any such ready-made context that would predetermine response in this way, they only have to work all the harder to provide a coherent emotional counter to the pervasive frontier ideology. In recent decades (no doubt encouraged by the temporary softening of the American masculine ideal that took place as an after-effect of sixties neo-primitivism) they have tended to fall back on a Jungian view of 'myth' as a mechanism for ordering and/or explicating experience to provide intellectual underpinnings to their fables of identity, usually validating the passive exemplar as a kind of anima figure. Unfortunately, such an imported schema tends to be somewhat less convincing for being imposed on rather than evolving from the material. In striking proof of this, although the fool-saint figure of Davies' Deptford trilogy is in *formal* terms a far more positive symbol than, say, either Mitchell's uncontexted Saint Sammy or Carrier's negatively contexted Boris Rataploffsky, the Jungian rationale does not permeate far enough below the surface to defuse the tensions implicit in the carnie association, or to explain the significance of Mrs Dempster's unhappy end, with its cautionary overtones. Even on the more overt levels of theme and character development in this series, in fact, there are difficulties that suggest that the author himself is not quite sure of the ramifications of his intellectual framework. For all his *talk* about the human value of myth and his supposed expertise in the subject, Dunstan Ramsay (Davies' obvious persona) seems oddly uncertain about what myth – or, indeed, the fool-saint herself – 'means' in personal terms. He himself, as a good Canadian, is a fatalist ('I rather liked the Greek notion of allowing Chance to take a formative hand in my affairs' a116); he plays a passive role in his relationships with women; further, he is explicitly self-identified with the abnormal ('the strangeness of my quest seemed to qualify me as a freak myself' a132) – but this demonstrated propensity for the unAmerican seems rooted far less in the elaborate, ostentatiously 'rational,' psycho-philosophical theory that he articulates throughout the trilogy ('belief in miracles and holy likenesses' is necessary in order to ensure that such humanistic values as 'mercy and divine compassion' will survive in a progressively dehumanized world, a178) than in a totally alogical and *a priori* personal bent for that stance. In any case, it should be noted that while the arbitrary – that is, consciously literary or philosophical – context may *affect* the moral/emotional status of the passive exemplar to a greater or lesser degree, compared to such 'natural' contexts as, say, the Québécois socio-political ambience it is of limited effectiveness in combatting the ambiguity that inheres in less accessible levels of response. This perhaps says something for the relative power of intentional and spontaneous, overt and covert components in literature.

Interestingly enough, there is one sub-group among Canadian writers that escapes both the Québécois' inherited negativism and the English Canadian's more diffuse uneasiness about the role exemplified by the fool-saint. There are no totally unambiguous versions of this figure in Canadian literature, but among all the examples mentioned there is one in which the exemplary role is at least not undermined to an extent that virtually negates any positive potential it may theoretically hold – where, in fact, passiveness is openly rewarded rather than punished or obscured. This, of course, is Wiseman's blind Danile. The explanation? If we think about it, it seems obvious that the key to Danile's anomalous success must lie in the fact that this novel was written out of a religio-cultural background that explicitly *approves* the tendency toward submission. The victim stance – if we can use this in its general rather than in its purely negative sense – is, quite simply, not only a *natural* (in so far as he has, since medieval times, become the very type of the scapegoat[12]) but also (in so far as he has in fact survived) an *efficacious* one for the Jew.

We see this clearly if we look at another Jewish-Canadian 'novel,' A.M. Klein's *The Second Scroll*. Uncle Melech, the exemplary figure in this book, is not technically speaking a fool-saint, but because his exceptional intellectual gifts are so narrowly unworldly (as his naive and futile campaign on behalf of the ghetto dwellers of Casablanca reveals, Melech's capacity to deal with the mundane realities of life is severely limited, his spontaneous response to problems being far more idealistic than practical), we may consider that he is at least functionally akin to the true idiot. When we notice, moreover, that his other identifying personality traits – his susceptibility to external influences, his self-identification with the disadvantaged and the suffering, his self-effacement (the only photo of him turns out to be a 'double, a multiple exposure' 61), especially, perhaps, his seeming impulsion toward martyrdom –

are all consonant with the features we have observed to be characteristic of the holy innocent, it seems quite plausible that Uncle Melech should be considered as a variant of the same figure. The really interesting thing about *The Second Scroll*, though, is the fact that the larger moral dynamic of the book, far from fighting against the sanctification of a passive model, actually reinforces the example of the iconic victim to the extent that public and private responses appear to converge. *Uncle Melech is no other than the whole Jewish people*:

Jewry had ceased as Existence. Among the nations it constituted an anomaly, in speech it was a solecism; the verb *to be* confined to the passive mood ... [Only] the Judaic Idea continued. It continued as Essence . The consequences of this separation of Essence from its typical Existence ... were early apparent. Jewry, leading in the lands of the Diaspora but a vestigial part-existence, moved of necessity between banality and suffering. Suffering, indeed, became the index of its viability, the mirror fogged at the seemingly breathless mouth. Jewry ceased to consider life as a reality to be experienced, but as a gauntlet to be run. The secret of the run gauntlet is to reduce yourself to as small a size as possible. [Only] Jewry turned inward ... was immune to death. This had been proved empirically; Jewry could not wholly die. (72)

With communal validation like this, it is no wonder that Danile escapes to a large extent from the problematic undertones so often carried by this particular literary role in Canada.

Despite our obvious ambivalence about him, it would be a mistake to underestimate the authority embodied (at least covertly) by the fool-saint even for non-Jewish Canadians. Inasmuch as we identify with the basic Jewish stance – the 'feminine' stance – far more strongly than we like to admit, our most strenuous efforts to be rational, to be American, are not in fact capable of dispelling his secret appeal. The concluding story of Munro's *Lives of Girls and Women*, 'Epilogue: The Photographer,' provides a particularly intriguing commentary on this communal peculiarity – albeit an oblique one that insinuates its message only very slyly. At first, indeed, it would seem that we are in the presence of an effective piece of *de*-mystification. Initially, that is, this short piece appears to be offering us no more nor less than yet another version of the ultra-conventional *Bildungsroman* theme wherein the protagonist, usually by means of some embarrassing social encounter, is confronted with his own naiveté and forced to recant all his 'romantic' notions about 'life.' In this case, the predictable ironic tension lies between Del Jordan's would-be-authorial fantasies about the 'tragic' Sherriff family, with its mysterious, self-destructive daughter ('She was a sacrifice, spread for sex on moldy uncomfortable tombstones, pushed against the cruel bark of trees' 204) and its beatific idiot son, and the reality of the rehabilitated Bobby Sherriff who, quiet-spoken, polite, and altogether unexceptional, invites the girl one afternoon to share a piece of very ordinary cake on the front porch of his very ordinary – *disconcertingly* ordinary – home. Counter to our conventional expectations, however, the breach is *not* healed, eradicated by recognition. At the last, just as Del is about to leave, Bobby offers her – quite gratuitously – a final, incontrovertible proof that reality is *not* merely ordinary; that people's lives, far from being accessible and explicable, are 'dull, simple, amazing and unfathomable – deep caves paved with kitchen linoleum' (210):

Bobby Sherriff spoke to me wistfully, relieving me of my fork, napkin, and empty plate.
'Believe me,' he said, 'I wish you luck in your life.'
Then he did the only special thing he ever did for me. With those things in his hands, he rose on his toes like a dancer, like a plump ballerina. This action, accompanied by his delicate smile, appeared to be a joke not shared with me so much as displayed for me, and it seemed also to have a concise meaning – to be a letter, or a whole word, in an alphabet I did not know. (210-11)

It is not the dis-illusionment the convention calls for that Del's experience catalyses, but re-cognition rather. And this it seems, judging by our literature, is exactly how it happens for us as well. Just when we think we have deflated him the fool-saint stands forth in all his mystery, offering us an epiphany. As Kroetsch puts it (perhaps remembering the mute importunities of his dying clown), the '"madman," come to a powerless wisdom, speaks his enigmatic dance' (Bix).

Is this the end of it, then – enigma? Probably – as long as we can never truly accept *or* repudiate our ambiguous alter ego. Are there, though, no plausible alternatives, no comfortable displacements by means of which we can mirror ourselves without flinching? If the fool-saint is so difficult to handle, in other words, are there no other vehicles to carry our burden of self-perception, no more palatable versions of the passive exemplar to be found in Canadian writing at all? Interestingly enough – for the displacement involved is both a wholly logical and a wholly unconventional one – the answer to this is yes. Although his symbolic functions are camouflaged to some extent by extrinsic literary and sub-literary associations, the fact is that the figure of the *Indian* seems almost always to be used in this country, intentionally or not, to illuminate, like the fool-saint, the exemplary submissive stance.

Traditionally, of course, the fictional savage in North America has most often bespoken, for good or ill, Rousseau's 'child of nature.' This being the case one may wonder why the Canadian Indian would not turn out simply to be a negative symbol rather than a positive one. For a number of reasons, the reaction was not that simple. To the early colonist the Indian represented not merely nature but, inevitably, man-in-nature – a phenomenon even more disquieting to contemplate than the naked face of the wilderness. In consequence, there was a general tendency simply to block him from consciousness. Equally far from both paean and vilification, early accounts of the natives in Canada more often than not treated them in purely negative terms: 'They have no religion; they have neither art nor literature; they have no civic life, no government; no clothing ... no beard!' (*Le sauvage* 28-9). Even in art, as François-Marc Gagnon points out, they were typically presented 'with no specific racial features. They look like unclothed Europeans' (13). The strategy had even greater psychological than aesthetic ramifications. Having rendered him invisible, the Canadian became incapable of 'seeing' the Indian at all, *except* in so far as he entered into white history.

Indicative of the Indian's historical position is the way in which he is first introduced into Canada's story and the order or preference followed with respect to other things or groups of people ... Typically a general history of Canada will begin with a description of Canada's physical features. Then the Vikings arrive, followed by John Cabot, and finally by Jacques Cartier, when Canada's history can be assumed truly to have started.

Suddenly with no prior notice, much like the wives of Cain and Abel, the Indians are mentioned as being there. They welcome Cartier or they materialize to kneel with him around the cross he has erected. In one account the kidnapped chief Donnacona appears already en route to France; in another the Indians make their entrance as 'other reasons which help to explain the slow growth of the colony' ...

Typically, Indian initiatives are ignored or emasculated ... Indians who are personally singled out as being worthy of praise, or even of mention, seldom go beyond Donnacona, Pontiac, Brant, Tecumseh, Big Bear and Poundmaker. All these men intruded on the white man's history, either as allies or as misguided obstacles, and only as such are they given consideration in most general accounts. (Walker 27-30)

The end result of this selective appropriation, somewhat paradoxically, was that the Indian, purged almost entirely of his alienness, became available to serve as a symbol not of 'other' but of 'self.'

This development was crucial. Leaving aside the question of whether the perceptual bias is either 'scientifically' defensible or fair to the Canadian native (the Indian as historical reality and the Indian as symbol are two entirely different entities in any case), there are obvious aspects of the Indian's existential condition that make such symbolic potential particularly attractive for the Canadian writer. In comparison with his relatively infrequent appearances in 'serious' modern American writing, the Indian has thus become one of the more important personae in the Canadian 'langscape.' Interestingly enough, his popularity has not, as in the United States, turned him into a pulp stereotype vitiated by retrospective sentimentalization. This is perhaps because the whole basis of his relevance – the key to his significatory function – has been and is quite different for the Canadian. In Canada, in Atwood's words, Indians are not valued because 'they are good or superior, but [because] they are persecuted' (F294). The Indian, in fact, even more than the madman or the cripple (who, being by definition mentally or physically 'abnormal,' may be dismissed as offering only anomalous experience), is the 'archetypal' victim.

Here we are brought up short by an apparent inconsistency. I have implied that the Canadian vision represents a departure from convention, yet this last point brings us right back to mainstream primitivism. After all, isn't the American noble savage commonly a victim too? The difference between the two usages lies in the fact that one images victimization as *event* and the other victimization as *state*. Where the American writer focuses on the catastrophe and the tragic decline from greatness, in other words, the Canadian is more likely to treat the Indian's condition as a fixed *donnée*. This distinction is not invariable, of course. Harold Horwood's *White Eskimo* demonstrates explicitly how white determination to 'save' the natives, to gather them into civilized, sanitized, church-centred villages, not only took the joy out of their lives but, by destroying the old, decentralized hunting and trapping culture, made them economically vulnerable. Most Canadian novels, however, don't offer the Indians even an *imaginative* alternative to degradation. More significantly, they generally don't carry the kind of indirect messages about solutions that are implied, of necessity, when one indicates cause or fixes blame. In David Williams's *The Burning Wood* and Rudy Wiebe's *Peace Shall Destroy Many*, it is because they are viewed as irredeemably corrupt by the godly that the natives are ostracised. Since in both books it turns out to be the iconic father rather than the community at large who is ultimately responsible for this lack of charity, though, it would be a mistake to put too much stress on the religious (or anti-religious) theme. Besides, if we survey the corpus it is clear that despite both general good will and the efforts of well-meaning individuals (there is plenty of ignorance and unconscious prejudice, but the out-and-out bigot or 'Indian-hater' is rare in Canadian literature) the Indian fares no better in secular communities. W.O. Mitchell's *The Vanishing Point*, Matt Cohen's *Wooden Hunters*, and Margaret Laurence's Manawaka novels, to mention only a few, are both unanimous and typical in presenting the Indians as above all casualties: victims not of some romantic decline *or* explicit, localized, white villainy, but simply of poverty, disease, ignorance, accident, anachronism. As Don Gutteridge says of *The Vanishing Point*, even when the tone is light, the message is not evaded:

A comic framework, but definitely dark comedy. The Stonys die from T.B., venereal disease and pneumonia; throughout we find them suffering cold, hunger, and innumerable minor afflictions. Mitchell has a clear and unsentimental eye upon these Stonys. Patronized for decades by white bureaucrats, they are helpless to provide themselves with food and shelter. Moreover, they suffer with patience the white teacher's futile attempts to 'civilize' them. But these are not noble savages. Such a life does not breed nobility. (B96)

These Indians are not victims only arbitrarily or accidentally or temporarily (the noble savage myth always titillates us with a tacit, rosy, wishful 'what if...?'), but because their victimization, like, indeed, our own, is built into the very nature of things.

Such a view has some interesting corollaries. We can see many parallels with the treatment of animals. The lack of any of that sense of communal guilt which colours most latterday American treatments of native peoples is once again linked directly with our tendency to identify ourselves with rather than against the Indian. Again, too, such self-identification reinforces our desire/need to divest the savage of any remaining traditional symbolic associations with nature. Even more so than with animals, consequently, the Canadian literary Indian tends to reflect our own discomfort with the wilds. Not surprisingly in view of her own ambivalence, Emily Carr, for instance, returns repeatedly in her book of short stories, *Klee Wyck*, to the twin topics of the Indians' vulnerability in the face of a strikingly inimical environment ('Black pine-covered mountains jagged up on both sides of the inlet like teeth' 37) and their consequent avoidance of a too-intimate relation with it ('The Indians forbade their children to go into the forest, not even into its edge' 11). Indeed, even in cases where the natives are actually living in a 'state of nature' – as in Peter Such's *Riverrun* – we find few romantic notions about primitive harmonies. The wilderness is an *antagonist* ('To guard its children the river, as all waters do, deceives a man's eyes and deflects his aim' 35), and as such always at least potentially dangerous. Inasmuch as his vulnerability is perceived as being all the greater for his closeness to nature, the Canadian Indian, unlike the noble savage, is actually shown as being *more* dependent on 'civilization' in its rudimentary forms than the white man. Far from Hollywood versions of primitive freedom, tribal life is marked – necessarily – by 'the strong, sure discipline of the seasons, the authorities worn smooth by long obedience, the regulated comings and goings' (Evans 269). The Canadian Indian may be permanently on the edge of the wilderness (just as he is on the edge of but excluded from white society), but he is certainly not self-identified *with* it.

This very circumstance makes him all the more effective as a symbolic alter ego. Not merely the *fact* but the form of his vulnerability reflects succinctly the Canadian's sense of his own condition. It is not surprising, therefore, that the terms used to describe the Indian's dilemma in Canadian fiction evoke those same iconic images we uncovered in earlier chapters. The Stonys in *The Vanishing Point*, for example, are identified as 'terminal cases' (91); they are said to be caught between the 'old Indian good-livin' and the new white way' (126); they are tied up 'in a sack' (378). The West Coast Indians of Hubert

Evans's *The Mist on the River*, similarly, are imprisoned by 'fences' of language, custom, and misunderstanding (56, 60, 71). Once again it is the interface that is the locus of both energy and anxiety. The latter book, in fact, is one of the most intensive explorations in Canadian fiction of the problems entailed by the border condition. Evans delineates in painful detail his young protagonist's desperate attempts either to reconcile or to choose between the equally unsatisfactory extremes of meagre and restrictive village life or dangerous and ofttimes degrading freedom in the city – and his failure to do so. No matter how hard he tries to break out, Cy is 'trapped between ... opposing wills' (73). '[H]e could not make up his mind and knew he could not' (74). He is '"one of those who weaken themselves by trying to go two ways"' (86). In the end, having first alienated his wife and her dying father by condemning their superstition, and then betrayed his own principles by backing down – too late – out of love and fear, he is left totally confused about whether the enemy he is battling is inside or out. 'Was the dark thing in his mind,' he asks himself, 'and had he yielded, not to her, but to it? He felt he would never know' (281). As for all of us, it turns out that the really critical interface for Cy – the one which, even in imagination, he is unable to transcend – is the 'between' (both link and cleavage) of self and other.

As with the other figures examined in this section, the Indian does not become a role model simply for the *fact* that he is a victim, even a particularly appropriate *kind* of victim, but because his *response* to his condition is exemplary. The title image of Evans's book is an important one. At first it seems only an allusion to Cy's confusion: 'Along the river bottom, mist clogged the lights, giving him the illusion of travelling a strange road toward a destination he did not know' (226-7). If we think about it, though, we realize that the key point to this image is not the mist in itself but the fact that the *road* – connoting a choice of 'ways' – is only a facsimile. *Despite appearances there is no question about which way the river is flowing.* Nor is there any necessity for Cy to 'see' that current. He need only submit himself to be carried in the proper direction. And this is what he does in the end. *Accepting* his incapacity to choose, he submits himself to the current of life that has been chosen for him. '"I cannot be certain of what I really do believe,"' he tells his wife with 'a new and tender understanding.' Then, 'he put her from him and went in. Around the walls of the big room all the chairs were filled. But one chair at the head of the room had been left empty and he went to it and sat down, taking his rightful place among his people' (282).

Acceptance. This it is that gives the Indian, in Gutteridge's words, 'his dazzling ability somehow, against all odds, to cope and survive and be human' (B96). Since the Indian's world is also our world, however, this is also the posture that we must, imitating him, learn to adopt. This is the whole point of Robert Kroetsch's *Gone Indian*. Jeremy Sadness (like many of us) starts out thinking like an American. Seeking freedom, self-certainty, a new, untrammelled 'natural' life, he escapes to the frontier in quest of a mythical Grey Owl, the ultimate self-created man. Here he realizes his dreams of heroism by winning a snow-shoe race – and is rewarded by being beaten up. This disillusionment lays the ground for the real lesson to be learned from the border experience: 'watching an Indian choose not to win a dog-team race, seeing there the absurd arbitrariness of a world in which "the difference of six feet, after those fifty miles, made one man a loser" and observing the "magnificent indifference" of the dogs to their loss[,] Jeremy relates this perception to the final transformation of Grey Owl: "The hunter who would not, finally, hunt. The killer refusing to kill"' (R.M. Brown c104). The insight prepares him for the final apotheosis which, though it loses his life, confirms his identity. Jeremy's mentor, Madham, an academic who has spent his life in flight from the 'bleak and haunted landscape' of his birth, where the 'wind-torn prairies meet the edge of [the] northern forest' (13), would undoubtedly view his protégé's ill-fated union with Bea in the end as, in Glenys Stow's words, 'a destructive longing to return to the womb.' The truth is, though, Stow continues, that Jeremy, having come to terms with his position as loser by identifying with the native is able to go 'willingly, actively, towards [his] conclusion, forward as a man, not backward as an infant,' accepting that the leap into manhood necessarily 'also involves a plunge into female irrationality, darkness, suffering and death' (b94). *To live authentically, Jeremy, like all of us, must learn how to die.*

The ultimate emblem of this critical surrender, translating Jeremy's act of empathy into physical terms, is the marriage or sexual union with the Indian. Again we find a striking divergence from American practice. Despite the fictional Indian's ostensible 'nobility,' miscegenistic marriages are rare in American literature in any case – the explicit nature association simply entails too many problems for a culture that fluctuates compulsively between raping and revering the landscape – but the few examples to be found (outside of those 'doomed' unions obviously intended to provide a negative object lesson) generally reveal at least two features that stand in marked contrast to the Canadian pattern. First of all, the white partner (virtually always a man) tends to play an aggressive role. Daniel Boone's legendary courtship of his Indian wife, for example, is commonly associated with the erotic/aggressive image of a panther pursuing a deer.[13] Presented in any such terms as this, the Indian/white marriage is simply a conventional confirmation of the white man's *conquest* of the wilderness. Secondly, and somewhat inconsistently, especially in twentieth-century versions the Indian partner typically represents passion, uninhibited life-force, primitive (especially sexual) vitality. He/she is, in other words, quite specifically the 'savage,' rather than the more homely primitive. This is an important distinction. Such a union is clearly *union with the 'other.'* As such it connotes self-transcendence, *escape* from the constrictions of the civilized 'I,' rather than any sort of empathy with and acceptance of a passive (that is, victim's) stance.

If we look at Canadian literature with these features in mind, we soon recognize how striking the difference is. To begin with, the sheer *number* of white/Indian 'marriages' to be found in our poetry and fiction, from the nineteenth century through to the present, is anomalously high from an American standpoint. Indeed, if we throw out all the unsuccessful combinations discussed above, the Indian/white union would have to vie for quantitative dominance with all the other heterosexual modes examined in Canadian writing. This is not surprising when we consider that it was the unconventional female-dominant pattern that turned out to offer the best chance of success among Canadian literary marriages. The Indian/white marriage is not quite the same in all respects to that particular model, of course, but the stance required of the formally 'active' partner is virtually identical. The only difference here is that the protagonist does not submit himself to a stronger consort, but, rather, *identifies* himself or (as it may be in this case) herself with a weaker one, submitting, as it were, to fate, necessity, life.

This explains why in nearly every case the Canadian protagonist's decision to commit himself to an Indian marriage is connected with a *general* change of attitude. Unlike the American's capitulation to raw emotion, the Canadian's discovery of tender feeling for the native is less a *cause* than a *result* of his realignment of personal stance. Usually there are two stages. First he (or she) gradually learns by observing the native lifestyle the advantages of passivity. This is generally a slow and reluctant process since it goes entirely against his 'American' prejudices. Finally, and usually abruptly, a point is reached where he makes an imaginative leap from sympathy to empathy. It is at this moment, the moment when he relinquishes self-assertion, that he is enabled truly to 'see,' and hence to love, his mate for the first time.

Does this sound like an oversimplification? The pattern is surprisingly ubiquitous, both early and late. Dick Harrison has mentioned (without endorsing) the possibility that those writers responsible for the more recent spate of Indian novels may simply have been 'capitalizing on the current wave of romantic primitivism' (E181) but both the popularity *and* the characteristic form of the numinous encounter with the primitive alter can be traced a long way back. If we look at Mazo de la Roche's 1923 novel, *Possession*, for instance, we can see the same dynamic at work that may be discerned in contemporary versions. Fawnie herself is a rather unconvincing creation, but her particular brand of shallowness is distinctly Canadian. More important, the message conveyed by the ending is exactly what we might predict on the basis of the outline above. Derek, the protagonist of the book, must renounce his restlessness and ambition, submit himself to the slow turn of the seasons, to rootedness, to the land, before he can overcome his contempt for the Indian girl (whose 'docility … almost put him asleep' 229) and live with her happily ever after. 'A great love for Grimstone surged over [him]. Grimstone and he were one. His own flesh that morning had become one with the soil. He could never leave it now. And there upstairs was Fawnie, little, weak, something to be cared for, protected, his own – after all. What a strange thing possession was! You thought you were the possessor when, in truth, you were the thing possessed' (288). The whole book is a demonstration of reorientation from the active to the passive mode.

Possession, admittedly, is hardly a great novel. In this kind of study, however, flawed or second-rate material may be even more useful than more successful productions, if only because conventional patterns tend to come through relatively untransformed. Once we are aware of its existence, on the other hand, whatever the idiom (and interestingly enough, Harrison's comments notwithstanding, modern practice is generally even *less* 'romantic,' less in tune with the times than de la Roche's), however eccentric the writer's intentions or individual his style, the base pattern is unmistakable. First the gradual realization of the value of the passive exemplar, then the leap to empathy, *then* the symbolic union. In Wiebe's *The Temptations of Big Bear*, for example, Kitty McLean's sexual initiation takes place not merely after, but in the immediate context of, that moment when the girl turns to Big Bear (the legendary leader who is so paradoxically powerless in fact, victim of both the white man's authoritarianism and the red man's lack of it) and announces that she wants to be more like him, 'A Person' (313).

Other examples, though varying widely in detail, carry the same implication. In Williams's *The Burning Wood*, under the influence of the shamanic figure of the Sun Dancer, Joshua must rid himself of both his romantic notions about primitivism ('Coming Day looked in surprise at him. "You don' figger dis place here is d' happy huntin' grounds, or even dat it use't' be, do you?"' 192) and his white man's exclusiveness ('Coming Day seemed to look right inside him … "I see you tryin't' stay like yer grandfad-der, always fightin' t'ings off, tryin' t' keep a distance."' 193) before he can finally decide where his loyalties and best interests lie. Much of the rhetoric Williams uses in speaking of the symbolic marriage here is 'American' (Lulu, despite her affinity for parked cars rather than leafy bowers, is a little too much the symbol of erotic vitality for the Canadian norm), but it is significant that the image that ends the book, the image that marks the conclusion to the dream quest through the wilderness in pursuit of the anima, is an image of perfect quiescence: '*his feet drumming drumming down through loam down into clay his headway mattering no longer and then only his heart beating wildly as the bark creeps up his ribs*' (204).[14] In *The Diviners*, Morag's flight to Jules Tonnerre marks her declaration of independence from Brooke's structured existence and her decision to let life carry her, to have a child, to exchange certainty for risk. In *The Vanishing*

Point, most strikingly of all, Carlyle is blind to Victoria's erotic potential (she has always been − simply and safely − the little lost lamb, his surrogate child) until the climactic evening when he symbolically gives up his paternal stance toward the community, his attempt to impose order, manipulate events, battle both natural chaos and native apathy, by submitting to the hypnotic appeal of the drums and the dance he has hitherto condemned as 'lobotomy' (204):

Who cared now − who cared now! Only the now remained to them − the now so great only death or love could greaten it. Greater than pain, stronger than hunger or their images paled with future − dimmed with past. Only the now − pulsing and placeless − now! Song and dancer and watching band were one, under the bruising drum that shattered time and self and all other things that bound them.
  Her hand took his as they stood up, held it as they walked to the tent flap. The drum followed them all the way to Beulah Creek bridge, then with one lambasting sound, it was stilled. (385-6)

If all these oddly echoing replications were not enough to confirm our view of the role of the Indian/white marriage in Canadian fiction, we also get the same message, backwards, from a number of negative examples. If such a union signals the adoption of a submissive stance, its *failure* is almost invariably rooted in the protagonist's stubborn refusal to relinquish finally the proud autonomy, the rigidity, the self-assertiveness of 'white' identity. In Matt Cohen's *Wooden Hunters* Laurel Hobson initially submits to the Indian musician who has rescued her from the woods but later feels uneasy about it. Almost as if her body knows better than she that the role is an inappropriate one, 'only twenty-four hours after she let Johnny Tulip into her sleeping bag [,] knowing even as she lost her balance ... that these two incidents were somehow related, that now whatever had been started on Johnny Tulip's porch was being finished,' Laurel falls off a cliff (51). Though she returns to the island after her convalescence, the sexual liaison is never renewed. Later we realize why. Laurel, in symbolic terms, is diametrically opposed to everything the Indian represents. Strong, self-contained, ruthless, like her father 'a truculent foreigner' in the wilderness (73), she rejects any possibility of identification with weakness. The repudiation of the friendly deer halfway through the book echoes her tacit repudiation of Johnny himself. '"You see," Johnny said. "She likes you." "Sure," Laurel said. "If I had my gun, I'd shoot it" ... She shouted as she approached it, clapping her hands and trying to scare it into the bush' (767).
  Another negative version, found in Wayland Drew's *The Wabeno Feast*, is interesting because of its connection with features examined earlier. Drummond McKay, the writer of the journal that forms one of the narrative strands of this book, is a young Scottish fur trader. A puritan, a stoic, a man of strong will and 'common sense,' he is determined to carve an empire for himself in the

wilderness. Due (at least in his own telling) to the persecution of his sinister, slovenly associate, he suffers a number of setbacks and ends up in his despair, much against his better judgment, setting up housekeeping with a beautiful young Indian girl. Like Laurel's brief affair with Johnny, though, this union is doomed from the start. Far from adapting himself to *her* lifestyle, adopting *her* attitudes and orientation, McKay, his moral strength having been undermined, is more determined than ever to maintain his white, civilized, *masculine* apartness – by building a house:

I informed her that I had commenced our dwelling, and that it would require many trees and much labour before it was completed ...

She answered as I had expected: That she anticipated nothing, besides the dwelling which was of the type which had served her well throughout her life, which was not a cage, which did not require the killing of great trees.

When we had eaten I again raised the matter of the building, more sharply than I had intended and was again nettled by her indifference ... I told her ... that I laboured for her benefit as well as my own. At this she laughed and came to kneel beside me, taking my head upon her breast. 'Ah no,' she said. 'No. It is not for my well-being that you would imprison me, and so imprison yourself. It is not for me that you must build such things to continue after you are gone, yet never live' ...

By the morning she had gone ...

I called for her, but my voice was lost in the mists above the lake. (258-61)

It is not long after this that McKay goes mad from his self-inflicted isolation. This is not the 'healthy' madness of the fool-saint, however. He dies by his own hand, still shouting defiantly (to the 'partner' who turns out to be nothing more than the imagined shadow of his own repressed self) that he is *not* an animal, he is a *man*. Because McKay refuses to recognize himself as a loser, he loses even more definitively in the end.

The numerous examples considered throughout this chapter are enough to establish both the importance of the passive role model to the Canadian imagination and the existence in our literature of specific, well-established conventions for handling that ambiguous figure. The work that best summarizes the whole phenomenon, though, has not yet been mentioned: Leonard Cohen's *Beautiful Losers*, a strange, intense prose-poem cycle wherein the primary locus of emotional energy is an iconic figure who is both an Indian *and* a saint.

The bulk of Cohen's novel is narrated in the first person by its two major characters, F., the mentor, and I., his protégé. In terms of the complex of attitudes we have been examining throughout this book, the former (for all that he is identified as a French-Canadian nationalist) is the archetypal American: self-made millionaire, political activist, sexual hero. I. would like to emulate his

friend ('I want F.'s experiences, his emotional extravagance' 58; 'I [want] to live
in a folk song like Joe Hill' 24), but he is, to his disgust, much too 'Canadian':
timid, self-conscious, terrified by an all-too-immediate sense of corporeality
('Why do I feel so lousy when I wake up every morning? Wondering if I'm
going to be able to shit or not. Is my body going to work? Will my bowels
churn? Has the old machine turned the food brown? Is it surprising that I've
tunneled through libraries after news about victims?' 7). Given these fundamental character differences, it is small wonder that these men also diverge
radically in their attitudes toward the Indian. F. believes wholeheartedly in the
noble savage (his theories about the parallels to be drawn between the American
native peoples and the ancient Greeks could have been lifted verbatim from an
early nineteenth-century romance by someone like William Gilmore Simms);
his idea of what to *do* with an Indian is hence classically erotic-aggressive. I., on
the other hand, even when trying consciously to follow F.'s example, is
incapable of doing so. In quest of life, fertility, reassurance, all he can see is
death:

The Indians are dying! The trails smell! They are pouring roads over the trails, it doesn't
help. Save the Indians! Serve them the hearts of Jesuits! I caught the Plague in my
butterfly net. I merely wanted to fuck a saint, as F. advised. I don't know why it seemed
like such a good idea. I barely understand it but it seemed like the only thing left to me.
Here I am courting with research, the only juggling I can do, waiting for the statues to
move – and what happens! I poisoned the air, I've lost my erection. (43)

As a result of this unwonted bias, I. is not only impelled to select as the special
object of his study a tribe whose 'brief history is characterized by an incessant
defeat' ('The very name of the tribe, A–, is the word for corpse in the language
of all the neighboring tribes. There is no record that this unfortunate people
ever won a single battle ... My interest in this pack of failures betrays my
character.' 5) but finds himself reluctantly obsessed with the greatest loser of
the group, a young woman who, even before her conversion sanctifies her
masochistic fascination with mutilation and death, embodies the absolute
opposite to primitive vitality (she is disease-pocked, allergic to the sun, frigid,
and melancholy).

The question that arises at this point, of course, is what the author means to
imply by the contrast he sets up. I have intimated that the novel presents a kind
of paradigm of the Canadian's wholesome affinity for the passive role, but one
could equally well claim it is a critique either of the unhealthy repressiveness of
modern society or, more specifically, of Canada's self-destructive political and
economic policies. Because Cohen's vision is a complex one, the answer is not
immediately apparent. Certainly the interpretive key is not contained in the

character of the saint herself. From the limited, contradictory, and inconclusive evidence we are given, Catherine may equally well be – as her name implies – 'She who puts things in order ... someone who proceeds in shadows, her arms held before her ... She who, advancing, arranges the shadows neatly' (55) *or* simply a pervert in love with pain. E.D. Blodgett, for one, inclines toward the latter view. 'Catherine's sainthood is metaphorically a "Nazi medical experiment" ... and while [I.] fantasizes that she is "fragrant as a birch sapling" ... she systematically flogs herself to death with the same birch stem' (a188). We have to keep in mind, on the other hand, that the facts Blodgett cites in support of this conclusion are drawn almost entirely from F.'s section of the narrative. But this is the whole problem. *Everything* we know of Catherine is subjectively derived. As a result, we have to recognize that the 'real' Catherine has nothing to do with Cohen's message. The only way to discover what the book 'means' – what is being implied about the worth or worthlessness of our national fixation on sainthood – is to unravel the text's judgment on the relative merits of the two divergent *attitudes* illustrated.

At first glance it would seem that F. wins hands down. Even if we manage to put aside our own *a priori* American biases, I.'s low opinion of himself, his sense of guilt and even shame that he is 'unnaturally' preoccupied with the unattractive Catherine instead of emulating F. in pursuit of a simple, light-hearted fuck, is bound to influence our assessment of his emotional health.

All the other girls ... wore rich pelts, embroidered leggings worked with beads and porcupine quills. Beautiful! Couldn't I love one of these? Can Catherine hear them dance? Oh, I'd like one of the dancers. I don't want to disturb Catherine, working in the long house, the muffled thud of leaping feet tracing perfect burning circles in her heart. The girls aren't spending too much time on tomorrow, but Catherine is gathering her days into a chain, linking the shadows. Her aunts insist. Here's a necklace, put it on dear, and why don't you paint your lousy complexion? She was very young, she allowed herself to be adorned, and never forgave herself. Twenty years later she wept over what she considered one of her gravest sins. What am I getting into? Is this my kind of woman? ... F., is this what you want from me? Is this my punishment ...? (56-7)

Even more damning than I.'s *feelings* of inferiority, moreover, is the fact that his *behaviour* seems to bear out his self-condemnation as well. In ironic contrast to his erotic obsession with his 'fictional victim,' he is unable to respond to his very real, very sexy Indian wife. Why? On the surface it would seem he is simply not 'man' enough. He is made uneasy by Edith's sexual passiveness because it seems to demand that he himself play a more aggressive role. F. suggests that he would be better off to treat women like 'servants,' 'With whips, with imperial commands, with a leap into her mouth and a lesson in choking'

(31), but I., of course, is incapable of this sort of approach. I. doesn't have the nerve to take what he wants. I. is a weakling.

Or is he?

Even now, having moved from simple fornication to more overt displays of machismo, the picture begins to waver a bit. Is the heroic F. really such a hero if his 'healthy' lust simply boils down to sexual bullying? Later discoveries reinforce our doubt. For one thing, we find out that for all Edith's formal status as an Indian (that is, a victim), by the time I. meets her she has been literally remade by F. The sex goddess, in other words, is totally unnatural – a product of the chauvinistic American imagination. Being, to his credit, incapable of either the detachment such a cold-blooded and manipulative strategy requires *or* the egocentricity necessary to play opposite to such a stereotyped pneumatic fantasy, it's hardly surprising that I. has difficulty relating to his wife. Even leaving aside the ethical problems implied by Edith's masquerade, the *kind* of persona F. has invented for her inevitably inhibits his response. Recreated, she now has nothing but sex ('primitive vitality') to offer. He on the other hand, being the archetypal Canadian, is temperamentally unsuited to play any role based on 'screwing the natives.' Even though he might *think* he envies F., in other words, I., like the men who tried to rape Edith back when she was still simply *sauvagesse*, is prevented by his essential humanity from following through on the aggressive 'American' impulse. 'Edith peed in fear and they heard the noise of it louder than their laughter,' he says, reconstructing the scene that is obviously a kind of epiphany for him. 'It was the pure sound of impregnable nature and it ate like acid at their plot. It was a sound so majestic and simple, a holy symbol of frailty which nothing could violate. They froze, each of them suddenly lonely, their erections collapsing like closed accordians as their blood poured upward like flowers out of a root ... They could not bear to learn that *Edith was no longer Other, that she was indeed, Sister*' (76-7, italics added). I.'s self-identification with these would-be and incapacitated rapists (despite F.'s urgings that he 'make nothing of this connection') not only explains but justifies his 'abnormal' rejection of the live Edith in favour of the dead Catherine. By doing so, he is only trying to find the beautiful loser his wife *should* have been.

Interestingly enough, Cohen's story does not stop with the moral contest between F. and I. In the last section, as Scobie points out, 'the boundaries between the individual characters disappear, as do the distinctions between their roles of saint, teacher, disciple. The old man of the final section shares the characteristics of both I. and F., and the narrative deliberately blurs the two into the "remote human possibility" of IF' (c19). At this point we suddenly realize that what we have isn't a nationalistic allegory at all but merely a kind of psycho-drama illuminating the inner conflict suffered by the Canadian as his home-grown 'instincts' battle for supremacy with his American 'superego.' If we have any doubts left as to the final moral alignment of the book we need only think of the concluding image of I/F in the movie theatre disintegrating corporeally and then, filtered through 'the point of Clear Light' (305), dissolving into the film on the screen. Linda Hutcheon detects a negative note in this ending. 'The epigraph of the novel begins: "Somebody said lift that bale," introducing the victim/victimizer theme which is then underlined by the continuation which identifies the line as Ray Charles singing "Ol' Man River." Although there is no logical sense in mentioning who is singing these written words, the link with the final vision of the novel would suggest that to become a Ray Charles movie is not liberation for the narrator, but perhaps symbolic capitulation to the victimizing forces' (A301). What Hutcheon doesn't consider is the possibility – indeed, judging by our literature, the certainty – that many Canadians believe, at least covertly, that for us, as for Fred Bodsworth's wise wolves, 'symbolic capitulation to the victimizing forces' *is* 'liberation.'

NOTES

1 Douglas, *The Feminization of American Culture* (Knopf 1977) 12
2 Hemingway, *In Our Time* (Scribners 1930) 81
3 In this connection we may recall Christiane Pflug's use of caged birds mentioned in chapter 5. Pflug's representativeness is further demonstrated by the fact that another motif frequently employed in her work to convey a sense of vulnerability and entrapment, the doll, also turns up frequently in Canadian literature, and with much the same implications. Blais' usage in *La belle bête* is typical. 'The image of dolls is repeated constantly with reference to both Louise and Lanz,' says Margot Northey. '... Thus Louise is referred to as a "frivolous doll" or "pretty doll," who never suspected that one day "she would lie battered and abandoned"; Lanz has "the graceful, congealed laughter of marionnettes"' (73).
4 See Northey 60 for a discussion of this feature in Hébert's *Kamouraska*; also Urbas, esp. 115-16 and 129, on Blais and Ferron.
5 It is interesting that when MacDonald wants an example of the kind of animal stories that served as the inspiration for Baden-Powell's 'woodcraft' movement, he turns to fiction written by the British Kipling and the American William Long.
6 According to David Levin, the development of these attitudes in post-Revolutionary America was due to the combination of transplanted romanticism with more practical, patriotic motives. 'What was effeminate in the [French, Spanish, or Italian courtier] ... was his self-indulgence, his use of subtlety and deceit, his "languor" or "torpor." The masculine virtues were courage, self-reliance, self-denial, endurance, candor, and vigorous activity ...

'Thus romantic admiration for honor and masculine vigor merged with bourgeois admiration for industry. The inactive person, the torpid society, could not progress. To a nineteenth-century American who knew that his continent had to be "improved," torpor and languor seemed subversive.' *History as Romantic Art* (Harbinger 1963) 39-40

7 There is just a hint toward the end of the book that the anguished George not only admires but *resents* his wife's equanimity in the face of her impending doom. 'There she was – so brave, so frail, her beauty being destroyed, her life chewed away. Why? There was I, torn by pity and grief, and loathing at what her plight did to me' (342).

8 Woolf, 'The Madman as Hero in Contemporary American Fiction,' *JAmS* 10 (1976) 257, 260

9 See Raymond Olderman, 'The Grail Knight Arrives,' chap. 1, *Beyond the Wasteland: A Study of the American Novel in the Nineteen-Sixties* (Yale 1972) 35-52.

10 Hassan, *Radical Innocence: Studies in the Contemporary American Novel* (Princeton 1961) 81

11 Fiedler, *Freaks: Myths and Images of the Secret Self* (Touchstone 1979) 137

12 See Otto Rank, *Beyond Psychology* (Dover 1958), 285 ff, for a discussion of the similarity between perceived female and Jewish roles. Interestingly, Rank claims that much of the misogyny built into Freudianism stems from Freud's Jewish biases: 'Freud's conception of the woman is not only derived from masculine psychology but more especially from the definite patriarchal attitude of Old Testament tradition. Scientifically, this means that even the man is not conceived of by him psychologically as the male – in spite of the overrating of the libidinal drive – but as the *father* or prospective father or prospective son; that is, in man's procreative role in the biological scheme of the species. Here, again, we meet the Old Testament emphasis on procreation as the only means of immortality for a culturally frustrated people. His conception of the woman is not of an independent individual in her own right but as an instrument for man's procreative ideology ... [In] Freudian doctrine ... the woman ... therefore is depicted as enslaved, inferior, castrated, whereas in the psychology of the male the masculine qualities appear exaggerated to the point of caricature in a libidinal superman.' This is not all. 'Since woman, in the course of history, actually has suffered from the very beginning a fate similar to that of the Jew, namely, suppression, slavery, confinement and subsequent persecution, one might say that the psychology which the Jew took on as a result of his early fate was essentially a feminine one. What Freud attempted unconsciously in his ideology therefore was the projection of those feminine characteristics of the Jew upon the woman, thereby achieving a kind of therapeutic self-healing for the Jewish race' (286-8).

13 See Richard Slotkin, *Regeneration through Violence: The Mythology of the American Frontier* (Wesleyan U. 1973), esp. 156-7, for an interesting discussion of this legend.

14 We find a fascinating – because more explicit – parallel to Williams' conclusion in John Newlove's poem 'The Hero around Me':

> Once heroes marched through my mind
> in solid ranks, the deeds
> shaped pointedly, and I knew
> I could never be one of them,
> though I desired it, wished for one sharp moment
> in my life – thinking
> of the hero as man in combat only ...
>
> The day came, but not as war.
> Fields of grain around me were crystal,
> the sky polished, endless gold and blue,
> and in the still heat a meadowlark
> twisted its sculptured tune around me
> once, quickly, a deft feat of superior magic,
> and all time stopped, world without end,
> and I was as a tree is, loathing nothing.

9

Hat Tricks

The Orient, says Joseph Campbell, is obsessed with 'the force of the cosmic order itself, the dark mystery of time ... the never-dying serpent, sloughing lives like skins, which pressing on, ever turning in its circle of eternal return, is to continue in this manner forever, as it has already cycled from all eternity, getting absolutely nowhere.' The West, on the other hand, sets against this undying power 'the warrior principle of the great deed of the individual that matters.' The victory of free will, 'together with its corollary of individual responsibility,' thus 'establishes the first distinguishing characteristic of specifically Occidental myth ... the lesson ... of a self-moving power greater than the force of any earthbound serpent destiny.' The result? '[T]he early Iron Age literatures both of Aryan Greece and Rome and of the neighbouring Semitic Levant are alive with variants of the conquest by a shining hero of the dark and – for one reason or another – disparaged monster of the earlier order of godhood, from whose coils some treasure was to be won: a fair land, a maid, a boon of gold, or simply freedom from the tyranny of the impugned monster itself.'[1] We have already observed the Canadian's affinity for the Oriental mode: acquiescence to rather than battle against the inevitable. The question remains whether the distinctively Western *active* role model on which Campbell comments has any place among our literary personae at all. The answer, perhaps surprisingly, is yes – but with reservations. For one thing, if Canada has an image of heroism it is not the American-style adventurer but the magician. Secondly, this figure, though powerful, is not viewed as entirely, or even primarily, positive. Nevertheless, our examination of Canadian literary roles and relations is incomplete without him.

Who is the magician? To start with, although there are an unusual number of 'real' magicians or shamanic figures to be found in the Canadian corpus, the term is meant here to designate a character type rather than (or as well as) a profession. A magician is simply one who *manipulates* the elements of his world rather than being manipulated *by* them. More important, he does so by the force of his own will. A priestly or messianic hero gains his powers by virtue of his connection with the extrapersonal realm, a scientist (or, for that matter, a pioneer) from nature,[2] a military or political leader from society, but though the magician may use or coerce supernatural as well as natural forces, the source of his ability to do so is purely internal. As is appropriate for the hero of a culture unable to credit transcendence, he is, in other words, above all self-contained. Indeed, he shares with some of those more problematic hybrid heroes of archaic myth (as Paul Zweig says of Achilles) a kind of indecorous greatness 'which cannot be apprehended in human terms; a quality whose natural outlet lies in self-directed, self-perpetuating actions. The inward necessity of such actions may parallel that of the moral order, but only by accident, or by ruse.'[3]

In naturalistic terms this bent produces a distinctive, easily recognized kind of personality. Even when a magician is in civilian dress, so to speak, he is unmistakable. If we survey Canadian literature, we may detect the type in (among others) Michael Hornyak of Robert Kroetsch's *But We Are Exiles*, Wayne Farrell of John Mills's *Skevington's Daughter*, Wesley Duivylbuis of Clark Blaise's *Lunar Attractions*, Roger Dork of Fred Bodsworth's *The Atonement of Ashley Morden*, Darcy Rushworth of Patricia Blondal's *A Candle to Light the Sun*, Esau Gillingham of Harold Horwood's *White Eskimo*, Howard O'Hagan's *Tay John*, Caspar Arkwright of Leo Simpson's *Arkwright*, and the tramp of Sylvia Fraser's *The Candy Factory*, as well as in the more explicit shamans or conjurers of Jack Hodgins's *The Invention of the World*, T.G. Roberts's *The Red Feathers*, James Houston's *Spirit Wrestler*, and Robertson Davies' Deptford trilogy. What makes this figure so distinctive? The answer is simple. Claiming, nay, demanding our attention is part of his stock in trade. Alone among typically timid and conservative Canadians the magician is *ambitious*, not merely willing but eager to stand out from the crowd (Keneally 'wanted to go down in history ... He would have liked to have the whole world looking at him' 258). Such an attitude naturally has consequences that make its exponent very hard to ignore. For one thing he tends to be much more of a *public* figure than is normal for a Canadian. For another, he is almost always *successful* in a worldly sense. This isn't mere luck. The details may vary from case to case, but the magician invariably has whatever traits will allow him to manipulate his environment most effectively, whether it is strength (Wise-as-a-she-wolf of *The Red Feathers* has 'a giant as tall as a pine and as broad as a hill [lurking] within his slender frame' 9), manual dexterity ('he was a master of all those sleights that had seemed so splendid and so impossible in my childhood,' says Dunstan Ramsay of Magnus Eisengrim in *Fifth Business*, 59), or, as in *Arkwright* and *But We Are Exiles*, simply business acumen. Often, indeed, it is this success that is our first and primary token of his identity. In *White Eskimo*, for instance, when Esau Gillingham arrives on the scene, even more than his imposing physical appearance it is his obvious competence in a practical sphere that marks him immediately as a man of power.

He descended upon Labrador as though from heaven. The Eskimos still talk of the morning the giant stranger came down out of the hills in the dead of winter dressed in the skin of a white bear, driving a team of white dogs with a long sled on the Eskimo pattern ... and bringing the biggest single load of white fox pelts anyone had ever seen.

Had he been aiming at a reputation for witchcraft, nothing he might dream up could have succeeded better than this. Eskimos have a great respect for the successful hunter, and a firm belief in magic as an element of such success. Shamans of the highest class – angekoks as they are called – are believed to be able to transport themselves, with the aid of their spirits, or torngaks, almost instantaneously from place to place. And here was one who, obviously, had come by no ordinary means, out of a land where mortals did not live but where spirits were abundant – that is to say, the interior mountains of Labrador. (8–9)

What this all boils down to is that the magician, as opposed to the saint, is a natural winner. It is this single fact that presupposes almost every other feature he exhibits.

What, aside from the success itself, are these distinguishing characteristics? First and foremost, both cause and comitant of his ascendency, the magician is an egotist. A lone wolf by nature, he neither wants nor needs anyone else. He may seem to put himself out to keep people around him – indeed, even when he lacks Keneally's formal oratorical skills, the magician, as evidenced by the fact that so many of the ilk are seducers, is generally notable for his powers of persuasion – but this is simply because his position demands a retinue. The affect, in other words, is only one-sided. Though he may *use* people ('"He consumed me the way he consumed everything,"' says Kettle of Hornyak, 54), he does not actually enter into relationship *with* them. There is no necessity for it. Egocentric to the point of obliviousness, the magician requires neither empathy nor love nor even approval. This independence, combined with an almost godlike (or childish) confidence in his own powers, makes him almost invulnerable. He is immune to social pressures ('"I've lived an Outsider's life,"' says Eisengrim with satisfaction, c247), to economic necessity ('Mike had only to write a cheque and say, "Hornyak would like some cash"' 10), to legal constraints ('"It's your duty to break a vicious law and to go on breaking it at every opportunity,"' says Horwood's Gillingham, 121), even, seemingly, to normal physical danger ('Ash began to see with a mounting incredulity that Dork had no expectation of dying in that crash – or any other crash. Dork was literally and unconditionally incapable of feeling fear for himself ... He couldn't conceive of a world that didn't have him at its center, therefore in the restricted confines of his perennially adolescent mind Dork was immortal' 77–8). The magician, in sum, is *self-validated*.

It's easy to see from this why the Canadian would find the figure fascinating. Davies suggests that the basis of his appeal is our modern hunger for enchantment ('"People want to marvel at something, and the whole spirit of our time is not to let them do it ... What we offer is ... an entertainment in which a hungry part of the spirit is fed."' a186), and undoubtedly this is at least a minor element in the equation. If we examine the responses to be found within the fictional worlds themselves, however, it seems obvious that much more important than his facility for stimulating our sense of wonder is the magician's capacity to incarnate for our vicarious titillation *freedom* from all the woes and limitations we feel ourselves to suffer: freedom from social inhibitions ('for the next nine days [after their meeting] Peter Guy was first scared and concerned and reluctantly drunk, and then fascinated, not only by Michael Hornyak but by himself, and then carefree and drunk with abandon, and after a while no longer some of the other things he had been, not a twenty-year-old virgin . and no longer a stranger to the police' 10); freedom from moral scruples ('Working on these illusions [with Eisengrim] was delightful but destructive of my character. I was aware I was recapturing the best of my childhood; my imagination had never known such glorious freedom; but as well as liberty and wonder I was regaining the untruthfulness, the lack of scruple, and the absorbing egotism of a child ... The day I found myself slapping one of the showgirls on the bottom and winking when she made her ritual protest, I knew that something was terribly wrong with Dunstan Ramsay' a192); freedom especially – through the contagiousness (we hope) of his own implausibly effective insouciance – from our anxiety about death. Glamour and enchantment notwithstanding, the magician indulges our wishful fantasies above all by escaping where escape is impossible. He becomes a kind of talisman of possibility. Even when we don't approve of him – even when we don't believe in him – this is a promise that's very difficult to resist. The emotion generated by the bearer is hence considerable. The scene in *White Eskimo* where Gillingham conducts the policeman over the Kiglapaites at mid-winter, for instance, demonstrates vividly the awe and envy he almost inevitably catalyses simply by virtue of his seeming proof against either exterior menace or human frailty:

I must've expressed some fears about what lay in front of us – no wonder if I did either, looking at that frightful mass of ice-sheathed rock – for I remember Gillingham saying while carefully laying strips of frozen bacon over caribou steaks in a pan, 'Corporal, there is no place on the face of this earth where a man can't survive' ...

The first hour wasn't too bad, but it got steeper as we went and began to snow lightly ... I went in constant fear of sliding down over the ice-covered boulders and breaking my neck. But in spite of his size, Gillingham seemed as sure-footed as a goat.

After we crested the first hill ... I was completely lost. You couldn't see back into the cove we'd left, or forward into the mountains, and there was no sense o' direction at all that I could lay hold of ... Left to myself at this point I'd surely have wandered over some god-awful cliff into a crevice where my body would never have been found. How Gillingham knew his way through the tangled and ungodly mess I had no idea, but he went forward without a second's hesitation. (204-6)

In a world permeated by danger, the magician is just such a one as we would wish ourselves to be.

Or is he?

The problem is – as this last quotation reveals – a magician is all too obviously 'other.' We may titillate ourselves with momentary fantasies of *sharing* his charmed existence, but even in our wildest dreams we cannot imagine *being* him. The reason for this may be traced at least partly to the covert sexual orientation pointed out in the last few chapters. In the masculine mode traditional to Western literature any heroic figure represents at best an ideal *self*, at worst the evil alter or *shadow*. When the symbolic ego is feminine, however, the heroic figure, being contrasexual, represents the self's *opposite*. And as such he naturally tends to evoke, even to merge with, every equivocal image of 'otherness' in our conceptual vocabulary. In consequence, not only is the active exemplar in Canadian literature typically 'American' (it's no surprise that it's F. rather than I. in *Beautiful Losers* who 'wanted to be a magician' 207), not only is he – as we observed of *Tay John* in chapter 5 – implicated with nature, but he tends to assume, by virtue of both his manipulativeness and his ascendency, a specifically paternal – that is, authoritarian – role. '"I am the Father of you all,"' says Keneally to his flock of colonists, '"and you are my children"' (111). This is not an entirely negative association, of course – just as the animus is not an entirely negative figure. As we have already noted, despite the fact the father is by definition a threat, he also has his strong points. If nothing else, as long as we ourselves prefer to play the safe, passive roles, it is necessary for our survival that someone else be prepared to take the risks, not merely tackling on our behalf the *exceptional* tasks, those forays into forbidden realms that have always been the function of the shaman ('His skill lies in his ability to enter the magic countries, and then return,' says Zweig of the questing hero [29]; 'He will be a ... spirit wrestler, a sickness fighter, and if you pay him, he will not fear to go on dangerous journeys for you,' echoes Houston of his more modern angekok, 57), but, in a world where danger is omnipresent, even those minor presumptions of day-to-day decision-making which could in any way pit the individual against the flow of events. Certainly it is because he relieves them of this disturbing necessity for *choice* that Keneally's Carrigdhoun villagers are willing to play the slave to his master. Once the fear disease has eaten deeply enough 'at the fiber of [their] self-esteem' (118), it becomes easier for them to believe in their own worthlessness than to wage the heart-breaking battle against it. 'It was as if they'd said, okay, we'll let you pretend to be a dictator and a tyrant and even a superhuman legend, we'll even let you go so far as to act like you really believe it and treat us like dirt, if you'll let us pretend, too, to be filthy ugly creatures of the earth who can't see anything higher than our fence-posts' (259). Why? *Because once you have fallen that low you don't have anything more to lose.*

The problems entailed by this stance are obvious. Even with the relation between Keneally and his colonists we have slipped over into the kind of masochistic self-abasement that has been such a bogey for Canadians ever since Margaret Atwood pointed out our predilection for victimization. The existential isolation we endure as houses on the prairie, garrisons in the wilderness, is hard enough for the psyche to bear up under without the superaddition of any element that would nudge us over the line between fear and love of death – especially since the latter offers at least one way, perhaps the only way, to escape from our anxiety. What is involved is more than simply a danger to our self-esteem. If heroes risk their lives, it's possible that too-willing victims risk their souls. Indeed, we see all too clearly what can happen if the tendency is given full reign in the deplorable fate suffered – indeed, *courted* – by Simon Mottley in *Skevington's Daughter*. So great is the professor's need for self-flagellation (*vide* his 'scholarly' fascination with the sadistic appetites of the title character of the book) that he not merely submits to but literally *invents for himself* an evil oppressor. Transforming a relatively ordinary and indeed rather vulgar malefactor (the Nazi-obsessed hippie, Wayne Farrell) into a kind of cross between Charles Manson and an Aztec priest, he first fantasizes his capture by and eventual, almost grateful acquiescence to this deliverer-cum-executioner ('I felt serene . it was as if there had been a subtle change ... the enclosure was no longer a prison but instead a refuge – a clearing in the jungle with a wall built sensibly to keep the things of the jungle out' 159), and then actually hallucinates himself to death:

I know there is nothing beyond but eternal darkness, the extinction of my consciousness and for this latter I am truly relieved. My death means one more dawn for you, and yours will mean morning for someone else, for it is by our deaths that the universe feeds and renews itself. It is only through our blood that this nightly victory over darkness is gained. Wayne has told me this and it is true. Do not therefore mourn me since they shall coat me with gold... the Golden One... El Dorado... and dispose of me as it should be done. (161)

As long as we believe there is a significant moral difference between *living with* (Heidegger's 'being toward') and *giving in to* death, we surely have to hold that Mottley's infatuation with oblivion is something to be avoided at all costs.

We can't hold Wayne Farrell to blame for Mottley's innate weakness, of course. He just happens to be conveniently on the spot – at most, a catalyst for the catastrophe. Like A.M. Klein's demagogues (the Orator of 'Political Meeting,' Shabbathai Zvi of 'Out of the Pulver and the Polished Lens,' even Hitler himself), this particular version of the magician is, as Zailig Pollock describes it, 'essentially passive and uncreative, a hollow personality construct-ed out of clichés, who, in the absence of the true hero, simply magnifies all that is ... least vital in the people he claims to lead' (54). Even aside from his tendency to reinforce our own worst nature, however, at least in the view of the Canadian the magician seems to pose a number of dangers peculiar to *his* character, rather than to ours. For one thing, there is a recurrent suspicion in this country that power is always going to bring evil in the long run, not merely because, as Roberts would have it in *The Red Feathers*, it invites envy ('"Magic is for gods and mighty chieftains,"' says the pragmatic Run-all-day when offered the gift of flight; '"it is too potent a thing for humble folks ... [for it] breeds powerful enemies"' 11), but because *by its very nature* it spawns cruelty and corruption. It seems almost inevitable to us that – as Keneally's foster-mother, old Lady Flynn, realizes of him when he returns to Carrigdhoun a full-blown prophet – the 'trickster child' will be 'nurtured into meanness, the unnatural strength ... developed into a danger, the immense knowledge ... twisted ... into a cynicism' (105). It is in this recognition – not in a fear of our own death-wish – that the Canadian's ambivalence about the hero seems to be rooted. Ambivalence? Oh, yes. Despite the strong sense we are given of how attractive, how almost irresistible he is, virtually every magician in the corpus, as if to warn us not to get too close, exudes an unmistakable whiff of brimstone.

As with so many other aspects of Canadian literature, the satanic side of the magician is elusive. The problem is, his negative qualities are so closely allied with the qualities that make him fascinating that it is hard to tell them apart. The amorality and social independence that constitute his enviable freedom also make him unreliable. Even if he is not villainous in any real sense of the term, far from being a social 'champion' he is simply one of those self-interested individuals whom Zweig calls 'adventurer': 'they are not loyal, nor are they disloyal. The question simply does not arise for them. Their loyalty is directed toward the turns and chances of their own destinies' [36]. He can't be counted on, in other words. The problem would be less severe if his lack of dependability had to do only with public functions (the Canadian, while a long way from the romantic American anarchist, is at least sceptical enough about the public realm to be dispassionate if not sympathetic toward a dereliction of 'official' duty), but in the magician's case the betrayal is as likely to be personal as not. Without love *or* scruple to restrain egotistic desires, emotional detachment turns out all too often to be indistinguishable from simple callousness. Darcy Rushworth doesn't care enough about his father's feelings even to lie about his reasons for dodging enlistment. Roger Dork doesn't think twice about using deceit to seduce a friend's girl. Magnus Eisengrim is indifferent to the fate of his mother.

If we extend this insensitivity to human suffering – the bland and cheerful readiness to pay for gratification in the coin of someone else's pain – from the single to the multiple case what we have is simply, as Rosemary Sullivan puts it, 'the shadow side or underbelly of the [American] myth of opportunity': that is, 'the reality of exploitation' (A146). T.G. Roberts hit on the true nature of the average magician back in 1907, long before the anti-capitalist stance became fashionable. Magicians, he said, were in general petty individuals who 'overthrew their enemies by provoking stronger people against them, working slyly, with many false tales and foolish antics. They had been at the bottom of most of the wars in the big island, and ... usually gained power and wealth at the cost of warriors's lives' (90-1).

This last quotation points to something a little more serious than simple callousness, to be sure. When we talk of war we are talking of a threat not merely to our feelings but to our lives. And the fact is, the magician seems to have an *affinity* for war, not merely because of the opportunity it presents for profiteering but because *there is something in his nature that actually thrives on battle*. This is the one thing about Roger Dork that Ashley Morden has the most trouble understanding. Dork was born to be a warrior. He is good at it – strong, lucky, fearless. What is more *he enjoys it*. The average Canadian has far too much empathy to be able to detach himself from the victim's point of view, but for Dork dealing death makes him feel alive:

Almost every building in thirty square miles of Hamburg was ablaze that night – the greatest havoc Ash saw during the war ... [He] was having a struggle to keep from being sick in his oxygen mask. And then, as they went in for the bomb run, he heard Dork's voice, gay and ebullient on the intercom: 'Jesus Christ, look at all the color! Isn't that a beautiful sight!'

That was Dork and *his* war. Seventy thousand people were dead or dying that night in the fire storm of Hamburg, and for Dork it was beautiful. He reveled in war's shattering of restraints and inhibitions – especially those regarding women. His war had no qualms or second thoughts. He was one of the fortunate ones who fought his war merely because his country *was* at war. (21)

Where does it come from, this apparent bloodthirstiness? Part of it is undoubtedly rooted in the emotional self-sufficiency of the magician – certainly this it is that makes him *capable* of killing so casually, without qualm or remorse – but what part of his character makes him enjoy it so much? Is it his competitiveness, his obsession with winning? – or perhaps just the joy of exercising a skill? Possibly. But it's possible, too, that there is something dark and irrational *built right in* to the magician's role. If we turn to mythic parallels, the connection may become clearer.

I have already said the magician is not a champion. His associations will not, therefore, be with those exemplary figures – Beowulf, Roland, St George – who battle evil on behalf of the common good. This means that we must look for his roots among what Zweig calls the 'equivocal heroes.' But what *kind* of equivocal hero is he? There are two distinct types to be found within the general category. The first is the trickster or wily opportunist like Odysseus; the second a more dangerous figure – Hercules, the Hindu god Indra, the Irish Cuchullin – whom we might call the 'wrathful hero.' The distinguishing feature of the latter, as the label suggests, is his predilection for violence. He is an incomparable warrior, but his fury is so undisciplined that once aroused he is a menace to friend and foe alike. Although his intentions may be good, all too often those who would take advantage of his skills discover – too late – that the 'energy which fed his triumph has blinded him to moral distinctions and family allegiance. He has become the intense berserker radiance of his acts' [Zweig 43].

Why the lack of control? One explanation would put the blame on the source or nature of his powers. Many mythic warriors are attributed with the characteristics of wild animals – in the *Iliad*, for instance, as Rosette Lamont points out, 'Hector is a wild boar, Aeneas a lion, Odysseus a deep-fleeced ram, Achilles a bull, a vulture, or eagle swooping down on its prey' [4] – as if to imply that in battle they *become* as beasts. Even when their animal association takes the form of a contest *against* some deadly creature – as is the case with Hercules and Sampson – it is, in Lamont's words, 'not only a way of dramatizing a great human's superiority to brute strength, but a *symbolic representation of the savage passions that enter into the hero's makeup*' [italics added]. If the warrior's passions are channelled by either exterior authority or a social commitment, the bestial aspect of his nature may be kept under control, but if, in his egotism, he resists such channelling, he takes on not merely the strength but the irrationality of the beast. The wrathful hero is dangerous, according to this view, simply because violence is by definition unhuman.

Other views are more pessimistic. The bestial theory, by making control the key, at least leaves open the *possibility* for a constructive use of force. One could argue, however, that the control itself exacerbates the danger. Pitting himself against not merely external enemies but the human weaknesses of pity and fear, the hero must repress some instincts and exaggerate others, become a creature of extremes. Any such departure from the golden mean can only upset his psychic balance. 'The tremendous discipline and self-control which allow brave men to carry out their purposes,' says Lamont, 'are defined by the very fact that they counterbalance a seething sea of emotions ... even a form of madness' [7]. Over-controlled or under-controlled, both of these explanations imply that aggressiveness is by its very nature dangerous. For whatever reason, the wrathful hero seems to be cursed by some inner blight that creates havoc wherever he goes: 'At the climax of risk and fury, this hero rises up in terrifying splendor, as a man of no society: drunkenly solitary, an embodiment of all risk, all transgression; as if the violence of his character had traced a boundary on all sides of him, which severed him from the world of social values, hierarchy and family' [Zweig 43].

What, you may ask, does this have to do with the Canadian magician? The very name we have given this figure implies that his ascendancy depends on wit rather than force of arms: surely he should be associated with the trickster rather than the berserker. Indeed, we have already seen some of his resemblances to Odysseus. If, however, we survey the corpus with this categorization in mind, we soon notice a disturbing discrepancy. Despite the fact that most Canadian magician figures are initially presented in terms suggesting that wiliness, not brute force, is their natural stock in trade (even Dork, the one real 'warrior' in the group, is shown most often to achieve his personal ends by conniving rather than open aggression), their almost invariable secondary implication in a kind of violent and destructive behaviour quite uncharacteristic of the role they would seem, overtly, to have been assigned suggests that they are seen to offer covertly the dangers of the wrathful hero *in addition to* their own more subtle brand of threat. Darcy Rushworth murders a retarded girl who threatens his plans for his protégé. Wesley Duivylbuis, the eagle scout of *Lunar Attractions*, kills a transvestite who offends his sense of personal rectitude. Wayne Farrell commits arson and murder in revenge for insults. Keneally is implicated in several murders, not to mention fights and beatings. Horwood's Esau Gillingham is accused of killing his song brother, and although the sympathetic presentation of his character is surely meant to convince us that he is innocent, no other even vaguely plausible explanation is given. Most interesting of all, James Houston's Shoona is credited with causing the 'magic' deaths of several people through unconscious malevolence, as if his innate destructiveness is so great that it acts without and even against his conscious intent. From all these examples it seems clear that the Canadian is so uncomfortable with the idea of heroism, *any* kind of heroism, that he tends to impute the worst aspects of *all* the mythic models to his home-grown magician. According to our literature, in fact, *any* aggressive behaviour, even when socially condoned and well intentioned, is likely to have the worst, most deadly effects conceivable. Unlike the saint, Tekakwitha, the shaman is '*tarijuk*, one who turns things into shadows' (Houston 71). It is thus hardly surprising that the Spirit Wrestler – swimmer in deadly seas – cannot use his power to heal no matter how hard he tries. To use it at all, he learns to his despair, is *always* to hurt or to kill.

Carrying the taint of violence as he does, the magician naturally comes to seem even more firmly 'other.' Here we get into another of those vicious circles that seem to plague the Canadian consciousness, because the more alien he is, the more dangerous he naturally seems. At this stage, indeed, the menace implied by the magician carries us into a whole new level of experience. The apparent instability of his identity, as Zweig says of Odysseus, invites 'a strange encroachment of unhuman definition' [30]. This points to the magician's tendency to develop in a direction that denies altogether the possibility of human identification. It's a question of constitution. The 'self,' as we know it, is a mixed entity, good and bad, strengths balanced with weaknesses. This condition is automatically entailed by the nature of the human animal. Any creature or thing which is *absolutely* other, however, can also be *absolutely* itself – a pure essence unalloyed by any tincture of humanity at all. The magician, from whom we are commonly so careful to dissociate ourselves, can thus be either all good, lacking human frailties – and this is obviously what we are hoping for when we create heroic figures like Esau Gillingham – *or* all bad. Unfortunately – as we might expect considering our suspicions of otherness generally – it seems to be the latter possibility that the Canadian finds most convincing. Out of all the dozens, perhaps hundreds, of magicians and would-be magicians on Roberts's fabulous Newfoundland in *The Red Feathers*, for instance, only *one* is beneficent. More interesting than the simple fact of our predilection for explicit villains, however, is a more insidious fear – the fear that the hero might well be only a kind of grotesque fragment or shadow of real humanity – implicit in our writers's habit of associating him with a motif of twins or doubles.

The twin symbol has a venerable history in myth and folklore. What is more important, changes in religious thinking have given it a built-in ambiguity that makes it a useful significatory element in a culture suffering from as many psychological confusions as ours evidently does. On the simplest level the twin symbol can be used to underline the magician's association with archaic heroes and thus reinforce our distance. In prehistoric periods, Otto Rank tells us, every individual was supposed to have an immaterial self that dwelt in the spirit world. When twins were born it was believed that the second was simply the incarnate soul of the first. This could be interpreted in various ways. In many cultures the spirit-twin was considered dangerous, evil (because 'out of place'), and thus had to be killed that the 'real' person might live. From a slightly different point of view, however, it could be maintained that twins, having no ghost-selves vulnerable to magic, were more powerful than ordinary mortals. Hence we get such twin heroes as Remus and Romulus, the founders of Rome, and Amphion and Zethod, the builders of Thebes. At the same time, we also find the ambivalent image of the split personality developing in such myths of good/bad 'twins' as Cain and Abel, Set and Horus, Prometheus and Epimetheus. These elaborations on the original ideal of twinship come together to produce, on the one hand, a 'conception of the hero as the type who combines in one person the mortal and immortal self'[5] (there are thus excellent precedents for Keneally's ability to create and then to destroy his own 'good' twin, suggesting as it does the self-completeness, the self-control, and the spiritual invulnerability which is one mark of the true hero) and, on the other, the myth of the doppelgänger, the self's twin or double. The latter is the aspect, provocatively enough, that has the most relevance to the Canadian practice. The fact is, the particular twinning motifs associated with the magician in Canadian fiction frequently suggest that this ambiguous figure, on the surface so clearly 'other,' is in truth some kind of alter ego.

What kind, though? What does this disquieting pairing actually imply? In folklore the double is generally viewed as an unequivocal threat to the self's survival (going back to the earlier, more homely view of the twin) but if we look at literary, especially Romantic and post-Romantic treatments of the theme, we see that the encounter with the 'other' self, while traumatic, has come to be widely considered a potentially beneficial and even necessary experience. Numerous negative examples showing what happens when one unnaturally 'splits off' – represses – undesirable aspects of the personality (Wilde's *The Portrait of Dorian Gray* for one; even more strikingly, Stevenson's *Dr Jekyll and Mr Hyde*), reinforced by a few positive examples that demonstrate the benefits to be gained from reconciliation with the double (Conrad's 'The Secret Sharer'), establish clearly in literary tradition the idea, codified by Jung, that the risks of ignoring the unassimilated monsters lurking in the depths of the unconscious are far greater than the risks of confronting them. According to this (now pervasive) view, we should all, in other words – as Liesl, with rather ambiguous results, tries to teach David Staunton in Davies' *The Manticore* – be prepared to face our own cave bears. Is this what the doppelgänger motif signifies in Canadian literature?

Certainly in some cases that would seem to be the appropriate inference. Although the moral dynamic of the book is an elusive one, the narrator of Hubert Aquin's *Prochain épisode* – who despite his self-appointed role as a revolutionary reveals more than a superficial resemblance to his quarry/persecutor, the financier H. Heutz – seems to reach some kind of enlightenment when he recognizes his kinship (shared guilt, shared innocence) with his enemy. Similarly, in *A Candle to Light the Sun*, it is only by giving up his attempt to dissociate himself from his 'evil' alter – by accepting that even though the physical evidence of 'the double man, four armed, four-legged beast' had 'dissolved ... in the hemp-woman's embrace,' the 'beast lived still' inside him (302) – that David Newman is able to achieve his full humanity. In this latter example especially, the message is elusive – in Laurence Ricou's words, 'the confused syntax suggests that [his] understanding is tenuous and incomplete at best, more charged with emotion than with reason' – but it is nevertheless clear from 'the hints of betrayal, purity, and even redemption in [Blondal's] understated analogy to Christ's death' that the author at least *intends* us to impute something positive to David's encounter with his doppelgänger (A67). The mere fact that both these books are so hesitant about pushing home the point of their themes, however, suggests a certain discomfort with the conventional implications of the doppelgänger motif. This is not surprising. However fearsome it may be to confront one's home-grown inner monsters, it is doubly frightening to have to identify oneself even symbolically with a figure so definitively alien.

As a result of this reluctance, the Canadian treatment of the doppelgänger motif typically evokes the older and more basic dead/alive duality preserved in folklore rather than – or at least, covertly, in addition to – the conventional Romantic theme of the good/evil alters. Rather than viewing the double as either the ghost (bad spirit) of the primitive or the guardian angel (good spirit) of the early Christian era, however, the Canadian, suffering from the 'exaggerated fear of death threatening the ... Self' that Rank associates with the archetypal artist, transforms the symbol into its precise opposite: a representation of 'the perishable and mortal part of the personality'; 'indeed, the announcer of death itself' [77, 82, 76]. Here, of course, is Wade Powers's Horseman. Here too – explaining much of our uneasiness with him – is the doppelgänger who lurks within many of our literary magicians. No other theory can explain the fact that for all the recent popularity of Jungian concepts, more often than not the confrontation with the double in Canadian literature leads not to enlightenment – even the qualified enlightenment David Newman attains – but to disaster. In Clark Blaise's *Lunar Attractions* the protagonist himself survives the trauma of his recognition of the soul-sickness that haunts Wesley Duivylbuis, the 'perfect' classmate and shadow who has stolen his name, but only because David's previous enforced empathy with an archetypal victim, the sexually ambivalent Larry/Laurel ('I felt closer and closer to Larry ... I thought of the pain he'd gone through for his strange compulsion. Such loneliness was more profound than any isolation or any loneliness I had ever experienced. It was on the other side of loneliness like the unknown side of the moon' 181), 'sets up' a scapegoat who may, with perfect symbolic decorum, be sacrificed in his place. Kroetsch's Peter Guy is less lucky. Indeed, *But We Are Exiles* could be viewed as a prototype for the Canadian version of the negative-archaic (as opposed to the positive-romantic) doppelgänger fable.

Many critics miss the point. Frank Davey, for instance, believes that Peter can achieve 'rebirth' by casting off the victim role he accepted when he allowed Hornyak to seduce Kettle; by *becoming*, in effect, the magician himself. 'The novel suggests that Guy's quest can end only when he has somehow re-enacted his moment of failure, challenged his usurper's right to occupy his bed, and successfully displaced him,' he says (F156). Since it is difficult to see the act of crawling into a coffin with someone as a triumph of self-assertion, however, I am reluctant to accept that this is what Kroetsch is trying to tell us. John Moss, I think, is far more correct in his reading when he claims that at the time of the story Kroetsch's protagonist has gone too far already toward becoming 'his mirror opposite' (D41). The truth is, rejecting Kettle's plea that he 'Break the mirror' (how different from the Jungian platitudes that David Staunton is offered!), Peter, prepared for the role by his symbolic conquest of the landscape, exchanging 'the terrors of human relationships' for 'a river [in] his head,' does turn into his antithesis – but the result, far from the conventional rebirth that critics like Davey evoke, is simply oblivion: spiritual and probably physical death (103, 124). 'In final surrender to the metamorphosis,' says Moss, 'he tips Hornyak's appropriately defaced corpse from the canoe where it lies ... and ... takes its place' (D41).

All these associations make the magician an even more ambiguous figure, of course. To the extent that, as doppelgänger, he is potentially 'self,' there is a tendency for us to inflate him even beyond what our 'American' wishful fantasies might suggest; not to redeem him exactly (his essential alienness is far too threatening for that) but to make his evil *grander* somehow, more glamorous if not more justifiable – like Simon Mottley, in fact, to transform a vision of merely human nastiness into 'the kind of high Gothic [demonic-quest romance] represented by *Melmoth*, or *Moby-Dick*, or *Heart of Darkness* ... in which a lonely, self-divided hero embarks on insane pursuit of the Absolute.'[6] To the extent that he is irredeemably 'other,' however, we are motivated to diminish rather than augment his power. One way we can maintain an illusion of satisfying both these impulses is to allow the magician's satanic attractiveness full rein but *to make sure that he is punished for it*. How? Not by our own hands, for that single act of aggression would be enough to transform us into *him*, but through the self-destructive effects of his own nature. By invoking Nemesis, in other words. Keneally catches the fear disease he has exploited all his life and in a frantic attempt to hide from the accusing faces of his colonists corkscrews himself into the ground. Roger Dork is killed by a wolf when he, wolfish in a much less admirable sense of the word, tries to rape its mistress. Shoona, the shamanic 'swimmer,' having angered by his presumption those same dangerous spirits from which/whom he has derived his power, is first isolated from the human community by the fear his apparent irrationality catalyses and then, when he is most vulnerable, killed, appropriately enough through his half-crazed, grateful submission to a literally lethal seduction by the goddess of the sea. Such manoeuvres dispose of the problem neatly.

Or do they?

Our punishment of the magician (does the circle ever end?) introduces new ambiguities to complicate an already complicated picture. It is possible, like the ancient Greeks, to see the hero's downfall as simply the appropriate and inevitable price that has to be paid for self-assertion. Trespassing against the crucial, ponderous choreography of nature, he arouses, in Zweig's words, a 'widespread anxiety that greatness itself [is] a crime against ... order' [54] which, like our own anxiety about the magician, can only be allayed by a demonstration that that order will always reassert itself against individual encroachments. Hence the belief – the almost relieved acceptance of the fact – that 'To be a man to the fullest is to *deserve*, along with immortality in song, the bitterness of punishment' [56, italics added]. Such a view does not belittle human greatness – indeed the hero is seen as even *more* heroic for his insistence on self-validation in the face of such consequences – but it does 'context' it in such a way as to minimize both its psychological dangers and its socially disruptive potential. If we backtrack beyond Aristotle to the primitive roots of the great myth cycles we know most notably from the plays, though, the relationship between the hero and his punishment seems a little more equivocal. In Rank's words:

Man's eternal need to control [the] super-individual power [of leadership] is born from the fear of 'chaos' which lurks beyond the self we know. Hence, the superman was singled out as the divine king who became endowed with this dangerous weapon, dangerous to the bearer himself as well as to the subjects exposed to it. Since it is at bottom a power of life and death, the divine king, as we saw in primitive tradition, had to prove himself fit for his task by killing his predecessor. This was a cultic performance for which, according to the human law, he had to pay with his own life ... This double danger of the divine power may explain why in mythical and subsequent historical tradition the leader in times of crisis appears as a foreigner who is allowed to assume might. First of all, being alien, he takes this dangerous burden off the community shoulders, and secondly, being a stranger, he makes this strange irrational power more acceptable. At the same time having – as did Jesus, Jeanne d'Arc and other historical figures – assumed this power illegitimately, the outsider, like the divine king after his term expires, is prematurely removed from the scene of action. [136-7]

Rank's analysis has some rather provocative implications for our complacent disposal of the magician – especially since our relationship with the *pharmakos*, judging at least by the way we treat his avatars in our fiction, comes closer to the terms implied by the original ritual than to the more abstracted and idealized version that found its way into the great tragedies. The fact is, just as much as Rank's primitive tribesman we *need* the magician (the 'American') to do our dirty work for us. Like Keneally's colonists we impose on him the stigma of aggression, willing to suffer his mastery, even his brutality, as long as we ourselves may remain passive and invisible.[7] We make him 'king,' moreover, knowing perfectly well what 'crime' that entails. Under the circumstances it seems rather unfair, for us as for the primitives, to punish him for being exactly what we require. To make matters worse, both our superimposed ideology and our reluctant recognition of the double pressure us toward identifying *ourselves* with the doomed hero. How do we deal with these ambiguities? As usual, by evasion. We may discern in Canadian fiction at least three formal strategies for neutralizing the emotional threat posed by the magician.

The first strategy is the traditional one for dealing with institutionalized ambivalence: mythicization. Perhaps, though, the term 'dealing with' implies too much conscious intent for what is, in fact, a spontaneous cultural effect. Keneally and his ilk, simply because they embody the unnatural aggressive instinct that both intrigues and terrifies the Canadian, become *taboo*. This term does not just mean, as many laymen (influenced by Hollywood versions of savage culture) tend to think, the *forbidden*, but, rather, the *numinous*. 'Whatever is taboo is a focus not only of special interest but also of anxiety,' says Edmund Leach. 'Whatever is taboo is sacred, valuable, powerful, dangerous, untouchable, filthy.'[8] It is also difficult to talk about. This is where myth comes in. Myth represents the community's way of exploring its own feelings about taboo subjects without the risk of contagion. It reinforces critical conventions and categories of behaviour by examining and then either punishing, transforming, or displacing cases of transgression. Primary myths 'are always centrally preoccupied with persons and creatures who are wrongly constructed or wrongly born or in the wrong place, and with such universal moral offences as homicide, sexual misdemeanours, and abnormal food behaviour,' says Leach. 'Such myths exhibit the limits of normality and the potent danger of otherness.'[9] It is easy to see how Keneally *et al.* fit this prescription.[10] It is thus hardly surprising that Canadian writers working with the magician figure tend not only to endow him with personal qualities that link him specifically with other mythic heroes (Keneally is compared to Cuchullin and Magnus Eisengrim to Mephistopheles, while one of Horwood's narrators says of Gillingham that 'He belonged to the age of gods and heroes, like Richard the Lion-Heart, or Jason, or Gilgamesh in the epic' 3) but to introduce, more or less explicitly, many conventional mythic plot elements as well (the virgin birth in *The Invention of the World*, the conquest of the beast in *Tay John*, the idea of rebirth through name-change in *Fifth Business*, the underworld – over-water – journey in *But We Are Exiles*, the wilderness ordeal in *The Atonement of Ashley Morden*, divine revenge in *Spirit Wrestler*, and so on). Most important of all, at least in their references to the taboo hero himself, they tend to use, even in ostensibly realistic works, an unusually elevated narrative tone. These devices allow us to indulge our fascination with the magician while simultaneously emphasizing his abnormality – and our own unlikeness, of course.

Unfortunately, while it does facilitate one kind of psychological distancing, myth also gives its personae more immediacy, more *reality*, by enhancing their numen. Normally the implied religious dimension would provide a means whereby this element may be kept in its proper perspective, but the Canadian, forced to juggle a far more complex set of ideas and emotions than his primitive forebears, is incapable of responding to his communal myths, no matter how deeply imbedded, in such a straightforward way. Even leaving aside the difficulty of reconciling the attitudes covertly entailed by the Canadian cultural ambience with the values more consciously espoused, his Western faith in free will and rationality insist that myths have only symbolic significance and therefore only nominal relevance to his own patterns of thought and behaviour. This stance has some rather disturbing consequences. Since, as we have seen, the magician *does in fact* play a very real and very threatening role in our communal consciousness, the literary 'myth' *does in fact* reinforce our awe/fear of him, but because we do not allow ourselves to take that myth seriously, it loses much of its power to protect us from our own unrecognized feelings. Which leaves the magician even more of a psychological threat than before.

What to do? Many Canadian writers, especially those who (a) deal most explicitly with the ambiguity of the taboo figure or (b) attempt to present him as unambiguously positive (which triggers unconscious anxiety), simply respond by embedding the myth in an obtrusive external narrative frame. In *Spirit Wrestler*, for instance, the tale of Shoona is told to us by a Northern Service Officer who heard it from the protagonist as he was dying. In *White Eskimo* Gillingham's story is related jointly by two men who had 'known him at the peak of his power [but] held widely differing views about him' (3). In *World of Wonders* Magnus Eisengrim speaks for himself, but the recital is given its context by Dunstan Ramsay's earlier recounting in *Fifth Business*, disguised as a letter written upon retirement to his headmaster. Tay John's story is presented partly as straight legend and partly as a retrospective reconstruction by an interested sometime observer. The important thing is that we always approach the myth obliquely. Even in more or less realistic treatments, like *Lunar Attractions*, *The Atonement of Ashley Morden*, and *A Candle to Light the Sun*, our impressions of the magician figure are largely coloured by if not explicitly filtered through the consciousness of the other protagonists. In *But We Are Exiles*, typically enough, we don't arrive on the scene until the ambiguous Hornyak is dead. What is the purpose of this manoeuvre? Very simple. Even aside from its artful deflation of the taboo figure (myth alone compels respect; myth in juxtaposition with naturalistic material is automatically relegated to the category of mere fantasy), because we see nothing or little of the magician directly, it saves us from the necessity of committing ourselves to either uncomfortable belief or dangerous disbelief.

The Invention of the World provides a striking illustration of the advantages of the strategy. Keneally's story is, apparently, compounded from different kinds of material 'collected' by Becker, some of it (we assume) reworked to produce the 'legend,' other parts presented in the words of the actual respondents. Leaving aside for now the implications of this technique *qua* technique, we see the effects the method has on our view of/response to the hero. Firstly, because he is by definition one step away from reality, Keneally can be built up into the great and sinister figure our intuition tells us the magician must be without offending either our credulity or our sense of decorum. Secondly, the mixed reactions of the observers (Keneally is described variously as brute and saviour, fool and genius, a giant of a man who 'took up a lot more space even than his big body seemed to' and a 'whipped child' 205, 202) allow us simultaneously to justify our fear/admiration of the hero (that is, the testimony of those who recognized his charisma goes to prove that such a type 'really is' as impressive, and as dangerous, as we suspect) *and* to disown it as simply 'ignorance and prejudice' (217). Finally, because Keneally's story is both logically undermined by its seeming inaccessibility ('None of us will ever know what really went on in that place') and emotionally defused by its progressive narrative subordination to the experience of the 'normal' people whose vision dominates the book, we can maintain the illusion that its significance for us is in any case strictly limited.[11] Such duplicity as Hodgins demonstrates here is both so effective and, considering our need to come to terms somehow with the aggressive model we find so disturbing, so *important*, that we might say the oblique perspective has been subsumed by the very myth that it was evolved to deprecate. The Canadian myth of the magician, in other words, is replaced implicitly by a more reassuring myth of *our immunity to His spell*.

This brings us to the final stage. Having achieved at least aesthetic dissociation from the aggressor we now attempt to remove the 'self' from the equation altogether. How? Easy. We simply *neutralize* our ambiguous hero. By introducing into the picture the figure of his formal opposite, the fool-saint type, the Canadian, like the young protagonist of *Lunar Attractions*, symbolically displaces his own potential role as victim into a third party. It works, too. In any book where the active and passive exemplars are explicitly paired the tensions inhere in the relation between the two rather than in the relation between the symbolic ego and its potential model. In *Arkwright*, for instance, one of the major themes concerns the arch-capitalist's fascination with the life of the archetypal loser, Timothy Elmtree. In *The Candy Factory*, alternately, the focus of the narrative frame is on the efforts of the virtually invisible Mary Moon to escape from her 'claustrophobic, unheroic, repetitive and purposeless existence' (10) by uniting with the radically aggressive and self-obsessed tramp: 'She addressed his ruined eye, staring into the milky centre of it as if into a crystal ball, saying she had just had a vision! a vision of the future! saying she and the tramp were the perfect coupling, the one made out of the bowels of the earth, the other from the clouds in the loft! saying together – with her faith and his knowing cynicism – they could occupy the loft and save the Candy Factory' (52). In each of these cases the basic emotional dynamic of the book is self-contained, complete in itself, without implicating the reader.

As we might have expected, of course, the process of withdrawal from the magician does not stop at this neat point of closure. As almost always happens when secondary elaborations or transformations are introduced into myth, the tension between old and new elements not only creates new sources of strain but also precipitates a re-emergence, in somewhat different form, of the original ambiguities the symbolic construct was formulated to mediate. The problem with pairing the saint with the magician is that sooner or later the manoeuvre is bound to suggest what is implicit in all mythical oppositions, that they are merely two faces on the same coin. The complications entailed by this development are obvious. What we end up with is a self-symbol seeming to *merge* with its absolute antithesis – and in doing so confirming exactly that disquieting conflation that all our evasive strategies have been mounted to avoid.

By this means we are brought to the last and possibly most significant aspect of the cast of primary role models found in Canadian literature. Underlying *all* the diverse responses to experience embodied in the literary personae examined in the last two chapters is the recognition that in the long run – not in any immediate sense, but potentially, theoretically, *ultimately* – the saint and the magician may, in truth, merely represent two aspects of the same character. Kip Caley is both criminal and victim. Jerome Martell, the exemplary, twice-born Christ figure of *The Watch that Ends the Night*, turns berserker in battle. Doctor Nelson, the murderer of *Kamouraska*, has always dreamed of being a saint. In Atwood's *Lady Oracle*, the protagonist perceives a sinister duplicity in *all* the men who have been part of her life, beginning with her father, 'healer and killer' (295). This seems to counter our assertions (or fears) of uniqueness. The recognition that active and passive – yin and yang – are not merely opposite but intimately yoked is hardly an original one. Again, though, there is an important difference in emphasis to be discerned between the Canadian view and the more typical Western usage.

The crucial point to be noted is the fact that whatever hypothetical equivalence of male and female principles may be suggested by the yin/yang symbol, in practice the modes are never actually viewed that way. In virtually all historic Western mythologies, moreover, it is the *male* mode which is presented as if not an ideal at least some kind of norm. Reorientation toward the female component of personality, whether this is considered to be a positive or negative development, is thus always seen as some kind of deviance. Generally, indeed, the motif tends to emerge only covertly. According to Zweig, in romance literature, as in most primitive myth, the anima figure is treated as the hero's antithesis, both the inspiration to his bravery and, less obviously, 'the adversary he needs to master' [62]. The more radically he repudiates *identification* with the female principle, however – and we see this effect quite strikingly not merely in archaic but in American literature – the more he seems to exhibit feminine traits himself. Even aside from the ambiguous sexual implications of the male bonding so common among undomesticated males from Gilgamesh and Enkidu through Leatherstocking and Chingachgook, the very form of the adventurer's career, being, as Zweig points out, 'sublimely nondirective' ('the world solicits him and he follows its occasions, as water follows the slope of a hill'), 'violates all standards of responsible "male" behavior' [71]. Notwithstanding these subversive undertones, however, it is quite clearly the masculine mode that such stories are *intended* to celebrate.

In the modern period, the picture becomes slightly more complicated, especially on the Continent, where existentialism has had its greatest influence. Indeed, since this school holds that impotence is the key feature of the human condition, it would seem that its exponents have already accepted an inverted world view, replacing the heroic (that is, masculine) with the anti-heroic (feminine?) vision. If we look closely at the literature, though, we realize two things: firstly, no matter how widespread the victim stance is perceived to be it is never viewed as a norm (the very term 'absurd' implies that it violates *human* if not *natural* order); secondly, it is still the masculine, assertive mode that is presented as a conscious ideal. Indeed, self-assertion becomes even *more* important than before. The result, interestingly enough, is that although the feminine mode *seems* more normalized than it is in the romance, it is actually more vigorously resisted than ever. If the criminal is as much of a victim as the saint (violence, says Ihab Hassan, is the 'ultimate form of introspection'[12]), the saint, as indeed we already noted in our discussion of the American mad-hero in the last chapter, is as much of a 'protestant' as his official foil. Not only are both of these types isolates, in other words, but in *both* cases – not just, as we might expect, in the formally 'active' criminal – the world-negating stance is a form of rebellion against, rather than an acquiescence to, the externally imposed passive mode. One of the most interesting explications of this rather complex vision is found in Sartre's *Saint-Genet, Actor and Martyr*. As Robert Detweiler describes it,

because he accepts what others have made of him, his being wicked is innocent, but because he does evil, which involves acting on free choice, he is guilty. From this contradiction Genet evolves a two-fold position: if evil is predetermined, he is a martyr and saint (with feminine connotations), but if he takes it freely upon himself, he is the prince of crime. Thus the dialectic of being and doing resolves itself into the two corresponding roles of saint and criminal ... Particularly through pederasty Genet confirms the paralyzing power of the gaze of others; he becomes the submissive partner, the martyr or 'female' saint who suffers the lust of others, but still reaffirms his identity *through a conscious choice of an involvement in a criminal sexuality*. [italics added][13]

Far from signalling a free relinquishment of assertiveness, the existentialist's confirmation of his victimization paradoxically changes its whole meaning by turning it into a wilful act of self-creation.

Even from these brief summaries, it's easy to see why and how the Canadian approach to the saint/magician pairing would tend to differ from both traditional *and* modern practice. In Canada, as we have already established, it is the passive mode which is viewed as exemplary – not necessarily wholly positive, any more than its opposite is viewed as wholly positive even in the most self-consciously hero-worshipping cultures, but in a very real sense *normative*. It is therefore the shift from saint into magician, whether this is presented as good (an escape) or bad (self-destructive), *not* the covert feminization of the hero, which is viewed here as the deviant development. How does this divergence in attitude affect our literary practice? Well, for one thing, whatever the singular implications of the familiar mythic motifs we find throughout the corpus, the changed perspective effects radical changes in the emotional dynamics of the larger picture. Most notably, to the extent that given works reflect communal response, it's obvious that it will now be the possibility of the victim turning victimizer that catalyzes anxiety, rather than the reverse.

This feature seems particularly anomalous if we view it in the context of conventions that are well-nigh canonical in the United States. American popular fiction is full of gleeful celebrations of the little guy who grows up to be a hero and gets his chance to punish the bully who pushed him around when he was a kid. This fellow, indeed – the skinny misfit who develops muscles or the poor boy who gets rich or the innocent who takes the grand prize on the TV show away from all the eggheads – is none other than the American Adam, everyone's favourite alter ego. Not so in Canada. The Canadian version of the same story, even aside from the fact that it is extremely rare, far from suggesting whole-hearted approbation of and identification with such a reversal, invariably presents the victor in an exceedingly dubious light. Look at Davies' Deptford trilogy, for instance. No one would deny that Paul Dempster's metamorphosis into Magnus Eisengrim – his self-transformation from the most degraded of victims into a charming Mephistopheles – is a positive one for aesthetic if for no other reasons. Eisengrim himself, however, is a disturbingly equivocal character. Even if we write off his naive arrogance as an irritating but harmless quirk of character, we are bound to feel at least some shock (accustomed as we are to the inevitable 'nobility' of his clean-cut American counterpart) at the sadistic way he savours his ascendency over his erstwhile persecutor. Even more profoundly disquieting is the unintentional but nonetheless devastating effect he has on his 'double,' the actor from whom he learns his theatrical skills. '"Your emulation, as you call it, sucked the pith out of that poor old ham, and gobbled it up, and made it part of yourself,"' says one of his co-workers in later years. '"It was a very nasty process." "Roly, I idolized him." "Yes, and to be idolized by you, as you were then, was a terrible, vampire-like feeding on his personality and his spirit ... You were a double, right enough, and such a double as Poe and Dostoyevsky would have understood"' (c212). *A vampire-like feeding!* The allusion is both apt and telling. Paul Dempster's experience may demonstrate that it is possible for even the most degraded of victims to escape – indeed that the *most* degraded, being on the one hand the most desperate and on the other the most dehumanized, are most likely to have the motivation and the means – but the sinister overtones carried by Davies' description of his born-again magician also make quite clear what such transformations cost, in terms of personal integrity.

It may be objected, particularly by those reluctant to relinquish the wishful vision of Horatio Alger and Cinderella-in-Hollywood and Abe Lincoln emerging from his log cabin, that Eisengrim is an extreme case, not merely because of the rather exceptional experience that stimulates his metamorphosis but more because in Davies' literary treatment the discontinuity between the young victim and the mature victimizer is so complete that, the flashbacks of *World of Wonders* notwithstanding, we actually respond to him/them as two entirely separate persons. Regardless of historical/biological identity, in other words, the magician here has apparently managed to dissociate himself so completely from his earlier self as to escape entirely whatever effects may have otherwise obtained if he were still able to empathize to any degree with the perspective of a passive exemplar. Must this always be the way things turn out, though? Even admitting that we do seem to have an ingrained antipathy toward the hero as a type, under other circumstances – circumstances more favourably designed to appease our prejudices than those Davies delineates – is it not possible for the conflation of role models, rather than exacerbating our sense of unease, by eliciting our identification with the saint persona to humanize and thus redeem the all-too-alien magician? On the basis of the evidence provided by the corpus itself, the answer to this, it would seem, is a flat no.

We see the problems quite clearly when we turn to Gwendolyn MacEwen's *King of Egypt, King of Dreams*. On the surface this book is conventional historical fiction, exotic, romantic, satisfyingly melodramatic – it is the story of Akhenaton, pharaoh of Egypt from 1367 to 1350 B.C. It is also, however, a very Canadian story. For one thing, Egypt itself – a culture obsessed with death, obsessed with the integrity of the corporeal body, obsessed most of all with transforming what is transcendent into pre-eminently effable concrete facts – is a much more appropriate correlative for Canada than one might suppose.[14] More important, I Neter Ay, the character who provides if not a consistent centre of consciousness at least a normative narrative viewpoint for the book, strikingly resembles the figure we have come to see as the prototypical Canadian: pragmatic ('I've never experienced anything remotely holy in my life' 232), unsure of his own identity ('I was always my own mystery ... My life was always a string of inner queries.' 235), haunted by his awareness of mortality ('I felt something deadly grip me as I crossed the floor. A sudden nostalgia, a horrid fear coming from deep in my belly. I realized I was aging.' 238), fearful of touching ('I have always loved to have my hands covered ... and when Haremheb took my old gloves I felt positively naked and vulnerable for months' 241), suspicious of absolutes ('Order is surely born of chaos ... I always distrusted the pure, the singular man. He is the river with no branches. He flows into the sea. He is a lie.' 235), and, most appositely, both fascinated and repelled by the magician who is his master. MacEwen thus presents her material from a very Canadian viewpoint.

As for the 'history' itself, for all its exoticism this too conforms well with the Canadian pattern. Akhenaton begins his career as an exemplary victim. As a child he is nearly incapacitated by a debilitating illness. Even after he achieves normal health, he remains a clumsy, ugly misfit, ignored by his father, despised by the Egyptian people, universally acclaimed as 'the Idiot.' Significantly enough he is also rumoured to be without sex. After he mounts the throne, however, Akhenaton, suddenly self-confident, is transformed into a ruler, indeed a tyrant – a well-meaning tyrant who wants only to break the oppressive power of the temples, to spread a message of love among his people, but a tyrant nonetheless. As such he spells disaster for the country. Not only do his 'saintly' intentions fail to counteract the dangers inherent in his magician's role, they *actually make the situation worse.*

How? Much of the problem simply stems from the irreconcilability of ego- and other-centred versions of reality. The young king represents a classic case of animus-possession. Appropriately exemplifying 'irrational thought' (as opposed to the 'irrational feeling' typically associated with the anima[15]), he gives himself over to metaphysical speculation. Beginning with an attempt to replace the simple, substantial folk-gods with a pure abstraction, he ends, carried away by convictions of his own self-creation ('I ... have only my own history. Nothing *preceded* me. *Amemhotep was not my father!'* 105-6), by identifying *himself* with the absolute power he has posited. At the same time, however, the victim identification he has inherited from his former self has degenerated into a false, dangerous sentimentality that not only warps his judgment when it comes to playing his public role (as if it weren't enough that the forcible imposition of his eccentric new religion should deprive his people of spiritual comfort, insisting on the goodness of human nature he forbids his generals to take arms against the enemies that besiege his borders, thus depriving them of physical protection as well) but also allows him to insulate himself from any recognition of the suffering he causes – to deny, in effect, that he is a magician at all.

[Akhenaton] never permitted himself to reveal that underworld full of the creeping crawling things like violence or bitterness which all men must contain. He distorted those evils and let them build up within him until they emerged in grotesque, insane disguises. He couldn't bring himself to imagine human suffering – but let a flower be trodden on or a useless alley-cat mistreated by children and he'd be depressed for hours. Once I spoke to him about my childhood in Ipu, and how I used to find rocks outside the town in which were embedded little spiral-shaped creatures with frail spines and odd, twisted shapes. They seemed to me like tiny ancient beasts doomed to spend all eternity trapped in the stone. Can you imagine – he almost wept at the cruelty of such a fate, and talked of nothing else for days! I imagined him climbing and sobbing all over the rocks of Ipu, trying to claw the silly beasts out of their prisons, while entire cities starved and burned around him. (235-6)

The self-deluded magician – the magician tainted with the fool-saint's naiveté and idealism – is hence far more dangerous than the one whose exploitative tendencies are at least 'honest.'

It's no wonder, then, that the Canadian would tend to display a certain amount of nervousness about the saint/magician pairing. If the magician's power must always corrupt the saint's innocence rather than vice versa, then any composite figure of this sort is bound to be perceived as threatening simply on the basis of his own nature. The story doesn't end here, though. Even above and beyond such more or less obvious explanations for our ambivalence, there is another element in *King of Egypt* – indeed, to a slightly lesser extent, in Davies' trilogy as well – that suggests there is yet another factor involved in our response. In both of these, and especially in the former, there is an indication that the magician's role, far from being freely chosen, *is imposed on the erstwhile victim by extrinsic circumstances.* Paul Dempster seems propelled almost every step of the way by fate, moulded into his final shape not by inner vision but by chance-met acquaintances. In Akhenaton's case, even more suggestively, there is actually a hint that some magical metamorphosis is effected by the coronation ritual: he 'felt cold ghastly hands touch the nape of his neck. The Hidden Wind of the god was all around him ... But when at last he sat enthroned in the holy-sounding silence of the Coronation Hall and received the Double Crown of the Two Lands on his head ... his face wore an expression of purity and utter relief. In accepting the weight of the Red and White Crowns, another weight had been lifted from him, and he shone with a secret triumph.' Afterwards 'He shocked everyone by assuming, from the very first day of his reign, an air of command which he couldn't possibly have learned, an authority which radiated from deep within him' (34). What are we to make of the odd implications here? Simply this. In Canada there is an inclination to suspect not merely that self *may* be changed into other, that saint *may* become magician, but that it is a process that might be initiated at any time, unexpectedly, inexplicably, without the subject's active co-operation, *perhaps even without his awareness and against his will.*

Why should we be haunted by such a fear? Part of it undoubtedly is just our exaggerated horror of otherness coupled with the uncomfortable intimation that the magician, as animus, in fact represents a suppressed part of our own psyche. Part too, however, is possibly attributable to our ingrained 'American' prejudices. One common assumption in our shared culture is that impotence not only invites but actually *produces* aggression. 'Deeds of violence in our society are performed largely by those trying to establish their self-esteem, to defend their self-image, and to demonstrate that they, too, are significant,' says psychologist Rollo May,[16] codifying what has come to be a truism. This doesn't, of course, make it true. There is ample evidence even in May's own explication that the phenomenon, far from representing a universal pattern of human behaviour, is rooted in a national cult of masculinity that makes passiveness shameful.[17] The speciousness of the generalization, however, does not affect its power. Justified or not, the causal link between powerlessness and aggression (*vide* Paul Dempster) is by now such a well-established item of our folk wisdom that it can hardly help but colour our conceptions of social roles. The result? Even aside from our susceptibility to symbolic contagion, the more we become convinced of our passiveness, the more we are likely to suspect ourselves of a perverse but natural propensity to turn at the slightest provocation into those very monsters and bullies we perceive as our greatest threat. Such a suspicion would explain why literary productions seeming to confirm such an inclination would tend to stimulate considerable anxiety. More significantly, perhaps, it also explains certain peculiarities of Canadian folk culture.

Numerous Canadian critics including Dick Harrison, Margaret Atwood, and George Woodcock have noted with puzzlement Canada's propensity to ignore the 'real' heroes out of her history and canonize instead the 'losers.'[18] Woodcock suggests that, as reasonable people, 'we suspect the sheer gigantic irrationalism of the heroic' (B10). Atwood, on the other hand, claims that as 'losers' ourselves we identify most easily with the scenario in which 'an individual defending the rights of a small group finds himself up against faceless authority ... and is overcome by it' (F170). Our taste in folk heroes is, in other words, predicated upon our natural tendency to single out for attention those whose experience, in psycho-symbolic terms, is most consonant with our own. Such an inference seems eminently plausible – especially in light of the pattern we have seen emerging in the last few chapters. Unfortunately it just doesn't bear up under scrutiny. For one thing, vis-à-vis Woodcock's supposition, those we fixate on are commonly much *less* rational than those we reject. In his own example, Gabriel Dumont – a neglected Métis leader considered by this author to have demonstrated 'all the qualities of the kind of folk or frontier hero who is a contemporary equivalent to the great braggart warriors of Homer and Shakespeare' (11) – for all that he was 'the natural man par excellence' and thus barred by necessity from the ranks of acceptable alter egos, emerges as less alien, less mysterious, than Riel, the man who ostensibly symbolizes our own 'inner condition' (15). Nor is this merely a flaw in Woodcock's rendition (which, being designed explicitly to redeem Dumont from obscurity, has an obvious axe to grind). Even in officially Riel-centred versions of the story – even without

Woodcock's stage management, that is – Dumont tends to appear as a simple, sensible, and direct individual with clearcut loyalties and a realistic apprehension of events, while Riel, whom Woodcock himself describes as 'more devious, with deeper ambiguities of intent' (14), comes across as not merely inexplicable but in many ways repellent. It hardly seems sufficient, then, to say that we pay more attention to the latter simply because we feel threatened by the former's 'irrational' vitality. As for the correlative possibility emphasized by Atwood – that we identify with the loser, the martyr, the archetypal victim who, as Woodcock describes him, embodies 'our consciousness of deprivation and alienation from meaningful existence, our sense of rebellion without hope' (15), because he is our most natural alter ego – this, too, breaks down under closer examination.

Why? Because if we look at him without these preconceptions it seems obvious that the Canadian folk hero, though he may be a loser, is *not* in fact the passive type, the fool-saint, that we have associated with the Canadian symbolic ego. On the other hand, he is obviously not the classic magician described at the beginning of this chapter, either. So where does he belong? For all the apparent critical confusion on this point, we do not in fact have to go very far to discover the answer. Examining the evidence of the artifacts themselves, the features we find to be characteristic of the historical anecdotes most avidly seized upon by the folk imagination in this country suggest clearly that the Canadian folk hero is just such a composite as we find in MacEwen's Akhenaton. Certainly the story in which he appears, simultaneously confirming and appeasing our worst fears, echoes uncannily the plotline of MacEwen's novel: (1) an 'ordinary' person is transformed into a magician, usually by some catastrophic means, (2) willingly or unwillingly he wreaks havoc on friend and foe alike, (3) he is punished for his presumption by death, not through 'accident' (which, as Atwood points out, is the prototypical ending for the normal, nature-haunted Canadian victim-type, F166-7) but through 'history,' that is, politically related action of some sort, whether legitimate or otherwise.

It is beyond the scope of this book to offer a full overview of Canadian folk tales, but if we look at a few of the better known examples the pattern shows up clearly. The story of Albert Johnson, the 'Mad Trapper of Rat River,' for instance, concerns (as Rudy Wiebe has detailed in his 'Collected notes on a possible legend') one of the most widely and diversely re-collected incidents of our national past. To offer only the barest bones of the narrative, the protagonist in question was apparently an eccentric hermit living in the Canadian Northwest who one day, absolutely unprovoked, shot a Mountie (who had come to his cabin on a matter of routine enquiry) and then fled into the wilderness. After a gruelling manhunt the miscreant was cornered and, choosing to fight to the end against impossible odds, forced his pursuers to kill him. Albert Johnson, in other words, was both an aggressor and the victim of his own aggression. What is most pertinent to our inquiry, however, is the fact that the three most constantly stressed motifs in the diverse songs, poems, and stories Johnson inspired are (1) the apparent irrationality and perhaps even insanity of the man's behaviour (the strong implication, in other words, that he wasn't responsible for his actions), (2) the extreme ferocity which, allied with his striking opaqueness (there is constant reference to his mysteriousness, as well as a recurrent refrain of his silence, his apparent total repudiation of speech), renders him bestial, alien, less or more than human, and (3) an air of fatality which makes him seem 'Like a figure in Greek tragedy ... doomed ... the shadows closing in on him' (O'Hagan in Wiebe B233). Johnson is obviously not an alter ego for us – even aside from the fact that he was reportedly a 'nasty, misanthropic, vicious little man,' we are, as Wiebe points out, incredulous that anyone should be 'so profligate with his single life' (246). The fascination he exerts is only explicable, therefore, if we postulate that his experience coincidentally assumes the shape of a therapeutic psychodrama which first forces us to confront and then allows us to repudiate something we view as a particularly immediate threat to our sense of self.

A second example of the same phenomenon is provided by the case of the Donnellys, a much publicized 'black Irish' family who, in the late nineteenth century, terrorized the countryside around Lucan, a small town in southwestern Ontario, and then were themselves brutally murdered, according to hearsay by their long-suffering neighbours. Once more we see the familiar pattern emerge. On the one hand, as the prototype requires, since their involvement in the generations-old feud between the Irish-Catholic 'Whiteboys' and the Protestant Orange Order was inherited along with their name, the Donnellys' aggressive role was in a sense thrust upon them rather than freely chosen. On the other hand, despite this extenuating factor it is clear even in the most sympathetic treatments that the family, as befits a clan of magicians, were ruthless and competent aggressors: thieves, barnburners, brawlers. In recent versions of the story, probably under the influence of the post-sixties upsurge of anti-establishment feeling in the United States and the consequent popular enshrinement of the 'bad guy' as hero (Butch Cassidy, Bonny and Clyde, Billy the Kid[19]), there has been some attempt to obscure this latter fact. Orlo Miller, for instance, claims that previous writers, in assuming 'the Donnelly family to be the principal instigators of the Biddulph feud,' were misled by slanders 'tirelessly and maliciously circulated by the assassins and their kin' (33, 41). Even Miller, however, can't disguise the fact that the Donnellys, though perhaps amply provoked, were the purveyors as much as the victims of violence. What is particularly interesting in his account is the way the remnants of folklore, for all his assiduous attempts at debunking, still spread an uneasy gothic pall over the ostensibly objective recital of events. It almost seems as if the folkloric sources exerted an influence on his imagination that he couldn't quite control. We get an inkling of why this might happen if we view Miller's version in a broader context. Looking at more 'popular' treatments (such as William Crichton's adaptation of Leonard Yakir and Murray Markowitz's screenplay) we realize that the very elements – such as Johannah's witchcraft and the boys' conscious criminality – Miller would excise from the text as prejudicial are in fact the features that comprise not only the Donnellys' interest but their *appeal*, the basis for the fascination they exert.[20] For all that Miller is intent on redeeming them, it seems clear that the Donnellys became folk heroes not despite but because they were magicians – and because they have already been definitively conquered for us.

A third example of the Canadian folk hero has already been touched upon. Of all available historical personages the one who has stimulated the most controversy and attention in this country is Louis Riel. So odd is his story, however, that even those who have been captivated by him seem unable to explain exactly *why* they find him so intriguing. Because of his racial background and its associations with the westering movement, many have attempted to put him in an 'American' context. Joseph Howard, for instance – who was, in fact, an American himself – devotes over five hundred pages in *Strange Empire* to recasting Riel into the mould of those doomed noble savages of the mythic American west who put up a courageous fight against 'science and the machine – and perished' (18). Unfortunately for Howard, Riel resists strenuously that kind of type-casting. As a result, one of the things that emerges most strongly from the book is the author's discomfort with and disappointment in the unheroic reality of his chosen hero ('He was a mediocre horseman. He was clumsy and his hands were undexterous; many men of his race caught in prairie blizzards with no tool save a knife could survive, but he would have committed his soul to God and died. He could not shoot straight; he knew nothing of firearms and he dreaded and shunned them all his life' 147) – especially in comparison with his lieutenant, Dumont, 'the most indomitable man that New Nation had produced,' 'the sort of man about whom legends grew' (458, 307). The American, in other words, is unable to identify with Riel no matter how hard he tries. On the Canadian side, conversely, we find an equally anomalous but opposite effect. Woodcock, who wants desperately to divert national attention and identification *away* from the 'loser' ends up demonstrating nothing quite so vividly as the completeness, and the irrationality, of Riel's *ascendancy* over the 'American' heroic principle embodied in Dumont.[21] Indeed, if it weren't for the obvious bias of the interpolated editorial comments, on the basis of focus alone we might easily conclude that Woodcock's book, its title notwithstanding, is as much 'about' Riel as, say, Howard's is. For the Canadian, it would seem, Riel *has to* be at the centre of that particular story, no matter what one starts out to write.

Despite this apparent public confusion about what the story 'means,' if we look at Riel himself we soon realize that here we have a figure who exemplifies our type pattern to an uncanny extent. Without claiming to do even minimal justice to either his career or his personality, both of which have been amply documented in literary as well as historical studies, I will merely point out that this notorious Métis is not merely formally akin to but amazingly like Akhenaton. Firstly, called by fate to an unsought public office he was apparently *stricken after the fact* with the mad conviction that he partook of divinity himself, having been appointed by God to play not just a priestly but a Messianic role. In Thomas Flanagan's words, 'Even the rumbling of his stomach, he said ... was the sound of the Holy Spirit at work in his body' (125). Secondly, for all his good intentions his ministrations had catastrophic results, not simply through bad luck but in consequence specifically of his combination of 'saintly' naiveté and outright *hubris*. In particular, his refusal to let Dumont employ guerrilla tactics against the Canadian forces even though, from any reasonable perspective, it was obvious that the Métis rebels had no chance in open combat (see Flanagan 138) was based equally on a misguided squeamishness (horrified himself by bloodshed, he was concerned lest public opinion would take him to be a 'savage') and on a determination to 'force' a miracle. As Flanagan explains it, 'As a prophet, Riel expected to triumph through divine intervention. His miraculous victory would be the sign needed to authenticate his new religion in the eyes of the world. The military weakness of his strategy was its religious strength, because it required a miracle to work' (140). Riel, in other words – clearly confirming his magician status – was quite willing to put his followers' survival on the line in order to authenticate his own transcendental identity. In the end, of course – just as we expect and require – Riel was defeated, appropriately, by history and his own monomania.

One interesting thing about all these culture heroes is that the more 'literary' the vehicle is in which they appear, the more the negative side of their character is played down, perhaps due to the intensity of the identification an author is forced to make with his material. In James Reaney's trilogy of plays based on the Donnellys, for instance, the author employs a wide variety of formal devices (including the use of a chorus to underline the family's vulnerability and isolation, the distortion of fact in order that the story might better conform with romantic conventions, and the yoking of diverse formal echoes to impart a ritual tone to the action) in order to make his subjects appear more heroic. In Don Gutteridge's *Riel*, the poet not only stimulates sympathy by setting his protagonist against a blatantly satirized 'public' backdrop of voices, but, associating him consistently (and judging by the man's diaries quite uncharacteristically) with a whole constellation of nature imagery, places him squarely in the tradition of American primitivism. [22] Even in the most concerted attempts to normalize these figures, however, the underlying ambivalence tends to make itself felt as surely as Reaney's Donnellys refuse to stay peaceably in their graves. In Wiebe's *The Scorched-Wood People*, for instance, Riel is made to seem so human in his pain and indecision, so *familiar* in his fool-saint's guise, that at many moments we are inclined to find ourselves wondering, with Dumont, is *this* the 'hero' we have been led to expect: 'Hesitant, surrounded by children, kneeling so small and worn'? (186) The enforced empathy, however, only makes it all the more disquieting when we are confronted with those *other* moments of absolute alienation, those troubling interludes of madness or ecstasy when we, in the persons of Riel's humble and hopeful brethren, are jolted into a sudden awareness of the 'terrifying voice' that transforms the mousy youth into a figure of 'incredible beauty' (223) – and at the same time labels him wholly, irrevocably *other*. It is the tension between these two irreconcilable visions, of course, that makes Wiebe's telling of the story so powerful, for in emphasizing this particular element he puts his finger on what is – for us – the most emotionally significant aspect of the tale. The fact is, in order for this story to 'work' on the level of psychodrama, the question of Riel's sanity, Riel's *identity*, has to be left unresolved. Or rather, it must be resolved – *ambivalently*. We must be allowed to see him, to believe him, both sane and unsane; the owner, quite simply, of a vision 'ungraspable by any but himself' (325). Fortunately, the facts themselves resist neat solutions. Historically, negative versions have tended to favour villainous sanity in order to justify the government's treatment of the case; positive ones to present the man, in the straightforward terms of victimization, as demented. More recently Flanagan has attempted to portray his protagonist as a conventional millenarian religious leader rather than a madman or a villain. None of the diverse commentators, however, have been able to banish the essential ambiguity from their texts. Wiebe does not, therefore, create a *new* Riel for us so much as simply refrain from arbitrating the enigma inherent in the original story. This novel, in other words, though ostensibly narrated in conventional terms, is, as much as the quasi-documentary *The Temptations of Big Bear*, constructed almost wholly out of 'found' components, the ineluctable 'givens' of history. The result? Notwithstanding a certain tension set up by his decision to mediate this facticity through the person of a decidedly *un*historical speaker,[23] Wiebe's self-restraint, his delicacy in the face of his protagonist's opaqueness, pays off in many ways. Indeed, it is only because he has tapped the true mythic ambivalence of his source material so effectively that he is able, without lapsing into sentimentality, to exploit fully Riel's obtrusive sense of doom, of inexorable fatality (the nightmares, the cryptic insistent visions, the ghostly gallows we keep glimpsing in the background[24]), and in doing so to elevate his anagnorisis from pathos to something very like tragedy.

Having reached this point it is interesting to consider how these national peculiarities of taste affect our selection of 'real' political leaders – if only because it offers us an incomparable opportunity to demonstrate what has heretofore, for the most part, simply been asserted, that the reactions and transformations traced throughout this book are not merely 'literary' but characterize culture on the broadest level. Actually there is a great deal more – and more explicit – continuity between *mythos* and *praxis* than might be considered possible. The only real difference between our favourite folk heroes and our favourite politicians, in fact, is that the former according to convention are *failed* magicians – magicians, that is, whose divers nemeses have already struck – while the latter are successful ones. Part of the explanation for our apparent willingness to let this one variant, the magician-as-politician, 'get away with it' (in contrast to the therapeutic purgation we insist upon for his brothers) is undoubtedly linked to our perceptions of our own self-interest. Political behaviour may reveal a substantial strain of *covert* irrationality, but it is rarely wholly self-destructive. Another part though, it seems likely, may be related to the specific role he plays in our lives. The folk hero is always one who transgresses, crosses boundaries, encroaches on tabooed areas. The political leader, on the other hand, by definition limits his activity to the public realm – a sphere both foreign and fearsome to us, but to which *he*, as magician, *properly* belongs. The magician-as-politician, in other words, may not only be allowed but *willed* to prosper in so far as he is identified with a public role. What is more, since it is *only* such a figure who can function in such a role, we are inclined to support our politicians only to the extent that we do perceive them as magicians. As a result, it's exactly those same characteristics, that pronounced 'otherness' we find so repellent and threatening in private encounters, which we are comforted to note in a political leader. Contrary to all normal – or at least 'American' – assumptions about political motivations, that is, we Canadians are inclined to elect political leaders we don't like or identify with, not despite but because of the often radical incompatibility they represent.

Is this true? It certainly isn't consistent with the town-meeting ideal of democracy that seems to dominate the North American public imagination, is it? Actually, the Americans' emphasis on the representativeness and the responsiveness of their politicians – the desire for the leader to be seen simply as an idealized self – is something of an historical oddity. According to Rank, a normal response to the perception of human vulnerability is the creation of an *in*vulnerable – that is, qualitatively different from the self – transference object. In Ernest Becker's words:

Realistically the universe contains overwhelming power. Beyond ourselves we sense chaos. We can't really do much about this unbelievable power, except for one thing: we can endow certain people with it. The child takes natural awe and terror and focusses them on individual beings, which allows him to find the power and the horror all in one place instead of diffused throughout a chaotic universe. *Mirabile*! The transference object, being endowed with the transcendent powers of the universe, now has in himself the power to control, order, and combat them.[25]

'It follows, of course,' Becker adds, 'that the less ego power one has and the more fear, the stronger the transference' [147]. In the light of our observations throughout this book, it's not surprising, then, that the Canadian should be impelled, despite his suspicions, to elect strong (and thus by definition non-representative) leaders. It is also not surprising, since the role model is ready to hand, that this leader would resemble our equivocal magician. In any case it is a fact that if we look at the men who have wielded the most power in Canada, we not only find a surprising consistency in character and approach quite independent of articulated philosophy or party line, but soon realize that there is no doubt the congeries of personality traits we are confronting fits, to a striking degree, our description of the prototype above. Consider, for example, Sir John A. Macdonald, William Lyon Mackenzie King, and Pierre Elliott Trudeau, three of our longest reigning prime ministers: both singly and as a group these men not merely accommodate but go far to prove the thesis that we only trust the capability of a politician to the extent that his dissociation from us is complete.

How? To begin with, all three of these men demonstrate strikingly that quality of 'otherness' we have found to be a characterizing feature of the magician. If this is often overlooked in public assessments, it's only because, again, our *conscious* perception of the situation tends to be based on American values. Popular interpretations of early Trudeaumania, for instance, generally accept as *given* that Trudeau was the kind of charismatic personality who invited identification. Made all the more aware of their own national drabness by the aura of glamour that clung to the American presidency in the early sixties, Canadian voters, says George Radwanski, 'found in him a reflection of how they would like to perceive themselves: the shimmering intelligence, the physical prowess, the much-reported taste for adventure and danger, the combination of toughness and grace, the appeal to women' (115). Unfortunately for the plausibility of such analyses, the Canadian, in his inner sense of self, is far more likely to identify *against* than with the American. Far from denoting a Canadian wishful self-image, therefore, the fact that Trudeau was openly compared to Kennedy, like the fact that Mackenzie King's political career took off after he had publicly established what was to be a lifelong connection with American millionaire John D. Rockefeller, is one of our best indicators that we are indeed dealing with a magician. And *that* makes him 'other' simply by definition.

Personal qualities tend to confirm the designation. Throughout his tenure Trudeau was often described even by close associates as opaque, unreadable, inaccessible. Sympathetic commentators speculated that this self-containment was at least partly illusory, a defence against over-sensitivity rather than a proof of coldness. It seems evident, nonetheless, that what the public *saw* was simply 'an impressive but hard loner sealed in an impenetrable shell, socially ungenerous in his reluctance to give anything of himself [or] ... to be touched' (Radwanski 29). This much-touted remoteness was exacerbated, moreover, by unpredictability. Going far beyond fluctuations in mood and manner, in his political conduct Trudeau ofttimes appeared downright capricious. 'He [had] no qualms about making decisions as prime minister which [fell] short of, or even appear[ed] to contradict some of his stated beliefs,' says Radwanski (120). More critical for present purposes, the *quality* of his inconsistency bespoke not weakness but simply a blatant disregard for propriety. Far from suggesting an all-too-human failure of wit, in other words, there was considerable evidence, including the word of Jim Coutts, his longtime aide, that even the most ill-considered and extravagant remarks were made deliberately to keep the electorate 'off balance.'[26] Was it a political liability, this frivolousness? One would certainly think so. If we look at the man's career, however, there is much to suggest that his penchant for evasion was not only tolerated but to some extent admired.

Why should this be so? What it comes down to is a question of the place in politics of sincerity. According to conventional wisdom any hint of playacting in a public figure should signal his unsuitability. As Leslie Miller points out, 'It is very difficult in these times for us to conceive of artifice as anything but a destructive and irresponsible temptation. Our impulse is to assert that artifice is only properly at home on the stage, and when it moves from the stage to (of all places) the political realm it can only result in frivolous mischief at best (like the Rhinocerous Party) and outright chicanery at worst. To us, the move which would link the actor and politician even metaphorically is regarded with great suspicion' (n.p.). Notwithstanding the *apparent* public stipulation of such a view, however, if we look at the political arena itself we have to suspect that the Canadian response is somewhat different from what conscious assumptions might lead us to expect. Canadians, oddly enough, seem to *like* artifice in their politicians. Indeed, surveying the public temper it's not at all surprising that Miller, a Canadian sociologist, should diverge from the conventional attitudes she cites above to present a *defence* of the role of theatricality in politics.

How do we explain this departure? Miller claims that theatricality, used properly (that is, 'productively'), can serve as a 'means of preserving the collective life' inasmuch as the politician's style, in its 'symbolic character as the imitation of the "life beautiful,"' may become an embodiment of and an inspiration to communal ideality (n.p.). On the basis of our discussion of the literary magician, however, I would venture to speculate that the motivations underlying this anomalous preference involve something a little more complex than this essentially aesthetic explanation. The key factor, I think, is the propensity already noted for the magician, and especially the saint-turned-magician (it's interesting that in our sample at least Trudeau, who was sickly during his childhood, and perhaps even Mackenzie King, who had to fight as a youth against what he himself perceived as a weak, perverse nature, fit into this category[27]) to embrace dangerous visionary 'schemes.' Under such circumstances the more sincere – the more dedicated – such a figure appears to be, the more nervous we become. And the more we are inclined to value any evidence that he *isn't* taken in by his own pose. Indeed, when Jim Coutts says that Trudeau is the best actor he has ever seen, far from being an indiscretion the statement merely confirms that we may safely accept this man as our leader.[28]

Assigning such a role to theatricality explains some puzzling aspects of Canadian political history. If the foregoing explanation is correct then the greater the perceived propensity in a national leader toward idealism, the more overt 'artifice' we would expect the public to allow or even demand. As it turns out, this, in fact, is what seems to be the case. Macdonald's obsession with such issues as Confederation and the transcontinental railway, for instance, was balanced by an almost frivolous tone ('He wore the dignity of a Prime Minister much too gaily,' says Creighton. 'Surely it was a mask and he an actor.' BII252) which, though deplored by his colleagues, was (judging by his political longevity) more likely viewed by the public as reassuring than otherwise. King's messianic presumptions,[29] even more extremely, were matched not merely by theatricality ('he strove to convert the sorrows which come to every man into things extraordinary, making himself thus a symbol of the tragedy of the people'; 'He had developed a singular talent for turning up where he thought history was being made'; '[T]he Cabinet's course [of non-interference in a labour dispute] would have left Mackenzie King out of the picture ... And so he stepped to the centre of the stage.') but by a blatant duplicity that at times approached outright dishonesty.[30] Of the three examples cited, in other words, King at least was a thoroughgoing opportunist. 'One of the baffling features of Mackenzie King's mind,' say Henry Ferns and Bernard Ostry, 'was its capacity to discover half-truths among the multitude of pressures bearing upon him ... [with which] to deceive others and, perhaps, even himself' (195).

How, we might wonder, did he get away with it? Theatricality is one thing: deliberate falsehood something else again. On the evidence of Ferns and Ostry, King was little more than a demagogue. Yet the public 'allowed' themselves to be fooled by him for over twenty years. Could Canadians really have been so naive as to take this man at face value? It doesn't seem likely – not, that is, unless they had a vested interest in doing so. And this, I would maintain, was in fact the case. King's moral flaws, his lack of substance, actually made him *more* attractive to the Canadian voter, not less. Canadians would far rather see a cynical and even frankly dishonest politician in power than an idealist. As long as a leader's actions are clearly based on self-interest, they know where they stand. For another thing – and this brings us full circle – to the extent that he is visibly ambitious, visibly exploitative, he confirms that he is indeed a magician, thus reassuring them that they have the right person for the job.

Next question: what features, besides inaccessibility and unaccountability, are characteristic of the magician-as-politician? Duplicity may be an *acceptable* feature, but surely it isn't enough in itself to put a man in and *keep* him in power. Actually, the putting and the keeping are two slightly different problems. In contrast to the United States, where a propensity for the electorate on the one hand to idolize and on the other to identify with the nation's top officials leads so easily to disillusionment and the demand for a new broom,[31] in Canada an incumbent always has a slight edge since the mere fact of *being* a winner goes some way to prove that he *should* be a winner. This doesn't hold universally, of course, but regardless of either policy or public events, chances are reasonably good that a politician having once got in will stay in – *as long as he can continue to appear to the voters as a magician*. This last point is the important one. If an incumbent begins to seem too easy-going, too ethical, too 'nice,' his constituents become uneasy, they find it difficult to believe he has the skills to navigate the dangerous waters of public life and politics. This is probably why Lester Pearson could never get the support he seemed to deserve. It is also why, in 1979, the voters dropped Joe Clark like a hot potato before he even had a chance to make his mistakes. Canadians clearly wanted to punish Trudeau that year, but in retrospect it seems obvious they didn't expect – or want – to be so successful in their demonstration that they'd be stuck with an amateur. Clark, in other words, won his place not by virtue of his own powers, but only by default. He thus had a strike against him from the outset. His behaviour in office only exacerbated the situation. He was earnest, hard-working, well-intentioned – but totally incapable of control. No magician this, Clark in fact was all too clearly one of *us*: dull, pedestrian, unlucky.[32] And that was the whole problem. Since Canadians are only too well aware of their *own* incapacities, the absolute impossibility of *them* filling adequately the hero's shoes, they found it incredibly nerve-wracking to sit back and wait for the inevitable crash. Naturally they turned him out with what seemed to be grossly unfair haste at the first opportunity.

Even victorious, then, Joe Clark was perceived as a loser – and this precipitated his downfall as a matter of course. Though winning is important, in other words, it only works for someone who looks like a winner. But just what comprises a plausible performance of a winner's role? Again if we look at our three examples the answer seems obvious. The winner – that is, the magician – behaves like a *father*. This means, to start with, that he is wholly self-sufficient and self-actuated. Like Macdonald he is thick-skinned enough to ignore public opinion and wise enough to take the long view, wait out the transitory excitements of the day, seek 'the certainty of the future' rather than courting the fleeting moment with elaborate apologies or explanations or defences (Creighton BII126). Like Mackenzie King he is so confident of both his mission and his capabilities that it never occurs to him he might *not* be a winner. Like Trudeau, ignoring both criticism and compliments – indeed, making it clear that any outside judgment passed on his behaviour is irrelevant and presumptuous – he assumes both the right and the responsibility to run the country *exactly as he sees fit*. In this last case the essentially authoritarian stance was at least for the first few years somewhat obscured by rhetoric. Although it was clear from the beginning that Trudeau was not frightened of public disapproval and had no intention of pandering to the electorate (' "if that's the kind of thing you want, you had better elect someone else" ' Westell 84), he did talk a great deal about participatory democracy. Contrary to what one might expect from his articulated political philosophy, however, once the dust settled it quickly became obvious that while, as an intellectual, he was genuinely interested in *hearing* alternate viewpoints, whether from laymen or from official advisers, he was not interested in 'sharing government's actual decision-making role with the public in any way – nor even necessarily allowing public opinion on any given issue to prevail' (Radwanski 135). ' "I'm pretty rigid and pretty set in things that I believe in deeply," ' he is quoted as saying. ' "[M]uch of my consultation and participation is done in the hopes that people will come in the end to see things as I do" ' (in *ibid.*). The confession is unAmerican in its ideological if not its practical implications. In its own context, however, it is not idiosyncratic at all. We need only compare Ferns's and Ostry's comments on King's attitude toward public opinion: 'It has often been supposed that Mackenzie King was one of those politicians who make up their minds by counting heads and headlines; that as a politician he was froth on the surface. This is quite a mistaken view ... When he joined forces with Rockefeller the public indignation about [the latter's labour policies] ... was immense ... And yet Mackenzie King was not deterred ... from joining the unpopular side. He understood the realities of power' (210-11). Trudeau's *non*-participatory democracy was clearly part of a genuine Canadian tradition.

What kind of regime results from this kind of quasi-autocratic stance? On the positive side Trudeau did give the country the strong leadership and political stability it wanted after years of minority governments and muddle. He was sure enough of himself to refuse to coddle the voters, warning them bluntly against unreasonable expectations of his ability to produce. Oblivious to public disapproval about his 'private army,' he took advantage of all the perquisites of his office to build the kind of strong administrative team which could help him use his time and resources to maximum effect. Finally, and most important, by gathering the reins of power firmly into his own hands he was able to minimize internal dissent (' "If they don't agree with cabinet decisions, they won't be ministers for long – not for very long at all," ' in Radwanski 109) and ensure that the business of decision-making was conducted in an orderly and sophisticated manner. Thanks to Trudeau's authoritarianism, in other words, Canada got the kind of leader who was thoughtful, even meticulous, in his management of day-to-day affairs; bold, decisive, and self-confident under pressure.

It all sounds very good, doesn't it. And why not? The magician has obvious advantages when it comes to handling power. Even Mackenzie King's slick ability to stage-manage events was, inasmuch as the country's interests and his own necessarily coincided much of the time, an asset not merely from his own point of view but from the public standpoint as well. There is an obvious negative side to this too, of course. Neither Macdonald nor King were well-liked – plagued by financial scandals and national disunity, Macdonald especially clung to power at times only by his fingertips. Trudeau, too, at times seemed so unpopular with both the press and the electorate as to make the idea of his re-election absurd. Interestingly enough the basis of his unpopularity would seem to be the *same* features that originally made him a winner; his condescension, his disdainful refusal to be held to account, his patent sense of superiority. The famous lack of tact, reassuring one moment, at another evidently convinced a frightened electorate that his indifference presented a threat to their personal well-being. As Anthony Westell describes it, barely a year after his election (which had been hailed as the dawn of a new age in Canada) 'Parliament was rocking to angry cries of "Heil Hitler" as Trudeau cut off debate in the House of Commons, and it was the wisdom of the day that the Prime Minister was contemptuous of Parliament, arrogant toward his critics and greedy for personal power' (83). With the country in this mood, Trudeau's baldly outspoken pragmatism ('"there are a lot of people who are bargaining that the Government can't act tough for too long because it will only get frightened if it sees employment go up to 6 per cent ... But if people think we are going to lose our nerve because of that, they should think again because we're not"' *ibid.* 147) became perceived, quite simply, as callousness. Trudeau, in other words, was now feared to be cruel rather than merely incomprehensible. Trudeau's wonder-working, super-efficient, ultra-rational political machine, further, now became widely perceived as 'too slow, too centralized and ... [oriented toward] coldly technical rather than warmly human answers to problems' (*ibid.* 113).

If this weren't enough, Trudeau's difficulties didn't stop with a disillusioned electorate, either. Exacerbating its negative effects on public morale, his egocentric attitude proved counterproductive in his governing role as well. His main problem was an unfortunate talent for antagonizing people. Not only did he succeed in stirring up a great deal of generalized hostility through his biting criticism of almost every segment of the public sector that failed to live up to his own high standards of integrity and rationality ('He didn't hesitate to savage, at one time or another, not only most political parties and politicians, but also French Canadians as a society' Radwanski 79), but he also showed himself incapable of establishing healthy mutual relationships even with his own followers. Why? Apparently, like so many of the fictional magicians we have seen, despite his *abstract* charisma the man was inept when it came to dealing with humans face to face. As Donald MacDonald put it, '"he's a very private person himself and he doesn't, I think, have a great deal of empathy for other people, and he can fail to comprehend or sympathize with other people's situations"' (in *ibid.* 214). As a result, 'his style fail[ed] to inspire ... any sense of loyalty or dedication to him *as a person*' (*ibid.* 221, italics added). This shows up particularly in the number of defections that took place during his tenure. Not all left for the same reason, of course. Some, like John Turner, were alienated not just by general differences in temperament but in particular by the prime minister's refusal to cater to or even recognize personal factors in his professional relationships.[33] Others fell by the wayside because they were too individualistic to fit easily into a system that, as Radwanski points out, was 'best suited not to the aggressive, independent, take-charge minister who decides what his department should be doing and battles it through to completion, but to a rather more bland, technocratic compromiser and team player' (164). Trudeau, in other words, brooked no individualists but himself. The result, aside from the loss of potentially valuable political material, was a change in the whole tenor of the government. '"As the influence within cabinet of ministers of a cerebral type increases," [said] one Trudeau associate, "then more and more ... [the government becomes an] emotionless, sometimes vapid, gentlemen's club ... in which no one raises voices and in which there has to be a consensus"' (in *ibid.* 165). Not a very inspiring picture. But perhaps this is always going to be the consequence of having a strong man – a magician – in charge: a weeding out of strength from the ranks. Both King and Macdonald conducted their governments much more informally than Trudeau, and certainly neither of them overemphasized the cerebral, 'collegial' approach, but it is a fact that at least part of the reason for their remarkable length of tenure, their reluctance to give up office despite, in both cases, the encroachment of old age and ill health, was the virtual absence of suitable heirs apparent.

The magician, then, even at his best, tends not only to invite popular misunderstanding, but to cut himself off from potential sources of personal support. The question then arises: how, in that case, does he manage to stay in power? Is it simply a matter of political skills? This is the answer Ferns and Ostry would give with regard to Mackenzie King. 'He was an impersonal, secretive political technician who depended for his success upon his capacity to understand both theoretically and practically the anatomy of society and the laws of its movement. He never invited men to love him, and very few did. Nor did he invite them to hate him, and very few did. But he knew how to manipulate them, and he did' (279). Despite the fact that this statement could apply almost as well to either of the other two in our sample, however, there is something more involved here than manipulative expertise. Again it comes down to the *role* in which we are wont to cast our politicians. The fact is, though we may not like it and even complain bitterly about it, we *expect* the magician to behave autocratically – and indeed would feel uncomfortable if he did not. Take our response to Trudeau's single most autocratic act, his invocation of emergency powers during the October Crisis of 1970. In the immediate aftermath of that event the widespread public outcry against such evidence of government tyranny, the almost unanimous media condemnation of 'Pierre Trudeau's stifling of dissent at bayonet point' (Peter Newman, in Westell 254) was deafening. Despite this, there is ample evidence that the Prime Minister's decision was *privately* applauded. 'The polls showed that 85 per cent of Canadians approved of the use of emergency powers and more than 80 per cent of the letters to Trudeau in October were favorable. He was widely praised as a resolute national leader who had stood firm against terrorism' (Westell 256). Why the discrepancy between real and apparent reaction? Even leaving aside the undoubted American component, one might speculate that Canadians, disturbed by any reminder that the father-within bears an uncomfortable resemblance to the magician-without (remember *Wacousta*), are bound to express their anxieties by making ritual public objection against any overt display of aggressiveness by a political leader. Notwithstanding, they are actually at the same time secretly relieved to have it confirmed that they have elected a man psychologically equipped to fight the forces of evil and irrationality on their own terms. 'The fact that the terrorists were capable of cold-blooded murder seemed ... proof that emergency powers were necessary to deal with them,' says Westell (251). Above and beyond any other function, 'The War Measures Act demonstrated that the established order of government was not helpless' (*ibid.* 255-6) – and this was exactly what the Canadian people needed to maintain their peace of mind.

In view of an example such as this (and it could be multiplied with no trouble at all), it seems unlikely that the Canadian's odd persistence in voting for men he ostensibly doesn't like or trust is an accident. The pattern of response we have uncovered here also hints at an explanation why the New Democratic Party, champion of the 'little man,' seems unable to stir up more than a token level of support; why, indeed, in a country where the strength of women is obviously so highly regarded, there are relatively few women politicians. Both these groups are too much 'us.' We want a magician up front.[34]

Even if we hate everything he represents.

This brings us to the last aspect of the Canadian magician-as-politician. Electoral support notwithstanding, it seems evident that this figure arouses exactly the same anxieties in the flesh as he does in fiction. Again it is the ambivalence of his character that disturbs us – the capacity for those same features that comprise his appeal to speak to us just as insistently of danger. The equivocality of his aggression is self-evident. Less obviously, his artifice, which on one level we find reassuring, also stimulates less comfortable feelings – and not merely, as in literary treatments, for 'symbolic' reasons. In Jungian terms, the politician is (or plays at being) an extravert. In marked contrast to our own obsessive subjectivity, by choice and necessity he 'thinks, feels, acts and actually lives in a way that is *directly* correlated with the objective conditions and their demands.'[35] Unfortunately, anticipating Jung, we cannot help suspecting that this rational alignment, this ostentatious objectivity, merely covers up an irrational underside which is ready to burst forth at any moment.

The more complete the conscious attitude of extraversion is, the more infantile and archaic the unconscious attitude will be. The egoism which characterizes the extravert's unconscious attitude goes far beyond mere childish selfishness; it verges on the ruthless and the brutal ... [Such traits] remain hidden ... so long as the extraversion of the conscious attitude is not extreme. But whenever it is exaggerated, the unconscious comes to light in symptomatic form; its egoism, infantilism, and archaism lose their original compensatory character and appear in more or less open opposition to the conscious attitude. [338-9]

The magician's nature being what it is, then, if we *expect* him to be strong, cold, controlled to the point of obnoxiousness it seems likely that at least covertly we will *expect* him to have a dangerously regressive aspect as well. How do we manage to suppress this disquieting recognition with respect to our political leaders?

Actually, we don't.

If we go back to our three examples we will see that each of these men displays blatant signs of the kind of inner turmoil suggested by Jung. Mackenzie King's well-known sexual problems, his addiction to spiritualism, his abnormal devotion to his mother and his dogs – all amply documented by C.P. Stacey – provide the most obvious case in point, but biographical examination of Macdonald or Trudeau yields equally suggestive hints of a latent 'infantilism' if only in their shared propensity for intemperate language and violent displays of temper.[36] The important question is not whether such aberrations constitute a 'real' danger, or even whether the attribution of instability is justified in any given case, but – inasmuch as they necessarily entered into public *perceptions* – how they affected the nation's *attitude toward* these men.

Again the findings are not quite what one might expect. Although Trudeau was often criticized for his outbursts, his occasional impatient obscenities, it was commonly done almost cheerfully, as if his auditors found their discovery of such a flaw quite gratifying. The reason for this, I would suggest, is linked with exactly those patterns of response mentioned with respect to both literary and legendary magicians. In the first place, Canadian observers probably *are* actually relieved when a political leader exposes himself this way. *Expecting irrationality*, they are reassured when it appears in such a relatively harmless guise as a temper tantrum. The same thing holds even for more serious flaws like Macdonald's notorious drunkenness, his tendency 'in moments of acute tension ... [to go] back to the bottle for escape,' to 'break out,' to abdicate all responsibility for days at a time and become 'an irresponsible stowaway' on his own ship (Creighton B1164, 67; 1330). Unlike, say, American voters, who require their politicians (as alter egos) to behave impeccably in private as much as in public circumstances, the Canadian will not only excuse but even welcome any flaw of irrationality *as long as it signals a personal rather than a professional weakness.* If danger is inevitable, such a preference seems to imply, at least we may insist on it being confined, symbolically, to a sphere where its effect may be dissipated with least public harm. This is not the whole of it, though. Since such a defect is pre-eminently self-destructive, detecting it also, we may speculate, allows us to indulge covertly our wish to see the magician punished without thereby punishing ourselves. Trudeau's domestic problems, his bad luck or sheer foolishness in selecting an unsuitable wife – which would have spelled disaster for him in an American arena – was thus here a considerable asset. On the one hand, since he was implicated not merely as object but as subject with her irrationality, if only by association or displacement, we could consider the marital failure a 'safe' flaw. On the other hand, we were secretly gratified to see him repaid for his hubris in such a way as would not impair his public performance unduly. Trudeau's domestic losses hence spelled almost certain *public* gains. How does this tie in with our broader political response? Simple. Exactly as we might predict from our equivocal attitude toward the magician as a type, Canadians, it would seem, are most likely to vote for and keep voting for those who confirm both their efficacy *and* their limitations, the full extent of their 'otherness,' by demonstrating characteristics that in rational terms would seem to make them *less* acceptable, less suitable altogether. This, then, evoking the puzzling willingness of Keneally's colonists to co-operate in their own enslavement, brings full circle our phenomenology of the Canadian magician and his exemplary role.[37]

What does it all mean? The most important thing we might derive from the foregoing survey, perhaps, is the recognition that our love-hate relationship with the active role model may provide a key not merely to our political biases but to much of our social distinctiveness as well. According to Leslie Fiedler, popular fiction, which he associates with myth, 'speaks for both oppressor and oppressed, joining together all elements of the community, no matter how embattled and disjoined.'[38] If Fiedler is right, it may explain why we find relatively little self-admittedly frivolous literature in Canada, and why we indulge ourselves in an imported product uneasily, with (judging by our virtually unanimous public condemnation of Hollywood and the 'tube') diffuse but palpable feelings of guilt and shame. For all that Fiedler thinks he is generalizing beyond a national experience, in Canada the communal mythology would seem to imply that we are most at ease when the oppressed and the oppressor *stay* 'hopelessly sundered.' This is the final message conveyed to us by the ambiguous relation of magician and saint.

NOTES

1 Campbell, *The Masks of God*, Vol. III, *Occidental Mythology* (Viking 1970) 24, 22
2 This could help explain the conjunction of what seem on the face of it to be oddly assorted (i.e., both 'advanced' and 'primitive') traits in the prototypical science fiction hero.
3 Zweig, *The Adventurer* (Basic Books 1974) 52
4 Lamont, 'From Hero to Anti-Hero,' *SLitI* 9, 1 (1976) 8
5 Otto Rank, *Beyond Psychology* (Dover 1958) 93
6 G.R. Thompson, 'Romanticism and the Gothic Tradition,' introduction to *The Gothic Imagination: Essays in Dark Romanticism* (Washington State U. 1974) 2
7 This tendency toward 'comfortable' abasement may well explain Canada's otherwise inexplicable readiness to sell out her national resources to her more aggressive neighbour. As W.L. Morton notes, the evidence points 'to an unusual situation in Canada. Why should a country with a history so distinctive, a position so happy, a natural endowment so great, be so ready a victim of a foreign take-over unparalleled in extent and degree? The question both lack[s] and require[s] extensive investigation, but answers might be divined with some assurance. One [is] that the situation was not created by Americans. It was the doing of Canadians, Canadian businessmen and Canadian politicians ... They were aided and abetted by the Canadian public, which until recently had not protested their performance, but rather applauded it. The political party, for example, which has been most prone to continentalism, the Liberal party, has been in power by the will of the Canadian electorate fifty-four out of the seventy-four years since 1896' (A143).
8 Leach, 'Anthropological Aspects of Language: Animal Categories and Verbal Abuse' in Pierre Maranda, ed., *Mythology* (Penguin 1972) 49
9 Leach, 'Structuralism in Social Anthropology' in David Robey, ed., *Structuralism: An Introduction* (Clarendon 1972) 52
10 It is interesting in this connection to note Jung's claim that anima/animus projections, to an even greater extent than the shadow (which is recognizable as an aspect of the self, albeit an unattractive one), have a natural tendency to 'mobilize prejudice and become taboo' simply because they are 'unexpected,' foreign, difficult to assimilate. See *Aion: Researches into the Phenomenology of the Self*, trans. R.F.C. Hull (Princeton 1979) 17-18.
11 As Theodore Ziolkowski speculates about the Victorian gothicist's preference for short over long fictions, another reason for 'boxing' the magician into small,

relatively self-contained sub-textual narrative units might have something to do with the formal qualities of the shorter prose forms. 'The intrusion of the supernatural into a world governed by rational laws of nature is one of the most violent acts of chaos imaginable, an offense to reason and order. If such an intrusion is to be fictionally acceptable, it must be presented in a context that embodies reason and order. Otherwise the chaos would be both aesthetically unsatisfactory and morally depressing. Among the various literary forms, the shorter forms of fiction – novella and short story – have long been regarded as models of aesthetic form. Since they exemplify order, they can afford to incorporate instances of chaos as fleeting moments of crisis. The order of the narrative itself – in contrast to the generally looser order of longer forms like the novel – functions as a consolation in the face of the chaos depicted within the story.' *Disenchanted Images: A Literary Iconology* (Princeton 1977) 253

12 Hassan, *Radical Innocence: Studies in the Contemporary American Novel* (Princeton 1961) 27

13 Detweiler, *Story, Sign and Self: Phenomenology and Structuralism as Literary Critical Methods* (Fortress/Scholars Press 1978) 82

14 It is interesting also that the role of the Sky-God in Egyptian mythology – usually a pre-eminently masculine function – is played by a female deity ('She covers the whole earth, a huge cow on whose belly all the stars are constellated, or a female figure towering over and bending across the earth') while the Earth-God, usually feminine, is Geb, a male. Marie-Louise Von Franz, *Creation Myths* (Spring Pub. 1972) 50

15 As Jung describes it, 'Whereas the cloud of "animosity" surrounding the man is composed chiefly of sentimentality and resentment, in woman it expresses itself in the form of opinionated views, interpretations, insinuations, and misconstructions' (*Aion*, 16).

16 May, *Power and Innocence: A Search for the Sources of Violence* (Delta 1976) 23

17 May points out, for instance, that police brutality may often be traced to the fact that when criminals fail to demonstrate proper respect for authority many officers, far from viewing this simply as a legal trespass, 'feel their manhood is being challenged and their reputation, on which their self-respect is based, is at stake' (29-30).

18 It is interesting that we show no such reluctance to give full recognition to *American* aggressive heroes. This is obviously partly because they are so well publicized, but it may also have something to do with the fact that, being 'other' by nationality as well as by nature, they have transgressed no boundaries, and thus are not taboo.

19 Actually, the process of renovating the 'bad guy' which had its most recent peak in the late sixties-early seventies was begun long before. As Stephen Scobie points out, 'For the first twenty years or so after Billy's death, writers strove to outdo each other in creating ever more extravagant pictures of his villainy; he became a devil incarnate, a paragon of evil. Then, about the beginning of this century, the trend reversed; Billy became sentimentalised into a poor, misunderstood kid, excuses and

justifications were found for his killings, he was transformed into a folk-hero of the
Robin Hood variety. In 1930, the first of Hollywood's film versions of Billy the Kid
starred the former All-American football star, Johnny Mack Brown; thirty years
later, Penn's film starred Paul Newman' (D38).

20 Miller is especially vehement in dismissing the witchcraft rumours. Around Mrs
Donnelly, he says, 'there has been built by the family's detractors a whole body of
false legend picturing her as the evil genius of the family, a backwoods Lady Macbeth
implacably urging her browbeaten husband and sons on to ever greater and ever
more outrageous deeds of rapine and cruelty. The portrait is absolutely without basis
and an unspeakably vicious and wanton tampering with the facts' (138). In Crichton,
in contrast, this element is treated both lengthily and with great relish, with the
result that Johannah, far from being as unattractive as Miller's defence implies,
appears as a powerful woman who does not hesitate to call on occult powers to protect
her family from their enemies: '"I'm on the side of the good God and his Holy Son
but what my mother told me and taught me I cannot forget. On this earth Satan
walks, even if a soul dies; he must be fought. The ways of the Church work – but
sometimes not fast enough to stave off ill"' (24).

21 '"I yielded to Riel's judgment,"' said Dumont, '"although I was convinced that from
a humane standpoint, mine was the better plan; but I had confidence in his faith and
his prayers, and that God would listen to him." There was obviously a division within
Dumont between the highly practical hunter and warrior, who never really
abandoned his view of the appropriate strategy for the situation, and the pious Métis
in whose eyes Riel had become a substitute for the missionaries who had lost credit by
refusing to support resistance to the established government. The balance between
these two opposing views was tipped partly by Dumont's almost feudal sense of
fealty ... and partly by a bond of affection that sprang up between the two'
(Woodcock B191).

22 At the beginning of the poem Riel, the man of two bloods, is suspended *between* the
natural world of the Indian and the constructed world of the white man, the
meandering dirt paths of the prairie and the straight 'steel tongue' of the railway. By
the time of his trial, however, he is almost entirely the conventional native exiled
from the life-giving sources of 'home':

> So, it had come down to this, not a valley,
> Or a wilderness, but this courtroom and these
> Faces that were strangers now, and this smell of wood
> Decaying (his hand on the box, feet on this floor),
> Though the varnishing gleamed like a second sun,
> He could smell wood rotting, at the pith, like earth
> Soured and no greenness to it, no scent of growing,
> Of stored sun springing into wheat and waiting sky;
> Had come to this town: squared to prairie with straight

Streets and houses angled, and the steel of railways
Like a bullet through the prairie's heart – land of
Rectangular fields and sun mitred to sky –
Intelligence of steel, and wood rotting on
The nostrils...

It had come to this: out of the sacramental morning
And dream of one Saskatchewan and midnight
At Duck Lake and twilight over Batoche, where
they had held true to the straightness of their heart,
Where they had gathered to themselves a last corner
Of north. (48-9)

23 Even aside from the 'omniscient' lapses that inhibit our response to what would otherwise seem a conventional 'first-person limited' style of narration, Pierre Falcon, the 'Métis bard' who celebrated in song the earlier, successful Métis rebellion of 1816, is a glaring anachronism as Wiebe's putative participant-reporter.

24 Just as Riel is about to set out on his last, fateful journey with Dumont, the pair of them share such an omen: 'they saw that hill again and in a glance knew that they had both seen that revelation: a gallows there and a man swinging from that gallows. Vision and certainty. Though it must have been no more than a heat mirage bending a dead or stunted cottonwood up near the edge of the river, the wavering blackness a momentary crow perhaps struggling in a downdraft against the open sky, struggling upward./ When you see that, you know' (188).

25 Becker, *The Denial of Death* (Free Press 1975) 45

26 '"He's the best actor I've ever seen. He's got more moves than Bobby Orr. You know, in the House one day he's baiting the Opposition, the next he's doing the mumbling number so you can hardly hear him, another he's doing the professor and giving a lecture. He does it to keep everybody off balance. The greatest weapon in a prime minister's arsenal is surprise"' (in Radwanski 14).

27 As C.P. Stacey reveals, King was unable to stay away from prostitutes in his early years despite all his efforts to discipline himself out of the habit. His diary demonstrates vividly how hard he had to work to turn himself into the kind of person he could be proud of. '"Wasted time till 5 came home on elevated.... I now feel terribly sorry & disgusted by my action.... I fought hard against temptation & this has broken my Chicago record. I cannot bear to think of it. – Why am I so weak? Why cannot I keep where I strive so hard to be? – I will try harder the next time"' (46).

28 To find artifice safer, or even morally preferable to sincerity is not idiosyncratic to Canada, of course. Arturo Fallico, in fact, connects it, somewhat paradoxically, with the existentialist concept of authenticity. 'It is when the purposing being *becomes* the role, or forces himself whole into it, holding back nothing of himself as free agent that bad faith arises; contrariwise, it is when he is self-possessed as the being who can

initiate any and every role that he can "play" the role sincerely and without bad faith. It makes more than just a moral sense to say that Hitler and Mussolini were "bad actors," or that a true actor-artist playing these same roles on the stage would be doing not at all "bad acting," but the genuine article. Also there are those who are inclined to temper their judgment of Mussolini with a note of pity, on the grounds that he *was* an actor – a "ham," to be sure – but who look upon Hitler as having been an evil and dangerous man precisely because he was no actor – he really believed himself to *be* the role.' *Art & Existentialism* (Prentice-Hall 1962) 98

29 Even as a youth Mackenzie King was sure that as a grandson of William Lyon Mackenzie he was destined to accomplish some 'great work'; later, in the course of his spiritualist activities, he became convinced that various 'spirits,' including Laurier and St John, had informed him that '"God had chosen [him] to shew men & nations how they should live"' (Stacey 67, 175, 183-4).

30 Ferns & Ostry 147, 160, 115; on the general question of duplicity, see also 127, 134.

31 As John Kenneth Galbraith commented with regard to the man who becomes the subject of the public's 'great expectations,' '"Such ... a career, is not especially secure. The job turnover is very high. That is because, while it is easy to place a man on a pedestal, it is not at all easy to keep him there. A pedestal is a peculiarly public place. Since the build-up is indiscriminate in its selections, some rather grievous shortcomings may thus be revealed ... to a public whose expectations are inordinately high"' (in Radwanski 117). Galbraith's implication that under such circumstances the process of disillusionment is well-nigh inevitable makes it all the more interesting that Trudeau, who was given as much of a build-up as the most glamorous of American politicians, *did* manage to hang onto power even after the romantic image was dissipated and the public no longer able to see him as the knight in shining armour.

32 Biographical study of Clark, as Donald Swainson points out, can only emphasize this aspect. 'David Humphreys' portrait of Joe Clark is flaccid and dull. That this is so constitutes real evidence concerning Clark, because Humphreys sets out to write a sympathetic study. He wants Canadians to "know the Joe Clark I know." His book does instruct the reader about Joe Clark, but the result is likely to be a feeling of profound disquietude. Clark came from a prosperous small town Alberta family. His experience is both limited and limiting: school in High River, brief service as a journalist, undergraduate training at the University of Alberta, extensive activity in the Progressive Conservative Youth movement, activity in the senior party, unsuccessful experiences in two law schools, graduate work at Alberta, brief employment with Robert Stanfield, travel abroad and election to the House of Commons in 1972.

'These activities were all important and interesting to Joe Clark, but can generate no larger interest in any but the most compulsive student of party politics. There was no brilliance as student or journalist. His interest in politics is confined to the tactical; no important ideas or policies are associated with him. Humphreys attempts to make

Clark appear more human by telling anecdotes about the man, but are we reassured to learn that he is passionately fond of "canned candied popcorn called Poppycock?"' (418-19).

33 'Trudeau's unwillingness to express appreciation is rooted in the basic elements of his personality,' says Radwanski. 'If the early Greek philosophers believed that man is the measure of all things, Trudeau too often believes that he is the measure of all men. Because he has trained himself to be inner-directed and not to depend on praise ... he assumes that others feel the same way. And even when he realizes that this is not the case, something still inhibits him from expressing appreciation' (218).

34 We may speculate that this dictum puts the NDP in a double bind. It is likely that most of those who support them now, since they obviously do so *knowing* that they have little chance of winning, are not electing potential 'leaders' at all, but, rather, 'critics' or 'watchdogs' – an embodied conscience for the country, as it were. They hence not only accept but *require* different characteristics in their candidates – characteristics consonant with an alter ego – than do those voting for possible 'winners.' If the NDP changed its image enough to be able to compete for real power, it is likely, therefore, that they would lose a great deal of this extant support and have to compete with the better-established magicians from a very weak if not non-existent base.

35 C.G. Jung, *Psychological Types*, trans. H.G. Baynes, revised R.F.C. Hull (Princeton 1976)

36 Macdonald's notorious temper was perhaps a little more flamboyant than Trudeau's ('he was ... a furious Highlander who was ready and willing for a fight. And for nearly a quarter of an hour he stood in his place, his face contorted with excitement, gesticulating violently, and shouting his denunciations at the top of his voice' Creighton B203), but by all reports Trudeau's colder rage was even more devastating in its effect. 'Trudeau slips into a combative mood the moment he feels directly challenged or invited to justify himself,' says Radwanski: 'his eyes narrow and become colder, his face hardens, his voice takes on an edgy impatience. If the other person persists, Trudeau's cold anger visibly compresses itself into an icy fury that becomes almost a physical force radiating out toward his antagonist' (200-1).

37 Our task in this chapter has been merely to trace the broad outlines of a pattern. As may be inferred from the short list of sources cited, the discussion of Canadian politics in particular was designed rather to pique the reader's curiosity than to exhaust, or even to suggest, the full socio-historical ramifications of the subject. There is, however, one additional piece of documentation that seems to demand mention if only because of its title. Richard Gwyn's biography of Trudeau was not available when this book was in the making. The fact makes it all the more interesting that *The Northern Magus*, while differing from the foregoing in its *interpretation* of the relationship between the leader and his electorate, nevertheless reinforces strikingly the *image* of leadership that I have inferred from our communal myths. Trudeau, says Gwyn, was a 'sorcerer,' a 'performer,' a 'Single Combat Warrior.' 'His

countenance, chilly and cerebral, flared nostrils hinting at a sneer, gives him a natural aristocratic quality of dominion over others' ('Prologue,' n.p.). Here is our Magician *par excellence*!

38 Fiedler, 'The Death and Rebirth of the Novel' in John Halperin, ed., *The Theory of the Novel: New Essays* (Oxford 1974) 193

10

'I'-Site

Every thesis and antithesis imply, perhaps entail, their own synthesis, the transcendent third. So it is with the saint and the magician. For all the obtrusiveness of these types in Canadian literature, there is still one predominant member of our *dramatis personae* who remains to be considered – and one who, in peculiar ways, subsumes key aspects of *both* the exemplary roles outlined above. Who is this motley figure? If one casts one's mind over the ranks of Canadian literary protagonists the answer must be obvious. *As* must the reason for his importance. It all comes down to the uncertainties of our national self-image. Because so many of the traditional patterns by which experience is comprehended are called into question in the Canadian 'closed system' world, but *without* the clear break away from the past/present British/American heritage that would complete the transformation – because, as Anthony Dawson points out, 'coming of age in Canada seems often to mean going from definiteness to indefiniteness, from conviction to hesitation, certainty to uncertainty' (47) – the problem of *finding* identity (as noted in chapter 4) becomes here almost a matter of *creating* identity. Hence the title of Jack Hodgins's book, *The Invention of the World*. Hence, too, Frederick Philip Grove's blatantly fictitious 'autobiography.' More important, hence the characteristic thrust of so much of our literature. 'The idea of writing about one's life in order to shape it, or to give it actuality,' Dawson notes (53), is a major preoccupation of Canadian writers, and the figure of the *artist*, in all his guises, is one of the most important problems posed by the Canadian oeuvre. Why 'problems'? Perhaps because, as Peter Stevens suggests, the artist's confrontation with terra incognita makes him by definition an *explorer*, a role which, as the questing poet-cum-*coureur de bois* of Douglas LePan's 'A Country Without a Mythology' discovers, is as dangerous for the nature-haunted Canadian in psychic as in physical terms.[1] Perhaps only because he *is* an artist. In any case it is certainly a fact that creative activity is commonly imaged in Canadian literature as not merely crucial but traumatic.

Actually there seem to be two kinds of fear associated with the artist's role in Canada. The first is the fear of being dehumanized and diminished by a commitment to art; not merely emotionally warped, cut off from normal human relations like the protagonist of Brian Moore's *The Great Victorian Collection* (a novel that Patricia Merivale categorizes as a 'Gothic artist-parable' with its thematic focus on the 'tension between "life" and "art"' 199), but, more extremely, implicated in some kind of broadly destructive psychic violence that creates havoc, causes harm, damages others almost inadvertently, as if (as Michael Ondaatje speculates) 'The making and destroying [came] from the same source, same lust' (B55). This is not an unusual theme in literature, of course, but in Canada it achieves unusual poignancy because of the radical ambivalence felt toward *any* aggressive act. Indeed, at its worst, the felt danger of dehumanization in this country images forth an artist who 'devours' his object, as in Harlow's *Scann*, where both Thrain, the town-maker, and Philippa Morten, the mad matriarch – interchangeable alter egos for the obsessed writer, Amory Scann – literally whittle away the physical extremities of their victims. In this mode the artist is at best a conjurer (MacEwen's Julian the Magician, whose art, neither quite pure magic nor pure craftsmanship, but in either case clearly a transgression against nature, can bring only the kind of enlightenment which in the long run is more likely to be destructive than wholesome), and at worst the explicit killer represented by Ondaatje's Billy the Kid, a dangerous amalgam of coldness and emotional turbulence which, significantly enough, suggests the deadly naiveté of the saint-turned-magician we examined in the last chapter.[2] This brings us to the second kind of apprehension. Both Julian (who practically forces his own crucifixion) and Billy are killed at the ends of their respective stories. This is no more than we expect. Though the artist may be a potent figure, an incomparable manipulator, should he fail he is doubly vulnerable because of the extent to which he has exposed himself. As the self-appointed agent of control, the man whose primary function, in Julian's words, ' "is to celebrate the ego," '[3] the artist according to all propriety must be prepared to accept punishment for his reckless self-assertion. The second and greater fear associated with the artist's role in Canada, therefore, is the fear not of destroying but of being destroyed. Perhaps, though, in this case 'conviction' would be a better word to use than 'fear.' The fact is – and here we come to the crux of the 'problem' mentioned above – a great deal of Canadian literature seems dedicated to the proposition not merely that an artist *deserves*, nor even that he *may* suffer, some kind of retribution, but that by virtue of his self-appointment to the creative task it is almost *inevitable* that he precipitates his own destruction.

Here is where we depart most particularly from convention. In the common 'psycho-social romantic parable' that Merivale invokes – and this sets the tone for most modern treatments of the theme – the artist's doom is predicated upon the fact of his rebellion against and persecution by 'society.' The gift of art is a 'fatal' one, in other words, specifically because 'despondency and madness' are the invariable result of a confrontation between 'the lonely artistic sensibility' and 'the crass, unfeeling world' (Merivale 199). This element is not entirely missing from the Canadian corpus – David Canaan's fate in Ernest Buckler's *The Mountain and the Valley*, for instance, is prepared for, if not immediately caused, by his insistence on holding himself aloof from the life of the community – but in general the artist's downfall seems to be viewed in this country as founded in something more basic than a mere social problem. Here, indeed, the greatest danger posed to the artist seems to be something inherent in the very nature of art. For all its importance and appeal, there is simply something about art, about the way it functions in our world, the quests it inspires and the stance it entails, that makes it deadly. Such, at least, would seem to be the implication of Moore's and MacEwen's and Ondaatje's artist parables; of Anne Hébert's *Les chambres de bois*, where art and order are opposed not merely to time but to life; of Robert Kroetsch's *The Studhorse Man*. As W.H. New points out with respect to this latter book, 'Hazard's quest – announced by one of Poseidon's nicknames – insists in such a civilized wasteland on the flesh-and-blood vitality of "Poesy." It is a deceptive belief, for ... Poesy kills him in the end' (A183).

Why, in the face of all traditional assumptions, should we view art in such a peculiar fashion? The answer to this critical question is already suggested by the classical echoes carried by our phrasing in the paragraph before last. In a country where even the most justified kind of aggressiveness is hubris, art, which in a sense sacralizes self-assertion, becomes an abomination, an act not merely of indiscretion but of blasphemy, based as it is on the assumption by its practitioners of magical, even divine powers. Does this seem extreme? We find a vivid illustration of such an attitude in Gabrielle Roy's exemplary fable, *La montagne secrète*. This novel, even more than those already cited, demonstrates many of the features characteristic of the Canadian handling of this motif. Indeed, Pierre Cadori, Roy's painter-protagonist, may be considered a kind of prototype for the Canadian doomed artist figure. What, then, we might ask, is the specific cause of his fall? Pierre Cadori makes his first mistake when he takes on nature. Undeterred by savage animals, starvation, killer storms – undeterred even by his 'apprehension' of the psychic dangers implied by his presumption (84) – he sets out to confront and to expropriate the landscape. What he *achieves* is something much riskier than mere expropriation. 'The mountain of his imagination had almost nothing in common with the mountain in Ungava. Or at least what he had been able to capture of the latter he had, at his own inner fires, softened, melted, cleansed, to cast it anew, in his own fashion, making of it a new raw material, henceforth entirely human' (185). *Cast anew!* Mythic allusions aside, this phrase points up the real problem. Cadori not only attempts to assume powers properly reserved for divinity but, worse, he succeeds. Unheeding in his humility, he crosses the imperceptible threshold between mimicking and making. At this point, as the book itself underlines, 'it [is] no longer [a] question of who [has] better succeeded with his mountain, God or Pierre, but merely that he, Pierre, [has] likewise created' (185). And this, of course, seals his fate. No hubris so outrageous can pass unnoticed: he *must* be punished. As indeed must his brothers-in-craft. Not all acts of creation in Canadian literature are presented in such melodramatic terms as Pierre's, whose heart-stoppage at the very moment of triumph underlines with unusual vividness the retributive nature of his downfall, but almost always there is the implication that to make art entails some kind of death.

If we can leave aside the question of doom for a moment, it is quite predictable on the basis of the psycho-symbolic propensities we have seen in the foregoing chapters that Canadians *should* localize a good deal of anxiety in art. Art, by definition, transcends the boundary between human and non-human. The artist, therefore, is by definition permanently poised – with 'hairspring balance,' as Dennis Lee puts it (20) – *right on that critical line.* Even aside from the fact that in human experience *any* significant boundary tends, as Edmund Leach points out, to become taboo ('A boundary separates two zones of social space-time which are *normal, time-bound, clear-cut, central, secular,* but the spatial and temporal markers which actually serve as boundaries are themselves *abnormal, timeless, ambiguous, at the edge, sacred*[4]), we have already observed that Canadians are more than normally sensitive to the problems posed by this particular conjunction. For this if for no other reason it is hardly surprising that we would be ambivalent about any role with such symbolic associations. It is also not surprising that the ambivalence should be most painfully felt by the artists and writers themselves, inasmuch as it is they who have to cross the dangerous threshold.[5] And this, in fact, is what appears to be the case. Judging by the oeuvre, the Canadian creator, going far beyond the normal national preoccupation with limits, most typically feels himself to be a person radically divided, chronically unsure whether he is – or wants to be – self or other, saint or magician; like Billy the Kid, 'Balanced between sanity and insanity, between human machines and mechanical men, between the gentle hunter and neutral assassin' (Mandel B116). Small wonder, then, that he tends – with Margaret Atwood's poetic persona – to be obsessed with 'edges,' those 'transitional slivers of doubt between hazard and security, the known and unknown'; haunted by (in John Nelson Foster's words) 'metaphors for mind and emotion pressing against the outer limits of those forms they are forced to inhabit, and simultaneously hugging those boundaries in exquisite fear of the chaos beyond them' (12). Small wonder, indeed, that he exhibits the classic symptoms of the Wacousta syndrome in their most extreme form. If even the most basic – the merely propaedeutic – existential interface is disquieting to the

Canadian, once we introduce into the picture a whole constellation of fuzzy, ill-assorted notions about art – once we attempt to balance, as the practitioner at least surely must, our conditioned reverence *for* it with our instinctive apprehension *of* it – the situation must inevitably seem more desperate by far. *And* even more incapable of solution.

This, in any case, is what the literature itself would seem to suggest. In Alden Nowlan's poem 'Survival' – to consider only one example – two of the poet's own personae, one 'wholly drunk' and the other 'wholly sober,' confronted with experience in the raw – a lion – react respectively in aesthetic and practical terms. The result is that the latter escapes unscathed while the former, 'transfixed by the indescribably beautiful/visions that he saw' (21), is devoured. Here is the Canadian artist's dilemma in brief. Here, too, is our most frequent response to that dilemma: ambivalence. 'While this is unquestionably one of Nowlan's finest poems,' says Marilyn Baxter, 'it is not immediately clear what the poet is saying about the visionary experience. Is he suggesting that it is better *not* to have it and survive ... or to have the vision and cease to exist?' (110-11). Baxter claims that the solution the poem itself implies is compromise between unnatural extremes, a kind of psychic integration ('Og's spiritual death is as tragic, if not more so, than his companion's physical death. But the two selves need not necessarily be divided in real life' 111). It is possible, however, that this reading depends on her own desire for reconciliation, her need, perhaps, to rationalize any poem she admires. In so far as it is, finally, inconclusive read in its own terms, what this poem really conveys, or at least contemplates, is the possibility that it is ultimately *impossible* to reconcile the discrepant aspects of the artist's existential position. No wonder the latter tends to think of himself as doomed!

In consequence of these conditions and predispositions it is appropriate that the Canadian creator should be preoccupied with the symbol of the window or doorway. 'The windowsill has ... become one of Miss Avison's favourite images to suggest the edge of perception, the moment when perception becomes necessary or possible' (New A237). 'The first lines [of Marlatt's book] acquaint us with the themes of imprisonment, escape, and search, while the book at large elaborates upon these themes by examining them in the context of restrictive private and aesthetic frames ... [beginning with] the frames of windows decorated with boxes of roses [through which the protagonists] watch each other watch each other' (Lecker B109). 'The "still windowledge" is the centre of [Klein's] meditation. Inside is space organized for human purposes, human safety; outside a vast seemingly limitless universe. It is the Canadian situation in a nutshell' (Marshall 103). If we turn to painting we find an even greater fondness for the device. Christiane Pflug is far from the only one to make an ambivalent identification with the structural correlatives of transition. Works as diverse as David Milne's *Window* (ca 1930), L.L. FitzGerald's *From an*

Upstairs Window (1948), Gordon Rayner's *River Window* (1965), Ernst Lindner's *The Window* (1969), and Hugh Mackenzie's *The Window* (1969) suggest the same divided experience Marshall infers from Klein's poem. More significantly, both writers and artists seem to view the window/door symbol or its functional equivalents not merely as a means of defining stance and perspective but as a source or nexus in itself of considerable anxiety. Indeed, if we compare the following two quotations, one focused on art (Michael Greenwood on Christopher Pratt) and one on literature (Margot Northey on the French-Canadian novel), we will see that the inside/outside motif is used with remarkable consistency by Canadian creators of quite diverse types to signal feelings of extreme if diffuse emotional and/or cognitive ambivalence.

There are certain recurrent motifs in [Pratt's] paintings that seem clearly related to the basic mental functions of introversion and extroversion – the acts of looking inward and outward. The doors, windows, walls and mirrors that are featured so insistently seem to represent symbolic thresholds distinguishing the orientation of his ideas toward one aspect of reality or another ...

In such a painting as *Landing* (1973), the essential qualities of [his] vision are epitomized. The typically austere setting composed of elemental geometries has all the claustrophobic atmosphere of an existential drama. The 'landing' is another threshold device offering two possible courses of psychological transition: to ascend the ghostly staircase to what must be an equally barren destination, or to proceed through the open door into a cell-like room whose boundaries are predetermined and whose silence is palpable. Partly concealed by the open door a curiously shaped settee upholstered in dark material stands against the far wall, a symbol not so much of relaxation as of consciousness suspended in time, a kind of death. Neither course is productive; no outcome to an unyielding situation can be expected. (33)

The view from the window in which a captive (usually a woman) looks out from her 'prison' is a repeated motif in gothic literature, but also has a special place in Quebec literature, where the captive spirit often symbolically represents the isolated containment of French-Canadian society, cut off from participation in the larger outside world. One remembers Elisabeth Rolland in *Kamouraska*, and the image of Maria Chapdelaine looking out both longingly and in fear upon the forest and its avenues of escape ... In *La Guerre, Yes Sir!*, [in contrast,] it is a nun standing outside in the cold who is cut off and who is left to gaze through an open window at the bustle of activity within. In this image Carrier does not seem to imply a reversal of customary meaning, that is, he does not seem to suggest that the inner group rather than the outer world is the source of vitality. After all, there is death inside the room as well as without, in the coffin as well as in the decayed teeth of the nun. The nun's puzzling question as to who is alive and who is dead would rather suggest that Carrier means simply to disrupt or disturb the customary image and its cluster of associations. (85)

As we may infer from these and numerous similar commentaries, the most significant thing that Pratt's and Hébert's and Carrier's windows (along with most other threshold images in the corpus) have in common is the sense not merely of tension-yoked antagonistic 'spaces' but of consciousness somehow trapped in the eternal twilight of 'between.' We may take the window symbol, then, to stand not only for the artist's position on the borderline, but even more for his unacknowledged apprehensions about the psychic dangers that position entails.

Unfortunately, the Canadian creator's exercises in self-imaging do not stop with the window – which, being an abstraction, at least offers the possibility of a certain degree of displacement of affect. When the interface in question is not just the formal division between inside and outside but, quite specifically, the fragile line between self and other, 'that membraneous edge' Foster finds to be such an obsession of Atwood's (12), the imagery spawned is much more disquieting. The problem is, as Mary Douglas demonstrates in her study of 'natural symbols,' the human preoccupation with categorization and the consequent tendency for one to cross-reference all possible aspects of life-experience means – as noted in our examination of Moira/Themis disorienta-tion above – that it is virtually impossible to keep anomalies in one kind of experience from contaminating all others. In particular, there is a general predisposition toward the metaphoric conflation of corporeal and social existence. 'The social body constrains the way the physical body is perceived. The physical experience of the body, always modified by the social categories through which it is known, sustains a particular view of society. There is a continual exchange of meanings between the two kinds of bodily experience so that each reinforces the categories of the other.' In the kind of social system that, according to Douglas's description, corresponds most closely to our own so-called garrison culture ('for the social type I have called small group, the universe is divided between warring forces of good and evil ... The group boundary is the main definer of rights: people are classed either as members or strangers. Magical danger is associated with the idea of boundary.'), this means, firstly, that there will typically be a great deal of concern about the integrity of the body ('The dangers to it will come ... from failure to control the quality of what it absorbs through the orifices; fear of poisoning, protection of boundaries, aversion to bodily waste products') and secondly, that problems of social transgression will commonly be translated into terms suggesting threats to this physical integrity.[6] Douglas's account explains much about the rather eccentric body imagery associated with the artist's (by definition transgressive) role in Canada. And this in turn explains – and no doubt exacerbates – the perceptible aura almost of terror catalysed by the creative act. Amory Scann notwithstand-ing, the process of 'making art' seems to be most often associated by the Canadian with the progressive shedding of little bits and pieces of one's self.

Creativity, in other words, is apparently viewed as quite literally deadly, involving *by necessity* a breach of personal discretion so serious as to invite annihilation; the image of the artist as devourer is hence always balanced by a vision of the artist as devoured.

The first evidence we find in confirmation of this interpretation is the Canadian writer's predilection for fecal imagery. Scatalogical metaphors are not unusual in literature, especially types with a satirical bent, but here the usage is given an unconventional thrust by its frequent association with artistry. Sylvia Fraser's *The Candy Factory* offers a striking example.

Defecation was his greatest pleasure.
... Far better than jacking off. More like child-birth, he imagined. A true act of creation, accessible to every man – God's wonders, mixed with man's juices, passed through a hazardous course of tubes and tribulation, then offered up, once more, to God
...
The tramp rolled his buttocks, coiling his spoor. He wondered what colours he had produced today: russet? mahogany? puce? maroon? khaki? dun? fuscous? saffron? purple-flecked? green tinged? The possibilities were as endless as the colours in oil, as the patterns in fire. (16-17)

What, exactly, does this analogy imply? Assuming, as I think we must, that it is something a little more profound than the graffito 'art is shit,' we may perhaps speculate that the overt connections are underlaid by a number of covert contra-messages suggesting, firstly, that creativity, like the tendency to metamorphose into a magician, is a natural, involuntary, and potentially traumatic reflex (it is significant that Timothy Findley, speaking of his own creativity, should use this same parallel to communicate his sense of compulsion: 'You've got to get it done. I mean it's like saying: Excuse me, I've got to go to the bathroom, and if everybody started to prevent you ... there would be disaster' B132), and secondly, inasmuch as faeces equals both fertilizer (life) and decay (death), that as act it is both personally and socially ambiguous.

At least one effect of this latter suggestion is to render the artist figure even more problematic than before. We see the type development even in Fraser, where the creator/defecator, a vital if repellent figure, at least demonstrates both dedication and vigour in the prosecution of his particular métier. For all his apparent success as effectuator, this man, we learn in an immediately succeeding passage, is so egocentric as to be unbalanced, perhaps even dangerous:

The tramp sniffed his spoor. He felt the usual craving to devour it, but resisted – not out of revulsion, but out of moral responsibility. He believed the day he dined on his own spoor would be the last day of his life, and – since everything in Creation was but an extension of his own imagination – the end of the Universe. It would be the Devil swallowing Himself by the tail. God feasting on His own body in remembrance of Himself. The supreme act of solipsism. (18)

If this is the conception of the artist carried implicitly by the excretion metaphor in Canadian literature, it is small wonder that its invocation tends to trigger a considerable sense of strain.[7] In Leonard Cohen's *Beautiful Losers*, I. is endlessly anxious about his tendency to constipation, associating this with a flawed psyche (46-50). In Robertson Davies' *The Manticore*, David Staunton's traumatic childhood experience with constipation remedies, and especially with the enemas administered by his insensitive nurse, are causally implicated with his adult rigidity (85-6). In W.O. Mitchell's *The Vanishing Point*, though the act of evacuation is used as a moral/emotional touchstone, it is primarily in a negative sense, the toilet behaviour of various characters signalling the flaws of both over- and under-socialization.[8] All of these usages reinforce our sense that creativity is viewed in Canada very ambivalently indeed.

Once we get beyond excretion, the picture becomes more complex and more disquieting. Evacuation – whatever its moral associations – is at least a *natural* function, and as such focuses less attention on the question of *whether* one should create than on the relatively minor problem of *how*. That the Canadian's body-anxiety goes much deeper than this is confirmed by the recurrent concern with the vulnerability of bodily extremities that may be discerned throughout the corpus. Even aside from the preoccupation with mutilation and amputation, again and again we are brought up short by images of sinister or threatening or at least ambiguous *hands*. Earl Birney's famous poem by that name is one of the most extended explorations of this subject. (The complexity of this piece lies not merely in the tension it sets up between the 'webbed claws' of balsam and the more overt violence of the weapon-bearing tool-making human hands, but in its subtle progression from the fear of being touched/victimized to the fear of touching/victimizing to the final hint, when the poet invokes the magnet that waits in Europe for 'our' steel-gloved fist, that to touch, even *as* victimizer, is perforce to become potential victim.) Similar complexity, similar undertones, may, however, be detected even in relatively casual usage. '"Girl!" Dr Gumm cried and Lilja froze ... A long bony finger, the massive thumb at right angles to it, found her. "The hand of God is on you!"' (Blondal 83). 'Ordinary hands that rustle and crablike reach, nobody ever notices hands. A pair for each, a brace of scuttling, suddenly hands that feed ... The Hands of Orlac ... Boy that's a. Pretty good story. Ha! Lucan loosening his tie just for now, relaxing, show them my ease. Before I. Cruel hands of strangers, prying fingers' (Gibson c94). '[I]t's odd we'd been talking about dismemberment because it turned out the foetus-faced man wore a hook in place of a right hand and he was using this hook to pluck at Harry's lapel, the better to argue with him ... Here's my favourite graduate student, Harry said, disentangling himself from this maniac's prosthesis and trying to give me a hug, whereupon his arm was snapped at in mid-air and caught like a gadfly by a trout' (Mills 90). 'She began to stimulate him with her hands and her long fingernails, and it occurred to him what vicious little hands they could be' (Helwig A16). 'Meals were a time of naked exposure. Hands reached out revealing trembling fingers. Faces met in grave collision' (Blais B22). It is clear from this recurrent uneasiness that for the Canadian touching and being touched are equally repellent, equally dangerous possibilities. Always, it seems, we see in hands (as Joan Coldwell says of *La belle bête*) 'physical destructiveness where love ought to be' (66). What does this have to do with creativity? Since art is the prototype of 'reaching out' – of 'love,' if you will – the risks not merely of meeting a rebuff but of actual dismemberment, of extreme physical and mental pain, are all the greater for an artist. 'Amputation,' by imbuing the victim with a certain air of 'otherness' – as Atwood notes of the charismatic one-handed shopkeeper in *Surfacing*[9] – asserts its own power, but the price paid in suffering for any such distinction is very high.

The artist, then, fears not just that his activity will compromise him in some way, but that it has the potential to cause him even more radical kinds of damage. Certainly this is what *Surfacing* suggests, playing as it does with images of amputated hands, severed sexual organs, sawn-up magician's assistants, and, especially, decapitations of all kinds. It's obvious that this latter motif is intended by the author to suggest that her protagonist/persona/artist figure suffers from some kind of 'dissociation of sensibility' ('At some point my neck must have closed over, pond freezing or a wound, shutting me into my head; since then everything had been glancing off me, it was like being in a vase' 105-6),[10] but the ubiquitousness and diverseness of dismemberment imagery to be found in this book implies a more broadly based kind of anxiety. As James Harrison points out, 'It is fragmentation rather than polarization which is the underlying nightmare of the novel' (76). To what extent are we justified in associating this unwholesome preoccupation with uneasiness about the role of the artist, though? Inasmuch as the key to this woman's entire neurosis would seem to be her distress about having undergone an abortion – birth being an obvious symbol for creativity – Atwood's parable, with its constant sounding of that archetypal fear of physical disintegration implicit in edge paranoia, elucidates not merely the dangers of love but the extent to which an artist can be crippled – that is, wounded – by those very functions that define her as such. In this respect *Surfacing* is less idiosyncratic than prototypical. Indeed, the connections we have drawn here suggest that the multitude of childbirth disasters I have noted in Canadian literature may well signify not merely the problems posed by Canadian familial relations but the extremely mixed feelings experienced by the Canadian artist confronted with his own creativity.[11]

If dismemberment metaphors speak of anxiety, this still falls significantly short of the 'fear of being devoured' – that is, totally consumed – cited above. We approach closer to this ultimate image of victimization, however, when we note, in addition to the fecal references, the missing fingers, and the dead babies, a further – and perhaps definitive – motif of cannibalism associated in Canadian literature with creative activity. Why definitive? With a fragmentation motif the affect is fairly straightforward. Like Alden Nowlan's poetic alters (who are of course merely the products of a different kind of splitting apart), one can either reach out and risk mutilation or stay closed up inside the self and suffer the consequences of somewhat different but equally painful varieties of psychic violence. The idea of cannibalism, on the other hand, points up *both* types of fear noted above: the fear of being consumed and the equally intense fear of consuming others. In Atwood's *The Edible Woman* – which, in its correlation of eating with objectification, turning subjects into 'things,' brings out some of the more important underlying implications of this motif – the second aspect is presented only obliquely, in so far as Marian's increasing identification with 'prey' makes it impossible any longer for her to be even an 'innocent' predator. More explicit in its handling of the theme is Audrey Thomas's *Blown Figures*. Bringing together all the strands we have been tracing in the last few pages, this latter work (which, as George Bowering points out, 'abounds with images, found and otherwise, of headless bodies and severed heads ... of eggs, of blindness and one-eye, of blood, menstrual and other' D88-9) juxtaposes the artist/narrator's quest into the past for her own identity with a subliminal quest for her miscarried child (lost creativity), and then implicates both with a cannibalism motif. Significantly, while the protagonist at first seems equally terrified of being eaten by witches and of becoming a witch herself, in the closing pages it is said that she goes to the witch tree (whether in dreams or in the flesh doesn't matter) and assumes the name ODI AKESE or SHE EATS GRAND PEOPLE (543). The artist can – and perhaps must – accept his destiny in the end, despite its dangers. *Blown Figures* makes it clear, however – and herein resides the real problem of the artist's role – that to do so is to become in some sense a monster.[12]

After going this far, the final question we might ask, as Marilyn Baxter felt compelled to ask of Nowlan's poem, is how, ultimately, does it all balance out? Is the Canadian artist, in general terms, as resigned to his monstrosity as Thomas's protagonist is? Actually, no. Which is hardly surprising. Burned fingers are daunting enough. Exacerbating matters, an implied corollary to all the diverse mutilation metaphors is the suggestion that it is not mere physical damage that the artist risks but *spiritual* disfigurement, perhaps obliteration.

The idea that Canadian poems about making poetry tend to be studded with symbolic mountains and oceans, indeed, that the poets themselves may, on the basis of the kind of poesis they practise, be classified as mountaineers or swimmers, has been so extensively discussed by such critics as Douglas Jones

(*Butterfly on Rock*) and Tom Marshall (*Harsh and Lovely Land*) that it may, I think, simply be stipulated. Most of those who have worked with this idea, and certainly the two cited, have, however, concerned themselves almost solely with the substantive aspects of the perspectival dichotomy ('Mountains evoke objectivity and a god's-eye view of the dangerous external world, water the ever-changing depths of the self, the collective unconscious and the racial and evolutionary past' Marshall 12), ignoring for the most part the equally obvious problems each stance entails. Ideals aside, in *Canadian* literature the mountain suggests far less readily the artist figure's 'objectivity' than his presumption. In almost every case where the motif is invoked, in fact, it turns out to be in some sense an instrument of doom: Pierre Cadori dies painting the mountain; David Canaan dies daydreaming on top of the mountain; Earle Birney's David dies climbing the mountain.

Ocean symbols in the Canadian oeuvre are similarly ambivalent, evoking an image of drowning just as easily and as often as the more neutral image of swimming. Jones, for one, tends to use both terms almost interchangeably, as if, with Jung, he considers the plunge, however traumatic its attendant effects, to be valuable for psychic health.[13] 'Thanatos overcomes Eros,' he says cheerfully of Duncan Campbell Scott's drowned Piper of Arll, doomed by his futile yearning to transcend merely earthly art. But, 'Negative as it may be, the conclusion remains haunting, rich, and beautiful' (19). Beautiful, maybe – but inasmuch as it symbolizes the central dilemma of the Canadian artist, it is also *disturbing*.[14] For this if for no other reason it is a mistake, I think, to minimize the negative side of all our submarine imagery. The truth of the matter is, in alternate mode even Irving Layton's 'breathless swimmer in that cold green element' is simply a 'dead poet' (170-1). And why not? What we are dealing with here is a wholly alien environment. No wonder Margaret Avison speaks of the swimmer's moment on the edge of the whirlpool not from the swimmer's point of view but from the vantage of one who will *not* 'dare the knowledge' of that 'ominous centre' (36). No wonder, too, that Atwood's persona in *Surfacing* is unhinged by her experience in the lake. Whether or not we see this woman's experience as ultimately therapeutic (we will return to this question in the next chapter), the fact is that what she confronts as a swimmer is quite clearly inimical to her sanity if not her life. There is, as Linda Hutcheon points out, 'no life-giving warmth in her metaphorical waters' (B85). And so it is with all those swimming poets. If cannibalism – being consumed – is the ultimate threat to physical integrity, *drowning is the ultimate symbol of mental dissolution*. This, then, is the last, most excruciating, and perhaps most inescapable element in the Canadian artist's fear of his own role.

The exemplary figure here is Buddy Bolden of Ondaatje's *Coming through Slaughter* – the other side, the swimmer version, of the killer-poet, Billy the Kid. Obsessed by death dreams, identified with windows, knives, and ambiguous hand imagery, Bolden, though appropriately enough (like Billy) an 'American,' is another prototypical Canadian artist figure. As Stephen Scobie points out, he is 'fascinated by the razor-edge balance between control and lack of control' (A8). More specifically, Ondaatje implies, he wants (presumptuous-ly) to get *beyond* order, at least in so far as that implies pattern artificially imposed ('John Robichaux! Playing his waltzes ... Every note part of the large curve, so carefully patterned that for the first time I appreciated the possibilities of a mind moving ahead of the instruments ... I loathed everything he stood for' 93), attempting instead to penetrate right to the essence of otherness, revealing – creating – a kind of reality that will *be* rather than merely *imitating* nature as does art. Unfortunately, like the iconic Audubon water turkey invoked earlier in the book,[15] Bolden plunges too deep. Giving himself up to the alien element – in this case his own music – he literally explodes into otherness, blows his mind, dissolves:

All my body moves to my throat and I speed again ... feel the blood that is real move up bringing fresh energy in its suitcase, it comes flooding past my heart in a mad parade, it is coming through my teeth, it is into the cornet, god can't stop god can't stop it can't stop the air the red force coming up can't remove it from my mouth, no intake gasp, so deep blooming it up god I can't choke it the music still pouring in a roughness I've never hit, watch it *listen* it *listen* it, can't see I CAN'T SEE. (131)

From this moment Bolden, having spent himself too liberally, lapses into the madness which, as Sam Solecki comments in an article aptly entitled 'Nets and Chaos' (see especially 40), is identified in the book with images of self-mutilation: 'Bolden's hand going up into the air/ in agony./ His brain driving it up into the/ path of the circling fan' (136).

If so many dangers are perceived to attend the creator's task, apart from influencing thematic concerns it will also naturally affect the way Canadian writers perceive and present *themselves*. In fact the authorial presence we may infer from Canadian literature manifests a number of what, from an international perspective, appear as striking peculiarities of stance and tone. In the modern world at large, the act of making art is now generally viewed as almost unequivocally positive, and the artist portrayed – indeed *self*-presented – as not merely significant but heroic. This state of affairs (to simplify somewhat) was an indirect result of the disillusionment and despair that spread in the wake of the crumbling of Victorian epistemological certainties. No longer capable of belief in an orderly universe, writers no longer looked for meaning – or even models – in 'the world.' 'The struggle to sustain meaning and pattern within the limits of realistic style, subject, structure, and theme became almost unbearable, and the novel slowly but inevitably shifted its focus inward and receded from contemplation of the social and contingent.'[16] The consequent emphasis on subjectivity only exacerbated the process of relativization (moral, cultural, psychological) and this in turn placed even greater importance on the writer's ability no longer simply to record but to *create* experience. The ultimate extension of this development was found in existentialism with its radical rejection of humanist absolutes and consequent claims that man not only could but must create *everything* that made up his personal reality, including himself. Art now became not merely a solace but a crucial, fragile stopgap against encroaching chaos.[17] 'What existentialism did ... was to promote a general feeling that man was alone in the world, was now detached from all systems of belief, and that the creator must find his salvation from art alone, reinventing it from the very beginning.'[18] Hence the artist as hero.

In America this trend had even more radical effects than in Europe. Even the existentialists, with their emphasis on self-validation, tend to recognize a social component in the artist's exemplary role – Camus' Dr Rieux, for instance, claims at the end of *La peste* to be writing in order to 'bear witness in favor of those plague-stricken people, so that some memorial of the injustice and outrage done them might endure; and to state quite simply what we learn in a time of pestilence: that there are more things to admire in men than to despise'[19] – but in America, right from the beginning, the artist, inasmuch as he seemed to offer a pre-eminent demonstration of the Adamic mode that typifies 'the' American, was above all else an individualist. From the Puritans through to Whitman – that prototypical namer of the world and singer of the self – the country thus witnessed not the growth of something new but merely the transformation of seeds already present: 'from an egocentrism sought after because it manifests an ultimate theocentrism, to an egocentrism sought after for its own sake ... from a poetry expressive of God's way with man, to a poetry expressive of man's way with himself and with the God which his sense of himself reveals.'[20] And after this – well, as Roy Harvey Pearce points out, 'All American poetry since is, in essence if not in substance, a series of arguments with Whitman' [57]. From Joel Barlow's crude attempts to 'make' a nation in *The Columbiad* through to Wallace Stevens' quest for the Supreme Fiction that would give 'God to reality,' American creators have had a propensity 'to conceive of the poetic act as the sole means of self-identification and self-preservation' [381, 130]. The American artist, in other words, has been self-perceived in pre-eminently heroic terms all along.

The development doesn't stop here. What happens when native egotism comes together with 'modern' pessimism[21] – and this is the point that must be borne in mind with respect to Canada – is that the artist figure, already marked by a mythically justified self-assertiveness, finds his self-chosen task of 'making' now has universal as well as personal significance. Not only does he 'make' *on behalf of* the world as does the exemplary European artist, but – like Fraser's maniacal tramp – by making himself he literally *makes the world*. With such validation the American artist feels no qualms about proclaiming himself quite openly. And does so. The most obvious examples are those writers like Norman Mailer who make no distinction between public and poetic acts, for whom creating is performing and 'Performance is an exercise of power,'[22] or those artists like Andy Warhol whose personalities become greater objects of popular interest than their art. Even where the individual creator shows no public sign of this kind of self-assertion, however, the works themselves tend not merely to reveal but to assert an unabashed egocentricity. Abstract impressionism in art, for instance, at least by implication makes the artist's sensibility the measure of all things. '[Jackson] Pollock was an intensely subjective artist. For him inner reality was the only reality ... [and] "the gesture on the canvas" was "a gesture of liberation from value – political, aesthetic, moral."'[23] In literature, similarly, the refusal of many post-modernists – Pynchon, Barthelme, Burroughs – to pay even lip service to either empirical verisimilitude or the reader's need to comprehend, their wilful spinning of apocalyptic fables and hallucinatory tales so inaccessible as to hide, nay, to *deny* meaning, speaks of an absolute confidence in the creator's authority. To an even greater extent than the American artist, therefore, the American writer tends to underline his own presence in his work. As Charles Glicksberg says of Sukenik, his refusal 'to play the game according to the rules of realism ... calls attention to his manhandling of the plot ... lets it be known that he is inventing characters and putting them in stories he has concocted.'[24] Just as much as Mailer this kind of writer is advertising himself – *and* his mastery. 'Underlying it all,' says Roger Sale, 'is a huge assertion of personal power, which leads to aggressive showmanship ... in other words, style used as a badge of personal authority, and personal authority having the ability to invent and master whole worlds.'[25]

In light of these trends outside the country it seems all the more significant that Canadian writers apparently take a most *un*heroic view of themselves. One might expect that an increased sense of the risk involved would enhance one's sense of value but the fact is that most of our creative compatriots seem more concerned to efface than to assert themselves. But wait a minute! – I can hear the objections forming already: *efface*, you say? That isn't the impression Douglas Jones would give. 'For [Jones] the Canadian poet is the hierophant, the liberator, the forger of the uncreated conscience of his race,' says D.J. Dooley (156). Such pronouncements seem to have considerable weight on their side, too, when we look at a writer like Layton whose self-assertive, Nietzschean stance – usually imaged as a mission to 'liberate' society from stifling convention – has been widely proclaimed both by critics (see, for instance, Kurt Van Wilt, Wynne Francis) and by the poet himself. For all assertions to the contrary, however, even Layton – his repetitive strident assertions of masculinity projecting 'a self threatened by images of castration or engulfment' (Mandel A96) – reveals a certain covert anxiety. Even Layton worries that if the poet 'offers his hand in friendship and love ... someone will try to chop it off at the shoulder' (B120). And once we get past Layton and a few of his ilk, we find little evidence in Canadian art or literature for the kind of phatic pose Jones invokes.

[Film-maker] Allan King tries as far as possible to let his material speak for itself. Whether it is the immense formality with which he interviews his winos at the time of *Skid Row* or his scrupulous fidelity to the original text in *Who Has Seen the Wind*, as a director King tends to make himself invisible, as if absent from his own films. (Harcourt 16)

In some ways [Audrey] Thomas resembles the collagist or found poet, squirrelling away funny advertisements, news stories, songs, & forming the narration of her stories around them. Thus chance combines with memory to create texts that are on the ridge between control and accommodation. (Bowering D86)

[W]e are able to recognize a strain of *documentary realism* that keeps re-asserting itself in early Canadian painting despite the comprador patrons' insistence on having things look European. *It is the practice of recording social reality as the artist finds it, with the artist preferring the discipline of his observed subject matter to any stylistic concern.* (Lord 101)

[Harold] Innis's concern with limitations, his inveterate tendency to search out biases, and his feeling for the tentativeness of his subject were all to a certain extent reflected in his style of writing. Or, more accurately, it may be said that his distrust of the dogmatic reinforced an elliptical form of expression. (Berger 107)

It is [Eli] Mandel's own predicament to be a writer and yet long to say with Agee, 'If I could, I'd do no writing here' – because like Agee he wants to direct his reader's attention to the thing itself, which for a critic means to the text itself ... Mandel's discomfort with the intermediary role ... can be seen throughout his 1966 series of lectures published as *Criticism: The Silent Speaking Words*, making them a series of warnings, a map of drawing back. (R.M. Brown A168)

This recurrent deferment to the 'thing seen,' the obvious reticence of the 'see-er,' is a far cry from the American view Schultz attributes to, for instance, Nabokov, that 'Raw data in and of itself is of no importance or concern.'[26] Indeed, Jones and Layton notwithstanding, judging by these comments Canadian creators would like not merely to *obscure* the question of authorial responsibility but perhaps to deny the really creative aspects of their function altogether. 'I believe in "story" as a fact beyond and outside the entity of its maker,' says Wiebe. 'Michelangelo's ... statement that he studied the rock for the shape that was inside it and then used his chisels not to create that shape out of the rock but rather to release ... it – that has always seemed to me profoundly true to the storymaker's art also' (D45). If it were only one or two or a few writers we were talking about here we could explain the bias on the basis of aesthetic preference, but the sheer ubiquitousness of this kind of implicit self-deprecation, the obtrusive presence in so many diverse productions of what even Jones recognizes as 'a certain inhibition and doubt, a lack of faith or a fear of heights' (A12), argues ineluctably that the Canadian is in fact unfashionably intimidated by the heroic implications of creation and thus reluctant to assume openly the elsewhere-acclaimed artistic role.

Such a departure might be expected to have considerable consequences for the style of literature produced. The fact is, numerous of the formal characteristics of the Canadian oeuvre are so inexplicable outside of a supposition of authorial paranoia that even if our speculations were not adequately substantiated on other grounds analysis of these alone would almost certainly lead us to the same conclusion. More concrete than the admittedly impressionistic evidence of a writer's general approach yet less susceptible to contrivance than the pre-eminently self-conscious level of explicit theme, one of the most unmistakable indicators of attitudes toward authorial stance is the tacit role model one may infer from trends in the presentation of authorial surrogates in literature. In Canada we find in the narrators employed by our writers a very general tendency to minimize rather than celebrate the writer's supposed power. At the very least, in contrast with the traditional romantic scenario, Canadian versions typically downplay the more aggressive aspects of the role. Further than this, however, there are a great many cases where the putative 'creative' function is carried out in such an oblique manner that *the artifact appears to evolve almost accidently*. If we examine the corpus we will note at least four common strategies for protecting the author-surrogate from not only the consequences but even the *appearance* of presumption.

THE ARTIST AS AMATEUR

One ploy often used by Canadian writers to this end is the presentation of the 'artist' as an 'ordinary' person with no pretensions about creating 'art.' In such cases the book is purportedly unpremeditated and uncontrived: a casual diary, memoir, collection of letters, or combination of such material. In this category we find such diverse novels as Mills's *Skevington's Daughter*, Davies' *Fifth Business* and *The Manticore*, Blais' *Les manuscrits de Pauline Archange*, Ross's *As for Me and My House*, Cohen's *Beautiful Losers*, Klein's *The Second Scroll*, Helwig's *The Day before Tomorrow*, Aquin's *Prochain épisode*, and Symons's *Place d'Armes*, where we have a novel pretending to be a journal purportedly intended to provide the basis for a different novel. Much recent poetry, similarly, though eschewing an explicit narrator figure, in Frank Davey's words 'claim[s] the unconditioned structure of the journal or ship's log, or of ongoing recollection, or even of speech made to fill the silence' (D100). The same sort of technique is even to be found in a few instances in art. Greg Curnoe, for example, as David Thompson describes it, often approaches his work 'like a kind of diarist, objectively recording both visual notations and his own stream of consciousness in a series of what he calls "lettered landscapes," mostly executed with marking ink and rubber stamps of a forty-year-old local type-face, and based on what he sees from the studio window' (72). The effect of all this is to avoid as much as possible the impression that the artifact is 'made up.' In most of these productions the narrator's artlessness is emphasized on the one hand by an unpolished or rambling style and an apparent randomness of arrangement and on the other by a specious facticity ('[T]his type of journal approximates most closely the "journalistic" impulse to take down history as it is made,' says Elspeth Cameron of Symons's ostensible model, the military journal. 'Accuracy is of utmost importance. Thus letters, lists, orders, enumerations, and treaties are often recorded *verbatim*, not paraphrased.' A268). Interestingly, the denial of secondary – and especially aesthetic – motivations, the pretence that the object alone determines both content and form, tends paradoxically to efface the first-person writer not merely as an artist but as an individual. Indeed, despite the fact that this particular narrative method has traditionally been viewed as offering greater immediacy, in Canadian versions the effect is primarily one of off-handedness, as if the material were repudiating both its own significance and the possibility of meaningful communication.

THE ARTIST AS DISINTERESTED COLLECTOR OF FACTS

A second popular technique for obscuring authorial responsibility involves the presentation of a facsimile artist figure who by definition is non-creative. Such personae are often types such as journalists (Harlow's *Scann*), social scientists (Marian McAlpin of Atwood's *The Edible Woman*), or academics (historians like Dunstan Ramsay of Davies' Deptford trilogy or Anthony Maloney of Moore's *The Great Victorian Collection*; archivists like Lou of Engel's *Bear*) who, according to convention,[27] do not 'make' fiction at all but merely report facts – a much less presumptuous business. If their official positions as disinterested observers were not enough to protect them from suspicions of self-assertion, the books in which these individuals appear very often address the question of what comprises reportorial accuracy, almost always with the effect of setting up their protagonists as champions of objectivity. In *Tay John*, for instance, as Ondaatje points out, O'Hagan's narrator is not only absolved before the fact by the very chapter titles ('Hearsay,' 'Evidence – Without a Finding') but on the level of story firmly dissociated from any unbecoming appearance of 'interest' by an ostentatious neutrality of tone. 'Denham is not the secure, more assured narrator of Conrad's Europe but a voice genuinely apt for describing an unfinished legend that is reshaping before his eyes. Tay John's life is seen only in the brief seconds of lightning in the night, the rest is tentative meditation. The source ... dominates our minds' (Ondaatje c282).[28] In Carol Shields's *Small Ceremonies* the narrator's 'innocence' is made even more explicit. The protagonist of this book, an historical biographer, reiterates again and again her inability to invent. '"It's your old Scarborough puritanism,"' one of the other characters, a novelist himself, tells her. '"Judith Gill, my girl, basically you believe fiction is wicked and timewasting. The devil's work. A web of lies"' (20). We might infer much the same of a great many writers in Canada. Judith Gill, indeed, strikes us as eminently representative in many of her attitudes – especially in so far as she emphasizes collection rather than interpretation in her approach to her work. 'I am setting out to exhume her, searching, prying into the small seams, counting stitches, adding, subtracting, keeping score,' she says of her most recent project (34). This brings us to a point where the 'amateur' and the 'professional' almost seem to converge. The fact is, going even beyond the conventional implications of his official role, the so-called disinterested narrator is typically presented as above all a *scavenger*, not merely distant kin but soulmate to the many artistic garbagemen we find in the corpus: Spiegel the Junkman of Martin Myers's *The Assignment*; Sylvia Fraser's tramp; especially Laurence's Christie Logan, a true 'diviner' who can 'read' garbage like a book [45].[29] Like the narrator of Hodgins' *The Invention of the World*, therefore, though guilty perhaps of curiosity he is not ultimately responsible for the material he presents: 'Trust me or not, believe what you want,' says Becker, 'by now the story exists without us in air. I am not its creator, nor is any one man; I did not invent it, only gathered its shreds and fragments together from the half-aware conversations of people around me, from the tales and hints and gossip and whispered threats and elaborate curses that float in the air like dust' (69).

THE ARTIST AS 'INNOCENT'

Yet a third way to protect a narrator from the stigma of creativity is for the writer to suggest that he lacks either judgment (like the child narrators who are so common in Quebec fiction: Blais' *Les manuscrits de Pauline Archange*, Hébert's *Le torrent*, Ducharme's *L'avalée des avalés*, Ferron's *L'amélanchier*, Langevin's *Une chaine dans le parc*, among others) or, more significantly, free will. There is thus a recurrent 'Aeolian Harp' motif running through Canadian literature. One is simply 'called' by his material as the water diviner is summoned by the hidden elements of the earth (Laurence, *The Diviners*), or has a vision 'imposed' on him unbidden (Moore, *The Great Victorian Collection*), or becomes 'possessed' by ghosts (Harlow, *Scann*), or 'receives' a poem as though it were 'dictated' by some spectral other (Bowering, *Allophanes*), or feels himself living out a fiction composed by a Greater Power (Lowry, *Dark as the*

Grave Wherein My Friend Is Laid). Again the important point is that the artist himself does not presume to create but merely *finds* or *reflects*.[30] The artist, therefore, is safe from retribution. Or at least *should* be. Unfortunately, while preserving the fiction of non-complicity all right, this third category also seems to imply a number of dangers we don't find in the previous two. If the artist is merely an instrument he is also, in a sense, a *victim* of his own work. At best he is *used*, often to his discomfort and detriment ('Moore shows what dangers imperil ... the man to whom art happens, the man who – the image is made literal in *The Great Victorian Collection* – "just dreams it up"' Merivale 202); at worst he may find himself *transformed*, as the art demands ever greater commitment, into exactly the monster he most fears. MacEwen's Julian the Magician, wishing only to be a skilful trickster, finds himself impelled jointly by the 'magic' that lurks within even the most pedestrian illusion ('"Inside the womb... of the art, my dear Peter... is a foetus, another art. The virgin craft... expands, feeds the other..."') and by the hunger of his audience ('"I don't want to be divine... I don't want them to make me divine... they force it, they force it..."') to embrace the messianic role that eventually leads to his de-struction (29-30). If the image of the artist as passive receptacle offers certain obvious attractions, it also localizes a good deal of ambivalence. The question is why?

If we turn to the field of art we see an interesting demonstration of this whole problem worked out in historical terms. For roughly a decade, from the early forties to the early fifties, the leading lights in the Canadian art scene were the Quebec Automatists. On the surface this is not surprising. Despite the revolutionary political orientation of these painters (which would tend, for obvious reasons, to catalyse a certain amount of alienation), the basic concept of Automatism, which stressed a wholly spontaneous, wholly undirected kind of activity, *should* have been particularly attractive for Canadians. This explains its initial success. But what explains its failure? For the fact is, although this movement (especially in the work of Borduas and Riopelle) was responsible for some of the most spectacular art ever produced in this country, in the long run it turned out to be relatively uninfluential as well as relatively short-lived. Indeed, a number of its own leading members, like Fernand Leduc, defected by the early fifties to join the Plasticiens, a school emphasizing a generally more disciplined approach leading eventually, in the work most notably of Guido Molinari, to radically simplified, hard-edge, surficial, geometric composi-tions.[31] This last point hints at an important consideration. It is possible, judging from the direction of departure, that Automatism was ultimately rejected for exactly the same reason it was taken up: its emphasis on the passivity of the creator. This seems even more probable when we look more closely at some elements in the art itself. Automatism was fraught with contradictions from the start. As Ann Davis points out, 'On one hand, drawing on the "romanticism" of Surrealism, the movement was emotive, individual, and intuitive. On the other hand, working with the ... stylistic concepts of Cubism, the group became disciplined, organized, and intellectual' (c22). The fact that trends subsequently moved in the direction of a *more* intellectual style seems to indicate rather strongly that it was the kind of experience implicit in the surrealistic component that the Canadian found suspect. Why? If we consider the definition of surrealism we may begin to grasp the nature of the problem.

Surrealism in art was a movement initiated in Paris in the early 1920's. Under the leadership of André Breton, the Surrealists set out to redefine 'reality.' Inspired to some extent by Freud and working in conjunction with poets, they shifted their attention away from the external world, as consciously perceived and understood, to an interior universe of mystery and surprise located within and approached through the unconscious mind. The mind's eye, in other words, replaced the man's eye, and 'reality,' though not actually rejected, was recast in terms of the illogic of dreams and fantasy. (Davis c17)

According to this, at least for the Automatists – and we might speculate that the same holds true for any passive creator – the artist's submission was submission to the unconscious. Why should this be a problem? Because the Canadian, quite simply, *distrusts his own inner self*.

What, we might ask, would account for such an odd circumstance as this? In the first place, since the ocean in all those 'swimming' poems is above all the realm of psychic reality, primeval impulse, phantasm and dream, there is simply the fear of 'drowning' – losing oneself – that we have already examined. In the second place, there is the more specific fear that the phenomena one will encounter in the submarine regions will be inimical ones. This assumption is rather out of step with some of the more fashionable dicta of modern psychology. According to Jung, for instance, though he might meet monsters on the way, it is always ultimately a treasure of great worth – a pearl, crown, a sleeping princess – that the 'diver' finds at the 'bottom of the ocean.' Very few Canadians, however, seem able to put much faith in this kind of promise – even when dealing with themes that are explicitly Jungian. In Davies' *The Manticore* David Staunton's confrontation in the bear cave, for all Liesl's high-flown talk of great mysteries and human nobility, seems, at least in comparison with the epiphany the Jungian machinery leads us to expect, both pointless and degrading. Certainly the encounter-trauma – in particular the loss of bowel control precipitated by the protagonist's primitive terror at being lost in the dark – is inadequately balanced by the off-hand, anti-climactic dénouement and the rather trivial reconciliation symbol we are presumably meant to recognize in the gingerbread bears. As a result, even leaving aside the problematic substitution of the brute symbol for the anima figure as object of the quest, this seems a rather ambiguous variant on the Jungian/gnostic fable which would seem to have provided Davies' model. Other renditions of the subterranean journey are even more blatantly negative. In Douglas LePan's *The Deserter* the underworld is a nightmare realm of 'pursuits and conspiracies and shocks ... captures and evasions ... [and] shifting entanglements,' a battlefield within the protagonist's 'own darkness' (258). The only results one can expect from a plunge into *this* element is death.

LePan seems more typical than not. Canadians, it would seem, are simply *afraid* of what they might find below the civilized surface of the mind. If we think of all the ambiguous mirror imagery in the corpus we will perhaps begin to realize why. Inasmuch as mirrors are the 'windows of the soul' the Canadian's ambivalence toward them clearly indicates that penetrating inward is viewed as somehow equivalent to penetrating *out*. There is nothing particularly odd about this. Indeed, if we look to Freud rather than Jung we will soon find ample explanation for such a feeling of self-alienation. 'Freud's essential discovery, Lacan tells us, was that man bears otherness within him. The schism between the unconscious and the preconscious-conscious system brings man face to face with his own radical "extraneousness to himself."'[32] *Otherness within!* No wonder we feel nervous. And to make matters even worse, there is a strong indication further that this will be no *ordinary* otherness, but the specific kind of otherness we most dread. In Nietzschean terms the Dionysian type – Jones's swimmer – is identified not only with *dreaming* and *intoxication* but also with the *primitive*. 'The Dionysian impulse ... means the liberation of unbounded instinct, the breaking loose of the unbridled dynamism of animal and divine nature.'[33] *The unknown landscape within, therefore, is exactly equivalent to the wilderness without.*[34] This is what Atwood's 'Journey to the Interior' is all about. Whereas (according to Foster) in *The Journals of Susanna Moodie,*

The wilderness outside the clearing represented danger and unfamiliarity and the clearing safety ... the coast in 'Journey to the Interior' represents the security of everyday life and the interior the unknown where there is a 'lack of reliable charts.' The interior is the metaphoric wilderness, that Atwoodesque landscape of lines broken by a curious metrical whim, familiar objects ('lucent/ white mushrooms and a paring knife/ on the kitchen table') suddenly highlighted and menacing, odd repetitions that are evidence not so much of a poet's laziness as of a journey become a circling in an undecipherable forest. (11)

In consequence of this disquieting correlation, even aside from the more obvious threats to both personal integrity and social order posed by irrationality, any 'submission' to the unconscious – and here is what lurks behind all those innocuous Aeolian harp motifs – is likely to put the artist at the mercy of, indeed actually aligns him *with*, the most dangerous forces the Canadian can imagine. In Marshall's words, the poet-as-swimmer 'plunges into elemental passions and realities: death, self-exposure, psychic deformity at the hands of the world, age, animal terror.' What is worse, he may '– in the underwater world of his deeper unconsciousness – *become* the landscape' (69). For the Canadian this is a *very* frightening thought.

THE ARTIST AS ENIGMA

The last category is a little different since it is based not so much on what a narrator *is* as on what he is *not*. That is to say, it covers all those authorial surrogates who are made to appear as possibly – though not certainly – *unreliable*, such that their relationship with and responsibility for the material comprising the artifact is difficult to pin down. In some cases a writer may go so far as to obscure which of his characters is in fact the narrator. In Fraser's *The Candy Factory*, for instance, we have two potential artist figures, both flawed: on the one hand, the aggressive and solipsistic tramp, an explicit 'collector'; on the other, Mary Moon, the invisible voyeur who makes up stories as a way of 'making up for the mistakes and disappointments of her own life' (7-8). Because of the abrupt, unbridged break between the introductory chapters in which these individuals appear and the stories comprising the rest of the book, however, we are not sure what kind of connection, if any, we are intended to infer. Are these the stories in Mary's Special Accounts Book? Are they the results of the collaboration between her and the tramp which is announced at the end of their section? Or are we simply to take all the stories, including the first, as discrete and equivalent fictional experiences? *The Candy Factory* is an unusual case. In most instances the *act* of writing is stipulated; it is merely the *meaning* of that act that is obscured. There is a variety of ways by which this effect may be achieved.

The Question of Veracity

The most obvious method of undermining reliability is simply to suggest that a narrator is lying. In its more basic form this strategy may simply open up the possibility of error by contrasting irreconcilable versions of the same story (Harold Horwood's *White Eskimo*), but taken to extremes it can produce a narrative construct as complex, and as problematic, as Hubert Aquin's *Trou de mémoire*, a novel in which we encounter, successively, a putative primary narrator who, though inclined to cast some doubt on his own stability ('I find my thoughts out of puff from trying to catch up with words that escape by whole platoons regardless of verisimilitude' 29), claims to be offering an honest account of first-person experience; an editor, who not only reveals a variety of neurotic biases of his own but challenges the facticity of at least parts of the 'found' manuscript ('Pierre X. Magnant has distorted the true story he is confessing' 57; 'this passage has been shamelessly retouched' 83); and a mysterious woman who claims to have invented the whole thing ('I made up out of whole cloth the pseudo-hallucinatory delirium of Pierre X. Magnant, who – please believe me – has no existence outside my imagination' 97). Such a strategy as the latter denies the reader any safe vantage at all. As Leonard Sugden points out, 'We are ... led a merry dance in a network of shifting scenes, narrators, and identities until, in the last pages, when RR denies her former assertion of having written the entire book we are once again on shaky ground' (88).

The Question of Intent

This strategy is closely related to the last in so far as it attacks the technical believability of the artifact, but in this case the effect is achieved by raising some question as to whether a given 'text' is or is not meant to assert some 'truth-value,' and if so, what 'kind' of truth it might be. Actually, such ambiguity is tacitly invoked every time an inner-fiction appears. In this regard it is interesting that books-within-books (Symons's *Place d'Armes* or Laurence's *The Diviners*) and also pictures-within-pictures (Hugh Mackenzie, D.P. Brown) are so common in the Canadian corpus. The impression of uncertainty is intensified, however, if components of different status are not merely mixed but deliberately confused (Matt Cohen, for example, admits to drawing 'almost no distinction' between reality and fantasy[35]) or if the integrity of the internal construct is overtly undermined. In Alice Munro's *Lives of Girls and Women* Del's story-making is bracketed, ambiguously, by her historian-uncle's cautious chronicling of trivial facts, the evil photographer of her own fantasy, and the 'true' mystery of Bobby Sherriff. In Shields's *Small Ceremonies* the author comments indirectly on the biographical task by setting up a thematic tension between fiction (lying) and plagiarism (copying). In James Reaney's *Listen to the Wind*, though the introduction of Victorian melodrama (the play-within-the-play) 'does give a heightened dimension to present-day reality' by pointing up its archetypal underpinnings (Dudek B23), the fact that the child-director manipulates the ending does reflect rather peculiarly on the whole problem of authorial discretion. Finally, in Davies' Deptford trilogy, Ramsay's sensational and frankly fictitious biography of Magnus Eisengrim undermines the reliability of his own memoir (see St Pierre, especially 129); more important, the film-making framework to the last section, with its emphasis on artificiality, its constant philosophizing about 'how to reflect reality,' about 'the nature of truth ... and whether one can define it' (Brennan 71), raises considerable doubt not only about Eisengrim's veracity but about Davies' aims and intentions as well.

The Question of Competence
In this category our attention is drawn to the narrator's existential limitations and thence to the accuracy of his observations. In some cases this is done quite overtly. The narrator of one of the stories in Munro's *Something I've Been Meaning to Tell You*, for instance, herself points out the implausibility of her pretended breadth of insight:

And how is anybody to know, I think as I put this down, how am I to know what I claim to know? I have used these people, not all of them, but some of them, before. I have tricked them out and altered them and shaped them any way at all, to suit my own purposes. I am not doing that now, I am being as careful as I can ... But that only takes care of the facts. I have said other things. I have said that my grandmother would choose a certain kind of love. I have implied that she would be stubbornly, secretly, destructively romantic. Nothing she ever said to me, or in my hearing, would bear this out ... (161)

In most cases, however, our realization of the inadequacy of the narrator's access comes gradually. In Wiebe's *The Scorched-Wood People* we begin to suspect Pierre Falcon when he appears to claim first-hand knowledge of events at which, in his own telling, he couldn't possibly have been present. This makes us wonder about Wiebe's motives for resurrecting this legendary bard out of the Métis past, and about what role – real participant or conventional omniscient narrator – he intends him to play. In *Kamouraska* the problem becomes even more serious due to the gothic trappings of the vehicle Hébert has chosen. We know from what we have been able to piece together of the story that Elisabeth was miles away when many of the key events occurred, yet she describes them as if she were remembering – not imagining – scenes that took place before her eyes. 'Ever so softly I pick up the thread of George Nelson's actual journey ... The road, till now so flat, hardly higher than the river. And now, hill after hill. Up one side, down the other ... And all that snow piled high in the ravines! If only I were sure that the road was well marked! Are those scraggy little fir trees there, along the side, stuck like fish bones into the snow?' (190-1). What does it mean, this eye witness effect? In most cases we would simply conclude that the narrator was faking, but in *Kamouraska* the hints of psychological abnormality prevent us from taking this easy way out by allowing at least the bare possibility of some extra-sensory mechanism.

The Question of Sanity
In the fourth category the question of competence is again raised, but here the focus is on mental rather than physical limitations. In the simplest terms, the question of the narrator's responsibility is obscured by a suggestion (rarely an outright assertion) that he may be insane. There are several ways this may be accomplished. In Audrey Thomas's *Mrs Blood* we make certain inferences

about the speaker's instability not merely from our knowledge of her stressful circumstances but more because of the surrealistic imagery, the lack of logical connection, the eccentricity of the style with its compulsive circling and repetitions. In Martin Myers's *The Assignment*, in contrast, the suspicion is voiced by the putative madman himself (361). In Robert Kroetsch's *The Studhorse Man*, finally, the narrator's incompetence – or *possible* incompetence – is implicit in the fact that he is resident in an insane asylum at the moment of writing. Actually, Demeter Proudfoot may exemplify the Canadian unreliable narrator inasmuch as he crosses several key categories: his view is oblique ('By a fortunate combination of light and reflection, I am able to see out of my window without leaving my bathtub. A mirror is so placed above my sink that I have been able to sit for hours, attempting to imagine what in fact did happen ... exactly where I imagine it' 85); though zealous in his commitment to 'fact,' he also confesses to an aesthetic intent ('I myself prefer an ordered world' 61); most important, perhaps, he is involved in the story to an extent that makes us doubt his objectivity. As Morton Ross describes it, 'Demeter's complex response to Hazard, even more than his violent participation in the climactic events of the plot, makes him an intrusive presence in his own narrative; his self-conscious efforts to escape the limits of disciplined biography with the licence claimed by the artist as extreme neurotic are engrossing enough so that Demeter's experience constantly threatens to supplant Hazard's as the novel's subject' (111).

The Question of Candour

In naming this strategy I mean to invoke not just those cases where an author implicitly impugns his narrator's sincerity or good will, the adequacy, as it were, of his disclosure, but a broader, more subtle kind of undermining whereby the whole philosophical/psychological orientation of the artist figure is called into question. One of the most effective ways of achieving this is to suggest problematic shadow narrators behind the more overt speakers, perhaps even – as in Ondaatje's *Coming through Slaughter* – multiple levels of displacement. If we examine this latter book carefully we realize that the real and implied narrative stances are by no means identical. Although the book opens in traditional third-person mode we are quickly encouraged to focus our attention on Webb, who in his quest for the missing Buddy Bolden serves as an explicit author-surrogate. This identification presents several problems, however. Inasmuch as Webb is a detective – that is, fact-finder – he approximates to the preferred model for the Canadian artist. On the other hand, both his methods and his morality are undermined by suggestions of, firstly, incompetence (the physical impossibility of his entry into Bolden's mind makes us question the validity of the subjective material); secondly, manipulativeness ('God he talked and sucked me through his brain so I was puppet,' says Bolden: 'He could reach

me ... could tilt me upside down till he was directing me like wayward traffic'
86); and thirdly, illegitimate 'interest' (the impression of voyeurism we pick up
through Webb's evident preference for the subjective mode in recounting
sexual or violent interludes connects him with the photographer Bellocq, whose
art is described as 'fetish, a joyless and private game' 64). We get an inkling as to
what all this apparent anxiety about the authorial function may imply when,
less than twenty-five pages from the end of the book, the narrator-
behind-the-narrator (Ondaatje himself?) suddenly emerges in his own person
and confesses his ambivalent, perhaps irrational identification with the subject:

When he went mad he was the same age as I am now.
    The photograph moves and becomes a mirror. When I read he stood in front of mirrors
and attacked himself, there was the shock of memory. For I had done that. Stood, and
with a razor-blade cut into cheeks and forehead, shaved hair. Defiling people we did not
wish to be ...
    The thin sheaf of information. Why did my senses stop at you? There was the
sentence, 'Buddy Bolden who became a legend when he went berserk in a parade...'
What was there in that, before I knew your nation your colour your age, that made me
push my arm forward and spill it through the front of your mirror and clutch myself?
(133-4)

Immediately following this disclosure – this *exposure* – the book retreats almost
entirely into facticity: interviews, chronologies, transcripts of tapes, quotations, bald recitations of events.

The Question of Identity

At last we come to the most basic ploy of all. Just as the reticent/unreliable
narrator is, in a sense, a mask for the author outside the fiction, artist figures *in*
fiction are commonly masked, camouflaged, or disguised as well. The longer the
creator's 'real' identity can be kept in doubt, the feeling seems to be, the longer
he can escape stray lightning bolts. The prototype here is Atwood's *Lady
Oracle*. Joan Foster, the protagonist of this book, is one of the most multiply
'disguised' characters in the corpus. On a personal level this means, primarily,
effacement: an almost grateful self-subordination to the bizarrely diverse
expectations of a series of love partners (see MacLean 183). In the professional
sphere, however – suggesting that this is the level localizing the most anxiety –
her attempts to avoid recognition are so extreme as to involve an actual
masquerade. More important, they also involve an eventual *un*masking. Going
significantly beyond any problems entailed by the simple evasion strategies we
have been examining, the collision between Joan's mutually exclusive identities
as a 'serious' poet and a writer of escapist fantasy points up the profound
ambivalence that underlies the Canadian artist's predilection for masks. Even

more than protecting her from an inimical 'other,' Joan's disguises, by allowing her to compartmentalize those incompatible (passive and active, saint and magician, wife and writer) aspects of her own personality, protect her from *herself*. It is only when she inadvertently opens up the channels to the unconscious through her experiments with 'automatic writing' that we see just how important such a compartmentalization can be. Defences down, Joan not only loses her mask; she loses *control*. Her poems begin to seem like a Costume Gothic 'gone wrong' ('It was upside-down somehow. There were the sufferings, the hero in the mask of the villain, the villain in the mask of a hero, the flights, the looming death, the sense of being imprisoned, but there was no happy ending' 234). Her current Costume Gothic, on the other hand, turns strange and recalcitrant, resisting her manipulation to become 'curiously interwoven with her own life, portraying [it] ... as if through a prism' (Mansbridge 115). The message is clear. There is no telling what may happen if one puts aside one's mask and becomes openly, in one's own person, a 'creator.'

These, then, are the characteristic manifestations of the 'artist-as-subject' in Canadian literature. Or perhaps, considering his elusiveness, *non-manifestations* would be more accurate. How, though, does all this relate to Canada's 'real' artists and writers? Presumably they must have come to terms with their vocational anxieties, or they wouldn't be producing paintings and poems and books. In fact, things aren't quite so simple. Whatever they may consciously feel about their high visibility, there is ample evidence that Canadian creators – and particularly fiction writers – habitually practise a kind of unconscious misdirection to protect themselves from their own hubris. Unmediated narratives, indeed, give an even greater impression of evasiveness than those that offer either a direct or indirect authorial persona. Lacking the surrogate, Canadians almost invariably opt for narrative techniques that create an illusion of non-intervention; that is, casualness, coolness, spontaneity.

What are these techniques? Most obviously, all those varieties of discontinuous narrative that have proven so popular with Canadian writers in recent decades foster anonymity simply by extension, inasmuch as they not only de-emphasize the impression of artifice or authorial manipulation associated with 'storytelling' but also appear to minimize the element of subjectivity altogether. A documentary effect is often achieved either through general tone and approach or – as in Moore's *The Great Victorian Collection* – by integrating into a third-person matrix a variety of types of ostensibly 'objective' supporting material such as interviews, reports, letters, and journal entries. The more these components are randomized, the more the whole gestalt works to deny aesthetic intent. The effect is most pronounced (a) when radically different kinds of fictional material are combined in such a manner that the significance of their interrelation is left undefined (bp Nichol's *Two Novels*, for instance, where a collection of letters, fantasies, and literary parodies, which may or may not be written by the same individual, 'Andy,' is juxtaposed with a gush of tortured subjectivity entitled 'For Jesus Lunatick'; Hodgins's *The Invention of the World*, with its mythical, realistic, and reportorial sections; Klein's *The Second Scroll*), or (b) when fragments of diverse fictional and factual material are mixed together more or less promiscuously, without any clear normative context (Thomas's *Blown Figures*; Ondaatje's 'historical' prose-poems, *The Collected Works of Billy the Kid* and *Coming through Slaughter*). Recent poetry uses much the same kind of approach, often carrying it to even greater extremes. '[I]n [Klein's] "Grain Elevator" all his worlds are yoked together in a cinematic flow of images flashing by at almost hallucinatory speed, a "montage/of inconsequent time and uncontiguous space"' (Marshall 58). 'The anatomy of [bissett's] books reflects [his anti-conventional] attitude: variations in the size of pages, inserts of advertisements and items clipped from magazines and newspapers, crayon drawings, inverted pages' (Early 145). 'Colombo has eschewed the hieratic and redeemed the demotic, the banal, the everyday, the ignored. Collector, beachcomber, encyclopedist, arranger, anatomist, compiler of an endless commonplace book, he celebrates the poetry which is all around us but which we often fail to notice' (Mallinson 67). 'Collage is a technique used by McFadden frequently in his later work. In particular, the visual media of the photograph ... and the sketch drawing ... are presented in collage with the written sight-sound medium ... The photographs in *Letters from the Earth to the Earth* are not the issue of either artistic or professional-commercial camera work. Rather, they have the quality of the family snap-shot album' (Kiverago 54). Both the feigned artlessness of the collector-of-facts and the apparent wish to shift attention from the interpreting observer to the self-order of the thing seen that we observed in connection with the fictional narrators above may easily be recognized in the practices indicated here.

It may be argued, to be sure, that the very features I am attempting to single out as distinctively Canadian are, in fact, the things that link our literary practice most obviously with international trends. Obliqueness, equivocation, and discontinuity are three of the key characterizing features of recent fiction. As André LeVot points out, the post-modernist proclaims it not merely his right but his duty to cut literature 'away from its utilitarian function of communication,' using 'various devices, automatic writing, aleatory games to make [it] a specific operation, an autonomous activity, non-descriptive, non-referential' [46]. Without denying that Canadian writers, and especially poets, have both deliberately and inadvertently turned for models to Europe (especially Quebec) and the United States – indeed, without attempting to claim that there is any single technical trick in current usage that cannot be explained and justified on the basis of such models – I would merely assert, as with art in earlier chapters, that because Canadians stress primarily those aspects of imported fashions which are particularly congenial to their own preconditioned biases, their borrowings not only tend to take on a new emphasis and implication here, but to change in the direction of greater consonance with patterned responses already built in to the cultural mix. Where an individual poet may seem to yield to explication entirely in terms of extra-national derivation, therefore, the corpus viewed as a whole will reveal consistent peculiarities, both qualitative and quantitative, in the way those same derivative features are combined and distributed such that there eventually emerges a difference of kind, not merely of degree. With respect to the techniques we have been discussing, such a difference may be discerned, firstly, in the *extent* to which they have influenced the habits not merely of our avant-garde writers but also of those whose practice and aims are otherwise relatively conventional; secondly, and more important, in the tacit assumptions they reveal about the author's role as mediator.

Let's backtrack a little to consider wider usage in this area. In the traditional novel the reader is guided to a 'correct' interpretation (as to both fact and value) by such means as authorial intrusion, normative characters, or univalence of theme. Even in the multivalent narrative structure (where multivalence 'applies equally to multiple ways of viewing and to multiple ways of being seen'[36]) which began to appear with increasing frequency concomitant with the subjectivization of art in the early twentieth century, the author typically directs the reader's assessment of the interpretive possibilities offered in the text by covertly manipulating affect. With the more recent exploding of narrative form, however, this sort of coercion has ostensibly been eschewed, multivalence being embraced not simply as a technique but as an ultimate goal. One of the major means adopted toward that end has been the popularization of what Sharon Spencer calls the 'architectonic novel,' a fictional construct in which linear connection (both temporal and logical) is abandoned in favour of juxtaposition, a principle of organization 'which abolishes all overt transitions as well as the suggestion of causality, and which renders possible the free creation of all sorts of relationships among the items [represented in order to]....
expose the subject from as many angles as possible.'[37] This sounds very much like the kind of approach produced by the Canadian writer's reticence, doesn't it? If the Canadian's reason for retreating to indeterminacy is less a *confusion* about the nature of reality than merely a *reluctance* to be so openly presumptuous as to put forward his beliefs and opinions undisguised, it is certainly true that the results are much the same:

The first characteristic [of the open novel] is the multiplication of perspectives that has already been mentioned: the perspectives may take the form of a great many narrative points of view focused on the same subject; of experimentation with the perspectives of the camera; or of the great variety of perspectives available through literary quotation, illustration, mixtures of prose and poetry, and typographical variation. The second characteristic is the deliberate rejection of the novel's 'frame,' of those literary conventions that have traditionally served to distinguish the novel from its surrounding context of reality. Third comes the naked exploration within the novel of the processes through which it came into being. [Spencer 52-3]

Sounds familiar, doesn't it? Despite all this weight of evidence for identity, I would still maintain that there is not merely a difference but a *significant* difference between Spencer's 'open novel' and typical Canadian writing.

Notwithstanding the apparent denial of norms, of closure, of *mediation* in post-modern fiction (a ploy which a number of recent commentators such as Alan Friedman proclaim as intellectually and morally preferable to the promulgation of a 'false' view of life entailed by conventional literary structure: 'the deliberate avoidance, in the depiction of an experience, of any resolution ... is ... an ethical statement in its own right. The flux of conscience remains unclosed; experience *is* not closed.' Dooley xi), it is still a fact that in almost all cases of such fiction it is possible to infer a voice, a stance, *behind* if not *in* the text. To be more specific, even if the narrator is absent, ambiguous, or incoherent we may – and, in our quest for determinacy, invariably *do* – reconstruct an authorial presence from the raw material of his product. This is Wayne Booth's 'implied author' – 'not the narrator, but rather the principle that invented the narrator, along with everything else in the narrative, that stacked the cards in this particular way, had these things happen to these characters, in these words or images.'[38] What does this have to do with our argument? Simply this: whereas even the most frenzied of, say, American fiction yields fairly easily this kind of implicit puppetmaster such that we may infer, if not specific conclusions, at least, observing his 'attitude' to the object itself, a fairly specific slant or outlook, Canadian writers, though they can't excise him entirely, tend to erect a great many barriers between the reader and this figure.

We see a clear demonstration of this phenomenon if we turn to representative individual cases. Vladimir Nabokov's *Pale Fire* shows certain obvious similarities to the kind of Canadian material we have been examining in that it poses not as a novel but as a collection of scholarly documents, that is, as Robert Ryf summarizes, 'a Foreword, a tedious poem in four cantos by John Frances Shade, and a series of notes written, as was the Foreword, and, apparently, the Index, by a visiting professor named Kinbote, intimated to be a fugitive from a country named Zembla.'[39] The thrust of the book, however, lies not in any intrinsic interest offered by the component parts but in the question of what relation either of the two radically divergent views represented bears to the other *or* to external 'reality.' This is not an easy question. The two things all commentators seem to agree on, however, are (a) that *neither* character can be considered reliable, and (b) that there is no way of determining the extent of their unreliability. 'Nabokov manages to obliterate the borderlines between fact and fancy ... to a degree where all certainties must crumble,' says Manfred Puetz.

'Neither the precise identities of Shade or Kinbote nor their exact relationship can be established beyond doubt. The only thing we can be sure of in *Pale Fire* is that we are never sure when and where the real ends and the mythic begins.'[40] This quotation raises an interesting point, though. For all its plausibility it isn't really quite true. This book *couldn't* resist judgment as completely as Puetz indicates, because if it did we would have no way of deciding (as the critics obviously have) that both narrators are unreliable rather than merely one or neither of them. More important, we would have no basis for concluding that the indeterminacy is intentional, and therefore interesting, rather than merely an aesthetic flaw. How, in the light of the intrinsic ambiguity, are we able to formulate such judgments? How, on the basis of an ostensibly 'valueless' text are we able to infer (as we most certainly do) a definite satiric thrust? Because we have a strong sense of a presence *behind* the text. 'What makes a narrator unreliable is that his values diverge strikingly from [those] of the implied author,' says Seymour Chatman; 'that is, the rest of the narrative – "the norm of the work" – conflicts with the narrator's presentation, and we become suspicious of his sincerity or competence to tell the "true version." The unreliable narrator is at virtual odds with the implied author; otherwise his unreliability could not emerge' [149].

In Canada things don't usually work this way. If we think about all those evasive narrators we will realize that we are generally unable to determine with any certainty *whether and to what degree they are reliable or not*. Sanity, competence, veracity: all are called into question but rarely is any indictment pressed home. In Canadian literature, if the narrators are difficult to credit with any confidence, they are difficult wholly to *dis*-credit as well. Some of this indeterminacy stems from the personality of our type artist figure. Some of it, though, points to the absence – or at least the ambiguity – of an implied author against whom we may measure reliability. We find much the same problem, moreover, in the kind of multivalent work mentioned above. In Wiebe's *The Temptations of Big Bear* not only does the mutually undermining juxtaposition of subjective and objective, 'found' and 'invented' material, explode the idea of definitive 'historical' truth ('His plot becomes the arrangement of these facts in such a way as to lead the reader to contemplate not the logical sequence of cause and effect in the lives of his characters, but rather to ponder the elusiveness of any clear literal understanding of life as a sequential inevitability,' says Stan McMullin. 'The ultimate approach is to leave the reader profoundly disturbed about the paradox and contradictions of the written word.' B249) but implicitly challenges the whole concept of authorial stance. As Ina Ferris says with regard to another of Wiebe's novels, the 'polyvocal technique, while reflecting the multiplicity and subjectivity of modern reality, functions primarily to focus the problem of point of view itself, to raise questions about the possibility of an authentic, integrated vision' (81). This is a critical factor. In setting himself specifically to the task of holding interpretation in abeyance – 'The question for the novelist is not "Will I find the facts?" It is rather, "Will I dare to fully contemplate with all my quintuplet senses the facts that I do find?"' he says in his methodological essay 'On the Trail of Big Bear' (47) – Wiebe is *choosing* not to arbitrate his own work. Many readers will not rest with indeterminacy, of course. Partly, one suspects, because of the influence of sixties-style American neo-primitivism and partly because in the lieu of any recognizable narrative voice one tends to identify with the most compelling personality *in* the fiction, many critics seem to read *Big Bear* as a kind of noble savage parable: 'Big Bear is ... credited with more enduring values than his Victorian adversaries who are so closely identified with the mechanical horror of the steam locomotive,' says Dick Harrison (E203). The book itself, however, resists such oversimplifications. Granted that we may perceive many 'tragic ironies' in the confrontation between the two cultures,[41] these properly belong to the realm of the *signified* rather than that of the *signifier*, a function of our own relationship with the reality pointed to by, but not contained in, the fiction. As far as imputing any special sympathy to an 'implied author,' the best reason for suspecting the validity of such an operation is implicit in the tone of the text. In marked contrast to both the hypocritical white rhetoric *and* the naturalness of the Indian, Wiebe's style in the 'omniscient' sections is cool, detached, above all abstracted, with an obtrusive graphic emphasis – a constant resolution of sensation into line, shape, colour, form: *surface* – which evokes of necessity an impermeable psychic barrier between the see-er and the thing seen:

The motion was so deliberate, so inevitable that each horse and rider seemed to hang still on the open ridge slanting to a cusp of poplars down, behind a fold in the earth. One by one, as if on parade, in single file they moved and when the lead horse with its moulded rider merged down into the trees even the seeming motion disappeared in relation to itself, in relation to the sky, the sage gleam of the river, the green land now tinged brown and gold in the September sun. One figure, another, and another, vanished but at the top of the ridge there was always one more so the line simply remained, drawn against those three elements and wavering a little but there, drawn, and only as they studied one bit of that line, squinted to almost see the thin spiral of dust rise like ashes upward from the poles of the travois, was there a flicker of motion downward from the notch of blue sky, downward into the earth beyond the water. (15)

To identify this 'voice' with any of the varying shades of resolution held suspended in the raw data of the book is both facile and misleading.

Is Wiebe anomalous in withholding himself in this way? If we think back over the numerous texts considered in this section, the answer must be no. Canadian writers in general have a tendency to shy away from the sorts of manipulativeness which allow a reader to infer an authorial presence. This holds for micro-elements as well as for major components like theme. When Rod Willmot comments on what he views as unnecessary obscurantism in bp Nichol's virtually unpunctuated 'Jesus Christ Lunatick' ('all too frequently when reading Nichol the reader's experience resembles an excursion into a snowbank' 99), the implication is that Nichol is both inept and eccentric, but when we note similar tendencies in much more conventional writers (when Earle Birney revised his work for the 1966 volume of *Selected Poems*, for instance, he removed almost all punctuation marks and replaced them with space or line breaks, thus forcing mute juxtaposition, a 'passive' technique, to take over much of the burden of explication normally carried by conventional author-imposed syntactic markers) we realize that Nichol's practice, while extreme, is consonant with the larger trend. One wouldn't want to mistake a 'leaning' for a rule, of course. Really radical strategies are far from commonplace across the board. If we were to generalize we might say that French-Canadian writers since the sixties have been *more* innovative (one common explanation for this is that the rejection of conventional forms was a revolutionary act, reflecting social breakdown [see Bourneuf], but one may also speculate that the revolutionary context, intensifying demands that the writer 'stick out his neck,' would tend to exacerbate residual anxieties about the creative act, thus prompting more extreme evasive strategies) and English-Canadian *women* (perhaps because of factors noted in chapter 6) generally less so. The corpus taken as a whole, however, yields a type 'implied author' who is surprisingly consistent with his overtly reluctant surrogates.

Having established this much it is interesting to examine some of the specific technical usages that help the Canadian writer maintain his putative anonymity. Besides textual discontinuity, another means to narrative disguise entails the general obfuscation of *viewpoint*. The simplest way to achieve this is by varying the narrative perspective of a book widely through time, often while blurring temporal distinction. In Hugh Hood's *White Figure, White Ground* and Margaret Laurence's *The Stone Angel* and *The Diviners*, for instance, two different chronological sequences – one based on memory, the other on present experience – are fragmented and juxtaposed. Wayland Drew's *The Wabeno Feast* goes one step further by paralleling sequences from the present and the personal past with historical material. This denial of a stable vantage, reminiscent of Faulkner's *Absalom! Absalom!* (though somewhat less complex), proves an effective means of building suspense. The variations are by no means always as orderly as in these particular cases, however, where at least the sequences all converge in the present. In Nowlan's *Various Persons Named Kevin O'Brien* and Thomas's *Blown Figures* the narrative jumps back and forth between past and present with erratic abandon, while Jacques Godbout's *Couteau sur la table* conflates both into one dream-like stream of consciousness. Most subtly of all, the text of Blais' *Les manuscrits de Pauline Archange* continually slides imperceptibly from past into past imperfect, from what was into what might have been. In this latter novel, says Dawson, 'past and present are molded together, each sentence expressing the potential to include other temporal perspectives, to move off in other directions' (61). Time here is as contingent as speech, as uncertain as whim. The effect is not an uncommon one. Matt Cohen's *The Disinherited*, though almost ostentatiously 'realistic' compared to the hallucinatory worlds of Blais and Godbout, not only strips time of its orderliness but, more disturbingly, by 'Replicating the mental processes of rumination,' as Moss puts it (cix), undermines the self-evidential quality of its objective existence. In doing so it also erodes our faith in authorial control. Even as we are being reassured by the 'roundness' of the characters, by the conventionality, not to say slickness, of the *progression d'effet*, the hinted possibility that the most extreme disjunctions may be connected in some way, even causally, with sex and/or violence (the past/present oscillation doesn't start until page 100, where Richard's near-fatal fight with his father is juxtaposed with a guilty sexual episode, and thenceforth the transitions seem stimulated most often in the context of Katherine) gives an air of neurotic compulsion to the narrative that keeps attention focused not on the stagemanager in the wings but on the text itself.

Obfuscation does not stop with such relatively minor feats of misdirection as this. Of considerably more significance for our topic than the loose time orientation is the tendency for the narrator to obscure the line as well between the subject and the object of his discourse. Again this may easily be taken to reflect recent trends in the United States. As with many other aspects of our putative cultural kinship, however, there is an important distinction to be made. For all the surficial similarity of effects, the implied posture is quite different in each case; where the Canadian will neither claim nor relinquish any of his options, the American's strategy is less to render boundaries equivocal than to erase them altogether. Judging by the oeuvre, in fact, he would like nothing better than to set himself up as both the speaker and the word spoken, the means and the end of his fictions. This is hardly self-effacement. Nor – despite the hovering ghost of post-modernism – is it anything new. One need only think once more of Whitman. Indeed, even in traditional, ostensibly impersonal productions like, say, *Moby-Dick*, there is often more than a slight hint that the 'invented' other is only an occasion for an exploration of the 'self.' 'Ishmael the visionary is often indistinguishable from the mind of the author himself,' notes Charles Feidelson. 'It is Melville's own voice that utters the passage on the heroic stature of Ahab. This apparent violation of narrative standpoint is really a natural consequence of the symbolic method of *Moby-Dick*. The distinction between the author and his alter ego is submerged in their common function as the voyaging mind.'[42] Such convergence, though perhaps noteworthy with respect to the conventions of realism, is by no means rare in American literature. It stems, in part, from the loss of usable history. '[T]he author of the American epic must be his own hero,' says Pearce, 'as his epic is the record of his struggle to make something of himself' [134]. Thus it is that we find Ronald Sukenik appearing in his own person in his first novel, *Up*, and Norman Mailer as the chief character of *Armies of the Night*; thus too the popularity during the last decade of conceptual art, art as 'happening,' art that desacralizes the artifact to display instead the mind and imagination of its creator.[43] The fact is, we might say of many contemporary Americans, artists and writers both, what Lucie-Smith comments of neo-Dadaist Yves Klein: 'Klein is an example of an artist who was important for what he did – the symbolic value of his actions – rather than for what he made. One sees in him an example of the increasing tendency for the personality of the artist to be his one true and complete creation' [128].

The Canadian practice, as we might expect, shows few signs of this kind of self-celebration. Indeed, strongly countering any sort of internationalist interpretation, if we look closely at patterns of narrative preference it would seem that the Canadian confuses subject and object simply because he doesn't want to be identified too firmly with *either*. At times the underlying anxiety is presented quite blatantly. In Audrey Thomas's *Mrs Blood*, for instance, the title character is torn between equally unbearable alternate versions of herself as 'Mrs Blood' (the compulsively subjective, experiencing 'I' trapped inside her own suffering psyche) and 'Mrs Thing' (self-perceived as object, this persona's identity is tied almost entirely to surfaces). In Atwood's *The Edible Woman*, similarly, Marian McAlpin is psychically deformed by an apparent incapacity to control – or to choose – that ground of being we might call the 'I'-Site. Horrified by her progressive metamorphosis into an object, yet afraid to take the self-responsibility of a subject, this woman's more-than-Kafkaesque predicament[44] demonstrates the Canadian's ambivalence in perhaps its most striking and unmistakable form. Numerous other examples where the subject/object problem is implicit only at the level of language appear to be underlined by the same existential dilemma, however. What it boils down to is this: the Canadian is uneasy about committing himself to the peculiar truth-value, the specific type of 'obligation,' implied by either a wholly subjective *or* a wholly objective stance.

In some cases (*Tay John, Beautiful Losers, The Second Scroll*) this reluctance remains largely repressed, showing up only in simple narrative alternations, where one mode is set against the other, modifying its evidentiary status with respect both to questions of intent – the *signifier* – and to questions of fact – the *signified*. In other cases, though, the discrepancies are more radical. Nowlan as Kevin O'Brien not only jumps around in time but explores fragments of his past from alternating first- and third-person perspectives; consistently neither subject nor object, he manages to suggest a severe disjunction within the human consciousness itself. In Matt Cohen's *Korsoniloff*, more explicitly, the protagonist, as Jon Kertzer points out, 'refers to himself in both first and third person in order to distance himself from his experience and so dramatize his schizophrenic condition' (95). In Leo Simpson's *Arkwright* and Graeme Gibson's *Five Legs* the technique is carried even further, such that the narrators, as if they lack even the vestiges of a stable ego-image, slip unobtrusively back and forth from one mode to the other throughout the whole course of their recapitulations. Most interesting of all, in Laurence's *The Fire-Dwellers* we are kept constantly just on the *verge*, neither wholly in nor wholly out, of Stacey McAndrew's mind.[45]

What does it mean, this compulsive equivocation? 'I did not want to write a novel entirely in the first person, but I did not want to write one entirely in the third person, either,' says Laurence. 'The inner and outer aspects of Stacey's life were so much at variance that it was essential to have her inner commentary in order to point up the frequent contrast between what she was thinking and what she was saying' (D59). Is this the whole answer? My own feeling is no. Laurence's explanation, though undoubtedly 'true,' is just a little too neat to be taken as adequately modelling the full complexity of *any* author's motivations – not to mention the fact that in this case at least, the convolutions of the method seem grossly underdetermined by any such 'rational' program. There are, after all, quite conventional ways for handling this sort of problem. Should we simply dismiss it as a kind of showmanship, then; a carefully crafted but entirely arbitrary literary *tour de force*? Maybe. It's possible, though, that Laurence's practice isn't quite as extreme or as idiosyncratic as it may at first seem. Perhaps, indeed, this ostentatious ambivalence of stance – along with Gibson's and Simpson's and Cohen's and Nowlan's 'neurotic' shiftiness – merely represents the logical extension of the Canadian propensity for evasion.

In this respect it is intriguing to note that a 'middle voice' was actually codified as a category in early Greek speech. Pierre Vernant's comments on this feature, which disappeared with the birth of the modern world, provide some provocative sidelights on Canadian preferences which may make our speculations about the covert psycho-social significance of what would normally be viewed as a purely technical dimension seem a little less far-fetched. In ancient Greece, he says (following Benveniste),

we see two cases, one in which the action is ascribed to the agent like an attribute to a subject, and another in which the action envelopes the agent and the agent remains immersed in the action – that is the case of the middle voice. The psychological conclusion that Benveniste doesn't draw, because he is not a psychologist, is that in thought as expressed in Greek or ancient Indo-European there is no idea of the agent being the *source* of his action. Or, if I may translate that, as a historian of Greek civilization, there is no category of *will* in Greece. But what we see in the Western world, through language, the evolution of law, the creation of a vocabulary of the will, is precisely the idea of the human subject as agent, the source of actions, creating them, assuming them, carrying responsibility for them.[46]

It can hardly be an accident that the particular cultural idiosyncracies – passiveness, a sense of personal impotence in the face of fate – that Vernant here connects (by implication causally) with this shared peculiarity of Greek and Canadian 'language' should be so central to the Canadian character delineated in the foregoing pages.

Leaving the intricacies of voice to return to the consideration of gross phenomena, a further by-product of the subject/object ambivalence – and one which is responsible for a number of distinctive trends in Canadian literature – is the blurring of the distinction not merely between *I* and *it* but between the normally non-contiguous (by definition) categories of fictional and non-fictional modes. I have already pointed out the popularity of 'found' materials such as historical documentation. Where the tendency becomes really problematic is when personal confession begins to be confused with more objective forms of discourse. This is not simply a matter of a writer 'using' pieces of his own experience to create fiction. Such a ploy is both common and conventional. The problem arises, rather, when the autobiographical component is presented in such a way as to be both self-announcing *and* self-effacing at the same time. This is what happens, for instance, in Klein's *The Second Scroll*. As Miriam Waddington points out,

Klein called his work a novel, but as a fictional narrative it presents serious problems. First of all, the line between fiction and autobiography is very wavering throughout, and Klein's use of a narrator who speaks in the first person does not help matters. There are occasions when the narrator slips unmistakably into the author's persona, such as when he describes life on the Avenue de l'Hôtel de Ville. The autobiographical impression is further strengthened when the narrator tells of his assignment to visit the newly founded State of Israel in order to discover and translate 'the poems and songs of Israel's latest nest of singing birds' ... One cannot help recalling that Klein too had translated both Yiddish and Hebrew poetry. (94)

Other cases are less glaring, but we need only think on the one hand of the number of Canadian writers whose work emerges quite obviously from a personal 'background' – Laurence, Wiebe, Richler, Munro, Nowlan, not to mention numerous poets – and on the other of the inclination on the part of the public to ferret out autobiographical elements as if that were where the only possible 'truth' of a book must lie ('If there is one question I have been asked more than any other since ... I started to write my fictions ... it is how autobiographical is my material,' says David Watmough 135; 'there's an almost sick desire to make every novel a roman à clef,' complains Marian Engel D95), to realize that Klein's failure or refusal to keep his categories straight very probably signals a *national* reluctance to draw too firm a line between art and life.

Is this perhaps nothing more than a basic anti-aesthetic bias, though; a covert neo-puritanistic discomfort with the idea that there is anything as resistant to logical categories, as self-assertive, as 'art' in our communal repertoire? Perhaps. Certainly there is plenty of evidence that the idea of art does disconcert us. But in this case what are we to make of transgressions in the opposite direction like Grove's wholly invented autobiography and Hugh Hood's facsimile memoir, *The Swing in the Garden*? This latter book in particular is a real oddity. First impressions notwithstanding, it is not simply the conventional mock journal that Daniel Defoe perfected as far back as the eighteenth century. Every aspect of style and presentation – the compendiousness, the exaggerated facticity, the exhaustive but indiscriminate nature of the observations recorded, the lack of any apparent story or structure, the extent to which the author defuses inappropriate emotional identification with the young protagonist by keeping to the forefront the obtrusive, rambling, slightly pedantic voice of his narrator, the putative adult rememberer – is designed to create the impression that this is 'real,' not invented. Indeed, on the basis at least of how it *reads* there is no reason why it should even occur to anyone to question its authenticity – except for one thing: we know it isn't true. *The Swing in the Garden* is the autobiography of a made-up person named Matthew Goderich, *not* of Hugh Hood. This discrepancy is a little bothersome. If the vehicle is a 'fake,' how much can we believe of the contents? The 'facts' seem plausible, but what about the protagonist's feelings, not to mention the narrator's superimposed interpretations? Because the confusion of genres inhibits our attitude toward the book we are prompted to ask questions that would never occur to us if it were clearly either fish or fowl: was life at that time and in that place 'really' like that? What we want, in other words, is either more or less art. So why, in view of these problems, should Hood have chosen this particular approach? It's quite possible that his decision stemmed specifically from the same ambivalence that produced Laurence's 'middle voice.' Against the suggestion made above that an anomalous emphasis on the autobiographical element in our fiction simply signals an anti-aesthetic bias – that it is only the 'making' which is suspect – we might rather speculate that Canadians, nervous about the whole problem of subject/object commitment, feel most comfortable writing (and perhaps, if we can judge by the popularity of quasi-non-fiction writers like Pierre Berton and Farley Mowat, even reading) literature which straddles the line such that – as Munro says of her own practice – it is 'difficult to sort out the real memories ... used in [a] story from those that are not "real" at all' (B183).

If the middle voice and the facsimile or fictionalized memoir represent two of the most distinctive responses to subject/object ambivalence, there is, of course, another, even more obvious strategy an author may use for disguising his own responsibility; that is, to invite or, better, to *force* the reader himself to become a participant. Not surprisingly, we find ample evidence of this dodge, too, throughout the Canadian corpus. 'The compulsion to establish ... conjunctions, when Aquin ... has made it both essential and impossible to do so, forces the reader into active collaboration in the writing process, into trying to bridge the gap between the antiphons and make a "unity,"' says Patricia Merivale (202-3). Reaney's '*Alphabet* is an exercise in the use of the imagination, because the form it takes is a mosaic of myth and documentary out of which ... the reader is invited to make his or her own patterns ... *Colours in the Dark* and the Donnelly plays have the same combination of mythic and documentary material, the same juxtaposition of various forms, and the reader or viewer of the plays has again to "rouse his faculties" to make himself the place where it all comes together,' echoes Stan Dragland (116). Wiebe's *The Blue Mountains of China*, 'multiple and fragmented, highlights the absence of [an] integrative vision and engages the reader in his own struggle in a narrative wilderness,' Ina Ferris adds (79). To what extent, however, is this sort of strategy merely conventional? Even in traditional novels the reader is usually implicated in the narrator's viewpoint in order to secure his complicity (a confessional tone or chatty asides, for instance, assert – in Jonathan Culler's words – 'that the meanings extracted from the scene are the common property of narrator and reader: wholly *vraisemblable*'[47]); more recently, the appeal to the reader has become almost a cliché of avant-garde fiction. 'The post-modernist,' says Bowering, 'invites his readers, & sometimes his characters, to take a hold somewhere & help him move the damned thing into position' (c7). Again, though, we can distinguish subtle but important differences between Canadian and other usages. The authors – largely American – invoked in this last quotation employ the technique in question for one of two reasons: to underline the artificiality of the text (and therefore draw attention to themselves as artists) or to emphasize reality's resistance to aesthetic ordering. The Canadian, in contrast – concerned above all to sidestep responsibility – tends not merely to implicate the reader in a purely formal sense but to put the *whole burden of interpretation* on his shoulders.

Part of the explanation for this defection probably relates to the practical problems entailed by our sense of existential isolation. E.H. Gombrich has pointed out the extent to which the evocative power of art depends less on present than on prior information, the viewer's capacity to *share* the artist's vision in so far as it is expressive as well of his *own* experience.[48] When a writer not only forces the beholder to work by withholding interpretation but also *draws his attention to the fact*, he may simply be signalling his lack of confidence in the possibility of this kind of intersubjectivity. Personal ambivalence undoubtedly has something to do with it, too, though. When Birney uses the second person plural in about half the poems in his 1948 *The Strait of Anian*; when Laurence, forcing us to 'respond and disclose in synchrony' with her characters, makes us see them directly, as we would 'real' people, rather than knowing them only through her telling (Labonté 170-1); when, especially, Timothy Findley in *The Wars* invokes the reader as researcher, conducting him step by step through a process of investigation that has no reality except in so far as it is taking place *now*, disclosing its essential form right under, and *only* under, our eyes – all of these strategies argue for an author who, like the narrators examined above, would like to dissociate himself at least symbolically from the act of creation. In the latter book, for instance, though in fact most of the 'story' is unobtrusively narrated in the third person, we are never allowed to forget for long our complicity in the task of deriving meaning from neutral data. The author-as-mediator is conspicuously absent. 'In the end, the only facts you have are public. Out of these you make what you can' (10). 'You begin at the archives with photographs' (11). 'There is no good picture of this except the one you can make in your mind' (71). '[Y]ou make your way by trial and error ...' (99). 'You begin to arrange your research in bundles – letters – photos – telegrams' (191). Surely this is the last step in the effacement of authorial presence.

If the reader is formally invoked as the ultimate arbiter in Canadian fiction, this doesn't mean he is free to 'make' anything he likes out of the proffered reality, of course. Or, indeed, that he would if he could. (Remember this is the champion of non-involvement we are talking about here.) Rather, there is a strong sense throughout the whole corpus – and this, not Findley's adroit footwork, or Hood's sleight of hand, or Laurence's edge-sitting (which are all merely symptomatic), is the real bottom line to our story – that from the point of view of both writer and reader the artifact, whatever that might be or represent, is simply *given*. Indeed, if we had to pick a single analogue to convey what Canadian literature is really 'like,' it would be film. Think about it. Of all kinds of creative activity, film-making best satisfies the criteria implicitly established by the Canadian world view. In the first place, far more convincingly than any written form it provides an illusion of non-aggressive, even impersonal creation. Despite recent *auteur* theories of the cinema that emphasize the inventiveness of the director, the *popular* impression of film-making focuses on the camera, betokening a mode of artistry that resolves the problem of subjectivity, as Stanley Cavell puts it, 'by removing the human agent from the task of reproduction.'[49] The film, therefore, is by convention if not by definition exactly the kind of artifact the Canadian writer would seem determined to pretend he is contriving. The film, moreover, caters uniquely to the type Canadian *reader's* fears and preferences, too, by allowing him a perfectly passive role. Early critics, including Wyndham Lewis, were disturbed by the extent to which film appealed to, and encouraged, a tyranny of the senses,[50] but tyranny is exactly what the Canadian wants. 'How do movies reproduce the world magically?' Cavell asks. 'Not by literally presenting us with the world, but by permitting us to view it unseen. This is not a wish for power over creation (as Pygmalion's was), but a wish not to need power, not to have to bear its burdens. It is, in this sense, the reverse of the myth of Faust' [40]. This is an approach very congenial to our communal psyche.[51]

If the *idea* of film is attractive to the Canadian, it seems clear when we turn to our literature that many of its tangible properties are equally so. 'Movies,' indeed, serve as one of the most frequently recurrent motifs in the corpus. At times the usage is occasional – the movie imagery at the end of *Beautiful Losers* signals the protagonist's shift, significantly enough, to a mode of total passivity – but often, and more interestingly, film is used by writers simultaneously as a metaphor and as a model for narrative technique. For both Morag of *The Diviners* and Min of Engel's *The Honeyman Festival* memories of the past – by implication both immediate *and* inaccessible – present themselves 'as a series of movies or film-strips' projected upon the passive screen of the mind (Parker 112). In Blais' *La belle bête*, alternately, an extended 'picture metaphor' ('enforced in the novel itself by reference to film') underlines the superficial and theatrical quality of present experience (Coldwell 64). The subject/object of Ondaatje's *Billy the Kid*, most strikingly, is 'not only the still subject of a photograph ... [but] also the recorder of visual impressions':

'I am very still/ I take in all the angles of a room' ... His perception is visual; a room is a picture; a day, a series of frames ... In many scenes, [he] waits in a dark room and looks out to a white landscape defined by the frames of windows and doors. Space throughout the sequence of prose and poetry is bordered by box frames: porch rails, windows, walls, barbed wire fences, and coffins ... [Billy] presents himself as a camera, recording the track of a fly across a white surface in a deliberate reversal of a white star's imprint against the night sky. (Blott 189)

Examples could be multiplied without effort. If we appropriate to the category not only works that make conscious use of film motifs but those as well that are cinematic by virtue of specific technical borrowings (Canadian writers are particularly fond of montage), a greater than usual visual emphasis, and/or the use of a 'camera's eye' type of narrative stance, the field becomes so broad as to take in a surprising proportion of the entire corpus. We have already discussed the outstandingly graphic quality of Wiebe's style; we have not yet observed the extent to which this writer's evocation of the thing-as-seen stands as a kind of normative model for Canadian literature. In Hébert's *Kamouraska*, for example, though film is never mentioned, much of the protagonist's dream-memories is presented in sharp and exhaustive detail exactly *as if* we were watching a cinematic presentation. And Hébert is far from exceptional.

Canadians, it would seem, are literally fixated on *appearances*.

We must be careful, on the other hand, not to misconstrue this fact. For all the striking emphasis on visual effects, there is nothing insubstantial about the phenomena thus revealed, in Hébert's novel or elsewhere. Nor, despite the narrow focus, the deliberately limited vision, is there any sense, as there is in a great deal of recent extra-national fiction, that the world, 'reality,' stops at the boundaries of the presently-experienced. In film, says Tiessen, 'the presently not-seen world itself always constitutes a form of presence, as well as a form of the unknown, and always seems prepared to become visible and intrude' (137) – and so it is in Canadian literature. In fact, our writers' passiveness, their refusal to impose meaning, only makes what Heidegger calls 'the objectness, the over-againstness'[52] of the material environment that much more palpable. As a result, the Canadian fictional universe seems above all to be full of *things*. Poets as different as E.J. Pratt ('[B]uilt on nouns and verbs ... His verses are crammed with things and actions. Not abstractions and aspects, but individual things and particular actions. The result is a poetry essentially concrete and direct.' MacKay 41), Paul-Marie Lapointe ('Lapointe's work exudes a happy and radiant sensuality: things such as salmon, furs, and cupboards are given a strong and simple existence and bask in the glow of an inventive embrace of the senses' Chamberlain 153), and Daphne Marlatt ('In these poems, Marlatt repeats her contention that the self can be understood only in relation to external phenomena, and insists that "Matter inserts relation." Much of the book is devoted to the painstaking examination of the objects surrounding the poet.' Lecker B120), as these quotations show, give objects a paramount importance rivalling the significance attributed by the romantic to feelings and by the classicist to ideas. Novelists are likewise object-oriented. Hood's *The Swing in the Garden* begins by evoking the physical presence suggested in the title ('In those days we used to have a red-and-white garden swing set up in the backyard beside the garage, a noisy outbuilding of rusty corrugated metal stamped in shivering, wave-like sheets, which rumbled with theatrical thunder when the wind blew hard' 5) and thence proceeds to catalogue in naturalistic and ofttimes tedious detail the multiplex physical facts that characterize his chosen setting. Is this a function, specifically, of this author's documentary purposes? Hardly. Think of Atwood's Lady Oracle with her passion for 'junk' – 'gilt spoons, sugar tongs in the shape of hen's feet or midget hands, clocks that didn't work, flowered china, [and] spotty mirrors' (160); think of Laurence's Manawaka, its solid, meticulously realized houses 'dense with objects seen and described' (C. Thomas D185); even more strikingly, think of the tangible, almost overwhelming clutter of Hazard's home in *The Studhorse Man*, where Kroetsch, seeming merely to count over the detritus of one man's existence, manages to suggest the overridingly materialistic, enigmatic/inconsequential as-it-is-knownness of a whole world:

currycombs, a broken hamestrap, a spoon wired to a stick for dropping poisoned wheat into the holes of offending gophers, saltpetre, gentian root, a scattering of copper rivets, black antimony, a schoolboy's ruler, three mousetraps in a matchbox, two chisels for trimming hoofs, Cornucrescine (for making horn grow), ginger, horse liniment and liniment for his back, Elliman's Royal Embrocation, blue vitriol, an electuary, nux vomica, saddle soap in a Spode (a simple blue and white) saucer. Spanish fly – (9-10)

The fact is, Canadian writers – and the propensity goes far beyond the few cited here – seem almost preternaturally preoccupied with (as Dawson says of Alice Munro) 'the utter solidity and yet curious vulnerability of the physical' (58). Munro, whose own work is pre-eminently rooted in concrete reality, goes so far as to suggest that this leaning may reveal not merely an aesthetic preference but a psychological necessity. 'I can't write about states of mind,' she says. 'I can't have anybody in a room without describing all the furniture. You know... I can't get into people or life ... without having all those other things around them' (c257). Munro seems to think of herself as an oddity ('God knows that isn't the way most people live any more'), but her difference from other Canadian writers, if any, is only one of degree. Canadians seem to place an unusual importance on the substantiality of the 'real.'

The question that arises, especially in the light of what I said earlier about Canadian introversion, is *why* there should be this stress on the external. One possible answer is that the tendency is entailed by the conventions within which Canadians write. Though there are many aspects of Canadian literature that seem anti-realistic, the mere fact of the writer's reluctance to tamper with the 'given' – which is, after all, the most *basic* identifying characteristic of realistic writing[53] – makes it seem 'realistic' almost in spite of itself. The film connection, moreover, would tend to exacerbate this impression, especially once it becomes consciously recognized. 'The medium of the movies is physical reality as such,' says Erwin Panofsky [in Cavell 16]. 'Cinema is committed to communicate only by way of what is real,' André Bazin adds. The Canadian would thus be predisposed to the presentation of a *real* world simply by association. Lacking the true realist's comprehensive 'program,' however, this predisposition would tend to devolve upon isolated 'symptoms' or segments of reality rather than reality-as-a-unified whole. Since (in Culler's words) 'Enumerations or descriptions of objects which seem determined by no thematic purpose enable the reader to recognize a world but prevent him from composing it' [193], this development in turn would account for the overwhelming impression of an environing world characterized by free-floating, enigmatic *things*.

A second possible explanation has to do less with the Canadian's conventionality than his uniqueness. In a new country, especially one as vast and vacant as

Canada, the writer's sense of his own isolation inclines him naturally toward those modes of writing that will help him to locate himself externally rather than those by means of which he may explicate his inner workings. Such writing, says Northrop Frye, 'does not start with a rhythmical movement, or an impetus caught from or encouraged by a group of contemporaries: it starts with reportage, a single mind reacting to what is set against it. Such a writer does not naturally think metaphorically but descriptively' (B233). What, though, do we make of the fact that Canadian writers seem to have become *more*, not less, thing-obsessed as time has passed? Part of it may be due to a lessened dependency on the kind of avoidance strategies discussed in chapter 3. Part, too, may relate to the fact that although the physical country, at least in its most immediate aspect, has been tamed, identified, the psychic landscape is still relatively featureless. The Canadian, culturally adrift, has a very weak sense of himself yet. What is more – as noted above – he has very little faith in the possibility of *shared* experience. This alone would be enough to turn the writer to what is incontrovertible, the *facts*; to filling in the multifarious details of mundane reality one would normally take for granted. 'You can afford to leave out a hand or an eye [from a painting],' says Gombrich, 'but you cannot ask the beholder to guess the design of a table-cloth of which he had no knowledge' [205].

Does this answer the question?

For all their plausibility, it is my guess that neither of these hypotheses, in itself, offers the whole explanation for Canada's thing-orientation. Each contains an important *part* of the truth but both fail to take into consideration the full complexity of the situation. Both the literary and the ethnological models suggest that the emphasis on objects signals a *reaction* of some sort. This much is probably true. It is a mistake, however, to infer further that the *things* themselves – whether facts or objects – are in consequence merely propaedeutic. What we realize if we look closer is that not only do Canadians utter *things* because this is the level of discourse stimulated by their environment but *their environment takes this particular form because, in a sense, the things utter themselves*. Why? Remember what was said about our recoil from otherness? According to Jung's description of psychological types this initial response could well explain not only our introversion, which seems quite logical, but our subsequent, apparently paradoxical preoccupation with physical reality as well.

To the extent that [a person's] consciousness is subjectivized and excessive importance attached to the ego, the object is put in a position which in the end becomes untenable. The object is a factor whose power cannot be denied, whereas the ego is a very limited and fragile thing ... [So] if the ego has usurped the claims of the subject, this naturally produces, by way of compensation, an unconscious reinforcement of the influence of the object. In spite of positively convulsive efforts to ensure the superiority of the ego, the object comes to exert an overwhelming influence, which is all the more invincible because it seizes on the individual unawares and forcibly obtrudes itself on his consciousness. As a result ... a compensation relation arises in the unconscious which makes itself felt as an absolute and irrepressible tie to the object. The more the ego struggles to preserve its independence, freedom from obligation, and superiority, the more it becomes enslaved ... The object assumes terrifying proportions in spite of the [introvert's] attempt to degrade it ... It continually imposes itself on him against his will, it arouses in him the most disagreeable and intractable affects and persecutes him at every step. [378-9]

Does this sound unduly extreme? Perhaps not when we notice how often the object-world in Canadian literature is made to seem not just obtrusive but positively *uncanny*.

The numinousness manifests itself with varying degrees of intensity. As a least common denominator it is significant that 'things' in Canadian literature are commonly deemed to have a definite existential status quite apart from the experiencing self. 'There is nothing uncertain about a rose,' says Sister Pelagia in Engel's *The Glassy Sea*, 'nothing tentative' (160). 'The absolute nature of things is independent of my senses,' adds Davies' David Staunton, more extremely (b269). What does this independence imply for the observer? For one thing it makes the object – man-made *or* natural – seem not merely strange but mysterious. Lady Oracle's fascinated sense of the secret lives of artifacts ('What amazed me was the sheer volume of objects, remnants of lives, and the way they circulated. The people died but their possessions did not, they went round and round as in a slow eddy ... How difficult these objects are to dispose of, I thought; they lurk passively, like vampire sheep, waiting for someone to buy them.' 160-1) suggests exactly the same half-alarming, half-thrilling shock of recognition that Richard Thomas of Matt Cohen's *The Disinherited* experiences in his confrontation with nature: 'The bird stepped forward then stopped again. It flexed its tail feathers and a shudder ran through its wings. Then, almost spastically, it flapped its wings again, twice, and landed on Richard Thomas's lap. They were both so surprised that they froze. Then it moved again. Its foot landed on Richard Thomas's hand and the feel of it, damp cold and spiny, startled him and he drew his hand away. Then the bird was gone, leaving more strange sensations where the feathers had brushed across his face' (7). Power to stimulate amazement in this way resides in phenomena only to the extent that they *resist* human comprehension. 'The mountain speaks' in Birney's 'Bushed,' 'but its "messages" proclaim words the trapper either cannot ... or doesn't wish to understand' (Robillard 45).

If things are incomprehensible in the Canadian fictional landscape, they are also inaccessible to other modes of approach. Indeed, inaccessibility may be their single most noticeable quality. This suggests another reason, besides the cinematic influence, why Canadian writers and artists put so much emphasis on *surface*. D.P. Brown's paintings, filled with walls, windows, inner-pictures, mirrors, shiny table-tops, reflecting artifacts – anything to call attention to the indirection of art and the surficiality of life – provides a striking visual correlative for Atwood's reflection-filled poetry. Hugh Hood approaches the same intuition somewhat more directly. While his artist protagonist in *White Figure, White Ground* is successful in capturing the phenomenal aspect of the object-world in his painting *Light Source No. 2*, he fails utterly in *Light Source No.1* to penetrate *inside* to its noumena (see Cloutier, especially 62).

Does this prove our case? If it went no further than such practices as these, the phenomenon of the Canadian's thing-orientation would still fall significantly short of at least the last phase of adaptation outlined by Jung. From a simple preoccupation with the external, the introvert's 'fear of objects develops into a peculiar kind of cowardliness,' he says; 'He is terrified of strong affects in others, and is hardly ever free from the dread of falling under hostile influences ... the relation with the object becomes primitive ... and the object [itself] seems endowed with magical powers' [379]. We are reminded that a distinguishing characteristic of Mary Douglas's 'small group' culture is an obsession with witchcraft (see note 12 below). Nevertheless, when we talk of objects being not merely mysterious but frightful, surely we are going a little too far. Or are we? If we look at Canadian art, Jung's evocation of a 'puissant and terrifying' thing-scape does not really seem all that improbable.

I already noted the disquieting undertones in many Group of Seven paintings; these have become more blatant in the work of, say, magic realists like Alex Colville. 'Colville's paintings present a study in paradox,' says William Withrow: 'most are casein tempera and oil on Masonite, meticulously faithful in detail, with a clear, cool surface feel to them. Their subject matter, like the medium in which they are done, is open and light: a tree, a dog, a couple at the beach, a woman looking through binoculars. But under this reassuring surface is a tension, a sense that is almost sinister' (58). In what does it consist, this undercurrent? There are no tattered trees, no 'incubus' – not this time. The fact is, though, despite its polish – despite the almost palpable absence of nature in the raw – the world Colville gives us is unmistakably 'other.' Why? For one thing, the subject matter is somewhat less innocuous than Withrow implies. Even aside from overtly enigmatic compositions like *Church and Horse* (1964) and *Horse and Train* (1954), with their unsettling hints of violence and irrationality, Colville's 'frequent allusions to space and travelling in the form of ships, the ocean itself, rivers, bridges, roads, [and] especially railroads,' as Michael Greenwood points out, signal 'an obsession with the idea of time as an irreversible drift toward eternity' (B36). More important, the super-realistic style, in much the same way that exaggerated rationality hints irresistibly at its opposite, repels rather than reassures.[54] The landscapes revealed, quite simply, are alien. The intensity of visual detail works to deny both the depth suggested by the careful delineation of perspective and the interrelation of forms (despite the eschewal of outline, the hard edges, the opaqueness and almost truculent solidity of each discrete element, make all surfaces, mental and physical, seem closed, impervious to penetration, mutually exclusive); the consequent lapidary effect typically gives the paintings, even when the matter presented is unexceptionable, a peculiarly lifeless – or even life-*denying* – quality that speaks of a world quiescent, stultified, stillborn, reeking of fatality.[55] If Colville's vision is representative – and I would claim that in many ways it is – then the Canadian's 'object,' at least in so far as it is writ large, blown up beyond the comfortable microfocus of potted plants and house furnishings, is as much of a repository for terror as anything Jung suggests. But this just takes us full circle to where we were several chapters back. The solidity, the absolute givenness of the object, is implicit in the gothic wilderness. Kierkegaard claims that since man truly exists only as a solitary individual, he can relate to reality only existentially, through *dread*.[56] Reversing this we might speculate that because the Canadian is *a priori* heir to existential dread, he has an *a priori* intimation of the realness, the incontrovertible over-againstness of the 'other.'

At this point it is perhaps necessary – as the reference to Kierkegaard suggests – to stop once again and consider whether the Canadian's thing-orientation, if not the subtle undertones of paranoia, may not be better explained in a context of world trends. Despite the rather striking similarities to be discerned in a number of areas, I would say not. In Europe, the ultimate orientation of both philosophers and writers is toward the realm of the subject. The phenomenologists, particularly Husserl and Heidegger, *theoretically* make much of both the human significance and the self-supportive nature of external phenomena (for Husserl, says Arturo Fallico, 'the primary fact about consciousness is its consciousness of *things*' [2]), but if we look more closely at their practice we realize that their real concern is not the object-in-itself but the relation *between* object and observer, Heidegger's *dasein*, a concept that implies both *being-in-the-world* and *being-together-with* [Choron 232]. '*The object scrutinized remains bound by his intentionality to the observer*,' Fallico points out. 'For this reason, inspection of the object must lead back to the intending observer whose thought about it defines the object he is observing' [8]. Both phenomenology and the later varieties of existentialism that drew so heavily upon it thus betray the object-in-itself even as they raise the battle cry, 'Let us get back to *things*!'[57] If we turn to contemporary European literature, moreover, we find very much the same situation.

But wait: the objection will surely be raised that we are overlooking Robbe-Grillet's *Nouveau Roman* and the recent popularity, at least in France, of *chosisme*. As its name implies, this movement was above all else concerned with the integrity of the 'thing.' 'Robbe-Grillet rejects what he calls the "humanist" equation: "le monde, c'est l'homme,"' says Sharon Spencer: 'He wishes to cleanse the world of objects of their impure and false human associations. Therefore, he shuns attributive adjectives and virtually all metaphors. His task is not to interpret the world but simply to see it fresh, to see it as it might be viewed through the lens of a camera. In order to do this, he abandons conventional description and, instead, enumerates dimensions, surfaces, and relationships among objects in their spatial situations' [108-9]. Could anything possibly sound more 'Canadian'? Unfortunately for its founder's impressive intentions, in practice the *chosiste* program reveals a number of significant inconsistencies. 'Robbe-Grillet's famous description of a tomato slice [in *Les Gommes*], which tells us first that it is perfect and then that it is flawed ... introduces uncertainties [about the referential function] and thus lifts our attention away from a supposed object to the process of writing itself,' says Culler [193]. The result does as much violence to the integrity of the 'real' object as does the most blatant subjectivism. Inasmuch as he speaks on the one hand of 'inventing freely' and on the other of the work's internal necessity, 'What Robbe-Grillet seems to be saying,' Alice Kaminsky concludes, 'is that the novelist uses his imagination to construct characters and events which have no necessary relationship to anything extrinsic to the novel itself.'[58] Why the marked divergence from apparent intent in a program that seems so explicit? Perhaps the reason is hinted in Spencer's description quoted above. If the Canadian's obsession with things is linked at least in part to his fear of otherness, the European intellectual, out of disillusionment with the false promises of optimistic humanism, has simply withdrawn affect from transcendent philosophies. 'Robbe-Grillet ... has affirmed that "essentialist" conceptions lie in ruins, that man cannot simply look on the world as a private possession set up to serve his needs,' says Victor Brombert. 'His insistence on the world of objects and of surfaces goes hand in hand with a deep-rooted suspicion of all anthropomorphic interpretations.'[59] Though *chosisme* may *sound* a lot like Canadian literary practice, therefore, the respective psychological grounds reveal an essential distinction. It is quite a different thing to *choose* thingness than to have thingness thrust upon one.[60]

What about the situation in the United States? Here, as we might expect, the subjective orientation is even more clear-cut. As noted above, the groundwork for a pre-eminently egocentric literature was laid more than a century ago ('By explicitly putting the question of the "conformity" between subject and object, idealism focused attention of the *forming* process and led to Emerson's feeling that "the state of the world at any one time was directly dependent on the intellectual classification then existing in the minds of men"' [Feidelson 114]), and matters have continued in this train ever since. Again, of course, there is bound to be the inevitable objection: we are ignoring those notably thing-centred literati, the imagists – a significant enough oversight considering the frequency with which this movement is cited in discussions of Canadian poetry.[61] Again, I will have to say very much what I said of the Europeans. *Articulated intentions are misleading*! The imagist manifesto was fraught with contradictions from the beginning. 'Its early promulgators ... wanted to have both a poetic style which would make for a poetry of particularist, ego-centred insight and also a system of belief, a dogma, which, in its concern for order and reason, would deny the validity of such an insight' [Pearce 422]. The result? Predictably, for the most part the former won out – even in the work of William Carlos Williams, the author of that celebrated declaration 'No ideas but in things.' The fact is, Williams uses his 'simple, separate things' above all as a way back to the *subject*. 'He assures himself that he is what he is by virtue of his power to collocate such objects into sharply annotated images,' says Pearce. 'He must feel himself into the things of his world; for he is ... dependent on them as occasions to be himself – as poet. Perhaps – and herein lies the pathos – they depend on him as much as he depends on them. "So much depends" ... on a poet's being there to make them what, at their best, they can be: objects in a poem' [339]. Pearce's last comment underlines succinctly where we can expect to find contemporary American writers taking their stand on the subject/object issue. The idea, not the object, is the repository of meaning[62] – and the ultimate idea is the 'poem.' Hence the recent movement toward self-reflectiveness in art, 'the conscious devaluation of the latent invisible ... [which] focuses attention on the figure in-itself and only secondarily on the automatic field it inhabits and imbues with value.'[63] Hence too – going back to an earlier topic – an emphasis on the importance of the 'maker' so marked as to comprise, in writers, outright solipsism.[64] This takes us a long way from 'thingness.' 'The "as if" quality of so many recent novels, the fact that they are so candidly *contrived*, so clearly *abstracted* from quotidian life, does not necessarily vitiate their effectiveness as works of art,' says Ihab Hassan; 'it merely enhances their distance from that brutishness of facts on which, say, *Moll Flanders* plumply rests.'[65]

If we turn back to the Canadian, we are now in a position to gauge his uniqueness. Should we not be concerned, though, to recognize that so many significant aspects of our creative practice seem causally related to some sort of neurotic symptom? Certainly not as far as the literature is concerned. Art in itself is amoral, impersonal, non-intending. As such, anything – good or bad, healthy or unhealthy – is grist for its mill. It can never judge; it can only express. Does this mean, then, that art is irrelevant to our own experience of the world? Not at all. Inasmuch as art swallows indiscriminately the most painful and divergent aspects of our experience, it has the power to neutralize our anxiety, transforming it into otherness, giving it back to us not as immanence but as recollection. Art, in other words, can take our 'symptoms' and change them into something very like myth. To note that certain aspects of Canadian art may have been catalysed by what would commonly be considered in individuals a psychological abnormality is not, therefore, to imply that it is either aesthetically flawed or culturally degenerate. Indeed, the very features we've been discussing are responsible for some of the most noteworthy characteristics of our recent oeuvre. To pull together our divers strands, what we find in recent Canadian art and literature is neither the feigned dehumanization of the *Nouveau Roman* nor the excessive self-obsession of American post-modernist fiction, but a *duality* of self and other eternally linked in uneasy equipoise, both equally inescapable, equally importunate, equally real. If the Canadian writer declines either subjective or objective responsibility, in other words, Canadian literature manages to encompass (using W.H. Harvey's categories) both Dickens's 'world of things sensed as living a life of its own' and Virginia Woolf's all-digesting, luminous interior sensibility.[66] This juxtaposition gives rise to at least two different kinds of tension which between them account for a number of striking literary effects.

The first and most obvious kind of tension we may expect to be generated by a dualistic vision like this is a tension within the world of the book itself between the subject and the object. We have already noted numerous instances of this effect with respect to Canadian thematic preferences, and especially in connection with our obsession about the inadequacies of the flesh. It doesn't take much imagination to see how it might be extended to elucidate certain stylistic choices as well. '[T]he utter rationality that is always implicit in the detective story serves as counter-point to the hallucinatory prose style [of Aquin's *Trou de mémoire*] … as well as to the madness which threatens all of his characters,' points out Russell Brown (D7). More interesting than cases like this latter, where the motif is an 'embedded' one, many works go so far as to exploit the duplicity overtly and exhaustively on both levels at once. In *Kamouraska*, Hébert uses a variety of techniques ranging from first/third-person narrative shifts to an exaggerated cinematic style – that is, both dreamlike (flowing) and object-oriented (graphic) – to convey the impression of a consciousness not just dissevered from but actually *afflicted by* the 'thingness' of the world she inhabits:

[T]here's something watching me, here in the petrified landscape of Kamouraska. Something motionless, agape… I never should have come back. The charred ruins of the manor, all black against a sky of stone. The front still seems to be intact. The door, wide open. Through the doorway you can see the wild weeds growing madly in massive clumps behind the house. The drawing room window has a few little panes in place, smoked black… Somewhere in the wall, one motionless speck of life, stony but alive, aims itself in my direction. Holding its fire. Stuck in the stone… All at once, it moves. A lizard, I suppose, hidden among the stones, now suddenly scurrying down the wall. In nimble zigzags. Falling at my feet. Good Lord! Now all the ruins seem to be coming to life. This living speck begins to budge and bit by bit it wakes up all the walls left standing. [73]

We will be returning to Elisabeth d'Aulnières in the next chapter. For now we might only note the representativeness (for all its extremity) of her predicament. More important, we might note the 'representativeness' of Hébert's mimesis. Quite apart from its contribution to characterization, this author's exemplary vision of the over-againstness of the inhuman also hints at an explanation for the surrealistic effects which, despite our uneasiness about diving too deep, seem such a striking component of Canadian and especially Quebec literature. Whatever our discussion of Automatism may have suggested, the term 'surrealism' can be used variously to denote either a method (creativity as a tapping of unconscious forces) *or* a type of content (especially incongruous and grotesque conjunctions and disjunctions such as we find in dreams). Canadian literature may seem surrealistic, therefore, not because it is particularly free or spontaneous (indeed, as we will see in the next chapter, it tends rather to be highly, and even quite conventionally, structured) but because, in the most basic terms, the whole oeuvre is predicated upon an image of self in explicit, uneasy juxtaposition with a world which, if only for its absolute resistance to anthropomorphic appropriation, all too often seems (as Clara Thomas says of Laurence's *The Fire-Dwellers*) 'like a vast canvas by Hieronymus Bosch' (D118).[67] The Canadian fictional universe, in other words, is surrealistic simply *de facto*.

If the tension *within* works (the object as 'seen') has some interesting implications, there is yet a more profound tension between work and world built into the Canadian's version of 'seeing.' In this case, we have a double discrepancy not merely between the subject and the artifact but also between the artifact and the object, where the former is not – as for the American – a means of mediation but rather a mysterious third presence that repels for what it withholds even as it consoles by uttering. '[T]he mysteriousness of the photography lies not in the machinery which produces it,' says Cavell, 'but in the unfathomable abyss between what it captures (its subject) and what is captured for us (*this* fixing of the subject), the metaphysical wait between exposure and exhibition, the absolute authority or finality of the fixed image' [185]. And so it is (for us) with art. Take the question of the landscape. I have just said that it is alien, wholly inaccessible. Yet a few chapters ago I claimed that it has been redeemed, made available for the poet to use as he willed. These two statements seem irreconcilable, yet both in a sense are absolutely – and crucially – true. What does this mean? Perhaps we can creep up on the matter indirectly. Take Marian Engel's *Bear*. There is a moment in this book when the protagonist experiences an epiphany that is very important for getting to the heart of the Canadian experience. After days of anthropomorphizing her animal lover, Lou finally realizes that 'she could paint any face on him that she wanted, while his actual range of expression was a mystery' (78-9). Exactly the same thing holds true for the landscape as a whole. Far from appropriating it to ourselves, the most we can hope is that, as for LePan's young deserter, 'a strip [will] sometimes peel off from the surface of things and impose itself on [our] perceptions' (167). What we take from the landscape, in other words, is nothing proper to its own being – from that point of view it is, as LePan points out, 'completely without meaning' – but simply a facsimile we have abstracted for our own purposes. As a result there is exactly the same absolute discrepancy between the landscape-as-code, which is accessible (it is hardly coincidental that Klein, in *The Second Scroll*, speaks of the landscape of Israel as 'an open slanted bible' 70), and the landscape-as-phenomenon which is *not*, as there is between the word-as-sign and the word-as-arbitrary-black-mark-on-a-piece-of-paper. What is more important, the naturalization of the one brings us not one step closer to the other – and indeed, as has been said, by confronting us with the mystery of its *own* presence, its reticence and transparency, may actually exacerbate our sense of estrangement. At the same time as it estranges, of course, this mystery also provides the means to its own validation. This is perhaps the one element, finally, that accounts for the odd and exciting quality of as-it-isness that characterizes the best of Canadian art.

But this leads us into another chapter.

NOTES

1 As John Ower describes it, 'The poet, like the voyageur before him, must leave behind the whole of the traditional civilized order of Europe, with its moral law and its religious ritualization of existence. His canoe becomes a "bateau ivre," swept through a wilderness in which the stark contrasts and the savagery of our country's "violent weathers" are mirrored psychologically in the sudden onset of wild appetites and passions. The poet has entered what Northrop Frye terms the "hyperphysical" world of Schopenhauer's will, a blind, violent and capricious life-force which inspires both untrammelled nature and the human unconscious. The traditional Romantic belief is ... that this terrible journey ... will paradoxically return man's lost innocence, bringing him into the "limpid gracious Presence" of the Divine and rendering nature once again the "garment innocent and lustrous" of the human spirit. This faith is evoked by LePan ... only to be ironically dismissed as out of keeping with the Canadian landscape. In the setting in which the poet-voyageur finds himself. The untamed energy of the life-force has produced a labyrinthine wasteland of "tangled struggling roots," "weeds, that clutch at the canoe" and "Wild birds hysterical in tangled trees." At the centre of this maze, in symbolic opposition to the "golden-haired Archangel" of the spiritual, there "teeters some lust-red manitou"' (84).

2 In T.D. MacLulich's words, 'Billy withdraws into emotional neutrality in order to avoid acknowledging his own susceptibility to emotional or physical weakness ... [He] does not like to witness events which remind him that a messy, vulnerable, organic layer exists beneath the surface appearance of the external world. Billy wishes he could ignore the after-effects of his killings and he takes offense at all instances of apparent disorder in the natural environment' (C111).

3 MacEwen amplifies: '"Whose ego?" asked Philip ... "Anyone's," was the slurred answer. "It takes a place normally occupied by small gods, large gods, etc. But the magician is basically the sole conscious agent in the course of things. All the elemental laws come under his hand; he manipulates; he controls... he is the true forerunner of every science, every religion..."' (47).

4 Leach, *Culture and Communication* (Cambridge 1976) 35

5 See chapter 12, 431-2, and especially footnote 24, for a discussion of the connections between art-as-ritual and boundaries.

6 Douglas, *Natural Symbols: Explorations in Cosmology* (Vintage 1973) 93, 169, 16

7 There are a few exceptions to this. In Kroetsch's novels urinary images are often, despite their vulgarity, unambiguously positive. As P.L. Surette says of such usage in *The Words of My Roaring* and *The Studhorse Man*, 'The rigorous critic will observe that neither Johnnie's nor Hazard's evacuation is essential to the plot, and the fastidious will note that their characters are so thinly offensive that such gratuitous bad taste is hardly needed. Those who are neither rigorous nor fastidious may hear the delicate tracery of Kroetsch's prose through the hyperbole and vulgarity of which it is composed. Since event is treated as metaphor in fabular fiction, police court logic (rules of relevance, based on rules of evidence) does not apply. Both Backstrom and Lepage reveal their benighted humanity in simple and humble acts of mere animality that are nonetheless redolent with human imagination and significance' (16).

8 See Gutteridge B for a Freudian interpretation – and a criticism – of Mitchell's evacuation imagery.

9 'Madame sold khaki-coloured penny candies which we were forbidden to eat, but her main source of power was that she had only one hand. Her other arm ended in a soft pink snout like an elephant's trunk and she broke the parcel string by wrapping it around her stump and pulling. This arm devoid of a hand was for me a great mystery, almost as puzzling as Jesus ... I try to remember what the rest of her was like, her face, but I can see only the potent candies, inaccessible in their glass reliquary, and the arm, miraculous in an unspecified way like the toes of saints or the cut-off pieces of early martyrs' (27).

10 This is the aspect emphasized by Catherine McLay. 'The problems of language and communication which affect personal relationships are ... closely related to the division in the novel between mind and body, language being associated solely with mind. R.D. Laing observes:

... Some persons do not have a sense of that basic unity which can abide through the most intense conflicts with oneself, but seem rather to have come to experience themselves as primarily split into a mind and a body. Usually they feel most closely identified with the "mind."

'He continues: *"The body is felt more as one object among other objects in the world than as the core of the individual's own being."*
'This is the dilemma of the narrator [of *Surfacing*]' (40).

11 In this regard it is interesting to note the connections made in Daphne Marlatt's *Rings* between physical and aesthetic creation and evacuation. According to Robert Lecker, 'As the woman meditates upon the child floating within her, a parallel is established between birth and creativity. The poet survives in the stream of experience only by continually relocating the origins of flow:

"delivered"
is a coming into THIS stream. You start at the beginning
& it keeps on beginning

'Although fragmented language and images continue to illustrate the presence of a multiphasic consciousness, the fourth section of *Rings* is primarily devoted to an examination of another relation: that between process, purgation, and birth. The metaphor is clear: creation can only be the product of a total release of consciousness. Spontaneity as a diarrhoea of words. The woman's desperate need for intestinal release is emphatically linked to the release provided by birth:

if only
it would all come out. But what if I had a baby in
the toilet!' (B118)

12 The connections implied here seem particularly appropriate when we note Mary Douglas's contention that when 'we have social units whose external boundaries are clearly marked, whose internal relations are confused ... then we should look for the active witchcraft type of cosmology.' Indeed, the symbolism of witchcraft in general reveals a great deal of overlap with the symbolism characteristic of Canadian literature. 'A closer look at the symbolism of witchcraft shows the dominance of symbols of inside and outside,' Douglas continues. 'The witch himself is someone whose inside is corrupt; he works harm on his victims by attacking their pure, innocent insides. Sometimes he sucks out their souls and leaves them with empty husks, sometimes he poisons their food, sometimes he throws darts which pierce their bodies. And then again, sometimes he needs access to their inner bodily juices, faeces, semen, spittle, before he can hurt them. Often such bodily excretions are the weapons of his craft' (138-9).

13 'Canadians, [T.E. Farley] contends, have ignored the implications of their actual experience to the point where their authentic identity lies stillborn in the unconscious, at any rate in the realm of the inarticulate, so that they remain divided within and against themselves. Precisely such a state of affairs is symbolized by the images we have been looking at, the images of the drowned poet, the sleeping shepherd, the dreaming Adam under the snow. One of the examples clearly implies that we shall continue to be plagued by feelings of guilt, by "an exquisite parching for the taste of completion," until we are willing to surrender ourselves to our authentic experience, until we are willing to be the tree and the stone and the thread of moss and the crystal of snow' (Jones A29).

14 In Tom Marshall's words, 'The piper succeeds in finding his place within the great tradition, but the strain costs him his life. Only in dream or death ... can the two worlds be joined' (25).

15 'The final stages of an evening's drunkenness would see her reaching into her suitcase to bring out the copies of Audubon drawings. Hardly able to talk around a slur now she'd interpret the damned birds, *damned*, as she saw them, for she was sure John James Audubon was attracted to psychologically neurotic creatures. She showed him the drawing of the Purple Gallinule ... the Prophet Ibis ... the Cerulean Wood Warbler drunk on Spanish Mulberry, and her favourite – the Anhinga, the Water Turkey, which she said would sit in the tree tops till disturbed and then plummet down into the river leaving hardly a ripple and swim off with just its eyes and beak cresting water – or if disturbed further would hide by submerging completely and walk along the river bottom, forgetting to breathe, and so drown' (25).

16 George Levine, 'Realism Reconsidered' in John Halperin, ed., *The Theory of the Novel: New Essays* (Oxford 1974) 249. André Malraux outlines the parallel development that took place in art: 'the distinguishing feature of modern art is that it *never* tells a story.' As Victorian certainties evaporated, 'the "subject" [that is, the historical fiction] was bound to disappear, because a new subject was coming to the fore, to the exclusion of all others, and this new subject was the presence of the artist himself upon his canvas.' *The Voices of Silence*, trans. Stuart Gilbert (Princeton 1978) 100, 101

17 'As Croce has said, "Before the work of art, we stand as if in the very presence of the creation of the world." In the perfect coalescence of feeling with image, the original aesthetic constructivity accomplishes perfectly what neither waking-state reality nor dream can accomplish separately – it lends wakeful reality to the dream, and dream-like liberating spontaneity to wakeful life. In this sense, the work of art implies that all reality is something that is *made*, or that the possibility of its free and unrestricted making and unmaking stands prior to any and all of its actual formations so that none can have ultimacy of being and meaning for the existent. The very presence of the presence which is art casts a veil of illusion over all the hard, fast, and pressing realities, even if only by comparison ... Who in the seizure of the musical

masterpiece has not felt with Schopenhauer the presence of the Will behind reality itself, and the surrounding world as only a representation of it.' Arturo Fallico, *Art & Existentialism* (Prentice-Hall 1962) 60-1

18 Edward Lucie-Smith, *Late Modern: The Visual Arts since 1945* (Oxford 1975) 10

19 Camus, *The Plague*, trans. Stuart Gilbert (Knopf 1977) 278

20 Pearce, *The Continuity of American Poetry* (Princeton 1967) 19

21 It is interesting that in describing reactions to the shock of modernity, André LeVot, for all his attempt to place American writing in a 'world' – that is, European – context, falls back on exactly the same terms that Pearce uses with respect to traditional American poets. 'Apparently as naked and guiltless as Adam, and as unburdened with memory, the writer starts naming his strange world, inventing a new syntax, a new way of telling his experience.' 'With the new fictionalists, from Burroughs to Barthelme, from Hawkes to Coover, one becomes aware of the disappearance of both the militant faith of naturalists like Dreiser or Steinbeck, and of the charismatic image of the Writer as the receptacle and defender of the essential cultural values' ('Disjunctive and Conjunctive Modes in Contemporary American Fiction,' *Forum* 14, 1 [1976] 46, 45). LeVot's writers may have been pushed to a new point of extremity by their world context, they may express themselves by way of new models, but this description makes it very clear that *in essence* they are merely playing the same game as Whitman.

22 Richard Poirier, *The Performing Self: Compositions and Decompositions in the Languages of Contemporary Life* (Oxford 1971) 87. In Mailer, adds Poirier, 'we have the case of a writer who really believes that when he is "working up the metaphor" he is involved in an act of historical as well as of self-transformation' (93).

23 Lucie-Smith, quoting Harold Rosenberg, the chief theorist of Abstract Expressionism, in *Late Modern*, 36

24 Glicksberg, 'Experimental Fiction: Innovation versus Form,' *CentR* 18 (1974) 146

25 Sale, 'The Golden Age of the American Novel,' *Ploughshares* 4, 3 (1978) 132

26 'Characters (Contra Characterization) in the Contemporary Novel' in Halperin 145. Schultz points out that 'For Nabokov the raw data of experience is not reality, is indeed at the farthest remove from reality. Hence the realistic novel which attempts verisimilitude is unreal paradoxically in direct ratio to its approximation to raw data. In actuality, as Nabokov knows, but which we conveniently forget, the realistic novel can never be anything other than a parody of the external world, no matter how hard it tries to imitate it, since the image of that world can never be equivalent to the object. Reality for Nabokov is rather the pattern which the imagination can discern in or create out of the raw data. Reality then is basically the product of a creative or imaginative act – an artistic act. And the more complex is the pattern the more "real," that is, the more comprehensive and inclusive, the "reality."'

27 In Louis Mink's words, 'Just as one conceptual presupposition of common sense has been that historiography consists of narratives which claim to be true, while fiction consists of imaginative narratives for which belief and therefore truth-claims are

suspended, so another presupposition has been that historical actuality itself has narrative form, which the historian does not invent but discovers, or attempts to discover.' 'Narrative Form as a Cognitive Instrument' in Robert H. Canary and Henry Kozicki, eds., *The Writing of History: Literary Form and Historical Understanding* (U. Wisconsin 1978) 134

28 As Glenys Stow points out, the implied propriety of maintaining a tentative – that is, non-aggressive – narrative stance is underlined by the author's treatment of Alf Dobble, the aggressive entrepreneur. 'The desire to manipulate the future is to O'Hagan the overpowering sin' (A178).

29 It is interesting that Wallace Stegner uses the town dump at Whitmund as a jumping-off place for his memoir-history of Canadian frontier life. See *Wolf Willow* 31-6.

30 A number of Canadian poets, and Frank Davey in particular, have elevated the idea that a writer should 'submit' himself to his material to the level of an aesthetic dictum. 'It is my view,' says the latter, '...that there is a place in the writing of poetry for *discipline* and *control*. And not at all a small one. But *discipline* and *control* are never in any way to be applied to the poem; rather they are to be applied to the poet himself. It is our view that the poem, like the short story, the novel, the dance, the piece of sculpture, has its own laws, its own directions, its own disciplines, and that these are to be strictly submitted to by the poet rather than ignored in favor of his own predilections' (E27).

31 It is possible to speculate that even Borduas felt some ambivalence about the tenets of his own school. Barry Lord claims that 'Borduas' example is that of colonial. He does not grasp this space with the confident sweep of a Pollock or a Kline; instead, he qualifies it with signs of tension all over his canvas' (163).

32 Malcolm Bowie, 'Jacques Lacan' in Geoffrey Sturrock, ed., *Structuralism and Since: From Lévi-Strauss to Derrida* (Oxford 1979) 136

33 C.G. Jung, *Psychological Types*, trans. H.G. Baynes, rev. R.F.C. Hull (Princeton 1976) 138. Jung continues: 'The Dionysian is the horror of the annihilation of the *principium individuationis* and at the same time "rapturous delight" in its destruction. It is therefore comparable to intoxication, which dissolves the individual into his collective instincts and components – an explosion of the isolated ego through the world. Hence, in the Dionysian orgy, man finds man: "alienated Nature, hostile or enslaved, celebrates once more her feast of reconciliation with her prodigal son – Man."' Very un-Canadian!

34 The symbolic conflation suggested here is not uniquely Canadian, of course – American neo-Freudian Norman O. Brown, for instance, describes the 'boundary between the self and the external world' as a 'model for the boundary between the ego and the id' (*Love's Body* [Vintage 1966] 148) – but rarely is the connection made so obsessively. Frye, indeed, claims that it is a primary distinguishing characteristic of recent Canadian poetry. 'Earlier Canadian poetry was full of solitude and loneliness, of the hostility or indifference of nature, of the fragility of human life and values in

such an environment. Contemporary Canadian poetry seems to think rather of this outer leviathan as a kind of objective correlative of some Minotaur that we find in our own mental labyrinths. The mind has become a dark chamber, or *camera obscura*, and its pictures are reflections of what is at once physical and human nature' (D42).

35 'I've decided that in some sense fantasy and reality share really a lot, and that the things they share are often much more important than their differences. As far as I'm concerned in my writing now, I draw almost no distinction between the two. There can be so-called fantasy experiences which are unreal, or they can be real, and the same with reality experiences. It all depends on how one is connected to it' (C81).

36 Alan Warren Friedman, 'The Modern Multivalent Novel: Form and Function' in Halperin, 123

37 Spencer, *Space, Time and Structure in the Modern Novel* (NYU 1971) xxi-xxii

38 Seymour Chatman, *Story and Discourse: Narrative Structure in Fiction and Film* (Cornell 1980) 148

39 Ryf, 'Character and Imagination in the Experimental Novel,' *MFS* 20, 3 (1974) 324

40 Puetz, 'Imagination and Self-Definition,' *PR* 14 (1977) 139

41 It is interesting that these ironies are conveyed most sharply through the 'found' elements of Wiebe's narration. As Patricia Morley describes it, for instance, 'Big Bear's sojourn in prison is told through pastiche, by juxtaposing three newspaper clippings from *The Globe* ... *The Saskatchewan Herald* ... and *The Toronto Mail* ... The writer of the first article appears to be impartial. He informs his reader that Big Bear is learning to be a carpenter and that the half-breeds are docile and contrite. The writer allows himself a few conjectures such as the longing for the Plains that must lurk in Big Bear's eyes. The second clipping states that Robert Hodson has been appointed public hangman for the Dominion. Hodson was cook to the McLean family and suffered the two months Indian captivity with them. (Hodson appears in Big Bear's nightmarish visions after the latter's release from prison.) The third newspaper article is obviously by someone who thinks, with Stanley "Pointnose" Simpson, that good Indians are dead ones. He describes Big Bear as a small "weazen-faced chap, with a cunning, restless look." The reporter's prejudices shape up some beautiful ironies, not the least of which is Poundmaker's comment that it was sometimes hard to say what the truth was' (A104-5).

42 Feidelson, *Symbolism and American Literature* (U. Chicago 1953) 31

43 Though it is popularly held that 'conceptual art' is self-validated on intellectual if not aesthetic grounds, the *practice* of such art, as Lucie-Smith points out, would seem rather to represent a new extreme of egocentricity. ' "Pure" conceptual art – an art of statements only, or an art in which the audience is asked to find its satisfaction by following the creator step by step in his thought processes, without asking that these should take a form more concrete than words or diagrams on paper ... seems to suffer from [a] kind of inappropriateness ... Indeed the public nature of an art exhibition too often seems hostile to what is being done by the conceptual artist. From the use of deliberately "inappropriate" materials and techniques, as with Dubuffet, twentieth-

century art has progressed to a deliberate mismatching of the means of expression and the framework within which it exists.

'In part, at least, this seems an inevitable consequence of the transference of interest from the art object to the artist' (275-6).

44 Such fables as *Metamorphosis*, where the protagonist is turned into an insect-object, illuminate Kafka's conviction that (in Michel Zéraffa's words) the 'radical transition from the personal to the impersonal ... signifies the death of civilization' (*Fictions: The Novel and Social Reality*, trans. Catherine and Tom Burns [Penguin 1976] 129). Atwood's heroine, while certainly sharing this particular fear, is equally terrified of the opposite possibility, the process of becoming a *person*.

45 Unfortunately, space does not permit a description that would do justice to the complex style of this book. To summarize very briefly, in Barbara Hehner's words, 'Stacey's story is told in blocks of third-person present-tense narrative, flush right and left; paragraphs of first-person present-tense thinking by Stacey, indented with a dash; passages of dialogue, without quotation marks, indented about an inch from the left margin; memories of Stacey's childhood, in third-person past tense, with smatterings of present participles (conversation within these memories is indicated by italics); and the interruption of radio and television broadcasts in block letters' (44).

46 Vernant, discussion following Roland Barthes' 'To Write: An Intransitive Verb?' in Richard Macksey and Eugenio Donato, ed., *The Structuralist Controversy: The Languages of Criticism and the Sciences of Man* (Johns Hopkins 1972) 152

47 Culler, *Structuralist Poetics: Structuralism, Linguistics, and the Study of Literature* (Cornell 1976) 196

48 'In contrasting information and evocation as two different functions of the image, I am merely reviving a distinction which was made by Sir Joshua Reynolds in his famous discussion of Gainsborough's portraits. As long as a portrait "in this undetermined manner" contains enough to remind the spectator of the sitter, "the imagination supplies the rest, and perhaps more satisfactorily ... than the artist, with all his care, could possibly have done." True, as Reynolds continues, the effect presupposes a knowledge of the sitter; in the absence of such knowledge the imagination may "assume almost what character or form it pleases." Evocation, in other words, relies even more on prior information than perspectival records.

'No doubt this is true. But the formula does not yet tell us what type of information we do need to bring the incomplete image to life. Perhaps it is less information than understanding that is involved. An intelligent woman who had her first baby relatively late in life observed that baby snapshots began to assume more vividness for her after she had experienced how babies move and react. It is this capacity to generalise, to move from the known to the less known, which must never be left out of account when discussing "the beholder's share."' Gombrich, 'Standards of Truth: The Arrested Image and the Moving Eye' in W.J.T. Mitchell, ed., *The Language of Images* (U. Chicago 1980) 211

49 Cavell, *The World Viewed: Reflections on the Ontology of Film* (Harvard 1979) 23

50 'Essay on the Objective of Plastic Art in Our Time' in Walter Michel & C.J. Fox, eds., *Wyndham Lewis on Art: Collected Writings 1913-1956* (Funk & Wagnalls 1969) 214-15

51 Adding to the illusion of narrative passivity implicit in film is the fact that Canadian film-makers have an anomalous proclivity, as Peter Harcourt points out, for 'films that create the world through the eyes of a young child. Claude Jutra's *Mon oncle Antoine* and Francis Mankiewicz's *Le temps d'une chasse* immediately spring to mind; but *Lies My Father Told Me* and *Lions for Breakfast* work in much the same way. If we extend the age to take in all the young, then the list of films is enormous – in terms of richness and productivity, virtually the Canadian equivalent of the American Western!' (14).

52 Heidegger, *Poetry, Language, and Thought* (Harper Colophon 1975) 67

53 As George Levine points out, 'romance can be stipulatively defined as a form in which pattern dominates over plausibility, in which the central figure achieves the fullest possible freedom from the limitations of a restricting context, in which ideal values are worked out and shown to be viable,' whereas 'Realism attempts to create the illusion of non-fiction as the writer struggles to come to terms with, as Frye puts it, "things as they are and not as the story-teller would like them to be for his convenience."' In Halperin 238-9

54 Significantly, Ortega y Gasset makes a connection between super-realism, which would seem to be pre-eminently objective, and surrealism, which is conventionally subjective. 'From the standpoint of ordinary human life things appear in a natural order, a definite hierarchy. Some seem very important, some less so, and some altogether negligible. To satisfy the desire for dehumanization one need not alter the inherent nature of things. It is enough to upset the value pattern and to produce an art in which the small events of life appear in the foreground with monumental dimensions.

   Here we have the connecting link between two seemingly very different manners of modern art, the surrealism of metaphors and what may be called infrarealism. Both satisfy the urge to escape and elude reality. Instead of soaring to poetical heights, art may dive beneath the level marked by the natural perspective. How it is possible to overcome realism by merely putting too fine a point on it and discovering, lens in hand, the micro-structure of life can be observed in Proust, Ramón Gómez de la Serna, Joyce.

   ... The procedure simply consists in letting the outskirts of attention, that which ordinarily escapes notice, perform the main part in life's drama.' *The Dehumanization of Art* (Doubleday 1956) 32-3

55 Much of the sinister undertone stems from the unnaturally complete accessibility of detail. It may be that magic realism simulates visual acuity to such an extent specifically because the artist wants to emphasize that the apparent enigma is an attribute of reality rather than a function of either the viewer's expectations or his

capacity to 'see.' Gombrich examines the problem of reconciling fidelity to fact with fidelity to vision in 'Standards of Truth.'

56 See Jacques Choron, *Death and Western Thought* (Collier 1963) 225 for a description of this aspect of Kierkegaard's thought.

57 It is interesting, considering what I have said of the self-aggrandizing tendencies not merely of the American but, more covertly, of the existentialist stance, that Karsten Harries finds a distinctly romantic strain in Heidegger. 'Such a view of authentic existence may suggest a heroic nihilism, a faith in the meaning of life in spite of, or perhaps rather because of a lucid awareness of the nothingness that governs human existence and that dooms man and all his projects ... to certain defeat. Perhaps this attempt to salvage victory from defeat, meaning from nothing, is particularly German. *Being and Time* reads in places as if Heidegger has been inspired by the *Nieblungenlied*, as if its hero were dark Hagen, who stands beyond good and evil, whose life is shadowed by death, who possesses the strength to accept the certainty of defeat, responding to it with an affirmation of the situation into which he has been cast, and who discovers meaning in this affirmation.' 'Fundamental Ontology and the Search for Man's Place' in Michael Murray, ed., *Heidegger and Modern Philosophy: Critical Essays* (Yale 1978) 78

58 Kaminsky, 'On Literary Realism' in Halperin 227

59 Brombert, *The Intellectual Hero: Studies in the French Novel 1880-1955* (U. Chicago 1964) 209

60 Many of the significant 'things' that do turn up in French literature – such as Roquentin's little snatch of jazz tune – are objects of art, not objects of nature. Jean Cocteau's remarkable film, *The Blood of a Poet*, with its self-animating portrait and statue, provides a striking demonstration of this propensity.

61 Hugh Hood claims the imagist program for himself (A, esp. 97-8); D.G. Jones proclaims it as a *donnée* for a significant proportion of the Canadian corpus: 'No ideas but in things, said William Carlos Williams. The current influence of American poetry on the younger generation of Canadian poets is not merely a fad, but stems from a common conviction. In varying degrees Bowering or Newlove, Nowlan or Purdy share with Williams a common distrust of conventional forms, rhythms, diction, and imagery, and a common desire to explore and articulate those aspects of their experience that are ignored or denied or simply distorted by the traditional matrix of language. Here is the reason for the continuing vitality of imagism ... among a number of the more recent Canadian writers. To tell it as it is, to name and define a world of inarticulate feeling ... the imagist program provides a basic method. Avoid the dictionaries groaning with lies; present an image, the thing in itself' (A168).

62 Geoffrey Hartman has some interesting comments on this phenomenon. 'There is meaning, there is an object focussed on, but there is also something cleaner than both: the very edge of the pen/knife that cuts or delineates these lines. "A word is a word most," Williams wrote, "when it is separated out by science, treated with acid to

remove the smudges, washed, dried and placed right side up on a clean surface.... It may be used not to smear it again with thinking (the attachments of thought) but in such a way that it will remain scrupulously itself, clean perfect, unnicked, beside other words in parade. There must be edges."

'The cleanliness, however, of Williams's phrasing depends so much on what is edged out that we become more interested in what is not there than in what is. The red wheelbarrow moves us into the forgetfulness of pure perception, but also suggests someone can't stand his own mind; it is as functional a carrier of the cultural surplus or whatever nonplusses clean thinking as Ford's slick cars and other vehicular gadgets made in America . The strength of *pure* poetry resides, then, like all poetry, in the impure elements it cuts out, elides, covers up, negates, represses.' *Criticism in the Wilderness* (Yale 1980) 120-1

63 Charles Russell, 'The Vault of Language: Self-Reflective Artifice in Contemporary American Fiction,' *MFS* 20, 3 (1974) 354

64 See Arlen J. Hansen, 'The Celebration of Solipsism: A New Trend in American Fiction' *MFS* 19, 1 (1973) 5-15.

65 Hassan, *Radical Innocence: Studies in the Contemporary American Novel* (Princeton 1961) 105

66 Harvey, 'Character and the Context of Things' in James Calderwood and Harold Toliver, eds., *Perspectives on Fiction* (Oxford 1968) 363

67 The 'grotesque' element that Margot Northey finds to be so pervasive throughout Canadian literature is obviously related to the same phenomenon inasmuch as this feature is rooted above all in unexpected or inappropriate juxtapositions. As Northey describes it, 'it is possible to provide a working definition of the grotesque as an aesthetic term, referring to a mode of writing rather than a condition or attribute of nature: the grotesque emphasizes incongruity, disorder, and deformity, and arises from the juxtaposition or clash of the ideal with the real, the psychic with the physical, or the concrete with the symbolic' (7).

11

The Writing on the Wall[1]

Robinson Crusoe may be a nerve without a shell; he may be afraid of his own shadow, but he has the instincts of his vulnerability. Like a mollusk, he knows how to secrete around him a thick wall-like skin. Robinson Crusoe never stops building walls. For twenty-eight years of the 'silent life,' he ramifies, reinforces, camouflages, and naturalizes the walls of his enclosure ... When [he] decides that he must protect his home base so that he can live with peace of mind, he plants a thicket of tall, pointed stakes in the ground in the form of a wide semicircle, spending months at the task. 'The piles or stakes, which were as heavy as I could well lift, were a long time in cutting and preparing in the woods, and more by far in bringing home, so that I spent sometimes two days in bringing home one of those posts, and a third day driving it into the ground ...' Here is Robinson Crusoe doing what he does best: laboring day in, day out, repeating his clumsy, persistent craftsmanship until it is almost ritualized, a psychic wall against loneliness.[2]

Note has already been made of the Canadian's family resemblance to Robinson Crusoe (see p 43; also C. Thomas B). We too build walls, not merely to keep danger out but to *mediate* between us and otherness. Walls, after all, are not only the limits of the interior but the inner edge of the exterior as well. That inner edge must be constructed with care to give a semblance of safety and familiarity to the alien element that environs us. How do we manage this job of construction? For Malcolm Lowry, says Geoffrey Durrant, 'meaninglessness and isolation are Hell, and ... the creation of a Paradise depends directly on the discovery or the attribution of significances ... For such a writer, the way out of solipsism cannot be a return to the common-sense world of solid objects and solid citizens; it must be sought in the interpretation of the world as a language' (64). Lowry's situation is the Canadian's situation. Only by *explicating* the raw data of our experience, by *pinning down* meaning and relation, can we establish the safe, familiar home which, paradoxically, may naturalize the other. 'The relationship between man and space is none other than dwelling,' explains Heidegger.[3] This is why, if the artist in our culture ventures little in his own voice, the speaking artifact, though hedged around with taboos, nevertheless achieves an importance for the Canadian process of self-identification even beyond the fairly conventional kinds of 'making,' persona-fication, invoked at the beginning of the last chapter.

The most basic phase of our world-constructive activity comprises simply a scrutinization – an almost compulsive counting over – of the conceptual components of our experiential set. Notwithstanding the object-obsession noted in the last chapter, we are concerned not merely to acknowledge 'things' in their diversity, but to *seize hold of* (if not penetrate into) the enigma of their presence, to *place* them, to determine how they *fit in*. The exemplary occasion for this kind of exercise is provided by the photograph. Even more than the film, the photograph stands as a uniquely appropriate iconic representation of phenomenal reality as it is apprehended by the Canadian: a set of discrete and almost wholly disconnected elements. Or rather, it expresses with particular vividness our *ideas* of that reality. The basis for this appeal lies with an apparently inherent ambivalence of signification. On the one hand the photograph seems to be ineluctably true-to-life. Photography, says Stanley Cavell, satisfies 'the human wish, intensifying in the West since the Reformation, to escape subjectivity and metaphysical isolation – a wish for the power to reach this world, having for so long tried, at last hopelessly, to manifest fidelity to another.' On the other hand, its self-evident transparency is matched by a reticence equivalent to the opaqueness of the object-in-itself. 'The image is not a likeness; it is not exactly a replica, or a relic, or a shadow, or an apparition either, though all of these natural candidates share a striking feature with photographs – an aura or history of magic surrounding them.' The photograph, indeed – and this, as Cavell notes, is at the root of its fascination – 'holds reality from us ... holds reality before us, i.e., withholds reality before us.'[4] This is exactly what life itself seems to do. It's no wonder, then, that the photograph has been seized upon by so many Canadian writers not merely as *representation* but, paradoxically, also as the very type of *non-representational* assertion.

It does not follow, mind you, that the photograph has simply become a kind of communal symbol – not if by this we intend to imply any homogeneity of meaning. Indeed, its literary functions are almost infinitely diverse. One can find major instances in the work of Margaret Atwood, Matt Cohen, Al Purdy, A.M. Klein, Daphne Marlatt, Robert Kroetsch, Margaret Laurence, Alice Munro, Alden Nowlan, Michael Ondaatje, Florence MacNeil, Audrey Thomas – well, the list could go on for half a page – where the photograph has been used in as many different ways as there are users: a point of departure, a sign of fulfilment, a clue, a denial, a promise, a nexus of meaning or emotion. The one thing that is consistent, though, is that *whatever* any particular photograph may seem overtly to represent, like the window symbol it generally carries along with it some suggestion of moral or emotional equivocation. The same duplicity that constitutes its appeal, that is, also renders the image extremely problematic. At times the ambivalence evoked seems merely connected with a kind of nostalgia, a sense of betrayal of or by the past. In MacNeil's 'Home Movies' the re-viewed film – which, in its artlessness and discontinuity, represents something closer to a snapshot album than the movie proper we have examined elsewhere – seems associated primarily with the speaker's feelings of guilt for neglect, for forgetfulness, maybe simply for growing up and away ('I am among them tentatively/ as a shadow wavering on the rocks/ then growing strong/ I am a hand/ that breaks into a rash of promises/ before the haloes dim/ and the promises merge into/ unaccountable dots' 130); in Thomas's *Mrs Blood*, alternately, it is the protagonist herself, bodied forth as 'A stranger. A face in a blurred mirror' (194), who is misconstrued. More significant, however, are those cases – and they are numerous – implying that some radical betrayal (whether of the observer or the observed is not always clear) is inherent in the nature of photography itself. At best this produces an uneasiness, as in Daphne Marlatt's *Frames*, about the photograph's facility in substituting verisimilitude for 'truth,' its susceptibility to trickery; at worst, as if the concept of *nature morte* were literal rather than figurative, by focusing on the photograph's tendency to freeze or fix its objects, draining them of life by lifting them unnaturally out of the flux of time, it produces a disquieting image of art as an act of violence against the world. This is the aspect emphasized in the motif of the photographer-as-killer, a category that would include not only Ondaatje's machine-like Billy (the most obvious example, amply elucidated by recent critics[5]) but also such figures as Del Jordan's evil Photographer ('People saw that in his pictures they had aged twenty or thirty years. Middle-aged people saw in their own features the terrible, growing, inescapable likeness of their dead parents; young fresh girls and men showed what gaunt or dulled or stupid faces they would have when they were fifty.' D205) and Marian McAlpin's gun-and-camera-crazy fiancé in *The Edible Woman*, that 'dark, intent marksman with his aiming eye ... a homicidal maniac with a lethal weapon in his hands' (257). The photograph, as a means of mediating experience, is evidently both effective *and* disturbing.

This two-sidedness sets the tone for a wide range of Canadian usages. The same fundamental ambivalence tends to be evoked, though not usually so openly, by a number of other iconic devices commonly employed by Canadian writers for symbolically organizing or explicating the raw data of perceptual/ conceptual experience. Since these features, though appearing for the most part as subsidiary and occasional motifs related to character development, are in fact propaedeutic to important larger structures of the Canadian oeuvre, it is worth taking the time for a brief survey of the basic types. These may be divided into three groups depending on whether the area of scrutiny is the relation between signs and things, things and things, or self and things, with a fourth group subsuming functions of all the other three.

WORDPLAY

Many Canadian writers reveal a gleeful fascination with different aspects of language or even isolated words, ranging from the *sensuous* ('I loved the sound of that word,' says Del Jordan of 'tomb,' '... I did not know what it was, or had got it mixed up with womb, and I saw us inside some sort of hollow marble egg, filled with blue light' Munro D45), through the *scholarly* (Earle Birney's interest in Old English; Klein's encyclopaedic sounding of semiotic resources from calligraphy through cabbalistic symbology), to the *political* (the use of *joual* by young Québécois writers in the late sixties–early seventies was interpreted as a 'radical protest against all the values of earlier generations' Falardeau 108). Under the enthusiasm, however, is a perceptible tension. One problem simply concerns the potential words reveal for betraying the speaker. Much of Laurence's work, as T.Q. Dombrowski points out, focuses on the conflict between, on the one hand, the terrible need her protagonists feel to *explain* themselves and, on the other, their inability – due either to speechlessness or, worse, ill-placed volubility – to do so. 'Despite their earnest efforts to control their speech, Laurence's characters again and again speak in a manner that defies their own intentions' (56). Another, more serious problem, though, is signalled by an apparent uncertainty about what it is exactly that words can or should *do*. A primary function is the ritual of *naming* necessary in a new land,[6] not exactly as an act of assimilation (as Dorothy Livesay's poem 'The Colour of God's Face' reveals, those who are truly at home in a place – who feel 'Between the land and themselves/ ... no difference' 58 – have no need to label it) but more as an attempt on the part of the *un*assimilated to control or coerce what is alien. 'A name is the magic to keep it within the horizons,' says Howard O'Hagan in *Tay John*. 'Put a name to it ... and you've got it' (80). Going one step beyond this is the attempt, by imposing a vision – like the railway builders of E.J. Pratt's *Towards the Last Spike*[7] – to use words not merely to name but to *transform*. Already at this stage we find predictable uneasiness about the consequences of manipulation, of introducing 'interest' to upset the natural correlation between signifier and signified. Finally, there is the ultimate presumption – as in bp Nichol's *The Martyrology* ('the document of a phenomenological quest to follow language ... on [a] voyage of discovery that is [a] life-long poem' Barbour A98) – of purporting to *replace* the object with the name, give the order of the signifier a reality quite independent of the signified. This is where the whole process blows up. The Canadian, for reasons we saw in the last chapter, cannot believe that reality will allow itself to be circumvented in this way. Reality is out there, waiting to pounce. And since words are one of our very limited means of relating to it, we cannot bear to have their mediating function undercut. *We cannot bear any suggestion that words don't mean something real.* On the other hand, this bias creates its own difficulties, because we also find it hard to believe that any extension of self such as language *can* comprehend otherness to any significant extent. 'How could that colour be caught in words?' asks Morag in *The Diviners.* 'A sort of rosy peach colour, but that sounded corny and was also inaccurate' (4). As a result of these seriously mixed feelings what we find is that a kind of nervous playing with or on or against the lexical-literal level of discourse occurs so consistently as to suggest that writers are trying to creep up obliquely on the whole stressful question of meaning. 'They use the word "cope" a lot,' muses the protagonist of *Mrs Blood*: ' "Oh we'll just have to cope." I see them all invested with a bishop's mantle or the conical cap of the Archbishop of Canterbury. Yet I'm not sure what a cope is. I must ask for a dictionary. I have no cope, I cannot cope. I have no hope! Skip rope. My doctor gives a little hop and skip, a sort of shy little dance as he advances into the ward every morning' (13).

CATALOGUES

Following quite naturally from the object-orientation discussed in the last chapter, even more than their preoccupation with words and images Canadian writers also show a penchant for lists, inventories, genealogies, and catalogues. Kroetsch, for instance, uses the device not just as a means of mediating between theme and content ('more often than not for him the lists gravitate, as his world does, toward a subsuming metaphoric vision,' says Eli Mandel A64) but in some cases – most notably *Seed Catalogue* – as the structural control to an entire work. What lies behind such a preference? One element obviously relates to the fact that lists, being conceptual rather than physical 'collections,' allow us a means of dealing with 'things' indirectly. More important, however, is that catalogues offer us the odd capacity to *arrange* reality without *manipulating* it. As Robert Harbison points out, the true catalogue is absolutely unhierarchical. Just as a 'sketch selects and magisterially directs; a catalogue abdicates responsibility, presents everything as of equal value, is not a moral form.'[8] It's easy to see how such a thing would appeal to an artist who wanted to eschew artistry in favour of the 'given.' At the same time, catalogues – for all their neutrality – do succeed in reducing chaos to consistency, blotting out the 'awful, anarchic inner voice' (as Marian Engel's Lou describes it when she turns to her own task of cataloguing as a defence against the creeping irrationality of her obsession with the bear, 92) and giving us at least an illusion of order. How? Subsuming everything – often quite arbitrarily – under one head, 'They take a mélange and make it into a consistent porridge, so that wherever we are in them we are in the same place' [Harbison 155]. The essence of the catalogue, in other words, is not the presumptuous imposition of an egocentric standard of value (if Dionysian spontaneity frightens us, so too – in a different sort of way – does the Apollonian vision with its 'paranoic desire for light,' its determination to 'control life as it were from the outside' Jones B19), but, rather, the almost ritual reduction of otherness to a state of belonging.

Such a contrivance has obvious advantages for an inadequately mythologized country. What better way to comprehend such an indigestible diversity as (in Kroetsch's poem) 'lives ... letters, documents, memories, speech, stories, big stories and little stories, invocations and epilogues, first and last words, loves and deaths, emptiness, all that the prairie wasn't, could not be, its absences, emptiness and fulfilment, the plenitude of being. Seeds and catalogues, the books we read' (Mandel B119)? From this point of view the catalogue simply offers a way of assimilating the vast experiential data we are confronted with. This isn't all, though. Beyond its basic function the catalogue also reveals a mysterious capacity to console. One of the first things we notice in surveying the field is that this second category of conceptual device lacks almost entirely the undercurrent of anxiety we detect elsewhere. That's because the ambivalence has already been mediated by the duplicity of the form. The key – as, indeed, I implied above when I mentioned 'illusion' – lies in the fact that while the *act* of ordering is noticeably lacking, the *appearance* of ordering is not. Like the young protagonist of Clark Blaise's *Lunar Attractions*, an amateur archaeologist, we are consequently enabled to pretend that we have the capacity – the nerve – to 'collect and not merely to gather,' to 'Pluck significance from chaos,' while at the same time reassuring ourselves that *without* our intervention everything may be accommodated, confirmed in its own importance, its own place: '"Everything is priceless," he said, "Sticks that the kids played with. Bones that they threw to their dogs. Everything is precious. Everything"' (202). Thus it is that Laurence's Morag, purporting to view Catharine Parr Traill as a desirable model of domestic discipline, in the end, far from learning any real lessons, finds solace in a ritual recitation of her idol's lists and catalogues.[9] Thus it is, too – and even more significantly – that Rudy Wiebe, numbering over his sources in 'On the Trail of Big Bear' (people; books and pamphlets; the Sessional Papers of the Parliament of Canada; the diaries, notes, speeches, personal letters, memoirs, interviews; the calendar; newspapers; pictures; maps and places, 47-8), can tacitly suggest, firstly, that all these data have meaningful interrelation, and secondly, somewhat inconsistently, that they are comprehensive, unselected, and entirely uncontrived. Simply to list is somehow, almost magically, to assert the presence of meaning.

GEOMETRIFICATION

The third and in some ways most interesting of the Canadian's tools for arranging his conceptual world – in this case for exploring the position of the self with relation to its field of action – is the graphic analogy. In particular, loaded references to lines and circles abound throughout the corpus, dragging in their wake a complicated vision of alternate and possibly antithetic philosophies of life. How does this work? In Jack Hodgins's *The Invention of the World*, to give one fairly simple example, the straight line is associated with Julius Champney, town planning, and order, while the circle suggests Wade Powers' dungeon. As the book sets them up, each of these symbolic poles has its own claims, its own pros and cons. The line represents not merely regimentation but poetry; the dungeon, as noted above, is both cage and cave. Together they irradiate the book with a healthy tension. This, then, is the line/circle game at its best. Unfortunately it doesn't always turn out this way. Usually, in fact, the invocation of opposites invokes as well anxiety, confusion, even – as in Robert Harlow's *Scann* – radical ambivalence: '[H]e is not obsessed. He does not push himself along straight lines' (39); '"Straight Lines Lead to Traps"' (210); 'He wonders with humility if he is going in circles again. Perhaps. But in the blind dark what difference is there between a circle and a straight line' (254); 'A good Linden grin is a straight line. *Via Dolorosas* are straight lines also' (292). Beyond the exploratory abstraction here, the personal uneasiness is palpable. Why?

Part of it, no doubt, is simply the built-in uncertainty of our own existential position. As has been amply demonstrated, Canadians relate most naturally to the circle position. On the other hand, recognizing our vulnerability, when it comes to regulating our relations with the world at large we are inclined to depend upon those people and principles representing line-like aggression. In the last decade this basic quandary has been both intensified and obscured by an overlay of imported American primitivism. As a result, instead of a neutralized vision of the natural and the social in dynamic juxtaposition (see Wiebe c30), what we frequently find in post-sixties fiction, at least on the surface, are moral fables like Don Gutteridge's *Riel*, in which the natural, the circular, has become almost wholly beneficent. *Underneath* the surface, however – as we might predict – a good deal of at least vestigial disquietude still lurks, not just because we are nervous of the 'American' alternative ('The imposition of the straight line on the curve tends to get seen by those doing the imposing as part of the Divine Plan, and that can lead to a good deal of intolerance and rigidity,' says Atwood; 'the American way, by contrast, can lead to a good deal of violence' f122) but more because our national tendency to identify the aggressive principle *with* rather than *against* nature upsets the whole symbolic equation. We see this clearly if we look at the emotional associations commonly evoked by the road or railway in our literature. To Gutteridge the iron rails cutting across the prairies are unequivocally evil, but to most others, even those otherwise primitivistically inclined, they represent not merely communication, human contact,[10] but *safety*. 'All his attention was concentrated on not straying off the road,' we are told of Anthyme in Roch Carrier's *Floralie, où es-tu?*. 'Because men just as solid as him, just as strong, had not followed the paths, they had been forced to remain in the forest forever and lumberjacks had found their clean white skeletons in the green grass with flowers growing inside them' (38). With this vision hovering in the background it is small wonder that Canadians, like Wallace Stegner's younger self, despite their ostensible circle-orientation tend to value highly the trails they are able to impose ('They were ceremonial,' says Stegner, 'an insistence not only that we had a right to be in sight on the prairie but that we owned and controlled a piece of it' 271) not despite but *because of* the fact that they violate nature.[11]

This feeling alters considerably the thrust of at least the more thoughtful treatments of the primitivistic theme. Wiebe's *The Temptations of Big Bear* appears at first to be quite unequivocally on the side of nature (the line-oriented white men are disorderly, devouring, frenetically restless[12]; their surveys slice open the land like a knife until 'broad lines of stark bleached bones ... [are] spread straight, pressed and flattened' as far as one can see, 409) but if we read closely we soon realize that the message is far from unequivocal. Not only are the natives, explicitly identified with the circle of the seasons, the all-embracing curve of earth and sky, dependent on the white man's Law, the 'word' of power that is 'always the same' (144), for protection and sustenance, but nature itself is frequently imaged, at least covertly, as brutal and unforgiving: 'The last red edge of the sun slashed across his closed, monolithic face' (388). Why the ambivalence? The problem is, the quiescence of the circle, of Wiebe's natives, suggests not merely nature but *death*, the ultimate still point in time, while violence, for all its threat, is, as John Moss indicates, at least *process*, a sign of 'the struggle for life and against death' (E27). Perhaps the Canadian's only real solution in the face of this conceptual dichotomy is Wiebe's solution, to reduce the irreconcilable linear and circular aspects of the human condition to the abstractions of pure pattern, language, style, where alone they may co-exist in harmony. As Tom Marshall points out, 'Technique can be a garrison too' (50).

MAPS

This last category not only completes the present listing but opens the subject up to a multitude of further ramifications. Even more than photographs, maps are probably *the* iconic artifact in the Canadian's conceptual vocabulary. We find them, or their equivalents, not merely as Atwood claims in 'exploration poems' (F115) but everywhere across the full spectrum of kinds in Canadian literature: Maggie's motley collection of highway maps, nautical charts, and timber survey maps in *The Invention of the World*; Peter Guy's mental river in *But We Are Exiles*; David Greenwood's treasured atlas in *Lunar Attractions*; the maps on the cover of Marlatt's *Steveston* and the frontispiece of Stegner's

Wolf Willow; perhaps even the 'concrete' maps implied by all the iconic cities that punctuate the oeuvre from Scott Symons's *Place d'Armes* to James Reaney's *Twelve Letters to a Small Town*. This is hardly surprising, of course. Even more than the act of naming the act of mapping is the first thing that is necessary in an unknown land. As Atwood puts it, 'Any map is better than no map as long as it is accurate, [because] knowing your starting points and your frame of reference is better than being suspended in a void' (F246). From this point of view the whole of fiction is in a sense a map, and its primary task the task of orienting us in our newfound world – an exercise for which *Wolf Willow* provides the definitive example. This fictionalized memoir, as Mandel describes it,

exercises a profound attraction ... not only because of [Stegner's] interest in defining west as a region, not always an easy thing to do, but for two other reasons: (1) his sense of definition as mapping, and (2) the place that is west for him. Like the miniature or model worlds that entrance other regional writers, I think of James Reaney, Robert Kroetsch and Clark Blaise in particular, for Stegner, maps provide boundaries; and boundaries are not only areas of rich interaction but of transformation too. His West ... lies at the center of, or on the edge of, extraordinary boundaries [such as] ... the line between past and present, the line between frontier culture and town culture, the line between north and south, the watershed of the rivers running to the Arctic and those running to the Gulf of Mexico, one of the great geographical and historical divisions of North America ... the ecological boundary of glaciated and unglaciated land, and the surveyor's boundary, the forty-ninth parallel; the book takes its definitions then in prehistory and history, in legend, romance, and personal memory. (B107)

The literary map thus facilitates and elucidates our relationship with otherness by naturalizing, quite literally, given portions of *terra incognita*. The significance of the map does not stop here, however. Indeed, by far its most important function is not to chart *particular* places but to provide an exemplary demonstration of how we may best conceptualize the self/other relation in a *general* sort of way.

What does this mean? Well, just as the catalogue, by modelling the relation between *things* and *things*, also implies a generalized model of the relationship elucidated by wordplay between *words* and *things*, the map generalizes the schematic relation between *self* and *things* examined in the last section. The map thus provides not merely an *instance of*, but a *pattern for* world construction. Indeed, we might go so far as to say, with Harbison, that in theory *as well as* in practice the map, as 'our main means of aligning ourselves with something bigger,' may actually be thought of as 'semireligious in nature' [124]. In this respect there are two features in particular that we should note. To begin with, inasmuch as they are deemed to be *isomorphic* with the terrain represented, maps are by convention 'true.' This makes us feel that we are dealing with reality in some form, rather than merely fiction. As Harbison points out, we place a faith in maps 'that we hardly ever do in ... paintings ... because we could follow the lines on the ground if we chose' [125]. Of course a map is obviously not 'really' a landscape, no matter how accurate it may be. What it provides us with, therefore – as in the case of the catalogue – is a conceptual tool that will allow us to deal with, indeed, literally to construct, a phenomenal world while simultaneously *dissociating ourselves from it.* Secondly, maps – again like catalogues – mediate the control/no control question. On the one hand they both confirm the general orderliness of the at-large ('the appearance of whimsy, of points labelled at random, is a cover for a rigidly determined order' [Harbison 125]) and rationalize our potential connection with all aspects of that realm. This creates the unalterable impression that we are integrated into an *a priori* network of processes and connections quite beyond our need or ability to manipulate. On the other hand, even while protecting us from the appearance of aggression, the map-as-model, by a kind of transference also suggests that the erstwhile resistant thing-world is in fact amenable to our desires. How? The element of 'planned similarity' in a map – the dictum that 'a "bend in a road" corresponds to a "bend in a line"'[13] – opens up the possibility that simply by changing the map (which isn't really coercion, since it belongs to the realm of self rather than other) we may actually change the world. This duplicity perhaps explains why Canadians, though they might disapprove of map-*makers* (line-imposers), seem universally intrigued by their product. 'She hated the maps, or what they showed her, says Hodgins of Maggie Kyle, 'and yet she could not have done without them' (44). Nor could any of us. '[C]onnect connect,' says Scann (Harlow 145) – in marked contrast to the 'American' F.'s 'Connect nothing' (L. Cohen 20). *It is exactly this that the map allows us to do!* Like the discredited humanist ideal of 'art,' it assures us of man's ability 'to turn chaos, disruption, meaninglessness into order, totality, significance.'[14]

Next question: if the map really is a model in the broad sense outlined here, how does this affect trends in Canadian literature? Actually, the connections revealed are both more direct and more highly visible than one might suppose. To put it simply, Canadians in general appear to prefer fictions that are 'like' maps to those that are not. What kinds of fictions are these? The answer to this may be inferred from a paper called 'The Rhetoric of Temporality' by Paul de Man which among other things demonstrates, or at least hints at, the extent to which a fundamentally anthropocentric world view – which Canada's obviously is – entails a specific, specialized literary response. As Anne Mellor summarizes,

Paul de Man begins his essay by calling into question the 'supremacy of the symbol, conceived as an expression of unity between the representative and the semantic function of language' ... between nature and language ... [He] later broadens his attack to include another, historically parallel, mystification: nineteenth-century realism ... For De Man, mimesis – the accurate reflection of nature in art – is no longer possible ... [because] there is an unbridgeable gulf between the subjective self that changes and dies and is thereby confined to a purely temporal condition – and that objective nature which endures and hence has a 'temporal stability' ... Trapped in the prisonhouse of language, the conscious mind can never cross over to the realm of unconsciousness.

On the basis of these ... assumptions, de Man then proceeds to *privilege one form of literary discourse, the allegoric*, over another, the symbolic ... [asserting] that allegory – whose signs refer to anterior signs, whose texts derive their meaning from other literary texts, and which thus inhabits a purely linguistic context – is 'the unveiling of an authentically temporal destiny' ... Symbolism, in contrast, attempts to embody linguistically the identification of the subject with an other, rather than the 'relationship of the subject with itself.' [italics added][15]

A chasm between self and other. An artifact that rehearses rather than ignoring this split. Doesn't this sound remarkably like our description of – and explanation for – the map-as-model? And other aspects of the situation only reinforce such an identification. Indeed, simply on the basis of its intrinsic character – its capacity, firstly, in Charles Feidelson's words, 'to beg the question of absolute reality' ('The allegorist avails himself of a formal correspondence between "ideas" and "things," both of which he assumes as given'), and secondly, to preserve 'a conventional order whose point of arrangement [is] easily defined'[16] – allegory may well be described as a *verbal map*, the map-as-fiction. What is more important, if we look at the corpus we will see that literary practice in this country, though not for the most part allegoric in any obvious sense, does in fact share many of the distinguishing features that Angus Fletcher attributes to the allegoric mode: discontinuity ('If reality is imaged in diagrammatic form, it necessarily presents objects in isolation from their normal surroundings'); radical surficiality ('The visual clarity of allegorical imagery is ... like the hyperdefinite sight that a drug such as mescaline produces'); passive or paratactic structure ('This term implies a structuring of sentences such that they do not convey any distinctions of higher or lower order'); a polarized world view ('another sort of dualism associated with allegory ... is not the dualism of double meanings, but dualism in its theological sense, where it implies the radical opposition of two independent, mutually irreducible, mutually antagonistic substances').[17] Reviewing this list in the light of our observations throughout this book, it's clear that if the typical Canadian fiction, taken by itself, is not necessarily an allegory *per se*, Canadian literature is allegorical in the most general sense of that word.

Having established this much we are now in a position to interpret a number of important characteristics of the Canadian oeuvre which taken in isolation may seem insignificant or at least unrelated. The fact is, just like the conceptual devices examined above, though on a far broader level, this implicit allegorical element entails a number of very particular advantages for the writer attempting to mediate some sort of relationship with otherness. In the first place, as with the map, the normalized duplicity of the form allows for a strategic dissociation of experiential levels. The most obvious effect of this mechanism is to provide psychic relief. Thanks to the abstracting process proper to allegory, that is, the writer (and by association the reader too) is able to distance himself not only from 'things' in the form of objects and other people, but even from disturbing aspects of himself. 'One way that writing is important to me is that it maintains my sanity,' confesses Matt Cohen; '... it is a means for me to articulate my own world and externalize it rather than having to turn in against myself' (c61). Beyond this simple displacement, however, once the characteristic conventions are invoked there is typically a secondary development whereby attention is not merely diffused but focused almost exclusively on the *vehicle* of the allegory – that is, the artist's construct – rather than on its *tenor*. How? Allegory, says Jonathan Culler, not only allows but 'flaunts the gap' between word and object, thus parading not what is meant, but the *means* of meaning.[18] Indeed, even far more casual metaphoric practice conduces to such a transference. As Sigurd Burkhardt points out, 'The first purpose of poetic language, and of metaphors in particular, is the very opposite of making language more transparent. Metaphors increase our awareness of the ... language by increasing the thickness and curvature of the lenses.'[19] One may speculate that when the writer/reader has good reasons for being ambivalent about the *signified* the displacing mechanism is even more likely to be triggered. Certainly this is what happens in a great deal of Canadian literature.

The result? At its most basic the process is responsible for such phenomena as a relative accentuation of 'formality' not merely in writing but, by association, in general culture. We find a good example of this in Leonard Cohen, whose work, in Frank Davey's words, argues 'for the importance of reducing life to ceremony, and transmuting its treacherous actualities into the trustworthy simplicities of mythology and art' (F68). Alternately, suggesting that 'connections' can be made only provisionally and obliquely, it also seems to encourage a predilection among authors (James Reaney is a pre-eminent example[20]) for intellectual/perceptual 'play.' Moving significantly beyond what are largely matters of emphasis, however, the displacement of affect can even go so far as to imply that the ideal *is* the real. We must be careful not to misinterpret, of course. This is not the sanctification of the 'made' object we see taking place in American fiction as more and more writers affirm the somewhat solipsistic dictum that '"reality" does not precede mimesis ... but rather ... the impulse to, and the act of, mimesis can be viewed as the reality itself.'[21] In the Canadian allegory – exactly as with the map – the convention of isomorphism implies that the vehicle is *by definition referential*. Far from preventing an idealizing tendency as one would think it should, though, what this means is simply that we find an even *more* radical transformation taking place than in the self-conscious New Novel. Again following the map analogy, implied shifts of meaning and value in the realm of the signifier may be taken to assert, at least symbolically, that the external world is modified magically through modifications in its representation. At the very least this produces a comforting ambiguity. In Klein's 'Autobiographical,' for instance, we are ultimately unsure whether the poem-construct invokes a 'real' Montreal, or Montreal-as-poem construes the ideal realm Mandel describes as 'a fabled city of Jewish lore, imagination, and scripture' (A118), or *the fabled city actually creates a new Montreal*. At best it conveys, *almost* unequivocally, that any order attributable to the vehicle, or model, may be transferred – *in*tended rather than merely *pre*tended – to the otherwise unorderable phenomenal realm as well.[22]

A second advantage of allegory lies in what we might call its proclivity for wholeness. Internally this feature produces a strong impression of both formal and emotional coherence. Simply through its conventional allusiveness, in other words, the total allegorical figure always lends what Fletcher describes as 'particular symbolic force' to its individual parts. 'The whole ... determine[s] the sense of the parts, and the parts [are] governed by the intention of the whole ... [which yields] a teleologically ordered speech' [85]. Already, therefore, the allegory strongly projects a sense of internal necessity. Beyond this, however, the covert assertions carried by its logical infrastructure imply not merely a limited, self-contained construct but a *generalized* order, a complete cosmos like the medieval world scheme Lovejoy examines in *The Great Chain of Being*, by which the present occasion – whether book or poem – is both entailed and explained. Allegory thus both creates and invokes a fully rationalized *system*.

Canadian literature, though allegoric only covertly, manages to achieve much the same effect, quite economically and without 'breaking silence,' as it were, simply by exploiting tendencies already inherent in the communal paradigm. On a fairly rudimentary level, with regard to the factor of internal coherence, the predilection for houses *in* fiction is matched by a bias toward fiction *like* houses. This implies that our writers, concerned 'to provide as literal a shelter as possible ... through a desire for the reassurance of clear definition' [Harbison 73], will tend to give high priority to communicating a strong sense of *place* (could this explain the obtrusive and largely illusory regionalism of Canadian literature, I wonder?) and on the other hand that elaborate structuring of a fairly conventional sort (like the 'four-times-four, or four-squared pattern' of Wiebe's *Peace Shall Destroy Many*, the elaborate multiplex dialectic commonly employed by Hubert Aquin, or the elemental/alchemical motifs that provide structural/thematic underpinnings for both Sheila Watson's *The Double Hook* and Margaret Laurence's Manawaka tetrology[23]), though due to its humanistic associations clearly anathema to avant-garde writers outside the country, will here be considered not merely acceptable but of special value. Alternately, balancing this architectural element – and here we come to the cosmic factor – there is also an evident desire to establish horizontal connections, that is, to locate given house-fictions explicitly within contiguous larger contexts, that leads Canadians, among other things, to produce interlocking sets of works, sometimes connected explicitly by geography (again Laurence's Manawaka provides a prototype, but several of Matt Cohen's books are similarly set in what George Woodcock calls 'a mythical small town of Salem which Cohen seems about to turn into a Canadian equivalent to Yoknapatawpha County' D149), sometimes – like Hood's proposed 'history of our time'[24] – merely by design. Subsuming both these tendencies is the rather sly strategy of manipulating cognitive/symbolic elements to produce an *illusion* of 'system.'

What does this involve? If we examine the corpus we will see that Canadians have a propensity not merely to make use of ready-made materials on the level of content but also to import ready-made informing structures from psycho-symbolic schemata through to pre-established metaphoric 'sets.' Phrased thus the approach may not sound particularly noteworthy – after all, as Culler points out, 'every "traditional" novel of any value will criticize or at least investigate [available] models of intelligibility' [190] – but careful consideration reveals that there is actually a subtle but important difference between the Canadian and the more general practice in this regard. The fact is, Canadians do not so much *investigate* these models, far less *apply* them, as simply use them as stage furniture, fixed standards of purely formal significance against which to set or within which to frame the by definition incoherent sense data yielded by 'real' experience. This technique has certain obvious advantages. Because 'mapping the terrain' implies discovery rather than creation, to avoid even the appearance of assertion in compiling our fictions we are constrained to approach not merely the 'world' but also the 'word' with only the most tentative preconceptions. Unfortunately, the result of this – as Daphne Marlatt illustrates vividly in *Steveston*, a poem in which, despite the invoked 'object,' the primary focus is actually the poet's process of 'trying out' alternate ways of constructing a town-as-poem coincident with her own provisional town-as-idea ('The matter of this poem is arrived at hesitantly,' says Douglas Barbour: 'the poet tells us some part of that multiplicity and then retreats, "That's not it" ... to begin again' B185) – is to focus more attention on the 'subject' than most Canadians are willing to risk.[25] Ready-made components, with their appearance of 'givenness,' relieve us to the highest degree possible of this problematic necessity of intervention. This is not all they do, however. The use of ready-made components also intensifies the allegoric effect, on the one hand underlining the conventionality of the vehicle while on the other increasing the impression of realistic reference. 'In proportion as in what [fiction] offers us we see life *without* arrangement do we feel that we are touching the truth,' writes Henry James in 'The Art of Fiction.'[26] Just like his use of 'found' story materials, the Canadian writer's passive employment of conventional forms (that is, as a means of suggesting rather than imposing order) conveys the impression that he is merely presenting without contrivance. Finally, and perhaps more important for our present topic, the kind of practice we have been discussing here, by pointing beyond the covers of the book to some kind of extrinsic order, creates the impression – as in allegory – that the individual instance may be 'placed' in the larger scheme of things.[27]

Although the *fact* of extrinsic reference is more important generally speaking than the object of it, it is obvious that the degree of borrowed authority asserted by the work will depend on the kind of order invoked. In Canadian practice the most popular structural/thematic packages tend to derive from either the literary[28] or the 'mythic' order. This latter would include both the explicit biblical analogues that inform such books as *The Stone Angel* and *The Sacrifice* and the somewhat more elusive classical echoes we may detect in the treatment of our heroes. It would also include the generalized Jungian symbology employed by poets like Jay Macpherson and James Reaney. Northrop Frye's theory of archetypes has, of course, been extremely influential in developing this latter area – perhaps even more for what it *is* than for what it *says*. As much as any poet in his train, Frye himself provides a fascinating example of 'Canadianness,' not just because his criticism emphasizes what is 'given' in literature – the eternal forms – over what is invented but because, more significantly, his oeuvre may be seen both to elucidate *and* to exemplify the whole allegorizing tendency examined in the last few pages. Indeed, if we put aside our preconceptions about 'criticism' long enough to give due notice to this exemplifying aspect, it may explain some of the problems presented by his theory *qua* theory. A number of critics have been irritated by the putative cosmic inclusiveness of Frye's schemata. 'Frye seeks for criticism what he finds in myth, a sense of all-encompassing form,' says Eric Gould, 'but he mistakes form for religious content and has few suggestions as to how mythic thought itself, the tangible evolution of archetypes in narrative, actually operates' (725). A plausible complaint. Yet from a slightly different perspective, those very features on which critics like Gould fix – and in particular the form/content conflation – seem to hint that it might be more fruitful to consider Frye as practising rather than preaching. Theory aside, in constructing his transcendentally validated catalogue of literary forms, what Frye actually produced was an aesthetic model of self/other relation – that is, a 'fiction.' In Geoffrey Hartman's words, Frye 'uses allegory ... to create accommodating archetypes and to achieve an integration *avant la lettre*.' It is easy to see why such a manoeuvre would bother those intent on deriving a purely logical formulation. This integration Hartman cites is of necessity achieved only at the cost of weakening the letter of the work to the extent that it tends to become merely 'catalyst or vanishing agent.' How, then, is the text redeemed? By exactly those same types of transference noted above. Frye, Hartman continues, 'comes close to understanding why theology, and now critical theory, is forced to break with representational values by means of the very instrument – traditionally denominated as allegory – that is also used to save appearances. But he continues to save the appearances, and to draw everything into an encyclopedic, monumental, totalizing system.'[29]

How does all this relate to the literature produced by Canadians? As we may read between Hartman's lines, one of the most important ramifications of Frye's practice, as of allegory in general, is tacitly to affirm the meaningfulness of the *signified* while focusing attention on the *signifier*. When he speaks of 'the total shape and structure of the Bible' as comprising its true importance, for instance, he is not merely discussing but mimicking myth, sidestepping both textual problems and truth-claims (c188). Frye does not, therefore, as Gould suggests, simply derive 'forms' and then imbue them with the numen properly belonging to content but, rather, asserts a referential linguistic structure isomorphic with – that is, by definition *separate from* but *informed by* – significant aspects of 'reality.' This is the key point. In so far as Frye's practice is prototypical – and I think we can stipulate that it is – it means that the Canadian, unlike the American, for whom myth is commonly either true or false,[30] may take the myth as both serious *and* playful. This element comes across with particular force, as we might expect, in Reaney – especially in those plays like *Colours in the Dark* and *Listen to the Wind* which present themselves as, equally, 'pure' fantasy *and* a reflection of 'real' life. The duplicity of allegory is, in fact, an explicit characterizing feature of Reaney's entire practice. 'That's how poetry works,' he says: 'it weaves street scenes and twins around swans in legendary pools. Let us make a form out of this: documentary on one side and myth on the other: Life & Art. Into this form we can put anything and the magnet we have set up will arrange it for us' (c4). Note the suggestion of passiveness here, the implication that the ready-made forms will do the work! It is significant that Reaney is fascinated with maps and diagrams (see Atwood D113), because it is clear that his own work, even more explicitly allegoric than most, comprises a *map of* rather than an *entry into* his chosen terrain.

The question that now arises takes us into another dimension. If allegory invokes an image of generalized, abstract order, what effect does this have on that basic feature of more 'realistic' kinds of fiction, the *story*? Here, one would think, is where we run into problems. Surely the static relations implied by the patterns we have been examining must militate against any convincing sense of process. Surprisingly enough, it doesn't work this way. In the first place, the intellectual orientation of allegory – in marked contrast to the 'inexpressibility, ineffability, [and] absolute *in*determinacy' of the symbol – produces an effect of cognitive transparency. 'Allegory offers a structure that [not only] ... rigidly separates surface and depth ... [but also] absolutely determines and verifies a single meaning,' says Patricia Tobin. 'In other words, in its unequivocal specification of duality and determinacy, allegory might be [said] ... to expose [both] ... the impossibility of unification and ... the needlessness of obscurity.'[31] The result is a kind of singlemindedness or *unidirectionality*. In the second place, the emphasis on logic implies *linearity* and even, by association, causal connections. And in the third place, the inner necessity of a 'structure that is forever legitimizing itself ... locking its elements into ... teleological relations,' by 'overdetermining the reading of the book [and] ... forcing the reader to proceed "straight through,"' speaks forcefully for the ideal of a *completed action* [Tobin 65]. Just as the iconic road 'moves' through the map, consequently, what we find within the subsumptive image of stasis offered by allegory is a persuasive countering image of self-contained process. Simply because 'fiction' implies 'story,' that is, there is a propensity for any systematic aggregate of images, no matter how neutrally conjoined, to present itself as a facsimile of *narrative*, animated by the convention of 'meaning,' oriented by the convention of form. J. Hillis Miller, in an essay entitled 'Ariadne's Thread,' evokes vividly the kind of metamorphosis involved. 'Narrative event follows narrative event in a purely metonymic line, but the series tends to organize itself or to be organized into a causal chain. The chase has a beast in view. The end of the story is the retrospective revelation of the ... underlying "truth" which ties all together in an inevitable sequence revealing a hitherto hidden figure in the carpet. The image of the line tends always to imply the norm of a single continuous unified structure determined by one external organizing principle.'[32]

This brings us to a problem. With all this talk of logic, linearity, and completion, what we are obviously talking about here is the traditional 'closed' form generated by the assumption (in Alice Kaminsky's words) 'that since individual life has the order of a beginning, middle, and end, the novel should reflect such order.'[33] While it is true that this kind of fiction offers the greatest relief to man's existential anxieties – after all, as Frank Kermode says, 'Men, like poets, rush "in to the middest," *in medias res*, when they are born; they also die *in mediis rebus*, and to make sense of their span they need fictive concords with origins and ends, such as give meaning to lives and to poems'[34] – it is also true that this is *not*, by and large, the kind of fiction that has been produced recently by serious writers in either Europe or the United States. Why? To some extent it is simply a matter of 'truth' versus 'realism.' As Kaminsky points out, 'for the writer who views life as being chaotic and disordered, the open form of fiction is more relevant' [225]. Aside from merely facilitating a more authentic mimesis, however, the new forms also represent an explicit rebellion against the false view of life buried in the old ones. Sartre, as Roy Pascal indicates, was one of the most forceful spokesmen for this approach.

[Sartre criticizes] the traditional form of the novel, the chief falsity of which lies for him in the narrator (personal or impersonal), who writes from the standpoint of the outcome of the events related, and who thereby profoundly distorts the nature of real experience. The whole pattern of a story, the coherence of its events, is built on this false premise of retrospection, for it is only in retrospect that we can recognize events to be significant or irrelevant and contingent. The nature of living, which Sartre powerfully illustrates from the experience of participating in the Resistance during the war, is quite opposite to that of fiction, since when acting we never know the outcome, we are unsure of effects, and we ignore what is happening elsewhere and in the minds of the people around us. Sartre considers this falsification of life to be a subtle form of self-assertion on the part of the bourgeois class.[35]

What happens once a view like this becomes consensual? The traditional novelist's faith in narrative, in the possibility or the morality of 'homogeneous action and coherent meaning' – what Tobin calls the genealogical imperative [201] – disappears, and with it the traditional temporally-oriented novel. 'Linear logic, founded on the development of time sequences, is abandoned,' says LeVot, 'and spatial planes become the new locus where transformational patterns are set to work' [46]. Lest the reader be tempted to import alternate, possibly static forms of order, moreover, horizontal connectivity is disrupted as well. 'The new narrative,' Tobin summarizes, '... goes comic and cosmic, allegorical interpretation is either a colossal hoax or a grim joke, and reader and character are left wallowing on the surface' [203].

How does the Canadian fit this pattern? We have observed elsewhere important temperamental differences between this country's writers and the 'new' novelists. There are also, however – notwithstanding the foregoing comments – obvious elements in our literature, such as its surficiality and discontinuity, that would seem as much at odds with linearity as Sartre's overt antagonism. It is easy to see why Canadians might prefer the traditional novel. In the first place, our fear of a disorderly universe inclines us to put a high value on any means for producing a convincing illusion of order. More important, our sense of irremediable isolation combined with a deep-seated fear of solipsism (for all our self-admitted dependence on 'architecture,' we are well aware of the unwholesomeness of that most conventional of literary houses, the gothic mansion[36]) gives us a strong motivation for favouring models of even formal connection. The question is, though, whether Canadians do – can – in fact produce this kind of fiction.

Actually, if we look at the oeuvre an interesting pattern begins to emerge. It has been widely remarked how much Canadian literature transgresses the line between literary modes, moving from, on the one hand, poetry that is documentary or narrative ('The anecdotal as opposed to the syntactical,' as

Mandel puts it; 'poetry as story not as form, and as prose' B118) to, on the other, novels that are strikingly poetic:

L'aquarium by Jacques Godbout might quite easily have taken the form of a collection of poems; writing in a very modern style and dealing with the combined themes of ennui, death, and love, the author would only have had to select from his raw material those moments of special keenness. (Robidoux 133-4)

Like Leonard Cohen's *Beautiful Losers* (a book to which it bears more than a passing resemblance), [*Coming through Slaughter*] is a 'novel' in which the real action takes place at the level of the poetic image. (Scobie A6)

[*Blown Figures*] is not a novel, Thomas once said, it is a book (though the title page says a novel). It is a lot like a big concrete poem, or better, a found poem. It is perhaps a found novel, at least half so, and that's interesting. (Bowering D86)

Sheila Watson's *The Double Hook* belongs to a genre which challenges form as the distinction between poetry and prose. This short novel seems easily divided into verse form and prose passages, yet its impact derives from the interaction and, more significantly, the fusion of the two modes. As prose poetry, it postulates inherent poetic and prosaic structures which transcend the disposition of language into stanza or paragraph form. (Marta 44)

What are we to make of this peculiar phenomenon? Perhaps it merely reflects on our borderline condition. If, on the other hand, one accepts David Lodge's contention that poetry is metaphoric by nature (that is, structured through juxtaposition of discrete elements) while prose is metonymic (linear),[37] our apparent inability – or unwillingness – clearly to differentiate between the two may well suggest something a little more telling about the Canadian character than that. If we go even further and speculate – as, looking at the great preponderance of poets-turned-novelist (Klein, LePan, Cohen, Atwood, Kroetsch, Ondaatje, *et al.*) over novelists-turned-poet, we might well do – that the dynamic *behind* the uneasy equipoise bespeaks an at least vestigial attempt to break out of our (metaphoric) isolation to make (metonymic) connection, it explains a good many of the anomalies in Canadian literature. What this view would assert, in other words, is that Canadians, despite their ambivalence and even fear, while accepting discontinuity as man's first and ultimate condition yet *postulate relation as a goal.*

This may seem like a rather extravagant conclusion to draw on such scanty grounds, but if we think of what has been said about the likelihood of an extravertive reaction to extreme introversion, the hypothesis takes on a certain amount of at least theoretical plausibility. While hard data are few and equivocal, moreover, there are at least a few substantive features in the oeuvre that may be taken as evidence that this kind of movement is in fact implicit in the Canadian response. Think back to the chapters on marital and familial relations. What I would suggest is that some of the peculiarities observed in that area both explain and are explained by exactly the same impulse signalled by the metaphor-to-metonymy model. The key to this is contained in Francis Hsu's 'Hypothesis on Kinship and Structure.' To summarize briefly, Hsu claims, firstly, that any nuclear family may be analysed in terms of its 'dyads,' that is, sets of 'two linked persons'; secondly, that different familial models give different relative prominence to their component dyads ('What actually occurs is that in each type of nuclear family one ... takes precedence over the others ... [and consequently] tends to modify, magnify, reduce, or even eliminate other dyads in the kinship group'); thirdly and most importantly, that *The dominant attributes of the dominant dyad in a given kinship system tend to determine the attitudes and action patterns that the individual in such a system develops towards other dyads in this system as well as towards his relationships outside of the system* (original italics).[38] Hsu then goes on to elucidate the particular attributes typically associated with each variety of dyad-dominancy. Those relevant here are as follows[39]:

Father-Child	1. Continuity	The condition of being, or the attitude of desiring to be, in an unbroken sequence, or connected with others.
	2. Inclusiveness	The act of incorporating or the attitude of wishing to be incorporated.
	3. Authority	Personal power that commands and enforces obedience, or the condition of being under such power.
	4. Asexuality	The condition of having no connection with sex.
Mother-Child	1. Discontinuity	The condition of not being, or the attitude of desiring not to be, in a sequence or connected with others.
	2. Inclusiveness	Already defined above.
	3. Dependence	The condition of being or the attitude of wishing to be reliant upon others.
	4. Diffuseness	The tendency to spread out in all directions.
	5. Libidinality	Diffused or potential sexuality.

It's easy to see from this list that the Canadian's most natural stance would be very close to that designated for the mother-child dyad. It's also easy to see why, in theory, he would desire a shift into the father-child mode with its promise of control, its repudiation of the threat of sex. The question is, however, whether we may discern any tangible sign in Canadian literature that such abstract preferences, no matter how plausible, actually do affect the way Canadians conceptualize their familial relations. Perhaps surprisingly, the answer to this would seem to be yes. *Only* by positing a willed and (at least vestigially) active orientation to the father-son dominant-dyad type can we explain our propensity, despite negative feelings toward the father himself, consistently to fill any vacuum left by the absence of a strong paternal presence in a given fiction by attributing to the mother the masculine dominance and aggressiveness that would *turn her into a 'father.'* Aside from anything else, this pattern seems to argue a strong urge to move from a condition of discontinuity to one of continuity. Which brings us back to our original question. Despite his natural predilection for the 'poetic,' it is actually quite predictable that the Canadian should demonstrate an equally strong wishful bias toward the linear form.

Establishing the relevance of allegory's affinity for 'story' does not, to be sure, explain or explain away the characterizing forms of Canadian fiction. So far we have been looking at 'linear pattern' only in its most academic sense. As long as we are talking strictly about allegory, moreover, this is the level on which our discussion must remain. Because allegory exudes such a strong impression of inevitability simply by virtue of its *a priori* associations, there isn't any felt need for rationalizing the connections between sub-elements of plot. 'The dramatis personae in allegorical fictions will not have to interact plausibly, or according to probability, as long as they interact with a certain logical necessity,' says Fletcher. 'This necessity in turn appears, as a result of the rhythms of allegory, to take on a magical force' [182]. Unfortunately, this sort of quasi-mystical mechanism isn't good enough for the Canadian. We have already noted the at least formal significance of 'reality' in his mental set. As a result of this he is inclined to believe that any novel not firmly grounded in 'history' is going to be irrelevant if not immoral. Though quite as ready as the American to suspect that 'there is an irrevocable distance between sign and referent,' in other words, the Canadian is reluctant to accept the logical implication of this intuition that 'meaning can refer only to its own linguistic system.'[40] Excepting, to some extent, the Québécois (who is more afraid of otherness than of introversion), the Canadian thus tends to eschew forms that lack an adequate realistic dimension. In this regard what Davey says of Margaret Atwood hints at not merely a personal but a communal peculiarity:

In ... seven books of poems ... [the] opposition between the static, the mythological, or the sculptural and the kinetic, the actual, or the temporal has been a central concern. Atwood's consideration of this opposition has been simultaneously ethical and aesthetic;

all attitudes toward form in her work have been subject to moral judgments. The sources of this antithesis lie in the earliest days of Anglo-American modernism. Its deepest roots are in T.E. Hulme's rejection of nineteenth-century empathetic realism for 'some geometrical shape which lifts him [man] out of the transience of the organic' and in the searches of Proust for 'the real without being of the present moment' and of Pound for 'a fragment of time in its pure state.' Throughout Margaret Atwood's poetry such goals are presented as attractive, attainable – in terms of both life and poetic form – but ultimately unsatisfying. The formal garden can be created and entered, but its marble flesh cannot be lifted from still dance into dancing life. (A172)

The Canadian, in short, wants not merely to connect but to connect with the real.

Such a consideration has repercussions for our literary practice on more than a purely thematic level. The desire for realism is not totally at odds with the allegoric component in our writing – remember that referential function – but in light of the trends toward psychic dissociation it does create a few problems. It's all very well to talk about a symbolic move from metaphor to metonymy, but the question remains as to how, on more overt levels, the Canadian responds to the incompatible urgings of his own nature. The most obvious solution is to reverse the allegoric process, stipulating that the referent with its borrowed transcendent order is in fact more wishful than real but countering any consequent impression of insubstantiality by ensuring that the *vehicle* will be ostentatiously realistic. One way of achieving such an effect is simply to fill the text to overflowing with things felt, smelt, *seen*. This is the practice of Hugh Hood, who calls himself both a *realist* and a *transcendental allegorist*[41]; it might also be designated the practice, though perhaps with less conscious allegoric intent, of any writer – like Kroetsch (*The Studhorse Man*) or Hébert (*Les chambres de bois*) – who combines an emphasis on the phenomenal surface of the world with an openly fantastic form. Aside from the invocation of thingness there is another strategy, however, which, inasmuch as it caters to our linear pretensions by focusing on plot, is ultimately more satisfying. The fact is, the best way to rid the allegorical construct of the stigma of unreality is to pretend that the story embedded in the vehicle represents a real (possible) rather than just an ideal (mental) operation. One simply presents the allegoric as mimetic, in other words, such that it is apparently no longer imaginary but derived. What kind of story allows for this sort of manoeuvre, satisfying simultaneously the demands of both allegory *and* realism? In allegory, as Fletcher points out, the two basic forms are the battle and the questing journey. The first of these is too apocalyptic for Canadian taste, but the latter may obviously be adapted to realistic story-making.

At this point another problem arises. Our basic introversion may allow for a certain degree of psychic readjustment, but we are still radically alienated by the landscape, the threatening realm of 'out there.' This would seem to militate decisively against the journey form. One plausible alternative is the quest that is intellectual rather than physical in nature. But does this sort of solution meet the Canadian's particular needs? Certainly it has been tried often enough. As Russell Brown notes in 'In Search of Lost Causes,' a surprising amount of Canadian literature, though stylistically distinct from conventional detective fiction, shows marked similarities to the mystery genre in its most general aspect. Davies' *The Manticore*, Kroetsch's *But We Are Exiles*, Richler's *St Urbain's Horseman*, and Kreisel's *The Betrayal*, for instance, all focus on the attempt to unravel or dis-cover what is hidden, all show the obsessive concern with guilt and innocence, the reversible flight-and-pursuit motif, the incremental revelation of truth which are identifying features of this form. Despite its appeal, though, the detective story *per se* is lacking in one important area. While it certainly offers all the satisfactions of the allegorical quest (suspense intensifies a linear impulse while the convention of solution affirms closure; the whole hermeneutic framework, moreover, catalyses a systematizing process fully equivalent to allegory's magic – 'the desire to see what happens next does not itself act as an important structuring force,' says Culler, '[but] the desire to see an enigma or a problem resolved does lead one to organize sequences so as to make them satisfy' [211]), the very fact that makes it so appropriate for a nation of introverts, its emphasis on the ratiocinative, also puts it in the realm of the inadequately 'real.' Indeed, it is significant that Québécois make the most extreme and open use of the mystery convention (*Prochain épisode, Kamouraska*); for the generality of Canadians, concerned to break out of rather than reinforce their existential isolation, the form smacks a little too much of solipsism. Detection is still an important motif in Canadian literature, but more often than not it is naturalized by integration into a different kind of plot. What is this new element? Just what we began with: a journey – but *not* a journey in space. In diametric opposition to the American with his compulsive questing after '"somewhere else," that forever distant place one can never attain' (Kattan 103), the Canadian prefers – indeed, is constrained – to do all his questing in *time*.

Or are we going a little far in suggesting a division as comprehensive as this? After all, look at the evidence. Item: 'Canadians are supremely at home when they travel,' claims Kroetsch. 'The departure, initiation and return of travel literature is basic to the narrative mode; the urban figures in Canadian literature, when we actually encounter them (in Davies, in Thomas, in Atwood, in Mordecai Richler) are, typically, travelling' (Bviii). Item: Americans *love*: westerns, pioneer sagas, civil war romances, G.I.-hero stories (any theatre, any period), and practically anything set during the Revolution. Both of these statements are self-evidently true. At the same time they are both profoundly misleading.

This is going to take a little explaining. Let's look at one side of the question at a time. We'll start with the United States – and we'll start by considering a random collection of critical statements.

1 Roy Harvey Pearce: 'The American epic is not *about* history; it *is* history – the history of men pondering what it might mean to be heroic enough to make history'; 'The strictly historical materials in *Paterson* are presented as so much *disjecta membra* and are allowed to have meaning only as they fit into the poet's scheme of things.'[42]

2 Max Westbrook: 'we Americans, 200 years later, like to tell the story again, to celebrate the story, and – most of all – to see the achievement repeated in specific events; for this shows that what we admire about the birth of our nation is not merely a worship of the past but is, rather, a moral achievement that has become a part of our national character' (in Lewis and Lee 9).

3 Peter Harcourt: 'In Hollywood films like *Bound for Glory, Thieves Like Us* and *Bonnie & Clyde*, while the *décor* is authentic, the thinking is modern. Especially in *Bonnie & Clyde* which, with its New Deal posters and sense of dusty streets, is the most meticulous of them all, the gestures are totally contemporary' (13).

4 David Levin: Nineteenth-century historian Francis Parkman was primarily interested in elucidating the psychological aspects of history. 'One reads of a battle, he said, with the "same kind of interest with which he beholds the grand destructive phenomena of nature" … In well-described skirmishes or single combats, however, "the reader is enlisted in the fray"; he shares the feelings of the participants and, instead of imagining a picture, seems actually to feel … "the tangible presence of rock, river, and forest." Parkman's control of point of view reveals the importance of this paragraph: again and again he tries to put the reader on the scene.'[43]

5 Dick Harrison: 'It may be that American writers, faced with an over-mythicized West, go back to find the facts, something solid, verifiable, and prosaic enough to draw that past into their known world' (A55).

By now we should be seeing a picture emerge. All these comments testify, in one way or another, to the American's interest in history. More covertly, however, they also reveal that this interest has very little to do with – and indeed is a kind of rejection of – the *past* as such. Judging by the evidence, in fact, the American is concerned primarily with bringing the past into the present, making all times contiguous with *now*. How can we explain this idiosyncracy?

In cutting ties with the mother country, the United States also, perforce, cut all ties with her own cultural progenitors, a pragmatic necessity later transformed into a patriotic duty through the promulgation after the Revolution of the self-exculpatory Adamic myth with its built-in assertion that Europe, and therefore 'history,' was the source of all that was degenerate and effete. As a result of this initial and continuing impulse, in Naim Kattan's words, 'the United States [became] a civilization of space without time ... [in which,] since there is neither past nor traditions, each generation begins the conquest of the world anew' (103). This, of course, explains the impulse to detemporalize, to rewrite history, over and over again, divesting it of its alienness, its *pastness* (think of the changing styles of movie westerns in the last fifty years!). Only so may it become psychologically accessible, safe. What it all adds up to is that the American does even his 'historical' voyaging in space.[44]

Turning to Canada now, we soon realize that superficial impressions are just as misleading here as in the United States. If the American is assiduous in his revisionism, the Canadian is equally assiduous at displacing his focus from space to time. This isn't really surprising, considering our national background. As observed in chapter 3, we have never been much taken with the idea of *exploring*. And why should we be? As Kattan points out, 'Surely ... the awareness of man's impotence before space [must] prevent any setting forth in search of an adventure that would be only an insane self-destruction' (110). On the testimony of our communal mythology, in fact, Canadians are purely and simply 'house-bound.' It is wholly predictable, for instance, that, in marked contrast to the Americans, whose first response to the necessity of developing a new self-image for the nation after the Revolution was to start celebrating the grandeur of their scenery, the sublimity of an untamed and untamable wilderness, the liberating influence of a forever-receding frontier, Canadians, even aside from the wilderness-denying gesture of a railway, asserted their independence primarily by an attempt to establish a unique cultural, political, and especially *historical* identity. 'The desire for a national culture that would reflect the culture of Canada in imaginative literature, art, and history became a master impulse in the intellectual life of the twenties,' says Berger. For many 'the quest for authentically Canadian modes of expression necessarily involved a critical attitude to the past' and an exploration of the specific means by which the country arrived at the 'state of things in the present' (54, 55). What, though – even stipulating, with Frye, that a *general* historical orientation was a natural and perhaps inevitable outgrowth of our initial garrison mentality[45] – are we to make of all those journeys on which Kroetsch commented above? Actually, if we look closely at Canadian 'travel literature,' taking a hint from the duplicity of its American counterpart, what we see is that *nearly every physical journey in the corpus is 'really' a trip in time.*[46]

Next question: how do we pull off such a feat of literary prestidigitation?

Simply by ensuring that the quest aspect of the journey, for all that it lures the protagonist physically away from home, is focused quite specifically in the past. The protagonist will not, in other words, achieve his goal (which, in line with its detective story associations, is usually intellectual in nature: an explanation, or a solution, or the answer to a question) merely by reaching some key location in space but, rather, by making a mental/emotional excursus into history. As a consequence, the 'travelling' is really irrelevant – or, rather, it has symbolic relevance only, affirming that the questor is in fact 'going somewhere,' making connections beyond the isolated ego. 'The trip home to Nova Scotia ... serves as a catalyst for the more important psychic journey in which the hero struggles with the past in order to meaningfully assimilate it with the fragmented present self,' says Douglas Parker of Alden Nowlan's *Various Persons Named Kevin O'Brien* (111). We might say exactly the same thing of the narrator's more exotic African trip in Thomas's *Blown Figures*. This raises another interesting point. We may, I think, speculate that it is significant that so many 'apparent' Canadian literary journeys do, like Thomas's, involve primitive cultures such as Africa or Mexico, inasmuch as this type of setting may be deemed to represent not merely a particular concept of personal or racial or symbolic past, but the very *idea* of pastness in all its absolute strangeness.[47] One novel that makes explicit use of a wide range of associations of this sort is Godfrey's *The New Ancestors*. Indeed, if we make note of all the 'temporal' features to be found in this book, with its extended exploration of political and cultural change, its demonstration of the importance of maintaining/renewing continuity, its elucidation, especially, of the pain of identity loss through loss of tradition, all the more poignant because of the conventional connotations of primitive wholeness provided by the setting (see Smiley 36), we will soon realize that the reader's putative quest-in-space here is given both its focus and its justification specifically by the author's *historical* concerns, while the complexity of the vehicle itself illuminates the subsuming problem of the enigmatic nature of *time*. The implications of such usage go far to confirm what we postulated above: the Canadian's evident desire for linearity, for connection, tends to be temporally rather than spatially oriented no matter what kind of 'journey' serves as its vehicle. As a result, as Mandel points out, 'it isn't just place we have to talk about but something more complicated and more compelling: remembered place – or beyond that – remembered self, something lost and recovered, a kind of memory, a kind of myth' (A70).

Transcribing this last quotation, I can't help thinking of Scott Symons's *Place d'Armes* – a celebration of 'placement' par excellence, but one which, predictably, turns out in the end to be a quest for the lost sense of tradition which the architecture merely crystallizes.[48] *Place d'Armes*, however, also suggests one further, final point that ought to be made about the timequest before we move on. The foregoing discussion has stressed the negative reasons why this particular form might tend to become a privileged vehicle in Canadian fiction. We should not overlook the fact that there are positive ones as well. Pulling together a number of elements we have so far merely glanced at in passing, we might fruitfully conclude this section by pointing out that whatever else it may offer, the journey into the past is (covertly) the perfect compromise between metaphor and metonymy. Inasmuch as it elucidates 'history' it provides us with at least an illusion of that connection we consider so crucial ('All of us need a pathway through the past,' says Robert Arn. 'A compass to the future is of no use if we have no idea from whence we came, any more than a compass to true north will lead us home if we have no idea if we came from east or west.' 38) but inasmuch as its implications of identity-search also lead us inward, simulating a descent into the belly of Leviathan (to borrow a concept from Reaney[49]), it also provides us with a means to evade or at least disguise that problematic confrontation with the other. Does this subversive contra-message reflect on the utility of the timequest as an instrument for combatting solipsism? An important question, but one which can be answered only through an examination of the effects actually achieved in a literary context. Our next task, therefore, must be to clarify how, in practice, the timequest actually works.

First step: ends before means. A quest implies a goal. If it is a 'real' quest, moreover, the goal has to be not merely a logically entailed but a naturalistically plausible one. Purely formal validation would mean that we were engaged only in ritual action, action-for-its-own-sake, rather than (as we want to pretend) action-toward. So what is the goal of the Canadian journey to the past? That's easy: *history* itself. An obvious answer – yet one that is so vague as to be virtually meaningless. If the exemplary journey really *is* a quest, we should be able to define what, specifically, *in* or *about* history the detective-protagonist is looking for. Perhaps we can get at this simply by asking what particular value is *ever* imputed to history.

In this regard there are two significant analogues which, elucidating as they do the general question of historical consciousness, should also elucidate the Canadian experience. Setting these forth in terms of dichotomies what we have is, firstly, the Old Testament in preference to the New Testament (that is, the Jewish emphasis on chronicle and genealogy versus the figural tradition[50] spawned by a Gospel which, in Otto Rank's words, 'does not speak of "progress" but of dying and rising again, thereby revealing the pattern of history not in terms of evolution but in a succession of crises'[51]), and secondly, Freud in preference to Jung (the hypothesis that the meaning of a life may be discovered by 'going back' through anamnesis to 'original' experience in the past[52] versus an emphasis on the manifestation in the present of timeless archetypes).

Already, of course, we can foresee difficulties in applying this particular double model. The Old Testament alignment is one we can accept readily enough. Our 'God,' after all, is an Old Testament God. And we have already had ample demonstration elsewhere in this book of our psychological kinship with the Jew. With respect to history in particular, moreover, we are, judging by our literature, at least half inclined to the Jewish view that it is the educational aspect of the past, and particularly its function as a repository of moral lessons ('Remember the days of old, consider the years of many generations: ask thy father, and he will show thee; thy elders, and they will tell thee' [Deuteronomy 32:7]), that comprises its primary importance. Take E.J. Pratt. In marked contrast to the prototypical Christian who, born again (like the American), 'starts his life ... on a secondary plane of experience, leaving behind him not only his own biological past but all past history before Christ' [Rank 167], this poet, *despite* his theological background, *despite* his explicit 'Christianity,' looks to history specifically for those exemplary 'heroic acts involving moral choice' which can 'equip man with an ethical guide for the struggle against nature' (Djwa A19, 5).[53] The question of Freud vs Jung, however, is another matter. Canadians, it would seem, are predisposed *against* that particular paradigm. Kroetsch, for instance, talking about the American cowboy in his ten-gallon hat as a manifestation of the id ('the good guy trying to free himself [from] ... the super ego') points out that there is in Canada 'much less excitement about that particular Freudian metaphor,' adding: 'I suspect we're more Jungian in some way' (F49).

Is Kroetsch right? Timothy Findley would certainly agree with him. 'I'm very Jung-oriented,' he says. 'I hate Freud but I love the old man sitting on his mountain' (B124). If we look at the mute evidence, though, such declamations seem a little anomalous. Even leaving aside the fact that the Freudian paradigm is so closely aligned with and indeed based upon the Old Testament vision that it is hard to see how one could accept the one and reject the other ('In accordance with the primitive moral code of the Decalogue,' says Rank, 'Freud put the emphasis on external restrictions and deprivations for the guidance of individual behavior, that is to say, on punishment and reward, rather than on the inner voice of the individual's conscience as indicated in the Christian religion' [274]), the Canadian *practice*, regardless of what we *say* about ourselves, seems to be far more Freudian than Jungian. Consider, for example, this description by Hayden White of the aims of Freudian psychotherapy: 'The problem is to get the patient to re-emplot his whole life history in such a way as to change the meaning of those events for him and their significance for the economy of the whole set of events that make up his life.'[54] *This is exactly the process David Staunton undergoes in* The Manticore *despite Davies' pretence that he is demonstrating a Jungian-style analysis.* How do we account for such a discrepancy? Part of it may simply be that Jung is more 'fashionable' in literary circles right now than Freud.[55] Undoubtedly, too, we are distressed by the extent to which Freud's Thanatos/Eros coupling exacerbates our own obsessions about sex and death. Most relevant to the discussion at hand, however, is the reason hinted at in the follow-up to Kroetsch's statement quoted above. 'We see opposites in necessary balance – maybe that becomes paralyzing, I don't know. If you accept the Freudian view there's lots of room for will.' Canadians, of course, are afraid of wilfulness. Yet without it they know they are never going to 'break out,' never going to move from the timeless Jungian realm of metaphor to the dynamism of metonymy. This ambivalence is bound to affect our attitude toward history, the value we impute to it – and by extension the way the timequest is framed.

What do we find when we turn to the oeuvre itself? Actually, there are two basic types of timequests in Canadian literature, public and private. The first stems from the desire of an individual to define not merely personal but communal identity. Here, not altogether surprisingly, is where we typically find the French Canadian. Why 'not surprisingly'? Because contemporary nationalism combined with a cultural bent for retrospectivity is bound to express itself as a concern with the public past. It is not coincidental, in other words, that the provincial motto of Quebec is *Je me souviens* – I remember. This very bias already introduces complications into the picture, however. Traditionally, 'remembering' for the Québécois has simply meant a repudiation of all change. 'It is both an appeal to the past to stay with us and a refusal of the future,' says Jean Ethier-Blais (309). Far from signalling an historical consciousness, therefore, the emphasis on memory invokes *only* the ahistorical, unaccented passage of days implied by the unchanging rhythms of the seasons, the cycle of life and death. '[W]e were surrendered to time,' says Anne Hébert. 'Time followed its course. By turns we were shaken or lulled by time. Like logs drifting down rivers, we slipped by. A defeat in the heart. A rosary between the fingers. Like the dead. Musing on the song of Lazarus ... "In Quebec nothing changes." Once this was truth. Immobile, peasant-like. Beneath the snow, or the summer sun' (c105). How did this happen? According to many recent French-Canadian views, history itself was the villain. Borduas 'visualized the history of the French-Canadian people as a huge conspiracy of the clerical and professional ruling classes designed to keep the people in a state of fear and ignorance,' says Ethier-Blais (309). Borduas was not the only one.

This posed a problem for the patriotic Québécois. New – and especially revolutionary – societies concerned to prove their legitimacy have even more need of cultural validation than most. '"A people without history,"' says Mircea Eliade (citing 'popular' opinion), '"is as if it did not exist"' [182]. It is hence quite natural that a significant number of recent Québécois works of fiction – Victor-Lévy Beaulieu's *Les grand-pères*, Jacques Ferron's *Le Saint-Elias*, Hébert's *Kamouraska* – should take their starting places in specific events from provincial history, affirming the vitality, even as they expose the grotesqueness, of Quebec's cultural heritage. Unfortunately, the perception that 'history' has been used as a weapon of oppression tends to undermine such efforts at self-identification. Besides, when the French Canadian looks backward he comes up against not merely betrayal *by* but betrayal *in* history. 'The basic ... trauma in the French-Canadian experience in North America,' says Max Dorsinville, 'is the termination, in 1760, of French rule in a country that had been named New France. Two resultant attitudes are usually assigned to this termination: one is that the French Canadian feels he was defeated, and that he is part of a "conquered people"; and the second is a sense of abandonment by the mother-country' (33). Even the most fervent patriot is likely to find small comfort in this.

How does the Québécois deal with such a painful discrepancy in his experience? One fairly straightforward response, like Freudian anamnesis, simply involves a cautionary re-enactment of the original trauma. Gérard Bessette's *L'incubation*, for instance, juxtaposes the two phases of an interrupted love affair to illustrate not merely the disjunction between past and present ('In recalling their adventure [Gordon] is puzzled as how to describe it,' notes Jeannette Urbas: 'was it madness, passion, an affair or just plain lust? Nina remarks at one point that their memories have something in common, they almost seem to fit in spots, but never quite match entirely.' 133) but also the disillusionment inevitably catalysed by the reflection of the former on the latter. 'Though the past and present are joined in many parallels, they are also irrevocably separated by important differences. The past, despite its associations with the dangers of war and bombardment, has become, ironically, the repository of joy and happiness, the seat of love' (Urbas 131). Just as the priestly version of Quebec's pastoral idyll did the most damage to those who most fervently subscribed to it, such fables imply, the more important history is seen to be, the more satisfying to one's sense of self, the more it is bound – as Nina and Gordon's 'grand passion,' mythicized beyond recognition, undermines any possibility of new relation – to have a deadening effect on the present.

Another strategy is more overtly evasive, inasmuch as it involves the attempt to substitute a less problematic means of self-identification for the discredited one. Like the initial impulse to reclaim the past, this response may be attributed at least partly to the specifics of the psychology of revolution. Historically there has always been a propensity for revolutionaries, lacking usable progenitors at home, to imitate and identify with such earlier cultures as can be seen as legitimizing models. 'The Jacobin fascination with the Roman republic, the Bolshevik miming of the French Revolution, can be seen both in their actions and still more in their utterances,' points out Bernard Lewis. 'The same kind of ritual reenactment of the past appears, in a grotesque form, in the restoration of beheading with the axe in Nazi Germany, and of penal mutilation in modern Libya.'[56] What does this have to do with the French Canadian? As unlikely as it may seem, I would suggest that we see the same mechanism at work in the identification of the *séparatiste* – like Cohen's F. (a man who, significantly enough, as Dennis Lee points out, has absolutely 'no interest in historical events' 67) – with the *American*. Unfortunately, inasmuch as the Québécois is even more radically introverted than his English-Canadian counterpart, this identification entails a considerable degree of anxiety. Whenever it is invoked, consequently – as in Claude Jasmin's *Ethel et le terroriste* – the fictional journey tends to take the form of frenetic, fruitless circlings lapsing always back into stasis and impotence.

The third means by which the Québécois attempts to negotiate his ambivalence about history involves a somewhat more radical manoeuvre. Like so many of the Canadian's more successful strategies for allaying his anxiety, this one is based on duplicity. Unwilling to give up his dream of ancestry, yet unable to come to terms with his 'real' past, the Québécois simply shifts his focus to what Paul Chamberlain calls 'the theme of origin, the *in illo tempore* of acts of foundation' (125). Time, in this mode, is expressed 'in terms of a dialectic relationship (often in the form of a reversal) between an idyllic, distant time and a more immediate, desolate time. Thus the idyllic past (golden age or primitive time) is opposed to the individual, historical past (which is stagnant and in ruins) and to the present (a time of poverty and nothingness)' (128). By this means the questor is enabled to have his cake and eat it too. Unfortunately, as often happens in strategies based on some variety of self-deception, in practice this displacement of affect entails secondary problems that tend to localize psycho-aesthetic tensions. In the usage of the poets upon whom Chamberlain focuses the undertones are kept largely under control if only because poetry itself, being pre-eminently metaphoric, tends implicitly to confirm the validity of an ahistorical mode. Fiction, however, is another story. The base theme, indeed, is nowadays rarely treated in prosaic forms – at least overtly. This may be partly because of the association of the *roman du terroir* with discredited traditions. More likely, though, it relates to the fact that while poets may idealize the 'process of founding, claiming, and exploring ... [the] act of settlement, of taking geographical possession of the territory' (128), the novelist must inevitably find it more difficult to escape the hard, unpalatable, historical *facts*. Two other prose forms, though, may be said to express the same impulse as the poetry of foundation. One is the novel of childhood which is so popular in Quebec ('The recapturing of childhood in an aesthetic form belongs to the pastoral mode wherein the creative imagination, finding present existence unsatisfactory, goes back into the past in quest of a more perfect world' Stouck A17); the other is the fairytale or fable.

If they sidestep the problems implicit in pastoral, neither of these provides a satisfactory solution to the problem of history, of course. Even leaving aside the drawback of the child's vulnerability – and our identification with it – both modes imply that one is leaving history behind entirely for the ahistorical realm of myth. '[T]he myth and fairy tale all operate through and represent this sense of the eternal,' remarks Andrew Lytle. '*Once upon a time; Long, long ago in a far kingdom* – these beginnings by their tone and meaning speak of no time, no country. They are outside time; they are always and forever about what is constant in human experience. The seeming tone of the far past is the announcement of the timeless held within the point of a moment.'[57] Why should this be a problem? For one thing, the realm of myth is pre-eminently the realm of the *natural*, the reconciliation of 'temporality, birth, death and resurrection, sexuality, fertility, rain, [and] vegetation' [Eliade 141]. More important for the present discussion, *the denial of time puts the Québécois right back in that static and stultifying state of cultural inertia he has mounted his revolution to escape*. In light of this crucial consideration it is no wonder that most Québécois fairytales are unpleasant ones, tainted with death, like the silent rooms of Hébert's *Les chambres de bois*, by virtue specifically of their timelessness. It is also hardly surprising that many of the writers caught up in this paradox – like the writer-revolutionary protagonists of Hubert Aquin's novels – turn to sex, violence, madness, any extreme of thought or conduct that might have the capacity to interrupt, to give accent and intensity to the deadening flux of time and the eternal.[58]

What about English-Canadian 'public' quests? Predictably – considering our uneasiness about the mesocosm – there are few of them. For all that one may discern almost across the board a concern about the broad *philosophical* aspects of history (a topic we will be discussing later), there seems to be little interest, outside Quebec, in its specifically *political* dimensions. Interestingly enough, one of the few English-Canadian novels to devote much attention to this aspect, Wayland Drew's *The Wabeno Feast*, addresses itself not to the problem of *recovering* the past but literally to *negating* history. The present-day plotline of this book (for it is one of the variety that interweaves a number of different temporal sequences) focuses on the exemplary journey into the past – that is, the wilderness – of a couple whose disgust with the contemporary world (which is painted in the conventional dystopic terms of sixties-style 'ecological' science fiction) is so extreme that they have decided to leave it, and with it 'history,' forever. Beyond this more or less naturalistic level, however, there is also the suggestion that their quest has a ritual and thus redemptive function. Progressively shedding maps and watches, they underline the significance of their regression by pausing along the way to read and then destroy the journals of a Hudson's Bay trader who long ago traversed the same route. The message is clear: modern man must undo the horrors he has wrought through his tampering with nature, go back to the beginning again.

What are we to make of this? The motif of ritual repetition, a common element in the religious practices of archaic (that is, myth-oriented) societies certainly provides an appropriate vehicle for communicating a specifically anti-historical vision. The idea of recapitulating to *undo* rather than to reconfirm, furthermore, while less common finds a parallel in, for instance, the Hindu technique of psychic 'regression' theoretically supposed to accomplish 'the annihilation of the Cosmos and hence [bring] about "emergence from Time," entrance into "immortality"' [Eliade 87]. Drew's story reveals certain serious inconsistencies, though, which suggest a covert temperamental bias *against* the implications carried by his explicit theme. At the same time as his plotline is arguing for the *need* to go back beyond history, the frame in which it is set seems to assert unequivocally that such a thing is impossible. The book both opens and closes with the senile ramblings of Charlie Redbird, a drunken Indian derelict whom we discover only at the last to be in some mysterious sense an alter ego for the Noble Savage invoked as the very spirit of nature in the journal whose course the voyagers are retracing, and if the opening hints at least barely at the possibility of redemption ('What was lost was found, and lost, and found again a thousand times among the filaments of wonder' 2), the ending unequivocally closes that door:

Soon they must come to take him home. They would receive him in great dignity and silence, and would wrap him in their best robes, as befits a chief. They would carry him home to the streams and the children playing ...

But the lone canoe which he saw at last, moving close to the forest in tricks of light and shadow, was not approaching as it should. It was passing him, passing so far away that he would not ... be seen ... Frightened, breathless, his mind floundering like a broken insect among the shards of litany which might once have brought them in, had the chief been potent and his medicine secure ... he seized from among the fragments of charm a name which he believed might once have been his own, although he could not be certain, so overgrown with whiteman's raillery had it become ... and he spoke this name softly outward, letting the wind cradle it from his lips like a child and a promise.

'Miskobenasa!'

His arms reached out, giving the name all the urgency and power at his command. But there came no response. The canoe, proceeding, was lost to him by degrees, and into his palms fell the first aimless flakes of snow. (279-80)

The Canadian, it seems, no matter how disillusioned he may be with 'history,' is unable to believe that 'myth' can really deliver all it promises.

Leaving the public arena we now come to the far more densely populated realm of the private timequest – a variety of fictional experience that at least initially *seems* a lot less troublesome. For one thing, unlike the public quest, this particular journey comes ready equipped with a sensible, and therefore suitable, *goal*. Here, hearkening back a few chapters, is where we find the search for the 'father.' The question still remains, of course, as to what we hope to gain by forging relation with the problematic paternal presence. It would be easiest simply to suppose that the act of evoking an ideal 'family' is part of the process of wall-building, of constructing our familiar place. Laurence's Hagar and Atwood's Lady Oracle are not alone in putting great store in their furniture, the arrangements of their rooms – the disposition of physical circumstances to facilitate recognition. 'I needed something familiar,' says Joan Foster. 'A place with no handholds, no landmarks, no past at all: that would have been too much like dying' (Atwood C7). Perhaps, then, it is necessary to recuperate the rejected father merely because the furniture of our lives would be incomplete without him. Unfortunately for this simple theory, the literature itself seems to suggest that behind this casual talk of furniture is a significantly more crucial kind of hunger. Canadians, as Dick Harrison points out, are obsessed with the idea of continuity, of establishing location in sequential terms. 'The current generation, looking for the ancestors who might help define their present identity, are shown like Pip in *Great Expectations*, searching the gravestones of lost parents' (E189). Far from simple furniture arrangement and even further from idle curiosity, the quest for the father, for the past, thus takes on an unmistakable urgency. The fact is, there seems to be an ineradicable need for Canadians to prove to themselves that he/it is there – and that he/it is *real*. The sense of crisis, unfortunately, only makes the quest that much more traumatic. 'I don't want to find ... that we have vanished without trace like a boat sunk in mid-ocean,' says Wallace Stegner in anticipation of a visit to the old homestead. '[T]o return hunting relics, to go down there armed only with memory and find every trace of our passage wiped away – that would be to reduce my family, myself, the hard effort of years, to solipsism, to make us as fictive as a dream' (9).

It is important to 'prove' the existence of the past, then, simply because we don't seem to be able to credit our own existence otherwise. 'It is essential I believe for us to know and understand what came before,' says Canadian artist John Boyle (34). Evidence suggests that his is the consensual view. *Without history man is lost*. This is why Wiebe's Big Bear is irredeemable – why, indeed, the Indian in general must be considered a hopeless case. Despite his compulsive and persuasive telling over of the past, again and again, as if in doing so he/they could somehow confirm an already lost future, we know from the beginning that Big Bear has lost his foothold in time: 'How a hunter can deny the rotting corpses and bones everywhere is beyond my comprehension,' writes Edgar Dewdney, 'but he insists [the buffalo] are being taken in to a hole in the ground and will reappear if and when the Indian has the land back. Such a superstition backing his platform ... should really elect him "prime minister" if Indians followed any logic discernible to us but fortunately their concept of individual liberty goes beyond all democracy; it is anarchic, and this the missionaries have not much affected [so] ... hopefully Big Bear soon finds himself out of tune both with the old freedom and newer logical beliefs' (121). Big Bear has been kicked out of history – and it is fatal. Matt Cohen implies much the same thing when he uses the image of a knife in both *Wooden Hunters* and *The Disinherited* to signal disjunction between generations, the loss of the past presaging the loss of the future. 'Six years ago everything had divided in half,' muses Johnny Tulip, thinking about the dead sister and the white girl who has stolen her place. 'His brother had given him the bone-handled knife and slashed it through the air, cutting the world into two parts' (E146).[59] To be cut off from history is to be cut off from life.

Why is it so important to us? Is it something about the father himself? For that matter, who or what exactly does this iconic figure represent. Convention – myth, history, literature, what have you – gives us lots of alternatives to choose from. Consider the following:

	absolute other		
1 magical father	father as	(magic)	primitive
	identical self		
2 intellectual father	father as exemplar (philosophy)		classical
(father-in-art)			
3 biological father	father as patriarch (law)		Old Testament
4 spiritual father	father as nurturer (religion)		New Testament

How does the Canadian relate to something like this? Actually – not well. We are afraid of 1 and incapable of believing in 4, so that rules out two possibilities right away. As for the other two, there are problems on both sides. The biological father is potent but repulsive. The intellectual father fulfils our wishful ideals, but unfortunately lacks credibility; we have trouble convincing ourselves that he is 'real.' It begins to seem as if the private timequest isn't so simple after all. Yet we still pursue it – with singleminded and at times absurd dedication. Perhaps Ernest Becker hits on the explanation when he points out that 'one's whole life is a style or a scenario with which one tries to deny oblivion and to extend oneself beyond death in symbolic ways, [for] one is [only] untouched by the fact of his death [when] he has been able to surround it by larger meanings.'[60] The 'father,' then, whatever else he represents, may perhaps be seen above all else as the symbol and occasion of a Proustian attempt 'to escape from the annihilating passage of time by trying to recapture the past in the vain hope that if [we] can do this 'the word "death" will have no more meaning."'[61] This would mean that, like Al Purdy, we launch our search for 'Owen Roblin,' that tutelary genius of 'place,' simply in order to 'prove' some kind of immortality. The 'father' himself, though providing both catalyst and goal for our quest, is finally irrelevant. '[A]ll I actually know of Roblin,' says Purdy, are

my own wild speculations
and some elusive unverified facts
add it all up and what do you have?
not very damn much –
and yet, as a result of my curiosity
or call it an obsession if you like
certain small rooms in my head are lighted up
the hall bedroom maybe
and definitely the downstairs hallway
I enter them unafraid of darkness or failure

In search of Owen Roblin
I discovered a whole era
that was really a backward extension of myself
built lines of communication across two centuries
recovered my past my own people
a long misty chain stretched through time
of which I am the last but not the final link (n.p.)

If Purdy is typical the whole thing can obviously be summed up in a few words: the father, quite simply, stands for *connection*.

Then again, perhaps all this makes it sound just a little too easy.

The problem is, though he might function as a symbol, the father is still a father. As such, he represents not merely 'parent' (which is bad enough) but otherness, *nature*. Which means that any quest involving him is bound to be dangerous. We see this clearly in Atwood's *Surfacing*. In this novel, which might be taken as a prototype for the personal timequest, a young woman takes a trip both *out* – away from civilization – and *back* – into her own past – in search of her father. Typically, as long as she stays with conventional means none of her goals are accessible. The father is missing; 'history' isn't there either. 'Her old home is in Quebec, in "foreign territory" where people speak a language not hers,' points out Catherine McLay. 'The road too is wrong; it "ought to be here" but there is a detour. "Nothing is the same, I don't know the way any more." As they approach the French-Canadian village, she expects to be filled with nostalgia and waits for "the cluster of nondescript buildings to be irradiated with inner light like a plug-in crèche." But the children are gone away to the cities, the little church is neglected, and "what I mean is dead"' (33). The solution? Atwood's protagonist, it seems, can find the missing continuity only if she goes beyond simple confrontation to *merge with* the landscape. 'She moves back through the layers of the past, the phases of evolution, first to the animal with "no need for speech," then to "a tree leaning." Finally she is "not an animal or a tree, I am a thing in which the trees and animals move and grow, I am a place"' (McLay 43). Does the strategy work? As Keith Garebian puts it, is the resulting epiphany – her madness, her visionary encounter with the missing parents – 'in fact, a breakthrough or a breakdown? Does she attain a positive anagnorisis or does she suffer from psychic or mental disintegration?' (7). She herself, Garebian comments, 'seems to think that she has broken through the old barriers: "I have to get up, I get up. Through the ground, break surface, I'm standing now; separate again"' (7). The question is whether *we* are able to believe her.

Actually – for all that Woodcock finds in this story, as in 'the purest, most intellectual forms of Buddhism ... a courageous coming into the light of reality' (A326) – the results of the quest here, as painted by Atwood are far from unequivocal. If the regressive exercise is unavoidable for this particular woman, it is also traumatic. Why? 'Nature is her norm, but in attempting to get closer to Nature she also gets closer to death,' comments Garebian, pointing out that 'when she laughs, after picturing herself as a "natural woman," a noise comes out "like something being killed"' (7). Granted, she *does* in fact survive, and in the end, with the possibility of a reunion with her lover in the offing, even seems to have reached some sort of accommodation with her emotional problems. So anticlimactic does this dénouement seem in comparison with the intensity of her earlier distress, though, that we have difficulty in accepting it as anything more than a kind of compromise, a scuttling back to safety after her attempt to 'become' otherness – whether fortunately or unfortunately – has failed. 'She records her disappointment when no fur appears on her skin,' says Garebian, 'for [this means] she is left a human (albeit an incomplete one) who must either immerse herself in the pattern of corrupt life or be destroyed' (7). In the light of our expectations, the pattern *seemingly* set up by the quest form, this ambivalent ending strikes us as rather anomalous.[62] Or does it?

If we look elsewhere in Atwood's work we will see that despite her apparent *desire*, perhaps above all else, to break out of isolation, she is very uneasy with what that action implies. In the title poem of *The Circle Game* the poet's persona, frustrated with the map-making, place-naming, objectifying practices of her partner, declares indignantly her intention 'to break/ these bones, your prisoning rhythms/ (winter,/ summer)/ all the glass cases,// erase all maps/ crack the protecting/ eggshell of your turning/ singing children:// I want the circle/ broken' (55). Elsewhere in the same collection, however, we find what is obviously the same speaker fervently looking for the lost key, the hidden 'huge and simple' pattern that 'informs, holds together/ this confusion, this largeness/ and dissolving' – building 'houses of ice ... in order to survive' (91, 87, italics added). Why the discrepancy? Quite simply because, for all her hatred of the 'panic of suburb,' the unhealthy rigidity of 'City Planners/ with the insane faces of political conspiracies,' Atwood evidently cannot help feeling that the 'landscape behind or under ... the plaster' is full of even deadlier threats

(36-7). Indeed, in this book – with implications amply elucidated in the last chapter – the landscape is almost always under water: 'I am in the lake, in the centre/ of the picture, just under the surface' ('This is a Photograph of Me' 71); 'the fish must be swimming/ down in the forest beneath us' ('After the Flood, We' 18); 'there are no/ sunken kingdoms no/ edens in the waste ocean/ ... only the cold jewelled symmetries/ of the voracious eater' ('A Descent through the Carpet' 30); 'Outside, the land/ is filled with drowning men' ('Winter Sleepers' 59); 'There is also a sea/ that refuses to stay in the harbour' ('Migration: C.P.R.' 69). Visualizing otherness in these terms, it is predictable that Atwood should be uneasy about the idea of anyone venturing 'out,' stepping off that safe, familiar 'lake-enclosed island/ with no bridges' which both defines and delimits the psyche (48). Connection is dangerous. '[T]o be aware is/ to know total/ fear' (30).

Is this a personal idiosyncracy, or is the problem a general one? To be more specific, is the quest for the father doomed to failure or are other writers able to negotiate the ambiguities that leave Atwood poised uncertainly on the water's edge? Purdy succeeds, in a sense, in finding Owen Roblin, but that particular timequest – a pursuit in which the validating function of the plot has been substantially displaced onto 'things' – is a little too much the intellectual puzzle, the questor a little too much the armchair detective, to satisfy our requirement that a 'real' journey be accomplished. What do we find if we look elsewhere? Unfortunately for our goal of 'breaking out,' Atwood's failure seems endemic. The following is only a brief and partial survey of representative examples:

ROBERTSON DAVIES, *THE MANTICORE*

In this novel David Staunton's journey to Switzerland represents his attempt, by unravelling the mystery of his father's death, to win posthumously all the love and approval the latter had withheld during life. Far from reconciling him with the long-desired paternal presence, however, the anamnesis climaxes with a decisive symbolic repudiation. Convincingly deflated in a dream – divest of both his power and his pants – the dead parent, it is implied, is forced to relinquish for once and for all his hold over the child-questor's mind. As David's Jungian mentor puts it, 'The old Troll King has lost his trappings' (264).

ROBERT KROETSCH, *BADLANDS*

The narrator in this novel tries to revivify an adored parent by recapitulating his journey into the interior. Just before she reaches the end of the trail, she experiences a kind of liberating epiphany at the sight of an old he-bear dangling undignifiedly from a helicopter sling (a vision that bears an interesting resemblance to David's dream cited in the last section), and decides to call off the search. 'I took that last field book with the last pompous sentence he ever wrote, the only poem he ever wrote, a love poem, to me, his daughter, and I threw it into the lake where it too might drown ... And ... did not once look back, not once, ever' (269-70). What has happened here? As Connie Harvey describes it, 'Through her recreation of Dawe's narrative, she is destroying, "uninventing," her vision of her father that has defined her. As she is freed from it, she is re-inventing her own vision in her commentaries. As she examines the final image, she comes to understand that the past is within her, that she does not need to look back' (51).

JACK HODGINS, *THE INVENTION OF THE WORLD*

Here the father is only symbolic, his place being filled by the ubiquitous magician; the search for him, moreover, is quite openly identified with the questor's need to expropriate not merely that one man's lifetime but the past in its entirety ('The debris of ... history is around him and he will reel it all in, he will store it in his head, he will control it; there will be no need, eventually, for anything else to exist; all of it will be inside, all of it will belong only to him' viii). Nevertheless, Becker's circumlocuitous progress around his island in search of scraps of information about the elusive Keneally is equivalent to the more conventional quests we have considered. The result is equivalent, too, for like Anna Dawe, Becker simply gives up. '*Donal Keneally is dead,*' he says at the last. '*His story has returned to the air where I found it, it will never belong to me, for all my gathering and hoarding*' (341, original italics).

A.M. KLEIN, *THE SECOND SCROLL*

In this last example, the role of the father figure is again played by a substitute, this time an uncle. In Klein's book, unlike Hodgins's, however, the quest itself is described from the beginning in the naturalistic terms of a dutiful search for missing kin. The realism does not, however, change the outcome of the fable. Despite the protagonist's increasing empathy with his fugitive kinsman as he pursues him – despite, too, the mythic underpinnings that allow Klein to present Uncle Melech in the kind of positive light usually denied to 'fathers'[63] – Klein's (overt) quest fails just like all the others. Arriving on the scene just after his uncle has been killed by terrorists, the young voyager admits his defeat: 'Across the continents I had looked and searched for my kinsman, and now that I had found him – I would not ever look upon his face. Forever would I have to bear in my mind my own conjured image of Uncle Melech' (91).

What are we to conclude from all these misfires? If nothing else, it seems to suggest that discontinuity is as inevitable in time as in space. If we look elsewhere, moreover, we find ample evidence that an unhappy intuition of this particular unpalatable fact is widespread even among those writers for whom the timequest seems most important. 'Proust had it easy with his tea and bun,' says Mrs Blood (103). Why the difficulties? At times the problem seems to be imputed mainly to human failings. 'However honest we try to be in our recollections we cannot help falsifying them in terms of later knowledge,' says one of the film-makers in Davies' *World of Wonders* (58). Often, however, some more radical juncture is indicated. In Atwood's *Lady Oracle* time is imaged as a labyrinth, easy to enter but impossible to retrace. The only way out is a door behind which waits the lover/villain, death. Such a view seems clearly to assert that the object of the quest is not merely in practice but *by definition* unattainable. Even symbolically. Like the well-meaning white men in Peter Such's *Riverrun* who misinterpret the primitive Demasduit's drawings because she has a different concept of perspective than they are used to, we have lost the key that would allow us to make historic experience our own. As a result, with the narrators of Munro's short stories, incapable of recreation, we are destined merely to remember, re-collect from a distance, view the past through the frail distorting lens of our own needs.[64] On the other hand, as with 'things' in space, the past is *there*, untouchable perhaps, but (weighty with the ponderousness of its own mystery) almost oppressively tangible. When 'I look at what I have done ... it is like a series of snapshots,' says one Munrovian persona of the results of her own timequest at the end of *Something I've Been Meaning to Tell You*,

like the brownish snapshots with fancy borders that my parents' old camera used to take. In these snapshots Aunt Dodie and Uncle James and even Aunt Lena, even her children, came out clear enough ... The problem, the only problem, is my mother. And she is the one of course that I am trying to get; it is to reach her that this whole journey has been undertaken. With what purpose? To mark her off, to describe, to illumine, to celebrate, to *get rid of* her; and it did not work, for she looms too close, just as she always did. She is heavy, as always, she weighs everything down, and yet she is indistinct, her edges melt and flow. Which means she has stuck to me as close as ever and refused to fall away, and I could go on, and on, applying what skills I have, using what tricks I know, and it would always be the same. (197)

With all this it would seem that our exemplary timequest is doomed to be a failure.

Or is it?

The problem with this interpretation is that although not one of the quests we have examined here achieves its formal goals, judging by the tone of the authors' attitudes, the way – typically – they handle their endings, not to mention the characters' own implicit reactions, the exercise on some level at least must be deemed to be *successful*. The obvious question that arises, then, is: if these seekers into the past prove unable to find the father, their explicit object, what exactly is it that they *do* discover? The obvious answer: the self.

This takes us full circle. Here again is the subversive underside I attributed to the temporal journey. Now, however, it seems to have emerged from obscurity to flaunt its true colours. The quest *beyond* turns out to have been the quest *within* all along. Unless, that is, our sample is biased. Unfortunately for our hopes of relation such would not seem to be the case. Even aside from books like *The Manticore* that address the theme of individuation directly, the fact is that *self*-discovery is almost always a concomitant of pilgrimages to the past. Klein's narrator and his Uncle Melech, for instance, merge at the end of the book into one symbolic personality combining 'incognito uncle and nephew unmet' (40): 'Each is a mirror image of the other,' says Miriam Waddington, 'and when the two images are brought together, we get, literally, a double exposure' (96). In *Surfacing*, with similar implications, when the protagonist examines the spot where she saw the 'ghosts' of her parents she finds only her own footsteps. Is this, though, *all* that may be achieved by our time-questor? – 'surfac[ing] into separateness,' as James Harrison puts it (80). On at least one level it would appear so. '[S]eeming to agree with Matthew Arnold rather than John Donne, yet without the former's melancholy resignation,' Harrison continues, 'Atwood almost claims it to be the inescapable human condition to be separate, to be alone, to be an island.' Yet – withal, in the end we are left with an image of the waiting Joe. Is there something in this fact, a message or a clue, that might help us salvage our timequest for the battle against solipsism? If we look at the other books on our list we will see that the same pattern, only vestigial in *Surfacing*, tends to appear again and again. Anna Dawe, in giving up on her father, joins in friendship and mutual misanthropy with her namesake, Anna Yellowbird. 'We walked out of there hand in hand, arm in arm, holding each other' (270). Becker joins in a nuptial celebration that confirms community. Klein's protagonist, most interesting of all, instead of finding the uncle who symbolizes both personal and racial past, finds the word that *creates* community. As Waddington describes it:

The figurative language of advertisements and daily transactions constituted the real miracle for Klein, who could find the only 'completely underivative poet' ... in language itself. Thus, language is at one and the same time both poetry and the source of poetic renewal; it is creation and creator together. The key image is miracle; but the miracle is language, and language, to the narrator, is poetry, and poetry is creation. (100)

If these questors fail to make contact with the past, *some* kind of connection clearly takes place.

What's going on here?

One way to explain the apparent paradox of a quest that is both a success and a failure is by hearkening back to features discussed earlier in this chapter. Despite the 'plausibility' of the timequest, the duplicity of the dénouement – the mechanism by which the displacement of affect from an approved but non-accessible goal (the absolute other) to one which is possible but prohibited (the self) is disguised by the introduction of a third formal alternative (the other self) which, though problematic, is viewed as less life-threatening – would seem merely to confirm the allegoric nature of the whole exercise. The intensity of affect, on the other hand, appears if not absolutely to rule out at least to resist such an eminently 'literary' explanation. The tone just doesn't fit. The evasive ending, far from 'contrived,' seems frequently to signal some kind of knee-jerk reaction, an unconscious response to an equally unconscious temperamental bias. In many books, indeed, the timequest carries such a strong air of compulsion as to suggest outright neurosis. The protagonist of Oonah McFee's *Sandbars* circles endlessly in an almost anguished attempt to focus on the precious, elusive parental figure ('"It's what I still don't know,"' she comments at her father's funeral: '"what I can't describe to myself – not being able to feel I am at last saying to him, "so that's what you saw and did! ..." That's what makes me sadder. All my life now, wherever I go, I'll never be free of that voice calling to me.' 93), but all that emerges clearly from her exploratory memoir are her own relentless, unanswered questions. 'Why am I forever being pulled to that pasture,' she asks. 'What is covered up in all that sky? ... Which mysteries are real? ... Or is it only my need?' (37, 104-5). There is neither rest nor comfort at the end of this quest; only a woman driven by a lack, a feeling of loss, a sense of mystery she can't even define. And what about Elisabeth d'Aulnières of *Kamouraska*, whose past not only haunts her but literally *drives* her to a frenzied nightmare recapitulation as if the punishment for her crime was to live it over and over, never let it end? Or the narrator/protagonist of Thomas's *Blown Figures*, moving deeper into madness even as, desperately ('Stuffing your hair into your mouth so you wouldn't scream' 134), she penetrates further back into time? Surely no journey that exudes such an air of irrational impulsion as this can be adequately compassed in terms of so conventional, so artificial a form as allegory?

The truth is that the impression of extreme anxiety we draw from these particular timequests only confirms all the more strongly the accuracy of our interpretation. Allegory itself, as Fletcher points out, strikingly resembles – indeed, may be considered a literary analogue for – the *compulsive syndrome* described by Freud. Consider – in the light of books like *Sandbars, Blown Figures*, and *Kamouraska* – the following description:

The commonest experience of the compulsive neurotic is that he is suddenly disturbed by impulses that have no apparent rational meaning, and thence are seen as arbitrary and external 'commands' [which, if ignored, generate anxiety] ... This anxiety is precisely the quality of the actions performed by the daemonic character [of allegory], since he is always determined to get to some goal, to reach home, to reach the Celestial City. Fear of not reaching that goal is even greater than fear of the particular terrors along the way. On the other hand, it is characteristic of allegorical plots that they preserve, on some level of literal meaning, a highly ordered sequence of events, which suggests that the anxiety does not usually break through the unbroken *surface* of compulsive fictions. The anxiety is kept in bounds by the rigid sequence of events leading to the winning of the quest. [Fletcher 287-8]

Following Fletcher's lead, then, the timequest as allegory, notwithstanding its feigned 'realism,' may perhaps be seen as both a manifestation of and an attempt to control, by symbolic means, the psychic distress that results from the enforced juggling of dangerous/designated and appealing/prohibited goals.

Let's examine this anxiety factor a little more closely. To start with, we should define more clearly how the allegory works. What we seem to have is an overt, unsuccessful attempt to penetrate and appropriate the past camouflaging a completed action focusing on horizontal connection. Does this mean that the two levels are mutually exclusive? Not at all. Here is where the allegory comes in. Although the primary quest for the father is by definition inconceivable inasmuch as it resolves itself into a confrontation with nature, it does serve as exemplary with respect to a more limited and strictly infra-human relation. More specifically, by demonstrating the ideal *value* if practical impossibility of self-submission to primeval otherness it both recommends and (by making it very clear which is the least of evils) facilitates the lesser opening of the self to the small othernesses that are other people. Beyond this it also asserts by elimination that this and this alone is what 'history' is for: to help us build *synapses*. The timequest, in other words, is simply a *model* of connection in its most basic form.

It sounds good, doesn't it? But if everything is so neatly rationalized, where – and why – does the anxiety come in?

Firstly, no matter that the possibility is covertly but definitively rejected, the very idea of the breaking down of barriers between self and other stimulates a certain amount of residual unease. This is hardly surprising. In Marian Engel's *Bear*, where the protagonist's historical excursus, eschewing for once the fiction of the lost father, is linked *explicitly* with the un-sane effort to make contact with nature, we find not only confirmation of the impossibility of such an endeavour but a clear indication that the attempt at transcendence must inevitably be repaid with pain. 'Lou assumes the stance of a female bear,' says Elspeth Cameron, 'only to be clawed and rejected. Nature itself draws the boundaries; the balance is righted; sanity resumes' (91). The 'moral' of this story is both predictable and revealing. Why? The one thing we must never lose sight of is the Canadian's conviction that the border between self and other –

any border between self and other – is simply, unalterably *taboo*. No matter what kinds of connectivity may be forged on a formal level, therefore, any suggestion that these may/should be translated into action is bound to set off negative reverberations, albeit inexplicit ones. In consequence of such problematic associations, even wholly inter-human connection, though self-evidently preferable to the primary option modelled by Engel, is disturbing enough to require very careful mediation. We will be looking further into this in the next chapter. In the meantime, it would be a mistake to underestimate the strength and persistence of the emotion it generates.

Secondly, and more important for our present subject, the transference of function to the horizontal level seems to discredit entirely the goal we started with, the establishment of relation through time. But why should this bother us so much? It's not as if we are thrown back, with Paul de Man and his recently not uncommon ilk, on the distressing conclusion that 'language is a self-enclosed system from which human consciousness cannot escape' [Mellor 218]. *Some* form of connection is implied to be possible, albeit an extremely limited one. What we are forgetting here, though, is the strong suggestion conveyed by some of our earlier examples that it is not merely history-as-occasion that focuses our need but history as the repository of some crucial if inexplicit good-in-itself: *real* history, that is.

Can we get any further now with our explication of the attitudes and expectations associated with this drive? The primary motivation is a desire for continuity, we said – continuity, and a symbolic escape from death. But given the timequest's duplicity, what exactly does this mean? Certainly our object is not, or not merely, the kind of abstract value invoked by historian George Wrong when he asserts, blandly, that 'history, like Christian teaching, heal[s] and conciliate[s]' (Berger 21). No – judging by the attendant concern, we have a much more personal stake invested in 'history' than this. Part of it, no doubt, is simply our conviction, being debarred from space, that the temporal dimension offers our last means of finding 'real' order in our world, order we can believe to be 'given' rather than imposed. 'Within the extended family,' says Patricia Tobin,

the individual member is guaranteed both identity and legitimacy through the tracing of his lineage back to the founding father, the family's origin and first cause. This project-in-retrospect of the children is matched in the prospective design of the father. He extends the paternal promise of purpose throughout his progeny, bestowing upon them a legacy that contains within this structural unity an entire history of meaning. By an analogy of function, events in time come to be perceived as begetting other events within a line of causality similar to the line of generations, [such that] ... all possibly random events and gratuitous details are brought into an alignment of relevance. [7]

Even beyond the obvious consolation offered by such a vision of regulated coherence, however, on the evidence of our literature Canadians clearly attach considerable importance to the ability not merely to *believe in* history passively but to *relate to* it actively. Again, why? Peter Stevens implies that it is simply a matter of ambition: 'It is as if the poet is suggesting that if he can rescue [his subjects] ... from oblivion, present them on paper in real language, then he will rescue himself as poet from oblivion' (195). Davies' Dunstan Ramsay would agree. 'Historians come and go,' he says, 'but the document remains, and it has the importance of a thing that cannot be changed or gainsaid ... I deeply wanted to create, or record, and leave behind me a document ... [in order that] so far as this world is concerned, I should not wholly die' (c21). Is this all there is to it, though? Countering – or at least complementing – Stevens's implication I would suggest, reviewing the corpus, that the obsession goes far beyond the need to see oneself immortalized in print. After all, if that were the whole of it, *any* topic of importance, not merely history, should serve the writer's purpose. The fact is, there is more than a hint of the superstitious, the not-quite-wholly-rational, to be detected in our dealings with history. Indeed, reading through these timequests, noting their sense of urgency, we may easily fancy the *sotto voce* assertion that if and only if we are able to redeem history, then by some magical retroactivity history – that is, posterity – will be able to redeem us. It is probably because of this that Canadian writers, even aside from their predilection for the timequest as a platform, devote a remarkable amount of attention in their fictions to the arbitration of such questions as the nature of time, the difference between history and myth, real and true: it is an attempt, quite simply, to come up with a view of history that will sidestep if not reconcile the ambiguities experience seems to reveal.

Before we examine some of the products of this exercise it might be useful to consider what kind of historical models the Canadian would find ready to hand if he looked elsewhere in the contemporary world. Actually, a quick survey suggests that history has fallen on hard times in the last few decades. In the United States its relevance is still generally assumed without too much question (though, predictably considering the observations above, if we look closely we will note that what the average American usually means when he talks of history is simply a collocation of local facts informed by myth), but in Europe, much as the Québécois have made history a whipping boy for their own loss of faith, the genealogical imperatives of previous generations are now commonly not only discarded for their failure to comprehend the true complexity of life ('Every corner of space conceals a multitude of individuals, each one of whom totalizes the trend of history in a manner which cannot be compared to the others,' says Lévi-Strauss; '... Even history which claims to be universal is still only a juxtaposition of a few local histories within which (and between which) very much more is left out than put in'[65]) but excoriated for their treachery in promulgating dangerous delusions, false expectations of 'meaning.' For Hegel, says Jacques Choron, 'history has an ultimate goal toward which it moves.' For Heidegger, in contrast, 'there is no comforting vision of history that can neutralize the meaninglessness of human existence that death, as final annihilation, seems to proclaim' [238]. On the basis of this perception, many European intellectuals, and especially the existentialists, would seemingly cast out the concept altogether. Sartre, for instance, taking up Nietszche's dictum that the best chance for human health and happiness lies in forgetfulness,[66] proclaims that the only important kind of time is *human* time, a time which (in Frank Kermode's description) is not imposed from without but generated from within as a kind of eternal momentousness 'faring forward irreversibly into a virgin future from ecstasy to ecstasy': 'The future is a fluid medium in which I try to actualize my potency, though the end is unattainable; the present is simply the *pour-soi*, "human consciousness in its flight out of the past into the future." The past is bundled into the *en-soi*, and has no relevance. "I was is not the foundation of what I am, any more than what I am is the foundation of what I shall be"' [139]. It is against and in specific reaction to this radical scepticism that all contemporary views of history must be seen as having evolved. Stipulating the common background, however, the corpus actually yields two apparently quite different styles of response which for convenience may be designated (though not without some risk of oversimplification) the subjective and the objective modes.

The first of these approaches derives ultimately from Romanticism. In its specifically modern version, though, it follows directly from Sartre's views mentioned above. The key, as with other aspects of existentialism we have observed, is self-actuation. If universal history is a fraud and history-as-given merely an unordered and unorderable aggregation of contingent details, man's only option is either to 'make up' a version of the past consonant with his own experience and needs or, more extremely, to step outside of history altogether by transferring his affect to the timeless aesthetic realm where alone – in Arturo Fallico's words – 'we find experience which endures, not by substitution and displacement, but by the kind of self-identical re-positing which keeps self-identity in being.'[67] Combining both these impulses, many recent European writers turn not merely to art but to an art that is explicitly anti-historical. This results on the one hand in priority being given to subjects and themes that confirm life's meaninglessness. More subtly, it implies that the significance traditionally imputed to temporal verisimilitude – the imitation of life through the creation of pseudo-histories – will now be reserved for those narrative shifts that *explode* the historical illusion. Once this happens, organization is no longer temporal but spatial; history is no longer embodied in but *replaced by* the wholly self-validated fiction.

We see much the same deliberate desanctification of the past among the

American avant-garde as well. '[T]he post-modernists,' says James Rother, 'when they deign to think of history at all, see it ... as "an aggregate of last moments," and there are countless millions of them. Or to put it another way, history is but a contrived *memento mori*, a slush fund of deceptions whose chimeras turn out inevitably to be just what E.L. Doctorow's *Ragtime* suggests they are, mirror images of our fictive selves.'[68] The question arises, of course – especially in view of my claim that Americans simply *assume* history – as to how representative the views expressed by this admittedly rather small group of writers really are. Oddly enough, if we put aside our preconceptions, we find what appears to be a paradox: with regard to his ahistoricism the American post-modernist both is and is not in the mainstream of his nation's thought. At first glance there would seem to be a tremendous gap between the work of people like Barthelme and Pynchon on the one hand and the vast quantity of contemporaneous pulp-to-best-sellers on the other if only because most of the latter is clearly based in a wholly conventional view of orderly historical process. If we turn to historical scholarship in the country – which, though slightly modified during the past quarter-century by the mild relativism of such individuals as Carl L. Becker and Charles A. Beard, has traditionally been strongly biased toward the practice of the nineteenth-century erudite school deriving from the work of von Ranke, with its emphasis on impartial fact and exhaustive documentation – the gap seems even wider. In the light of other propensities to be discerned in American historiography, however, we might speculate that this ostentatious facticity in both scholarship and fiction is founded less in a von Rankean passion for objectivity than in that same uniquely American dread of mechanistic determinism we find expressed so vividly in literary vehicles ranging from Dos Passos' *U.S.A.* through Heller's *Catch-22* to thousands of volumes of dystopic science fiction. In direct contrast to propensities we have observed in Canada, in other words, one may speculate that the ultra-individualistic American has been motivated to minimize 'connections' simply because of the sense of coercion carried by any concept of historical determinacy. We find much the same implication, moreover, if we probe below the surface of the apparent democratization of American history which has taken place this century under the influence especially of James Harvey Robinson and the school of 'New Historians.' For all the much-touted aims of achieving a more 'realistic' reconstruction of the past, the fact is, the shift of attention from political to industrial leaders and thence to the 'little man' one may perceive not merely in scholarly historiography but even more strikingly in aspects of folk culture (just think of the classic American war movie with its focus on the 'regular' G.I.) is really nothing but a progressively more blatant exemplification of the wishful Promethean myth that in America everyman can – indeed, must – be a *hero*, that is, an 'individual to whom we can justifiably attribute preponderant influence in determining an issue or event whose consequences would have been profoundly different if he had not acted as he did.'[69] Lurking beneath the rational surface of American views of 'history,' therefore, is an assumption fully as egocentric as that which the avant-garde novelist expresses explicitly: the individual-as-American, it is believed, just like Wallace Stevens's jar on the hill in Tennessee, *gives point and meaning to history simply by virtue of his presence in it.* This, for all that it is evidently unintentional and even unrecognized, is subjectivity par excellence.

Crossing to the other side of the fence, we move from the generally aesthetic to the self-consciously scientific. The second response one can make to the perception that traditional historical explanations are inadequate is not to proclaim, with the existentialists, that all order is fictional but – and here the exemplary stance is demonstrated by the structuralists[70] – to insist that it is immanent in phenomena-at-large, if apparently inaccessible on a purely individual level. Discrediting both the humanist notion of transcendent authority *and* the phenomenological notion of subject, in other words, this stance implies that the historian will address himself to those aspects, and *only* those aspects of reality for which he can reasonably postulate objective existence. According to Claude Lévi-Strauss, there are two basic routes by which one can approach this task:

The historian's relative choice, with respect to each domain of history he gives up, is always confined to the choice between history which teaches us more and explains less, and history which explains more and teaches less. The only way he can avoid the dilemma is by getting outside history: either by the bottom, if the pursuit of information leads him from the consideration of groups to that of individuals and then to their motivations which depend on their personal history and temperament, that is to say to an infra-historical domain in the realms of psychology and physiology; or by the top, if the need to understand incites him to put history back into prehistory and the latter into the general evolution of organized beings, which is itself explicable only in terms of biology, geology, and finally cosmology. [262]

The latter of these approaches, the macroscopic, is the one embraced both by Lévi-Strauss himself and by Freudian interpreter Jacques Lacan, both of whom, as Geoffrey Sturrock points out, 'are concerned with the operations performed by the human mind in general, not just with the workings of particular minds at particular times' [4]. The former and more radically 'objective,' on the other hand, is demonstrated variously in the work of Roland Barthes, Jacques Derrida, and Michel Foucault. The last named of these writers offers the most interesting standard of comparison for our present study inasmuch as his books in a sense represent the ultimate catalogue. Approaching his subject matter inductively or, as he calls it, *archeologically*, Foucault seeks to replace *total history* ('The project ... that seeks to reconstitute the overall form of a civilization, the principle – material or spiritual – of a society, the significance common to all the phenomena of a period, the law that accounts for their cohesion'[71]) with *general history*, that is, a kind of critical activity which would infer patterns and correlations, if any, *only* from the observed characteristics of the data itself, thus reconstituting the edifice of historical meaning not from an idealized set of blueprints but literally from the ground up. This, then, as against Sartrean self-creation, is the new 'objective' approach to history.

Next step: assuming that the Canadian were going to pick his view rationally from the range of available alternatives in much the same way as he would choose a new car, let's consider briefly how he might respond to these various theoretical possibilities. It's obvious from our foregoing observations that he will not be content to rest with complete ahistoricism, but what about the existentialist/American response versus the structuralists' claims? This is a hard one to call. With regard to subjectivity, for instance, although it is undeniable that fiction, by making experience more coherent, may be, if not quite 'real,' truer to the *heart* than fact, it is also evident that our almost morbid consciousness of the recalcitrance of 'things' makes us uncomfortable with either European-style subjectivization or American egocentricity. History for us (in Louis O. Mink's words) 'is still a matter of what "everyone knows" that the events and actions of past actuality happened *just as they did*, and there is therefore something for historiography, however fallible, to be about, something which makes it true or false even though we have no access to that something.'[72] We can't believe, therefore, that one has the moral right, let alone the ability, to change the facts, whether physical or temporal, just by wishing. The objective approach, alternately, poses even greater problems for the Canadian psyche. On the one hand it satisfies, or at least purports to satisfy, the reality requirement, but on the other it denies us that sense of meaningful connection that catalysed our quest into history in the first place. 'This supreme anti-teleologist resists the lure of any definitive ending,' says Hayden White of Foucault, 'just as he delights in beginnings that open in "free play," discoveries of paradoxes, and intimations of the folly underlying any "will to know."'[73] For all our thing-obsession, any confirmation that nothing *but* the contingent is available to human comprehension also disturbs us deeply inasmuch as it appears to mock our already painful sense of embeddedness in the natural. Nor is this the worst of it. The Foucault-style solution is even more seriously compromised by the fact that, judging by our literature, Canadians have serious doubts about whether the project it purports to achieve is *possible*. Our faith in the potential of any brand of trans-personal 'knowing' is notoriously small. Our scepticism is not without basis, either. By some quirk of chance or human nature, it was the most impersonal, objective, and outright mechanical theories of 'history' produced by the nineteenth century – Darwinism, Freudianism, and, especially, Marxism, with its millennialist promise that the *end* of history is at hand – which sparked the greatest *myths* of the twentieth.[74] Even Foucault, despite, or perhaps because of, his celebrated aim of demythicizing discourse, his determination to 'expose the dark underside of every discursive formation purporting to serve "the will of truth"' [White in Sturrock 90], does not escape this taint. As Vincent Descombes points out:

The conjunction of positivism and nihilism in the same intelligence produces a surprising mixture. Every one of Foucault's affirmations is ringed with a formidable critical apparatus (documents, quotations, intricate references), and yet it would be possible to construct alternative accounts using the same data – variations which Foucault himself is the first to sound. As certain historians have said, Foucault's work properly belongs to the genre of fiction ('Once upon a time...', 'If I were King...'). His histories are novels. [117]

Theoretically at least, then, both subjectivity *and* objectivity leave a lot to be desired.

Turning to the corpus itself, the next question we have to consider is whether the Canadian manages to achieve any better accommodation between the extremes in practice than seems possible in theory. A good number of works, judging by the radical ambivalence they reveal, would suggest that the endeavour is difficult if not impossible. In Harlow's *Scann*, for instance, the title character asserts again and again that to impose form on life is fraudulent ('This is memory as memory always is: fixed like light on film, and denying the rational need for connection, movement, culmination' 40; 'There are no beginnings or endings' 40; '[L]ife is a discontinuous narrative surrounded and made durative by the habit of mere existence ...' 237), but countering strongly this post-modernist refrain the whole book is a demonstration of the writer's desperate efforts to find and/or create that very meaning in history which his common sense assures him is non-existent. In the end, defeated by his own project, forced to relinquish the hope of any existential certainty whatsoever, he is left with only one thought, one hope: '"There are no beginnings and endings ..." he says, stuffing his briefcase and closing it. "*But there are responsibilities*"' (306, italics added). What this means is that Scann – and I think we might extend this dictum to cover a substantial number of Canadian writers – while unable to relinquish either fact *or* meaning, understands that each of us has an obligation to grapple with rather than surrender to the paradox of history.

This, then, is what we find in most of the books dealing with the problem: grappling, not resolution. Interestingly enough, the metaphors employed most frequently to explore the differential claims of the two basic modes of historiography are the *still photograph* and the *movie*. It's worth taking the time to look at these at least briefly once more from this point of view, inasmuch as between them they illuminate not merely the polarities but the peculiarities of the Canadian response.

HISTORY-AS-FILM

The consensus seems to be that film is essentially untrustworthy. Despite the ostentatious givenness of its visual components, and perhaps all the more disturbing in the context of this illusive realism, the sequence, the arrangement, the *flow* which, duplicitously, give a film both its great verisimilitude and its fabricated meaning are all self-evidently contrived. As a result, whenever the film image is invoked, even casually, in fiction or poetry, the problem of artifice is invoked as well. One of the most extended treatments of the theme is found in Davies' *World of Wonders* where the lengthy and explicit discussions of the theatricality of the art, the camera's ability to lie by misdirection, and, most of all, the film's problematic subjectivity ('[T]he skill of the cutting, and the juxtapositions, and the varieties of pace that had been achieved, were marvels to me. Clearly much of what had been done owed its power to the art of [the cameraman], but the unmistakable impress of [the director's] mind was on it, as well. His films possessed a weight of implication – in St Pierre's phrase, "the evidence of things not seen" – that was entirely his own.' 152) are largely, though not quite entirely, neutralized by the author's strong suggestion that the plausibility achieved by an 'artful' imitation of life is actually more 'true-to-history' than the 'dead things' presented passively in museums (58-60). This is usually the defence offered for explicit artifice in Canadian fiction: the possibility that it offers more rather than less authenticity. 'Anything I could have said would have been implausible,' says Atwood's Lady Oracle. 'This was the reason I fabricated my life, time after time: the truth was not convincing' (150). Unfortunately, this rationale isn't entirely convincing either. Even in *World of Wonders*, with Ramsay's (and Davies') assertions about the capacity of myth to enrich human life forming a persuasive sub-text to the story, the artifice of the film, juxtaposed as it is with the rather nastier 'gaff' of Eisengrim's carnie days, retains a certain air of moral equivocality. In other versions, like a number of the poems in Florence MacNeil's *Ghost Towns*, the ambiguous undertones come right out in the open.

'Newsreel'

My face made of barbed wire
is amplified silently
between Charlie Chaplin and the serial
Before I die
ladies will remove their hats

the shells will explode like paper flowers
I will run insubstantially
out of
my celluloid trench
my hands parrying the smoke
will accompany the piano player
in a gesture
of unconscious entertainment
and the gas searing my printed lungs
will be orchestrated on stage
to accompany
the slow march
out of the theatre. (13)

HISTORY-AS-PHOTO-ALBUM

Both the ubiquity of the photograph and the ambivalence of its symbolic connotations have been discussed. It remains only to see what specific relevance it has to the problem of history. The most extended development of this theme is found in Kroetsch's *Badlands*, a novel that, as most commentators have noted, appears to be explicitly and intentionally anti-historical. Perhaps, though, the message isn't quite as simple as it seems. What we have, in fact, are a number of mutually reflective and/or exclusive ideas about history revolving around the iconic role of paleontologist William Dawe. 'A man of rationality, he wishes to classify and order the material world in a logical pattern of moral implications,' explains Connie Harvey. 'He will not accept randomness and uncontrolled phenomena [because he] ... is afraid of the irrational force of life ... His maniacal compulsion to recover the past is prompted by this fear. He wants to prove that there is something permanent that is not touched by man's transitory lust for life' (345). He sounds like an only slightly exaggerated version of the prototypical Canadian, doesn't he? Bracketing Dawe's response are the alternate possibilities of, on the one hand, total subjectivity, represented by the ahistorical Web ('Web does not believe in the past. He is homeless because he burnt his father out.' Harvey 37), a man whose immediate response to experience is to transmute it into myth ('Priapic Web,' says Arnold Davidson, '... is the man most given to, in Anna's terms, the "mythologies of the flesh" ... So Web invents himself too. he turns his fiasco in the whorehouse "into magnificent success"; his modest success with Anna Yellowbird ... into an X-rated exploit of an amorous Pecos Bill.' 132), and on the other, total objectivity, represented by the photographer Sinnott. Critical opinion is almost unanimous in assuming that the latter is meant to provide an unambiguously negative model, largely due to the same problematic connotations of photography discussed above. There are at least a few points, however, that such an interpretation fails to account for. Firstly, although Sinnott's habit of 'giving his photographs portentous and cynically "naive" titles' is indeed a kind of fakery aimed at exploiting 'the romance of the past' (see D.P. Thomas 128-9), we note that his 'tainted' view of reality is enthusiastically confirmed by his models, often even at the cost of their own dignity, as if in their eyes 'fake' meaning – especially 'fake' meaning as convincingly 'real' as a photograph – is far better than none. Secondly, Sinnott's art gives at least a semblance of life to the otherwise wholly dead Tune. Finally, and perhaps most importantly, Sinnott is the only questor in the story who gets exactly what he wants and makes a clean getaway. Complementing this, it is obvious that Web, for all his retrospective fictionalizing, is quite helpless when it comes to, and indeed is rather badly tyrannized by, the *facts* of life. Leaving aside primitivistic assumptions about the value of 'naturalness,' therefore, it is not entirely clear that either of these polarities is presented as unequivocally preferable. So what is left? Kroetsch seems to suggest that there are really only two possibilities. One can give up on the past altogether as Anna does or one can settle, like Dawe, for a compromise version: a *glimpse* of history, a *token* posterity.

THE DIVINERS

Approaching the theme more explicitly than any other Canadian work of literature, this novel explores at length the differential modes of retrospectivity betokened by both photographs and movies. Interestingly enough, as exemplified in Laurence's stylistic innovations the book actually suggests three rather than merely two possibilities. Representing the objective option, predictably, are the snapshots Morag retains from her early childhood. The most significant aspect of these totemic artifacts is the fact that although they may not communicate much they are ultimately resistant to falsification, retaining an integrity and mystery all their own which is only made to seem more palpable – and more compelling – by the inadequacy of Morag's obviously (and self-confessedly) invented explanations. '*I keep the snapshots not for what they show but for what is hidden in them*' (6). At the opposite extreme from the snapshots, representing radical subjectivity, are the hallucinatory film-like fragments into which Morag's mind compulsively translates experience during emotional crises or daydreaming episodes. Finally, mediating between these two are the Memorybank Movies, an explicitly formalized (hence the title) stream of recollection and/or narration which is both 'composed' and, judging by its emotional authority, at least in terms of the text itself, 'true.' Emotions aside, the question is what kind of *general* significance are we intended to impute to this mediating category. Most critics assume that it is a normative and therefore wholly positive representation of the re-creative powers of the imagination. Laurence's Memorybank Movies, claims Barbara Hehner, 'are meant to illustrate her belief that every person, writer and non-writer alike, makes a fiction of his past truth, and by doing so, transmutes it into new truth. And the new truth is myth' (53). While I would not deny that the Memorybank Movies do indeed represent the fictionalizing process, there is ample evidence in the book that Laurence doesn't view this activity totally unequivocally. To counter Morag's quasi-climactic recognition of the non-factual and mutually contradictory legends of Piper Gunn and Rider Tonnerre as both 'true' and valuable, for instance, the novel returns again and again to a concerned questioning of the propriety and even morality of invention ('A daft profession. Wordsmith. Liar, more likely. Weaving fabrications.' 25). If this weren't enough, the final and subsuming image of divining, as noted earlier, by suggesting *the passive discovery of what is given* clearly counters any apparent approbation of the explicitly creative act. As far as the possibility of retrieving history is concerned, furthermore, though we know from Laurence's comments both in and outside her fiction that she considers the assimilation of the past to be a crucial aspect of identity-building, this is something, too, which *The Diviners* fails in the end to settle. One wonders whether the book's famous opening image of a river flowing two ways at once ('The current moved from north to south, but the wind usually came from the south, rippling the bronze-green water in the opposite direction') shouldn't be taken as the author's final comment on the subject. If so, the implications are far from reassuring. If the forward-moving current of history is not only invisible but irresistible, it is unfortunately clear that the backward-looking winds of myth only provide an *illusion* of movement in the water. If Laurence may be taken as representative, it would seem that the Canadian's attempt to normalize his relationship with history is a hopeless failure.

But then things are so rarely what they appear.

What happens if we move back a step or two? Actually, if the Canadian remains unable to resolve the photo/movie question with any degree of assurance on the level of individual books, we may infer from the oeuvre as a whole that he *has* managed to devise a set of techniques for living with and even exploiting the split. It is with a brief survey of these that both this chapter and our whole case for Canadian historicism must ultimately rest.

So – last question: how do we pull it off? The answer (we knew it all along): by sleight of hand! Or, to be more specific, by sleight of *word*.

The first of the key adaptive mechanisms by which the Canadian seeks to rationalize his quandary is simply a kind of *displacement*. The inaccessibility of the past is camouflaged by mentally integrating specifically temporal relations into a general network of objective, quasi-causal connections unifying human and non-human experience on all levels. History-as-progression-of-temporal-events is thus transformed into history-as-condition. The result? The allegoric and 'real' quests become mutually entailed rather than antagonistic. Treating connections *in* time implicitly confirms those harder-to-elucidate connections *through* time. This is undoubtedly why even in non-fictional historical writing there is a tendency to emphasize such connections. Harold Innis's example is pre-eminent in this regard. As Berger points out with reference to *The Fur Trade in Canada*, in contrast to the American school of Parkman with its emphasis on 'the activity of heroic figures and the adventure of exploration,' Innis's approach accentuated 'the interplay of geographical, technological, and economic forces. At every turn the tempo and direction of expansion, the very efforts of men involved in the trade, were depicted as reflections of inescapable and anonymous forces' (94). Relation with the past is thus guaranteed at least indirectly by means of an implication that *everything* is related.

The second strategy, though in some ways just a logical extension of the first, also involves a kind of cultural *regression*. Inasmuch as he is naturally predisposed in this way to a unified view of temporal phenomena – a propensity strikingly reinforced by an 'Old Testament' ethical orientation, since the latter (in Auerbach's words) already implies 'an unchangeable system of categories'[75] – the Canadian is inclined to endorse or at least, implicitly, to assume exactly that kind of humanistic historical thinking so despised by the existentialist. The Canadian, in other words, though he may never articulate such an idea *acts as though he believed* in the existence and the operation of the kind of regulatory mechanism a faith in which both motivated and justified the late-eighteenth-century project of devising or discovering within or behind diverse historical phenomena a single theme or (as Kant described it) ' "regular movement" ' such that ' "what seems complex and chaotic in the single individual may be seen from the standpoint of the human race as a whole to be steady and progressive though slow evolution of its original endowment" ' [in Mink 136]; that is, a *Universal History*. It may be objected, of course, that having repudiated the possibility of transcendental verifications, whether Christian or otherwise, we lack the assurance of progress, of purpose, seemingly implicit in such a concept.[76] As Mink points out, however, Universal History, at its most basic, by no means requires such a narrow interpretation. 'Universal History was not the idea that there is a particular plot in the movement of history but the assumption that underlays all proposals to display one sort of plot or another,' he says [136]. As a result, though one must necessarily accept that there is a single (though perhaps locally unintelligible) theme uniting all diverse particulars, the form in which that theme manifests itself in any given period is at least theoretically variable: 'it does not imply that there is a *law* of historical development or that the detailed course of events is inexorable' [137]. It is quite possible therefore to conceive of Universal History not as rationalizing and certainly not as predetermining specific instances of historical development but, rather, as simply providing 'the grid on which any of them might be traced'

[138]. It is this kind of invisible grid which, I would maintain, the Canadian seems to assume. How does this affect literary usage? Well, for one thing it rules out entirely the kind of Carlylean self-actuated romantic hero who, as Georg Lukács describes it, stands as a specific 'literary expression of ... social eccentricity and superfluity.'[77] Accepting the tenets of Universal History, at best we may posit a 'representative' hero à la Sir Walter Scott who both exemplifies and is created by specific 'social trends and historical forces'[78]; at worst we are forced to embrace a quasi-Tolstoyan notion that history has nothing to do with heroes of any sort, being merely enacted, unconsciously and spontaneously, by aggregates of individuals living out 'their normal, private and egoistic lives' [Lukács 98]. But all this is quite congenial to the Canadian temperament anyway. Indeed, numerous other aspects of literary preference and practice observed throughout this book go far to confirm the inference that Universal Historical assumptions do indeed underlie the Canadian world view.

The third and final strategy for normalizing our relationship with history is a little more complicated than these first two. Not surprisingly in view of the tendencies apparently inherent in our national character, it comprises a kind of literary *duplicity*. Notwithstanding their ambivalence, Canadian writers do seem to share a common intuition that the fictional aspect of literature is important. For all its dubious and even sinister implications of presumption (which threatens the writer) and deceitfulness (which threatens the reader) it seems highly possible that it is the only means of making sense out of life that we do or ever will have. Does this mean we give up on history? Not at all. It only means that we have to accept the possibility that it is only through fiction that history can be redeemed. Indeed, inasmuch as 'history,' especially the sort mentioned in the last paragraph, is itself merely a kind of 'fictive substitute for authority and tradition, a maker of concords between past, present, and future, a provider of significance to mere chronicity' [Kermode 56], we are forced to recognize that it is ultimately impossible to draw a line between the two. On the other hand, we still stop short of Kermode's assertion that fictions actually work for us 'better than history, perhaps better than theology, *largely because they are consciously false*' [64, italics added]. In marked contrast to this American-style affirmation of personal freedom what the Canadian wants above all, circumventing the problem he can't resolve, is a fiction *like a map* which is both 'made' and 'found,' a fiction that may be treated *as if* it were reality.

The question is: how does fiction achieve this sort of status? The hovering presence of a vague faith in Universal History helps (as Kermode points out, there is a significant difference between 'a literature which assume[s] that it [is] imitating an order [and] a literature which assumes that it has to create an order' [167]), but it is not really enough. For one thing, rather than continuing to set 'reality' and 'invention' at eternal odds, we have to come up with a vehicle that can accommodate the two quite different varieties of 'truth' which, as Gerald Mast points out, are implicit in our photography metaphor:

[T]he term 'realist' means one thing in its common application to a painting or photograph and quite another thing in its equally common application to a novel or play. A realistic visual image is one that is said to 'look like,' 'resemble,' 'reproduce,' 'iconically represent' the surfaces of the visual world. We see – or think we see, or have learned how to see, or are fooled into thinking we see – in a painting what we see – or think we see – in the real world. But a realistic story is one that is said to chronicle 'credibly,' 'probably,' and 'believably' the way we think people feel, think, or act, the way things happen, and the reasons they happen, all of which are consistent with the reader-audience-society's beliefs about psychology, motivation, and probability. The standard of one sense of realism is primarily visual while the standard of the other is primarily psychological.[79]

How does Canadian literature achieve this sort of integration? One fairly primitive means is simply that passive juxtaposition of unresolved alternatives on the level of theme or content which we have seen already in the work – and, indeed, the theory – of such writers as Kroetsch.[80] More structured approaches, however, demonstrate the potential for a far higher degree of resolution. Canadian writers have always tended to make some sort of functional discrimination between form and content, not wrenching them apart exactly but endowing the former with an unusual autonomy and authority of presence that prevents it from serving simply as the passive container of the latter. This means on the one hand that the innate duplicity of 'given' experience is automatically both expressed and exposed by virtue of its simultaneous participation in the signifying or referential order and the self-sufficient order of things. '[E]vents occur not only as a causal series, each step leading toward a conclusion, but also as a series of tableaux, icons, moments,' says Helwig of one of his own stories (c81). More radically, it gives form a semantic weight of its own equal to and independent of the conventional information-carrying function of fact. Form, in a sense, actually becomes a kind of counter-content.[81] Why is this important? In the first place it provides a supplementary means of assertion which by its very nature is non-negatable and therefore immune to the depredations of any form of reality criterion – a characteristic which, according to Hayden White, is common to both literary and historical 'classics.'[82] In the second place, it means that two virtually independent levels of signification can be carried by the same vehicle. How does this work out in practice? Think of *The Temptations of Big Bear*, where a wide range of unreconciled and irreconcilable material is contained by the single integrating factor of Wiebe's style. Think of Findley's *The Wars*, even more extremely, where an obtrusive denial of authorial mediation is balanced by a dramatic, confrontational mode of presentation which literally forces the reader to impose a 'plot.' What we have in both these novels, as indeed in a substantial number of Canada's most successful literary productions, is an artful arrangement of constituent elements such that *while the content of a given work (symbolized by photographs) asserts the discontinuity of experience, the form (symbolized by movies) asserts a counterbalancing and palliative wholeness.*

This brings us right back to allegory again as providing the best conventional structure within which to comprehend a double reality. Philosophy aside, in the end the Canadian manages to unify his divided response by utilizing forms in which the signifier (both unsystematic and opaque) and the signified (an ideal of order possibly but not necessarily corresponding to anything real) may be simultaneously dissociated and conjoined.

NOTES

1 In view of the fact that the title of this chapter seems to allude so pointedly to Timothy Findley's *Famous Last Words*, the reader may wonder why the latter is not even mentioned in the text. Oddly enough, the reference was purely unintentional – I did not come across Findley's book until my manuscript had been packed off to the publishers. If I *had* been looking for a pre-eminent illustration of the propensities on which this chapter focuses, however, I could not have made a better choice than the item thus accidentally invoked. Indeed, it is remarkable how close this novel comes – not merely in narrative technique but in numerous idiosyncrasies of stance and thrust, form and content – to 'the' Canadian novel which by now we should see emerging, slowly but surely, from the cultural ground.

2 Paul Zweig, *The Adventurer* (Basic Books 1974) 116

3 Heidegger, 'Building Dwelling Thinking' in *Poetry, Language, Thought*, trans. Albert Hostadter (Harper Colophon 1971) 157

4 Cavell, *The World Viewed: Reflections on the Ontology of Film*, (Harvard 1979) 21, 18, 189

5 In Ondaatje's book, as Anne Blott points out, 'Machines – guns, camera, and pencil – are shown to fragment and isolate single impressions out of the movement of life. This disintegration of living things is also seen in metaphors drawn from the still photo and the motion picture, conceived of as a series of stills infinitely arrangeable. Fixing, one metaphor from photography, runs throughout the book in the recurrences of madness and of hypnosis, a term defined once as "animal magnetism" and used in the text to explore the mentalities of killers: Billy, Garrett, and Livingstone. In this way, the transformation of nature to machine is linked through metaphor to the theme of madness' (188).

6 This idea forms the basic premise of Dick Harrison's *Unnamed Country: The Struggle for a Canadian Prairie Fiction*, for instance.

7 It is Reaney who offers the classic interpretation of this aspect. 'In this poem Pratt is always careful to show the struggle against Nature, against the Rockies and the

North Shore of Lake Superior as a struggle against something inside the human mind as well as something outside it,' he says. 'John A. Macdonald and Van Horne are always struggling with their own inability to express their vision in words so that other minds will be persuaded of its truth. This is the real struggle, the attempt to make words conquer all that is unknown. The transcontinental railroad has to be built painfully in people's minds as well as in their country. The poet's success in showing how the railroad grew in and out of human minds – Macdonald's mind, Van Horne's mind – removes the poem from the bank mural category, a category in which thousands of brawny young men hack away at large mountains of rock and the general effect is one of rock cutting away at rock' (G75).

8 Harbison, *Eccentric Spaces* (Knopf 1977) 159

9 ' "You look engrossed, Ma," Pique said. "What you got there? Hardcore porn? Hey, a *weed* book?" ...

'"I think it's marvellous, to find out all about them, Morag."

' "Oh, she doesn't," Pique said, laughing. "I'll bet she couldn't identify more than half a dozen. She just likes the names. Isn't that so, Ma?"

'*This girl knows me.*

' "Yeh," Morag admitted. "I guess so ..." ' (407).

10 As Elizabeth Marsland describes it, many fictional roads and railroads, 'far from being fragments in the middle of nowhere, are obviously parts of a continuous system, and because of such connectedness the sense of isolation of the remote community is reduced. The technique used by several authors – Roy, Constantin-Weyer, Primeau – to introduce the reader to the settlement, relying on those same travel facilities, has similar effect. Portage-des-Prés may be a "petit village insignifiant," far away "dans la mélancholique région des lacs et des canards sauvages," but we are shown how the village is linked with Rorketon, the end of the railway – albeit only by "un mauvais *trail* raboteux" – as well as the four stages by which one reaches the even more remote island' (75).

11 Harbison has some interesting comments to make about this aspect of our line symbol when he discusses the Roman road. 'The roads which ran from Rome in various directions till they hit the coast were ... ideal rays, radiations of Roman power. "All roads lead to Rome" coerces more than we think, means that the center has absolutely been ordained by human will, that all journeys have been plotted at the start, that the quality of clockwork has been imparted to human affairs. Roman roads were laid perfectly straight in an outlying place like Britain not because it was easy to do it that way but to show that even this wild did not defeat the Roman mind, which could treat it as if it were a plane. These roads stated clearly that the power came from man, who did not mean to respect the land' (45-6).

12 Significantly, Ondaatje's aggressive Billy the Kid is also, Stephen Scobie points out, 'constantly in motion both literally (the finger exercises) and ontologically (as his image shifts between historical fact, legendary accretion, and the creations of Ondaatje's personal imagination)' (B16).

13 Edmund Leach, *Culture and Communication* (Cambridge 1976) 51
14 André LeVot, 'Disjunctive and Conjunctive Modes in Contemporary American Fiction,' *Forum* 14, 1 (1976) 44-5
15 Mellor, 'On Romantic Irony Symbolism and Allegory,' *Criticism* 21 (1979) 217-19
16 Feidelson, *Symbolism and American Literature* (U. Chicago 1953) 8, 15
17 Fletcher, *Allegory: The Theory of a Symbolic Mode* (Cornell 1970) 99-100, 102, 162, 222
18 Culler, *Structuralist Poetics: Structuralism, Linguistics, and the Study of Literature* (Cornell 1976) 229
19 Burkhardt, *Shakespearean Meanings* (Princeton 1968) 27
20 Life, he says in an author's note to *Colours in the Dark*, should be 'an endless procession of stories, an endless coloured comic strip, things to listen to and look at, a bottomless play box' (4).
21 Myron Greenman, 'Understanding New Fiction,' *MFS* 20, 3 (1974) 316
22 All metaphor carries a covert suggestion of manipulation; allegory merely crystallizes the propensity. As C.M. Turbayne describes it, 'when I say that man is a wolf (metaphorically speaking) I am actually giving him a name shared by all other wolves just as if I believe that he is another sort of wolf like the timber wolf or the Tasmanian wolf, sharing with them all the defining properties of "wolf," or sharing with them inclusion in the denotation of "wolf." But though I give him the same name I do not believe he is another sort of wolf. I only make believe he is. My words are not to be taken literally but only metaphorically. That is, I pretend that something is the case when it is not, and I implicitly ask my audience to do the same. 'But more clarity is needed on the matter of what is pretense and what is not. Certainly when I use a metaphor there is no pretense about the name-transference. Man actually shares the name "wolf." But it is pretense that man is a sort of wolf. However, something besides the name is transferred from wolves to men. I do not merely *pretend* that man shares the properties of wolves; I *intend* it. What these properties are I may, but need not, specify. They cannot be all the properties common to wolves, otherwise I should intend that man is actually a wolf. Thus when I say that man is a wolf (metaphorically speaking) I intend that he shares some of the properties of wolves' (*The Myth of Metaphor* [U. South Carolina 1971] 14-15). The mechanism Turbayne describes here tacitly energizes much Canadian literature.
23 Morley A64 on Wiebe. For discussion of the latter two features see Sugden or Merivale on Aquin, Moss D166 ff on Watson, Woodcock C on Laurence.
24 Actually, to the extent that 'things' create 'place,' this work is house-like in both senses of the term. As George Woodcock describes it, 'Hood's present project is a series of twelve novels, to be entitled *The New Age*, about Canada during the mid-twentieth century. He has let it be known that he is emulating Proust, but in fact the detailed and almost obsessive preoccupation with material aspects of daily life, as distinct from the Proustian nuances of feeling and impression ... reminds one more strongly of Balzac' (D151).

25 The reason why the practice of Marlatt and a number of other recent Canadian poets diverges somewhat from the norm in this area is no doubt related to their conscious allegiance to the post-modernist theories of the American poet Charles Olson. It is interesting that Douglas Barbour, in his essay on Marlatt, makes a connection between Olson and the phenomenologists despite the fact that the former was apparently unfamiliar with phenomenological writings. 'It is from Olson, mainly, and through Olson from Whitehead, that "the central concept of attention before the mysteries of process" has entered postmodern poetics; it is a concept very similar to the "attentiveness and wonder, the ... demand for awareness, the ... will to seize the meaning of the world or of history as that meaning comes into being" which Merleau-Ponty argues is the phenomenological endeavour' (B177). We have already noted that the phenomenological position differs from the Canadian one specifically on that issue of subjectivity which is also the mark of Marlatt's divergence.

26 In *Selected Literary Criticism,* ed. Morris Shapiro (Heinemann 1963) 61

27 The capacity to 'borrow' successfully obviously depends on the writer's intellectual resources. This, rather than the somewhat superficial 'sociological' reasons cited by Dudek ('Canada is ... a conventional, narrow, and materialistic country; and in such a country, where there is no public, there can be no people's poets or artists' A105), perhaps explains the anomalously obtrusive 'academic' element in Canadian literature. 'In looking over [*The Book of Canadian Poetry*] ... one is struck immediately by the predominance of university and professional people,' says Frye, 'and it is in the classical scholarship of Lampman, the encyclopaedic erudition of Crémazie which is said to have included Sanscrit, and the patient research and documentation of Pratt's *Brébeuf* and sea narratives, that Canadian poetry has become most articulate' (C91). If we think about the characteristics that emerged in the last chapter – the obsession with fact, the insistence on impersonality – the trends Frye comments on here seem less noteworthy than predictable.

28 One example of this would be Sheila Watson's *The Double Hook*, with its adaptation of the formal elements of the 'western' (see Mandel A, esp. 62-3). More interesting because more farreaching, however, is the trend invoked by E.D. Blodgett in 'Cold Pastorals: A Prolegomenon.' For all our antipathy to the world vision implicit in primitivistic fantasy, Canadian writers frequently employ – that is, play with or on or against – numerous structures and motifs conventionally associated with pastoral.

29 Hartman, *Criticism in the Wilderness* (Yale 1980) 113

30 The fact that myth is made an object of both ridicule and reverence in much recent American fiction suggests that the American's much-touted hard-headed pragmatism actually makes him more susceptible to subsumptive/transcendent mystical explanations. This phenomenon is discussed in some detail in chapter 12 below.

31 Tobin, *Time and the Novel: The Genealogical Imperative* (Princeton 1978) 200

32 Miller, 'Ariadne's Thread: Repetition and the Narrative Line' in Mario J. Valdés & Owen J. Miller, eds., *Interpretation of Narrative* (U. Toronto 1978) 158

33 Kaminsky, 'On Literary Realism' in John Halperin, ed., *The Theory of the Novel: New Essays* (Oxford 1974) 225

34 Frank Kermode, *The Sense of an Ending: Studies in the Theory of Fiction* (Oxford 1968) 7

35 Pascal, 'Narrative Fictions and Reality: A Comment on Frank Kermode's *The Sense of an Ending*,' *Novel* 2 (1977) 40

36 See Harbison, *Eccentric Spaces*, 73-88; also Frederick Karl, 'Enclosure, the Adversary Culture, and the Nature of the Novel,' *Mosaic* 7, 3 (1974) 8-10.

37 Lodge, 'The Language of Modern Fiction' in Malcolm Bradbury & James McFarlane, eds., *Modernism* (Penguin 1976) 483

38 Introduction to *Kinship and Culture*, ed. L.K. Hsu (Aldine 1971) 8, 9, 10

39 Page 11. In Hsu's original, the dyads are labelled 'Father-Son' and 'Mother-Son,' but since the author does not appear to intend any significant differentiation along sex lines, I have substituted the more neutral term, 'Child.'

40 Charles Russell, 'The Vault of Language: Self-Reflective Artifice in Contemporary American Fiction,' *MFS* 20, 3 (1974) 351

41 As Dennis Duffy describes it, Hood's 'narrative contains the stuff of realistic fiction, the goods and speech and relationships of ordinary life [but i]n addition, like Wordsworth's accounts of boyhood ... [it] seeks always to place events within the larger powers sustaining them' (c141).

42 Pearce, *The Continuity of American Poetry* (Princeton 1961) 132, 336

43 Levin, *History as Romantic Art* (Harbinger 1963) 18

44 The exception to this general orientation is, of course, the American South, a region notoriously preoccupied with its own past. Far from weakening our argument, however, the anomaly actually strengthens it. The South, like Canada, is a garrison culture. In its case the original beseiging element was a politico-historical enemy rather than nature (indeed, nature for the southerner offers a primary source of consolation), but the effect – the recoil from otherness and the consequent introversion – was strikingly similar. In proof of this we need only note the extent to which Southern literature shares the formal characteristics of the Canadian oeuvre. This parallel will be treated more fully in a study of the mechanics of cultural change planned for the future, but in the meantime we need only think of Faulkner's explorations of the problems entailed by subjective versus objective modes of 'knowing,' of Tennessee Williams's doomed dynasties, of the strong gothic strain in Truman Capote, of Flannery O'Connor's fatalism, of Carson McCuller's fascination with the physically or mentally handicapped, of Walker Percy's preoccupation with human isolation, of the obtrusive grotesque element to be found throughout the whole corpus (see Lewis A. Lawson, 'The Grotesque in Recent Southern Fiction' in Marston LaFrance, ed., *Patterns of Commitment in American Literature* 165-80), to realize that the two literatures, for all the surficial differences between the environments that spawned them, covertly express much the same world view.

45 Frye, it must be admitted, does not draw quite the same conclusions from his

observations, implying that the Canadian's obsession with continuity in time is simply *equivalent to* rather than a *substitute for* continuity in space. Indeed, he goes so far as to claim that Canadians have a habit 'of probing into the distance, of fixing the eyes on the skyline ... inherited from the *voyageurs.'* Since, however, the evidence he cites in support of this supposed propensity speaks merely of a national preoccupation with modes of communication and transportation – i.e., *formal* networks of connection (see also note 46) – *not* of actual physical journeyings, his interpretation obscures the all-important distinction between 'real' and 'conceptual' extension (B222-3).

46 Supporting Frye, in Donald Creighton's studies of the role of the seaway and the railway in the country's development and, even more, in Harold Innis's writings on Canadian economic history, the breadth of vision and emphasis on geographic features create the illusion that a spatial orientation was in fact a major factor in national growth. When we look more closely at such works, however, we will note, as with Frye, that extension in 'real' space is once again being used as a metaphor for communication networks, or purely *formal* extension. This conclusion is reinforced by the fact that at least in Innis the emphasis is on the movement of information rather than of bodies. Far from invoking a mobile population as, say, Turner's frontier thesis does, Innis's concern is with the connection between political power and the capacity to communicate over distances, that is, to establish and maintain contact between separate segments of a population. 'His analysis of Near Eastern, Mediterranean, and European empires,' says Pamela McCallum, 'correlated the extent of imperial control over space and its duration through time in terms of communication technology' (5).

47 As Mandel points out, 'When the poet seeks to discover life in a threatening landscape and to create a usable past, both space and time tend to become esoteric, exotic, and ultimately primitive. Certainly, as often as not in modern Canadian poetry, "the orient eye decides geography," a place remote from the poet's "natural country." So it is that Earle Birney turns up in Mexico, in South America, in Japan, in India; and Al Purdy, with suit-case full of wine bottles, sends his messages from Cuba or Baffin-Land or Greece; Leonard Cohen journeys to and from Montreal, to Hydra, and, "the only tourist," sends poems from Havana to Canada, while Irving Layton discovers allegories of poet and critic in elephants and trees in Ceylon, or comments on sun-bathers, politicans, poets and lizards in Portugal, Spain, Greece, and Israel' (A82).

48 This is perhaps a good time to point out that when I speak here of a spatial as opposed to a temporal orientation in a novel I am talking about the spatial component of the *action*, not the spatial component of the *aesthetic form*. Whether or not spatiality in this latter sense is, indeed (as has been widely assumed ever since the appearance in 1945 in *The Sewanee Review* of Joseph Frank's seminal essay, 'Spatial Form in Modern Literature'), an identifying characteristic of modern writing (see W.J.T. Mitchell, 'Spatial Form in Literature' in *The Language of Images* [U. Chicago 1980], for a refutation of Frank's view), this is *not* the aspect I intend to invoke when I make

a distinction between the American's journey in space and the Canadian's journey in time.

49 Reaney's view reflects his conviction that myth represents the 'truest' and most effective means for organizing human experience. In the September section of *A Suit of Nettles* history is both the lowest level of the ferris wheel and, inasmuch as it offers only the barest advance on total chaos, the lowest form of order. The idea that historical recapitulation is a kind of descent into the maelstrom is not unique to Reaney, however. *Vide*, for instance, Hagar's long descent to the cannery where, though suffering the torments of the damned, she experiences the epiphany that allows her finally to achieve reconciliation with the past. See Dennis Cooley 140 ff.

50 As Erich Auerbach points out, 'Figural interpretation "establishes a connection between two events or persons in such a way that the first signifies not only itself but also the second, while the second involves or fulfils the first ... "

'This type of interpretation obviously introduces an entirely new and alien element into the antique conception of history. For example, if an occurrence like the sacrifice of Isaac is interpreted as prefiguring the sacrifice of Christ, so that in the former the latter is as it were announced and promised, and the latter "fulfils" (the technical term is *figuram implere*) the former, then a connection is established between two events which are linked neither temporally nor causally – a connection which it is impossible to establish by reason in the horizontal dimension (if I may be permitted to use this term for a temporal extension). It can be established only if both occurrences are vertically linked to Divine Providence, which alone is able to devise such a plan of history and supply the key to its understanding. The horizontal, that is the temporal and causal, connection of occurrences is dissolved; the here and now is no longer a mere link in an earthly chain of events, it is simultaneously something which has always been, and which will be fulfilled in the future; and strictly, in the eyes of God, it is something eternal, something omni-temporal, something already consummated in the realm of fragmentary earthly event.' *Mimesis: The Representation of Reality of Western Literature*, trans. Willard. R. Trask (Princeton 1968) 73-4

51 Rank, *Beyond Psychology* (Dover 1958) 156

52 Mircea Eliade, *Myth and Reality*, trans. Willard R. Trask (Harper Torchbooks 1968) 88-91

53 The struggle against nature as much as the ethical orientation finds a parallel in Hebraic thought. According to John F. Priest, 'Nature as a personified Thou is normally assumed to be an indispensable element in mythopoeic formulations. Those Old Testament scholars who so strongly stress the centrality of history at the same time find themselves obliged to denigrate the extent of Israelite concern for and reflection upon nature. Not nature but history is the familiar battle cry. With this I would agree, but for quite different reasons. I am prepared to argue that the Israelite did not ignore nature as a result of his apparent preoccupation with history, but that

he reoriented his understanding of nature to make it congruent with his reoriented mythology. Israel early "desacralized" nature to relate it to the human situation, just as he "demythologized" theogony and cosmogony to make them relate to the human situation' ('Myth and Dream in Hebrew Scripture' in Joseph Campbell, ed., *Myths, Dreams, and Religion* [Dutton 1970] 57). It is obvious how compatible such a trend would be with Canadian propensities.

54 White, 'The Historical Text as Literary Artifact' in Robert H. Canary & Henry Kozicki, eds., *The Writing of History: Literary Form and Historical Understanding* (U. Wisconsin 1978) 50

55 This is truer of the myth-oriented u.s. (*vide* influential critics like Richard Chase and Richard Slotkin, for instance) than it is of Europe, where recent work by such notable neo-Freudians as Paul Ricoeur and Jacques Lacan testifies to the continuing vigour as well as influence enjoyed by the Freudian tradition on that continent.

56 Lewis, *History – Remembered, Recovered, Invented* (Princeton 1976) 60-1

57 Lytle, 'The Working Novelist and the Mythmaking Process' in Henry A. Murray, ed., *Myth and Mythmaking* (Beacon Press 1960) 152

58 Leonard Sugden draws an explicit connection, for instance, between Aquin's violent sex imagery and his discomfort with conventional assumptions about temporal progression. 'The spasms of love serve Aquin, in the first instance, as repeated examples in his criticism of the traditional view of reality: that is to say, a belief in the continuity of time and, consequently, in the laws of cause and effect which sustain the hypothesis of an ordered universe. It is for this reason that the love act is always metaphorically associated with the theme of time. These convulsions or breaks in the psychic flow which show discontinuity in our lives are commonly experienced by human beings. And so it is in all nature' (82).

59 In *The Disinherited*, similarly, the fact that it is an attack by Richard on his father with a knife that triggers the narrative disjunctions (see chapter 10, 314) underlines the radical disjunction between generations on which this novel focuses. Interestingly, Timothy Findley uses exactly the same image in *The Wars* to suggest the same endemic discontinuity. ' "We're all cut off at birth with a knife and left at the mercy of strangers" ' (28).

60 Becker, *Denial of Death* (Free Press 1975) 104-5

61 Jacques Choron, *Death and Western Thought* (Collier 1963) 269

62 Writers who approach the novel in terms of 'myth' seem more likely than others to view the quest as successfully concluded. Catherine Ross, for instance, winds up her Jungian analysis with the assertion that 'In the last chapters the narrator achieves her animal form ... [and becomes] one with the sacred place of the gods' (B16). Frances Mansbridge, who takes a generally similar approach, although stipulating that even at the end of the book 'The barriers between the narrator and those around her [remain] much greater' than in the author's first novel, also asserts quite unequivocally that 'she achieves a mystical intuition into nature' (113, 111).

Considering the evidence of the text itself, however, it seems possible that such commentators import the affirmative ending they are led to expect by their 'archetypal' models.

63 Phyllis Gotlieb claims that this shift signals Klein's discomfort with the idea of deity. 'Klein with all his passion ... can only approach God roundabout at the end, for all other appeals have failed. He has made Him not a father but an uncle.' Why? 'However it may be, and however God and the Jewish people may have been reincarnated in Israel ... it seems clear that throughout Klein's work he found no solution for his angst. Melech's nephew will never truly believe in God. There is no epiphany in this work, no mystic union' (62-3).

64 'Munro is not a simple writer,' says John Moss. 'Her evocations of the personal past are warm but haunting. The small details of time and place are disconcerting to the reader, because they are exactly right – and therefore belong to another world. Her small-town Ontario is not what actually was, but what has been precisely remembered. Her past, her worlds of girls and women, she opens for us not through confession or revelation but directly as experience shared in recollection' (Aa8). Moss's description is at once accurate and misleading, however. Notwithstanding the preciseness, the graphic detail, our strong and constant awareness of a narrator detached in time from the recollected events makes our own access to those events a very indirect one. To some extent, in fact, the meticulousness of Munro's prose – like the meticulousness of Colville's painting – actually accentuates the barrier between the experiencing subject and the object experienced. Significantly, Moss makes this comparison explicit. '[T]he quality of heightened realism, or magic realism, or, as the late artist Jack Chambers called it, "perceptual realism," is the distinguishing characteristic of Munro's writing.'

65 Lévi-Strauss, *The Savage Mind* (U. Chicago 1966) 257

66 See *On the Genealogy of Morals and Ecce Homo*, ed. Walter Kaufmann & R.J. Hollingdale (Random House 1969), esp. 57-8.

67 Fallico, *Art & Existentialism* (Prentice-Hall 1962) 80

68 Rother, 'Parafiction: The Adjacent Universe of Barth, Barthelme, Pynchon, and Nabokov,' *Boundary 2* 5, 1 (1976) 32

69 Sidney Hook, *The Hero in History: A Study in Limitation and Possibility* (Beacon Press 1955) 153

70 In so far as at least two of my exemplars of objectivity explicitly deny any connections with structuralism, it may be objected that I am using this term rather too loosely when I adopt it as a group denominator. Indeed, judging by at least some aspects of recent usage, I could be accused of misconceiving the word altogether. In this respect it is important to note what has unfortunately been obscured of late by the tendency of scholars to appropriate only such aspects of 'new' theory as are congenial to the biases of their own areas of specialization, that on the basis of both its roots and its applications 'structuralism' can be taken to denote a whole number of quite different and even incompatible concepts: a kind of analytic method, a branch of or progenitor

to semiology, a general philosophical 'orientation' (Vincent Descombes, *Modern French Philosophy*, trans. L. Scott-Fox & J.M. Harding [Cambridge 1980] 77-82). In the light of such confusion, one might wonder whether the label might be better simply avoided. To this I would reply that as a means merely of invoking a particular stance – 'a particular field of enquiry,' as Geoffrey Sturrock puts it – the term seems to me, not despite but because of its fuzziness, to offer certain definite advantages for the present discussion. To be more specific, since I am attempting to suggest a significant degree of continuity between a number of writers who not only *appear* but, in some cases, *see themselves* as occupying quite distinct philosophical positions it seems useful to underline the fact, through the use of the structuralist label, that at least to the extent that they evince a common opposition to the ego-centricity of the phenomenologist, they are, in fact, working within the same methodological tradition. For a full discussion of this aspect, see Sturrock's introduction to *Structuralism and Since: From Lévi-Strauss to Derrida* (Oxford 1979) – a book which, as the title suggests, applies the structuralist cognomen to the same broad range of practice that my own usage here may be deemed to presuppose.

71 Foucault, *The Archaeology of Knowledge & the Discourse on Language*, trans. A.M. Sheridan Smith (Harper & Row 1972) 9

72 Mink, 'Narrative Form as a Cognitive Instrument' in Canary & Kozicki, 131

73 White, 'Michel Foucault' in Sturrock, 84

74 Hans-Georg Gadamer, interestingly enough, draws an explicit parallel between Marxism and Romanticism. 'The concept of the "society close to nature" is probably another case of a romantic mirror image [of the Enlightenment belief in perfectibility], whose origin ought to be investigated. In Karl Marx it appears as a kind of relic of natural law that limits the validity of his socioeconomic theory of the class struggle. Does the idea go back to Rousseau's description of society before the division of labor and the introduction of property? At any rate, Plato has already demonstrated the illusory nature of this political theory in the ironical account he gives of a "state of nature" in the third book of the *Republic*' ('The Historicity of Understanding as Hermeneutic Principle' in Michael Murray, ed., *Heidegger and Modern Philosophy* [Yale 1978] 169). For further discussion of the irrationality – the 'nostalgia' – that lurks beneath the ultra-rational Marxist rhetoric, see Victor Brombert, *The Intellectual Hero: Studies in the French Novel 1880-1955* (U. Chicago 1964), esp. 152-3. See also chapter 12, note 11 below.

75 'An ethically oriented historiography, which also on the whole proceeds in strict chronological order, is bound to use an unchangeable system of categories and hence cannot produce synthetic-dynamic concepts of the kind we are accustomed to employ' (Auerbach 38).

76 As J. Hillis Miller points out in 'Narrative and History,' *ELH* 41 (1974), '*Hegel* says: "That at the bottom of history, and particularly of world history, there is a final aim, and that this has actually been realized in it and is being realized – the plan of Providence – that there is *reason* in history: that is to be shown philosophically and

thus as altogether necessary." And: "A history without such an aim and without such a point of view would be merely a feeble-minded pastime of the imagination, not even a children's fairy tale, for even children demand some interest in stories, i.e., some aim one can at least feel, and the relation of the occurrences and actions to it" ' (455). Since Hegel's thought is so generally considered to exemplify the whole concept of Universal History, there is a widespread assumption that this kind of Christian optimism is not merely invited but entailed by the mode.

77 Lukács, *The Historical Novel*, trans. Hannah & Stanley Mitchell (Penguin 1969) 33. This is the same figure of whom Rank says, though he 'may not be historical himself ... historically speaking he is more real than history because he made it, shaped it, according to mythical pattern' (170).

78 Lukács 33. This latter type, in quite marked contrast to the Carlylean hero, has more in common with the exemplary Canadian than simply his relation to history. The fact is, despite all his obvious differences from the iconic fool-saint, Scott's protagonist is above all *submissive*. As George Levine puts it, 'the true heroes of the Waverley novels are passive figures who submit to history rather than create it. In the long run these heroes do not triumph over circumstances but, with the help of Scott's blatant manipulations of plot, retreat from history into the comfort of obscurity.' 'Realism Reconsidered' in Halperin 247

79 Mast, 'Kracauer's Two Tendencies and the Early History of Film Narrative' in Mitchell, *The Language of Images* 133

80 Kroetsch claims explicitly that the paradigm of the double hook – the image of 'equally matched opposites' – contains the key to the Canadian consciousness. 'The total ambiguity that is so essentially Canadian: be it in terms of two solitudes, the bush garden, Jungian opposites, or the raw and the cooked binary structures of Lévi-Strauss. Behind the multiplying theories of Canadian literature is always the pattern of equally matched opposites:

Coyote	:	God
Self	:	Community
Energy	:	Stasis

The balance, whatever the specifics, is always so equal that one wonders how paradigm can possibly issue into story' (E16).

81 It is interesting that this phenomenon can be detected in Canadian art as well as literature. 'The step from practical form to symbolic content is such a short one that we see that all form is incipiently formal in the social or ritual sense,' says Robert Arn of Ronald Bloore's work. 'Form becomes content in social function' (42). 'The total surround of "histories" determines "content" but form is unique: and this is true content,' echoes west coast artist Jack Shadbolt (A31).

82 'Our knowledge of the past may increase incrementally, but our understanding of it does not. Nor does our understanding of the past progress by the kind of

revolutionary breakthroughs that we associate with the development of the physical sciences. Like literature, history progresses by the production of classics, the nature of which is such that they cannot be disconfirmed or negated in the way that the principal conceptual schemata of the sciences are. And it is their non-confirmability that testifies to the essentially literary nature of historical classics. There is something in a historical masterpiece that cannot be negated, and this non-negatable element is its form, the form which is its fiction.' White, 'The Historical Text as Literary Artifact' 43

12

In Medias Res

Now we come to the hard part. In earlier chapters we focused on the recoil from nature – the 'Wacousta Syndrome' – that historically backdropped the Canadian sense of self, and on the iconography in terms of which that critical initial reaction came, covertly, to be expressed. This allowed us to define the conceptual underpinnings of the Canadian imagination. We then proceeded to analyse some of the particulars of the fictional worlds that have been constructed on this foundation: character types, relational models, recurrent themes and motifs. We ended by examining more general propensities: narrative reticence, a penchant for allegory, historical consciousness. It now remains only to take the results of our farreaching and ofttimes circuitous dissections and put the pieces back together in an attempt to discover what kind of literature, considered generally, emerges from this meld; to define more specifically, in other words, the type of 'map' our Canadian writers actually produce.

Perhaps we can best approach this endeavour by turning once more to a comparative mode. For all its demonstrated peculiarity, Canadian culture is not a wholly unique or isolated phenomenon, and in the present regard we may find it useful to consider points of resemblance as well as those more striking points of departure on which the argument has focused thus far. It is important to remember, for instance, what we noted in chapter 4, that however significant the differences between the Canadian world view and European existentialism, there is still a wide basic area of overlap. We must also not lose sight of the well-nigh seamless veneer of 'Americanness' that overlays our 'Canadian' foundations. More important than fairly obvious considerations like this, though, are the archaic echoes one can detect in the corpus. If a modern analogue to the Canadian communal voice may be found in the photography metaphor, with the snapshot and the film respectively representing the polarities of our critically divided mode of vision, an even more suggestive basis of comparison may be inferred from the general, methodical *cultural* biases we reveal. I have already underlined our Old Testament connections. What I have perhaps not elucidated explicitly enough – despite the copious hints encountered in the course of our perambulations through the 'langscape' – is that this particular component represents only half of the operative dichotomy. Opposed to the Hebraic aspect of the Canadian psyche is an equally strong element we might identify as Hellenic. What does this mean? If the Old Testament view emphasizes above all the coherence and continuity of experience (as Erich Auerbach points out, Jewish historicism implies that nothing has any importance except in so far as it can 'be conceived as an element in [the] sequence ... [of] the history of the Jews' [1]), the Greek mode, early exemplified by the *Iliad* and the *Odyssey* (in which, in Paul Zweig's words, 'scenes simply follow like hypnotic stills, with no complicated sequential links'[2]), suggests that life comprises a complex of unique, unrelated events 'whose boundaries in space and time are clearly delimited' [Auerbach 16][3]. This contrast, like the film/photo dichotomy, is both critical and basic. What is more, if – as the last chapter makes clear – the former alternative represents the Canadian's most hopeful *aspirations*, the latter obviously provides a more apt correlative for the anguished sense of existential isolation from which he *begins*. With this in mind we might make rather more of the 'Greek' element in Canadian culture than our observations on such specialized and occasional usages as the 'middle voice' have heretofore prompted.

The next question that arises is, of course, where this new intuition leads us. Certainly it seems unavoidably true that modern Canadian and ancient Greek literature, lacking the mythic-cum-historical connections Christianity forges for us with the Hebraic, are separated by such a vast historical chasm as to make any sort of detailed comparison seem either artificial or futile. Despite this problem, it is nevertheless possible that considered in *general* terms the Greek model may help us to pin down some important features of (if there *is* such a thing) the characteristic mode of Canadian literary expression. Chapter 9 discusses several features in the Canadian treatment of the aggressive role that seem to reveal similarities with some aspects of the classical oeuvre. It is here, I think, that we find a crucial clue as to what kind of literature the Canadian writer is – albeit unintentionally – really producing. To be more explicit, what we realize if we review the material covered in that chapter is that not only does the magician himself demonstrate a striking kinship with the equivocal epic hero but, more interestingly, the way his career – the exemplary rise and fall – is handled in our fiction is strongly suggestive of certain conventions of classical tragedy. This in itself would be small evidence for any particular bent, but there are other elements in the Canadian cultural ambience that would seem to be conducive to a tragic vision too. Indeed, taking all factors into account we might well say that Canada offers as fruitful a ground for tragedy as has existed since the golden age of Greece. Does this, considering the unheroic reality of

Canadian society, seem an absurd claim? Let's examine the whole question of tragedy a little more closely.

The trend toward modernity has not, in general, augured well for the tragic mode. Numerous twentieth-century critics (most notably George Steiner and I.A. Richards) have held, in fact, that the 'true' tragic impulse died with paganism. The reason for this, in Auerbach's words, is rooted in the 'Christian figural view of human life':

> However serious the events of earthly existence might be, high above them stood the towering and all-embracing dignity of a single event, the appearance of Christ, and everything tragic was but figure or reflection of a single complex of events, into which it necessarily flowed at last: the complex of the Fall, of Christ's birth and passion, and of the Last Judgment. This implies a transposition of the center of gravity from life on earth into a life beyond, with the result that no tragedy ever reached its conclusion here below. To be sure ... this by no means signifies a devaluation of life on earth or of human individuality; but it did bring with it a blunting of tragic climaxes here on earth and a transposition of catharsis into the other world. [317]

The demise was not total or immediate, to be sure. Shakespeare, for one, circumvented the problem posed by Christianity by, firstly, providing more explicit contexts that would tend to *particularize* the erstwhile abstract dramatic conflict, and secondly, emphasizing the *subjective* element in both causes and results. Unfortunately, these two strategies themselves dealt the death blow to that same tragic vision they were formulated to protect. On the one hand, the specificity of event militates against the sense of fatedness characteristic of Greek tragedy by suggesting that the 'world of realities ... is broader, richer in possibilities, limitless ... The sphere of life represented in a particular instance is no longer the only one possible' [Auerbach 321]. On the other hand, as a logical corollary to the freer consciousness implied by the insurgent relativism and the exuberant, distinctively *un*classical mixture of styles, the individual emphasis opened the way for the optimism to which Nietzsche attributed the disappearance of tragic heroism. The fact is, once Renaissance humanism had begun, covertly, to detach man from his supernatural ground,[4] it was only a short step to that total faith in the power of the individual will that came, for the moderns, to comprise a bulwark against, if not a solution to, the age-old tragic dilemma.

In Canada, in contrast, this whole trend is reversed. The sense of being engulfed by an inimical universe, the emphasis on human limitation, and the covert determinism to be discerned in our literature undercut any illusion of freedom ostensibly offered by our modernity, while our suspicion of transcendence rules out both the explicitly religious and the romantic-transcendental varieties of consolation. What is more, certain peculiarities of our national psyche may be interpreted to imply that there is in fact considerably more than pure coincidence involved in the apparent resemblance between the Canadian orientation and that of classical Greece. Tragedy, says Jean-Pierre Vernant, results from a conflict between two different views of the human condition. Its appearance in Greece marked the moment in time when there was 'a distance established between ... the religious thought proper to an earlier epoch and the juridical and political thought which is that of the City performing the tragedy ... great enough for the conflict of values to be painfully felt, but ... small enough so that the heroic past is not liquidated, rejected, so that the confrontation does not cease.'[5] Canadian experience obviously does not parallel that of the Greeks in any strict historical sense but there is evidence to suggest that the omnipresent conflict between the American romantic/heroic view of life and our innate conservatism reproduces the *psychological* conditions that characterized that critical moment. It is at least possible, therefore, that the Canadian, like the Greek, does have a temperamental bent toward the tragic and its complement the comic vision. The question is whether this bent is carried through into our modes of literary expression.

My answer to this is yes.

Suppose we posit two sets of polarities at right angles to one another. Romance and irony (from top to bottom) delimit the vertical axis of this particular model, while tragedy and comedy (left to right) are in horizontal opposition. Notwithstanding the gross resemblance to Frye's seasonal cycle, these positions – which represent the alternative conceptual sets out of which literature grows, abstracted categories of experiential referent rather than specific aesthetic projects – are related to one another not in terms of sequence but diametrically, in terms of their differential relations with a 'neutral' centre that we will take as defining a norm of *ordinariness*, that is, what the symbolic ego would hold to be the mean of actual human experience. In particular we may postulate as a primary distinction the very fact of a horizontal versus a vertical perspective. What this means, among other things, is that the romantic/ironic axis is characterized by a radical disjunction between the real and the ideal (these are imaged as *levels*, different in kind) while on the comic/tragic axis they are contiguous (imaged as *directions*, that is, relatively, and therefore different only in degree). In terms at least of these two categories (which are, of course, only playful) I think we may hypothesize that Canadian literature inclines toward tragedy/comedy while American literature tends to be variously romantic and/or ironic.[6]

Fine. But what, leaving aside abstractions, does this really mean?

Let's start with the United States. The important point for the present discussion is that the American does in fact tend to view experience as 'layered.' He expresses this perception in terms of either wish-fulfilling fantasies of personal freedom (including not only such naive creations as Davy Crockett or Conan the Barbarian but also many ostensibly realistic but larger-than-life urban heroes from Ayn Rand's self-made capitalists through to Wouk's Youngblood Hawk) which posit, in Frye's words, 'a world in which the ordinary laws of nature are slightly suspended: [where] prodigies of courage and endurance, unnatural to us, are natural' A33) *or* (especially in recent decades) ironic fables of entrapment in a world of terrifying incongruity. What is not generally admitted, however, is that the latter mode is simply a 'slipped' version of the former. Romance juxtaposes the idyllic with 'real' life; irony does the same thing on a lower level. Irony, at its most basic, is, in other words, built on the discrepancy between an unsatisfactory vision of what *is* and various wishful conceptions of what might or should or could be if life were less unreasonable. As D.C. Muecke says:

General irony lies in those contradictions, apparently fundamental and irremediable, that confront men when they speculate upon such topics as the origins and purpose of the universe, free will and determinism, reason and instinct, the scientific and the imaginative, ends and means, society and the individual, art and life, knowing and being, self-consciousness (what is conscious of what?), the meaning of meaning, and the value of value. Most of these, it may be said, are reducible to one great incongruity, the appearance of free and self-valued but temporally finite egos in a universe that seems to be utterly alien, utterly purposeless, completely deterministic, and incomprehensibly vast.[7]

Irony thus in a sense actually presupposes romance. It emerges when man recognizes the limitations of his condition *without* relinquishing the vision of something better. Where romance suspends disbelief to play the game of 'what if,' irony simply expresses the shock or anger or confusion consequent on the realization that despite either will or wishes, one is powerless to reconcile the golden world of imagination with the grotesquely inferior world of corporeal existence.

Irony and romance are not, therefore, merely opposites in mood (Frye images them as winter and summer) but functional complements. As such – and this is the important point – *each always has the tendency to turn into its alter.* This isn't as unlikely as it may seem. The more discrepant from experience the fantasy world, and especially the more important to one's sense of self (as the Adamic fantasy of new beginnings is so important to the Americans), the more likelihood there naturally is that one will suffer disillusionment and recoil into bitterness or self-mockery. This is the case, in Muecke's words, of 'the real ironizing the ideal, or more precisely, the ineluctable realities of life ironizing man's compelling need to reach toward perfection' [192]. That same unshakeable commitment to the dream responsible for this fall, however, *also* produces in its adherents a stubborn disinclination 'to accept the immitigable rule of reality, including death' – that quality Ihab Hassan calls Radical Innocence[8] –

which provides both the motivation and the means to reverse this process. Beginning with a mere symbolic triumph over oppression – using the ideal this time to undercut the real, thus expressing 'his spirit's independence of the world with disdainful or insouciant irony' [Muecke 192] – the vertically oriented hero soon convinces himself that the external world has no 'real' power over him at all; that in fact (as Sartre, according to Charles Glicksberg, proclaims lengthily and often) he 'makes himself just as he invents his gods and shapes the course of history.'[9] The consequence of this development is obvious. As Manfred Puetz points out, if – or perhaps because – the absolute experiential discrepancies entailed by the modern ironic/romantic vision rule out any sort of *synthesis*, there is a widespread belief in the possibility 'of transcending experience altogether, of passing into realms beyond it.'[10]

This wishful belief reveals itself in numerous ways in American literature. For one thing, according to Puetz, it is at least one of the factors responsible for the great spate of literary experimentation during the seventies. While seeming to 'strive desperately for verisimilitude in their works,' many contemporary writers 'actually make up new forms of experience after the old ones have failed and disappointed them' [242]. Even more pointedly, however, it reveals itself in some of the more peculiar characteristics demonstrated by the prototypical, ostensibly 'ironic,' contemporary American hero – in particular his optimism, his resilience, his irrepressibility. The anomalies stand out especially with respect to endings. While some recent novelists have been content to rest with stasis, to accept as final that irreconcilability of real and ideal experience which the ironic vision properly implies (Kurt Vonnegut's *Cat's Cradle* with its concluding image of a frozen world springs to mind as a pre-eminent example), a greater number of them – as, indeed, we have already noted (see p. 111 above) – evidently feel constrained to devise some kind of escape for their protagonists. Others, treating the ironic dimension as pure play, go so far as to nudge their entire fictional worlds into a higher – that is, less determined – level. 'In the latter case – approached as closely as possible today in Barth's *The Sot-Weed Factor* or in Brautigan's *In Watermelon Sugar* – the American novel,' says Puetz, 'has turned full circle to become again what Richard Chase maintained it has been all along; romance, the genre of suspended probability, miraculous endings, and exalted meanings' [244].[11]

It is easy to see from this description – and especially Puetz's invocation of 'transcendence' – why Canadians would have a natural antipathy to the vertical mode. If we examine the corpus, moreover, there is plenty of evidence to show that this antipathy does affect our literary practice and preference – at least when it comes to the romance end of the spectrum. Canadian writers, for reasons suggested in the last chapter, may use the forms and language and motifs of fabulation but both the mood and the values that distinguish romance are missing. Indeed, even leaving aside the special case of the magician, the prototypical Canadian – judging by our fiction – would seem to be firmly opposed to wishful fantasies of every kind. Thus it is that in overt Canadian literary usage an inclination toward romanticizing is commonly presented as at best naiveté (the protagonist of Marian Engel's *The Honeyman Festival*, for instance, having hoped that her paper theatre with its elegant little pretend-people might provide some sort of inspiration or release for her, that she might 'fly away on their backs to a personal never-never-land,' soon discovers that her innate pragmatism ultimately makes it impossible for her to give herself up to such fancies no matter how appealing: 'Growing up in orthopaedic shoes and school uniforms and being fed shepherd's pie and Lancashire hot-pot kept her from flying' 105); at worst a serious character flaw, a sign of radical retardation. The process of or capacity for dis-illusionment is hence often used as a means of revealing or measuring personal worth. In Adele Wiseman's *Crackpot*, for example, Hoda's commonsensical reassessment of her erstwhile idol, the Prince of Wales, is a key indicator that she has achieved a degree of maturity. Where once she dreamed of miraculous elevation, she comes, to her own moral advantage, to recognize and accept a humbler yet more humane version of reality which encourages reconciliation rather than, as the wishful dream tends to do, reinforcing her alienation. In Robertson Davies' Deptford trilogy, conversely, it is Boy Staunton's *inability* to make this particular renunciation that dooms him to live out his life as a kind of spoilt child. Morley Torgov's novel *The Abramsky Variations* makes the point even more explicitly. Goldie Brahms's obsession with Lindbergh so completely warps her sense of values that she loses touch with reality.

'What's to envy?' Louis asked.

'What's not to envy?' Goldie replied. 'A rich famous man for a husband; handsome, influential. They'll live like a king and queen there. You like it better the way we live?'

Louis looked at her in disbelief. 'We've got our son. He's alive for Godsake. Don't you think Lindbergh would give anything just to get his kid back? ...'

Goldie was silent.

'Well, don't you?' Louis insisted. 'Wouldn't you, if you were Charles Lindbergh?'

Where do the answers to such questions come from? From the heart? The mind? From both? Not always. Sometimes answers come from a worn-out linoleum ... from cracked plaster in the ceiling; a toilet that constantly overflows; an icebox that leaks; a sofa that has to be covered with a blanket and doilies to conceal rips and stains ...

A child is kidnapped and slain? The world is full of children. Lose one, make another. (23)

In the end, shattered by the revelation that her hero is a Nazi sympathizer, Goldie kills herself. We are neither surprised nor shocked; in terms of the emotional dynamic of the book this outcome, or something very like it, seems inevitable. Goldie is *already* dead in every way that matters before she takes the pills. This, in the Canadian view, is what romance does to people – and why it must be avoided at all costs. [12] Does that mean irony is avoided too? If my claims about the interdependency of the two modes are valid it would seem that it must. Opposed to this is the fact that the single adjective most often applied to Canadian literature by critics is probably 'ironic.' The question is whether this imputation is accurate, and if so, what it means.

Actually, the challenge posed to our interpretation is not as formidable as it first might appear. If we take a careful look at the criticism, we realize that the term 'irony' (perhaps because it has become such a catchword in modern fiction studies that it now tends to be assumed as a virtual *donnée*) is often applied too broadly in this country, or used incorrectly altogether. In the first place many critics are not as careful as they might be in distinguishing between ironies *of* the work and ironies that are merely *in* it. The latter would include (a) minor ironies of situation or event (arising when ignorance or accident produces a discrepancy in knowledge either among the characters or between the characters and the reader); (b) major ironies of theme or structure (found in books, for instance, where the 'education' or 'enlightenment' of a character initially deluded in his view of the world and/or himself is central to the plot and/or moral schema); and (c) narrative ironies (produced where the existential limitations of a controlling consciousness allow – or indeed force – the reader to reach certain conclusions about the relationship between the fictional and the real worlds which are suggested by but never stated explicitly in the text itself). As long as the discrepancy is localized in particulars, a book may contain any or all of these kinds of ironies without communicating an essentially ironic vision. Secondly, many critics confuse the object seen with the mode of seeing. There appears to be a general misapprehension, in fact, that *whenever* a meaning is left inexplicit or a situation ambiguous or a character ambivalent, especially if either the condition itself or the character's response is such as conventionally invites ironic treatment in contemporary American or European fiction, that the circumstance is inevitably ironic. Not so. Irony involves discrepancy, but not every discrepancy involves irony. The thing that makes the difference is perspective.

The fact is, nothing is ironic unless it is juxtaposed with a countering ideal or at least set against a *relatively* preferable state of affairs. This referent need not be explicit (as Jonathan Culler points out, the ironist cannot 'criticize one point of view or attitude for being excessively limited without asserting the completeness and truth of his own view'[13]), but it does have to be accessible *in terms of the work itself*. The book in other words must necessarily imply an observer (whether this figure is embodied in the persona of the narrator or merely entailed by the moral dynamics of the fictional world) who is normative, self-conscious, and – most important – detached from and therefore capable of recognizing the discrepancy responsible for the ironic situation.

The ironist and the object or victim of his irony are related as observer and observed ...

The ironist's awareness of himself as the unobserved observer tends to enhance his feeling of freedom and induce a mood perhaps of serenity, or joyfulness, or even exultation. His awareness of the victim's unawareness invites him to see the victim as committed where he feels disengaged; bound or trapped where he feels free; swayed by emotions, harassed, or miserable where he is dispassionate, serene, or even moved to laughter; trustful, credulous, or naive where he is critical, sceptical, or content to suspend judgement. And where his own attitude is that of a man whose world appears real and meaningful, he will see the victim's world as illusory and absurd. [Muecke 218]

But wait a minute – with all this stress on the ironist's superiority to his object, surely what Muecke is talking about here is the kind of particular or 'literary' irony we have already ruled out. To speak of ironic *vision* is to invoke the kind of General Irony in which by definition *all* are equally implicated, equally victims – is it not? Yes, and no. On the one hand, the ironist must recognize his own involvement or the contradictions he perceives would not be 'fundamental and irremediable.' On the other hand, since even to recognize that the condition *is* ironic necessitates distance, he must be 'detached from life itself or at least from that general aspect of life in which he perceives [the] fundamental contradiction' [Muecke 122]. Even General Irony, in other words, implies an observer with the ability to step back from his dilemma and view it dispassionately, albeit only momentarily. Furthermore, though such an observer may theoretically share the incapacity of the ironized victims to reconcile disparate aspects of experience, the very fact of his willed dissociation, by implying that such an incapacity is *ab*-normal or wrong, also invokes at least covertly an alternative reality in which such reconciliation would be possible. *Without this tacit alternative his ambivalence would not involve irony.* For a book to *be* ironic (as opposed to merely *containing* ironic elements) it must hence have a kind of built-in duplicity that connotes a complementary romantic countervision.

If we look at Canadian literature with these considerations in mind, we will soon see that the 'irony' cited by the critics is almost always of the literary, more limited kind. Take Sinclair Ross's *As for Me and My House*, for instance. Despite general critical opinion, this is a novel of which we might well say what Michael Ondaatje says of *Tay John*: 'if there is irony and qualification [here] ... it is directed not towards the source of the myth but to the story-teller's need for order' (c281). *As for Me and My House*, far from exposing in its protagonist(s) an ironically inadequate capacity for judgment, actually details the process by which the narrator *escapes from* her compulsively ironic vision of the world.

Why hasn't this been generally recognized? Perhaps because our American conditioning makes us more prone to see ironic than anti-ironic fables. Besides, the way Ross's novel is constructed, it *seems* to be setting up a classic ironic theme. Mrs Bentley is preoccupied with the discrepancy between false fronts and dowdy interiors, between social decorum and true feeling. Indeed, most of her diary is given to the attempt to arbitrate between the mutually exclusive exigencies of dream and reality. At the same time, her self-righteousness leads us to suspect that her ability to 'see through' the pretence, to comprehend what is truly 'real,' may be substantially more fallible than she believes. This, of course, sets us up for the conventional ironic reversal. What we get, however, is something quite different: a kind of dialectic progression whereby the ironic antithesis is superseded by a third term that deflates the possibility of deflation. It all comes down to Mrs Bentley's changing *attitudes toward* the discrepancies she is confronted with. In the earlier stages she cultivates detachment. When, bemused by the drought-stricken farmers' implausibly persistent belief in the efficacy of prayer, she comments to Paul Kirby that it must surely 'be a very great faith that such indifference on the part of its deity cannot weaken – a very great faith, or a very foolish one' (84), she is using simple irony to establish her own moral and intellectual ascendancy. When she later begins to wonder whether it is she herself 'who's never grown up, who can't see life for illusions' (125), she has progressed from simple to general irony by implicating *herself* in the apparent contradiction. This is obviously a step in the right direction. Not the final step, though. Departing now from the conventional pattern, Mrs Bentley is carried beyond irony entirely to the realization that her salvation lies not in discriminating between sense and foolishness but in accepting that such evaluative terms, being relative to the eye of the beholder, cannot alter the *human experience* which subsumes both 'reality' and 'dream.' Recognizing that the very flaws of self-deception for which she has castigated Philip also constitute the finest part of his character she perforce recognizes as well the interchangeability of her own strengths and weaknesses. Shaken in her sense of self, she then moves on to the far more important discovery that the whole issue of true and false is irrelevant since it has nothing to do with necessity. 'I must believe … Because I need him,' she says. Mrs Bentley gives up her grasp on discrepancy; she compromises; she *accepts*. This is no longer irony because it no longer asserts any value beyond what *is*. As W.H. New points out, because Ross blurs the edges of all his images, 'Absolutes do not exist' (B187).

Ross's example is not an unusual one. Indeed, when we look closely enough at most so-called ironic fiction in the Canadian corpus, the irony tends to evaporate. In Ernest Buckler's *The Mountain and the Valley*, for instance, there is no doubt that David Canaan is presented ironically, but because his moral authority is undercut so radically during the climactic scene on the hilltop by his childishly self-important fantasies, his dilemma is rendered personal and particular, drained of its capacity to implicate the observer. In other cases, like Mordecai Richler's *The Apprenticeship of Duddy Kravitz*, we are so deeply implicated that we lose our detachment. Most often, however, the ironic element in Canadian fiction is simply *contained* or neutralized, as it is in *As for Me and My House*, by a non-ironic resolution.

Margaret Laurence's practice is typical in this regard – and typically misunderstood. 'The terrible laughter of God is a strain which runs through all of Laurence's work,' says Sandra Djwa; 'Hagar listens for it at the abandoned fish cannery by the sea and Rachel recognizes that she too, ultimately but not unmercifully, has been a victim of a "jest of God" ... [This is] the irony of human existence: man, from his restricted vantage point, can almost never fully understand his own condition' (B45). A very neat interpretation. Unfortunately it distorts, subtly but significantly, what Laurence is actually doing. Perhaps because she *expects* irony, and knows how irony is supposed to operate, Djwa seems to have projected something on Laurence's novels that isn't there at all. Indeed, even if we go no further than those elements on which she herself comments, we can see an almost diametrically opposed dynamic at work. It is true that Laurence's protagonists are generally brought to realize that they have in some sense been victimized, but far from simply confirming their vulnerability this recognition (Laurence implies) is valuable primarily in so far as it teaches them that the whole concept of 'God,' connoting some kind of meaningful correspondence between man and 'otherness,' whether good or bad, is in the long run simply irrelevant. The 'box' is there, certainly. It entails limitation and even victimization; again, certainly. But *discrepancy* is something else again. Discrepancy lies entirely in attitude, point of view, mode of vision – and these are *not* externally imposed. The choice of whether to measure oneself against the problematic infinite (which is what irony implies) or to let that be, to turn inwards, to define oneself always and only in terms of the human centre, is a choice that every man may and indeed must make for himself. The whole point about Hagar's stone angel, in other words, is not that it represents a blind, cold, indifferent otherness but that it has been erected by human will. *This* – not the mere fact of their limitation (a *donnée* that once having been recognized and accepted may best be ignored) – is what Laurence's protagonists must learn. And they do. 'If You have spoken, I am not aware of having heard,' says Rachel Cameron. 'No omens. No burning bush, no pillar of sand by day or pillar of flame by night' (E171). Eschewing both the wish for and the fear of divine intervention, Rachel takes control over her own life.

We find this kind of accommodation everywhere in Canadian literature. Indeed, it seems to represent by far the *preferred* mode of fictional resolution. The keynote is compromise. If there is little faith evinced in the power of the individual or the possibility of heroism, there is also a disinclination in this country for one to beat one's breast unduly over the constraints built into the human condition. The Canadian, in other words, seems capable of accepting the absolute existential bounds to his freedom *without* allowing that these necessarily either define or delimit his human possibility. Though obsessed with the idea that he is (in Ofelia Cohn-Sfetcu's words) 'a finite creature surrounded by an indifferent universe,' that is, he nevertheless remains paradoxically convinced that he is 'capable of scoring victories ... in spite of his frailty' (25). This dual awareness, 'equally opposed to both facile optimism and facile despair,' permits him to be tolerant with both self and others, cognizant of but not cowed by human weakness. Thus it is that Duncan in *The Fire-Dwellers* is able to acknowledge his fear of drowning without letting himself be diminished by it. '[H]e keeps on walking outward until he reaches what he judges to be a decent and to himself acceptable distance. Then he turns and swims back to shore' (268). Thus too that Thom of Rudy Wiebe's *Peace Shall Destroy Many*, musing on the question of guilt and innocence, can grant full weight to the effect of environmental influences on human behaviour – social, historical, biological – yet not feel obliged to believe that his moral being is wholly determined thereby. 'Following [heredity] back, you arrived at Adam: what then? You blame God. And you go through life doing what you do because you can do no else. No. There was no need to follow your body with its every impulse' (231). Thom, it would appear, has come to terms with, if not solved (which is quite another thing), the very dilemma that causes the true ironist so much anguish. *How is it possible to reconcile the irreconcilable without deluding oneself?* Simple. By changing the terms of reference. This, at least, is the process that most Canadian fiction seems to recommend. One simply compartmentalizes finite and infinite, and then assumes that everything with human relevance – 'dream' and 'reality' both – derives its meaning solely from the human space.

Once such a balance is achieved, the chasm *within* experience disappears. There is no longer any necessity for wrestling with discrepancy. One controls what can be controlled, accepts what must be accepted, and simply doesn't concern oneself about the rest. Accommodation. Without guilt or bitterness. This, it would seem, is the Canadian way, the lesson that is embedded in much of our most powerful literature. Disdaining to waste his time hurling deprecations at an unseeing sky the prototypical Canadian, like Hershey Brahms of *The Abramsky Variations* (who fortunately inherits his father's aptitude for life as well as his mother's weakness for fantasy), sets himself to 'discover how to go on living where he is, with the things that make sense and the things that are crazy, with the lovable and the detestable, the genuine and the false' (117). In no uncertain terms, that is, *he repudiates the ironic vision.* 'Marian does not change her society (how could she?) or escape from it; the proof of her sanity is that she has learned to live effectively within it' (John Lauber on Atwood's *The Edible Woman* 30). 'Addison's final epiphany ... is his realization that the duality on which he has based his actions has no basis. He no more needs to kill off old Addison than Charlton needed to turn off the Squeasy ad; instead he must harness the undirected energies which he had incorrectly assumed were undesirable, thereby finding salvation in the fallen state itself' (Russell Brown on Simpson's *Arkwright* B96). '[T]he final effect of the passage is to suggest that the creative and destructive forms of power, embodied as they are in a single object, are expressions of the same principle and inherently related to one another' (John Sutherland on Pratt's *The Titanic* 57). 'In ... acceptance or acquiescence lies true tragic greatness: it mirrors the indomitable spirit of mankind. All great endeavour, great ambition, great love, great pride, great thought disturb the placid order of the flow of events. That order is restored when failure is accepted and when it is seen and acknowledged that life proceeds by compromise only' (F.P. Grove on *Settlers of the Marsh* in J.L. Thompson B87). 'Although Wiebe's comedy ... shades into satire exposing the hollowness of contemporary society, he militates against this clear and simplifying direction of decision through the central Quixotic concept that allows a more complex confrontation of real and ideal. Quixotic comedy admits both our materiality and our longing to transcend it but resists a simple alternative, denying escape from the material even as it refuses to dismiss the ideal' (Ina Ferris on *The Blue Mountains of China* 83). 'In Birney's latest poems ... a new detachment about both himself and the world modifies his humanism further into simply a tolerant amusement at man's foibles and resignation about his doom' (Frank Davey on *Rag and Bone Shop* C75). 'She [Naomie] is a realist in every sense ... She doesn't just let [things] happen, she strives, and where she meets a wall and realizes it's too big for her to climb she doesn't bother to try and climb over it. When she comes to the age she can no longer be a film star of the kind that she was, she very gracefully withdraws. That is over . When they say there is nothing [they] can do [for her haemophilic child], she says: "We must live with this." She's dying of cancer, it's the same thing, the whole thing, she accepts the reality ... I see that that is what we must learn to do as a race, to live within the bounds' (Timothy Findley on *The Butterfly Plague* B147).

If, as these quotations seem to confirm, Canadian literature is not ironic/romantic, it might be expected to diverge from mainstream contemporary fiction in other ways than mode of resolution. And it does. For one thing, as we might have predicted, it assumes for the most part an entirely different relation between man and men. The vertical perspective fosters almost by necessity an emphasis on individualism. The romantic hero, as Lilian Furst points out, 'is undeniably "the hero" of the works portraying him ... His overwhelming presence is the expression of that total self-absorption that makes his universe – and that of the work in which he appears – pivot entirely on his idiosyncratic ego'[14]; the ironic hero is equally if not more egocentric, having simply been driven in on himself by his sense of alienation. As a result, the protagonists of romantic/ironic literature seem frequently to exist in a vacuum, divorced entirely from *context*, whether social, historical, or moral. On the horizontal axis, in contrast, context is crucial, not only serving as a background to the action but providing the standard against which all individual experience is defined. Pure comedy and pure tragedy both deal (in different ways) with instances of isolation, but it is the transpersonal element that gives the aberrancies their meaning. Though it may be less explicit in modern than in classical variants, there is always a social milieu, a tacit communal voice, that fulfils the function of the chorus. Tragedy and comedy in fact not only accommodate but *presuppose* the social.[15] This being the case we will not be surprised to note that despite, and possibly as a direct consequence of, the Canadian's· *a priori* sense of isolation, there are many indications in our literature, even above and beyond the general metaphor-to-metonymy impetus mentioned in the last chapter, that contemporary artists in this country seem to be 'seeking images of wholeness rather than aloneness' (see 'Reason over Passion' 79). Indeed, all signs point to the fact that, unlike the Americans, Canadians believe their salvation will be worked out not in terms of the individual but of the group. Certainly this is the message of A.M. Klein's *The Second Scroll*. 'Our tale intends to suggest that the Messiah is, or is of, or is in, the ubiquitous anonymity of universal Jewry's all-inclusive generation,' says the author; 'he is the resurgent creativity of the incognitos of the folk' (B25). Klein's vehicle may be idiosyncratic, but the view it puts forth is peculiarly representative of the larger culture from which it emerged. As Dave Godfrey pointed out in a 1972 interview with Don Cameron, where the American now tends to identify the Holy City with the individual himself, for the Canadian it is still a Holy City, a symbol of *social* ideality (A11).

If there is an undeniable horizontal impulse in Canada, there are also – even aside from the ineptitude for interpersonal relation that seems to plague us in practice – a number of serious problems revolving around the search for fictional vehicles to express that particular orientation. Canada's attitudes may be at right angles to modern thought in some fundamental ways, but we are still largely constrained to work in modern conventions and idioms. For this if for no other reason, the question of social intercourse becomes a very delicate matter. The individualist emphasis in the United States is closely related to the Adamic pioneering myth, but modern literature even outside America has tended to be anti-social, not merely as a corollary to the alienation theme but at least to some extent as its ground. Where in classical literature 'society' could simply be assumed as a tacit norm,[16] now, unless a writer makes a deliberate attempt to suggest otherwise, it will usually be preconceived as negative. Why? Fiction, as Georg Lukács and others have demonstrated, has always taken as its starting point the problem of reconciling 'actual social relationships ... with the ideals or values which the individual hopes to realize in his own life,'[17] and since this task is problematic if not impossible, a covert anti-social bias is built into the novel form. During the twentieth century this potential has blossomed into a sense of estrangement so pervasive and so radical that the social/individual dichotomy is now commonly held to represent not merely an abstract or propaedeutic opposition but a virulent, unavoidable antithesis. Even if the difficulties went no further such an assumption would work against the expression of an impulse toward integration – at least by way of conventional vehicles. On top of this, the Canadian also has to deal with the innate suspicion of the public sphere inculcated by the Moira/Themis reorientation, a suspicion *persistently reinforced on a subliminal level by the very iconographic preferences imprinted on our communal psyche*. How, in the face of such detriments, can the pro-social bias survive? Conventions notwithstanding, there are other, countering influences at work that carry even more weight in shaping Canadian proclivities than either extrinsic literary pressures or our home-grown ambivalence toward the domain of Themis.

The factors fostering a pro-social bent in Canada fall into three categories: philosophical, political, and psychological. In the first place and in a sense underlying all the rest is the tendency arising from our perceptions of the man/nature relation toward belief in some kind of environmental determinism. As noted in our discussion of Universal History, whether the subject is man the individual or man the aggregate, Canadian writing of many different kinds seems simply to *assume* the existence and the primacy of a network of complex historical and social links that makes the concept of independent action seem laughable. Social relations are thus deemed important in Canada first of all simply because they are inevitable.

The second factor relates more directly to value. Confronting the problems of a northern frontier, Canadians have had it drummed into them that even if they *could* achieve the kind of escape from social connection and constraint that the American westering myth implies, they would be foolish to do so. Co-operative effort is the only way one can survive, let alone thrive, in an environment like ours. In Wallace Stegner's words:

Beginning with an individualism that on occasion was so complete as to be irritable, settlers soon enough found the semi-arid Plains a place where no man and no family could do it alone ... That single-handed assault on the wilderness might have worked in wooded country with plenty of water and game; nothing even approaching it should have been attempted on the Plains. So what began in individual effort remained – *if* it remained – to cooperate. The progress from the formation of the Grain Growers Association in 1915, and the gradual evolution of cooperative elevators, buying clubs, and banks, went its inevitable course to political flowering in a society militantly cooperative, even socialist. It is so because the country tolerated settlement on no other terms. (300-1)

Social scientists have put forth numerous theories to explain the significant socialist component in the Canadian as opposed to the American political spectrum,[18] but it seems obvious from such more homely recitals as Stegner's that there is ample explanation for the trend to collectivity simply in necessity. Stegner is not exceptional. Canadian accounts of the pioneering experience almost always emphasize not merely the propriety but the utility of co-operative action. Indeed, the trend goes well beyond the purview of the 'western.' The fact is, as against the strikingly equivocal treatment of the wilful individualist, from T.G. Roberts's *The Red Feathers*, with its pointed demonstration of the 'banding' process among primitives ('During the summer, six more families joined Run-all-day's band ... They had been without a leader for several seasons, moving as the whim suggested, hunting or fishing when need drove them to it, and constantly being bullied or robbed by more united families.' 127), to Pratt's *Towards the Last Spike* we find the pragmatic advantages of co-operation rung consistently throughout the corpus. Canadians, in other words, are socially predisposed, despite their ambivalence about 'society' in the abstract, simply because it is so demonstrably to their advantage to be so.

Thirdly and most important we find a psychological proclivity for the social among Canadians which would seem to have a number of plausible bases. To begin with, because, in Otto Rank's words, woman is 'more collective by nature than man,'[19] the feminization of the symbolic ego is almost certain to entail a corresponding socialization. As well, the preoccupation with death would tend to accentuate this orientation by displacing egocentric wishful hopes of futurity onto the group: faced with the incontrovertible fact of his own mortality man accepts 'immortality collectively, that is, through his children in the tribe, community or nation' [Rank 227]. Finally, awareness of the inevitability of isolation coupled with a sense of its dangers (one of the most disquieting characteristics of the magician, you may recall, is his self-containment) makes the idea of institutionalized interpersonal relations, standing in for more immediate varieties of exchange, seem all the more desirable for the risks they involve. Though this sounds paradoxical, the reversal is perhaps no more than predictable. The impulse to congregate surely begins with a heightened sense of one's fragility and exposure – and this, as we have seen, is a sense almost omnipresent to the Canadian. If, like young Brian in W.O. Mitchell's *Who Has Seen the Wind*, the moment we step beyond the noise and distraction of the community we are confronted with the overwhelming power of the infinite ('He was filled now with a feeling of nakedness and vulnerability that terrified him. As the wind mounted in intensity, so too the feeling of defenselessness rose in him. It was as though he listened to the drearing wind and in the spread darkness of the prairie night was being drained of his very self.' 236), it is small wonder that we are for the most part quite happy to garrison ourselves securely within social structures. When we go beyond fear to actual suffering, the need for communion becomes even more intense. Thus it is that the forced recognition of her own impending death jars even the grimly reticent Hagar from her solitude ('I want to take hold of her arm, force her attention. *Listen. You must listen. It's – quite an event.*' 215); thus, too, the news of her son's calamity finally impels the 'single-minded' and 'marvellously cruel' Mrs Ross of *The Wars*, after years of guarding her privacy so jealously from the potential assaults of need and love, to appeal to her husband for help (compare pp 137 and 179-80). The conclusion to which this equation points is obvious. If suffering is inevitable, then it is inevitable that we will *all*, sooner or later, be forced to reach out; to join with our fellow victims – to affirm our *social* identities. It is consequently the *return home*, not the withdrawal of the alienated hero we find in so much contemporary American and continental fiction, that structurally defines the prototypical Canadian novel. Douglas LePan's Deserter, shocked out of his naive idealism by visions of death, finds that the meaning he has sought in the dark landscape of his own psyche actually derives from the sunlit world of social roles and obligations he has thought to leave behind. Pique in *The Diviners* ends her journey by rejoining the tribe she has always needed but never known. The diverse questors of *The Invention of the World* all come home to the House of Revelations.

The question is, what does 'coming home' actually mean to a Canadian?

Here we get into trickier territory. It must be obvious from the trends delineated throughout this book that whatever the Canadian believes to be proper – even necessary – in theory, when it comes to application he is bound to feel considerable ambivalence about both the act and the object of relation. As all the ambiguous hand imagery reveals, 'touching' – attempting to reach beyond the self by any means whatsoever – is almost always viewed here as potentially, and quite literally, fatal. How does one get around such a fear? In some cultures it would be possible to retreat from one's sense of vulnerability into such grand abstractions as Mankind or The Nation, but in Canada, as we have seen, the diffuse and inexplicable dangers of the socio-political arena are viewed as even more menacing than the relatively predictable brutality of the egocentric individual. On the other hand, be it somewhat less fearsome the realm of personal intercourse is obviously full of pitfalls in practice. So what is the alternative? There is only one possibility left: to compromise, to strike a fine balance between private and impersonal. Thus it is that the Canadian's social reference group, as we might have predicted from our apparent alignment with Mary Douglas's boundary-obsessed 'small group' cultural category (see pp 286-7), is neither family nor society, but *community* – that is, any formally self-defined aggregate small enough for face-to-face communication but large enough to make social norms rather than emotion the standard basis for interpersonal relation.[20] Even if the isolated settlement had not played such an important role in the historical Canadian experience, there is consequently ample explanation for the much-commented-upon predominance of the small town (the modern version of the fort in the wilderness) in Canadian literature. The small town does not merely define our roots, but illuminates our *ongoing* sense of identity, our place in the world. Indeed, quite above and beyond its indubitable historical relevance the small town – what it represents – both reflects and is presupposed by the specific terms of the Canadian psyche. It is the house writ large. It is the outer limit of self versus other. Although numerous Canadian writers have played with the possibilities of less obvious kinds of symbolic communities in their explorations of the intangible but ineradicable connections between man and man, man and men, the small town is the most natural expression of the kind of normative social reality to which the Canadian relates.

What exactly do we mean when we say 'small town,' though? Certainly it is nothing like the American's predictable ironic or romantic stereotypes, neither Peyton Place nor Walton's Mountain. Whatever other characteristics may be revealed by any specific Canadian fictional community, its identifying feature – as, very often, its protagonists must discover for themselves – is always the fact that it comprises a *mixed* reality. Though few have expressed it quite so explicitly, Robertson Davies strikes a typical note.

Once it was the fashion to represent villages as places inhabited by laughable, lovable simpletons, unspotted by the worldliness of city life, though occasionally shrewd in rural concerns. Later it was the popular thing to show villages as rotten with vice, and especially such sexual vice as Krafft-Ebing might have been surprised to uncover in Vienna; incest, sodomy, bestiality, sadism, and masochism were supposed to rage behind the lace curtains and in the haylofts, while a rigid piety was professed in the streets. Our village never seemed to me to be like that. It was more varied in what it offered to the observer than people from bigger and more sophisticated places generally think, and if it had sins and follies and roughnesses, it also had much to show of virtue, dignity, and even of nobility. (a15-16)

Since the Canadian small town is relatively unidealized – that is to say concrete, particular, arbitrary, and mutable – it resists mythicization, strikes neither a consistently positive nor a consistently negative chord in our literature. In what respect, then, does it function as a social referent? The key obviously has to lie in the mode of action it suggests rather than in any particular abstract value it possesses. Just as the saint/magician pairing provides a touchstone for our exploration of the problem of how to live alone, the small town provides the other side of the picture, a prescription for living together.

But what exactly does this 'prescription' prescribe? If we start with what the town actually seems to mean to its inhabitants, fictional and historical both, the first word that springs to mind is *safety*. What kind of safety, though? Obviously at least part of the significance of the fictional community is still based on the old garrison function of protecting us from an inimical 'outside,' for even if the wilderness is under control, in a psychological sense we are no less besieged than ever. Certainly this is the message to be gleaned from (undercutting quite effectively its conventional ironic/romantic implications) *Who Has Seen the Wind*. No matter how bad the town is, Mitchell suggests, no matter how stultifying the manners and how indefensible the morality, it is preferable in the long run to the chaos beyond its borders. 'If,' says Warren Tallman, 'the town is presided over by Mrs Abercrombie, an incarnation of community enmity toward personality – let them be citizens instead – the prairie is presided over by old Sammy, an incarnation of the disintegration which is likely to overtake all but the most resourceful personalities when the individual self wanders beyond the sphere of human community ... And despite her overt hatred of the diversity and freedom that are essential for self-nurture, [the former] is less fearsome than is [the latter] ... with his mad, mumbled incantations over psychic chaos and old night. Or let us say that the open emptiness of the prairie is humanly more fearsome than the huddled pettiness of the town' (236). We find the same implication in Roch Carrier's trilogy. If the concept of 'otherness' has now become more diffuse – projected into a contest not merely against an inimical nature but against the 'big guys' as well – it seems evident from the cautionary tale of Philibert's flight from the brutality of his rural home to the much more terrifying because faceless malignance of the big city, his disillusionment and eventual death, that the village for all its limitations, for all its connection with oppressive cultural and religious traditions, still offers safety to the individual by keeping him cloistered. For Mitchell and Carrier explicitly as for other writers implicitly, therefore, the basic function of the pioneer settlement is obviously still a primary function of the modern literary town.

The matter doesn't stop here, though. If it did, once one uttered the talismanic words 'garrison mentality' there would be nothing more to say. In recent fiction the notion of safety tends to go far beyond the purely extrinsic – and it is in this realm we begin to find hints as to the basis of the town's real significance as a model. The fact is, the community also (and more importantly) shields the Canadian from the consequences of *his own inadequacies*. It protects him in the first place from the loneliness that would normally be the lot of anyone so inept in the area of human relations by providing a structured context in which each and every individual has a guaranteed niche determined by formal ascriptive processes rather than by his own efforts. Unlike the American who yearns for the opportunity freely to exercise his own will, that is, the Canadian (in the words of sociologist Kaspar Naegele) typically demonstrates 'a greater acceptance of *limitation*, of hierarchical patterns' (27) not merely because, as is often implied, of the continuing influence of British political traditions, but in return for the security of *belonging.* '"My own people" is the key to all the small-town literature,' says Clara Thomas. 'Narrow and constraining to the individual as the town may be, it was our kind of community, where everyone had his place – even the slot called "outsider" is better than no place at all – and where nobody's child could be lost' (D177). Secondly, the town offers the ultimate out for the man trying to negotiate the alternate perils of aggressiveness and introversion by providing him with a ready-made public identity – such as the reluctant writer's well-disguised authorial persona – that spares him the necessity of any real 'touching.' Finally, and most important, the town shields its inhabitants from the disastrous potential of spontaneous, uninhibited, and/or irrational behaviour by providing extensive prescriptive formulae for regulating interpersonal relations. Once again the pattern runs completely counter to American ideals of personal freedom. While no fonder of 'government' than their neighbours, Canadians are apparently willing to accept restrictions as the price paid for a higher good, holding with Philip Rieff (in Ernest Becker's words) 'that in order to have a truly human existence there must be limits; and what we call culture or superego sets such limits.'[21] In any case it is certainly true that although even Canadian literature offers a few conventional demonstrations of what happens when 'rules' become so rigid as to replace human considerations (Wiebe's *Peace Shall Destroy Many* is a pre-eminent example), the average individual in this country not only demonstrates the greater respect for codified *law* that numerous social and political scientists nave noted (see Lipset, for instance), but seems also to believe with Davies' David Staunton that social rituals, from major ceremonies through to the minor intricacies of parlour games, are not mere gratuitous fripperies but the mainstay of secular order, to be violated only 'at our peril' (b37).[22]

This last observation is a critical one inasmuch as it is here, in the concept of extrinsically regulated activity, that we find not only a final confirmation of our divergence from contemporary norms (in the existentialist's view, according to Arturo Fallico, 'Freedom and *spontaneity* are ... synonymous'[23]) but also the one element that brings together the whole gamut of Canadian cultural propensities. Ritual not only links the *personal* ('I was alone with an unknown country spread out around me, unknown people, and if I had ever felt suicidal this was the time,' says John Newlove of his experience in writing one poem. 'That feeling of complete despair somehow fostered a formality in me, perhaps the formal manners of a person who has no hope left, rather than a wildness.' Bowering B15) with the *public* (institutionalized ritualism, as Mary Douglas indicates, is a natural response both where 'power' is perceived as problematic and where culture contains significant covert elements which, being irreconcilable with conscious communal aspirations, require symbolic mediation: 'At first sight all ritual would seem to be a form of restricted code. It is a form of verbal utterance whose meanings are largely implicit.'[24]), and both of these in turn with the *aesthetic* ('The central characteristic of the compulsive response to ambivalence [expressed in allegory] is the ordered ritual ...' says Angus Fletcher. 'Its effect is to allow a degree of certainty in a world of flux.'[25]), but even reconciles the polarities with which this chapter opened by linking the Old Testament emphasis on *observance* ('The Jewish creed rested on righteousness,' Rank points out: 'if you follow the commands of your God, that is, respect his laws, you are good' [176]) with the classical penchant for *propriety* ('Because of his nature, man must be subject to rules, discipline, and decorum, for a precivilized vent and expression of the self is a release of the beast.'[26]). Ritual – the key feature represented by the small town in Canadian literature – hence stands simultaneously as a pre-eminent expression of Canadian psycho-symbolic predispositions *and* as a means of relieving the distress catalysed by those predispositions. The impulse to externalize experience ritually as 'image and symbol,' whether comprehended under the name of religion or of art, as Jerome Bruner describes it, both provides 'a basis for communion between men' ('What is "out there" can be named and shared in a manner beyond the sharing of subjectivity') *and* 'makes possible the containment of terror ... by . decorum.'[27]

Far from the American quasi-primitivistic image of community, then, it follows from this that it is an ideal of social regulation that provides a foundation to the Canadian's 'horizontal' reference. The next question we have to ask – since we have spoken of a 'behavioural prescription' – is what this means translated into specific values. In the first place, as we might expect, the Canadian orientation is pre-eminently humanistic, but the humanism implied is a rather peculiar kind since it is explicitly anti-idealistic. That is to say, the Canadian (judging by our literature) spurns all absolutes, including even those absolute virtues associated by Milton with the Golden Mean, as essentially *un*human. Thus it is that Abraham of Wiseman's *The Sacrifice* is doomed not by his weakness but by an excess of strength, by a disproportionate faith in human capacity that makes him blind to the equal reality of human frailty. Indeed, as Helene Rosenthal points out, 'the novel confirms ... that pure goodness cannot be borne by man, since he is a carnal as well as a spiritual being. Pure goodness invokes its opposite (either polarity cannot exist without the other) and so, since they are abstracts of a human admixture, nature itself tips the scales to establish a balance' (83). The same message is conveyed even more emphatically by Douglas LePan's *The Deserter*. The young protagonist of this allegorical novel, far from experiencing the Jungian epiphany we are led to expect by the mandala symbolism, is brought almost to despair by on the one hand his memory of a 'perfect' love and on the other his recurrent dream of a crystal sun-dial. Why? 'Rusty believes that if he were to surrender his vision of perfection, there would be only "waste, tundra, dying stars, apathy, meaning-

lessness spreading everywhere,"' says D.G. Jones. 'But what he discovers is
that the more he measures the world against his vision of heaven, the more
apathy and meaninglessness spread around him anyway' (A154). The consequence of this insight? Rusty, like Abraham, learns the hard way that to survive
he must relinquish his irrational, even 'criminal,' idealism:

It is the implacable imperfectability of life, in any final sense, its irreducible suffering,
guilt, and threat of absurdity that have driven Rusty to the recognition that value lies in
love and not in perfection. Perfection of whatever kind tends to be relatively impersonal.
What makes life personal is the recognition of each individual thing or creature as unique
and, however imperfect, as of value in itself. What is demanded is a reversal of the
Platonic pilgrimage. Instead of moving from the love of earthly things to a love of
universals, we are asked to move from the love of universals, those pure eternal forms, to
the love of the evanescent and mortal particulars. The love of heaven is replaced by the
love of persons, of a perishing imperfect world. (156)

LePan's young deserter is even less than Wiseman's inadvertent murderer an
anomaly. Canadian humanism is predicated specifically upon a vision which,
allowing that the human individual is by definition not merely by deficiency a
mixed entity (remember our observations in chapter 5 on the inextricability of
flaws and defences), focuses not on some idealized Man but on men. On the
other hand, too narrow a particularity has dangers of its own. The *special* case,
carried too far, is as destructive of social equilibrium as the ideal one. Hence the
propensity in Canada for both literary writers and historians, eschewing any
celebration of anarchic aggressiveness, to focus on collective – that is,
'aggregate' – rather than individual heroism. Which brings us back to the small
town again. In this feature as in many others E.J. Pratt provides a normative
example.[28] Even in his most heroic poem, *Brébeuf and His Brethren*, this poet
opposes the barbarism of nature not by the resolve of the isolated individual (the
Brethren, though subsidiary perhaps, are always very much part of the picture)
or by some kind of anterior transcendental validation, but, in Atwood's words,
'with an *ordered human society*' (F93, italics added). Other productions in his
oeuvre go even further toward a kind of depersonalization, lacking even a token
carrier for the conventional function. In poems like *The Cachalot*, for instance,
the standard or type of heroic behaviour (if any) becomes abstracted into pure
symbol – an unfocused energy devoid of either cognitive or moral content. In
Towards the Last Spike, on the other hand, it is identified specifically with
co-operative action and the common weal. 'The real hero of the poem is a
society's will to take intelligible form,' says Frye; 'the real quest is for physical
and spiritual communication within that society' (F98). Pratt's practice in this
regard is perhaps a little more extreme than most, but in line with their social
orientation (anti-ideal and anti-individualistic) Canadians on the whole seem to

localize an unusual amount of value not in exemplary persons at all but in more or less abstract representations of that middle ground between the purely private (idiosyncratic) and the purely public (ideal).

The result of this bias, predictably, is that the 'virtues' emphasized tend to be those that are consonant with communal rather than individual interests. In particular the ideal of selflessness is one that often seems to intrigue Canadian writers. Predisposed as we are to value compromise, not many would go so far as to advocate such suspiciously audacious acts of self-sacrifice as exemplified by Pratt's martyrs, but there is a general feeling abroad that it is a good thing to live if not to die for something larger than oneself. The pro-social doctrine Dave Godfrey states explicitly ('my basic premise is that everyone has a responsibility to society and the only way you can really lead a full life is in doing things with people and for people' B157) summarizes aptly, in fact, the tacit moral assumption that seems most often to underlie the work of Canadian authors. The phenomenon is hardly surprising, of course. As Stanley McMullin points out with reference to Grove, 'emphasis on man as a social creature' almost automatically gives precedence to such values and behaviour as contribute to the welfare of the community. Committed to the kind of compromise that allows man to 'over-rule his egotism and identify himself with others,' Grove is by necessity dedicated also to some kind of social *action*:

Commitment to the service of mankind is basic to [Grove's] view of life. In *A Search for America*, Phil Branden goes forth to assist fellow immigrants. Abe Spalding commits himself to public service in his district. Niels Lindstedt must learn to live as a social man. The two Clarks, Sam and Edmund, have idealistic visions of freeing man from toil by supplying them with their daily bread. Grove himself lived a life of commitment to mankind. He taught, often using his own funds to establish classes and equip laboratories. In 1943 he ran for the Ontario legislature as a c.c.f. candidate. His aim as a writer reflects his desire to serve mankind. (A35)

A desire to serve mankind! One of the more commendable responses one might make to intimations of mortality. But wait a minute. Having followed our conclusions this far are we not brought up short by the Canadian fear of the 'public' arena? Indeed we are. This is why, Godfrey and Grove notwithstanding, the Canadian's more typical way of demonstrating his social consciousness is not to *do* but merely to *be*; to make up for his reluctance to act by accepting all the more willingly the essentially passive stance imposed upon him as a 'good' citizen of the community. Though 'social' in the most basic sense, the real Canadian virtues are not, therefore, virtues on a grand scale, but those smaller, more equivocal virtues we might call *domestic* virtues: tolerance, reticence, decency, a clean house. What it boils down to is keeping a low profile. The fact is, like Engel's Min, rejecting (as dubious, dangerous, or simply inappropriate taken as a basis for regulating conduct) both the too-general (philosophy) and the too-particular (feeling), the Canadian has a very modest view indeed of what comprises acceptable social behaviour. 'The awesome thing ... is that if you push away Moses and the ancient Greeks at once, you are left with the Girl Guides. "To do my best to do my duty to God and the King (really????) and help other people every day, especially those-at-home?" Will it do? Better than the Beatles pewling love-love-love' (c54-5).

Accepting the general standpoint, what does this prescription imply for the individual? Aside from the well-documented emphasis on such useful survival traits as patience, perseverance, acquiescence ('Unlike Huckleberry Finn, the characteristic American hero who determines "to light out for the territory" when civilization becomes too pressing, the characteristic Canadian hero,' says Djwa, 'is the one who stays and endures – the farmers of Ross's prairie' c143), at the centre of the Canadian vision is the acceptance of the concept of role not merely as *mask* but as *model*. This is a key fact. Where the American seeks liberation through self-discovery, self-expression, even self-creation, the prototypical Canadian in quest of self-definition sets himself not merely to learn but to *become* the role that is projected on him by others. Such a manoeuvre – yet another form of 'disguise' – is no doubt stimulated at least partly by our instinct for self-preservation. As Wiseman's Hoda discovers from bitter experience, gearing one's expectations to the expectations of others is a sure way to minimize one's vulnerability. '[S]he had gradually learned never to draw attention while she was paying attention, never to demand comfort while she was giving comfort. And from the early pain of realization that nobody really wanted to know her, had grown her pride that nobody did know her, not really, not who she was, underneath, not nearly as well as she knew them, even though they talked about her and laughed at her and looked down on her' (292). Above and beyond this essentially negative value, however, the yielding of oneself to external pressure is often projected in Canadian literature as a positive good in itself. In the simplest sense, in lieu of rousing ideals and grand abstractions the encouragement of the individual to identify himself not merely passively but profoundly with his social role is the best means possible of guaranteeing the kind of self-sacrifice demanded by community welfare. In Pratt's *The Titanic*, for instance, the incentives for heroism are not, by and large, idealistic ones. The wife who is too proud to leave her husband's side, the young aristocrats who cede their places in the lifeboat to the women from steerage, the ten-year-old boy who insists on being categorized as a 'man': all of these make their choices out of a desire to appear well in the eyes of the world. With a slightly different emphasis the delineation of motives could undercut the sacrifice involved, but Pratt's affectionate handling of human foibles, far from diminishing his characters, only serves to confirm that a quite unheroic susceptibility to extrinsic validation can actually make for a better person.

Once this association is made, the ramifications go far beyond the purely public level of socially approved behaviour. In *The Stone Angel*, for instance, the key to both Hagar's failure as a human being and her final redemption is not so much her capacity to feel, or even the pride that prevents her from *revealing* those feelings (as we have seen, her self-containment is as much of a strength as a weakness), but her *willingness to play the roles required of her regardless of how these reflect or conflict with her feelings*. As W.H. New describes it,

[Hagar] will not bend to play a role ... even when roleplaying would bring relief to another person. When her brother Dan is dying, it is not Hagar but another brother, Matt, who pretends to be their mother in order to give the boy some comfort ... Similarly she refuses, early in the book, ever to be a housekeeper like Auntie Doll. But ironically these refusals all reverse themselves. In time Hagar finds herself playing the wounded mother, playing at being in a rage, keeping house for another and then, when she is very old ... playing house by the sea like a child again ...

'How can one person know another?' Hagar is constantly asking; but 'How can a person know himself?' is the deeper question that Margaret Laurence asks by implication. Even the first of these questions is double-edged. Hagar is not really known by the people around her, nor can Hagar really know them. Only late in her life ... does she come really to see her very self, and hence to see and know her role in life. Only then can she accept for even a moment, for the sake of others, a role that is out of character for her, and discover in it some degree of that capacity for love which she had always craved. (A211-12)

While the American's greatest fear is the loss of identity consequent upon acquiescence to social definition, the Canadian, it seems, perhaps because he is so sceptical about the kinds of resolutions that can be achieved by means of more spontaneous – that is, unstructured – relationships, believes that it is in terms of social definition that he is most likely to find himself.

This brings us back to our hypothetical modes again. If Canadian literature is clearly oriented on the horizontal (that is, social) axis of our diagram, why is it that the corpus includes very little of what could, by any stretch of the imagination, be called pure tragedy or pure comedy? The magician and his ilk, for instance, demonstrate some of the most important characteristics traditionally associated with the tragic hero: why, then, are they not tragic heroes in fact? The most obvious answer is that the magician, as a type, is predominantly *negative*, but many – indeed most – conventional tragic heroes are almost as morally ambiguous as he. Their culpability is particularly evident in Shakespearian tragedy where, in accordance with Aristotle's much-bruited theory of *hamartia*, the tragic flaw, the hero is typically and demonstrably responsible for his own downfall not by accident or by circumstance but by virtue of the fact that, in St John Irvine's words, 'there is a unique essence in him that makes him incapable of behaving in any other way' [in Auerbach 318]. As Walter Kaufmann summarizes it, 'Not only is *Macbeth* the tragedy of a noble man who was excessively ambitious, Othello was noble but too jealous, Hamlet was noble but unable to make up his mind, Coriolanus noble but too proud, Richard II noble but too soft, Antony and Cleopatra noble but – perhaps too much in love? – Timon noble but excessively generous, and Lear noble but too proud, uncompromising, blind, impatient, arbitrary, unjust, and imprudent, not to say insufferable.'[29] Even in earlier classical works, however, where – Aristotle notwithstanding – the tragic decline is often precipitated not by fault but by fate,[30] the tragic hero is still equivocal to the extent that he is 'a strong character in an exposed position' (Frye A38). Sinning or sinned against, his 'activity' alone is enough to convict him of *hubris*, that insolent presumption of divine power which comprises by definition a violation of both the natural and the social order.[31] This is not really so far from the magician after all. If we do not see our home-grown hero as 'tragic,' therefore, the fact must obviously relate less to his intrinsic qualities than to our own attitudes.

The Aristotelian association of pity and terror with tragedy implies that the hero's fate stimulates both the audience's detachment (the capacity to take pleasure in 'knowing, and seeing the inevitability of what works itself out'[32]) and its sense of identification (when he suffers for nothing more than the nobility, the presumption, the *wilful humanity* that we ourselves have admired and coveted, we realize how close we are at least in imagination to committing the fatal act of self-assertion; when, even more, 'he falls suddenly and unexpectedly into utter misery and destruction ... this teaches us that none of us can be sure how he may end' [Kaufmann 134]). Such a dichotomy evokes vividly the terms of our own ambivalence toward the magician, but with this difference: in the Canadian context the charisma of the hero, his power to stir us, is so threatening to our sense of self that we are inclined to use art to baffle rather than to augment our impulse to identify with him. As noted in chapter 9, we hence employ a variety of techniques to diminish the emotional authority of the type. Most important for the question at hand, we usually construct our fictional vehicles in such a way as to minimize any suggestion of the conventional tragic dynamic. We avoid moral absolutes. We focus on the experience not of the hero but of the 'chorus.'[33] We disguise the tragic elements of the plot by embedding them in a matrix of comic diction. This last is the key strategy. Too often dismissed as a mere stylistic idiosyncrasy borrowed from contemporary ironists, it has the effect of denying if not the inevitability at least the seriousness of the fall – and in doing so, defusing the terror. As R.B. Martin points out, 'Style alone may be used [as] a ... way of imbuing a comic work with a sense of impunity ... After the establishment by language of that tone of deliberate artificiality, catastrophe cannot really threaten.'[34] What Martin doesn't mention is that the ploy has the same effect in a 'tragic' work. This is what happens in many of Kroetsch's books, for example. If we reduce it to its bare bones, Hazard Lepage's fate is totally logical (like the tragic hero's, his downfall is predicated upon the terms of the world he inhabits, the irreconcilability of his masculine will with the 'box' in which he is forced to function), but all the more appalling for that fact. At the same time, the style – the narrative tone – ensures that its terror will not touch us except subliminally. Thus distanced, the magician may be dominated rather than dominating the reader's reality. The starkness of tragedy is avoided.

Is this a flaw in our literature, not to mention our national character – this backing off from confrontation? Not necessarily. The Canadian is almost inevitably going to be biased toward comedy in any case, not merely because our pessimism makes us all the more hungry for the affirmation it seems to offer ('Traditionally, tragedy ends in death,' says Maurice Charney, 'whereas comedy ends in marriage, feasting, dancing, the promise of babies, and a general mood of reconciliation'[35]), but even more because its conventional grounds, its mood and its focus, answer better than tragedy to the peculiarities of our native vision. Why? For one thing, comedy not only recognizes but actually exploits that felt duplicity of self and other, spirit and corporeality which, as we have seen, forms such an insistent substratum to Canadian perceptions of the world. 'There are, it seems, two limiting envelopes,' Kerr writes of the universe presented by comedy: 'even when I have regained my strength by feeding my body I cannot walk through board fences. One prison meets another, and though my own private person is quite mobile, the one it meets is fixed, stolid, impermeable. The material universe outside me can be kicked, and beaten upon, and even – to a degree – budged. But it cannot be dissolved. It will be there to confront me again when I come back' [192]. Comedy at its most basic is thus designed to reinforce our own most basic assumptions about our relations with reality. More to the point for the present issue, it is also designed to reinforce our assumptions about our relations with society. Comedy, even more than tragedy, speaks from and for the community. In the first place, it typically *addresses itself* to that same middle ground of human experience with which we ourselves identify. As Kerr points out, 'Comedy insists not upon the uniqueness of its hero's qualities but upon their commonness. It is tragedy that attends to the unique man, to the self-assertive plunger who isolates himself from his fellows in order to rise above them' [176]. Secondly, and more significant, *it moves to confirm* the social status quo rather than delineating and in some sense (albeit only aesthetic) justifying, cases of radical divergence. 'The true subject of comedy is manners rather than morals,' Charney says: '... in tragedy we are almost immediately engaged in questions of good and evil ... [but] comedy, as it is usually practiced, serves rather to enforce the prevailing mores than to establish any new society based on ... the claims of the ideal' [96]. From this outline it should be readily apparent why Canadians would have a *natural* proclivity for the comic mode. Even aside from these considerations, however, the preference is also quite defensible in purely philosophic terms. Indeed, with only a slight shift in perspective it is possible to see our practice of confounding comedy and tragedy not as an evasive manoeuvre at all, but as a positive statement, expressing an important intuition about the nature of reality.

The fact is, in life if not in art, comedy and tragedy are *always* mixed. One is not merely the obverse but the complement and fulfilment of the other. Furthermore, whatever convention may suggest about happy endings, it is actually comedy that communicates the bleaker vision. Where 'tragedy suggests that nobility is possible, that courage is admirable, and that even defeat can be glorious,' says Kaufmann, '... comedy suggests that nobility is a sham, that courage is preposterous, and that triumphs no less than defeats are ridiculous' [349-50]. Comedy is thus more profoundly despairing than the most cataclysmic tragedy. Indeed, for all its compensatory humour and ostensible reconciliations, there is at its heart an impermeable darkness that finds echoes in man's most anguished intimations. Kerr evokes vividly the ambiguity, the horror even, that lurks behind the cheerful mask. '*Something* inside comedy is not funny,' he says. '... It does more than acknowledge an ache; it wishes to insist bluntly, even callously, on its often overlooked secret nature ... To be funny is to have been where agony was' [16]. 'He [the comic protagonist] has abandoned hope and settled for what is here. He has chosen, for the time being, the lesser of two possible values, the ephemeral, the actual, the present and the passing, that which will leave him with no more than a rind. In the reflection of man's choices which drama gives off, tragedy is the positive and comedy is the negative' [20]. 'Comedy's first aching thought is about the personal ballast everyman carries with him. Its second thought is about the barrier to freedom thrown up by the rest of the tangible world. Everything from a mud puddle to a mountain is hostile' [190]. 'Death, whether inadvertent or intended, is a constant theme of comedy ... Because to contemplate any true ending for a comedy is to contemplate death. Only death will end the joke. Man cannot ever be free of the matter that impedes, annoys, and limits him until he is in fact severed from that matter, until his consciousness is cut free of the machinery that clogs it' [170-1]. 'The happy endings of comedy are no more than mere pretences. Or, rather, they are more. They are frauds' [58]. Far from embodying the naive wish to avoid or transform the unpleasant facts of human existence, comedy expresses man's profound fear that *there is no way out*.

And this, of course – bringing us full circle – suggests why, if there is no pure tragedy in Canadian literature, there is very little pure comedy either. It strikes too close to home. What are we left with? Not 'tragi-comedy,' which (at least as the term has traditionally been used) trends over into romance on the one hand and melodrama on the other. Not, in fact, any 'mixed' mode at all, if by that we mean a *synthesis* of both comic and tragic. Despite the Canadian's amply demonstrated predilection for compromise, for obvious reasons having to do with our national temperament we typically approach the problems of navigating unassimilable alternatives in this country by means of accommodating rather than transforming the terms of the given. If we examine the corpus itself, therefore, we will find that the prototypical Canadian 'fiction' (using that term in the broad sense to mean any imaginative construct) simply juxtaposes unameliorated modal alternatives rather than pretending to reconcile them. This may be achieved by vertical layering of overt and covert possibilities, by semantic duplicity, by serial inversion, by compartmentalization – indeed, by any of the psycho-symbolic mechanisms by which myth achieves its formal ambi-valence. The result – and here is where we find that prototypical 'allegory' cited at the end of the last chapter – is very often an extremely complex aesthetic object which is simultaneously despairing and affirmative. This is not simply a matter of balancing equal opposites, though. Indeed, if we had to generalize we might well say that Canadian literature starts from a bleak, uncompromising comic vision and strives for the uplifting optimism of tragedy.

How does this general orientation translate into the particularity of actual books and poems? A surprising proportion of Canadian writing, even when technically pessimistic on the level of plot or theme, strikes a final note of limited or 'contained' affirmation based (to pull together a number of diverse threads that have emerged during the foregoing discussion) on a recognition of the double necessity imposed upon every individual simply by his own humanity of, firstly, accepting without either illusion or recrimination the existential 'box' into which he is born ('What is, is,' says Kerr. 'And whatever perfectly satisfies its own requirements must be said to possess perfect rectitude. That man should sometimes be crushed by the requirements of a rectitude he can neither anticipate nor fully understand is very hard; but the fact has been observed and so must be recorded. "It may be hard," Kitto says in discussing the burdening of innocents, "but Aeschylus never pretended that life was easy, or that Zeus was simple, or that only the guilty are tortured."' [130]), and secondly, like Camus' Dr Rieux, taking full and free responsibility for what goes on inside the limited human space. According to what can be inferred from our literature, in other words, although the Canadian is well aware that man cannot choose his circumstances, he believes that one *can and must* choose how he will react to them; what, given his undeniable finitude, he will see, feel, *be*. Since value is subjective even if fact is not, it is up to the individual himself whether his life will be *worth* living.[36] This assumption is what gives Canadian literature a unique, almost puritanistic flavour oddly combining tolerance with high moral purpose.[37] It is also the feature largely responsible for the perverse cheerfulness which, repudiating definitively the institutionalized schizophrenia of the contemporary ironic stance,[38] lies behind much that seems superficially facile or 'soft' or old-fashioned in the Canadian voice. What Dennis Duffy says of Hugh Hood is true of many of our authors. 'Hood is not a post-modern in his sense of life – he sees it as grim, joyous, brutal, peaceful, but never as merely silly or absurd. His characters are haunted by the past, they are prone to fantasizing their way around reality, but they possess minds and bodies which struggle, at times successfully, to live really and presently. *It is not that they or their creator are unaware of the Horror or the Void; it is that they do not often dwell there'* (A243, italics added). The fact is, Canadians believe that it is just as self-indulgent to bemoan man's limitations, to use them as an excuse for unhappiness – 'to take refuge in tragedy,' as a disapproving Lady Juliette d'Orsey phrases it in *The Wars* (103) – as it is to pretend that they do not exist. We are thus required, before all else, *to live with our consequences*, to take moral responsibility for ourselves. As Birney points out, indeed, though man might be 'a spark beleaguered by darkness,' no one binds Prometheus but himself (Ag172).

And then what?

Why then, having accepted the terms – and obligations – of our discretionary powers, we may not merely affirm but *celebrate* what is.

Does this, in the light of the decidedly ambiguous patterns we have delineated in the foregoing chapters, seem like an extravagant claim? Perhaps. We shouldn't rule out the possibility, though, that our innate pessimism, by protecting us from the American's naive and fragile hopefulness, actually lays the groundwork for a more profound contentment.[39] In any case, for whatever reasons, if we turn to the corpus itself we will see that despite the obsession with boundaries and walls, within the admittedly small degree of freedom the Canadian allows himself he is inclined to be as optimistic, as hopeful, as *joyful* as the circumstances will permit. In the first place, though bombarded with constant reminders of his pain and frustration and impotence he still stubbornly clings to the view fostered by tragedy 'that suffering is no insuperable objection to life, that even the worst misfortunes are compatible with the greatest beauty' [Kaufmann 347]. As a result he is able, with Torgov's Lou, with Wiseman's Hoda, with Brian Moore's Ginger Coffey, to affirm that – win or lose – being alive is its own reward. Secondly, though constantly disappointed if not actually injured in his attempts to relate, he continues (albeit nervously) to seek for some contact beyond himself. Thus it is that for all the ambiguous hand imagery in Canadian literature, some of the most positive, most triumphant images in the corpus – like this one from *The Sacrifice* (interestingly enough, at once the most 'purely' tragic and unambiguously affirmative novel that this country has produced) – focus on hands as well:

He could neither move his own hand nor look away from his grandfather's. This was the hand of a murderer. His eyes, fascinated, saw that the hands were not really different in shape, one from the other. And for a moment so conscious was he of his grandfather's hand on his own, of its penetrating warmth, of its very texture, that he felt not as though it merely lay superimposed on his own but that it was becoming one with his hand, nerve of his nerve, sinew of his sinew; that the distinct outlines had disappeared. It was with the strangest feeling of awakening that he saw their hands fused together – one hand, the hand of a murderer, hero, artist, the hand of a man. He could not for the life of him pull his hand away, nor did he want to. It was as though he stood suddenly within the threshold of a different kind of understanding ... Impulsively he brought his other hand down on the hand that held his own. (345)

Finally, though fully cognizant of the behavioural constrictions entailed by his acceptance of communal definition, the Canadian is always ready to make the best of necessity. David Williams's Sundance; the war's-end celebration in Blondal's Mouse Bluffs; Gwendolyn MacEwen's *Breakfast for Barbarians* where, unredeemed, we are nevertheless invited (in Jones's words) 'to rejoice, to celebrate life in its mortal variety' (A183); the climactic Montreal cocktail party in *White Figure, White Ground*; David Staunton's Christmas at Sorgenfrei; 'the famous "fête sauvage" around Corriveau's coffin' where, 'As the villagers pray, then slip off to eat, drink, blaspheme, eye the women and tell salacious stories, they are affirming life' (Bond 129); Pratt's *The Witches' Brew*, 'a comic litany of the delights of rum-inspired eating, drinking and fighting' (Djwa A48); Hoda's weddings and funerals; Hazard Lepage's wake; the dance at which Carlyle finally lets loose in *The Vanishing Point* – it is amazing how many Canadian fictions evoke, or revolve around, or climax with some form of public occasion, festivity, or celebration. The meaning of these diverse types of gathering is perhaps made most explicit in Hodgins' treatment of the wedding reception that ends *The Invention of the World*. 'Containing' every conceivable human activity and artifact, interpreted one way this astoundingly Rabelaisian event could simply signify life-in-a-box; interpreted another, it asserts quite unequivocally that life *is* a party. Even allowing that it is no more than conventional to end a comedy with a marriage (signifying, as Kerr describes it, 'a coming together of black and white and of wisdom and folly, a fusing of forces that have been playing tricks upon one another, a settlement, a subsiding, a silencing, which may mean gratification or may as readily mean a kind of death' [64]), the incredible inclusiveness of Hodgins' hymenal celebration gives it, I think, a more-than-merely-conventional affirmative value to balance the emphasis on limitations elsewhere in the book.

Where does all this lead us? If in conclusion we wanted once more to 'place' Canada's orientation in a world context, we might suggest the following breakdown: in Europe, where the social context is simply assumed, albeit now for the most part negatively, the main concern of both writers and philosophers is 'being-with' (Heidegger's *dasein*); in America, where the social context is assumed but offset by a dream of freedom, of escape, we might say the preoccupation is with transforming 'being-with' into 'being-without'; in Canada, on the other hand, where 'being-without' has apparently been so forcibly imprinted on the psyche as almost to efface the European inheritance altogether, the American thrust is reversed to become, in a nutshell, 'being-toward.' The prototypical Canadian novel, whatever its other features, is thus very likely to have a shape resembling Sheila Watson's *The Double Hook* where, having learned the dangers of ambition ('when you fish for the glory you catch the darkness too' 15), the impossibility of escape ('I ran away, he said, but I circled and ended here the way a man does when he's lost' 132), and the vulnerability of man alone ('She wanted to cram the empty space with hate ... Die suffering so that James would remember the pain of her' 85), an aggregate of isolates comes together in mutual need and forms a new community. The final affirmation, appropriately enough, is ritually signalled when a child is born, named, accepted – and if Coyote's last speech ('I have set his feet on soft ground; I have set his feet on the sloping shoulders of the world' 134) reminds us that the future is likely to bring new problems we also have the sense, now the rain has restored the parched land, that these people, united, will have a firm enough grasp on life to survive them.

NOTES

1 Auerbach, *Mimesis: The Representation of Reality in Western Literature*, trans. Willard Trask (Princeton 1968) 16

2 Zweig, *The Adventurer* (Basic Books 1974) 32

3 Lest this seem rather scanty evidence for designating a *general* cultural proclivity, Suzi Gablik's art-historical studies demonstrate vividly that discontinuity was a key characterizing feature not merely of Homer but of Greek art as a whole: 'Perspective ... presupposes transformational relations and an operational system of "putting in relation"; it is just such an ability to order relations relative to a point of view which we do not find in Greek art. Despite their sublime conquest of sculptural form, despite the quite sophisticated foreshortenings achieved by some Athenian vase painters ... the Greeks basically did not represent objects relative to each other ... The figures themselves are of a dazzling beauty, each one posed in an attitude of sheer expectancy, but they do not really interact. There is an undertow of isolation; despite the grouping, each figure remains in a private space of its own.' *Progress in Art* (Rizzoli 1979) 14

4 For a discussion of this development, see Mario Praz, *Mnemosyne: The Parallel between Literature and Visual Arts* (Princeton 1967), esp. chapter 4. Interestingly, just as the increasingly individualistic focus in literature was associated with the increased mixing of high and low styles, the propensity toward subjectivization undercut old precepts of order in art as well. As Praz describes it, 'the possibility of

objective truth, which was the foundation of Renaissance aesthetics, came to be generally denied. Particularly in England the whole structure of classical aesthetics collapsed, owing to Hogarth, Hume ("Beauty is no quality in things themselves: It exists merely in the mind which contemplates them; and each mind perceives a different beauty"), Lord Kames, and Alison (for whom the beauty of forms was produced solely by association), until Julien Gaudet, in *Eléments et théorie de l'architecture* declared that mathematical ratios were chimerical and "les proportions, c'est l'infini."

'But already the anti-Renaissance movement which goes by the name of mannerism, attracted as it was by the picturesque, the bizarre, and – in a word – the particular, rather than by the Platonic ideal and the universal, had sought effects which implied a reversal of classical usage, and resulted in disquieting arrangements in [both] literature and the visual arts' (90-1).

5 Vernant, 'Greek Tragedy: Problems of Interpretation' in Richard Macksey & Eugenio Donato, eds., *The Structuralist Controversy: The Languages of Criticism and the Sciences of Man* (Johns Hopkins 1972) 288

6 It is interesting that Auerbach, as we have already seen (chapter 11, note 50), uses a horizontal/vertical schema to delineate certain historical developments in Western culture, since his categories have considerable bearing for our present, more general ones. As Eric LaGuardia describes it, Auerbach employs 'metaphors of the vertical and horizontal lines [to help define] ... the shift from the figural to the secular representation of reality ... The vertical (figural) line signifies a continuity of nature and spirit based on the acceptance of the temporal as well as the eternal, but a continuity in which a divine reality ultimately supersedes (or fulfills) the earthly. In the Renaissance there is a dissolution of this vertical, figural line in the direction of the horizontal or secular, signifying the more thoroughly temporal destiny of human life.' 'Chastity, Regeneration, and World Order in *All's Well that Ends Well*' in Bernice Slote, ed., *Myth and Symbol: Critical Approaches and Applications* (U. Nebraska 1963) 130

7 Muecke, *The Compass of Irony* (Methuen 1969) 121

8 Hassan, *Radical Innocence: Studies in the Contemporary American Novel* (Princeton 1961) 6

9 Glicksberg, *The Tragic Vision in Twentieth-Century Literature* (Delta 1970) 35

10 Puetz, 'Imagination and Self-Definition,' PR 14 (1977) 242

11 The propensity of the last two generations of European and especially French intellectuals to identify themselves with transcendent social philosophies such as Marxism, though less frivolous than recent American neo-Romanticism, nevertheless argues much the same kind of recoil. To some extent the phenomenon may be explained as symptomatic of the social guilt experienced in times of crisis by those who are the passive observers of history (Victor Brombert discusses this possibility at some length in *The Intellectual Hero: Studies in the French Novel 1880-1955* [U. Chicago 1964]), but, as Brombert himself concludes, an equally important ingredient

in the motivations behind this trend is the individual's need to rise above the despair catalysed by his recognition of the 'lie' of humanism and his consequent, terrifying conviction of self-responsibility. 'To lose oneself in a great Party,' exclaims Simone de Beauvoir, 'to fuse one's will with an enormous collective will: what peace and what strength!' [in Brombert 153]. There is more than a slight element of escapism here.

12 Further to this topic, it is an odd fact that despite their predilection for a camera's eye perspective on experience, Canadians tend to associate a fascination with 'real' movies with emotional and even mental weakness. It is significant, for instance, that one of the identifying characteristics of the unwholesomely independent young wife of André Langevin's *Poussière sur la ville* is her susceptibility to Hollywood-style versions of reality. Madeleine, as Jeannette Urbas points out, 'has a passion for movies and love-songs in the popular vein, not so much because of what they express, but because they open up for her a world of dreams and possible adventures closer to her desires than the everyday world she inhabits' (72).

13 Culler, *Structuralist Poetics: Structuralism, Linguistics, and the Study of Literature* (Cornell 1976) 157

14 Furst, 'The Hero or Is He an Anti-Hero?,' *SLitI* 9, 1 (1976) 56

15 At least part of the reason for this obtrusive social component is the fact that tragedy and comedy were in a sense designed specifically to mediate the opposing principles implied by the individual and his social setting. They would therefore not exist *without* that social setting. It all started with the rise of the City back in ancient Greece. As Jean-Pierre Vernant points out, once the process of urbanization reached a certain point, to maintain civic order the heroic world had to be repudiated. Unfortunately this was easier said than done. 'The ideal of the City is for citizens to be equal, whereas the heroic ideal is to be always first. The heroic ideal is kept alive in the City in order to maintain a dialogue. The past is rejected as *hubris*. But it is a surprising paradox that there is no cult of the hero in Homer or Hesiod ... The cult of the hero is a civic cult, instituted by the City. The City is the frame of reference in which heroes ... [are] assigned to places in their Pantheon. These heroes and heroic legends, while they are relegated to the past, condemned, called into doubt, still do not cease to stimulate certain questions, precisely insofar as they represent mental attitudes, values, patterns of behavior, a religious thought, a human ideal which is opposed to that of the City' (183). This is where art comes in. Tragedy and comedy each provide a means of dealing with – *distancing* – those dangerous anarchic impulses which can neither be assimilated nor forgotten.

16 As Auerbach points out, 'In the realistic literature of antiquity, the existence of society poses no historical problem: it may at best pose a problem in ethics, but even then the ethical question is more concerned with the individual members of society than with the social whole. No matter how many persons may be branded as given to vice or as ridiculous, criticism of vices and excesses poses the problem as one for the individual; consequently, social criticism never leads to a definition of the motive forces within society' (32).

17 Michel Zéraffa, *Fictions: The Novel and Social Reality*, trans. Catherine & Tom Burns (Penguin 1976) 44

18 G. Horowitz, for instance, claims that during the Revolution there was a splitting off of the loyalist Tory faction (which eventually stimulates socialism, its complement and alter) from the republican Liberal faction (which in a sense neutralizes by *subsuming* the basic socialistic impulse), with the result that both Canada and the u.s. started with a political bias built into their respective populations.

19 Rank, *Beyond Psychology* (Dover 1958) 258

20 In this respect it is interesting to speculate on the covert sources for Marshall McLuhan's famous metaphor of the global village. The fact is, in spite of the potential for almost instantaneous world-wide communication modern society is *not* getting more village-like. Indeed, it is possible that our increased awareness of the immanence of the 'other' may be responsible for what seems recently to be a greater insistence on formal geo-political divisions, a more rigorous delineation of 'sides.' It is quite possible, though, that it was McLuhan's subliminal 'Canadianness' that made him seize upon this particular image to project his intuitions.

21 Ernest Becker, *The Denial of Death* (Free Press 1975) 265

22 Ronald Sutherland, linking this bent for authoritarian structure explicitly with the puritanistic tendencies of the Canadian religious establishment, implies that with recent increased secularization the trend has been stemmed or even reversed ('*until very recently*, Canadians have tended to depend upon and to trust systems which control their lives' B3), but the continued importance of the 'small town' in our fiction clearly indicates that the phenomenon is much more broadly based.

23 Fallico, *Art & Existentialism* (Prentice-Hall 1962) 6

24 Douglas, *Natural Symbols: Explorations in Cosmology* (Vintage 1973) 54. With regard specifically to the mediating function, it is interesting to note the connection Geoffrey Leach draws between ritual and boundaries: 'in all human societies, the great majority of ceremonial occasions are "rites of transition," which mark the crossing of boundaries between one social category and another: puberty ceremonies, weddings, funerals, initiation rites of all kinds.' *Culture and Communication* (Cambridge 1976) 35

25 Fletcher, *Allegory: The Theory of a Symbolic Mode* (Cornell 1970) 344

26 Milton R. Stern, 'American Values and Romantic Fiction,' *SAF* 5, 1 (1977) 23, citing T.E. Hulme

27 Bruner, 'Myth and Identity' in Henry A. Murray, ed., *Myth and Mythmaking* (Beacon Press 1968) 277

28 Pratt is not only a pre-eminently 'public' poet in terms of his general *stance* ('In his writing Pratt adopts the point of view of the impersonal spokesman for mankind, adopts group values, and writes social epics,' says Frank Davey, B77-8), but his style, too, as Earle Birney notes, exemplifies particularly well the impersonal mode described in chapter 10 as characteristic of so much Canadian writing ('He has simply remained faithful to reasonably plain dramatic narrative and epic in an era of extremely subtle, introspective lyric' B91).

29 Kaufmann, *Tragedy and Philosophy* (Princeton 1979) 322

30 In many classical tragedies – *Antigone* is a pre-eminent example – the catastrophe is brought about by a clash not between good and evil, but between equally admirable but irreconcilable ideals. In others, more poignantly, the protagonist, despite his technical 'guilt,' is less villain than victim. Though Oedipus' 'blindness' may in the strictest sense be seen as a flaw, the action of the play, and especially the fact that he is doomed equally by his ignorance *and* his quest for enlightenment, his limitation *and* his attempt to transcend it, makes us feel that here is simply finite man at the mercy of a capricious fate. See Kaufmann's discussion of the relationship between man's finitude and his doubts about morality, both divine and human, as linked tragic themes (esp. 153-4).

31 Note that *hubris* or *hybris* does not simply mean pride or arrogance as is often assumed. As Kaufmann summarizes it, 'The Greek verb *hybrizein*, found in Homer, means to wax wanton or run riot and is also used of rivers, of plants that grow rank, and of overfed asses that bray and prance about. The noun, *hybris* means wanton violence and insolence and is frequently used in the *Odyssey*, mostly of Penelope's suitors. It also means lust and lewdness; and the noun, too, can be applied to animal violence. *Hybrisma*, finally, means an outrage, violation, rape; and in law this term is used to cover all the more serious injuries done to a person. It can also refer to a loss by sea.

'*Hybris* can be contrasted with *dike* and *sophrosyne*, two words that are notoriously hard to translate; but the former suggests established usage, order and right, the latter moderation, temperance, (self-) control. *Hybris* is emphatically not pride in one's own accomplishments and worth, nor even making a point of one's desert. It is not, like pride, something one feels (or "takes") but rather something that involves action. H.J. Rose puts the point well when he speaks in passing of "those who practice *hybris*, wanton disregard for the rights of others"' (74-5).

32 Richard Kuhns, *Structures of Experience: Essays on the Affinity between Philosophy and Literature* (Harper Torch 1970) 10

33 'The chorus … is – nearly always – the *inactive* agent in a Greek play. The chorus is not the hero; it is all the rest of us, those of us who lead lives of relative security because we dare nothing. The chorus may well praise the mean because – in its passive, reflective, undecided way – it is hoping for stability, frightened when great deeds are done.' Walter Kerr, *Tragedy and Comedy* (Simon & Schuster 1969) 125

34 Martin, 'Notes Toward a Comic Fiction' in John Halperin, ed., *The Theory of the Novel: New Essays* (Oxford 1974) 82

35 Charney, *Comedy High and Low: An Introduction to the Experience of Comedy* (Oxford 1978) 175-6

36 Considering our observations in chapter 11, it is interesting that Cohn-Sfetcu makes an explicit causal connection between the Canadian's acceptance of self-responsibility ('Canadian authors try to contend with the awareness that man's reason for existence is not supplied by an external agency, but is consubstantial with the individual who thinks. It is, therefore, to man himself that the task to create living value is set.') and

his propensity for temporal questing ('But, where to look for the redeeming feature of the life of man? In man's uniqueness, comes the unequivocal answer: in man's possibility to engage mentally in a vertical temporal movement, rather than follow a merely horizontal sequence of moments.')(26).

37 With the unappetizing example of Faulknerian-style relict Calvinism in mind, we do not commonly consider Puritanism to be an unduly 'tolerant' persuasion, but we need only consider Milton, with his advanced views on free speech and divorce, his disdain for a 'cloistered virtue,' to realize that the grim version is not the only possible one.

38 As Robert Detweiler points out, 'Because Western culture has rigorously divorced reality and fantasy, sane and insane, and forced these modes to exist in mutually exclusive fashion, human being-in-the-world has been distorted, and schizophrenia as a dominant form of illness has emerged to disclose a fundamentally mad dimension to our dividing of the world of experience' (Story, Sign and Self: Phenomenology and Structuralism as Literary Critical Methods [Fortress/Scholars Press 1978] 54). The Canadian view, evolved to accommodate those extremes which, in the absence of a transcendent 'leap' of some kind, cannot be bridged, avoids this problem.

39 We get an interesting sidelight on this discrepancy when we note the relatively greater success during the last decade of the work of Herbert Marcuse in the United States (especially among the intellectuals and 'counter-cultural' elements) than in his native Europe. As Vincent Descombes comments, 'Marcuse's brew of Freudo-Marxism was too thin for the appetite of the French reader, on two counts. Philosophically, the return to Hegelian Marxism appeared regressive; but above all, Marcuse's revised Freudianism was unacceptable to anyone who had learned from Lacan that desire is in no way a natural drive which society – and not reality itself – impedes. The likening of repression to social repression, the very principle of "Freudo-Marxism," appeared as a reissue of eighteenth-century inanities: nature is good, the savage noble, society evil. According to Lacan, repression precedes and accounts for all forms of social oppression. Desire, he says, has its beginnings in the impossible, and is condemned to find its satisfaction only in dreams. Such is the lesson of psychoanalysis, from which an ethics might have been developed, he adds, "if our age were were not so prodigiously tormented with idyllic imperatives"' (Modern French Philosophy [Cambridge 1980] 172). It seems evident from this description that this is at least one area where Canada comes closer to the European than the American pattern.

Catalogue of 'Primary' Sources

The list below represents an overview of the 'evidence' on which the foregoing argument is based. If its constitution is unconventional, the departure from standard form is dictated at least partly by the constitution of the text itself. Since this book is not 'about' art or literature in any ordinary sense but, rather, focuses on the cultural ground from which these arise, considered as raw data both the articulated statements of specialists of every variety *and* the tacit opinions of the public at large carry equal weight with the formal artifact as 'expressions' of the communal vision. As a result, it will be noted that a great many items are herein classified as 'primary' which one would normally consider 'secondary' or 'supporting' or 'background' material. For the reader's convenience the list is framed in such a way that it may serve as a functional index as well as a catalogue/bibliography. Listings at the end of each entry indicate the pages on which given authors/artists and/or texts are cited, analysed, and/or quoted. Specific editions are designated only in the latter case (and these, for ease of reference, are almost always the most 'popular' – often paperback – editions). Otherwise the date given is the original date of publication. Specificity of entries varies with the specificity of the referenced discussion. Abbreviations of periodical titles follow the usage of the *MLA* bibliography; M&S denotes McClelland and Stewart.

Aquin, Hubert 80, 175, 190, 319, 355, 402, 407
  A *Blackout (Trou de mémoire)* trans. Alan Brown (Anansi 1974) 302–3, 330
  B *Prochain épisode* (1967) 243, 296, 365
Arn, Robert, 'The Uses and Transformation of History in the Work of Bloore and Snow' *artscanada* 32, 198/9 (1975) 369, 410
Arnason, David, ed. *Nineteenth Century Canadian Stories* (Macmillan 1976)
Atwood, Margaret 286, 310, 326, 344, 361, 363–4, 365
  A *The Circle Game* (Anansi 1978) 379–80
  B *The Edible Woman* (Seal 1978) 106, 138, 142–3, 290, 297, 315, 345, 423
  C *Lady Oracle* (Seal 1977) 250, 306–7, 322, 376, 382, 393
  D 'Reaney Collected' *CanL* 57 (1973) 358

B   Interview in Gibson B 434

C   *The New Ancestors* (New Press 1972) 368

Godwin, Ted, 'G' CORNERS (1964) 96

Gose, E.B., 'They Shall Have Arcana' in Woodcock A 212

Gotlieb, Phyllis, 'Hassidic Influences in the Work of A.M. Klein' in Mayne 408

Gould, Eric, 'The Gap between Myth and Literature' *DR* 58, 4 (1978–9) 357–8

Grainger, M. Allerdale, *Woodsmen of the West* (M&S 1964) 29, 45–6

Green, Terence M., 'Future Imperfect' in *Books in Canada* (Jan. 1981) 92

Greenstein, Michael, 'Beyond the Ghetto and the Garrison: Jewish-Canadian Boundaries' *Mosaic* 14, 2 (1981) 65–6

Greenwood, Michael

A   'The Canadian Canvas' *artscanada* 32, 196/7 (1975–6) 93

B   'Christopher Pratt/Alex Colville/Jack Chambers' *artscanada* 210/11 (1976–7) 186, 285, 326

C   'Some Nationalist Facets of Canadian Art' *artscanada* 232/3 (1979–80) 98

Grove, Frederick Philip 45, 103–4, 185, 434

A   *In Search of Myself* (M&S 1974) 31, 46, 76, 137, 280, 318

B   *Settlers of the Marsh* (M&S 1966) 74, 103–4, 130, 148–9, 151, 474

C   'Snow' in Lucas 59–60

Guèvremont, Germaine 45

Gutteridge, Don

A   *Riel: A Poem for Voices* (Fiddlehead 1968) 260, 275–6, 349

B   'Surviving Paradise' *JCF* 3, 1 (1974) 218–19, 220, 333

Gwynn, Richard, *The Northern Magus* (1980) 278–9

Hanham, H.J., 'Canadian History in the 1970s' *CHistR* 55, 1 (1977) 70

Harcourt, Peter, 'Allan King: Film-Maker' in Helwig B 340, 366

Harlow, Robert, *Scann* (M&S 1977) 72–3, 206, 281, 286, 296, 298, 349, 352, 392

Harper, J. Russell, *Painting in Canada* (U. Toronto 1977) 56

Harris, Lawren 54–8

A   ABOVE LAKE SUPERIOR (ca 1922) 56

B   ALGOMA FOREST (1920) 55

C   ALGOMA WOODLAND (1920) 55

D   NORTH SHORE, LAKE SUPERIOR (1926) 57

Harris, Moses 11–12

Harrison, Charles Yale, *Generals Die in Bed* (Potlatch 1975) 117

Harrison, Dick 256

A   'Across the Medicine Line: Problems in Comparing Canadian and American Fiction' in Lewis and Lee 69, 366

B   'The Beginnings of Prairie Fiction' *JCF* 4, 1 (1975) 32

C   Introduction to *Best Mounted Police Stories* (U. Alberta 1978) 69

D   ed. *Crossing Frontiers: Papers in American and Canadian Western Literature* (U. Alberta 1979)
E   *Unnamed Country: The Struggle for a Canadian Prairie Fiction* (U. Alberta 1977) 30, 33, 35, 100, 103–4, 173, 222, 312, 376
Harrison, James, 'The 20,000,000 Solitudes of *Surfacing*' DR 59, 1 (1979) 289, 383
Harvey, Connie, 'Tear-Glazed Vision of Laughter' ECW 11 (1978) 381, 394
Heath, James, Illustrations in James Vancouver, *A Voyage of Discovery* (1798) 13
Hébert, Anne 80
A   *Kamouraska* trans. Norman Shapiro (Paperjacks 1974) 106, 108, 129, 131, 229, 250, 285, 303, 321, 330–1, 365, 371, 384
B   *The Silent Rooms* (*Les chambres de bois*) trans. Kathy Mezei (Paperjacks 1975) 103, 105, 223–4, 149–50, 152, 282, 364, 374
C   'Quebec: The Original Heart' in Kilbourn A 371
D   *Le torrent* (1950) 298
Hehner, Barbara, 'River of Now and Then: Margaret Laurence's Narratives' CanL 74 (1977) 339, 396
Helwig, David 80
A   *The Day before Tomorrow* (Oberon 1971) 87–8, 109–10, 153, 174, 184, 200, 289, 296
B   *The Human Elements: Critical Essays* (Oberon 1978)
C   'Time in Fiction' in Metcalf 399
Hémon, Louis, *Maria Chapdelaine* (1916) 44, 285
Henry, Alexander, *Travels and Adventures in Canada and the Indian Territories between the Years 1760 and 1776* (1901), excerpt in J. Warkentin 33
Hind, H.Y., *Report on the Exploration of the Country between Lake Superior and the Red River Settlement* (1858), excerpt in J. Warkentin 35–6
Hind, W.G.R.
A   BUFFALO ON THE PRAIRIE (1862) 13
B   CAMPING ON THE PRAIRIE (1862) 13
C   FOOT OF THE ROCKY MOUNTAINS (1862) 20
Hodgins, Jack 65
A   *The Invention of the World* (Signet 1977) 80–5, 103, 134, 136–7, 177, 206, 233–49, 280, 298, 308, 349, 350, 352, 380–3, 442
B   *Spit Delaney's Island* (Macmillan 1977) 104–5, 125, 155
Hood, Hugh 364, 402, 404, 441
A   'Sober Coloring: The Ontology of Super-realism' in Metcalf 341
B   *The Swing in the Garden* (Oberon 1975) 157, 318, 322
C   *White Figure, White Ground* (Ryerson 1964) 77, 147, 183, 313, 326, 442
Horowitz, G., 'Conservatism, Liberalism, and Socialism in Canada' CJEco&PoliSci 32, 2 (1966) 446
Horwood, Harold, *White Eskimo* (Paperjacks 1973) 153, 184, 218, 233–49, 302
Houston, James, *Spirit Wrestler* (Seal 1981) 233–49

Marsland, Elizabeth, 'La Chaine Tenue: Roads and Railways in the Prairie Novel' *CanL* 77 (1978) 401

Marta, Jan, 'Poetic Structures in the Prose Fiction of Sheila Watson' *ECW* 17 (1980) 361

Martin, Claire, *In an Iron Glove* (*Dans un gant de fer*) trans. Philip Stratford (Ryerson 1968) 177

Mayne, Seymour, ed. *The A.M. Klein Symposium* (U. Ottawa 1975)

Meares, John, *Voyages Made in the Years 1788 and 1789* (1790) 26

Melnyk, George, 'The Western Canadian Imagination: An Interview with Rudy Wiebe' *CFM* 12 (1974)

Meredith, John
  A SEEKER (1966) 95
  B PAINTING #1 (1962) 97

Merivale, Patricia, 'Neo-Modernism in the Canadian Artist-Parable: Hubert Aquin and Brian Moore' *CRCL* 6, 2 (1979) 281, 299, 318, 402

Metcalf, John, ed. *The Narrative Voice: Short Stories and Reflections by Canadian Authors* (McGraw-Hill Ryerson 1972)

Mezei, Kathy
  A 'Anne Hébert: A Pattern Repeated' *CanL* 72 (1977) 102
  B 'The Literature of Quebec in Revolution' in Helwig B 174, 175

Miller, Leslie 264

Miller, Orlo, *The Donnellys Must Die* (Macmillan 1962) 258–9, 275

Mills, John, *Skevington's Daughter* (Oberon 1978) 137, 233–49, 288–9, 296

Milne, David 55, 74; WINDOW (ca 1930) 284

Mitcham, Allison
  A 'The Northern Innocent in the Fiction of Gabrielle Roy' *HAB* 24, 1 (1973) 193
  B 'Northern Utopia' *CanL* 51 (1975) 52

Mitchell, W.O. 85
  A *The Vanishing Point* (Macmillan 1973) 72, 164, 177, 184, 206, 218, 219, 223–4, 288, 333, 442
  B *Who Has Seen the Wind* (Macmillan 1972) 153, 163, 178, 186–7, 196, 207, 427, 430

Molinari, Guido 299

Moodie, Susanna 48, 52, 63, 78, 79; *Roughing It in the Bush* (M&S 1962) 27–8, 37–9, 43, 56

Moore, Brian
  A *The Great Victorian Collection* (1975) 281, 297, 298–9, 307
  B *The Lonely Passion of Judith Hearne* (1955) 110–11
  C *The Luck of Ginger Coffey* (1960) 441

Morley, Patricia
  A *The Comedians: Hugh Hood and Rudy Wiebe* (Clarke Irwin 1977) 166, 338, 402
  B 'Survival, Affirmation, and Joy' *LakeheadUR* 7, 1 (1974) 194, 197–8

B   'His Legend a Jungle Sleep: Michael Ondaatje and Henri Rousseau' *CanL* 76 (1978) 401

C   'Scenes from the Lives of the Saints: A Hagiography of Canadian Literature' *LakeheadUR* 7, 1 (1974) 200, 204, 228

D   'Two Authors in Search of a Character' *CanL* 54 (1972) 274–5

Schaefer, Carl 57

Scott, Duncan Campbell 37

A   'Vengeance Is Mine' in *In the Village of Viger and Other Stories* (M&S 1973) 34–5

B   'The Piper of Arll' in *The Selected Poems of Duncan Campbell Scott* (1951) 291

Sears, Dennis T. Patrick, *The Lark in the Clear Air* (M&S 1974) 130

Seton, Ernest Thompson 51, 194, 198; *The Biography of a Grizzly* (1899) 192, 198

Shadbolt, Jack 93

A   'The Activity of Art: A Personal Response to History' *artscanada* 32, 198 (1975) 94, 410

B   MAN OF SYMBOLS (1971) 99

C   THE WAY IN (1973) 93

D   WINTER THEME NO. 7 (1961) 95

Shek, Ben-Zion, *Social Realism in the French-Canadian Novel* (Harvest House 1977) 85–6

Sheppard, Gordon, 'Violence and the French-Canadian Male' in Kilbourn A 150

Shields, Carol, *Small Ceremonies* (Totem 1978) 298, 303

Short, Richard 12

Shouldice, Larry, ed. and trans. *Contemporary Quebec Criticism* (U. Toronto 1979)

Simpson, Leo, *Arkwright* (Macmillan 1971) 233–49, 316, 424

Smiley, Calvin L., 'Godfrey's Progress' *CanL* 75 (1977) 368

Smith, A.J.M. 119

A   *The Book of Canadian Poetry: A Critical and Historical Anthology* (U. Chicago 1943) 36, 40, 403

B   *Masks of Fiction: Canadian Critics on Canadian Prose* (M&S 1961)

C   *Masks of Poetry: Canadian Critics on Canadian Verse* (M&S 1962)

Smith, Allan, 'Metaphor and Nationality in North America' *CHistR* 51, 3 (1970) 70

Snow, Michael 104, 106

A   BEACH-HCAEB (1963) 95, 105

B   BLIND (1967) 105

C   LAC CLAIR (1960) 98

Solecki, Sam, 'Nets and Chaos: The Poetry of Michael Ondaatje' *SCL* 2 (1977) 292

Souster, Raymond 200

Sparling, Mary Christine, 'The British Vision in Nova Scotia 1749–1848: What Views the Artists Reflected and Reinforced' (MA diss. Dalhousie 1978) 11–12

Stacey, C.P., *A Very Double Life: The Private Life of Mackenzie King* (Macmillan 1976) 271, 276

Staines, David, ed. *The Canadian Imagination: Dimensions of a Literary Culture* (Harvard 1977)

Stegner, Wallace, *Wolf Willow: A History, a Story, and a Memoir of the Last Plains Frontier* (Macmillan 1977) 36, 60–1, 63, 140, 337, 350–1, 376, 426–7

Stephens, Donald G., ed. *Writers of the Prairies* (U. British Columbia 1973)

Stevens, Peter, 'Explorer/Settler/Poet' in Lewis and Lee 280, 287

Stevenson, Warren, 'A Neglected Theme in *Two Solitudes*' CanL 75 (1977) 112

Stouck, David
    A 'Notes on the Canadian Imagination' *CanL* 54 (1972) 46, 48, 50, 373
    B ' "Secrets of the Prison-House": Mrs Moodie and the Canadian Imagination' *DR* 54, 3 (1974) 27–8

Stow, Glenys
    A 'A Discordant Heritage' *JCF* 16 (1976) 337
    B 'The Trickster Reborn' *JCF* 3, 1 (1974) 221

Such, Peter, *Riverrun* (Clarke Irwin 1973) 113, 117–18, 199, 219, 382

Sugden, Leonard, 'Hubert Aquin: Proteus in Despair' ECW 11 (1978) 131, 175, 303, 402, 407

Sullivan, Rosemary
    A Summing Up in D. Harrison D 53, 153–4, 239
    B 'World of Two Faces' *CanL* 63 (1975) 186

Surette, P.L., 'The Fabular Fiction of Robert Kroetsch' *CanL* 77 (1978) 333

Sutherland, John, 'The Poetry of E.J. Pratt' in Pitt 424

Sutherland, Ronald
    A 'The Calvinist-Jansenist Pantomime' *JCF* 5 (1970) 188–9
    B *The New Hero: Essays in Comparative Quebec-Canadian Literature* (Macmillan 1977) 446

Swainson, Donald, 'Trends in Canadian Biography: Recent Historical Writing' QQ 87, 3 (1980) 277–8

Symons, Scott, *Combat Journal for Place d'Armes* (M&S 1977) 124, 296, 303, 350, 368

Tallman, Warren, 'Wolf in the Snow' in Mandel C 187, 430

Teague, Frances, 'Prisons and Imprisonment in Canadian Drama' JCF 19 (1977) 102–3, 125

Thacker, Robert, 'The Mountie as Metaphor' DR 59, 3 (1979) 69–70

Thériault, Yves, *Agaguk* trans. Miriam Chapin (McGraw-Hill Ryerson 1967) 63–4, 70, 149, 157

Thomas, Audrey 344, 365
    A *Blown Figures* (Talonbooks 1974) 184, 290, 295, 313, 368
    B *Mrs Blood* (Talonbooks 1970) 106, 212, 304–5, 308, 315, 345, 346, 382, 384

Wilson, Ethel, *Swamp Angel* (M&S 1962) 84, 184

Wiseman, Adele 65

  A *Crackpot* (M&S 1978) 106, 202–14, 418, 435, 441, 442

  B *The Sacrifice* (Macmillan 1968) 115, 177, 434, 441–2

Withrow, William, *Contemporary Canadian Painting* (M&S 1972) 326

Wood, Susan, 'Ralph Connor and the Tamed West' in Lewis and Lee 59, 61

Woodcock, George

  A ed. *The Canadian Novel in the Twentieth Century: Essays from Canadian Literature* (M&S 1975): 'Margaret Atwood: Poet as Novelist' 379

  B *Gabriel Dumont: The Métis Chief and His Lost World* (Hurtig 1976) 256–7, 259, 275

  C 'The Human Elements: Margaret Laurence's Fiction' in Helwig B 402

  D 'The Meeting of the Muses: Recent Canadian Fiction and the Historical Viewpoint' *CHistR* 60, 2 (1979) 402

  E *Mordecai Richler* (M&S 1970) 65

  F 'There Are No Universal Landscapes' *artscanada* 222/3 (1978) 57, 93

Woodman, Ross, *James Reaney* (M&S 1971) 129

Wrong, George 386

Young, Dennis 104

Zezulka, J.M., 'The Pastoral Vision in Nineteenth-Century Canada' *DR* 55, 2 (1977) 25

Author's Note

The Wacousta Syndrome was written as part of a series of comparative culture studies focusing on the four grossly similar (in language, in derivation, in geohistorical terms) 'frontier' cultures of the United States, Canada, Australia, and New Zealand. This series (working title: 'Voice in the Wilderness') is collectively intended to elucidate the phenomenon termed the *Weltanschauung*, first, by isolating and explaining the mechanics of cultural change; secondly, by rationalizing the relations between culture-at-large and various kinds of cultural expression; and thirdly, by devising a portable methodology for 'mapping' culture by means of selected 'marker' traits.